CLASSICAL ANTIQUITIES OF

ALGERIA

A SELECTIVE GUIDE

by

Jean-Marie Blas de Roblès and Claude Sintès

translated into English and revised by

Philip Kenrick

CLASSICAL ANTIQUITIES OF ALGERIA

by Jean-Marie Blas de Roblès and Claude Sintès

translated into English and revised by Philip Kenrick

Originally published in 2003 by Édisud, Aix-en-Provence, as *Sites et monuments antiques de L'Algérie*

Published in 2018 by:
The Society for Libyan Studies
c/o The British Academy
10–11 Carlton House Terrace
London SW1Y 5AH

www.societyforlibyanstudies.org

Cover design: cbdesign and Philip Kenrick

ISBN 978-1-900971-54-6

Designed by Chris Bell, cbdesign

Printed in India by Imprint Press

CONTENTS

SOURCES OF ILLUSTRATIONS

1 Blas de Roblès/Kenrick
2 Philip Kenrick
3 Philip Kenrick
4 Philip Kenrick
5 Philip Kenrick
6 Philip Kenrick
7 J.-M. Blas de Roblès
8 Philip Kenrick
9 J.-M. Blas de Roblès
10 Title page of T. Shaw, *Travels, or, Observations relating to several parts of Barbary and the Levant: Illustrated with cuts* (2nd ed., with great improvements) (London 1757).
11 Photothèque du Centre Camille Jullian, fonds Paul-Albert Février
12 Photothèque du Centre Camille Jullian, fonds Paul-Albert Février
13 Blas de Roblès/Kenrick
14 Nacéra Benseddik
15 J.-C. Golvin
16 Google Earth: image © 2018 Digital Globe.
17 Blas de Roblès/Kenrick after H. B. Horn & C. B. Rüger, *Die Numider: Reiter und Könige nördlich der Sahara* (Bonn 1979), 144 fig. 66.
18 J.-C. Golvin/J.-M. Blas de Roblès
19 Wikimedia Commons, by 'Mus52'
20 Photothèque du Centre Camille Jullian, fonds Paul-Albert Février
21 Blas de Roblès/Kenrick, after N. Benseddik, S. Ferdi & Ph. Leveau, *Cherchel* (Algiers 1983) 72–73.
22 Philip Kenrick
23 Blas de Roblès/Kenrick, after S. Gsell, *Cherchel, antique Iol-Caesarea* (Algiers 1952) 105.
24 Philip Kenrick
25 Philip Kenrick
26 Blas de Roblès/Kenrick, after S. Gsell, *Cherchel, antique Iol-Caesarea* (Algiers 1952) 111.
27 Google Earth: image © 2018 CNES/ Airbus
28 Philip Kenrick
29 Philip Kenrick
30 Philip Kenrick
31 Philip Kenrick
32 Philip Kenrick
33 Philip Kenrick
34 Philip Kenrick
35 J.-M. Blas de Roblès
36 J.-M. Blas de Roblès
37 J.-M. Blas de Roblès
38 Philip Kenrick
39 Photothèque du Centre Camille Jullian, fonds Paul-Albert Février
40 Philip Kenrick
41 Philip Kenrick
42 Philip Kenrick
43 J.-M. Blas de Roblès
44 J.-M. Blas de Roblès
45 J.-M. Blas de Roblès
46 J.-C. Golvin/J.-M. Blas de Roblès
47 Photothèque du Centre Camille Jullian, fonds Paul-Albert Février
48 Philip Kenrick, after S. Raven, *Rome in Africa* (London & New York 1984), p. 252, with additions.

49 Philip Kenrick
50 Philip Kenrick
51 Philip Kenrick
52 Blas de Roblès/Kenrick, after A. Boëthius & J. B. Ward-Perkins, *Etruscan and Roman Architecture* (Harmondsworth 1970) 489 fig. 186.
53 Philip Kenrick
54 Blas de Roblès/Kenrick, after S. Lancel, *Tipasa de Maurétanie* (Algiers 1966) 44 fig. 23.
55 Philip Kenrick
56 Philip Kenrick
57 Blas de Roblès/Kenrick, after S. Lancel, *Tipasa de Maurétanie* (Algiers 1966) 48 fig. 25.
58 Philip Kenrick
59 Philip Kenrick
60 Philip Kenrick
61 Philip Kenrick
62 Kenrick, after J. Christern, Basilika und Memorie der heiligen Salsa in Tipasa. *Bulletin d'Archéologie Algérienne* 3 (1968) 193–258: fig. 4.
63 Philip Kenrick
64 Philip Kenrick
65 J.-M. Blas de Roblès
66 Philip Kenrick
67 Michel Lacanaud/Musée de L'Arles antique
68 Philip Kenrick
69 Philip Kenrick
70 J.-M. Blas de Roblès
71 Blas de Roblès/Kenrick after drawing by F. Rakob in H. B. Horn & C. B. Rüger, *Die Numider: Reiter und Könige nördlich der Sahara* (Bonn 1979), 138 fig. 59.
72 Philip Kenrick
73 Philip Kenrick
74 Philip Kenrick
75 Philip Kenrick
76 Philip Kenrick
77 Philip Kenrick
78 Philip Kenrick
79 Philip Kenrick
80 Philip Kenrick
81 Philip Kenrick
82 Philip Kenrick
83 Philip Kenrick
84 Philip Kenrick
85 Philip Kenrick
86 Philip Kenrick
87 Philip Kenrick
88 Philip Kenrick
89 Kenrick, after J.-P. Laporte, *Rapidum: Le camp de la cohorte des Sardes en Maurétanie Césarienne* (Sassari 1989) 26 fig. 4.
90 Philip Kenrick
91 Philip Kenrick
92 Kenrick, after P.-A. Février, Fouilles de Sétif: les basiliques chrétiennes du quartier nord-ouest (Paris 1965) fig. 3.
93 Philip Kenrick
94 Philip Kenrick
95 Philip Kenrick
96 Philip Kenrick
97 Photothèque du Centre Camille Jullian, fonds Paul-Albert Février
98 Blas de Roblès/Kenrick
99 Blas de Roblès/Kenrick, after P. A. Février, *Djémila* (Algiers 1968) end-plan.
100 Philip Kenrick
101 Philip Kenrick
102 Kenrick, after M. Blanchard-Lemée, *Maisons à mosaïques du quartier central de Djemila (Cuicul)* (Aix-en-Provence 1975), facing p. 153.
103 Kenrick, after M. Blanchard-Lemée, *Maisons à mosaïques du quartier central de Djemila (Cuicul)* (Aix-en-Provence 1975), 62 fig. 41.
104 Blas de Roblès/Kenrick, after P. A. Février, *Djémila* (Algiers 1968) 32 fig. 13.
105 Philip Kenrick
106 Philip Kenrick
107 Philip Kenrick
108 Blas de Roblès/Kenrick, after P. A. Février, *Djémila* (Algiers 1968) 38.
109 Philip Kenrick
110 Philip Kenrick

111 Philip Kenrick
112 Philip Kenrick
113 Philip Kenrick
114 Kenrick, after P.A. Février, *Djémila* (Algiers 1968) 46 fig. 24.
115 Philip Kenrick
116 Philip Kenrick
117 Blas de Roblès/Kenrick, after M. Blanchard-Lemée, *Maisons à mosaïques du quartier central de Djemila (Cuicul)* (Aix-en-Provence 1975), 175 fig. 79.
118 Blas de Roblès/Kenrick, after M. Blanchard-Lemée, *Maisons à mosaïques du quartier central de Djemila (Cuicul)* (Aix-en-Provence 1975), 108 fig. 43.
119 Kenrick, after Y. Allais, Les greniers publics de Djemila (Cuicul). *Revue Africaine* 74 (1933) 259–68, pl. II.
120 Philip Kenrick
121 Blas de Roblès/Kenrick, after M. Blanchard-Lemée, *Maisons à mosaïques du quartier central de Djemila (Cuicul)* (Aix-en-Provence 1975), 170 fig. 77.
122 Philip Kenrick
123 Philip Kenrick
124 Philip Kenrick
125 Blas de Roblès/Kenrick, after P.A. Février, *Djémila* (Algiers 1968) 69 fig. 40.
126 Philip Kenrick
127 Kenrick, after M. Christofle, *Rapport sur les travaux de fouilles et consolidations effectués en 1930–1931–1932* (Algiers 1935) 251.
128 Philip Kenrick
129 Blas de Roblès/Kenrick, after P.A. Février, *Djémila* (Algiers 1968) 77.
130 Philip Kenrick
131 Philip Kenrick
132 J.-M. Blas de Roblès
133 Philip Kenrick
134 Philip Kenrick
135 Philip Kenrick
136 J.-M. Blas de Roblès
137 J.-M. Blas de Roblès
138 Philip Kenrick
139 Philip Kenrick
140 J.-M. Blas de Roblès
141 Blas de Roblès/Kenrick, after A. Berthier, *Tiddis: antique Castellum Tidditanorum* (Algiers 1972), end-plan 2.
142 Philip Kenrick
143 J.-M. Blas de Roblès
144 Philip Kenrick
145 Philip Kenrick
146 Philip Kenrick
147 Philip Kenrick
148 Philip Kenrick
149 Philip Kenrick
150 Philip Kenrick
151 Philip Kenrick
152 Philip Kenrick
153 Blas de Roblès/Kenrick, after A. Berthier, *Tiddis: antique Castellum Tidditanorum* (Algiers 1972), end-plans.
154 Philip Kenrick
155 Philip Kenrick
156 Philip Kenrick
157 Blas de Roblès/Kenrick
158 Philip Kenrick
159 J.-M. Blas de Roblès
160 J.-M. Blas de Roblès
161 J.-M. Blas de Roblès
162 Photothèque du Centre Camille Jullian, fonds Paul-Albert Février
163 J.-M. Blas de Roblès
164 O. Boucher
165 Philip Kenrick
166 Drawing by F. Rakob in H. B. Horn & C. B. Rüger, *Die Numider: Reiter und Könige nördlich der Sahara* (Bonn 1979), 160 Abb. 87.
167 Philip Kenrick
168 Kenrick, after S. Gsell & A. Joly, *Khamissa, Mdaourouch, Announa : fouilles exécutées par le Service des monuments historique de l'Algérie* part 3 (Algiers 1918), pl. 12.
169 Philip Kenrick
170 Philip Kenrick

171 Philip Kenrick
172 Philip Kenrick
173 Philip Kenrick
174 Kenrick, after reconstruction by J.-C. Golvin and plan in S. Gsell, *Les monuments antiques de l'Algérie* (Paris 1901) 66 fig. 20.
175 H. B. Horn & C. B. Rüger, *Die Numider: Reiter und Könige nördlich der Sahara* (Bonn 1979), 144 fig. 67.
176 Blas de Roblès/Kenrick, after R. Cagnat, *Lambèse* (Paris 1893) end-plan, with additions.
177 Blas de Roblès/Kenrick, after F. Rakob & S. Storz, Die Principia des römischen Legionlagers in Lambaesis. *Mitteilungen des deutchen archäologischen Instituts, römische Abteilung* 81 (1974) 253–80: 260 Abb. 4.
178 Philip Kenrick
179 Philip Kenrick
180 Kenrick, after R. Cagnat, *Les deux camps de la Légion IIIe Auguste à Lambèse d'après les fouilles récentes* (Paris 1908) 19 fig. 2.
181 Philip Kenrick
182 Philip Kenrick
183 Philip Kenrick
184 Drawing by J.-L. Carbuccia in *Revue archéologique* 7 (1850), pl. 140.
185 Philip Kenrick
186 Drawing by J.-M. Gassend
187 Blas de Roblès/Kenrick, after M. Janon, Recherches à Lambèse III: essais sur le temple d'Esculape. *Antiquités Africaines* 21 (1985) 35–102, facing p. 36.
188 Philip Kenrick
189 Philip Kenrick
190 Philip Kenrick
191 Blas de Roblès/Kenrick after Y. Le Bohec, L'architecture militaire à Lambèse (Numidie). *Archäologisches Korrespondenzblatt* 38.2 (2008) 247–62: 258 fig. 8.
192 Philip Kenrick
193 Philip Kenrick
194 Blas de Roblès/Kenrick, after J. Lassus, *visite à Timgad* (Algiers 1969), end-plan, with additions.
195 Blas de Roblès/Kenrick, after J. Lassus, *visite à Timgad* (Algiers 1969), end-plan.
196 Philip Kenrick
197 Kenrick, after P. Romanelli, *Topografia e archeologia dell'Africa romana* (Torino 1970) pl. 153.
198 Philip Kenrick
199 Philip Kenrick
200 Blas de Roblès/Kenrick, after a plan by A. Ballu.
201 Philip Kenrick
202 Philip Kenrick
203 Philip Kenrick
204 Philip Kenrick
205 Philip Kenrick
206 Kenrick, after A. Ballu, *Les ruines de Timgad, antique Thamugadi* (Paris 1911) 14.
207 Philip Kenrick
208 Philip Kenrick
209 Philip Kenrick
210 Blas de Roblès/Kenrick, after a plan by A. Ballu.
211 Kenrick, after A. Ballu, *Les ruines de Timgad, antique Thamugadi* (Paris 1911) 22.
212 Philip Kenrick
213 Philip Kenrick
214 Blas de Roblès/Kenrick, after C. Courtois, *Timgad, antique Thamugadi* (Algiers 1951) 57.
215 Philip Kenrick
216 Philip Kenrick
217 Blas de Roblès/Kenrick, after a plan by S. Tourrenc reproduced in V. Blanc-Bijon (Ed.), *Lieux de cultes: aires votives, temples, églises, mosquées: IXe Colloque international sur l'histoire et l'archéologie de l'Afrique du Nord, Tripoli, 19-25 février 2005* (Paris 2008) 156 fig. 2.
218 Philip Kenrick
219 Philip Kenrick

220 Philip Kenrick
221 Philip Kenrick
222 Kenrick, after A. Ballu, *Les ruines de Timgad, antique Thamugadi* (Paris 1911), plan facing p. 32, with modifications.
223 Philip Kenrick
224 Kenrick, after After S. Gsell, *Les monuments antiques de l'Algérie* (Paris 1901) I, 207, fig. 66.
225 Philip Kenrick
226 Philip Kenrick
227 Blas de Roblès/Kenrick, after C. Courtois, *Timgad, antique Thamugadi* (Algiers 1951) 89.
228 Philip Kenrick
229 Philip Kenrick
230 J.-M. Blas de Roblès
231 J.-M. Blas de Roblès
232 J.-M. Blas de Roblès
233 J.-M. Blas de Roblès
234 J.-M. Blas de Roblès
235 J.-M. Blas de Roblès
236 J.-M. Blas de Roblès
237 Philip Kenrick
238 Philip Kenrick
239 Philip Kenrick
240 Philip Kenrick
241 Philip Kenrick
242 Philip Kenrick
243 Philip Kenrick
244 Philip Kenrick
245 Kenrick, after P. Trousset, Le camp de Gemellae sur le Limes de Numidie d'après les fouilles du Colonel Baradez (1947-1950). *Akten des XI Internationalen Limeskongresses* (1976) 559-75, figs. 1 and 2.
246 Philip Kenrick
247 Blas de Roblès/Kenrick
248 J.-M. Blas de Roblès
249 Blas de Roblès/Kenrick, after E. Marec, *Hippone la royale, antique Hippo Regius* (Algiers 1954) 117, with additions from V. Delestre, *Hippone* (Aix-en-Provence 2005) 15.
250 Philip Kenrick
251 Philip Kenrick
252 Blas de Roblès/Kenrick, after E. Marec, *Hippone la royale, antique Hippo Regius* (Algiers 1954) 125.
253 Philip Kenrick
254 Blas de Roblès/Kenrick, after E. Marec, *Hippone la royale, antique Hippo Regius* (Algiers 1954) 123 and X. Delestre, *Hippone* (Aix-en-Provence 2005) 197.
255 Philip Kenrick
256 Kenrick, after A. Boëthius & J. B. Ward-Perkins, *Etruscan and Roman Architecture* (Harmondsworth 1970) 482 fig. 181A.
257 Philip Kenrick
258 Philip Kenrick
259 Blas de Roblès/Kenrick, after E. Marec, *Hippone la royale, antique Hippo Regius* (Algiers 1954) 127.
260 Blas de Roblès/Kenrick, after E. Marec, *Hippone la royale, antique Hippo Regius* (Algiers 1954) 119.
261 Blas de Roblès/Kenrick, after E. Marec, *Hippone la royale, antique Hippo Regius* (Algiers 1954) 121.
262 Philip Kenrick
263 Philip Kenrick
264 Philip Kenrick
265 Philip Kenrick
266 J.-M. Blas de Roblès
267 J.-M. Blas de Roblès
268 J.-M. Blas de Roblès
269 J.-M. Blas de Roblès
270 J.-M. Blas de Roblès
271 Philip Kenrick
272 Philip Kenrick
273 Philip Kenrick
274 Philip Kenrick
275 Philip Kenrick
276 J.-M. Blas de Roblès
277 Kenrick, after S. Gsell & A. Joly, *Khamissa, Mdaourouch, Announa : fouilles exécutées par le Service des monuments historique de l'Algérie* part I (Algiers 1914) pl. I.
278 Philip Kenrick

279 Philip Kenrick
280 Kenrick, after S. Gsell & A. Joly, *Khamissa, Mdaourouch, Announa : fouilles exécutées par le Service des monuments historique de l'Algérie* (Algiers 1914) pl. II.
281 Philip Kenrick
282 Philip Kenrick
283 Philip Kenrick
284 Kenrick, after A. Ballu in *Bulletin archéologique du Comité de travaux historiques et scientifiques* (1919) 59 fig. 1.
285 Philip Kenrick
286 Kenrick, after S. Gsell & A. Joly, *Khamissa, Mdaourouch, Announa : fouilles exécutées par le Service des monuments historique de l'Algérie* part 2 (Algiers 1922) pl. 16 and N. Duval, I. Gui & J.-P. Caillet, *Basiliques chrétiennes d'Afrique du Nord. I, Inventaire de l'Algérie* (Paris 1992) pl. 164.
287 Blas de Roblès/Kenrick, after M. Christofle, *Essai de restitution d'un moulin à huile de l'époque romaine à Madaure (Constantine)* (Algiers 1930) end-drawings.
288 Philip Kenrick
289 Philip Kenrick
290 Philip Kenrick
291 Philip Kenrick
292 Philip Kenrick
293 Blas de Roblès/Kenrick, after E. Sérée de Roch, *Tébessa: antique Theveste* (Algiers 1952), end-plan.
294 A. Héron de Villefosse, Tébessa et ses monuments. *Le Tour du Monde* (1880) 1–32. This illustration on p. 9.
295 Philip Kenrick
296 Philip Kenrick
297 Philip Kenrick
298 Philip Kenrick
299 Blas de Roblès/Kenrick, after E. Sérée de Roch, *Tébessa: antique Theveste* (Algiers 1952), end-plan.
300 J.-C. Golvin
301 Philip Kenrick
302 Philip Kenrick
303 Philip Kenrick
304 Philip Kenrick
305 Philip Kenrick
306 Philip Kenrick
307 J.-M. Blas de Roblès
308 J. Chabassière, in *Recueil de la Société Archéologique de Constantine* (1888), hors-texte, pl. XIX.
309 Kenrick, after J. Christern & E. Müller, *Das frühchristliche Pilgerheiligtum von Tebessa: Architektur und Ornamentik einer spätantiken Bauhütte in Nordafrika* (Wiesbaden 1976) fig. 31.
310 Philip Kenrick
311 Philip Kenrick
312 Philip Kenrick
313 S. Gsell, *Les Monuments Antiques De L'Algérie* (Paris, 1901) vol. 2, pl. 75 (facing p. 30).
314 Kenrick, after S. Gsell, *Les Monuments Antiques De L'Algérie* (Paris, 1901) vol. 2, 29 fig. 89 and 31 fig. 90.
315 Philip Kenrick

TRANSLATOR'S PREFACE AND ACKNOWLEDGEMENTS

The reissue of the work *Sites et monuments antiques de L'Algérie* in an English edition was suggested to me by two factors. The first was that I was regularly taking to Algeria groups of English-speaking tourists who wanted to read something authoritative in English about the antiquities they were going to see; the second was that the illustrated French volume named above, which I had myself used with profit, had gone out of print and could no longer even be suggested for its rich illustration.

I did not feel myself competent to compose a new guidebook from scratch, but on the other hand, to produce a translation of the book of messieurs Blas de Roblès and Sintès some fifteen years after it was written might justify (and indeed call for) some revision and updating at the same time. I was greatly encouraged when the authors and Equinoxe, the publisher which had in the meantime inherited the titles of Édisud, placed no obstacles in my way, and indeed encouraged me in my project. I am deeply grateful to M. Jean-Marie Blas de Roblès who supplied me with digital copies of all the line drawings he had made, in a format in which I could replace the French legends with English text with a minimum of difficulty. He also made available to me many digital photographs which he had taken in museums, adding significantly to those which I had been able to take myself. On the other hand, the site photographs which he had used in the French edition, along with those taken by Odile Boucher (all colour slides) were deemed not to have survived the passage of time sufficiently well to be used again. Thus the site photographs are mostly new ones taken by myself, and have sometimes suffered from an increase in vegetation around the monuments. I am grateful to the Centre Camille Jullian, Aix-en-Provence and to their photographer and IT Manager M. Bruno Baudoin for the scanning and provision of various historic photographs, and to the Musée de L'Arles antique (directed by Dr. Claude Sintès) for permission to use fig. 67.

As I worked on the translation, I came to feel increasingly strongly that the new edition should not adopt the same format as before: this had leant itself to stunning illustrations but is not readily portable on site as a pocket guide. An early expression of interest by the Society for Libyan Studies led to the adoption of the same format as their *Libyan Archaeological Guides*. The resulting smaller format has of course meant that the illustrations cannot be so large, but I have as far as possible retained their extent, since the antiquities of Algeria deserve to be known to a much wider public than has hitherto been the case (at least in the English-speaking world).

The fieldwork which I have been able to do has been very limited, and in many instances I have been on the sites only in the company of tour groups, when it has not been appropriate to excuse myself to check some subtle detail. However, in February 2018 it was possible for me to carry out a brief independent reconnaissance. For this I am deeply indebted to my friend Ahcicene Segouini, who has not only taken exemplary care of my tour groups through his company *Expert Algeria*, but also, at his expense, facilitated this journey. I was driven skilfully and with good humour over very large distances by Mustapha Gueraini and was accompanied for much of the time by Abdelkader Bensalah, whom I have also long counted as a friend and whose acquaintance with antiquities staff throughout the country greatly facilitated my task.

I have been very conscious of the limitations of my familiarity with the Algerian sites and of the need for good advice from someone with a closer acquaintance with the material. I am grateful to Dr. Nacéra Benseddik for her help in this regard, but also particularly to Dr. Touatia Amraoui, author of a wide-ranging study of craft production in the Roman cities of Algeria. Her work, and her comments on a first draft of my text, have saved me in many places from repeating the hasty, and now discredited, interpretations of earlier generations of archaeologists. I have also received very useful feedback from Dr. Lisa Fentress and Dr. Corisande Fenwick. As on previous occasions, I have much to thank my wife Sue for. Apart from her patience with what might have seemed an obsessive hobby, as a 'general reader' she has insisted that I subdivide or simplify occasional over-long sentences; she has also pointed out instances where I have too readily used without explanation some technical term or Latin title. The text has undoubtedly been improved as a result.

I am deeply grateful to the Society for Libyan Studies, its officers and its Publications Manager Victoria Leitch for their support and encouragement. Finally, it has been a pleasure to work with the designer Christine Bell, who has once more skillfully blended my vision into a visually attractive whole.

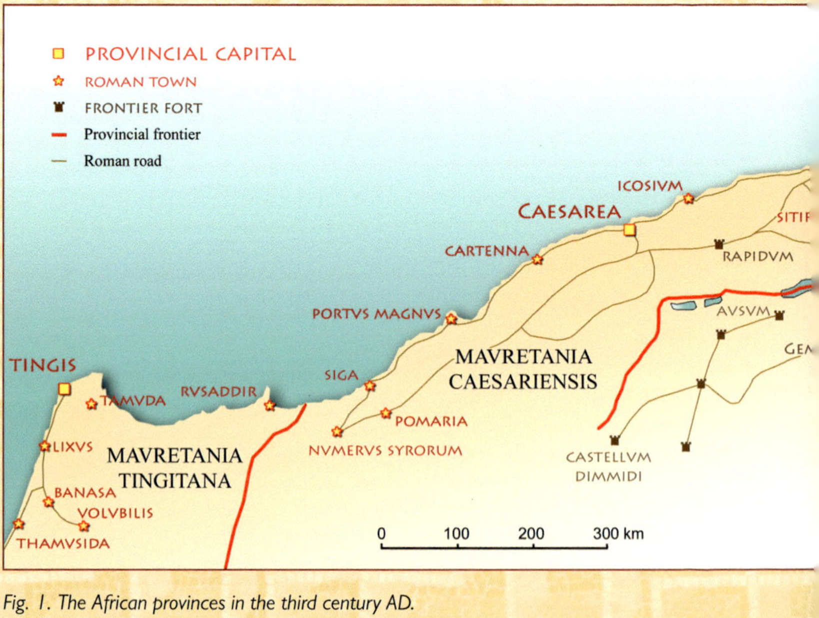

Fig. 1. The African provinces in the third century AD.

I. HISTORICAL INTRODUCTION

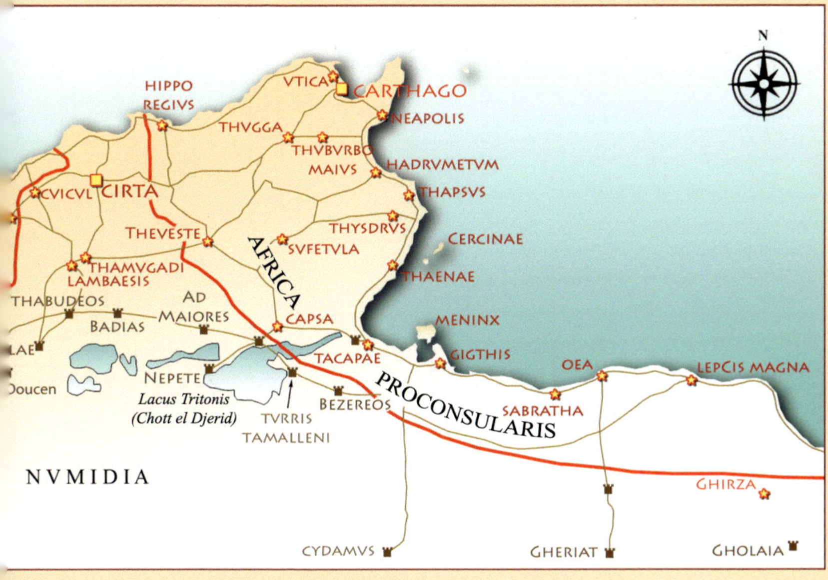

Before the Roman conquest

Two ancient sources tell us about the establishment of Phoenician settlements in North Africa. According to Diodorus Siculus, it was essentially for purposes of trade that certain inhabitants of Tyre and Sidon established colonies on these distant coasts. According to Sallust on the other hand, these commercial interests were accompanied by other motives: it was also to relieve population pressures and to satisfy the Phoenicians' desire for control which 'drove people of their race and others eager for novelty to found the coastal settlements of Hippo, Hadrumetum, Lepcis and other cities.' A few centuries later, the placing of Carthaginian settlements was motivated in part by similar factors.

The exposure of the African coast to strong northerly winds is such that these traders sought out, for their temporary trading-posts and for their permanent settlements, any site that would give them at least some shelter for their ships: offshore islands, rocky inlets or river estuaries. These undertakings seem not to have aroused any serious opposition on the part of the local inhabitants – who surely gained something from the new trade – and this led in turn to the development of more formal establishments. This has been demonstrated archaeologically through the discovery of artefacts and the excavation of cemeteries dated from the seventh century BC onwards. We know very little of the administrative or political structures which governed the relations between these cities or between the foreigners and the 'punicised' native settlements, of which Cirta (Constantine: see p. 152) is a good example. It is clear however that the new arrivals brought about permanent changes in the trades, skills and religions of the peoples with whom they came into contact.

There must have been pre-existing indigenous societies, but it is impossible to say anything about them before the fourth century BC. We are hampered by ill-defined and changing geographical boundaries and by unknown kings and alliances. Just one glimpse is given by the attempt at that time of the Carthaginian general Hanno to obtain the support of a 'king of the Moors.' From the third century onwards, the sources are much more specific and we find, in addition to Mauretania (of the Moors), the two Numidian kingdoms of the Masaesyli and the Massyli, readily distinguishable even if we cannot identify their traditions and their original organisation. We have a list of kings of Mauretania – albeit with gaps – from Baga at the end of the third century to Bocchus at the end of the second and Bocchus II and Bogud who shared the kingdom after that. The Masaesyli appear in the record from the

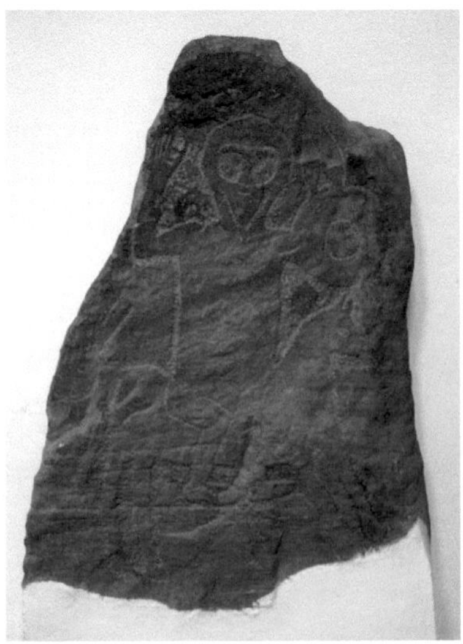

Fig. 2. Algiers, National Museum of Antiquities: Libyan stele showing a bearded warrior on horseback.

end of the third century, with Siga as their western capital and Cirta as their eastern one; their most emblematic king was Syphax, who appears in the sources in 213 BC. Towards the modern frontier between Algeria and Tunisia was the kingdom of the Massyli, whose first king was (possibly) Ailymas, then (definitely) Gaïa, father of Masinissa. Their capital is not known, but their territory included several large towns, such as Tébessa and Dougga. These kingdoms (often described as 'Berber', though this is a term which did not exist before the medieval period) constituted an agglomeration of entities with varied forms of administration, who would see their destinies fluctuate as they came into ever closer contact with the new power dominating the region: Rome. This was an upheaval which was far from painless, and was attended by incessant revolts and resistance, associated most notably with the names of Syphax, Jugurtha and Tacfarinas.

The progressive imposition of Roman control

As in other parts of the Roman Empire, the territory of what is now Algeria was subdivided into provinces, the boundaries of which do not always correspond to the political divisions of today. (See fig. 1.) While our primary interest may be in *Mauretania Caesariensis*, *Numidia* and part of *Africa Proconsularis*, these exist within the context of a wider geographical region, extending from the sands of Tripolitania to the shores of the Atlantic.

Of all Rome's possessions, the African provinces were undoubtedly those which took longest to achieve a settled administrative structure. It took three-and-a-half centuries, from the destruction of Carthage in 146 BC to the reforms of AD 197 (when Septimius Severus carved out part of Africa Proconsularis to create the province of Numidia) for the territory to reach its greatest extent; even then, the desert frontier remained a somewhat fluid concept. In simple terms, this expansion may be characterized by six specific episodes.

In the immediate aftermath of the destruction of Carthage in 146 BC, the Romans took possession of the ancient Punic (= Carthaginian) homeland (the North and East of Tunisia), enclosed it within a continuous ditch, known as the *fossa regia*, dug by the soldiers of Scipio Aemilianus, and divided it into regular plots of fifty hectares. This 'centuriation', traditionally dated to the end of the second century BC but possibly derived from an earlier land distribution, facilitated the organization of the land together with the raising of taxes. Since everything associated with Carthage was execrated, the capital of the new *provincia Africa* was established at Utica, a site in a geographically less favourable position, but symbolically more neutral. The political agenda of the time was not yet expansionist: the Roman state was interested in holding a strategic position, a bastion ideally placed to keep watch over a zone, the control of which was essential to the security of Rome. At the same time, it would prevent the old enemy, Carthage, from reinventing itself in another form or under another name.

At the end of the Roman Republic, in Africa (as elsewhere) the civil war of 48–46 BC split in two the supporters of Caesar and those of Pompey. King Juba I of Numidia made the mistake of allying himself with the Pompeians. He withdrew his army in flight after the battle of Pharsalus, but then assembled twenty thousand cavalry and thirty thousand foot-soldiers to oppose Caesar. Caesar landed in Africa, crushed Juba I at Thapsus – resulting in his suicide at Hippo together with that of Metellus Scipio – and annexed the kingdom of the Massyli in 46 BC. He thus brought under Roman rule a vast area, corresponding to Tripolitania and part of Tunisia, which he named *Africa Nova*, 'New Africa', in order to distinguish it from *Africa Vetus*, 'Old Africa', which had already been held by Rome for a hundred years. Caesar also revived Carthage, which became the capital of the province, and set up a buffer zone to the west under the fiction of an independent Numidian kingdom (actually entrusted to his lieutenant Publius Sittius from 46 BC until he was murdered two years later). He sent the young son of Juba (also Juba) to Rome, where he was brought up to admire Rome and its culture.

In 27 BC, Caesar's adopted successor Octavian (who at that point changed his name to Augustus) reformed the administration of Africa into the single province of *Africa Proconsularis*, so called because it was under the authority of the Roman Senate, which appointed a governor with the rank of proconsul. The territory comprised the Tripolitanian (western) part of modern Libya, the whole of Tunisia and part of Algeria, to a point just to the west of Hippo Regius (Annaba: p. 232). Calama (Guelma: p. 252), Thagaste (Souk Ahras) and Theveste (Tébessa: p. 271), for example, fell within this region which was essentially peaceful and urbanized and which did not justify the presence of a permanent military garrison. The environs of Cirta (Constantine) alone retained a special status, as a confederation of four cities – Cirta, Milev (Mila), Chullu (Collo) and Rusicade (Skikda) – under the title of *Respublica IV Coloniarum Cirtensium*.

Two years later, Augustus strengthened his control over regions further to the west, entrusting the kingdom of Mauretania (as a buffer state) to Juba II. This young man had been educated in Rome and had become a close friend of the emperor, whom he regarded as his benefactor; he was thoroughly indoctrinated into Roman ways, was highly literate and wrote extensively on a variety of subjects. Juba contributed strongly to the pacification and 'Romanisation' of tribes previously considered barbaric. The lifestyle and creature comforts of the conquering power were imported: Juba's capital at Iol was renamed

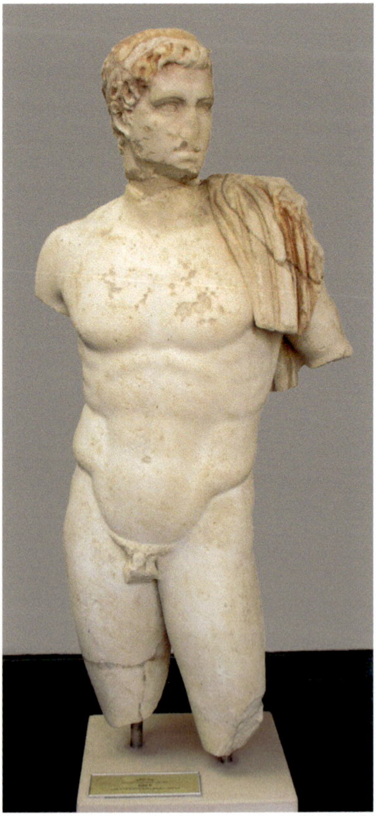

Fig. 3. Cherchel, Old Museum: Juba II rendered in the style of a Greek hero.

Caesarea in honour of Caesar Augustus and was equipped with all the public monuments appropriate to a city of the Empire: amphitheatre, theatre, baths, circus etc. (See p. 29 ff.)

In AD 40, the Roman takeover took a more brutal turn with the murder of Ptolemy, the son and successor of Juba II, on the orders of Caligula. A freedman of the dead king, Aedemon, attempted to avenge his death and to resist the imposition of direct control by Rome. However, his supporters were few (suggesting that most were already reconciled to the new reality), and by 44 the emperor Claudius had put down the revolt and re-established control. This vast region (amounting to the north-western part of Algeria and most of Morocco) was too large to be managed by a single administration, nor does it seem that there was any continuous communication by road throughout its extent. Claudius created two provinces, *Mauretania Tingitana* in the west, ruled from Tingis (Tangier), and *Mauretania Caesariensis* in the east, still ruled from Caesarea. These changes were accompanied by advances in juridical status, and cities such as Caesarea (p. 29), Tipasa (p. 52) and Rusuccuru (Dellys: see fig. 13) became *municipia* or *coloniae*. Archaeological and epigraphic evidence has also shown that there was a push by the Romans towards the south and the west around the end of the first century and the beginning of the second. It is difficult to determine whether this was the result of a large-scale military offensive, or whether it was driven by over-population of the coastal region and a search for new ground to bring under cultivation. A number of cities were either founded at this time or enjoyed an advance in status: Madauros (p. 265) became a colony under the Flavians; Aquae Flavianae (near Khenchela) was a new foundation; Thamugadi (Timgad: p. 185) was founded by Trajan in 100 as a colony for military veterans, and several other towns grew up in the vicinity of Lambaesis where the Third Augustan Legion had its headquarters. The same phenomenon can be detected in the western part of the region from the reign of Nerva (96–98) onwards, with the foundation of colonies at Sitifis (Sétif: p. 92) and Cuicul (Djémila: p. 100) and the establishment of a military post in the Hadrianic period at Rapidum (Sour Djouab: p. 88).

From the Severans to Constantine

The general configuration of Roman North Africa had been established in the first century AD, with three provinces – Africa Proconsularis, Mauretania Caesariensis and Mauretania Tingitana – covering the ground between the Syrtic Gulf and the Atlantic. Numidia at this time had a somewhat anomalous status: while it was theoretically part of Africa Proconsularis, it constituted a military frontier zone under the command of a *Legatus Augusti* appointed by the emperor (rather than the Senate). This situation was regularized in or around 197 by Septimius Severus (himself a Libyan), who created an official province of Numidia composed of the former military zone, the territory of the *Respublica IV Coloniarum Cirtensium* and the land of the *Suburbures* together with the colony of Cuicul. The capital of the new province was at Lambaesis, the site of the legionary headquarters (p. 169).

Under the Severan dynasty, a deliberate effort was made to consolidate control of the southern frontier or *limes* (whence the English word 'limit') by a further southward expansion. The goals were multiple: to increase the amount of

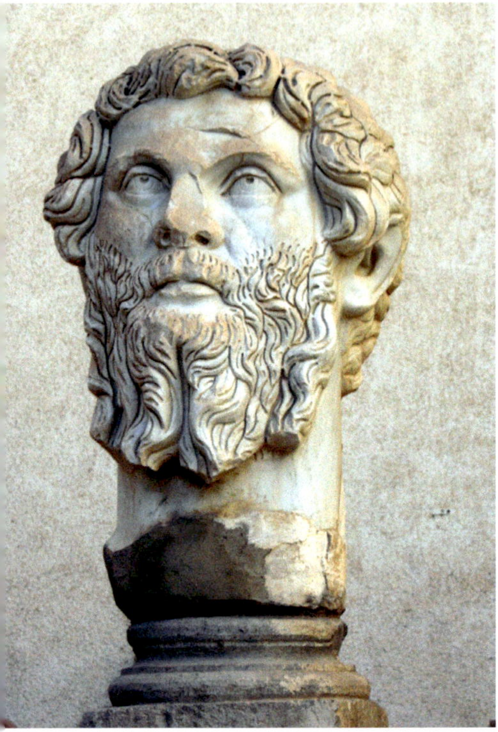

Fig. 4. Djémila Museum: colossal head of Septimius Severus.

agricultural land; to manage the transhumant pastoralists by controlling their seasonal migrations and to exploit the trans-Saharan trade and the riches of the tropics by controlling the major routes and watering-points. The remains of camps and of water-control systems show that the Romans penetrated deep into the interior, particularly in the eastern part of what is now Algeria. The veterans and colonists could, at the expense of huge effort, bring into cultivation the land on the desert margins while at the same time guarding the frontier. This was a very different pattern of occupation from previous centuries, when operations against the nomads never took the form of real battles, but more of raids, intimidations and skirmishes which sometimes led Roman troops a long way to the south. In 21–20 BC, for example, Cornelius Balbus pursued the Garamantes into the Fazzan and the cavalry was sent into the open desert to repel the Gaetuli. Later, there were permanent camps on the very edge of the desert (see fig. 1), at Gemellae (p. 227) in 126 and at Castellum Dimmidi in 198. (Gemellae, and neighbouring Thabudeos, seem to have been among the locations previously visited by Balbus.)

The administrative structure which was now established lasted until the time of Diocletian (284–305), when a wholesale revision of the government of the empire was carried out and the provinces were grouped into dioceses. The former Africa was divided into Zeugitana (capital: Carthage), Byzacena (capital: Sousse) and Tripolitana (capital: Lepcis Magna). Numidia was divided into Northern (or Cirtan) Numidia (capital: Cirta) and Military Numidia (capital: Lambaesis). Mauretania Tingitana was henceforth grouped with the provinces of Spain, while Mauretania Caesariensis was reduced to its western part, the eastern half becoming Mauretania Sitifensis (capital: Sitifis). Soon after, under Constantine, the two Numidian provinces were reunited, with Cirta, now 'refounded' as Constantina, as the capital. In the Diocletianic reforms, civil and military authority were also separated, with a *praeses* as provincial governor responsible for the administration of justice and a *dux* in command of the military forces. This stabilization, following the chaos of the later third century, ushered in a new period of prosperity with renewed building work in the cities and a better management of the countryside, described by some modern historians as a 'renaissance'.

The Vandals

The prosperity which followed the administrative reforms of Diocletian at the end of the third century did not last long, for new dangers arose with the revolt of the Moorish prince Firmus in 371. Firmus held a position (not clearly identified) in the Roman army, as did several of his brothers. He fell foul of the corrupt *Comes Africae* Romanus. (This position was a military command, independent of the provincial governors.) The opposition of Romanus drove Firmus to declare independence from Rome and to be acclaimed as emperor. In the course of his attempt to carve out an independent principality he sacked several cities, including Caesarea; his skill and the tenacity of his troops meant that it would take four years of fighting for the renowned general Theodosius to put an end to the uprising. In 386 Gildo, the brother of Firmus (who had endeared himself to Theodosius by remaining loyal to Rome), was appointed *Comes Africae* by the general's son, who was now the emperor Theodosius I. But Gildo soon made his own bid for independence, using his stranglehold on the grain supply in an attempt to enhance his power by playing off the eastern and western emperors against one another. The ensuing conflict ended only in 396 with Gildo's defeat and suicide. Whatever the hardships caused by these troubles, they paled into insignificance beside the next problem that the Africans had to face: it was the very unity of the empire that was threatened by the arrival of the Vandals.

The Vandals were a people from eastern Germany who had migrated into Spain at the beginning of the fifth century. In 429, the *Comes Africae* Bonifatius was in dispute with Rome and unwisely asked for their help. Their leader Gaiseric crossed the Straits of Gibraltar with a force of 80,000 and advanced eastwards. Bonifatius, who had by now made peace with Rome, was unable to make terms with Gaiseric and found himself under attack. Hippo Regius was taken in 431 and three years later the Vandals were formally recognized as *foederati* (allies) and charged with the defence of Numidia. In 439 Gaiseric again pressed eastwards and took Carthage without opposition: the contemporary historian Prosper wrote that the country was 'shared' between Gaiseric and the emperor Valentinian III. From then on, using their African bastion as a base, the Vandals set about raiding the western Mediterranean, with attacks on the Balearic Isles, Sicily, Corsica, Sardinia and even Rome, which was sacked in 455. The Catholic writers of the time described them as unimaginably cruel, bloodthirsty wreckers: this

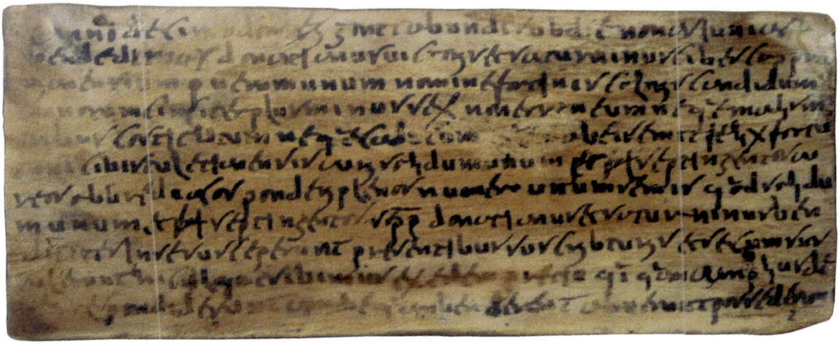

Fig. 5. Algiers, National Museum of Antiquities: one of the Albertini tablets, recording sales of land according to Roman law in the Vandal period (see p. 85).

reputation, possibly somewhat exaggerated, has become inseparable from their very name, which still carries this negative connotation today.

Once installed, the Vandals organized their society by retaining some parts of the pre-existing imperial legislation and by imposing certain new laws. They created separate jurisdictions, so that the Romans could live by their own laws, while the Vandals could only be held to account by Vandal judges in special courts; they set up mints; they promulgated edicts which persecuted both Catholics and Donatists in the name of their own Arian version of Christianity (for these divisions within the church, see p. 14); they established simple lines of inheritance in order to avoid the endless subdivision of property. This system underpinned Vandal rule for around a century, from Gaiseric to their last king, Gelimer.

The Byzantine reconquest

The eastern emperors, henceforth the only upholders of the Roman empire, did not give up the vision of recovering the rich provinces of Africa. Many attempts at reconquest – in 468 and 470, for example – failed and it was not until the time of Justinian that this enterprise was crowned with success. This emperor (who came to power in 527), having made an 'eternal' peace with the Persians, was free to send a substantial expeditionary force to Carthage in 533. The strength of this force, and particularly the leadership of the Byzantine generals Belisarius and later Solomon, was sufficient to defeat the troops of the occupiers. In March 534 King Gelimer surrendered, putting an end to Vandal rule. This was not, however, the end of the story, for various uprisings and revolts of Moorish tribes resulted in continued fighting until 546. In the light of this, one may question whether the Byzantines (claiming to be Roman but now speaking Greek) were in any sense welcomed, or whether they were seen as yet another foreign invader. Some inscriptions suggest hopes of a return to the prosperity of a century ago, but interludes of peace were interspersed with sporadic but ceaseless troubles.

The Byzantine administration restored the old administrative and legislative structures. The Diocese of Africa was re-established with seven provinces – Tripolitana, Zeugitana, Byzacena, Numidia, Mauretania Sitifensis, Mauretania Caesariensis, Sardinia – while the military command was reorganized with the arrival of military provincial governors (*duces*) in residence at Caesarea and Constantina. The task in hand was immense, but embarked upon with zeal: Solomon undertook a substantial reinforcement of lines of communication, with the creation or restoration of defensive works. Several cities, such as Theveste, Madauros, Thamugadi and Sitifis were now provided with massive ramparts enclosing a small central core of the previous built-up area. It is notable that at Thamugadi, the fortress was exclusively military in character and was built outside the town, around the principal water source. This suggests that in other locations too, the new strongpoints may have been intended primarily to protect the newcomers rather than the local population (who may not have seen them as friendly, and who may actually have been expelled from these areas). New churches were built and lavishly decorated with mosaics, not only in the principal cities but also in rural areas; and towns were reborn. But despite their efforts, the Byzantines were unable to hold their gains for long: weakened by an exhausting struggle with the tribes of the interior and undermined internally by religious and political squabbles, the heirs of Rome were no match for the challenge of the Arabs. The progress of the Arab armies was unstoppable: they were in Libya Pentapolis (Cyrenaica) in 642, in Tripolitania in 643 and in Byzacena in 647. The heroic resistance of the Moors, led by Koseila and then by a legendary woman, the powerful queen Kahena of the Aurès, delayed their advance for a while, but Carthage fell in 698, reducing the Byzantines to a last stronghold at Septem (Ceuta), from which they were driven in 709.

This sequence of events represented the final extinction of Roman rule in Africa. The cultural period from then until the present day is characterized as 'Islamic', but this obscures what is likely to have been an extended phase of adjustment in which, certainly, new values were introduced. But there was undoubtedly a continuity alongside this. Unfortunately, the enthusiasm of colonial archaeologists for Classical Antiquity has on many sites swept away evidence of continued vitality in the ancient cities after the end of Roman/Byzantine rule without record. This is an area of study which is only now beginning to receive an appropriate evaluation.

The organization of agriculture in the Roman period

The patron souses his fish with Venafran oil, but the sallow cabbage they offer to poor you stinks of the lamp. The oil provided for your dishes is brought upstream in one of Micipsa's beak-nosed reed-boats, which is why no one at Rome shares the bath with Bocchus: the oil he uses keeps even venomous snakes at bay!

Juvenal, *Satire* V, 86–91

The great wealth of Africa lay in its agricultural potential. The systematic exploitation of these fertile terrains and the resulting economic growth led Tertullian, in the third century, to be already concerned for the progressive exhaustion of natural resources:

Most pleasant farms have obliterated all traces of what were once dreary and dangerous wastes; cultivated fields have subdued forests; flocks and herds have expelled wild beasts; sandy deserts are sown; rocks are planted; marshes are drained; and where once were hardly solitary cottages, there are now large cities. … What most frequently meets our view (and occasions complaint), is our teeming population: our numbers are burdensome to the world, which can hardly supply us from its natural elements; our wants grow more and more keen, and our complaints more bitter in all mouths, whilst Nature fails in affording us her usual sustenance.

De anima 30, tr. P. Holmes

Immediately after the Roman conquest, the pattern of exploitation was still varied, including both modest native landowners or settlers, large aristocratic estates known as *saltus* and imperial property. But the small holdings were progressively absorbed into the larger, corresponding to a concentration of capital and leading to a pattern of management based on the *latifundium* ('large farm'). In the first century AD, for example, six families owned between them half the area of the province, resulting in recurrent problems. Not all of the land was cultivated, direct management required the maintenance of an army of slaves and the yields were by

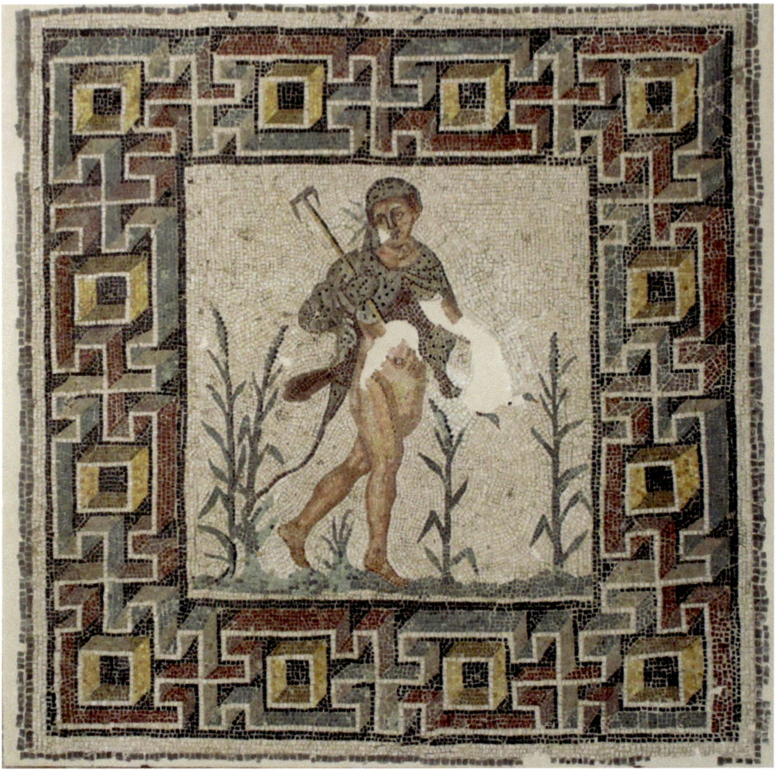

Fig. 6. Algiers, National Museum of Antiquities: Winter, from a mosaic of the Seasons (see p. 86). The Spirit of Winter is shown wearing a nebris (the skin of a fawn) and with a crown of reeds. He holds a pair of ducks (symbolic of winter hunting) and carries a two-pronged hoe, which is used in the same season to hoe between the vines.

no means as high as they could be. At the same time, the poverty of other settlers caused friction and unrest.

Nero (emperor 54–68), who cast a covetous eye on the power of these aristocrats, summoned the six family heads and had them put to death in order to lay hands on all their property and to add it to the imperial inheritance. In a less brutal fashion, legislative measures were taken by Vespasian (the *lex Manciana*), Trajan and Hadrian to promote the cultivation of every square inch of the land: peasants who, through their own efforts, bought into cultivation abandoned or previously uncultivated pieces of public land were given formal title to them. All of this led to positive improvements: the planting of vines and olives significantly increased production and the standard of living improved for ordinary people. Everyone could thus look forward to a better life, like the farmer of Mactar, who wrote proudly on his tombstone that, after working hard all his life, he had become owner of his property and had even held public office in his home town.

Grain and oil, the riches of Africa

If the agricultural output of Carthage was fairly balanced, involving both wheat, barley, grapes, olives, fruits and vegetables, it seems that the monoculture of wheat became the rule in the first century of the Roman occupation, as described by the Elder Pliny in his *Historia Naturalis*: 'The soil of Africa has been given by nature entirely to Ceres, while oil and wine are almost absent: the whole glory of the land is in its harvests.' It is true that cereals grow particularly well in these prolific soils, despite the poverty of rainfall. Pliny (again) cites yields of 150:1, while the most fertile soils elsewhere in the empire did not exceed 100:1; he reports a story of a lump of earth which was presented to the emperor because it had produced four hundred stems from a single grain!

Given that African wine and oil were despised for their poor quality, it was understood that the principal aim should be to develop the monoculture of wheat. This meant that Italy could retain a cost-effective production of wine and oil, while the *annona* (the state food subsidy for Rome) could be sustained largely from African grain. This service was responsible for the regular supply of grain to Rome – an essential prop to social stability – which it maintained through an army of functionaries, a fleet of ships and a huge organization. In the time of Augustus, for example, two hundred thousand citizens (a third of the free men) were registered to receive the free hand-outs, which have been estimated to have amounted to about 16,000 tons per month! It was Egypt that initially provided the bulk of the grain, though it was sometimes irregular because of climatic conditions; but the advantages of African grain rapidly became

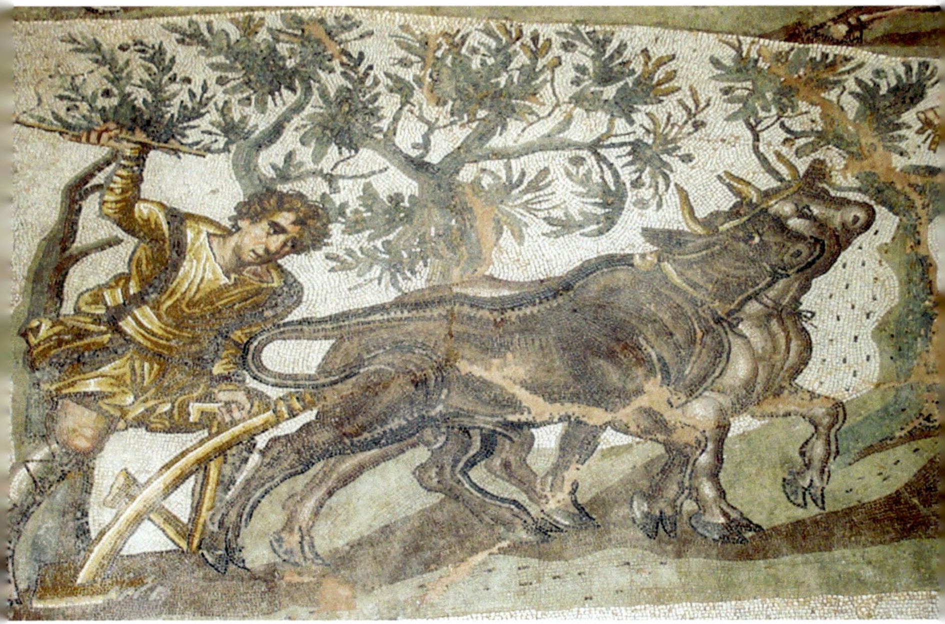

Fig. 7. Cherchel, Old Museum: ploughing in the seed beneath olive trees: detail from the mosaic of the Labours of the Fields (see p. 43).

apparent – large-scale production, reliable harvests, geographical proximity allowing a faster turn-round of the ships and lower transport costs. It has been calculated that up to a third of the grain requirement of Rome was satisfied by the African *annona* alone.

From the second century, the objectives of authority changed noticeably: the soils of the North, which had been over-exploited, began to be exhausted, while the many terrains previously unfit for cereal-growing were brought into cultivation in the mountainous and pre-desert zones as land-reclamation proceeded. A more appropriate agricultural policy was needed, and so a balanced polyculture of vineyards, cereals and olive groves was developed. Early-cropping fruits and vegetables were also grown, but for local consumption, while only a few luxury varieties, such as the jujube, pomegranate or truffle were exported.

African oil, on the other hand, rapidly established itself in empire-wide markets as a primary product, in the first place as a fuel for lighting, but also as a food product, once a more refined production process had improved the flavour. Processing plants of an industrial character were built on the farm estates: one of the most striking of these is at Bir Sgaoun, some 40 km to the S of Tébessa, which was built at the beginning of the third century AD (see fig. 8 and p. 288). The skeleton of this structure still stands, in the middle of nowhere, with massive blocks of dressed stone and flat lintels supported by arcades. Divided into four aisles some twenty metres long, the factory was equipped with crushing mills, six counterweighted presses and two settling tanks in a wholly functional unit. Many other traces of intensive olive cultivation may be seen on the high plateaux of Numidia and across Africa Proconsularis; the largest such establishment yet recorded, with seventeen presses, is in the hinterland of Lepcis Magna in Tripolitania.

Africans and the passion for literature

For we made selection of the Platonists, justly esteemed the noblest of the philosophers, because they had the wit to perceive that the human soul, immortal and rational, or intellectual, as it is, cannot be happy except by partaking of the light of that God by whom both itself and the world were made; and also that the happy life which all men desire cannot be reached by any who does not cleave with a pure and holy love to that one supreme good, the unchangeable God.

Saint Augustine, *City of God*, x.1, tr. M. Dods (1871)

The Africans did not differ greatly from inhabitants of other parts of the Roman Empire in terms of their occupations or their leisure activities, which they spent in hunting and at the baths, the arena and particularly the circus (for chariot races). They were distinguished, however, across all echelons of society by a singular appetite for literature – symbolized amongst other things by the fine public library at Thamugadi.

African literature held an eminent position in the Roman empire from the second century onwards. It could boast such prestigious practitioners as Florus, the orator Cornelius Fronto of Cirta (tutor to Marcus Aurelius and considered in his time to have been superior to Cicero), the jurist Salvius Julianus, Apuleius of Madauros, or indeed the pagan writers of late antiquity Aurelius Victor and Macrobius. There were also the great Christian writers Tertullian, Cyprian of Carthage and

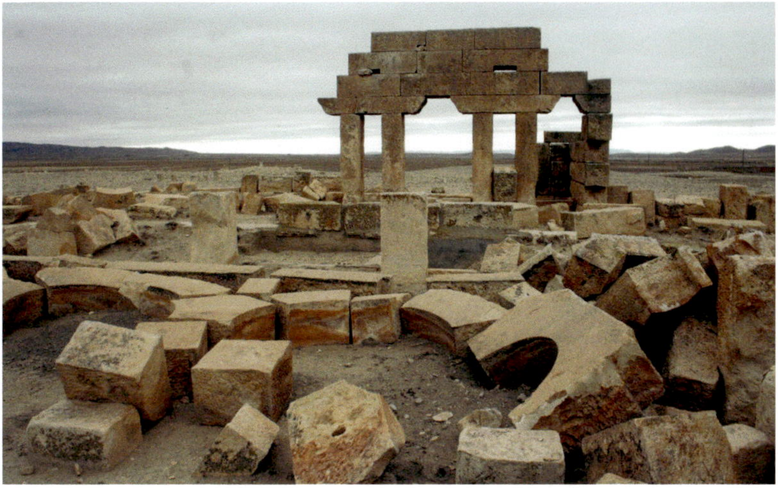

Fig. 8. Two surviving sets of oil-press uprights and fallen arcades of the oilery at Bir Sgaoun, S of Tébessa (see also p. 288).

Augustine of Hippo. The last-named, in particular, made reference – often appreciatively – to pagan writers; this was directly responsible for the respect in which ancient texts were held in the libraries of monasteries, thus contributing to the preservation of the Greco-Latin heritage. At the time when the intellectual triumph of Athens resulted in Greek becoming a threat to Latin culture, the Africans introduced new blood, breaking free of the rigid classical tongue and fostering a brilliant genre. The historian P. Monceaux has attempted to characterize this in the following terms: 'first of all, a richness of imagination, a sensitivity which is very lively but slightly morbid, and an acute awareness of the grand spectacles of nature. Then a mystic turn of mind often linked, in surprising contrast but already detectable in ancient Carthage, with much practical sense, a preoccupation with the useful and an obsessive determination to impart something, to persuade, to convert.' The style is very picturesque, with a sophisticated vocabulary, an undue enthusiasm for rare words, clever archaisms and complicated expressions which would have delighted the most pretentious stylist and a taste for puns which the greatest did not escape: Augustine himself is guilty of this when, for example, he describes Carthage (*Carthago*) as a sizzling 'frying-pan' (*sartago*) of shameful loves. Monceaux is again to the point: 'in sum, the style has plenty of punch, of depth, of imagery, but also a lot of exaggeration, a mania for hyperbole and plenty of bad taste.' This 'African baroque' – this mannerism which Juvenal called the *tumor africus* – had its attractions well beyond the provinces of Africa, finding imitators even in Severan Rome.

The people at large were not immune and it is touching to see the naïve popular expressions of admiration for the great authors and the body of classical literature. Numerous inscriptions include recognizable quotations, pieces 'in the style of …' and personal compositions: at Timgad a widower, Julius Silvanus, created a funerary garden for his wife, describing himself in a plaque on the wall as 'the Cicero of

Thabudeos'! Another remembered only the plays on words of the great advocate and filled the epitaph of his wife with allusions and puns in doubtful taste. Virgil, above all, enjoyed popular favour. We know that his poems were learnt by heart and his texts put to all kinds of uses: literary contests, bits of poetry based on his works, epigrams mixing hexameters from the Aeneid with topical verses. Quotations could be applied to all occasions, including the most banal, as in the inscription lauding the intervention of a procurator in the repair of a water-supply: the modest pipe is compared in Virgilian style to the cavern of a nymph! This popular culture was well understood by contemporaries, who were proud of it. Apuleius turns to the Africans and declares, 'I see amongst you in the whole city only cultivated people, who are all versed in all the sciences: children in how to acquire them, young men in how to display them and their elders in how to teach them.'

Christianity and the conflicts that came with it: Catholics, Donatists and Arians

In Africa, Christianity took hold with rapidity, as is graphically portrayed by a famous text of Tertullian, writing in 197:

We are but of yesterday, and by to-day are grown up, and overspread your empire; your cities, your islands, your forts, towns, assemblies, and your very camps, wards, companies, palace, senate, forum, all swarm with Christians. ... We could also make a terrible war upon you without arms, or fighting a stroke, by being so passively revengeful as only to leave you; for if such a numerous host of Christians should but retire from the empire into some remote region of the world, the loss of so many men of all ranks and degrees would leave a hideous gap, and a shameful scar upon the government; and the very evacuation would be abundant revenge. You would stand aghast at your desolation, and be struck dumb at the general silence and horror of nature, as if the whole world was departed. You would be at a loss for men to govern, and in the pitiful remains you would find more enemies than citizens.

(*Apologeticum*, chap. 37, tr. W. Reeve 1709)

For the empire as a whole, the formal turning-point was the Edict of Milan, issued in 313 jointly by the emperors Constantine and Licinius, which gave freedom of worship to Christians and no longer obliged them to do sacrifice to pagan gods.

The Donatist schism

Immediately before this, however, the steady expansion of the Church encountered a dramatic schism with the appearance of Donatism. This movement arose from the consecration in 311–12 of Caecilianus as bishop of Carthage. There was at the time a vicious debate within the established (i.e. 'Catholic') church over whether those who had compromised their standing – by handing over church treasures to the authorities during the persecutions of Diocletian a few years earlier – (*traditores*) should be readmitted and forgiven. Caecilianus was in favour of clemency, but those who were hostile (including the bishops of Numidia, who had not been consulted in his election) denounced his election as invalid on the basis that one of the consecrating bishops had been a *traditor*. The opposing party elected

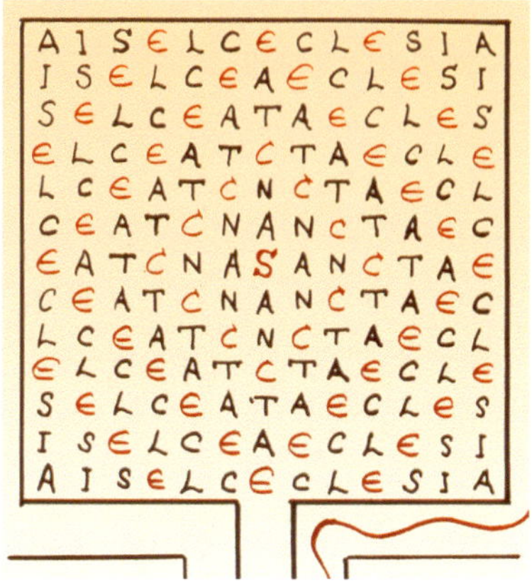

Fig. 9. Drawing of the lettering found in the centre of a labyrinth mosaic in a church at El Asnam (Castellum Tingitanum), dated to around 324 and now displayed in the Cathedral of Sacré Coeur in Algiers. Starting from the centre of the pattern, the words Sancta ec(c)lesia may be read in any horizontal and vertical combination, indicating the reach of the Church in every direction.

one Majorinus as bishop instead. Rome continued to recognize Caecilianus as bishop, but when Majorinus died within a year, he was succeeded by Donatus, who became the leader of the 'purist' cause and gave his name to the movement. A church council was held to resolve the debate at Arles in 314, where the Donatists were rejected. They appealed to the emperor and were again rejected in 316. During the debates, a theatrical coup was announced: justice showed that the accusation of treachery brought against the Catholic Church was a defamation, based on false documents, whereas the real apostates were the Donatists!

These revelations, which should have put an end to the schism, had no effect on its growth. Constantine declared that the Donatists were outlaws in 317, and then ordered their banishment and the seizure of their property. These measures only reinforced the conviction of the followers of Donatus that they were being persecuted by the 'Great Church' and that in this regard they were following in the footsteps of the early martyrs. Disconcerted by the continuation of the troubles, the emperor changed direction and re-established religious freedom by an Edict of Toleration in 321. Despite this, the advance of Donatism, seen as an anti-establishment movement, continued with ever greater vigour; its popular acclaim was augmented by an alliance with a violent group of disaffected agricultural workers, the *circumcelliones*.

In 347, the sending by the emperor Constans of officials charged with re-establishing the unity of the Church only inflamed the situation: the obligatory merging of the churches resulted in a religious war and in serial massacres, with each side accusing the other of the worst atrocities. Donatus was exiled and died in 355, and this seemed to bring an end to the movement. A few years later, however, the religious environment was drastically changed with the accession to power of a pagan emperor, Julian the Apostate. He restored the Donatists to their rights (in order deliberately to create dissension amongst the Christians) and the sect once again flourished under his reign (360–363).

In the time of Augustine, who became bishop of Hippo Regius in 395 when around half the population was loyal to Donatism, the quarrel took a more theological turn. Through his writings and sermons, he turned the issue decisively to concern the sanctity of the sacraments. In 405, a synod at Carthage appealed to Honorius for penal sanctions against the Donatists, which the emperor approved. In 411 a

The *circumcelliones*

This movement (possibly deriving its name from 'those who hang around the grain-stores' – *circum cellas* – i.e. seasonal workers) seems to have sprung from the poor who worked on the country estates. Forming themselves into roving bands, these exploited people took advantage of the religious struggles between the Donatists and the Catholics to hold landowners to ransom, to humiliate or mistreat members of the Catholic clergy and to ravage the countryside with blood and fire. These 'soldiers of Christ' (as they called themselves) were sometimes encouraged or even instructed by Donatist bishops. Mystics to the point of suicide, they accompanied their attacks and slaughter with cries of Deo laudes ('Praise the Lord', in the same manner as has been heard more recently in another tongue: 'Allahu akbar'). Saint Augustine reported that this cry was more feared than the roaring of a lion. But, as even their opponents admitted, these poor wretches set out to defend the poor and the oppressed: 'They hate their overlords and the rich,' wrote Saint Optatus of Milev (*De schismate Donatistarum*), 'And when they encounter a lord mounted on a carriage and surrounded by his slaves, they make him get down, load the slaves into the carriage and make the lord run on foot. They claim that they have come to restore equality to the Earth and they summon the slaves to freedom.' This perhaps explains why, having been massacred by the public authorities, around 340, the insurgents were venerated as martyrs. At Jebel Nif en-Nser near Ain M'lila (43 km to the S of Constantine), at the foot of a cliff, have been found 65 tombstones of persons (possibly *circumcelliones*) who had thrown themselves into the void in pursuit of martyrdom. Yet other fanatics preferred to drown themselves in lakes or to burn themselves to death on pyres which they had themselves lighted. Some of the more sophisticated sought to give a more obvious sheen of martyrdom to their deaths. They went unarmed to attack provincial governors on tour, so that they would be killed by the accompanying military escort. Certain governors countered their guile by arresting them and subsequently releasing them, thus depriving them of the glorious end they sought. Sometimes, on one of the main roads, they would approach an armed traveller and force him to kill them, on pain of being killed himself if he did not oblige.

great council was summoned at Carthage itself and was attended by around 280 bishops on either side. No agreement was reached, but the imperial commissioner declared the Donatists vanquished and their properties confiscated. It was barely twenty years later, however, that both Catholics and Donatists alike were persecuted equally by new masters, the Vandals, who followed the Arian heresy.

The Arian heresy

The religious adherence of the Vandals (see below) is named after Arius, a priest who lived in Alexandria at the beginning of the fourth century and who in 320 propagated a doctrine that was more philosophical than theological. Based on the subordinationist writings of Paul of Samosata and Origen, Arius defended the idea that the three persons of the Trinity cannot be equal or assimilated to one another. God the Father, uncreated and unbegotten, is alone eternal, whereas the

Son, begotten of the Father, is not eternal but had a finite beginning. Through this radical monotheism, Arius, seeking thus a logical explanation of the mystery of the Incarnation, arrived at the necessary subordination of the Son to the Father, who had existed before him.

To what extent the Christian community as a whole concerned itself with (or understood) such subtleties may be doubted, but they gave rise to heated debates. The Council of Nicaea in 325 gave rise to the Nicene creed, which asserted the consubstantiality of Father and Son (that they are 'of one being') and the error of those who asserted any difference between them. Arius was condemned and sent into exile, but the controversy grew, drawing in philosophers and theologians from East and West to argue over more and more subtle shades of meaning: the famous Eusebius of Caesarea, for instance, argued with Marcellus of Ancyra in distinguishing divine persons from divine actions. The situation was also complicated following the death of Constantine, for his son and successor, Constantius II (337–361) favoured the Arians. The accession to power in 361 of Julian the Apostate encouraged all dissensions in the Church: in the West the anti-Arians, under the leadership of energetic bishops such as Hilary of Arles, followed the Nicene creed, which attained the ascendancy, while in the East the Arians profited from the fragmentation of their opponents to strengthen their influence. The emperor Theodosius, who came to power in 378, was an adherent of the Nicene creed and, by means of a council held in Constantinople in 381, succeeded in obtaining general acceptance of a revised version of the creed of 325. This resolved the issue for a while. However, the Germanic peoples in the North had been evangelized by an Arian Goth, Ulfila. As a result, the Vandals considered the Arian faith as a distinctive attribute of their race, and were particularly repressive of both Catholics and Donatists in Africa.

The history of research

Prior to the French invasion in 1830, only occasional travellers ventured into the Maghreb (the term used by the Arabs to designate North Africa west of the Syrtic Gulf); the interest of their accounts for archaeology is sadly limited, since they mainly had an eyes for geography or natural history. The first to give an account of antiquities was Thomas Shaw, an Englishman who lived in Algiers for thirteen years as 'chaplain to the English factory' (1720–33). He identified Tipasa (Tefessad), described the ruins of Cherchel as 'almost as extensive as those of Carthage' and published a work at Oxford in 1738 (see fig. 10) in which he argued that the customs and traditions of the Arabs of his time were a survival from the Classical period: 'The Arabs retain a great many of those manners and customs which we read of in sacred and profane history. For, if we except their religion, they are the very same people that they were two or three thousand years ago' – a concept whose popularity has only recently begun to diminish.

Following the capture of Algiers, and once the military demands of the conquest had been satisfied, it was the military which began to record the archaeological riches of the country. Many officers, educated in the Classical tradition, found this a pleasant way to pass the time, like the Captain De Montgravier who mentioned in one of his letters the archaeological researches which he sometimes embarked

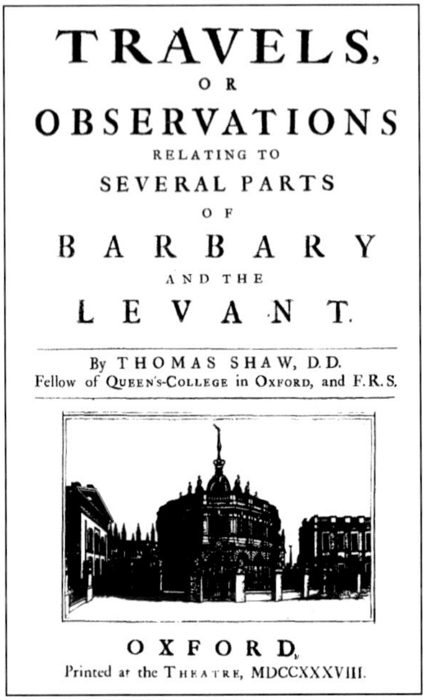

TRAVELS,
OR
OBSERVATIONS
RELATING TO
SEVERAL PARTS
OF
BARBARY
AND THE
LEVANT.

By THOMAS SHAW, D.D.
Fellow of QUEEN'S-COLLEGE in OXFORD, and F.R.S.

OXFORD,
Printed at the THEATRE, MDCCXXXVIII.

Fig. 10. The title page of Thomas Shaw's work, dedicated to King George I.

upon 'to enliven the leisure of the camp.' At the same time, other motivations may be detected in the political wish to find a symbolic justification for the presence of the French. Rome and its heritage – pacification and civilization of tribes described as 'retarded' – are never far from their discourse and statements of intent: '[archaeological] science can contribute to the task of civilization which is beginning in Africa under the protection of our arms ... I have felt myself the benefits ... of the history of Roman colonization in this land, of the institutions that they created and of the relationships which they established between themselves and the natives,' said Maréchal Soult in 1833. Military and scientific interests were intertwined, sometimes so closely that the dispatch of General Négrier on the taking of Tébessa gives an account not only of the movements of his troops, but also of the antiquities visible in the captured town. This activity was not always documented as one would have wished, when irreparable destruction was carried out in order to build barracks on ancient sites which offered 'an immense quantity of ancient material, ideally suited to new constructions.' The scholars who travelled in the wagons of the army worked hard, however, alongside many soldiers bitten by the archaeological bug: memoirs, descriptions and notes were made on many sites met with on their advance, such as Lambaesis, Sitifis, Hippo and Calama. Engravings and sketches were published, *objets d'art* and antiquities brought to light and hundreds of inscriptions recorded.

At a time when the protection of heritage was a low priority, this harvest generated a certain covetousness, with some generals going so far as to offer capitals or carved reliefs to their friends. On the other hand, Captain Delamare was sending antiquities back to the Louvre (which was far from keen to receive them) for their protection. The Duc d'Orléans went so far as planning to dismantle the triumphal arch of Caracalla on the site of Cuicul (Djémila: p. 120), stone by stone, and to rebuild it in Paris! Many shiploads of mosaics – for instance, that of Amphitrite and Neptune from Constantine – arrived in the Louvre, along with inscribed blocks and carved reliefs. These awaited the creation of the Algerian Museum in Paris, decided on by the Minister in 1845. Voices of protest were, however, soon heard: Adrien Berbrugger who was secretary to General Clauzel, a *chartiste* (historian and palaeographer) by training, and future curator of the library and museum of Algiers, complained that 'Africa, on becoming French territory, should not be stripped of its archaeological treasures as if it was still a pashalik of the Ottoman Porte.' In fact, the protection and development of the most notable discoveries began to take shape with the gathering of collections into places where they were accessible, both to researchers and to the curious. In Sétif, a hundred and forty-three architectural or inscribed blocks were lined up along a promenade, while romantic *jardins de vestiges* ('gardens of antiquities') were created at Guelma, Hammam Meskoutine, Tébessa and elsewhere. On the initiative of new learned societies, the first public museums were founded: at Algiers in 1858, in the theatre at Philippeville (now Skikda) in 1859, in the town hall of Constantine in 1877 and in Tébessa in the same year, where the surviving ancient temple was refurbished by Father Delapart. Some rich landowners, such as M. de Trémault at Tipasa or M. de Lhotellerie at Cherchel, made presentations of the discoveries made on their land, before handing them over to the community. The museum at Cherchel was not at all acceptable to the Inspector of Historic Monuments M. La Blanchère, who shrilled during a visit in 1890, 'The museum of Cherchel is a heap of junk in a wretched yard, apart from a few superb sculptures collected up by chance and lumped together like rocks in a miserable barn which provides a bare minimum of shelter.' Curiously, the great city of Oran, undoubtedly more concerned with its commercial development than with culture, was the last to establish a learned society: it opened its museum only in 1891, thirty-three years after Algiers.

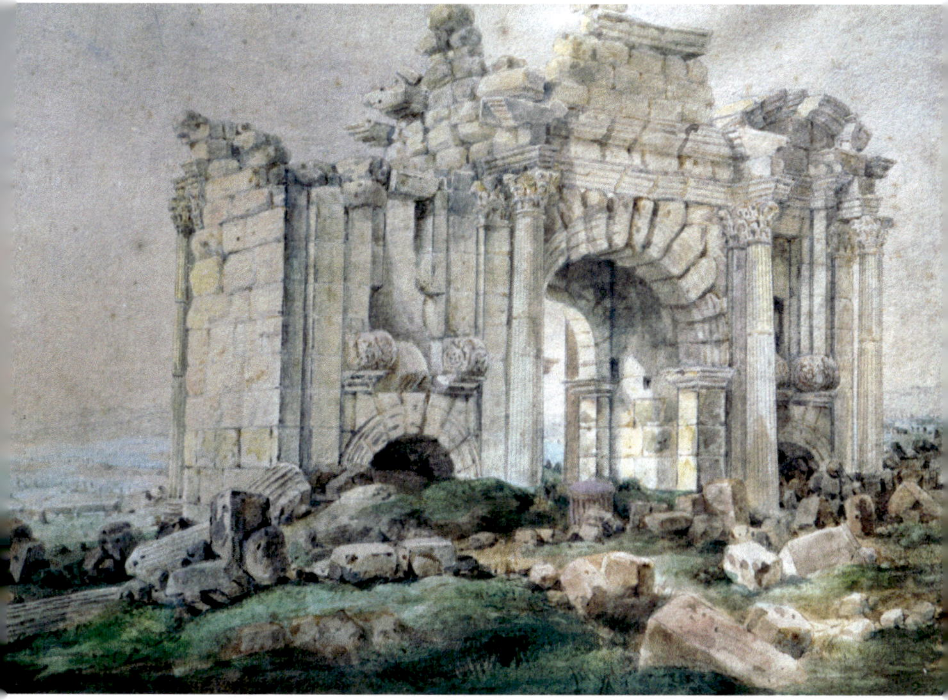

Fig. 11. The 'Arch of Trajan' at Thamugadi (Timgad) at the time of its discovery.

In parallel with the development of these repositories, publications multiplied: catalogues of museums, inventories, monographs on sites, excavation reports – all aspects were treated with greater or lesser enthusiasm, depending on the level of understanding of the writers. The settlement of the countryside alone is almost completely absent from these articles, while epigraphic studies were prolific. Citing the richness of the epigraphic record brought to light in Africa since the beginning of the colonization, the prestigious Academy of Berlin commissioned G. Wilmans, in 1875, to compile volume VIII of the *Corpus Inscriptionum Latinarum*; the work was completed by the great scholar Theodor Mommsen (with the collaboration of René Cagnat) and was published in 1881. This was followed shortly after the end of the First World War by the publication by the French alone (essentially S. Gsell) of *Inscriptions latines de l'Algérie*, at a time when the previous type of international collaboration was no longer possible.

The administration of the antiquities also gradually took shape. After a simple reconnaissance of historic sites in 1847 which had no immediate follow-up, the *Inspection générale de Monuments historiques et des Musées archéologiques* was created in 1854. This was subsequently split between the *Service des Monuments historiques* (1880) and the *Direction des Antiquités du Gouvernement général* (1923). The remit of these bodies was the maintenance and restoration of the monuments, together with the conduct of the large-scale excavations which began at this time. A number of the major sites, such as Timgad, Lambaesis, Djémila and Tipasa were systematically explored and exposed from 1880 onwards. The most significant

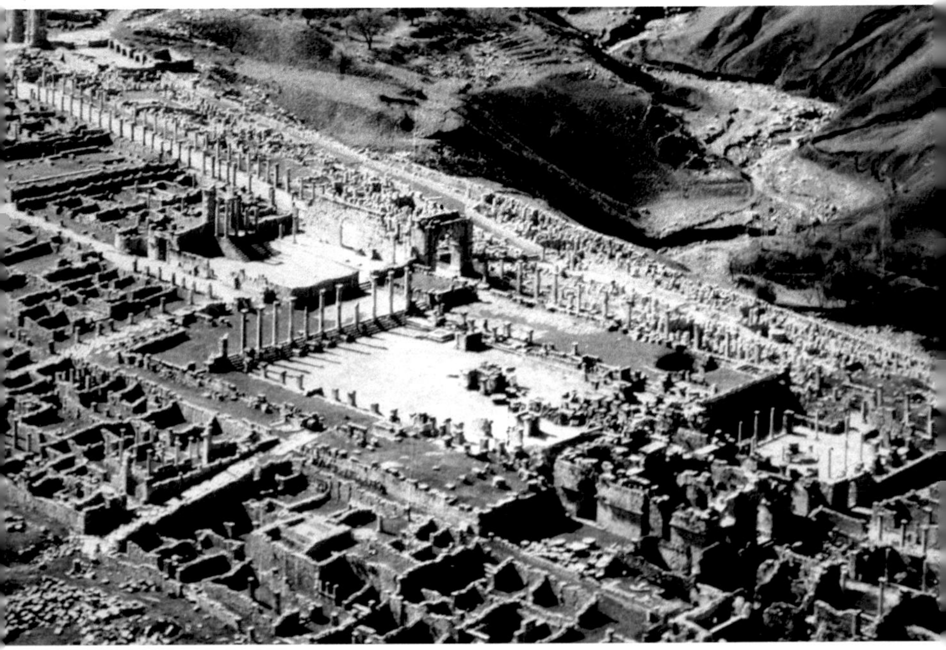

Fig. 12. An aerial view of the excavations at Cuicul (Djémila) in the 1950s.

individual in Algerian archaeology from the 1890s onwards was Stéphane Gsell, whose many publications are still of fundamental importance. His name will be referred to repeatedly in this book. The Service des Monuments and the Direction des Antiquités continued to function until the granting of independence in 1962. In due course, the young Republic passed a law in 1967 which placed the natural and cultural heritage under the guardianship of the State and created an executive body, the *Direction des musées, de l'archéologie, des monuments et des sites historiques.* On the basis of this legislation, the Direction embarked on a series of researches into areas which were considered to have been neglected in the colonial period: the monuments of the Libyco-Punic period (the Medracen, the mausoleum at Le Khroub, the royal mausoleum known as the 'Tombeau de la Chrétienne', the mausoleum of Beni Rhénane) and the sites of the Islamic period (Qala'at Bani Hammad, Tlemcen, Agadir, Tahert, Sédrata). In the decade 1970–80, the authorities also set in place a programme conforming to the National Charter with the aim of 'taking account of the necessity to re-write the national history and to rescue the remains which are visible in the towns and the countryside.' Today, the archaeological heritage is managed by the *Direction du Patrimoine* of the Ministère de la Culture. The Ministry has two public institutions under its supervision: *The Office de Gestion et exploitation des Biens Culturels* (OGEBC) which manages archaeological parks, historic monuments and their museums; and the *Centre National de la Recherche en Archéologie* (CNRA) which is in charge of leading scientific research.

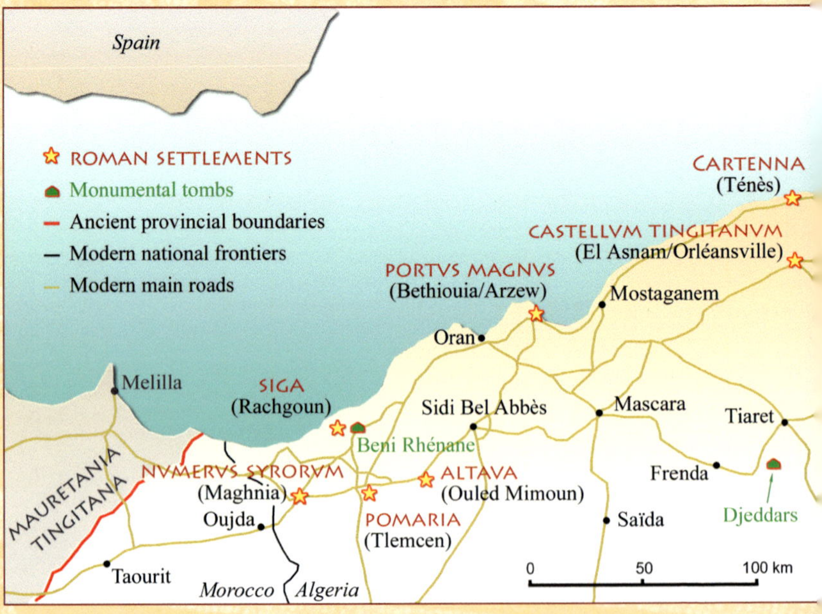

Fig. 13. Mauretania Caesariensis in the third century AD.

2. MAURETANIA CAESARIENSIS

The monuments described in this chapter are predominantly in the eastern part of this vast territory. Those in the western part are more widely separated and have been less extensively explored; they generally do not have enough to offer the tourist to justify the long journeys to see them on their own account. Mention is therefore limited here to only a few highlights.

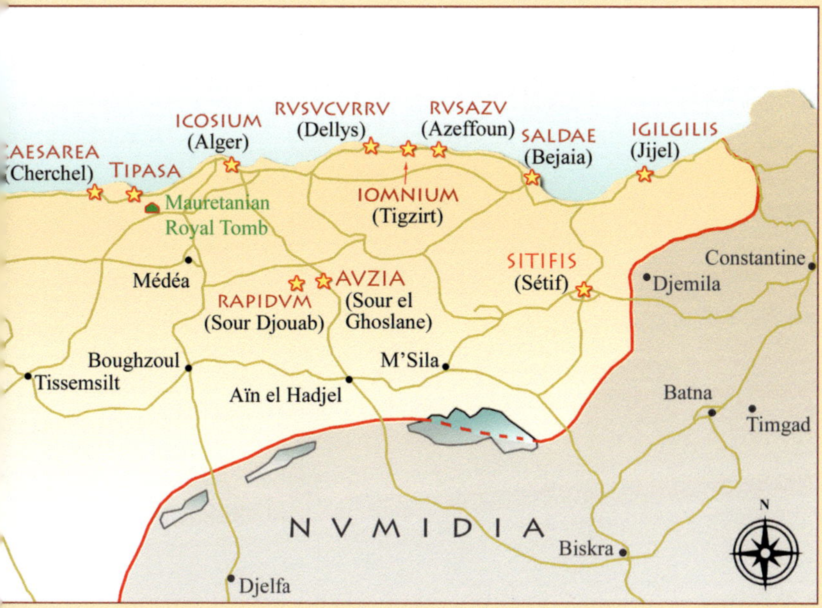

THE MAUSOLEUM OF BENI RHÉNANE

Just 4 km from the coast to the N of Tlemcen and close to the mouth of the Oued Tafna lie the meagre remains of *Siga*, the capital of the kingdom of Syphax. This king, who was initially an ally of the Romans during the Second Punic War, joined the Carthaginians in opposing the landing of Scipio; following his defeat near Cirta in 203, part of his kingdom was granted to Masinissa. The wife of Syphax was Sophonisba, daughter of the Carthaginian Hasdrubal; after the capture of her husband by the Romans, she married Masinissa, to whom she had been engaged before her first marriage and with whom she had always been in love. When Scipio Africanus insisted that the vanquished queen should be made to appear in his triumph in Rome, Masinissa chose to sacrifice her rather than to offend his powerful allies. The historian Livy recounts that he sent Sophonisba a cup of poison which she drank, declaring 'I accept this wedding gift.'

On high ground across the river from the site of Siga and to the N of the village of Beni Rhénane, excavations in 1960–61 revealed the remains of a large hexagonal obelisk-tomb built up in ashlar masonry, which must originally have been some 30 m high. (See figs. 14 and 15.) It was embellished with semi-columns with Ionic capitals; ten linked funerary chambers excavated in the rock beneath had vaulted ceilings, but had been robbed in antiquity and visited again in the Middle Ages. The closest known parallel is Mausoleum B at Sabratha in Libya (dated to the early second century BC). The few identifiable fragments of ancient pottery found in the vaults ranged in date between the end of the third century BC and the end of the second; the well-preserved surfaces of the tumbled blocks suggested that the monument

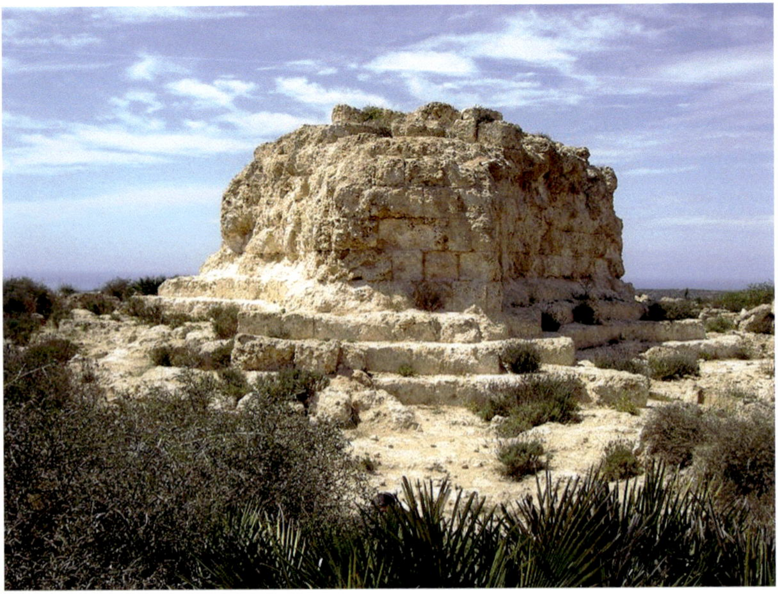

Fig. 14. The remaining core of the mausoleum of Beni Rhénane.

had then been deliberately demolished. It is possible that this was the tomb of Vermina, the son of Syphax, who died in 191 BC, and that it was dismantled when the kingdom of the Masaesyli fell under the control of Numidia (at the end of the second century?).

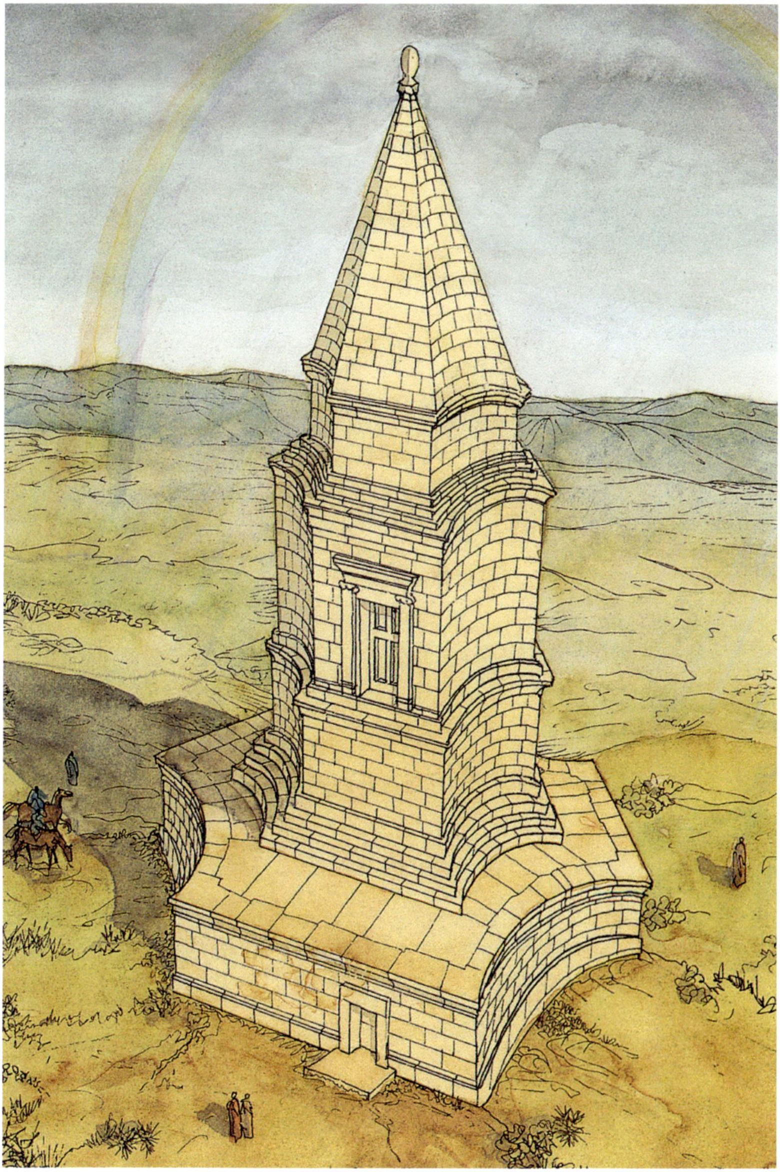

Fig. 15. A reconstruction drawing by J.-C. Golvin of the original appearance of the monument.

PORTUS MAGNUS (Bethioua, formerly Saint-Leu)

Portus Magnus was built on a cliff above the sea, 40 km to the E of Oran: the 'Great Port' that the name refers to is presumed to have been the Gulf of Arzew. Mentioned by Pliny the Elder and by Pomponius Mela in the first century AD, recorded by El-Bekri in the eleventh century and seen by Thomas Shaw in 1743, the site now lies almost a kilometre from the water's edge, immediately behind the coastal petrochemical complex. It is partly covered by the eastern edge of the village of Bethioua. Excavations in 1950–63 exposed a forum of 50 x 40 m with stuccoed columns and cisterns in the corners beneath the porticoes. The square was paved only in part, the remainder consisting of an artificial levelling of the natural rock surface. On the W side of the forum can be made out a little *curia* in the form of a rectangular building with a projecting apse in the middle of the W side. It was once paved with mosaic and its walls were veneered with marble. A temple of unknown dedication has been identified behind the *curia*, and another larger one 120 m to the W of the forum. There are also some traces of a defensive wall and, to the E of the forum, remains of houses along a street. Elsewhere were found two mosaics, now in the museum of Oran: a Triumph of Dionysus and a large panel of mythological scenes.

Finds of pottery have shown that the site was occupied before the establishment of Roman rule, though the excavated remains belong to the Roman period. The inscriptions found on the site come to an end after the middle of the third century, and we know of no bishop from Portus Magnus attending church councils in the fourth century or later. It may be that Diocletian abandoned this part of Mauretania towards the end of the third century – but the archaeological evidence is still too meagre for us to be sure one way or the other.

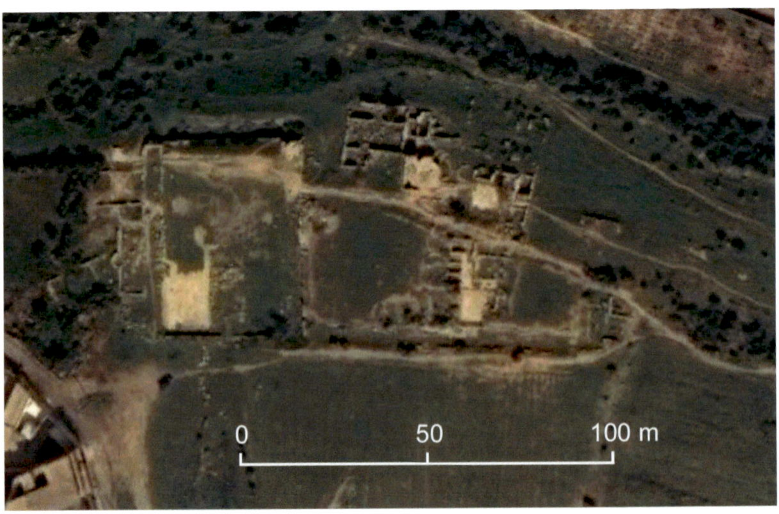

Fig. 16. Satellite image of the excavations on the edge of Bethioua, from Google Earth (dated 16 March 2015).

THE DJEDDARS

This singular group of monuments lies 250 km to the SW of Algiers, between Frenda and Tiaret. It is composed of thirteen mausolea attributed to the fifth and sixth centuries AD, a surprisingly late period. They seem to represent the last expression of the line of great monumental tombs that starts with the Numidian bazinas and includes the Medracen (p. 166) and the Mauretanian Royal Tomb (p. 75). The mausolea have square bases, above which rise low pyramids, faced in dressed stone (sometime reused); some have enclosing walls and additional structures. They are found in two separate cemeteries: the northerly group on Djebel Lakhdar (Djeddars A, B and C) are attributed to the late fifth century and are the earlier examples; the second group, of ten mausolea (D to M), is situated further to the S on Djebel Araoui and is thought to have been built about a century later.

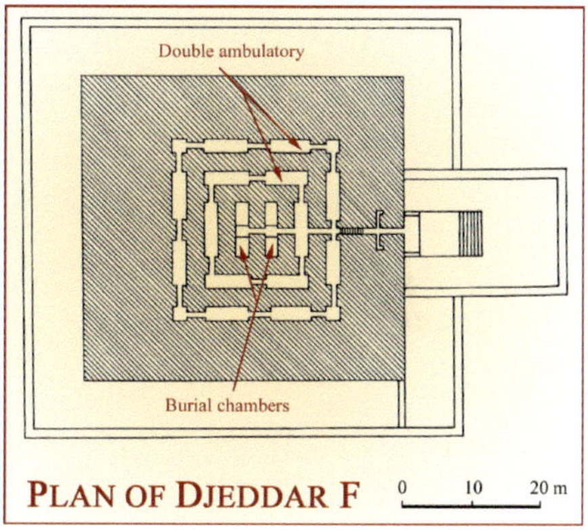

Fig. 17. Plan of Djeddar F.

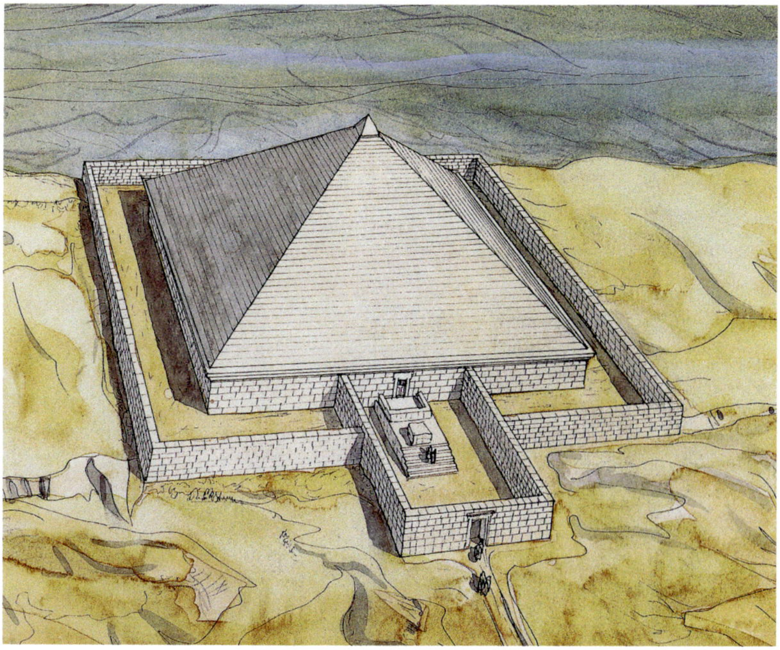

Fig. 18. Reconstruction drawing by J.-C. Golvin of Djeddar F.

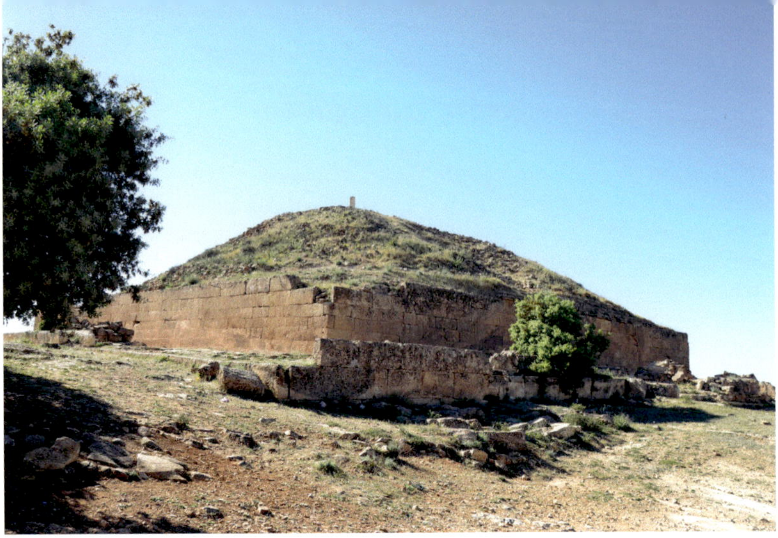

Fig. 19. Djeddar A.

Within the central core of each tomb was a funerary chamber surrounded by a complex of corridors and rooms, the purpose of which is unclear: chapels, associated burials? See the drawings of Djeddar F (figs. 17, 18). The façades are simple, with a false cornice and a few rare decorative elements in low relief distributed irregularly (reused?): animals (fig. 20), hunting scenes and Christian symbols (on Djeddar A). The tombs have all been robbed, depriving any investigators of clear evidence of date or of the identity of the occupants; these must, however, be the tombs of local Moorish chiefs or princes (at least partly Christianized).

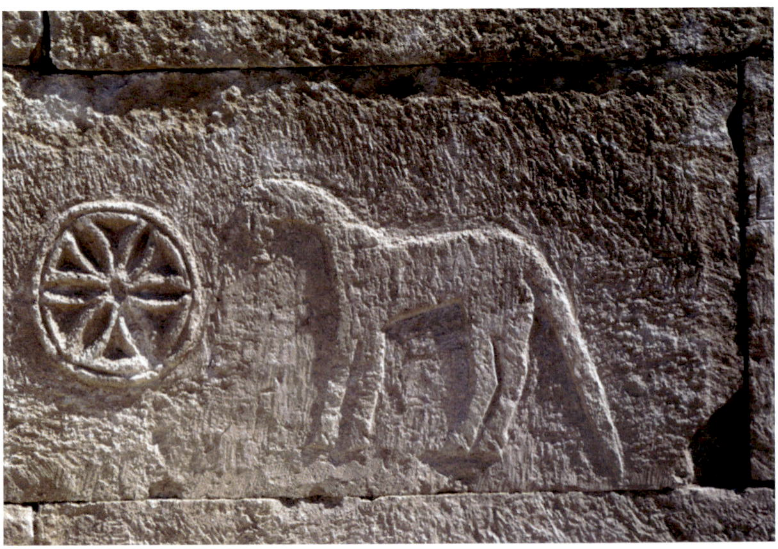

Fig. 20. Djeddar A: horse and rosette in low relief.

CAESAREA (Cherchel)

When at Caesarea in Mauretania I was dissuading the people from that civil, or worse than civil, war which they called Caterva (for it was not fellow-citizens merely, but neighbors, brothers, fathers and sons even, who, divided into two factions and armed with stones, fought annually at a certain season of the year for several days continuously, every one killing whomsoever he could), I strove with all the vehemence of speech that I could command to root out and drive from their hearts and lives an evil so cruel and inveterate; it was not, however, when I heard their applause, but when I saw their tears, that I thought I had produced an effect. For the applause showed that they were instructed and delighted, but the tears that they were subdued. And when I saw their tears I was confident even before the event proved it, that this horrible and barbarous custom (which had been handed down to them from their fathers and their ancestors of generations long gone by and which like an enemy was besieging their hearts, or rather had complete possession of them) was overthrown.

Saint Augustine, *On Christian Doctrine*, bk. IV, ch. 24, 53 (translation from P. Schaff, and H. Wace, *A Select Library of the Nicene and post-Nicene Fathers of the Christian Church*: Second series. Oxford and New York 1890).

It was because of a particular aspect of its geography – an islet lying a few tens of metres off the coast – that the site of Cherchel was noticed at a very early date by Phoenician sailors. The archaeologist G. Vuillemot discovered there Punic pottery of the fifth century BC, demonstrating its use as a staging-post or market. The African coastline is, on the whole, so inhospitable that this modest shelter was judged sufficient to warrant a permanent settlement, although the site was not particularly favourable either to commerce (being the outlet of no land route) or to urban development (it is cut off from the rich plains of the Chélif by a mountain ridge). The name of the settlement is first recorded in a source of the fourth century BC, the *Periplus* of Pseudo-Scylax. This was a portolan or mariner's guide, listing anchorages and coastal resources): it includes a promontory, a town and a port by the name of *Ioliou*, surely a corruption of *Iol*.

We know almost nothing of its initial layout – all we have is the location of a necropolis, on Cap Tizerine – but the town must have been of sufficient importance, and its advantages sufficiently obvious, for Bocchus to have made it one of his capitals. This Moorish king took up arms alongside his son-in-law Jugurtha, against the Romans. Twice defeated by Marius, he entered into talks with Sulla and agreed to hand over Jugurtha in 106 BC. The reward for his treason was the territory of the Masaesyli: thus Iol became one of the most important cities of Mauretania.

The most memorable resident of Iol was, however, Juba II, son of Juba I who was defeated by the Romans and committed suicide in 46 BC. This prince was deported to Italy at about the age of five, and was brought up carefully by Octavian (later Augustus) to espouse a deep affection for Rome. His patron, whose goodwill he had earned, had him married to Cleopatra Selene (daughter of Mark Anthony and the famous Cleopatra VII) and bestowed on him, around 30 BC, a kingdom composed of the two Mauretanias and of part of Gaetulia (an ill-defined area to the S of Mauretania, supposedly occupied by the nomadic *Gaetuli*). Juba II then reorganised the old city of Iol, the necropolis of which was partly abandoned, to create a new city of refined urban design and grandiose scale: the king named it *Caesarea* in honour of Augustus Caesar. One of the longest defensive circuits of the Roman world enclosed an area of 370 hectares, composed of the coastal plateau and the surrounding hills, not unlike the plan of certain Hellenistic cities, such as Ptolemais in Cyrenaica. The intersections of the grid plan can be made out from the junctions in the centre and in the eastern part of the plateau, where the streets cross one another at right angles, following axes aligned parallel to and at right-angles to the coast. Nothing was spared in the adornment of the city (shown by the surviving statuary) and in equipping it from the outset with all the facilities of a great city of the period. The monumental programme is characteristic of the process of 'Romanisation': a theatre (contemporary with the Theatre of Marcellus in Rome), an amphitheatre with a very curious rectangular central arena, the provision of a lighthouse for the port, perhaps also a circus – all of these were built during a very short space of time, demonstrating (if it were necessary) the dedication of Juba II. Juba enjoyed a very long reign; he was learned and widely read, and compiled a miscellany (of which virtually nothing survives, though it was extensively quoted by other writers) written in Greek on such diverse topics as the histories of Libya, Assyria and Arabia, with essays on painting, dramatic art, physiology and synonymy.

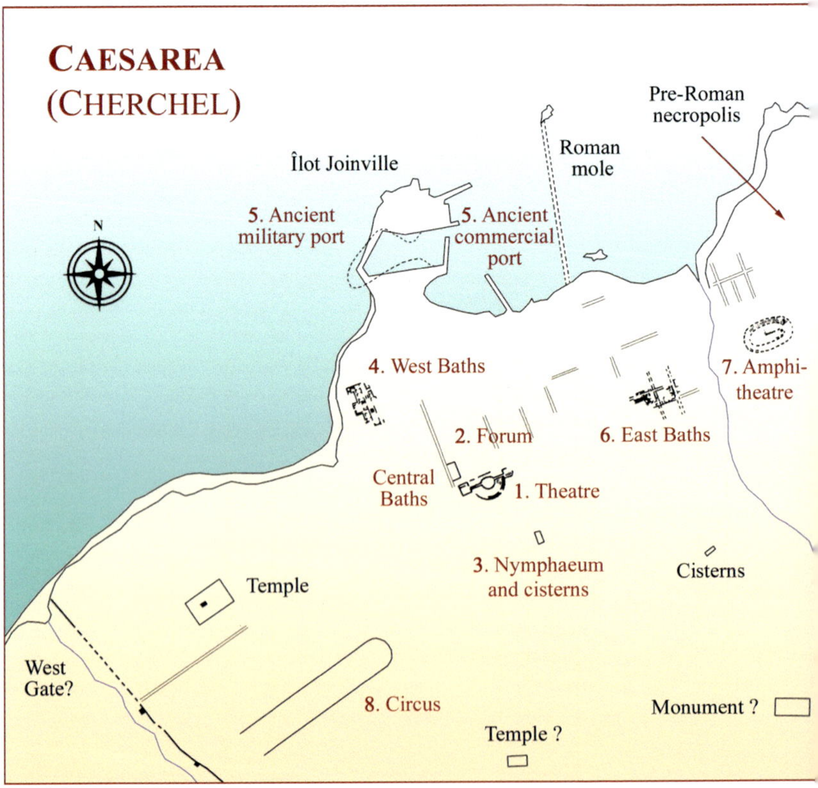

Juba died in AD 23, shortly after adopting his son Ptolemy as joint ruler. Ptolemy, of weak character and mediocre intelligence, provoked the enmity of Caligula by his ostentatious excess and his vanity, thus hastening his downfall. An imperial policy which now sought full annexation led the emperor to hasten a promised succession: he had Ptolemy assassinated in August 40, and this brought the kingdom of Mauretania to an end. In 42 Caligula's successor, Claudius, created the new province of *Mauretania Caesariensis* and confirmed Caesarea as its capital, with the status of *colonia*. Now populated with administrators and troops, the city also experienced an important development of its port facilities, sheltering merchant ships in its commercial port – protected by a new jetty on the east side – and the African Squadron of the fleet in a basin laid out behind the islet. It is, however, difficult when looking today at the modest fishing harbour of Cherchel, to imagine with Stéphane Gsell that Caesarea could once have been the second port of Africa after Carthage.

One has glimpses, rather than a full understanding, of the physiognomy of the city under the high empire. Apart from the West Baths, which can be attributed to the end of the second century, the successive phases of modification, embellishment or enlargement have not always been established in detail. These changes concern particularly the public monuments inherited from Juba II. The theatre and amphitheatre were both enlarged and the defences were refurbished; the circus acquired a triumphal arch in the Severan period, while the forum was renovated at the same time. The aqueduct on the E side of the city, perhaps built in the first years of the Roman administration, was improved during the second century. The city was certainly prosperous: the decurions (the principal magistrates) at the beginning of the third century boasted in an inscription of the 'splendour of their homeland.' A good part of this prosperity must be linked to the development of the land around the city: the studies of the archaeologist Philippe Leveau have shed light on the organisation of the surrounding countryside, with a dense network of farms, some specialising in olive cultivation.

In the year 217, a native of Caesarea, M. Opellius Macrinus, briefly became emperor of Rome. He was the Prefect of the Praetorian Guard under Caracalla, and arranged the emperor's assassination

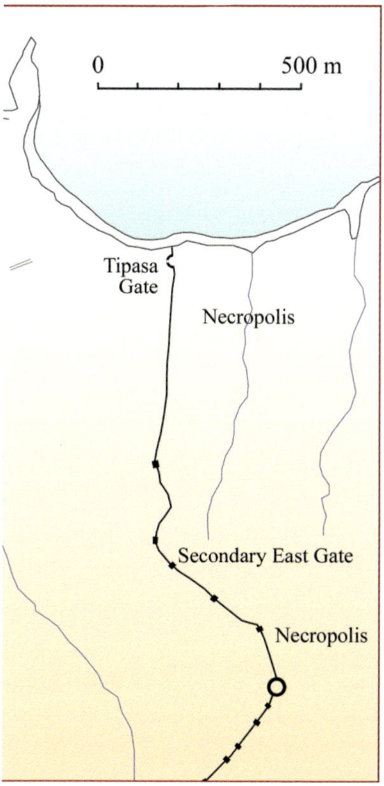

Fig. 21. Caesarea (Cherchel): disposition of ancient monuments.

in order to protect his own life. Macrinus then ruled, together with his son Diadumenianus, for just over a year before he too was overthrown. Both were executed.

This prosperity must have persisted until the early fourth century, despite administrative reforms and religious disputes; but it was seriously damaged by the revolt of Firmus, a Moorish chieftain, who invested and sacked the city in 371 or 372 (see p. 32). Ammianus Marcellinus described the city (probably with exaggeration) as totally devastated and the prefect of Rome Symmachus recorded an appeal by the inhabitants for a remission of taxes 'so that the exchequer should not complete the work of Firmus.' Caesarea was still a provincial capital when it was visited by Saint Augustine in 418, on the occasion of a dispute with the Donatist bishop Emeritus. The saint witnessed a curious local custom, the annual *caterva*, in which two parties of citizens pelted each other with stones! (See the quotation at the head of this section.)

After the Vandal period, Caesarea became the capital of a Byzantine province and the seat of a military command. Following the Arab conquest in the seventh century, the city must have dwindled away, though it probably never disappeared completely. The next description is that of the Arab historian Ibn Haukal, who wrote in the tenth century that 'Cherchel is a city of great antiquity; it is now in ruins, but its port survives. One can see there the ruins of ancient buildings, together with some colossal structures and stone idols.' Muslim refugees from Andalusia in 1492 revived the settlement, and in 1518 the Ottoman Turks built a fort (which no longer exists). There are still some fifteenth-century town houses, and many buildings incorporate large squared blocks from the Roman period.

EXPLORING THE TOWN

As Gsell warned in his guidebook of 1926, it is in the Museum of Cherchel that the glory of Caesarea lives on. 'The site of Iol-Caesarea,' he wrote, 'has never been abandoned. Many of its ancient buildings have been destroyed over the centuries in the search for building material; others have become buried beneath houses, gardens, vines, vegetable beds … But the ruins from which one can recover statues, mosaics, architectural fragments and inscriptions can rarely be explored in their entirety and kept accessible. There is no point in dreaming of uncovering vast complexes: Caesarea will never be reborn like Cuicul (Djémila) or Thamugadi (Timgad).' Some ninety years later, this statement is more true than ever.

The defences

Constructed by Juba II, the walls of Caesarea were 4,460 m long and protected an area of 370 ha, including several hills. The extent of this perimeter – one of the longest in Africa – is already impressive, but if one accepts, as suggested by Gsell, that the defences extended also along the coast, one arrives at a figure of 7,000 m, the same length as the walls of Rome in the Augustan period. Juba II was therefore doubly honouring Augustus, both by the choice of the name *Caesarea* and by ostentatiously mimicking the capital of the empire. (He was, however, also making best use of the lie of the land by placing the walls on the crests of the enclosing ridges.)

The wall varied in thickness (from 1.50 to 4.70 m) and incorporated some forty towers, mostly square, but sometimes round or octagonal. On the south side, three massive circular bastions reinforced the wall at strategic points, while six gates provided passage for roads leading east towards Tipasa and Aquae Calidae (Hammam Righa), west towards Gunugu (Gouraya) and south towards Zucchabar (Miliana).

The defences were refurbished in the middle of the second century, when those of Tipasa were constructed, and restored several times in the second half of the third century. In 371, Firmus dismantled part of the circuit, following which it was demolished by the Vandals.

Notable sections of the wall can still be seen on the surrounding hills, as can the South Gate – the only one to have survived. This is represented by its two octagonal towers flanking a forecourt, which is terminated 30 m towards the interior of the city in a triple archway.

1. Theatre

Set into the side of a hill, like a Greek theatre and in accordance with practice of the first century BC (figs. 22, 23), this building belongs probably to the time of Juba II; this would make it one of the earliest theatres in North Africa, alongside those at Utica and Lepcis Magna. Its cavea was composed of 27 tiers of seats, crowned by a curved portico and dominated on the central axis by a small shrine to an unknown divinity. The stage-building was embellished with three storeys of fluted columns, of white marble from Paros and Carrara, but also using granite and red and green porphyry. Following shameless depredations by the French military in the 1840s to build the barracks that overlook the site, all that now remains is foundations and decorative fragments on site, or in the square in front of the Old Museum. In the latter, however, are two colossal statues of Muses, which stood in the niches between the columns. Against the rear of the stage-building there was a portico with a Corinthian colonnade in the green and white marble of the nearby Djebel Chenoua: this must have been the southern edge of the forum.

Towards the end of the second or the beginning of the third century AD, when there was a growing fashion for the spectacle of gladiatorial combat, the building was converted into an amphitheatre. The five lowest tiers of seating were removed, together with the *orchestra*, stage and stage building in order to create an elliptical arena

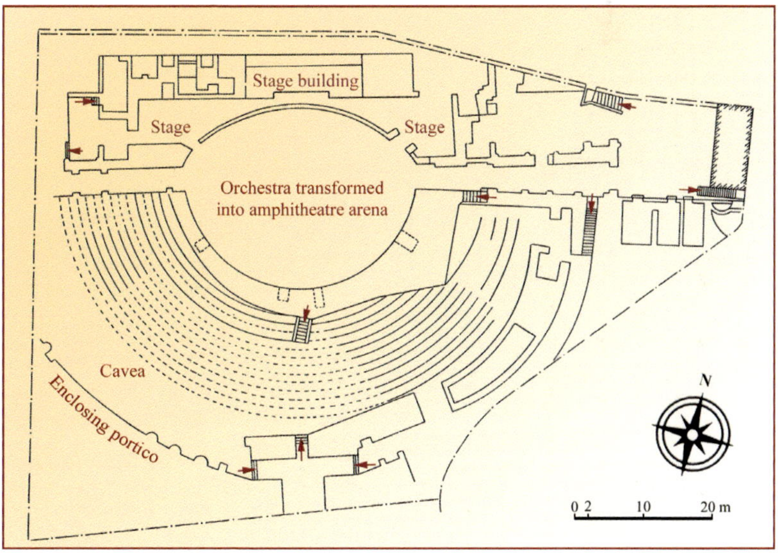

Fig. 22. Cherchel: plan of the theatre.

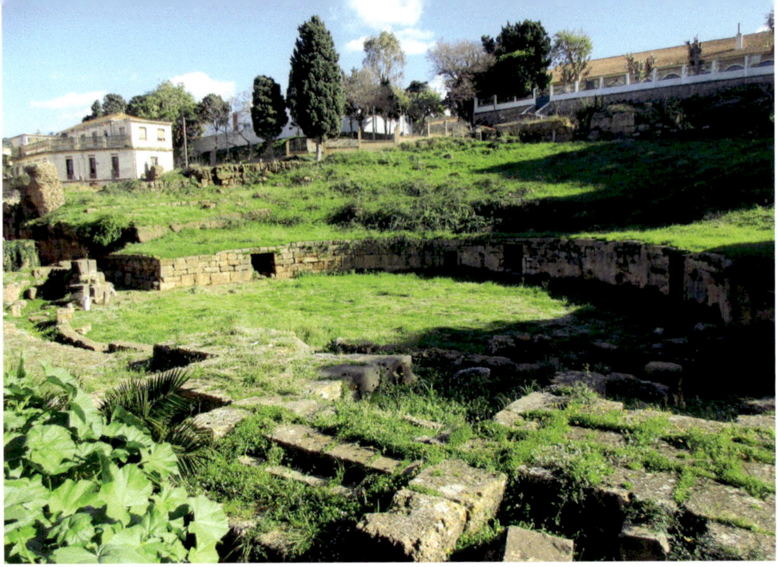

Fig. 23. The theatre of Cherchel.

(33 x 26 m) surrounded by a perimeter wall 3 m high to protect the spectators; into this were set four cells for animals. The east–west passageways (*parascaenia*), which had previously provided access to the theatre seats, became the entrances to the arena: the *porta triumphalis* for the entry of the inaugural procession and the *porta libitinensis* for the removal of corpses.

Immediately to the NW of the theatre were found the ***Central Baths***, but these have completely disappeared.

2. Forum

This was a paved square of 100 sq.m, once surrounded by porticoes (of which the bases of the columns on the N side are still in place). Only the NE corner has been exposed, as a result of rescue excavations by a British-Algerian team in the 1970s (fig. 24). The earliest structures revealed here were dated to around 200 BC, followed by a major change on a new alignment in the late first century, surely part of Juba's redevelopment of the city. The visible part, with a civil basilica along the

Fig. 24. Cherchel: the NE corner of the forum, discovered in the 1970s.

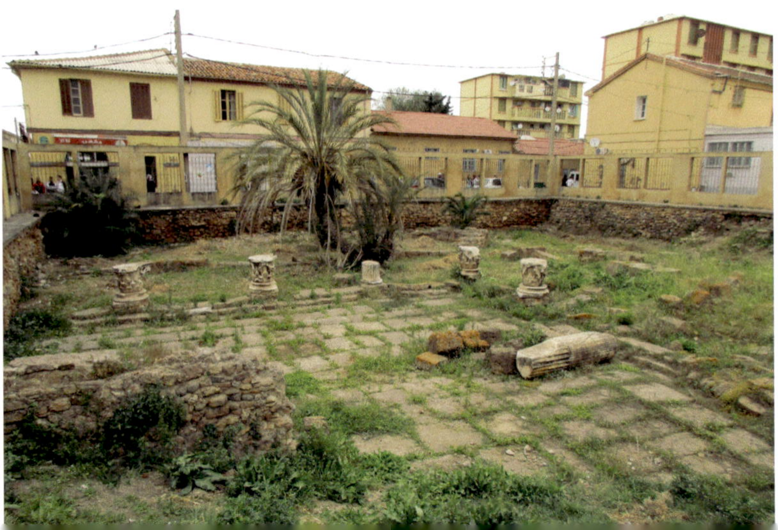

E side, belongs however to about AD 200. Subsequently, in the late fourth or early fifth century, wooden stalls were established in the portico, possibly following destruction during the revolt of Firmus. A black-and-white mosaic in the basilica (visible from the street on the N side) belongs to this period. Of similar date is a small apsed church on the N side of the area, which was destroyed by fire in the early sixth century, when it appears that the rest of the buildings were also abandoned.

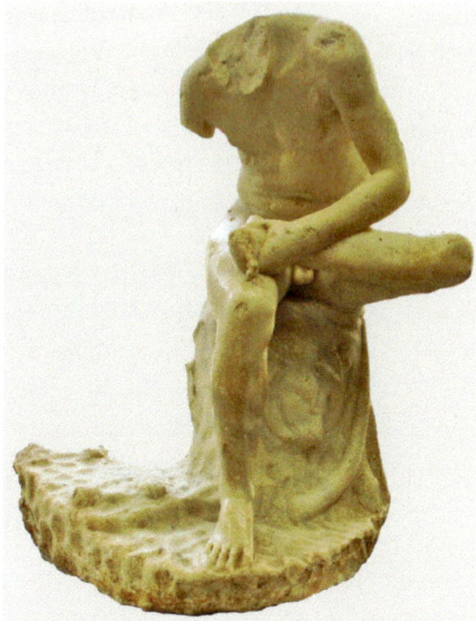

Fig. 25. Cherchel, Old Museum: marble copy of the Spinario *found in the West Baths.*

3. Nymphaeum and cisterns

To the SE of the theatre was found the hemicycle (15 m in diameter) of a stone-built nymphaeum, faced in marble, which served as a water tower. The building can no longer be seen; the barracks built here by the French also overlie six vaulted cisterns (each 19.0 x 4.5 m in plan and 8 m high), which were formerly fed by the aqueduct and supplied water to the city.

4. West Baths

This bath building, of the second century AD (115 x 70 m; 8,050 sq.m), is partly obscured by modern buildings. It conforms to a classical plan and is perfectly symmetrical (fig. 26). It is built of mortared brickwork, but the walls were veneered in marble while the vaults and ceilings were decorated with a combination of painted stucco and mosaic. All the floors were paved with marble slabs or with mosaic. Despite the poor state of preservation of the complex, it is still possible to make out the familiar sequence of cold and heated rooms, together with the plunge-baths or pools associated with them. The entrance

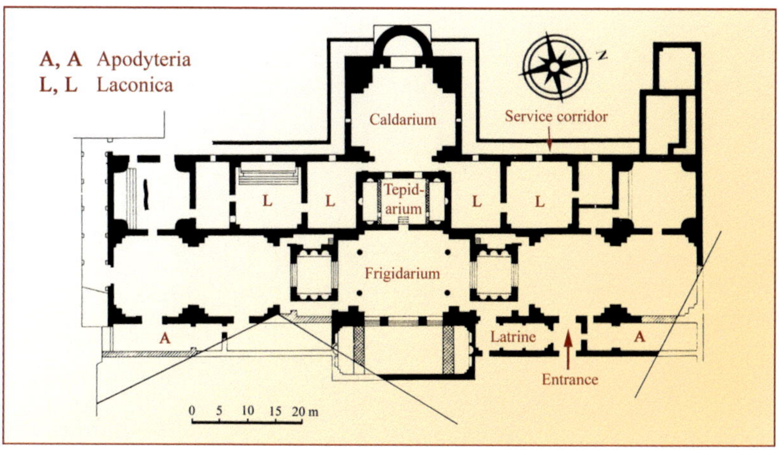

Fig. 26. Cherchel: plan of the West Baths.

portico was defined by an Ionic colonnade in granite, 8 m high. The *frigidarium* was paved with slabs of onyx from the present-day region of Oran, veined in yellow, brown and white; traces alone have been found of four granite columns from Hadjret-en-Nouss near Cherchel, 1 m in diameter.

Some fifty statues were found within the building, including a Venus (p. 86 fig. 87) and a Neptune now in the National Museum in Algiers, a Jupiter now in the Louvre in Paris and several hermaphrodites; also a copy of the bronze *Spinario* which is preserved in the Capitoline Museums in Rome (see fig. 25 and p. 44). This profusion derives from the fact that, towards the end of Roman rule, the West Baths became a sort of repository or museum for statues of fallen gods: they were no longer objects of veneration, but merely works of art. Several re-used pedestals found in the excavations (one of which is visible in the courtyard of the Old Museum) are inscribed *translata de sordentibus locis* ('transferred from derelict locations') – an expression which probably signifies abandoned temples.

Between the West Baths and the port, an ancient pool (36 x 10 m) was still visible in 1952. It had a triangular central refuge and two lateral plunge-baths.

5. Port

The ancient port of Caesarea consisted of two basins. One entered first a huge anchorage protected on the east side by an artificial mole, and on the west by a mole extending the Îlot (Islet) Joinville. From this mercantile harbour, a narrow canal led to a second, well-sheltered basin where warships were docked. Largely overlaid by the present port, this basin was enclosed on the W by a mole joining the Îlot Joinville to the shore. Nothing survives of the ancient superstructure of this military port, but in the eighteenth century an English traveller, Thomas Shaw, could still detect its former layout, as well as traces of the warehouses and porticoes which surrounded it. Having said that, as already outlined, the city owed its prosperity less to its port facilities than to the wealth of its agricultural hinterland, and particularly to the extent of olive cultivation.

Recent excavations on the islet have revealed the octagonal foundations of the ancient lighthouse, reported in ancient tradition to have been 36 m high and built on the model of the Pharos of Alexandria. Also found there were traces of Punic occupation in the fifth century BC – a century before the appearance of Iol in the list of emporia along this coast by Pseudo-Scylax – which indicate a very early occupation of the site. The forum excavations have subsequently produced pottery of the sixth century BC.

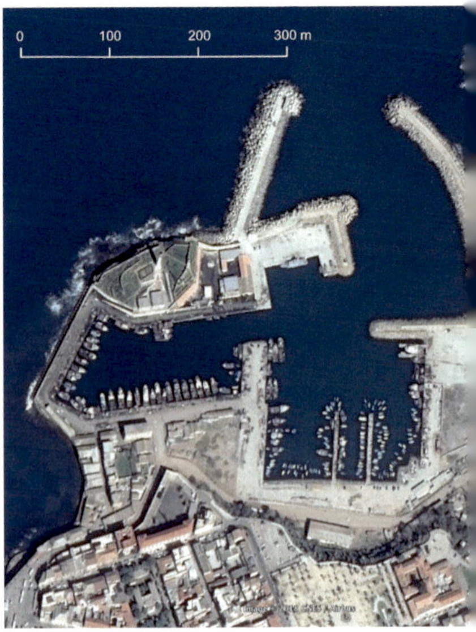

Fig. 27. Satellite image of the port of Cherchel, showing the two harbours and the Îlot Joinville which encloses the westerly one. On the E side, the straight line of the Roman mole, now beneath the surface of the water, is clearly detectable. The modern mole on this side was deliberately built on a curve in order not to obscure it. Image from Google Earth, dated 4 March 2016.

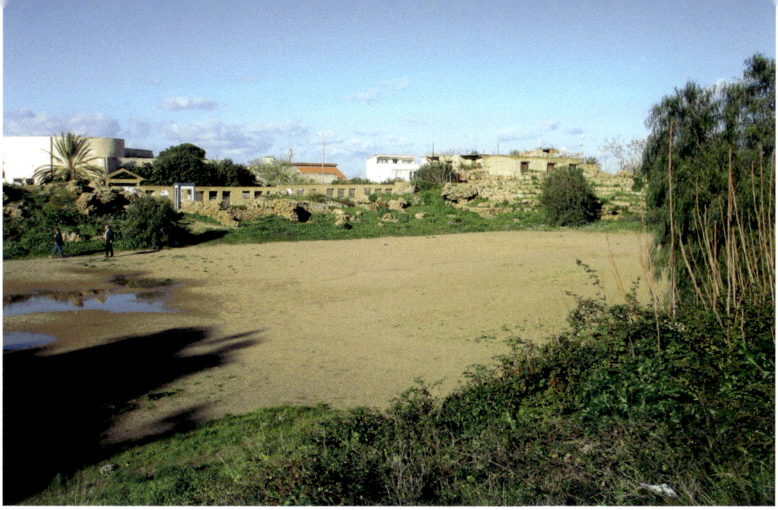

Fig. 28. Cherchel: the Roman amphitheatre.

6. East Baths

Smaller and less well preserved than the West Baths (4), a two-apsed *frigidarium* veneered with marble can be made out, together with a circular basin paved with mosaic. This cold pool was overlooked by three niches destined to house statues. One of these, a magistrate in a toga (*togatus*), has been found. The other rooms are too collapsed for easy identification, but fragments of painted decoration have been recovered; also a mosaic pavement illustrating the Judgement of Paris.

Not far from here, the former Parc Bocquet has yielded several mosaics and a superb statue of Isis, which implies the presence of a temple dedicated to this goddess.

7. Amphitheatre

Built by Juba II on the site of a former necropolis, this building has the very rare characteristic of being, not elliptical in plan, but composed of a rectangle (101 x 44 m) with semicircles on the short sides (fig. 28). With a surface area of 4,082 sq.m – thus significantly larger than the Colosseum – the amphitheatre of Caesarea had a capacity of only 14,400 spectators, in contrast to the 50,000 capacity of the Colosseum of Vespasian in Rome. Designed originally for 9,900 spectators, the *cavea* was heightened in the second century in order to achieve the capacity mentioned above. The seats were supported on banks of spoil on the straight edges, and on radial vaults around the ends. Beneath the arena, now buried to the height of the podium wall, ran two service corridors at right angles to each other. On the outside, the long sides were faced with a simple wall in large masonry, while the rounded ends were embellished with arcades.

The singular design of this building is surely an imitation of the temporary amphitheatre erected by Julius Caesar in the Roman Forum to celebrate his quadruple triumph in 46 BC. The provisions made there – excavation of underground annexes fitted with trapdoors and adjustment of the outline to enable the inclusion of wooden tribunes – allowed the creation of a more or less rectangular arena. Caesar, and subsequently Augustus, staged tremendous wild-beast hunts and battles between armed troops, which greatly entertained the Roman public. In his youth, Juba II would have had the opportunity to attend these games; it is therefore highly likely that he would have wished to provide Caesarea with an amphitheatre like that in Rome, but on a monumental scale. The building was not very well suited to gladiatorial combat, given its non-elliptical shape; and it was doubtless

Martyrs at Caesarea

Born at Rusuccuru (Dellys), Marciana belonged to an aristocratic family. Despite her great beauty, she dedicated herself to God and retreated to a cell not far from Caesarea. Around 303, during the persecutions of Diocletian, she came to the city to make a public profession of her faith and she smashed a statue of Diana. She was thrown to the wild beasts and died in the amphitheatre of Caesarea in the claws of a leopard. There were other martyrs who perished at Caesarea: Arcadius, who was dismembered; Severianus and his wife Aquila, who were burned alive; Theodota together with her seven children; and Fabius, who was a standard-bearer (*vexillifer*) and who died sometime between 293 and 304.

this failing which led in the third century to the transformation of the former theatre into an arena which then provided a better space for the games which were popular at the time.

The amphitheatre has suffered greatly from being used as a quarry during the French colonial period. It is now enclosed within a wall, with access in the middle of the N side.

8. Circus

Probably built in the time of Juba II, the dimensions of this hippodrome (400 x 90 m) are comparable to that at Lepcis Magna in Libya. The *spina* was refurbished in the second century and the *porta triumphalis* which led through the centre of the curved end is attributable to the third century. The outline alone remains as a level open space.

OLD MUSEUM

Built in 1908, this building contains an extraordinary collection of sculptures and mosaics displayed in the rooms around four sides of a central courtyard. This is impossible to list fully in the present context, besides which, the display has been undergoing progressive renovation during the last few years, with changes in those parts accessible to the public. At the time of writing this edition, there is a plan to incorporate into the museum the present town hall next door, and then to transfer to that part of the building the contents of the 'new' museum described below. The following is therefore a provisional list of some of the most important works, and the locations in which they are currently displayed (described in a clockwise direction from the entrance).

West wing

The sculpture and panels on this side are devoted mainly to the family of Juba II, who was responsible for the renaming of the city (from Iol to Caesarea) in the time of Augustus, and for its lavish development and ornamentation.

Personification of Caesarea (on the left): found in the West Baths in 1888, this head crowned by the skin of a marine creature – surely a dolphin – has a dense head of hair, parted in front into wavy locks. According to some historians this is a personification of Caesarea, but one would normally expect her to be wearing a mural crown (resembling battlements).

Personification of Africa (on the right): this piece comes from the theatre. Displaying her usual attributes, the goddess has an elephant's head for her headdress, with the trunk raised above her head and with sockets for two ivory tusks.

Head of a personification of Africa on the right, wearing an elephant headdress (with sockets for the tusks).

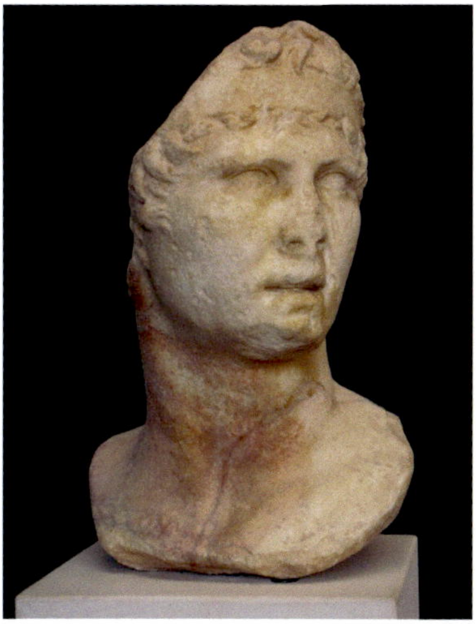

Fig. 29. Cherchel, Old Museum: portrait of Juba II in middle age.

Portraits of Juba II: there are several portraits here of Juba II, at different ages (see fig. 29). One of the heads is a cast of an original which is now in the Louvre in Paris. Another represents him in the style of a Classical Greek hero (fig. 3).

Portrait of Cleopatra Selene: head, also encircled by a royal fillet (fig. 30). The wife of Juba II has been reproduced magnificently by the sculptor, but with a realism that does not flatter his model. It is difficult to see in this hardly attractive young lady the daughter of Cleopatra VII and Mark Anthony. (Beginning of first century AD.)

Portrait of Cleopatra VII (not seen): one of the very rare portraits of the famous queen of Egypt who reigned from 51 to 30 BC and was the last of the Lagid dynasty. The head is covered, in the Roman style, and once had earrings. Finely executed, but idealised. (Beginning of first century AD.)

Portraits of Ptolemy: the son of Juba II and Cleopatra Selene is represented in several fragmentary pieces. A better-preserved portrait which was found at Cherchel is today in the Louvre. (Beginning of first century AD.)

Hercules: found in the West Baths and probably dating from the time of Juba II, who claimed him as an ancestor.

On the wall, the ***Mosaic of the Triumph of Dionysus*** was found in a private house and has been attributed to the mid to late third century AD. Within a wide and elaborate border of geometric and vegetal motifs, a central panel portrays a robed figure (Dionysus or Ariadne) holding a thyrsus, riding in a chariot drawn by two reluctant tigers and encouraged by a satyr. This is a cut-down version of a familiar motif, the most impressive rendering of which may be seen in the museum in Sétif (see p. 96 and fig. 96).

To the right of this mosaic are displayed the modest and poignant funerary memorials to several freedmen and women of the royal household, including C(aius) Iulius Niceros, who was Juba's cook.

NW corner

Kanephoros (= basket-carrier, labelled as a 'caryatid', which would have served as a weight-bearing column): a young girl, once

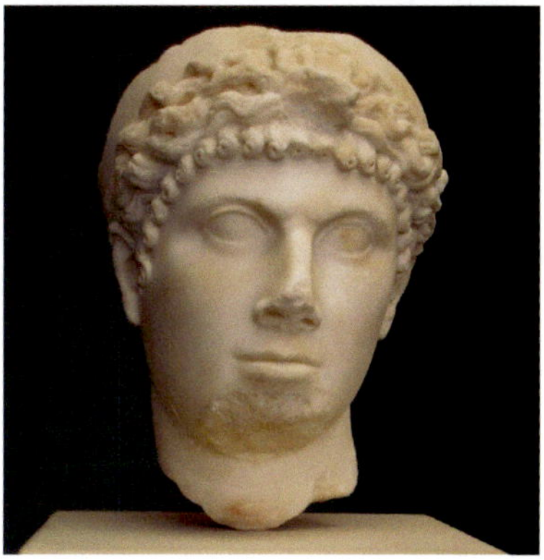

Fig. 30. Cherchel, Old Museum: head of Cleopatra Selene.

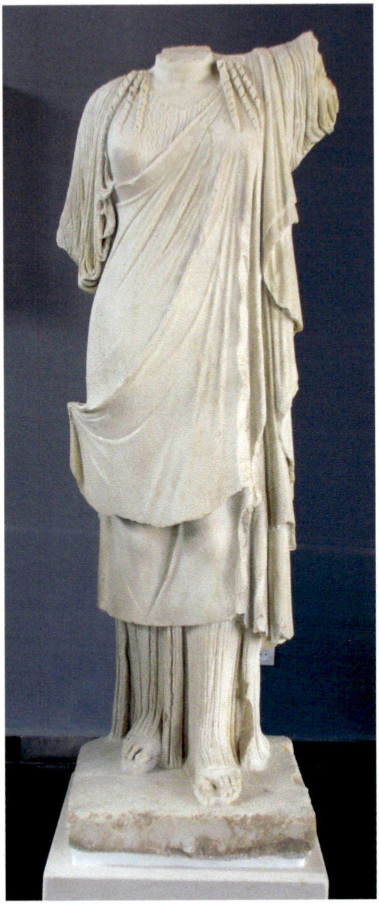

Fig. 31. Cherchel, Old Museum: Kanephoros, copy of a Greek original.

carrying on her head a sacred basket steadied by her left hand (all missing), wears a finely pleated woollen tunic and a cloak over her shoulders (fig. 31). The stiffness of the body and the treatment of the tresses of hair falling on her chest recall the archaism of the *korai* which inspired this work. (Excellent copy of a Greek original of 470–450 BC.)

North wing

Series of ***four colossal heads***, of a bearded man and three women, which must once have adorned the façade of a building, high above the ground (perhaps a temple of Neptune or even the palace of Juba). Found near the museum; probably of the time of Juba II.

Series of ***square marble pilasters***, with elaborate vegetal ornament, surely belonging to the time of Juba II; also several other architectural elements, relief carvings and marble table-legs which suggest the luxury of that time.

NE corner

This is given over largely to cult statues and objects associated with cult.

Isis: the goddess is identified by her attributes (fig. 32). On her head are the horns of a cow, behind which one should doubtless imagine a disc embellished with a uraeus (cobra) or with rays. In her left hand she holds a ritual bucket, and the right was probably shaking a sistrum (bronze rattle). Of high quality, this statue must have occupied a position of honour in a sanctuary – and indeed, it is known that Isis was revered very early at Caesarea. Pliny the Elder (writing in the first century AD) reported that he had seen in the temple of Isis there a crocodile which Juba II had captured south of the Atlas in Morocco: a decisive proof, in his eyes, that the source of the Nile lay within his kingdom. (Second century.)

Priestess of Isis (on the wall nearby): this small rectangular relief shows a priestess, identified by the ritual objects of the cult of Isis – the sistrum and the bucket.

Gallus (priest of Cybele, fig. 33): originally from Asia Minor, the *galli* belonged to a fraternity of eunuchs which accompanied the worship of the Great Goddess throughout the Roman Empire. This example is portrayed standing by an altar. He wears a laurel crown with a central rose; the two ends of the braided woollen cord which passes across his forehead fall from his shoulders as far as his knees. This striking figure is of the second or third century.

Aesculapius: found close to the theatre, this colossal seated statue is a copy of a work of the fourth century BC, perhaps by Bryaxis. (Beginning of first century AD.)

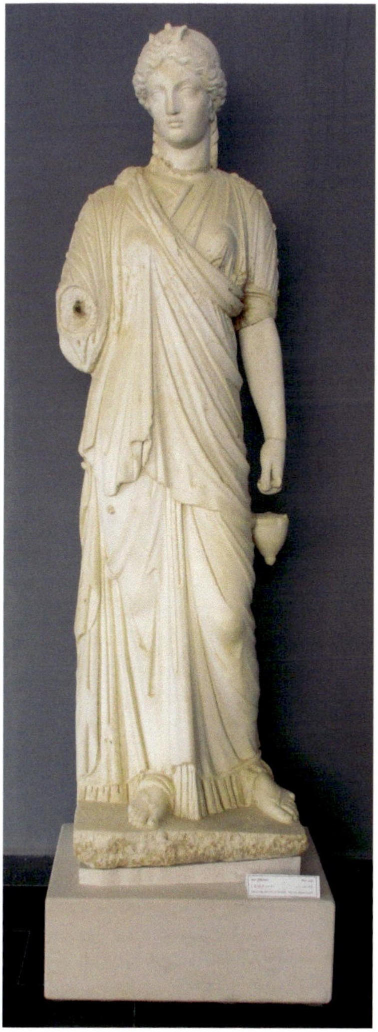

Fig. 32. Cherchel, Old Museum: statue of Isis.

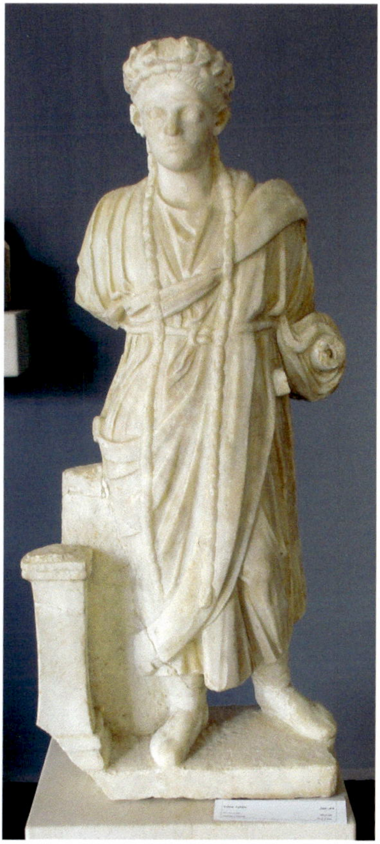

Fig. 33. Cherchel, Old Museum: statue of a gallus *(priest of Cybele).*

Also in this corner are two fragments of Egyptian statuary in polished black stone: legs and base only of a statue of ***Tuthmosis I***, of the 18th Dynasty (sixteenth century BC), and a headless statuette of the priest ***Petubastis***. These are surely antiquities brought to Caesarea from Egypt by Cleopatra Selene.

East wing

This side was still in a state of transition in 2018, and was not accessible to the public. Amongst other items, it contains the notable statue described below.

The goddess Cybele

This goddess, of Phrygian origin, was known to the Romans as Mother of the Gods, Great Mother, Rhea, Idaean Mother etc.

In contrast to many other oriental cults, the cult of Cybele was brought formally to Rome in 204 BC and installed in the Temple of Victory on the Palatine, in order to sustain the flagging fortunes of Rome in the Second Punic War. The retreat of Hannibal and the defeat of the Carthaginians at Zama two years later were attributed in part to her arrival; however, the rowdy and savage rites held in honour of the goddess offended austere Romans of the republican period. It was not until the time of Augustus that the cult really flourished, in conjunction with the worship of Attis. It was Antoninus Pius who introduced the rite of the *taurobolium* in the form of the sacrifice of a bull for the health of the emperor – thus reinforcing the 'imperial' credentials of the cult of Cybele. (The sacrifice of a bull would have represented an exceptional expense, beyond the range of many.) The priests of Cybele, *galli*, were eunuchs clad in colourful effeminate dress: they carried the statue of the goddess in processions, while playing the tambourine, beating their breasts and demanding alms. They could not be (or have been) Roman citizens. At a later date, they were replaced by *archigalli*, who were Roman citizens and who were not emasculated.

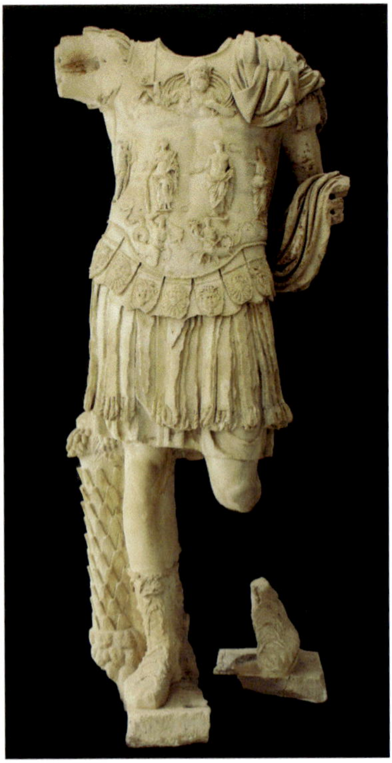

Emperor Augustus: this colossal statue may have represented the emperor Augustus with his arm raised, addressing his troops (figs. 34, 35). The execution is highly detailed, and the breastplate of the figure reproduces a parade item with repoussé decoration. The uppermost register is composed of the bearded bust of Mars Ultor (Mars the Avenger: during the civil war undertaken to avenge the murder of his adopted father Caesar, Augustus had vowed to erect a temple to *Mars Ultor* in the Roman Forum.) A second register shows, to the right, the deified Julius Caesar being crowned by a Victory and, to the left, the archer Cupid facing *Venus Victrix et Genetrix* (Victorious and Mother), whom Caesar had chosen as his ancestor. The goddess is armed with sword and shield. The third register is filled by a centaur and a triton. (Found at the NE corner of the theatre, and therefore perhaps once standing in the forum. Beginning of first century AD.)

Fig. 34. Cherchel, Old Museum: colossal statue of the emperor Augustus.

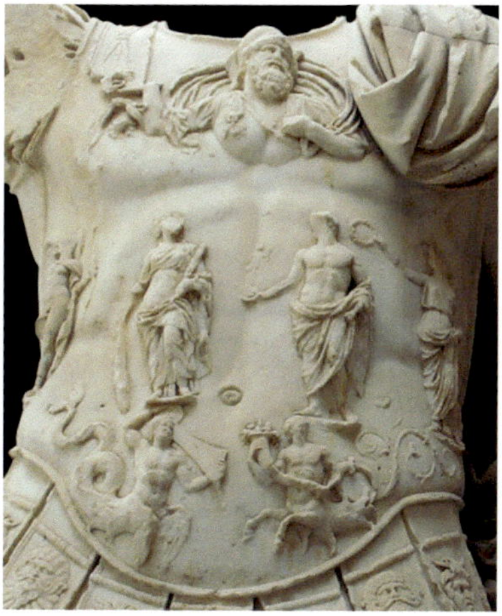

Fig. 35. Detail of breastplate of the preceding.

SE corner

Torso of Dionysus, a bearded figure with a goatskin over his shoulder.

Mosaic of the Labours of the Fields: admired for its virtuosity and its use of colour, this huge mosaic (figs. 7, 37) was found in the ruins of a private house, to the W of the town. The uppermost register shows a man driving a plough between olive trees, while a second goads the oxen. In the second register, a sower is followed by another ploughman, turning the soil lightly to bury the seed. The third register shows work in the vineyard: three men are hoeing the ground in between the trellised vines. In the lowest register, a labourer draws up soil around the roots of a vine, under the eyes

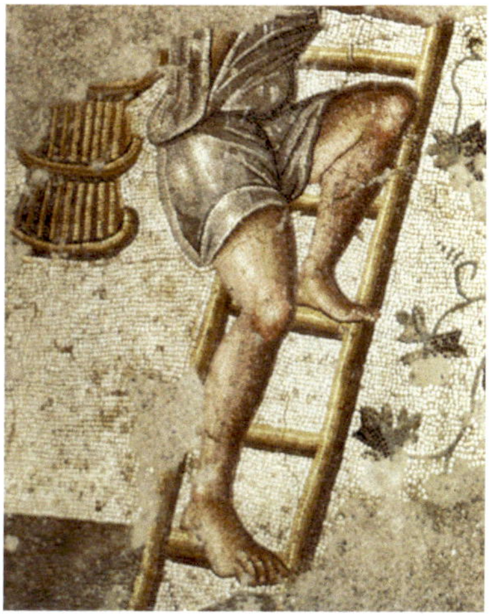

Fig. 36. Cherchel, Old Museum: mosaic of the Labours of the Fields, fragment of vintage scene.

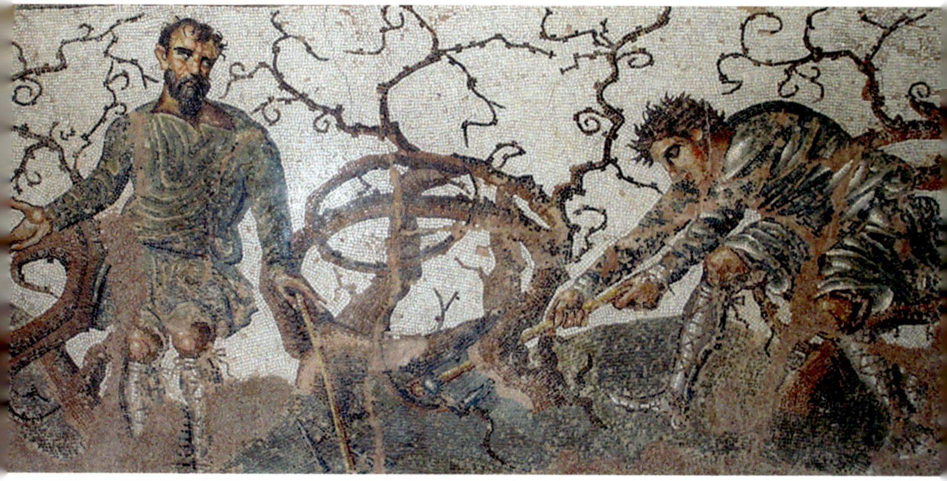

Fig. 37. Cherchel, Old Museum: mosaic of the Labours of the Fields, third register.

of a supervisor. A further fragment of the same mosaic (fig. 36, on another wall nearby) shows a harvester climbing a ladder in order to gather the grapes from a vine trellis. Apart from their aesthetic value, these images give us a useful insight into the agricultural tools and practices in use in Roman Africa. (No direct evidence of date, but probably end of third century AD.)

Mosaic of the Three Graces: in these figures, supposedly the embodiment of beauty, the demands of the theme have substantially exceeded the skills of the artist, and the effect is emphasized by the placing of the mosaic next to the greatly superior Labours of the Fields. (From the so-called House of the Julii, fourth century.)

South Wing

This wing (also in a state of transition in 2018) displays a number of more-or-less fragmentary mosaics, with mythological scenes or purely ornamental designs. Note the very different colour palette from the more dramatic designs on display in the museums of Djémila and Timgad (e.g. pp. 129, 214). There are also numerous marble sculptures of high quality, mostly Roman copies of famous Greek mythological subjects. These include a young satyr playing the flute; a satyr teasing a panther by holding its tail and preventing it from reaching a bunch of grapes; a seated boy looking for a thorn in his foot (fig. 25: this is a copy of a Hellenistic original, of which the most famous version, in bronze, is the *Spinario* in the Capitoline Museums in Rome); the goddess Diana, hunting with dogs (fig. 38); Pan with a satyr (very fragmentary).

Apollo: executed in a white marble of the highest quality, this statue is undoubtedly one of the finest in the museum (figs. 39, 40). The god is shown standing, with his weight slightly on his left leg. Wound around the trunk of a tree, on which a falcon perches, the serpent Python is dying, transfixed by an arrow. This is an ancient copy of an original

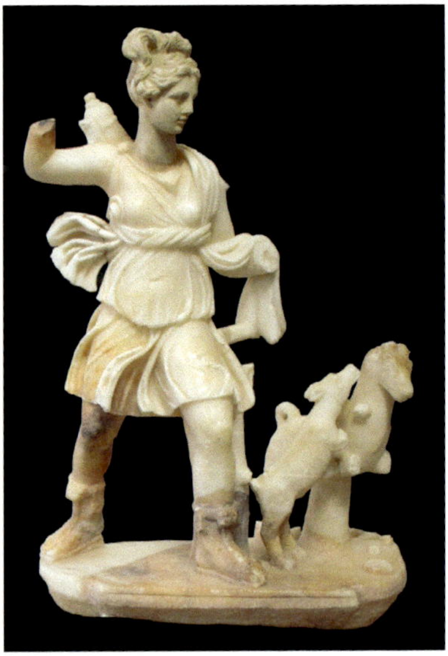

Fig. 38. Cherchel, Old Museum: marble statuette of the goddess Artemis/Diana hunting.

Representations in bronze – and marble

A marble copy of a human figure does not have the same centre of gravity or physical characteristics as its counterpart in bronze. While, therefore, the bronze may without difficulty be stable and able to stand on its own, the marble version may require added support in order not to topple, or break at the ankles. In this case, the support takes the form of a tree trunk on one side, and Apollo's quiver, resting on the ground, on the other.

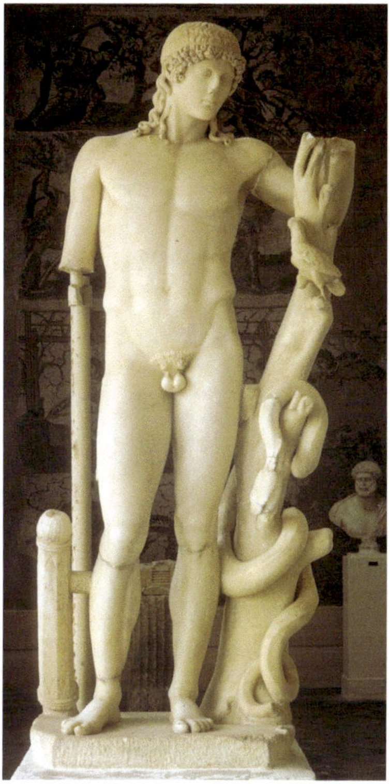

Fig. 39. Cherchel, Old Museum: statue of Apollo, a Roman copy of a Greek original.

in bronze of 460–450 BC attributed to the Greek sculptor Phidias. This example is very close to the Tiber Apollo (in the Museo Nazionale in Rome) which is also a copy, though less fine and less complete. The Cherchel example is distinguished by the precision of the modelling – note particularly the musculature of the back – and the serene gravity of the face, which recalls that of the Kassel Apollo in the National Museum in Athens. This was probably a cult statue, but it was found in a private house of the fourth century belonging to the enigmatic Thybridii Basiliani (so named in a mosaic), a time when it had already become an *objet d'art* for the pleasure of a rich collector. (Beginning of first century AD.)

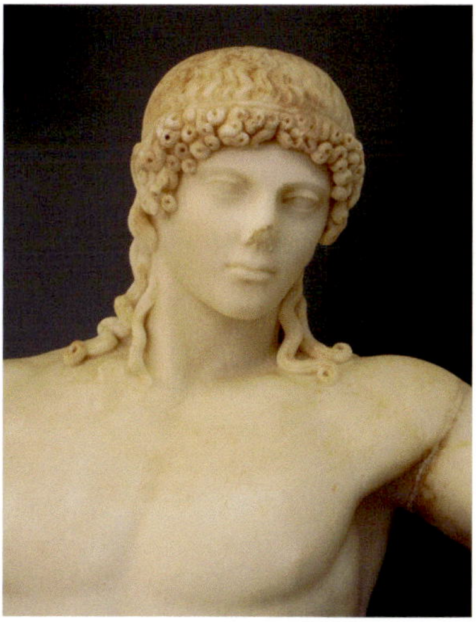

Fig. 40. Detail of the head of Apollo.

Courtyard

Here may be seen two mosaic-decorated semi-circular fountains from the peristyle of a Roman house.

Ulysses and the Sirens (W side): the curved side is surmounted by a statue of a winged Eros riding a dolphin, the mouth of the animal serving as a waterspout (fig. 41). Within the basin, the walls are covered by a mosaic which illustrates one of the most famous episodes of the Odyssey: lashed voluntarily to the mast of his ship, Ulysses/Odysseus listens without risk to the song of the sirens, while his companions, whose ears have been stopped with wax, continue to sail the vessel. Dolphins play on either side of the ship (where whelks and bivalves are also shown), while on the bank may be seen three of the seductive figures – half woman and half bird – who lured sailors by their singing and their beautiful playing. Unfailingly drawn into shipwreck on the rocky shore, the wretches would then be devoured. The designer of the mosaic seems to have followed the account of Diodorus with regard to the number of the sirens (Homer mentions two, other

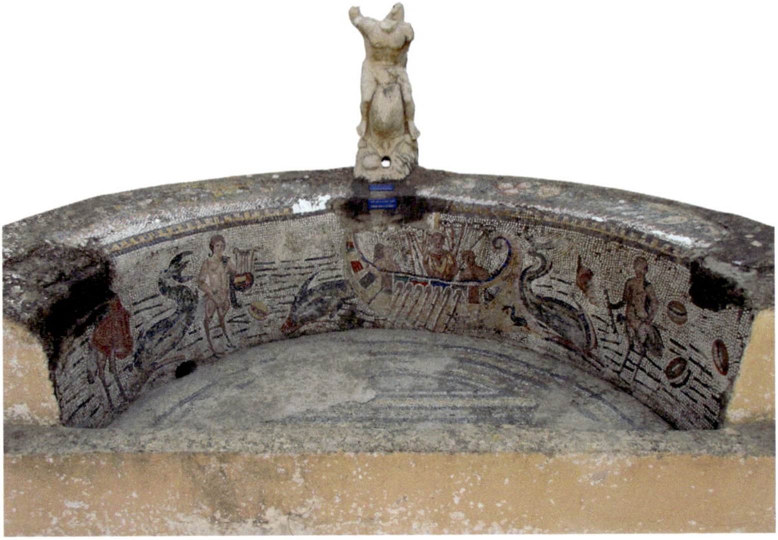

Fig. 41. Cherchel, Old Museum: fountain of Ulysses and the Sirens.

sources indicate four) and the instrumentation of the lethal trio: Parthenope played the lyre, Ligeia the flute, while Leucosia sang. (Second to fourth century AD.)

The Triumph of Neptune (N side): this is a similar fountain, but less well preserved. In the centre of the mosaic may be seen the head of Neptune with his trident, seated on the back of a hippocamp and flanked by nereids.

The courtyard also serves as a ***jardin lapidaire*** for carved stone architectural elements, sarcophagi and inscriptions. Amongst these, a statue-base on the W side is of special interest. This was found, together with many fine pieces of statuary, in the West Baths: it has been re-used at a late date, and shows clear evidence of Caesarea in decline. The original inscription has been very crudely obliterated, and over this tortured surface has been carved *TRANSLATA DE SORDENTIBVS LOCIS* ('Transferred from derelict locations'). (See p. 36.)

NEW MUSEUM

Added in 1977, this museum houses further mosaics (many displayed in the open air), together with small objects in cases and some statuary. The construction of the building was not of good quality, and there are plans (see p. 38) to enlarge the Old Museum and to transfer the additional materials there. The displays are distributed between two upstairs rooms and the garden.

Main (west) room

Cases around the walls display small objects, mostly pottery, in an approximately chronological sequence running anti-clockwise from the entrance, from Punic times through to the medieval period. The pottery is divided into storage wares, kitchen wares and fine (table) wares; there are also displays of glassware.

On the wall at the far end of the room are two funerary reliefs.

Stele of Balaterus: tombstone of Balaterus, son of Melus, an auxiliary soldier of the Sixth Cohort of Dalmatians (fig. 42). The portrayal of the dead man shows interesting details of his equipment: he has two javelins in his left hand, sword and dagger at his belt and an unidentifiable weapon in his right hand. He died at the age of 28, having served in the army for eight years.

Stele of Dazas: tombstone of a cavalryman in the same unit.

On the floor are two mosaics.

Mosaic of the Vintage: like the panel of the Labours of the Fields, this pavement deserves our attention not just for its aesthetic qualities, but also for the many naturalistic details which enhance our understanding of African customs in the Roman world. The centre of the mosaic is filled with a vine trellis, seen

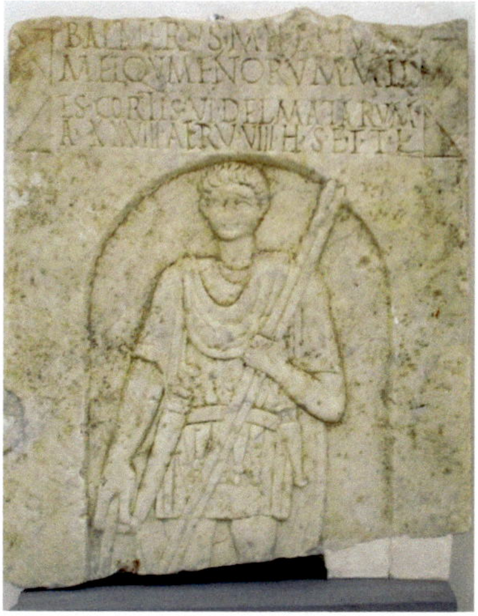

Fig. 42. Cherchel, New Museum: tombstone of Balaterus.

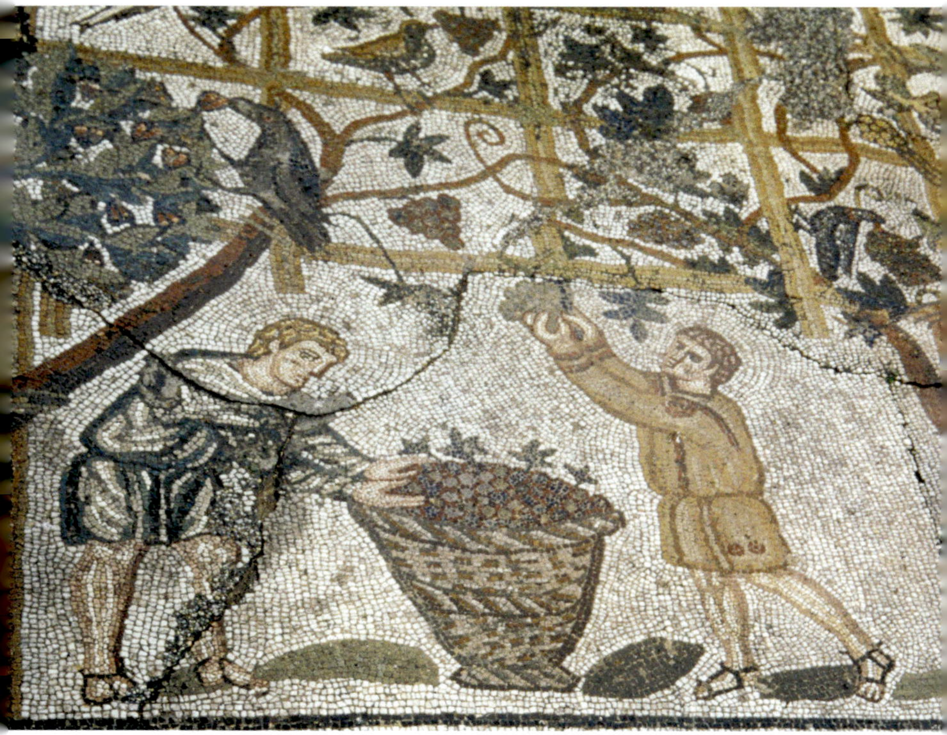

Fig. 43. Cherchel, New Museum: mosaic of the Vintage, grape-pickers.

from above; the wooden trellis is sustained by six timber uprights, five of which support vine stems. Birds flit amongst the branches and the bunches of grapes. Around this surprising composition, one harvester is cutting a bunch, while another drops his into a willow basket (fig. 43). Further on, a man is gutting the carcase of a sheep, which is hung by its hind legs from a tree (fig. 44). Blood pours from the neck where the head (lying on a rock behind him) has been cut off, while a dog has managed to get hold of the entrails. To the left of this scene, a cart drawn by a pair of oxen is carrying away its load of grapes, led by a harvester with a loaded basket on his shoulders. Another worker has succeeded in catching a hare amongst the vines. He seems to be offering it to the cook, who is stirring a huge cauldron, capable of feeding all the workers in the vineyard. On one side of the trellis, three men in loincloths have set about the treading of the grapes. (Discovered in 1958 in the E part of the town; late fourth or early fifth century.)

Mosaic of Minerva: this apsed mosaic was found in 1959 in a bath building on the 'Îlot Joinville', close to the lighthouse. The major part of it is covered with a design of wave patterns and floral motifs arranged in ellipses; in the apse is a decorated chalice from which floral tendrils spring, and in the centre is a small square panel showing the helmeted head of Minerva. (Second century AD.)

Lesser (east) room

Here are displayed some further fragments of mosaics, also fragments of painted wall-plaster recovered from private houses and a number of small sculptures, including an Aesculapius and heads of Janus, Mercury and Venus.

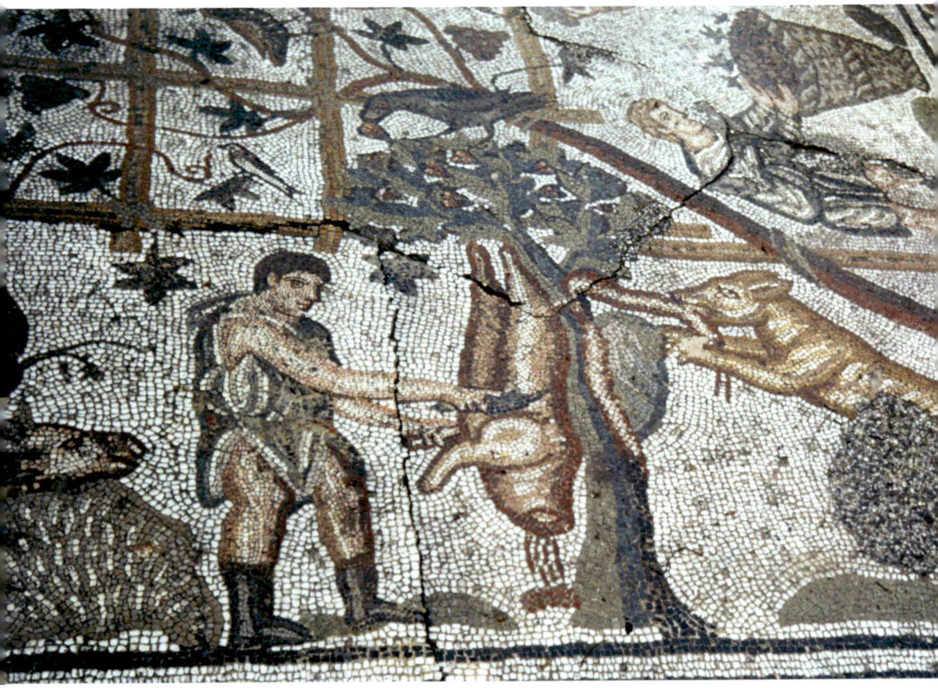

Fig. 44. Cherchel, New Museum: Mosaic of the Vintage, man gutting sheep.

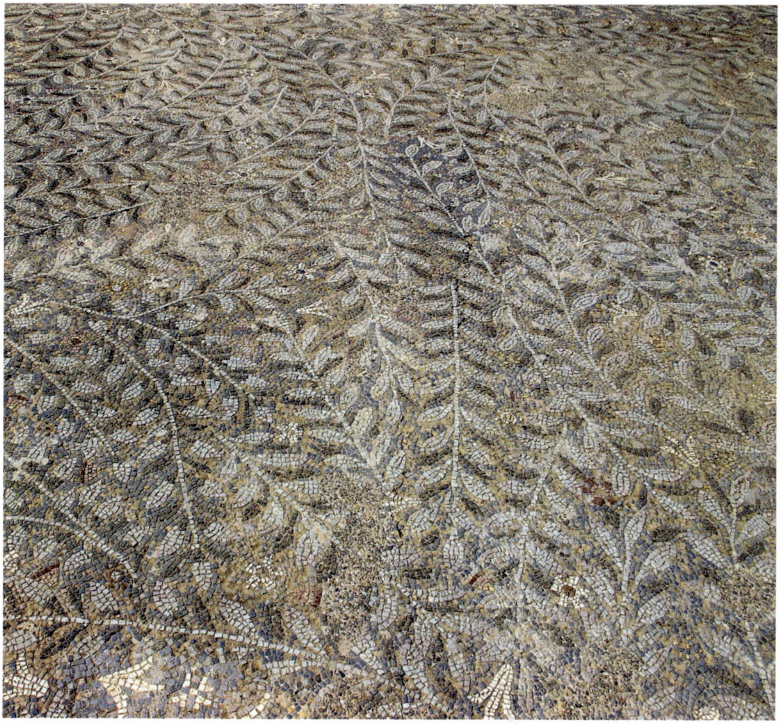

Fig. 45. Cherchel, New Museum: Mosaic of The Scattering.

Garden

Here are displayed mosaics ranging in date from the first to the fourth century, derived from excavations on the Îlot Joinville or from suburban villas. The following are of note.

The Scattering: this trompe-l'oeil pavement (fig. 45) portrays a floor scattered with laurel branches, little flowers and white, pink and yellow rose-petals.

Peacock mosaic: the apsidal shape and the choice of theme seem to suggest that this mosaic comes from a Christian basilica. Two peacocks face one another across a chalice, from which spring two vine-stems, whose curling branches are populated with birds, a deer and a hare. (Fourth century, displayed in the church facing the Place des Martyrs, until this was converted after independence into a mosque. The bright blue glass tesserae are modern.)

Marriage of Peleus and Thetis: this very damaged mosaic was found in the apsed *aula* (audience hall) of a Roman house, the outline of which has been recreated here. It portrays the occasion, attended by all the gods of Olympus, when Eris ('Discord') threw into the gathering a golden apple, declaring that it should go to the most beautiful woman present. This led to the Judgement of Paris (between Hera, Athena and Aphrodite) and hence to the Trojan War. (Second quarter of fourth century.)

THE AQUEDUCT OF CAESAREA

As for most ancient cities, an adequate supply of drinking water was crucial for Caesarea. The city had six vast, parallel cisterns (p. 35), fed by a complex array of channels. The aqueduct, which brought to the city the waters of a spring and a river 45 km to the SE (the longest aqueduct in Algeria) is difficult to date, but its initial

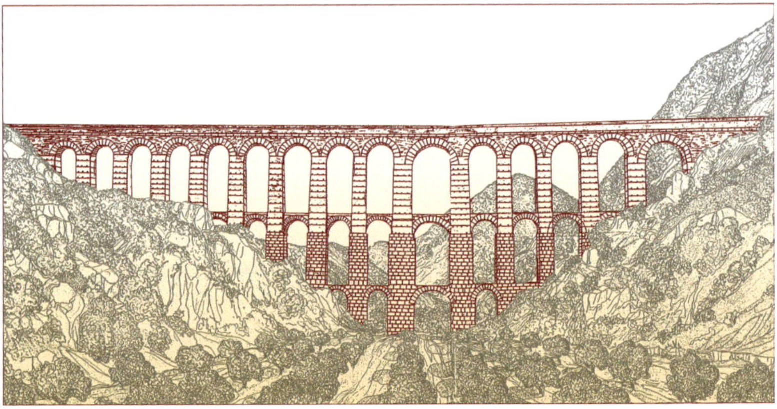

Fig. 46. Cherchel: reconstruction of the aqueduct bridge at Oued Bellah.

It is a commonplace today to admire Roman water engineering, but it was by no means always as clever as we like to think. Most above-ground aqueducts required constant maintenance, and a letter from the Younger Pliny (when Governor of Bithynia in 103) to the emperor Trajan makes the point.

'The citizens of Nicomedia, Sir, have spent 3.3 million sesterces on an aqueduct which they abandoned before it was finished and finally demolished. Then they made a grant of 200,000 sesterces towards another one, but this too was abandoned, so that even after squandering such enormous sums they must still spend more money if they are to have a water supply.

'I have been myself to look at the spring which could supply pure water to be brought along an aqueduct, as originally intended, if the supply is not to be confined to the lower-lying parts of the town. There are very few arches still standing, but others could be built out of the blocks of stone taken from the earlier construction, and I think some ought to be made of brick-faced concrete, which would be easier and cheaper.

'But the first essential is for you to send out a water-engineer or an architect to prevent a third failure. I will add only that the finished work will combine utility with beauty, and will be well worthy of your reign.'

Pliny the Younger, *Letters* X.37, tr. Betty Radice (Loeb Classical Library)

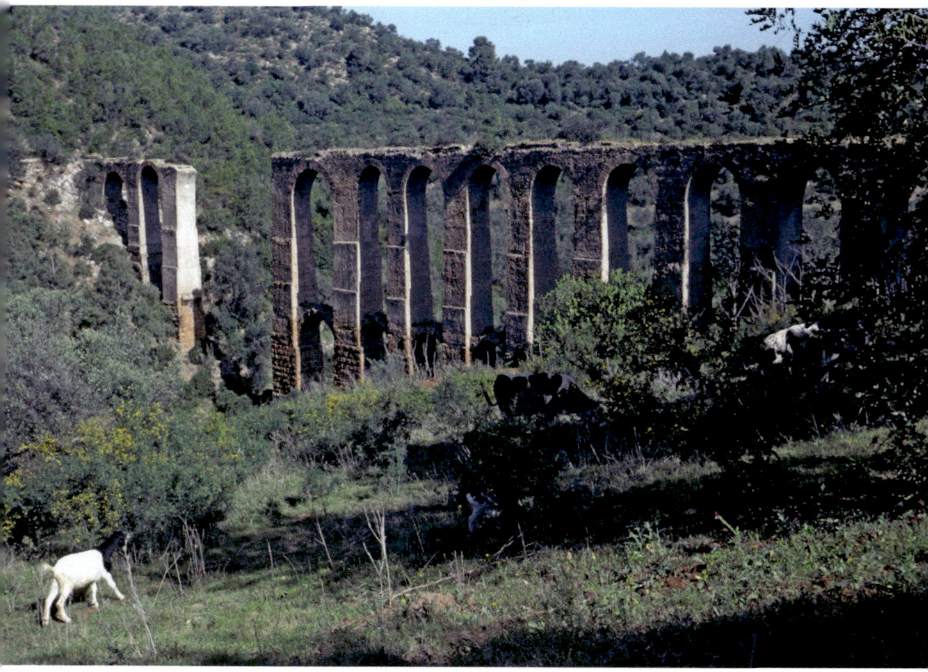

Fig. 47. Cherchel: the aqueduct crossing the Oued Bellah.

construction is tentatively placed in the mid-first century AD. The original design followed the contours of the land. In the second century, perhaps under Antoninus Pius, the course was shortened by some 10 km, cutting out the loops around the Oued Bellah and the Chabet Ilelouîne. The first bridge of this spectacular engineering project can still be seen to the left of the old road (N11) shortly before arriving at Cherchel from the direction of Algiers (see figs. 46, 47). It is 136 m long and 33 m above the valley bottom, with individual vertical piers, strengthened by bracing arches at two intermediate levels. Six km further on, the modern road passes through the more ruinous second bridge.

TIPASA

How many hours have I spent crushing the absinthes, caressing the ruins, trying to synchronize my breathing with the tumultuous sighs of the world! Immersed in the wild odours and the concerts of somnolent insects, I open my eyes and my heart to the unbearable grandeur of a sky soaked with heat. It is not so easy to become what one is, to rediscover one's deeper measure. But gazing at the solid backbone of the Chenoua, my heart quieted with a strange sense of certainty. I learned to breathe, I became whole, and I fulfilled myself.

Albert Camus, *Nuptials at Tipasa.* Translation by Sara Lott.

In contrast to Iol, Tipasa does not appear in the ancient *periploi* (mariners' manuals); only the etymology of the name, which means 'point of passage' in Punic, justifies an inference that this was a stopping-point on the great sea route from Carthage to the Pillars of Hercules (Straits of Gibraltar). Very little remains of the early settlement, apart from traces of a necropolis of the sixth or fifth century BC close to the port and a second necropolis close to the beach of Matarès, which has yielded prolific finds ranging from the fifth to the second century BC. Some historians have concluded that this was an urban dependency of Carthage rather than a simple trading-post. Equally, we know nothing of Tipasa during the time of the Mauretanian kingdom, notably under Bocchus II (46–33 BC), who made Iol one of his principal

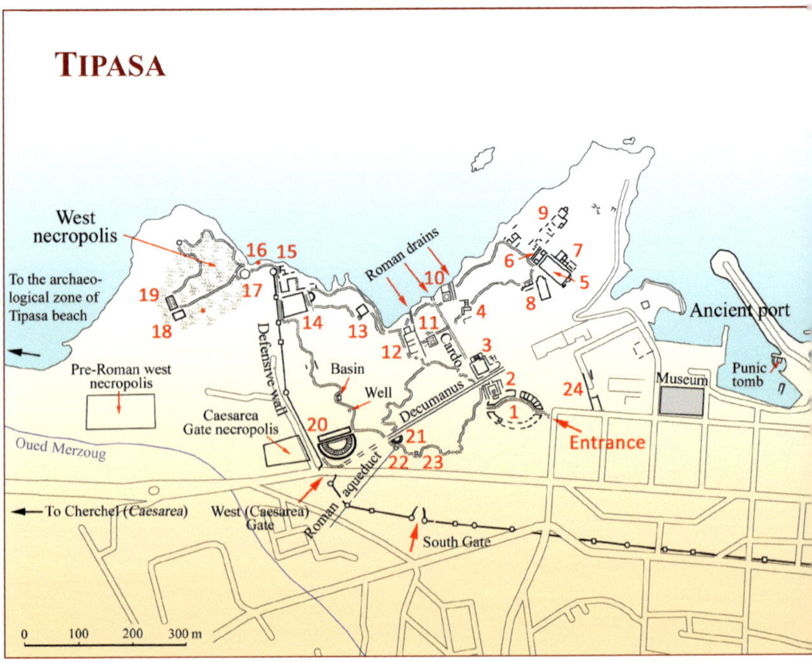

Fig. 48. Tipasa: plan of the site.

cities. It is only in the first century AD that we find any textual sources referring to it: Pliny the Elder reports that, after the annexation of Mauretania, Claudius gave Latin Rights (*ius latinum*) to Tipasa in 46, shortly ahead of Icosium. This privilege, though inferior to the Roman Rights of a colony, entitled the local élite to obtain Roman citizenship, which represented a positive step towards assimilation.

The layout was determined by a promontory which overlooks the old Punic port, with a first defensive circuit enclosing buildings of which we have almost no knowledge. It seems that the city expanded rapidly during the Roman period, since a much more extensive circuit was built under Antoninus Pius: the dedication, found in the excavation of the East Gate, places this in 146–7. Articulated by 31 towers, this impressive wall, 2.3 km long, enclosed a space which extended from the eastern headland as far as the hill on the west; it was outside these walls that cemeteries grew up in both the pagan and Christian periods. Some historians have linked this expansion – and the economic prosperity which it implies – to the rights and prerogatives associated with Roman citizenship which were conferred (under Hadrian?) to the free citizens of what became the new *colonia Aelia Tipasensis*.

In the middle of the third century, under the Severans, Moorish rebels were kept at bay and the cities of Africa, under this protection, achieved their greatest prosperity. The wealth of Tipasa came from trade, but also from the exploitation of the fertile agricultural resources of its hinterland. A number of the public buildings which

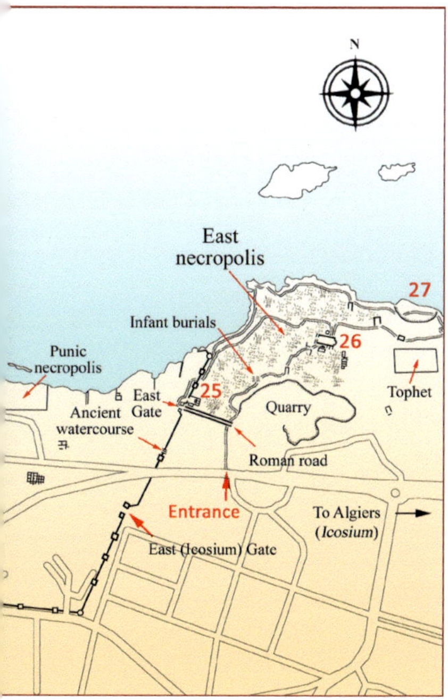

1. *Amphitheatre*
2. *Unidentified temple*
3. *New temple*
4. *Traces of early defences*
5. *Forum*
6. *Capitolium*
7. *Curia*
8. *Civil basilica*
9. *Private house*
10. *Villa of the Frescoes*
11. *Industrial establishment*
12. *Small baths*
13. *Private baths?*
14. *Large Christian basilica*
15. *Tower and postern gate*
16. *Rock tombs*
17. *Circular mausoleum*
18. *Basilica of Alexander*
19. *Martyrs' enclosure*
20. *Theatre*
21. *Nymphaeum*
22. *Header/distribution tank*
23. *Mausoleum*
24. *Great Baths*
25. *Basilica of Saints Peter and Paul*
26. *Basilica of Saint Salsa*
27. *Roman quarry and tophet*

can now be seen must have been built at this time, though they did not attain the level of luxury seen at Caesarea – a city which had, of course, benefited at an earlier period from royal favour and was a provincial capital. The use of marble veneer was less widespread and there were fewer statues of high quality, as may easily be judged by comparing the displays in the respective museums.

The physiognomy of the city changed with the ascendance of Christianity in the first half of the fourth century: the older buildings fell out of use and some were demolished. A new basilica with nine aisles (the largest in ancient Africa) thus made extensive use of masonry taken from pagan temples. Cemeteries developed around the sacred sites, and included enclosures in which the sarcophagi could be piled up in several tiers. This can be seen around the basilica of bishop Alexander and the funerary chapel which housed the remains of Saint Salsa in the later fourth century.

In 371–2, the assault during the revolt of the Moorish leader Firmus was fended off by the stout walls of the city thanks – so the legend says – to the intervention of Saint Salsa. The misfortunes of Caesarea and Icosium, which were sacked in this episode, seem to have favoured the prosperity of Tipasa for a few years longer: its population has been estimated to have been twenty thousand at this time. During the fifth century, much more serious difficulties were encountered with the annexation of Africa by the Vandals. The city was taken by siege and the walls, which had so successfully repulsed Firmus, were dismantled by the new rulers around 430–450. The divisions of the church were cast into new relief, with the Vandals (who had been converted to the Arian heresy: see p. 16) persecuting with equal vigour both Catholics and Donatists.

The recovery of the region in the sixth century to Roman (now 'Byzantine') power led to a modest renaissance, with repairs and enlargements to several churches. But Tipasa itself received no new defences and the respite was of brief duration. Like other cities in the region, it was gradually abandoned; many centuries later, its stones and its marbles were quarried by various authorities for the construction of other coastal cities, notably El Djezaïr (Algiers). Later still, the invading French army would continue this activity until more scholarly interests prevailed.

The core of the site of Tipasa is now a wooded public park; it was inscribed in 1982 in the list of UNESCO World Heritage Sites.

Saint Salsa

The history of this child, recorded by a citizen of Tipasa in the fifth century, is characteristic of the legends of early Christianity. Salsa, a young Christian, fourteen years old and incensed by idolatry, seized a bronze statue of a Roman god – 'a dragon with a gilded head and with shining eyes of polished red stone' – and threw its head into the sea. Pursued by the enraged pagans, she was stoned and cast in turn into the waves. The sea arose in tumult, until a passing Gaulish sailor (!) miraculously recovered the body. The waves instantly abated, which made it possible to bring the dead girl to shore and to bury her in a little chapel above the port.

EXPLORING THE SITE: WEST PART

1. Amphitheatre

The major (E–W) axis of this building (fig. 49) measures 80 m, and it has the unusual property that the elliptical arena is inscribed in a rectangle. Unfortunately very ruinous, all that remains is the podium wall and part of the vaulted substructures which once supported the seating. There were two principal portals at E and W, and three secondary entrances along each of the other sides. Just to the N of the portal at the W end may be seen a water-channel, which was perhaps used to flood the arena for mock sea-battles (*naumachiae*).

Clearly built at a late date, the amphitheatre encroaches on the neighbouring temple and makes use of various re-used materials. In the fourth or fifth century the W portal was reduced in width. Amongst the re-used materials found in this vicinity was a tombstone of a *Caninefas* (a tribal group in the Rhine delta) charging the enemy on horseback (see fig. 68); there are still a number of other tombstones and sarcophagi here. A little columbarium has been excavated to the S of this portal: it is unclear whether this has been incorporated from an earlier pagan necropolis or whether it was a repository for gladiators killed in the arena.

2. Unidentified temple

This temple, of which only the podium and the frontal stairway leading to the cella survive (a leg from a colossal marble statue was found there), stood in a precinct surrounded by a triple portico. The rear of the precinct was cut into when the amphitheatre was constructed and the W portico is a late restoration. The N portico opened through three entrances onto the *decumanus maximus*. This street was 14 m wide and bordered by raised porticoes continuing those of the temples. At the adjoining intersection, it was spanned by a four-way arch (*tetrapylon*) of which only the footings remain. Wealthy properties flanked it as far as the Caesarea (W) Gate.

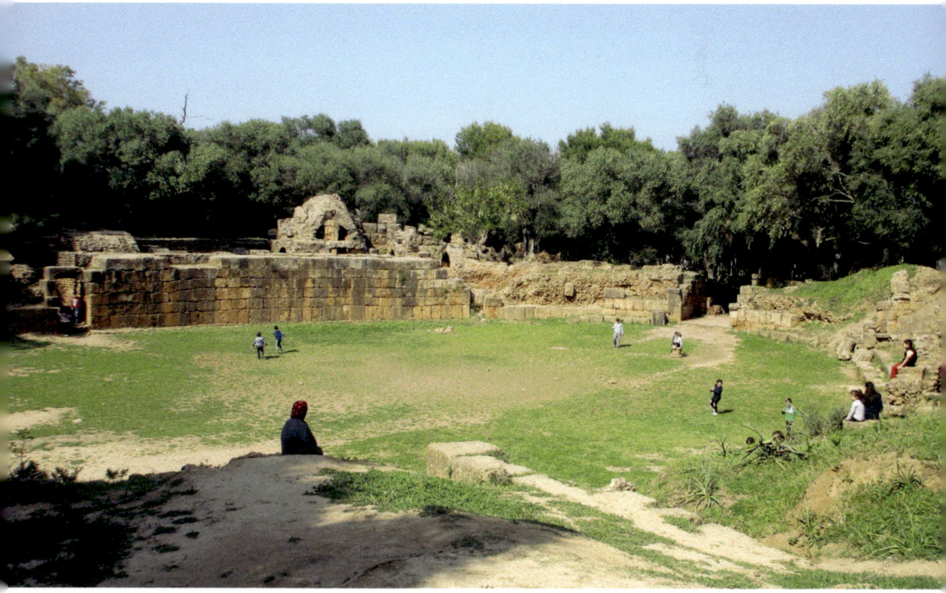

Fig. 49. Tipasa: the amphitheatre.

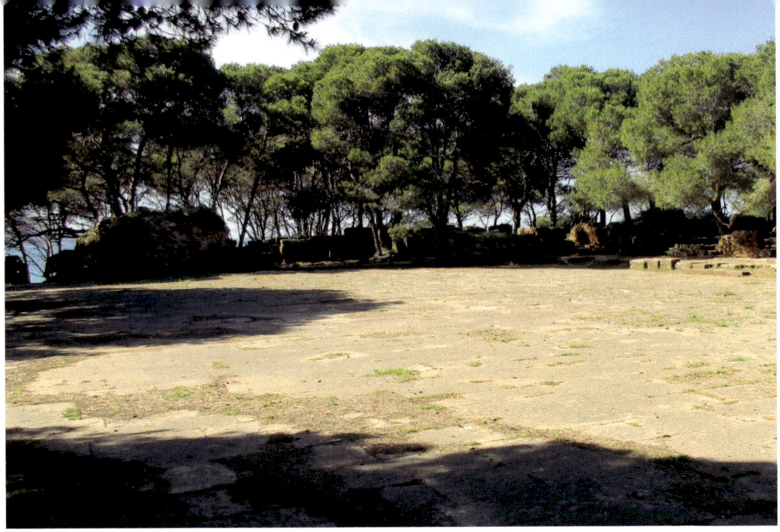

Fig. 50. Tipasa: the Forum.

3. New temple (unidentified)

Dated to the end of the second century or the beginning of the third, this temple also stood on a podium within a porticoed precinct. From the S portico, three doorways gave access to the *decumanus*. Within the precinct, a repair to the paving marks the original position of the sacrificial altar. A monumental stairway between flanking walls led up to the *cella*. The architect of the complex used subtle adjustments to absorb the irregularities of the site: the stairway is out of alignment with the axis of the precinct, there is not actually a right-angle in the design or any symmetry with the temple across the street. Even the four-way arch, planted at a point where there is a slight inflexion in the *decumanus*, contributed to the apparent harmony of the whole.

At a late date, the sanctuary went out of use. The S portico of the precinct became the right aisle of a Christian church inserted into the courtyard and aligned E–W. Its apse and part of the crypt beneath can be made out on the outer side of the E portico. The rest of the precinct became a market in the Byzantine period.

Descending towards the sea, the *cardo* was bordered by porticoes supported by rows of piers. The presence of wealthy private houses along this street is announced by their imposing portals.

4. Traces of the early defences

A first defensive circuit enclosed the promontory on which were sited the forum and the pre-Roman settlement. It was replaced in the second century by the much larger circuit, to which the E Gate (25) and a well-preserved tower on the W (15) belong.

5. Forum

Measuring 50 x 25 m, this paved square (fig. 50) was bordered on three sides by porticoes, while the *capitolium* occupied that on the N. A *cryptoporticus* illuminated by skylights ran beneath the western portico. Since the whole was quarried for building materials at various later dates, sadly little remains of its former grandeur.

The forum of Tipasa is sited at the summit of an eminence which is described in the *Passion of Saint Salsa*. It was here, where half-collapsed sanctuaries were already no more than 'shadows of ancient buildings' that she came in order to throw down the serpent that was still venerated: 'There was there a temple, at a well-chosen spot on a hill which rises above the rocks on which the city is built, with solid foundations of stone. This hill is as if in the centre of the city, which it dominates completely from both sides. Towards the sea, where it drops in steep slopes, it throws out a spur which separates the gulfs, resisting the waves which bathe it on both sides with clouds of spray. … This hill, since the beginning, since the very foundation of the city when the veneration of idols reigned unchallenged amongst the population, was known as the *Hill of the Temples*. It was indeed there that all the sanctuaries were built, as if to isolate them as fully as possible from the quarters of habitation.' The narrator of the *Passion* specifies that, at the time of writing (in the fifth century), where once had been the temples and where the Devil had later arranged a synagogue for the Jews, 'in this place where two sacrilegious cults had formerly reigned in succession, today the Church reigns supreme, in honour of a martyr.'

6. Capitolium

Nothing remains of this building apart from the foundations of the stairway which once led to the podium and the substructures of the three chapels which were dedicated to the Capitoline Triad.

7. Curia

This building was the political heart of the city, and lay on the E side of the forum. Its remains can barely be made out today; the same applies to the tribune for public addresses, which was a little further to the N along the same side.

8. Civil basilica

This building is divided by colonnades into three aisles; at the N end was a raised apse (*tribunal*) flanked by two pilasters and once separated from the central nave by a grille (fig. 51). The apse was paved with an

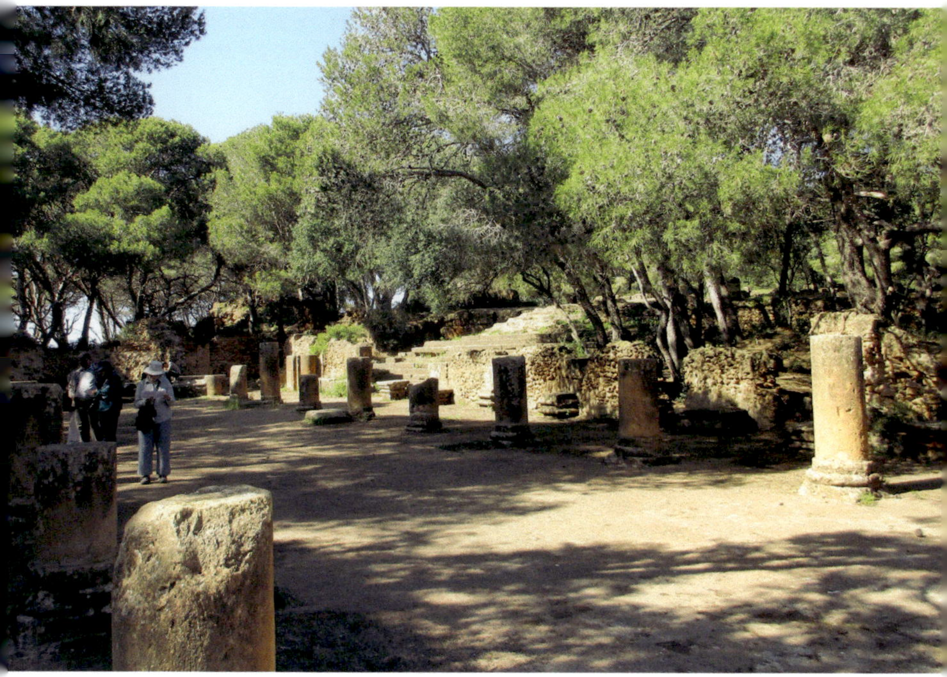

Fig. 51. Tipasa: the civil basilica.

extraordinary mosaic (which may be seen in the museum: fig. 66) showing a cowering captive family of three and a dozen portraits of Africans. The presence of such a theme, in an eminently symbolic location, doubtless underlines the Roman intention to impress on local populations the victorious power of the empire, and so to discourage any thoughts of resistance.

The basilica was built substantially later than the forum, for its NE wall impinges on the flight of steps which leads to the square; likewise the steps leading into the building overlie the paving of the *decumanus*; it is probably to be dated to the end of the second century or the beginning of the third. Despite the presence of a capital decorated with a chi-rho symbol, and of some traces on the floor which might suggest the foundations of an altar, the conversion of the building into a church remains largely hypothetical.

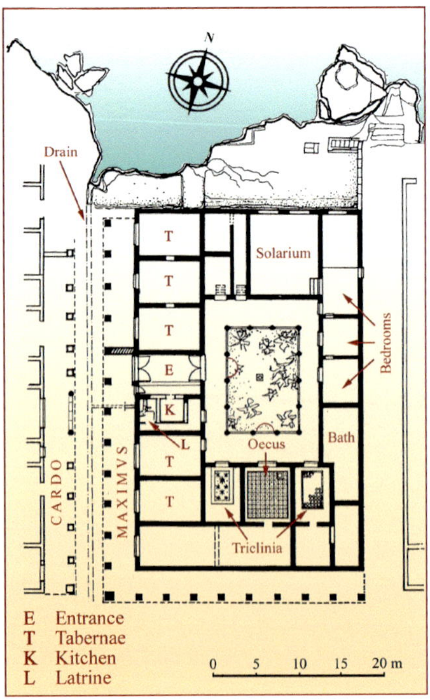

9. Private house

It is possible to make out here the apse of an *oecus* which was later converted into a Christian chapel. In the entrance corridor, a verse inscription in mosaic (now in the museum: see p. 72) was surmounted by two pigeons in a floral frieze and framed by a laurel-border. It predicted happiness and recognition to he who had built and decorated such a fine house.

10. Villa of the Frescoes

This wealthy town-house of 1,000 sq.m (figs. 52, 53), built over a former cemetery when the city expanded, is named after the painted wall-decoration which it once boasted, and of which fragments were found when it was excavated. The burials found beneath belong to the first century AD, but the villa seems to have been built in the middle of the second century, roughly at the time when the new defensive walls were laid out.

On the W side of the building, a grand portal led from the street into a central peristyle, off which opened the various different parts of the house. A large *oecus* (or summer dining-room?) occupied the centre of the S side, and was decorated with floral and geometric mosaic. This was flanked by two smaller reception rooms, also with mosaic floors. There was probably an upper floor on this side of the building. The house had its own bath suite in the SE corner, and another large reception room on the N side overlooking the sea. In the centre of the peristyle, a simple opening provided for water to be drawn from a rock-cut cistern beneath. At a later date, this opening was replaced by a tall stone well-head, and two semi-circular fountains were added to the porticoes of the peristyle, one facing the *oecus* and the other the main entrance.

The valuable city-centre frontage was not wasted, and the rooms on the W side were

Fig. 52. Tipasa: Villa of the Frescoes, plan.

mostly shops, open only to the street. The room immediately to the S of the entrance housed both the kitchen and a latrine!

11. Industrial establishment

This consists of four square tanks with rounded corners, a rectangular basin and a large space which was originally covered and was presumably a warehouse. The presence of a raised water-tank (half collapsed on top of the adjoining baths), that of a drain emptying directly into the sea, the discovery of giant storage jars (*dolia*), of numerous amphora fragments and of water-channels all suggest the production of salted fish or of *garum* (see p. 60).

12. Small baths

These modest public baths are very ruinous: the collapsed masses of concrete suggest earthquake damage, after which they were not repaired. Nonetheless it is possible to make out without difficulty the usual succession of cold and heated rooms that one expects in such an establishment, and there are still traces of painted decoration on the walls.

At a much later date, a creek below the baths, on the waterfront, provided an embarkation-point for the exportation of building stone to Algiers.

13. Private baths?

The plan is clear: one can readily understand the circulation of hot air from a furnace with external access, through the well-preserved heated rooms; there are also several plunge-baths and a latrine. The baths probably belonged to the adjoining building, the nature of which (public or private) is still unclear, though certainly of late date. There are mangers for stabling animals.

14. Large Christian basilica (cathedral)

Built in the fourth century, using elements taken from the Capitolium and the two unidentified temples, this church is, at 58 x 42 m, one of the largest in Roman Africa (figs. 54, 55). Six rows of columns defined a central

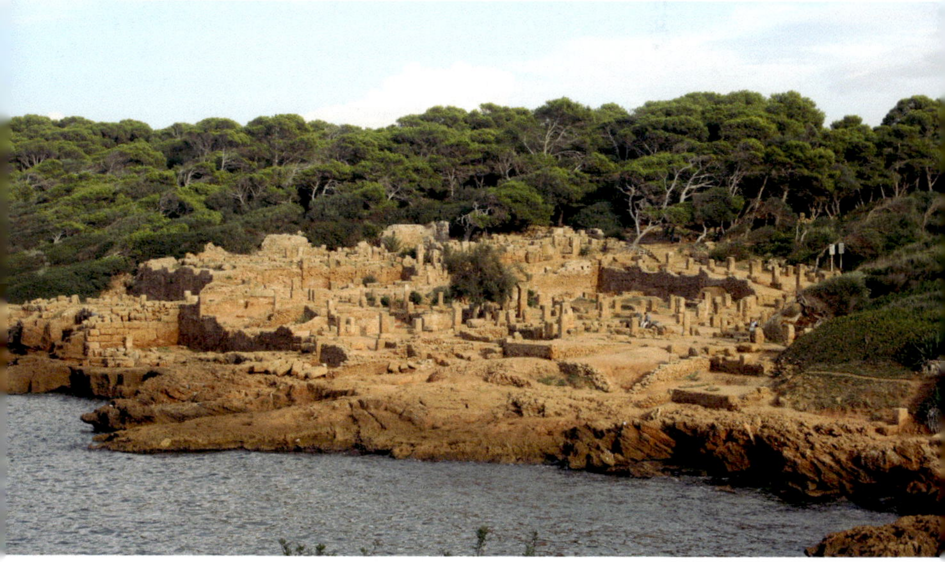

Fig. 53. Tipasa: Villa of the Frescoes from the W.

Garum

Garum 'is prepared from the intestines of fish and various parts which would otherwise be thrown away, macerated in salt; so that it is, in fact, the result of their putrefaction. Garum was formerly prepared from a fish, called *garos* by the Greeks; who assert, also, that a fumigation made with its head has the effect of bringing away the afterbirth. At the present day, however, the most esteemed kind of garum is that prepared from the *scomber* [mackerel?] in the fisheries of Carthago Spartaria [Cartagena in Spain] it is known as "garum of the allies", and for a couple of *congii* [6½ l.] we have to pay but little less than one thousand sesterces. Indeed, there is no liquid hardly, with the exception of the unguents, that has sold at higher prices of late; so much so, that the nations which produce it have become quite ennobled thereby. There are fisheries, too, of the *scomber* on the coasts of Mauretania and at Carteia in Bætica, near the Straits which lie at the entrance to the Ocean; this being the only use that is made of the fish. For the production of garum, Clazomenæ is also famed, Pompeii, too, and Leptis; while for their muria, Antipolis, Thurii, and of late, Dalmatia, enjoy a high reputation.'

Pliny the Elder, *Natural History* 31.43, tr. John Bostock & H.T. Riley (London 1855)

nave 13 m wide, flanked by three narrower aisles on either side. In a later restoration, the nave was further divided into three by the insertion of two additional colonnades, possibly because it had become difficult to obtain roof timbers of sufficient length. The principal entrance, flanked by two smaller ones, led directly into the nave, facing the chancel. At the E end, the apse of the basilica projected over the cliff, and was reinforced by massive buttresses. Some 700 sq.m of mosaic cover the floor of the church, but of this only fragments remain.

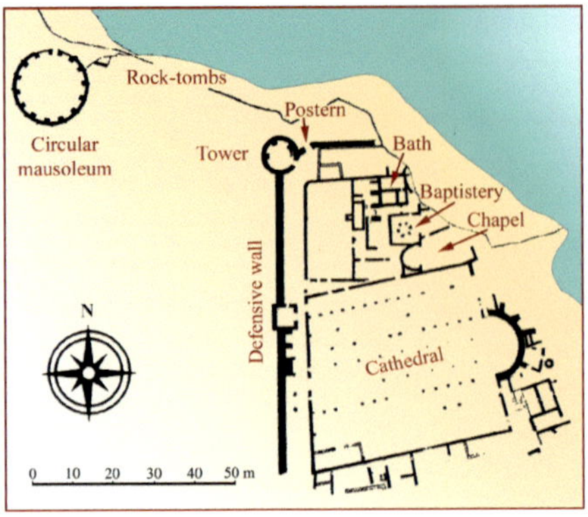

To the N of the basilica, a complex of structures included a baptistery with a stepped circular basin, a little chapel (perhaps a *consignatorium*, in which the newly baptised were confirmed in their vows), a small bath suite for the use of the *catechumenoi* (as at Cuicul: see p. 127) and – between these buildings and the rampart – the bishop's residence. It was reported by S. Gsell that, in the little chapel, 'a mosaic, found in poor condition and now destroyed, portrayed sheep grazing amongst asphodels: perhaps a metaphor for Christians living in peace under the rule of Christ, who had himself been compared to a Good Shepherd.' A room close to the baptistery yielded another mosaic which is now in the National Museum in Algiers: a verse inscription exhorts 'those who wish to acquire true knowledge of life to come and bathe here in the water of baptism, that heavenly gift.'

Fig. 54. Tipasa: plan of the cathedral and other buildings next to the western defences of the city.

15. Tower and postern

This circular tower marks the NW extremity of the defensive walls. Within, the base and supporting arches of a curving staircase leading to an upper level can still be seen. Next to the adjoining postern gate there is a bench for the gate-keepers. Built in the middle of the second century, the wall-circuit was 2.3 km long and 8 or 9 m high, incorporating 31 round or square defensive towers. Like all the other defences of Roman cities in Africa, it was demolished by the Vandals. The manner of demolition can be seen next to the Christian basilica: the walls were undermined before being toppled outwards by means of crowbars.

16. Rock-tombs

Pre-Roman cuttings in the rock, either vertical shafts or true chambers facing the sea, belong to a style of burial (*Hanout*) originating in Sicily and commonly found in North Africa. Two of the *haouanet* (plural) of Tipasa have the particular distinction of having been reused for Christian burials.

17. Circular mausoleum

This funerary monument takes the form of an unroofed stone-built circular enclosure, 20 m in diameter, decorated with engaged columns around the exterior (fig. 56). The internal face of the perimeter wall is articulated by fourteen vaulted recesses (*arcosolia*) which accommodated the sarcophagi of venerated persons. The presence of a further burial in the centre suggests that of a particularly revered saint. The structure is therefore probably a *martyrium*, i.e. a place dedicated to the cult of a martyr. The faithful then came to bury their dead *ad sanctos*, next to the saints, in order to 'protect them from the evils beyond the tomb' (Saint Ambrose). This was a custom which Saint Augustine criticised obliquely, explaining that 'the proximity of the

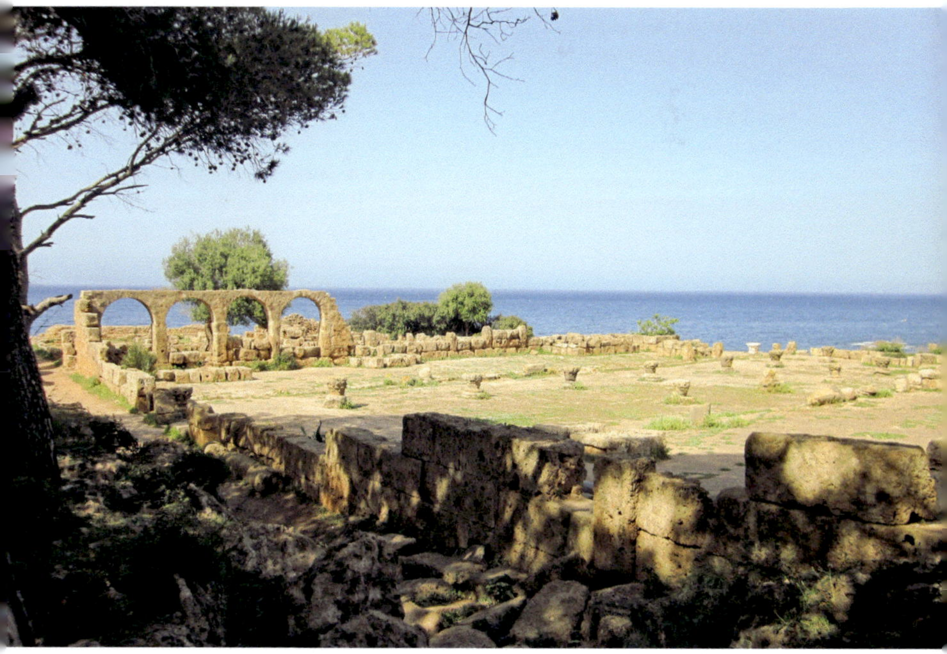

Fig. 55. Tipasa: the large western basilica, from the SW.

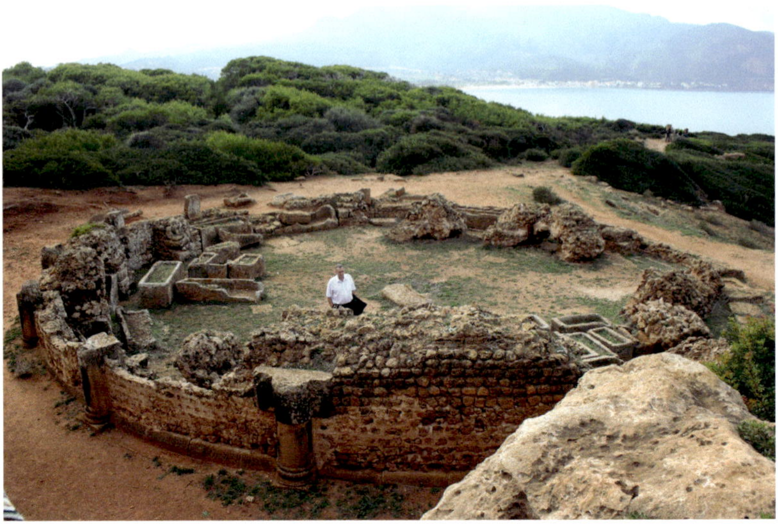

Fig. 56. Tipasa: the circular mausoleum next to the western defences.

tombs had no value apart from inciting the living to pray more fervently for their dead.'

18. Basilica of Alexander

Built in 400 in the heart of the West Necropolis (figs. 57, 58), the church was divided by two ranges of piers into a nave and two aisles. Its trapezoidal shape and the absence of an apse at the E end, behind the chancel, were determined by the rocky nature of the terrain.

At the W end, an apse housed four sarcophagi: those of (presumably) the founder of the church, bishop Alexander, and three chosen companions. At the opposite end, on a raised platform of stone, nine sarcophagi once contained the remains of ecclesiastical dignitaries or venerated martyrs who were dead long before the construction of the church. Previously buried elsewhere – perhaps in the crypt which opened off the SE corner of the building and which contains ten rock-cut cist-graves – these 'just forebears' (*iusti priores*) were installed in this position by bishop Alexander, who dedicated the foundation of the new sanctuary to them. A mosaic (now in the National Museum in Algiers: see p. 82) in front of the platform recorded, in thirteen verses, this honorific disposition. Indeed, the whole church was paved with mosaics, of which the finest examples – notably a large panel with seven tiers of fishes, lobsters and shells – have been transferred to Algiers (p. 87; a simpler geometric mosaic is on the floor of the museum at Tipasa). The words of Alexander have the interesting characteristic of being almost identical to those used by Cresconius in his basilica at Cuicul (see p. 128).

In the S aisle of the basilica may be seen a semicircular *mensa* (dining bench) and tombs of those who had obtained the privilege of being buried inside the church, close to the blessed. In the N aisle, a mosaic inscription in blue lettering on a white background recorded that Tiberinus, deacon to bishop Alexander, had obtained from the holy man permission to bury here his very dear mother, Rogata.

In front of the principal entrance to the church, at the NW corner, another mosaic called upon the faithful to choose martyrdom (*clausula iustitiae est martyrium votis optare*) and to give alms (*habes et aliam similem aelemosinam viris facere*). Two further mosaics, discovered in the narthex, permit a reconstruction of the sequence of moral exhortations which the faithful encountered when entering the church: 'first they entered the narthex where, as was normal in a funerary church, one evoked the resurrection of the flesh and a promise for the

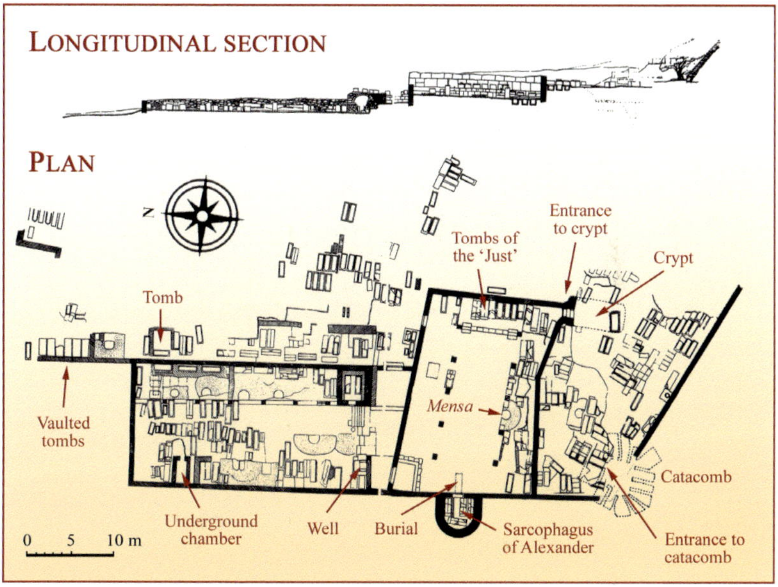

Fig. 57. Tipasa: plan and section of the Basilica of Alexander and adjoining structures.

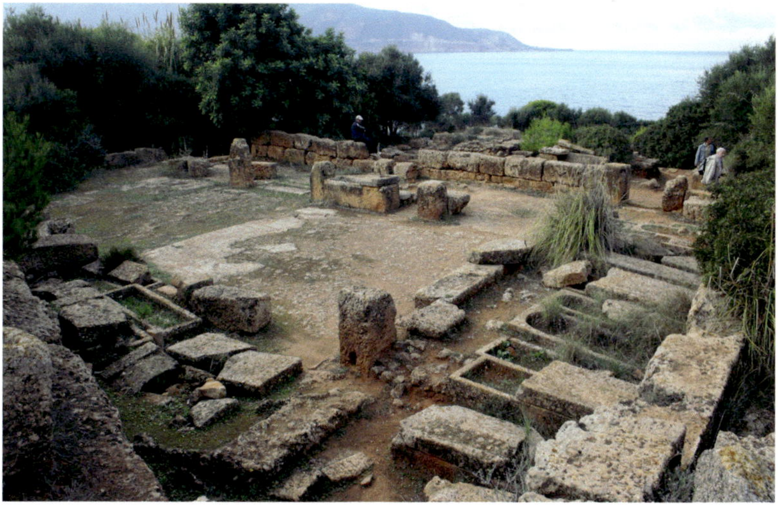

Fig. 58. Tipasa: the Basilica of Alexander.

believer of eternal joy. Then, after crossing the threshold and having been reminded of those for whom the church was built and whose memory was venerated, they were invited to practise charity, the true virtue of a Christian and his guarantee of eternal life. They would then ascend two steps, to be greeted in the body of the church by the sentence which extolled martyrdom and charity as the two ways of entering among the Just' (L. Leschi).

Outside, in a part of the early enclosure in which bishop Alexander had chosen to build his church, there is a circular catacomb amongst the tombs which press up against the S wall of the building: twelve funerary recesses (*loculi*) radiate around four cists cut in the rock. The walls of the cave were once decorated with red-painted plaster, but of this almost nothing remains.

19. Martyrs' enclosure

To the N of the basilica and below it is a rectangular walled enclosure where persecuted martyrs of the Christian faith were buried: some eighty graves have been counted. Predating the church and contemporary with the crypt, which surely held the 'Just' before their translation, the walls of the enclosure are of coursed masonry; it shared a common entrance with the approach to the later church. Along the E side, beneath the traces of a late portico, are six *mensae*, corresponding to tombs of martyrs. Only two of them have been identified: Rogatus and Vitalis. Cut into the rock beneath the northernmost *mensa*, a recess held the remains of a Christian named Maxima.

Along the W side of the enclosure, many other tombs lie in a row, including further examples of benches for funerary banquets.

Funerary rites: *mensae*

African cemeteries, and notably those of Tipasa, often show facilities for a particular rite, the funerary banquet. On the occasion of a burial, the ancients were in the habit of taking a meal in common, the *refrigerium*, in which the deceased notionally took part. Food and drink for the deceased were either spread on the ground or passed into the tomb itself by means of a funnel or 'libation tube' in the cover. These banquets would take place on occasions such as the *novendialis*, nine days after the funeral, or the *parentalia*, the equivalent of our All Souls Day. 'When the food has been brought,' recorded the children of a certain Aelia Secundula, 'the cups filled, the cushions laid out late in the evening, we shall speak with honour of our revered mother in order to soften our injury and our grief.' As an aid to the conduct of this convivial rite, the tombstone was often accompanied in the pagan period by a stone slab laid in front of it, carved to represent a table laid for dinner, with dishes and spoons (either hollow to receive real food, or with food also in the carving: see p. 215, fig. 229). In the Christian period, some tombs were equipped with dining couches in masonry or banqueting tables covered in mosaic which portrayed appropriate motifs, such as fish, victuals or mottoes like that now in the Tipasa museum (fig. 67). This commemorative banquet was inclined to degenerate in character. The ecclesiastical historian A.-G. Hamman has written, 'The Africans organized real festivals, with orchestra, lyre-players and dancing women. The tipsy participants took up with drunken shouts the most bawdy of couplets. Never mind the dead: the living amused themselves thoroughly and the occasion became a bacchanal.' Bishops and councils multiplied their warnings, and then their prohibitions (in 329 for Africa), but the custom was suppressed only with great difficulty.

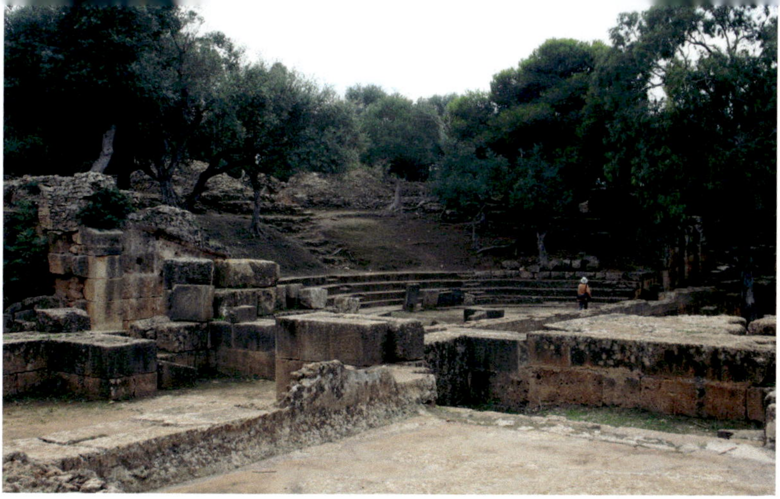

Fig. 59. Tipasa: the theatre.

An epitaph of one Victorinus was found here, 'martyred on Sunday the eighth of May, towards two in the afternoon' (*marture professum, octavo idus Maias die solis ore octava*) in a year towards the end of the third century. Close by, another *mensa* commemorates the priest Amantius and his companion Hilara, probably set up by their daughter at a time before the two Councils of Carthage (390 and 401) at which celibacy was prescribed for priests and deacons after their ordination.

20. Theatre

On returning inland from the large basilica (14), one reaches the theatre after passing by a semicircular plunge-bath belonging to a private house and, a little further on, the head of a Roman well. As at Madauros (p. 270) and Sabratha in Libya, the theatre of Tipasa (fig. 59) was built on flat ground which did not offer a slope to support the seating. This was therefore raised upon radial vaults and piers, as was also done for amphitheatres; the imprint of the timber shuttering over which the concrete vaults were laid can still be clearly seen in places. Designed to accommodate 3,000 spectators, the building conforms to the classical type and is carefully designed. Unfortunately, it has been reduced to little more than its foundations, since the stage building and almost all of the seating was dismantled in 1847 by the French military in order to build the cholera hospital nearby at Marengo (now Hadjout).

To the S of the theatre a gate, set in a semicircular forecourt flanked by two round towers, marked the road to Caesarea (Cherchel). This is now bisected by the modern road, but the lowest courses of the towers may be seen on either side. Outside the walls, the so-called Caesarea Gate Necropolis consists of cremation burials of the first and second centuries, together with collective chamber-tombs and *columbaria*. The fine collection of glassware on display in the Tipasa museum comes from these tombs.

Some 200 m further to the W, a necropolis, composed of rectangular tombs aligned in rows and covered by huge slabs, has yielded a series of Punic vases dated to the sixth or fifth centuries BC. Along with the archaic chamber-tomb which perches above the port (this Phoenician/Punic tomb was spared when the surrounding burial ground became a quarry), these represent the earliest evidence for the pre-Roman settlement.

Eight hundred metres further to the W, another necropolis was revealed during the construction of the seaside resort of Tipasa-Matarès at the mouth of the Oued Merzoug.

A wide range of burial types has been found there – burials beneath jars, *capuccina* burials (beneath a pitched covering of tiles), sarcophagi, domed tombs, *columbaria*, funerary enclosures, Christian hypogea with painted walls – but also *mensae* (dining-benches). One of these *mensae* was covered with a Christian mosaic, with a chi-rho symbol, fishes and marine animals, and an inscription dedicating the funerary celebration in memory of the dead 'in God: may there be peace and concord in our banquet' (in the local museum: fig. 67). The sarcophagus of Nereids and marine monsters on display in the museum (fig. 70) was also found in one of the hypogea in this cemetery.

21. Nymphaeum

This monumental fountain (fig. 60), in the form of a hemicycle, was decorated with statues between columns of the bluish marble from the Chenoua massif which dominates the W side of the bay. The water descended in cascades along the length of a wall veneered in multicoloured marbles, trickled down from step to step and then flowed from a single spout between each pair of columns (evident from accretions of scale in these positions, and from the surviving spout at the right-hand end) into a row of lower basins. A central sluice gate provided for these to be drained on occasion. The fountain had a practical as well as an ornamental purpose: the signs of heavy wear on the parapet of the lower basins shows that the inhabitants came there to draw water, as from a spring. Above and to the right of the main structure, one can see the remains of the open channel which brought the water; behind the nymphaeum, the aqueduct was conveyed on piers to the header tank (22) from which the fountain was supplied.

To the E of the nymphaeum, on the *decumanus maximus*, may be seen the foundations of a triple arch. This arch is thought to have carried an aqueduct across the road

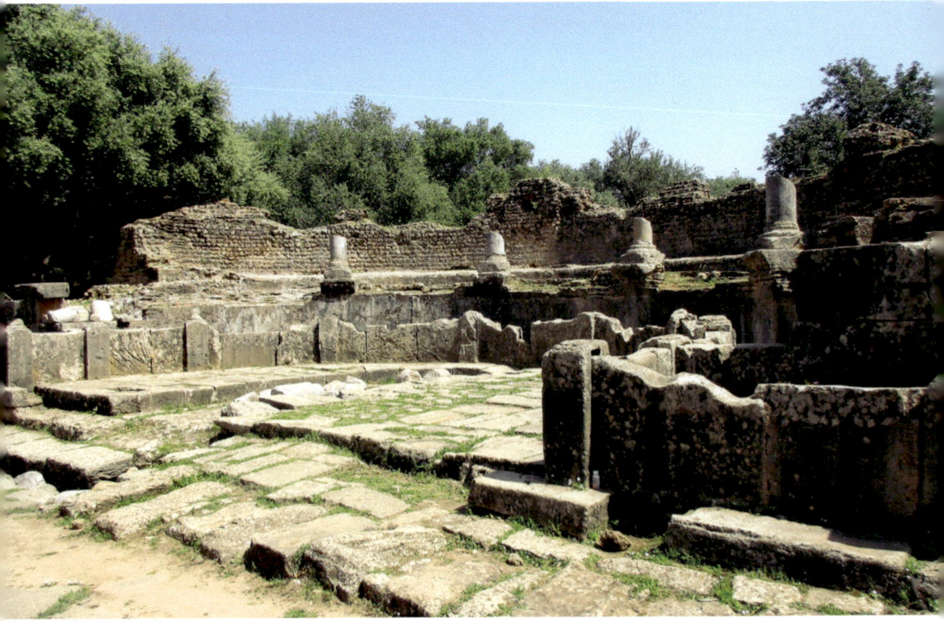

Fig. 60. Tipasa: the Nymphaeum.

in order to deliver water to the northern part of the city.

22. Header/distribution tank

This water tank is the termination-point of an aqueduct more than 10 km long, which brought water from a source to the SW of the city. From here, various channels delivered the water to different destinations, including the nymphaeum.

23. Mausoleum

This is a monumental tomb of the first century AD. The lower storey was square in plan and embellished with fluted pilasters; this supported an octagonal pyramid (now collapsed to one side) in a style which is Punic in origin (compare Le Khroub, p. 161). Inside the tomb was a chamber with niches for funerary urns.

24. Great Baths

Covering a similar area to the amphitheatre, this two-storey bath complex was one of the most important assets of the city. Extensively invaded by the modern village, one can see now only part of the *frigidarium*, obscured by luxuriant vegetation, and some imposing masses of upstanding walls. These are composed of a combination of brick-faced concrete and heavy ashlar masonry.

The garden immediately to the west of the Great Baths and in front of the excavation house (formerly the Hôtel du Rivage) is not generally accessible to the public. It houses a number of pieces of sculpture and architectural ornament, including two Roman sarcophagi of note.

Sarcophagus of the Kriophoros: This is a fine strigilated sarcophagus with rounded ends. ('Strigilated refers to the 'S'-shaped fluted pattern, the shape of which resembles a Roman *strigil*, a tool used in the baths for scraping oil and dirt off the skin.) In the centre of the long side is a standing figure of a beardless man carrying a ram on his shoulders, flanked by two other sheep (fig. 61). This has been interpreted as a representation of Christ as the Good Shepherd, but this seems to be belied by the images at either end of lions vigorously devouring gazelles (not lying down with lambs!). The image of Hermes carrying a ram on his shoulders goes back a long way in Greek mythology, but it was certainly adopted at a later date by Christians. While this sarcophagus is of Roman date, it is impossible to tell whether any allusion to Christianity would have been deliberate. (West necropolis, fourth century.)

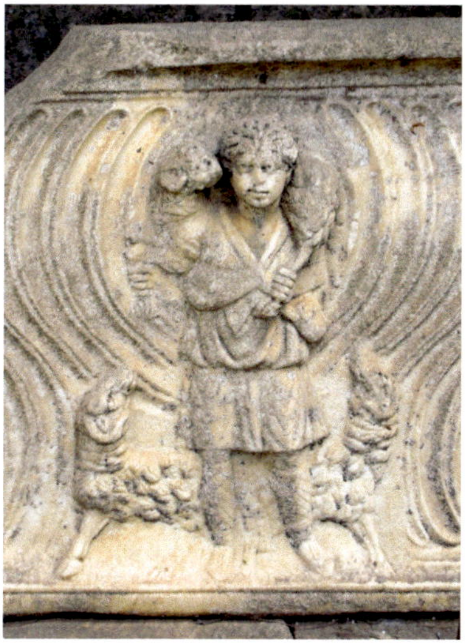

Fig. 61. Tipasa: sarcophagus of the Kriophoros ('ram-bearer').

Sarcophagus of the Dioscuri: beneath arcades supported by columns with spiral fluting, the central scenes (stolen) portrayed a couple at their wedding (attended by Juno and Hymen, carrying a torch), then the same couple celebrating a farewell sacrifice. These two images are framed by the guardian deities Castor and Pollux, while on the short sides are two scenes of sacrifice of a bull. (West necropolis, third century.)

EXPLORING THE SITE: EAST (EXTRA-MURAL) PART

25. Eastern defences and Basilica of Saints Peter and Paul

On the E side of the ancient city, a separate entrance leads into the archaeological zone from the main road through the modern village (N11). Here may be seen part of the eastern defences of the city, and one of two east gates facing in the direction of Icosium (Algiers). (The second lies to the S of the modern road and is just detectable where the line of the defences rises up the slope.) The sill of the gate is worn and there are evident ruts from wheeled traffic. An inscription found at one of these gates, which would have been placed above the opening, records its construction (i.e. completion) in 146–7. When the defences were demolished by the Vandals, the collapse of a gate tower blocked the passage through the more northerly gate, so the inhabitants cut a new opening in the N flank. The remains of the staircase leading to the tower and rampart walk, once supported on two arches, may be made out against the inner face of the wall.

The sixth-century church of Saints Peter and Paul was built *extra muros* (its entrance was cut through the rampart, which provided its W wall), to the NE of the gate, in the angle between the defensive wall and the road. The building consists of a nave and two aisles, separated by rows of piers, with a raised apse between two sacristies. The nave was cut off from the aisles by chancel screens, of which the sockets can still be seen. A fragmentary marble dedication to the 'Blessed martyrs Peter and Paul' (in the courtyard of the museum) explains the reason for the particular veneration of this church, and the profusion of tombs which surrounds it. Some of these lie within a funerary enclosure attached to the S side of the church.

To the NE of the church may be seen two towers of the defences with external

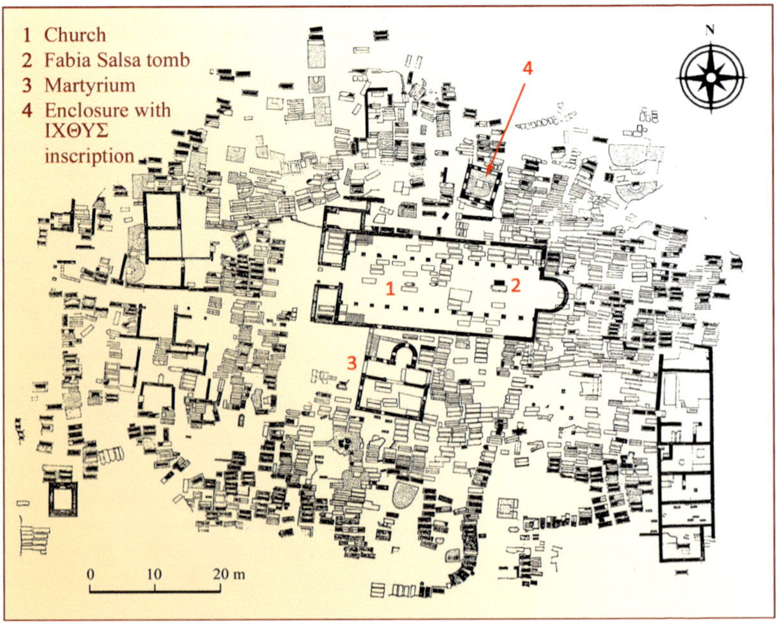

Fig. 62. Tipasa: plan of the church and martyrium of Saint Salsa.

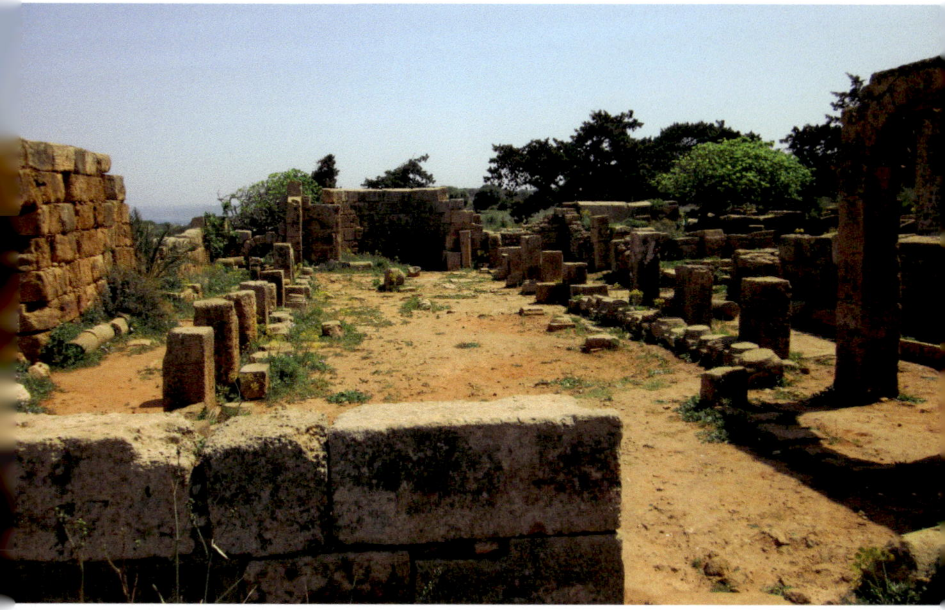

Fig. 63. Tipasa: the church of Saint Salsa.

staircases, and then a round tower like that on the W (15), which marks the eastern end of the rampart.

26. Basilica of Saint Salsa

Built in the late fourth century on the presumed site of the tomb of Saint Salsa, the first chapel was no more than some 15 m long. It was enlarged, then rebuilt, in the course of the fifth and sixth centuries. As seen (figs. 62, 63), the church is 30 m long. It was entered through a porch opening into a nave and aisles, separated by stone piers. The aisles carried galleries which were reached by means of staircases on either side at the W end. The many mosaics which once decorated the floor of the building included the dedication of Potentius to Saint Salsa (now lost) which stated that the remains of the saint were interred beneath the altar: 'The gifts that you see are the work of Potentius, who rejoices to have completed the task which he was set. Where the holy altar shines, there lies the martyr Salsa, sweeter than nectar, who has earned eternal life in Heaven, in full blessedness. Happy to grant to pious Potentius a favour which will reward him for his pains, she will bear witness to his merits in the Kingdom of Heaven.' At a later date, a reused marble sarcophagus was placed in front of the altar. It portrayed the legend of Diana and Endymion, but was later seriously damaged. In the same position, one can see today a tomb cover with a cylindrical top carved with rose-coffering, dedicated to a Fabia Salsa. The rare family name and the pagan inscription suggest that this belonged to an ancestor of the young martyr.

Immediately to the S of the church, a small rectangular building with a separate apse on the N side (fig. 64) has been identified as a *martyrium*: this was surely the original burial-place of Saint Salsa, built before the first church. A passage decorated with engaged columns carrying Corinthian capitals

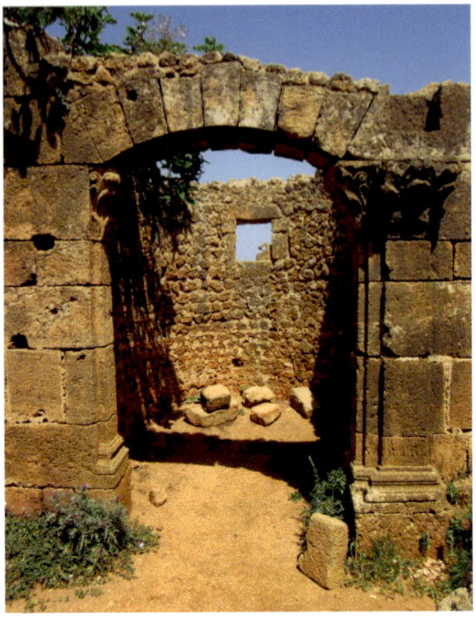

Fig. 64. Tipasa: apse of the martyrium *of Saint Salsa.*

enabled the faithful to visit the tomb, without entering it. According to the legend of Saint Salsa, in 371 the rebellious Firmus, having sacked Caesarea, came here to implore the assistance of the martyr in taking Tipasa, which was resisting his attack. 'He lit candles, but they went out, refusing to burn on behalf of a sacrilege. He offered a cup, with bread and wine, but the cup overturned and the holy offerings did not permit the impious man, under the pretence of piety, to make his vows ... The wretch did not understand that he was going to die and that there was no escape. ... That same day, and the following night, he had to fight again. He saw the crushing defeat of the fine chieftains whom he had summoned to aid him against the citizens. Defeated and disabled himself, he had to withdraw and lift the siege of the city, routed by the intervention of the martyr and the help of God. He died soon after, destined for Divine judgement before the accusation of Saint Salsa.'

In the vast necropolis which extends all around the church, a number of funerary enclosures (*areae*) can be seen. One of them, to the N of the church, still has its enclosing wall and fretwork windows. On the outside, to the left of the doorway, is inscribed *Ichthus* in Greek letters (ΙΧΘΥΣ), an acrostic symbolising ***I****esous* ***C****hristos* ***T****heou* ***U****ios* ***S****oter* (Jesus Christ, son of God, saviour). Within is a sarcophagus with a dining-couch on top.

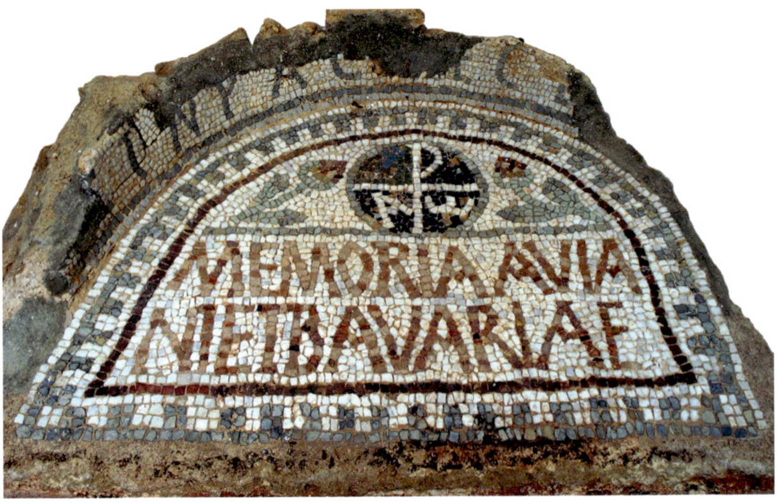

Fig. 65. Tipasa museum: decorated mensa *above the burial of Avianus and Bavaria.*

Amongst the hundreds of burials which crowded around the basilica and its saint, many were decorated with figured mosaics or inscriptions (see fig. 65). Many of these, and other inscriptions, remind us of the distant origins of the inhabitants of Tipasa, since they invoke southern Numidia, Italy or even Asia Minor.

27. Roman quarry and tophet

A few tens of metres to the S of this coastal quarry, excavations by Serge Lancel brought to light a zone of uninscribed *stelai*, offering tables and terracotta cinerary urns containing ashes of animals. This was a little tophet where a substitution rite (*molchomor*) was performed, consisting of sacrificing to the god Baal-Saturn infant animals in place of infant children. This sacrificial precinct, dated by Lancel to the first century, 'provides clear proof that, in an advanced stage of Romanisation, the most characteristic aspects of local Punic tradition were still alive and flourishing.'

MUSEUM

Courtyard

Here are displayed various Punic *stelai* and Christian commemorative inscriptions (*memoriae*) in mosaic or on marble slabs. Amongst these are the *mensa* illustrated in fig. 65 and (on the wall opposite the entrance) the fragmentary marble tablet recording the dedication of the church of Saints Peter and Paul (see p. 68).

Main hall

Mosaic of the captives: on the wall opposite the doorway is a mosaic which once occupied the apse of the civil basilica (18) (fig. 66). In the centre of a field of peltas and lozenges is a square panel depicting a captive family – father, mother and son – crouching with their hands tied; a shield rests on the ground beneath the father. This poignant scene is surrounded by a dozen portraits of Africans, representing either inhabitants of Tipasa or different ethnic

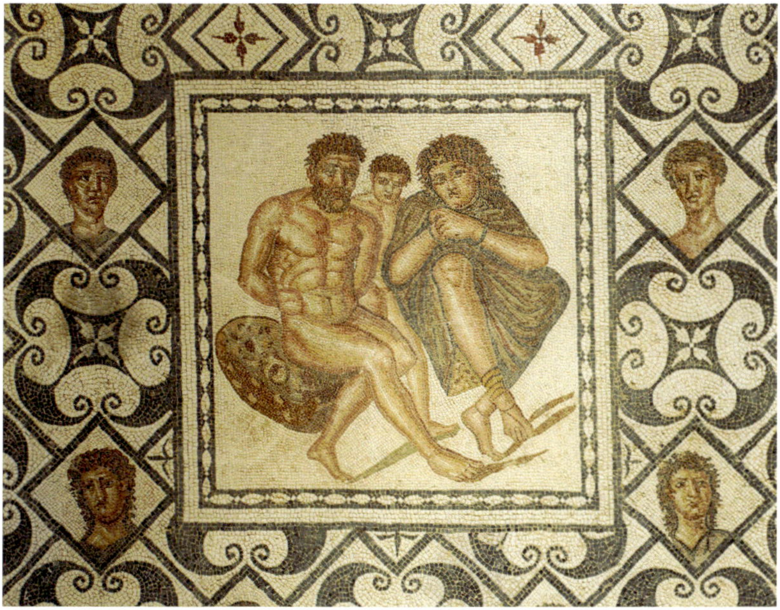

Fig. 66. Tipasa museum: mosaic of captives, from the civil basilica.

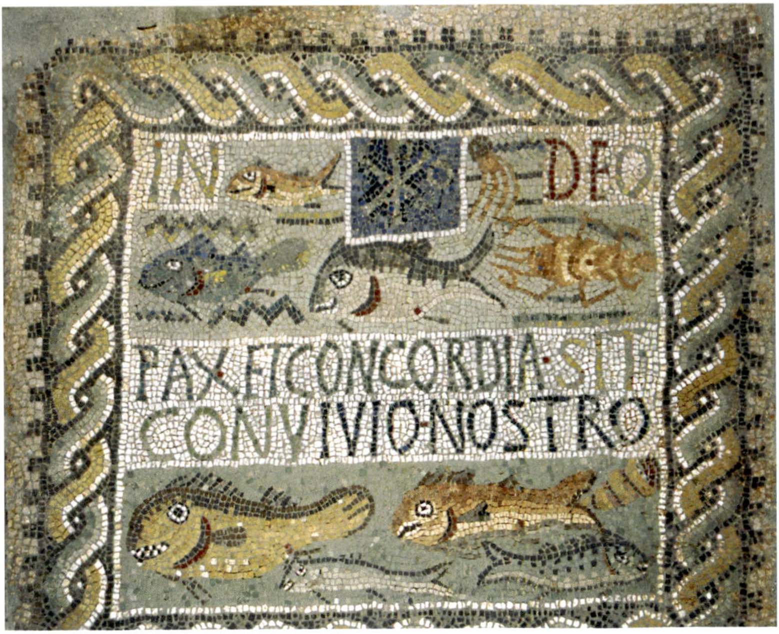

Fig. 67. Tipasa museum: mosaic tomb-cover from the necropolis of Tipasa-Matarès.

groups conquered and then assimilated by the Romans. (Late second century or later.)

Pax et Concordia mosaic (right-hand wall): see p. 64 and fig. 67. (Necropolis of Tipasa-Matarès.)

Verse inscription in mosaic: (above the door) from a private house, see p. 58.

Geometric mosaic on the floor. (Basilica of Alexander: see p. 62.)

Tombstones of soldiers: this fine collection includes four tombstones dedicated to foreign cavalrymen enrolled in the auxiliary forces of the Roman army stationed at Tipasa. The upper register of each stone shows the individual in action. From left to right, they are a Briton between two horses (fig. 68a); a Caninefas from the Rhine delta (see fig. 68b); an Iturian archer from the Middle East and, after a dedication to Victory found in the civil basilica, a Central European lancer. (Second or third centuries.)

Sarcophagus of Pelops and Hippodameia (left-hand end-wall, fig. 69, Pentelic marble): damaged, but of much higher quality than

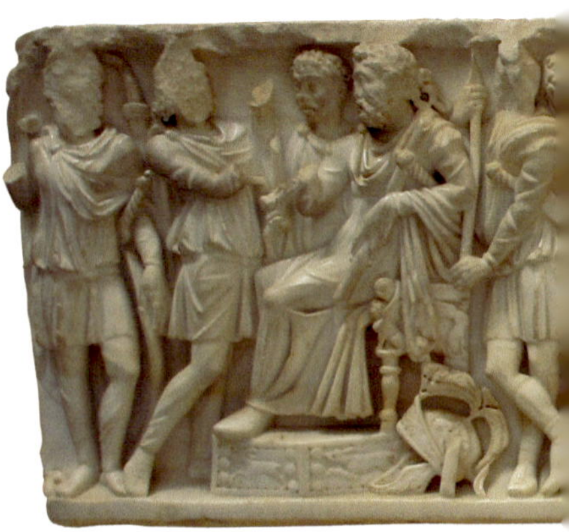

a

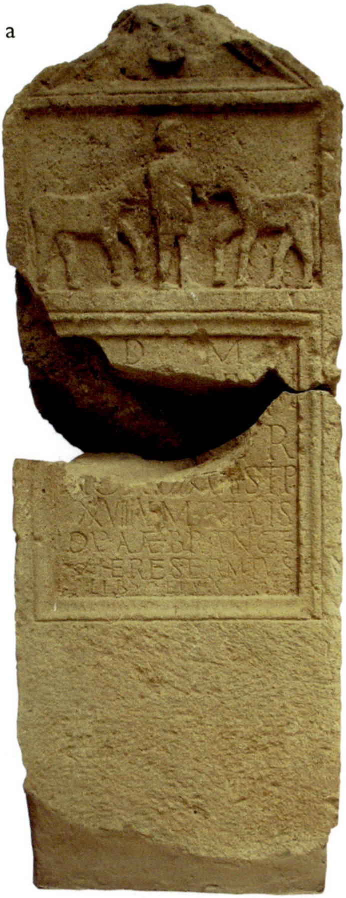

b

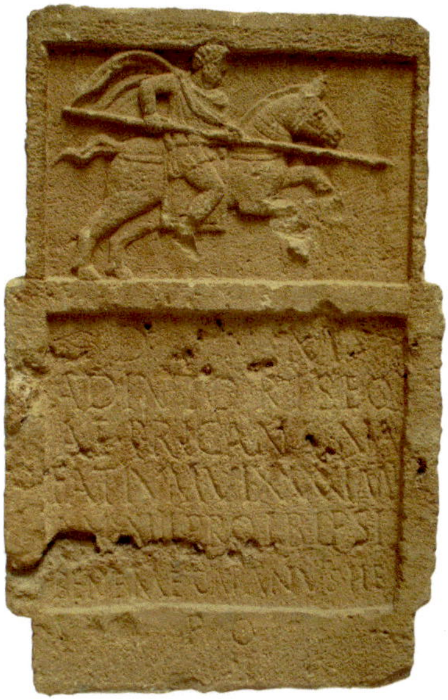

Fig. 68 (above right and left). Tipasa museum: tombstones of cavalrymen. (a) a Briton; (b) a Caninefas.

Fig. 69 (below). Tipasa museum: sarcophagus of Pelops and Hippodameia.

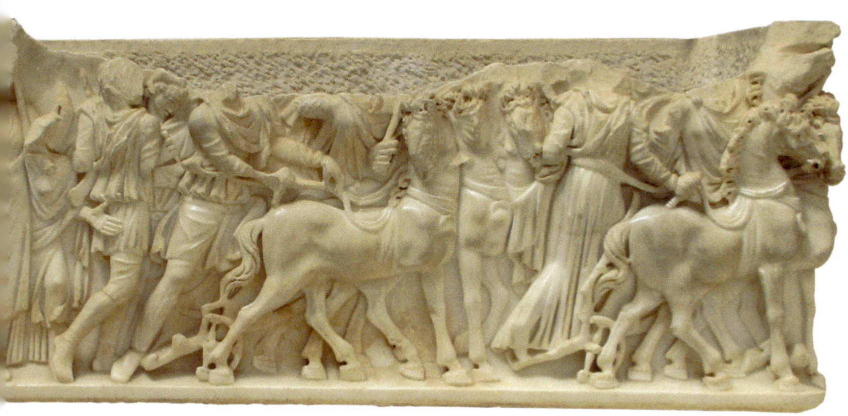

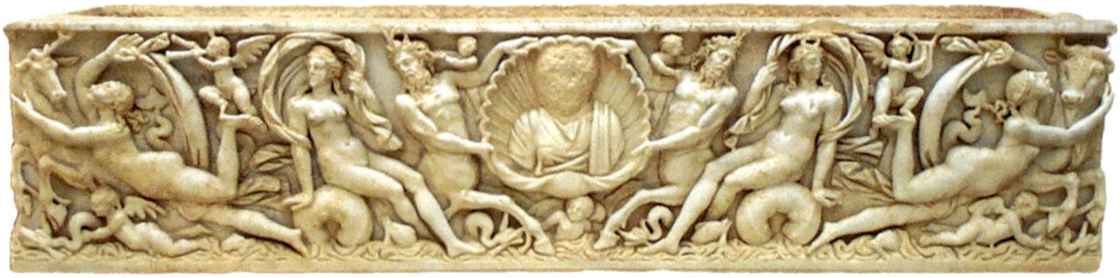

Fig. 70. Tipasa museum: sarcophagus of nereids and marine centaurs.

the other sarcophagi here, the reliefs on this item show part of the legend of Pelops. Son of Tantalus, Pelops came to Pisa in Greece to ask King Oenomaus for the hand of his daughter Hippodameia in marriage. The king used to challenge her suitors to a chariot race and then kill them, in order to evade an oracle which had predicted that he would be assassinated by his son-in-law. Thanks to the complicity of Myrtilus, the king's driver, Pelops won the race, married Hippodameia, killed his father-in-law and became king of Pisa in his turn. Revered for having founded the Olympic Games, the hero gave his name to the Peloponnese ('Island of Pelops'). The sarcophagus of Tipasa shows the early part of this story: at the left, Pelops approaches the throned King Oenomaus, while Hippodameia, to the right, appears to supervise the preparation of the chariots for the race.

Sarcophagus of nereids and marine centaurs (right-hand end-wall, fig. 70, marble, possibly Pentelic): a central shell, within which is an unfinished portrait of the deceased, is supported on either side by a marine centaur with a nereid seated on his back; the scene is framed by two further nereids, who are pursuing a deer and a bull respectively. The sea provides a ground-line and the spaces in the field are filled by winged cupids playing instruments or pursuing sea creatures. The reason for the unfinished portrait is that the incumbent would have ordered the sarcophagus from the quarry during his lifetime and specified the decoration; the sculptors in the distant quarry (near Athens), would have had no idea of his appearance, and would therefore have left the face roughed out, so that a local sculptor could eventually fill in the detail. When the time came for this, either there was no one locally with the necessary skill, or the heirs were not prepared to spend the additional outlay on their father's burial. (West necropolis, found reused and with its face to the wall, in a Christian burial; third century.)

Statuary: on pedestals on the right are a torso of a *Venus pudica* and a marble head of Aesculapius or Jupiter.

Display cases: the cemeteries around Tipasa have yielded large quantities of grave goods, which are well represented here. They include pottery vessels, glass cinerary urns and unguent bottles and many other small objects, ranging in date from the fourth century BC to perhaps the fifth century AD.

THE MAURETANIAN ROYAL TOMB

This singular monument, also known as the *tombeau de la Chrétienne* (Tomb of the Christian Woman, figs. 71, 72), stands above the coast of the Sahel, at an altitude of 261 m. Clearly visible from the Mitidja plain, from Tipasa and from the sea, where it served as an important landmark, this monumental tomb (64 m in diameter and 33 m high) raises many questions. Its fictitious association with a Christian woman derives from the cruciform pattern (imitating woodwork) on its four false doors (see fig. 73), and from a novel written by an officer in the army of the emperor Charles V during his captivity in the sixteenth century. In this, he invented the story that the daughter of Count Julian, who was seduced by the king of the Visigoths, was buried there.

The tomb is mentioned only once in ancient literature, in a text of Pomponius Mela written around AD 40: 'beyond [Iol-Caesarea], the communal mausoleum of the royal family ... then [comes] Icosium' (Algiers). This brief reference and the difficulties of architectural interpretation have left the field open for all sorts of hypotheses. The fact that it is stylistically more 'Hellenized' than the mausoleum of the Medracen (see p. 166, dated to the end of the fourth century BC) and that it was known in the first century AD as a royal tomb suggests that – when mentioned by Mela – it may have been

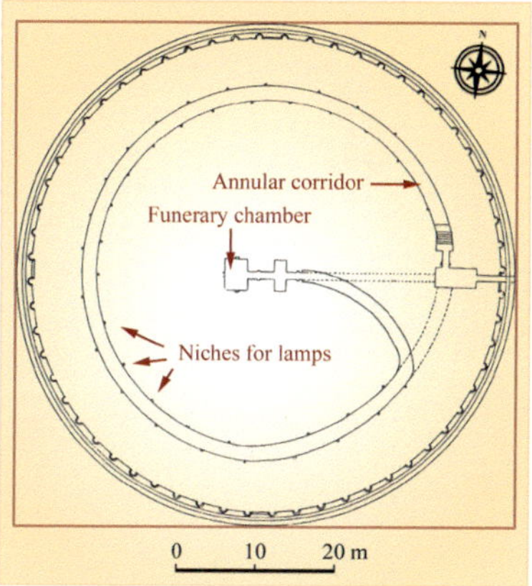

Fig. 71. Mauretanian Royal Tomb: ground-plan.

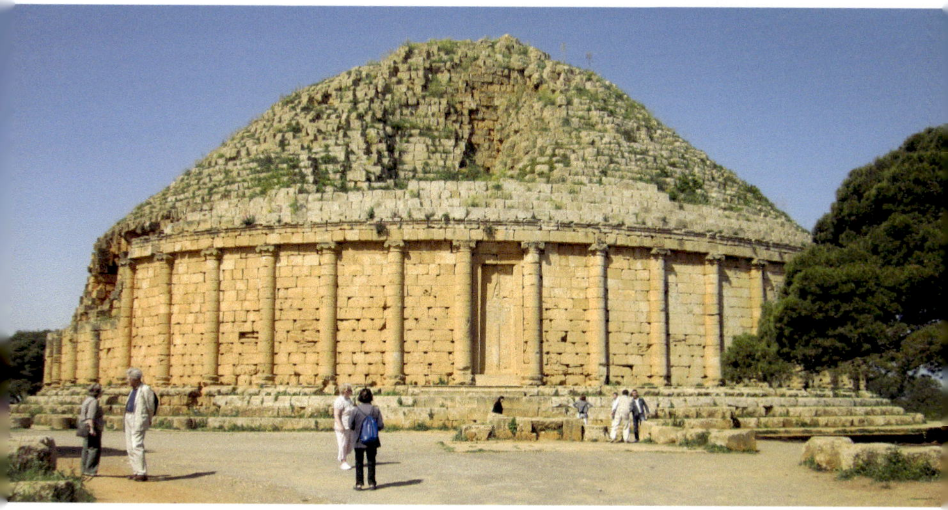

Fig. 72. Mauretanian Royal Tomb.

constructed only recently by Juba II, who died in AD 23. It would therefore be closely contemporary with the mausoleum built in Rome by his close friend, the emperor Augustus. The style of monument is North African, though the engaged Ionic columns show strong Greek influence.

Pillaged at various times, partly dismantled and bombarded by cannons by an eighteenth-century governor of Algiers, the monument has repeatedly excited the greed of those who hoped to find treasure within. This fantasy is behind an array of legends: a cowherd who became rich after following one of his cows into the tomb, a magician who made precious stones leap from its apex, howling ghosts or mosquitoes as large as birds sent by the dead to discourage treasure-hunters, and so on.

The first archaeological researches were carried out by A. Berbrugger, Inspector-General of the Monuments and Museums of Algeria, whose studies were published in 1866–67. This indefatigable scholar found the secret entrance hidden in the substructures beneath the false door on the E: an ante-chamber with animal carvings (fig. 74), annular corridor and central chambers, long since robbed. His work was succeeded by that of the Chief Architect, M. Christofle, who continued the study of the interior and restored the external facings in the 1920s. The entrance to the interior was sealed with concrete during the 1990s in order to prevent its use as a hideout during the troubles of those years, but the concrete has now been replaced by an iron gate.

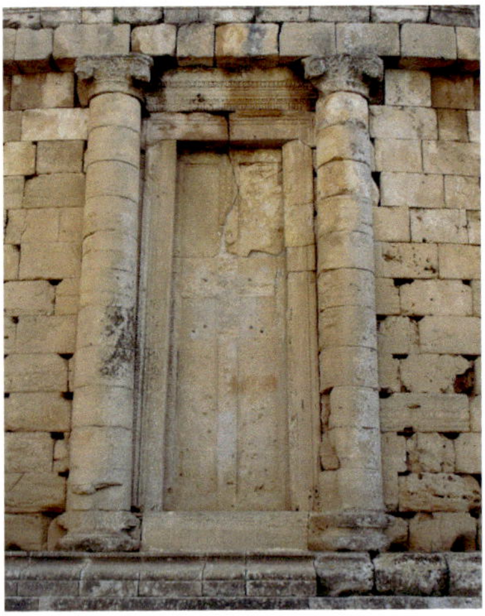

Fig. 73 (left). Mauretanian Royal Tomb: false door on the E side.

Fig. 74 (below). Mauretanian Royal Tomb: ante-chamber and entrance to annular corridor.

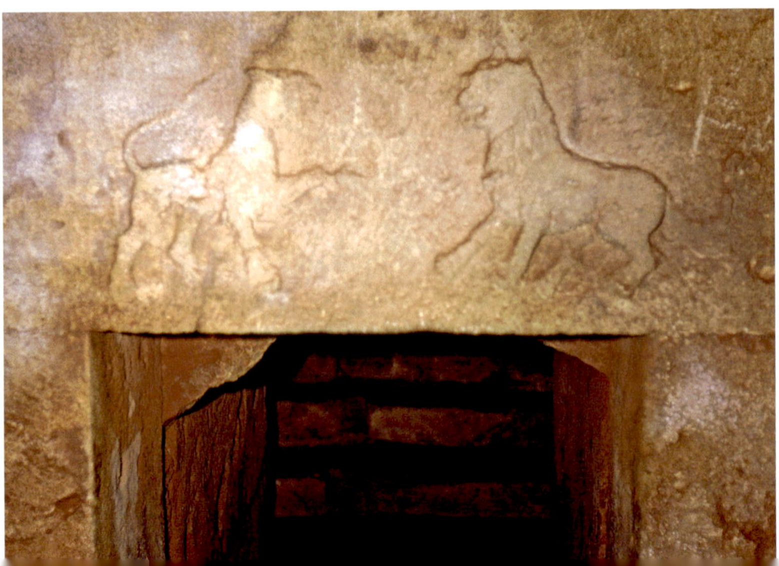

ICOSIUM (Algiers)

This little Punic trading-post took its name, according to the fantastical etymology of Solinus, from the twenty (*eikosi* in Greek) companions of Herakles who founded it. The name is, however, of Punic origin, in the form *Ikosim*. The present-day city of Algiers has left almost nothing visible of this ancient settlement, which was situated in the lower part of the Casbah. Until recently, discoveries had been limited to a series of inscriptions, a few fragments of sculpture, some coins and some old reports of ancient buildings (particularly through the attentions of A. Berbrugger). Now the construction of a metro station in the Place des Martyrs has occasioned deep and extensive excavation, and has brought to light a substantial Byzantine church, decorated with mosaics. The station is now in operation; it is hoped that in due course the mosaics will be put on display and public information will be provided. Ancient texts provide us with the information that Icosium had become a town with Latin rights in the time of Vespasian, that, like Caesarea, it was sacked by the rebel Firmus in 372, recovered by Theodosius in 373 and that it had a significant Christian community: we know the names of three bishops in the fifth century. After that, there are no further literary references until the tenth century, when the Zirid emir Buluggin founded the new settlement of el-Djezaïr ('The Islands') on the site.

NATIONAL MUSEUM OF CLASSICAL AND ISLAMIC ANTIQUITIES

The Classical and Islamic sections of the museum occupy separate buildings within the same enclosure; the Classical section alone is described here. The present building was inaugurated in 1897 and much of the display has been unchanged for many years (after all, the mosaics and large sculptures are not easy to move), but the arrangement of some of the smaller objects is subject to gradual change and may not conform exactly to that described below. In line with many other national museums, the collection is a mixture of older finds from scattered sites, assembled here before any of those locations had their own museums, while more recent finds have come here only if they are exceptional or do not have a more appropriate local museum to go to. There are also sometimes displays of looted objects which have been recovered.

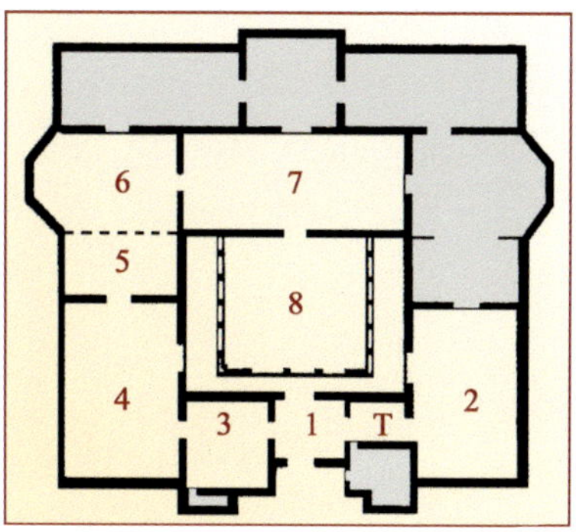

Fig. 75. Sketch-plan of the National Museum of Classical Antiquities, Algiers. For the numbering of the rooms, see the text below.

1. Vestibule

Here are four casts of monumental statues, the originals of which are elsewhere (a magistrate, from Calama; Dionysus, from Cirta/Constantina; the Lady of Djémila, from Cuicul and Ceres, from Caesarea). Placed over the doorway to the courtyard is the semi-circular ***Mosaic of the Good Shepherd*** from Bordj El-Bahri (former Cap Matifou, the eastern tip of the Bay of Algiers and the site of ancient

Rusguniae), found in 1899 and dated to the late fourth or early fifth century. Interestingly, while there is a shepherd with a sheep across his shoulders, the scene includes a second figure – almost lost – who is milking a ewe.

T. Ticket office and bookstall

2. 'Pagan cults'

The designation of this room is a little misleading, since few of the objects here now have explicit religious significance. The following items are of note.

Mosaic of the Four Seasons, on the floor, possibly from Aïn Beida (but its label is lost).

Mosaic of Amphitrite on (or falling off?) a hippocamp, with a wide geometric border, from the vicinity of the Qalaa of the Beni Hammad. (Fourth century?)

Mosaic fragment of a hunting scene from Ténès (*Cartennae*, late fourth century?).

Bellerophon sarcophagus: found at Azzefoun in the Kabylie, in the middle of a Roman wine-making installation, where it was presumably in secondary use (fig. 76). It is carved in marble, thought to be from Djebel Filfila and therefore of African origin, with a lavish scene from Greek mythology. (The workmanship suggests, however, a sculptor from a metropolitan Roman background.) The story of Bellerophon runs approximately as follows. Bellerophon left home because he had accidentally murdered his brother. At the court of Proitos, King of Argos, the king's wife Stheneboia fell in love with him. He rebuffed her; she accused him to Proitos of seducing her. Proitos (not wishing to kill his own guest) sent Bellerophon to his father-in-law Iobates, with a letter asking the latter to kill him. (Nice, how the laws of hospitality are observed in Greek myth!) Iobates in turn sent him to fight the Chimaera (a monster that was mostly lion, but with a goat's head growing out of the middle of its back and a serpent for a tail); but, with the aid of the winged horse Pegasus, Bellerophon succeeded in killing the Chimaera. Bellerophon married the daughter of Iobates and had children, some of whom died prematurely, and he lived thereafter miserably, far from the ways of men.

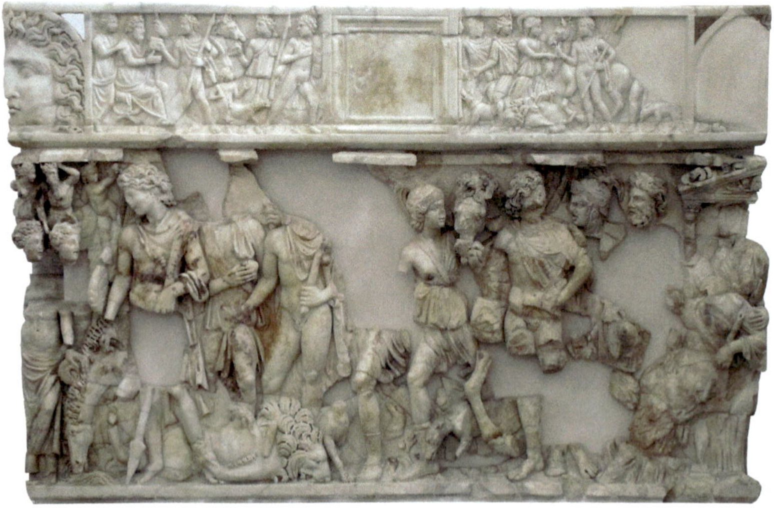

Fig. 76. Algiers, National Museum of Antiquities: Bellerophon sarcophagus.

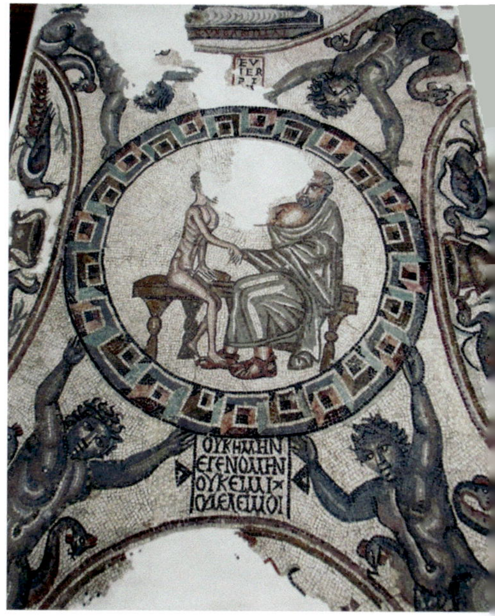

Fig. 77. Algiers, National Museum of Antiquities: funerary mosaic of Cornelia Urbanilla.

The story starts with the small left-hand panel on the lid. Here, Bellerophon (with Pegasus) takes leave of the seated king Proitos, who is giving him a tablet for delivery to Iobates; the rejected Stheneboia looks on from behind the king. This scene of departure is, however, conflated with the later departure of Bellerophon for the hunt of the Chimaera: this is indicated by the presence of a hunting dog, a man carrying a net, and a boy with a torch to drive the prey into the net. The corresponding panel on the right shows Bellerophon in repose, holding Pegasus by the bridle, with the dead Chimaera before his feet and tired huntsmen and dogs on either side. Bellerophon appears to be being addressed by an Amazon, interpreted as Virtue.

The body of the sarcophagus displays further scenes. At the left-hand end, Bellerophon is seen capturing/taming the winged Pegasus, who is drinking at the fountain of Peirene at Corinth. Next, Bellerophon and a companion once again stand over the dead Chimaera. The right-hand half of the front is occupied by a single scene: Bellerophon, holding Pegasus and again being addressed by an Amazon (Virtue?) is taking leave of a king and queen (Proitos and Stheneboia?), with a temple behind. (Approximately mid third century AD.)

Sarcophagus and funerary mosaic of Cornelia Urbanilla: these come from a tomb discovered in 1918 at Khirbet Ouled Arif (ancient *Lambiridi*). The mosaic (fig. 77) was on the floor of the tomb, which contained three sarcophagi, one of which is on display here. The sarcophagus is inscribed in Greek and records that Cornelia Urbanilla died at the age of 28 years, ten months, twelve days and nine hours, and that the tomb was dedicated by her husband Ti. Claudius Vitalis. The central panel of the mosaic is in the form of a circular medallion supported by four dusky tritons. This encloses a somewhat enigmatic scene of two men sitting on a couch. One is naked and is only skin-and-bone while the other, a more portly and distinguished figure, fully clothed, appears to be taking his pulse. It has been suggested, imaginatively, that this illustrates the story of the Macedonian prince Perdiccas, who claimed to be suffering from consumption. His doctor, the famous Hippocrates, observed that his pulse quickened in the presence of his mother and deduced an incestuous love as the cause. (Why this story should have been chosen in this context remains obscure.) Pairs of peacocks and geese, heraldically opposed on either side of chalices, fill the sides of the mosaic; the image at the bottom is lost while, at the top, we see the mummified Urbanilla in her coffin, with her name written beneath in Latin. There are two other inscriptions. Above the medallion is the unexplained name *Euterpius* (also in Latin characters); while below it is a Greek quatrain of Stoic content: 'I was not; I became; I am not; it doesn't bother me.' (Early fourth century?)

Aesculapius and Isis: two casts of statues, said to be from Caesarea.

Stelai dedicated to Baal-Saturn: these are typically carved in three registers, with Saturn at the top (a bearded and veiled figure), then the dedicators of the stone (often a married couple standing on either side of an altar), and in the lowest register images of the sacrificial animals being offered (fig. 78). Saturn is a barely disguised 'Romanization' of the Phoenician god Baal. (From Sillègue/Beni Fouda, to the W of Djemila; found when building a road-station in the late nineteenth century.)

Carvings of 'Libyan' type on irregular pieces of rock, mostly from the Kabylie, showing 'indigenous' warriors. Notable amongst these is the ***Stele of Abizar*** (fig. 79), representing a naked horseman holding three javelins and a shield in his left hand, while his right is raised in salutation or command. His thick hair and pointed beard resemble representations of rulers on the earliest Numidian coinage. The rider is accompanied by a tiny figure standing on the croup of the horse, a hunting dog, a bird and a Libyan inscription.

Marble fountain-head in the form of a Gorgon mask: this fine piece of white marble (fig. 80) once adorned a fountain close to the forum of *Hippo Regius* (see p. 243), from which it was stolen in 1996. In the upheavals of 2011 it was rediscovered in Tunis, in the house of

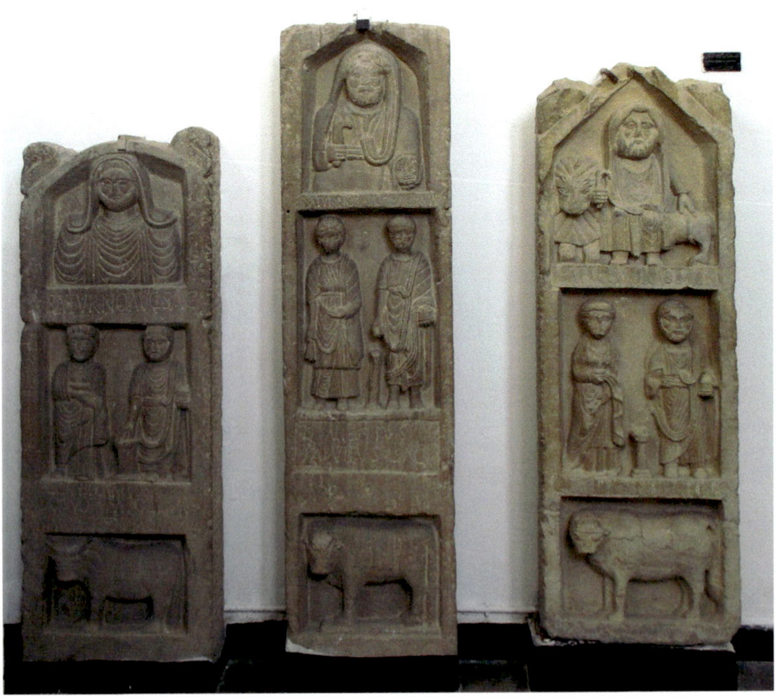

Fig. 78. Algiers, National Museum of Antiquities: stelai dedicated to Baal-Saturn.

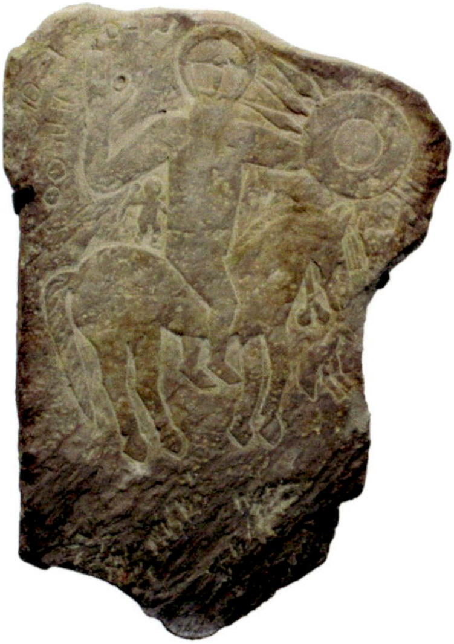

Fig. 79. Algiers, National Museum of Antiquities: Stele of Abizar.

the son-in-law of President Zine el-Abdine Ben Ali of Tunisia, and was in due course returned to Algeria.

Carved ivory plaques in a wall-case are from Sétif (*Sitifis*); they would have decorated pieces of furniture or boxes. Another wall-case contains some very modest fragments of painted wall-plaster, stucco and other finds from *Castellum Dimmidi*. (This must be one of the oldest displays in the museum.)

3. Bronzes

Cases here display small objects in bronze. There are items of practical utility such as oil lamps, surgical instruments and weighing scales, pieces of armour and cult statues and figurines. Of particular note are the following.

Child with eagle: a figurine of a naked child fighting an eaglet with its wings outspread. (*Lambaesis*, third century.)

Life-size ***foreleg of a horse***. (*Lambaesis*, Roman.)

Parade helmet in the form of a face of a beardless young man (or god) with short hair. (Ain el-Grimidi, from a tomb of the second or third century).

Fighting helmet, composed of an iron cap, to which are fastened decorative bronze plaques. Four of these form a cross descending from the top, while a fifth, horizontal element anchors them together around the circumference. The visor is composed, like the neck-piece, of a plate of beaten bronze; the lateral protections (*bucculae*) are missing, and on top is a circular seating, presumably for some kind of crest. (*Caesarea*, second or third century.)

A case dedicated to Egyptian deities, including a fitting from an Isiac altar decorated with busts of Isis, Serapis and Horus. (*Lambaesis*, Roman.)

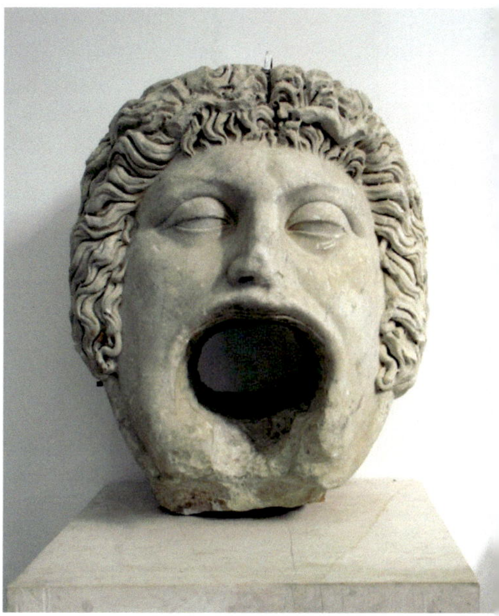

Fig. 80. Algiers, National Museum of Antiquities: Gorgon fountain-head.

Two busts of ***Africa***, with elephant headdress and holding a cornucopia.

Hand of Sabazios, an extremely powerful symbol of protection against evil (fig. 81). Sabazios was a Phrygian god, later identified with Dionysus. The hand is equipped with the attributes of an extensive pantheon of gods: note the presence of a bust of Mercury, a pine-cone, a serpent, an eagle, a ram, a frog, a tortoise and a lizard. (*Tipasa*, Roman.)

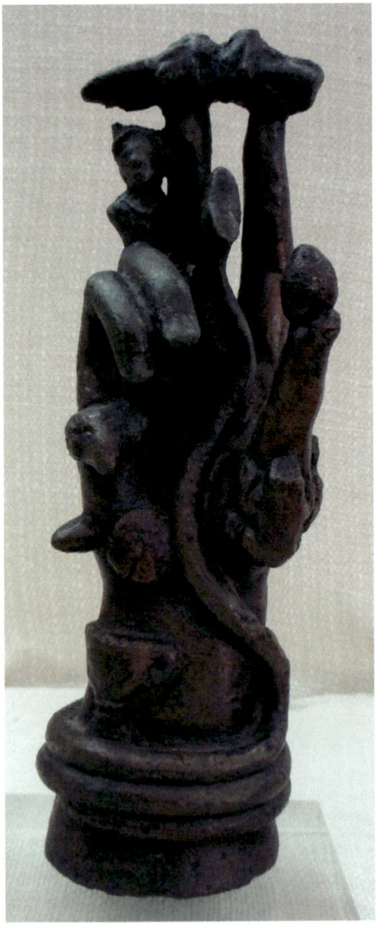

Fig. 81. Algiers, National Museum of Antiquities: Hand of Sabazios.

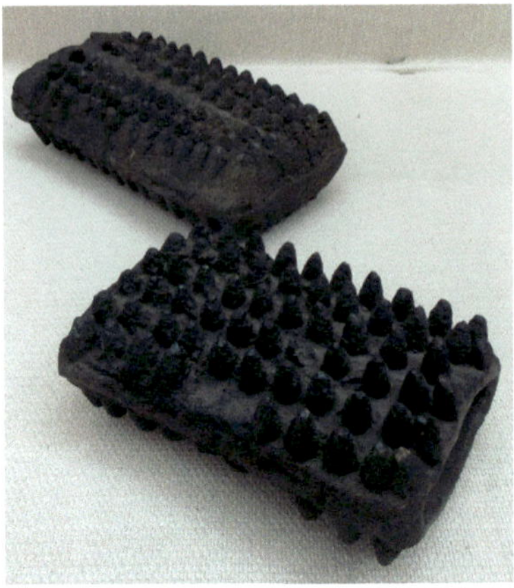

Fig. 82. Algiers, National Museum of Antiquities: tudiculae *for crushing olives.*

Two* tudiculae*: it is thought that these spiked heads (fig. 82), attached to a wooden handle and resembling a meat tenderizer, were used for crushing olives prior to placing them in a press. (El-Hadjeb, Mouzaïa, Blida province, Roman.)

4. Christian art

Here are displayed several important mosaics, many inscriptions and tombstones of the Christian period (fourth to seventh centuries), decorative and architectural elements from churches and a monumental sarcophagus.

Mosaics from the Basilica of Alexander at Tipasa (see p. 62): on the RH wall and the far wall as you enter the room. These are numerous: of the two large texts on the RH wall, that on the R records the foundation of the church and the bishop's translation into the church of the remains of the *Iusti Priores* (just forebears). The text is almost identical to that of bishop Cresconius at Cuicul (see p. 132), but the two are probably of very different date, implying that they share a common source (and that other bishops at other times may have commemorated themselves in the same words). The text on the L commemorates the bishop himself.

Sarcophagus of the Miracles of Christ (fig. 83). The cover of the sarcophagus is crudely decorated with dolphins swimming through the waves, flanking a *tabula ansata* intended to receive the name of the deceased (never carved). The front of the sarcophagus itself (the only carved face) is divided into seven individual scenes by arcades, as follows (from left to right): Christ, holding a scroll (and prefigured in this Old Testament story) attends Daniel who kills the dragon of Babylon by feeding it cakes made of pitch; the wedding at Cana; the healing of the woman with a haemorrhage; Christ enthroned in Paradise (flanked by palm trees); the miracle of the loaves and fishes; the healing of the blind man; the prediction of the denial of Peter. (Dellys, ancient *Rusuccuru*; mid fourth century, considered an import from Rome).

Daniel in the Lions' Den: two blocks on the RH wall, perhaps from a ciborium above a baptismal basin, are crudely carved to show the prophet Daniel amongst ravening lions. The inscription reads *Daniel in lacu leonum.* (Sillègue/Beni Fouda, to the W of Djémila.)

5. Reliquaries and small Christian cult objects

These come mainly from Henchir el-Khrib, near N'Gaous (W of Batna).

6. Glass, pottery, Albertini tablets

At the time of writing, this room has cases of pottery, oil lamps and glass, ranging from the fifth century BC to the Roman period, together with mosaics and a case of the inscribed wooden Albertini Tablets.

Mosaic of Achilles on Skyros: beneath a fancy awning are depicted two scenes from the legend of Achilles (fig. 84). In the upper register is a scene from his infancy, which is too damaged for definite identification – Achilles being washed for the first time? Being handed over to his nurse? A beardless man to the right is holding a shield, while to the left the scene is observed by the centaur Chiron, who is to become the child's tutor. The scene below is more intelligible. Thetis, the mother of Achilles, had been told in a prophecy that if Achilles took part in the Trojan War he would die there. In order, therefore, to avoid him being enlisted in the venture, she packed him off to the court of King Lycomedes of Skyros, where he was hidden in women's clothing in the king's harem (!). Odysseus, however (representing the Intelligence Service of the Greek expedition), discovered where Achilles had been hidden and devised a cunning plan. He arrived at the court with a trumpeter, who sounded the call to arms. The women fled in panic, while Achilles instinctively threw off his women's clothes and called for his arms, thus disclosing himself! This is what we see here: Achilles

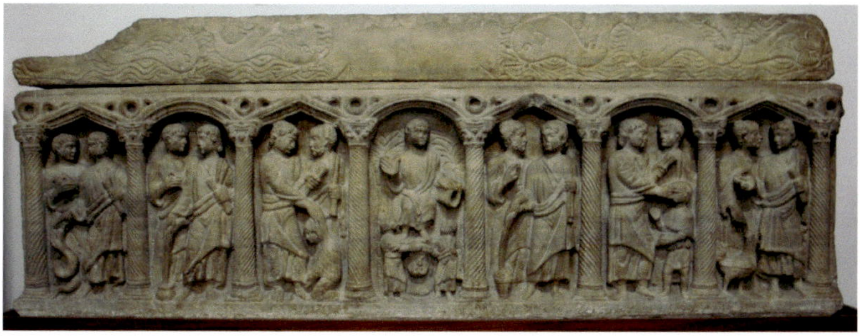

Fig. 83. Algiers, National Museum of Antiquities: sarcophagus of the Miracles of Christ.

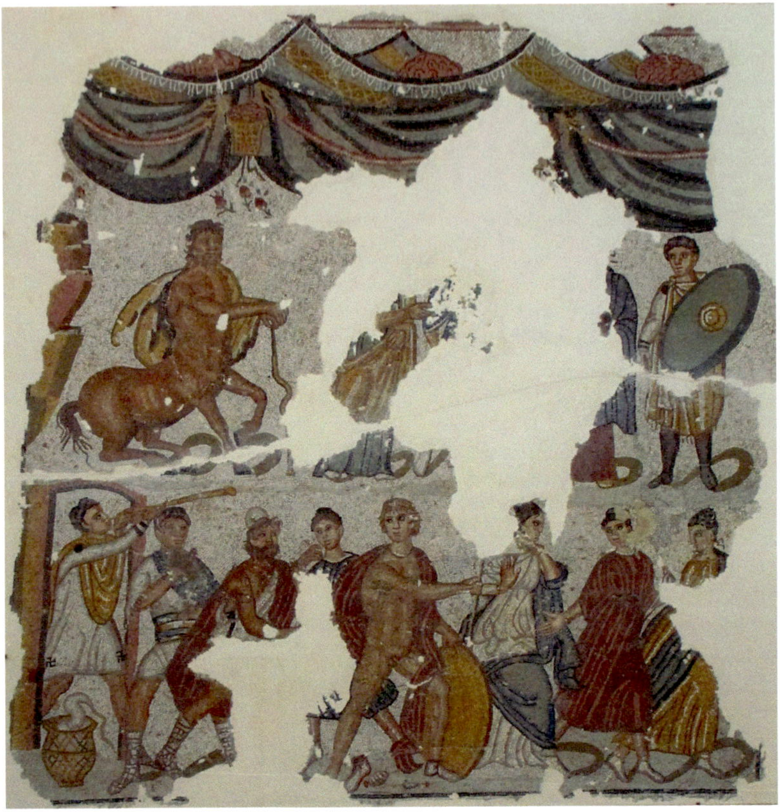

Fig. 84. Algiers, National Museum of Antiquities: mosaic of Achilles on Skyros.

in the centre, semi-naked, is seizing his arms, while the women to the right make their way out of the picture. To the left, we see Odysseus, bearded and wearing a traveller's felt cap, while behind him, in the doorway, the herald is sounding his trumpet. (Tipasa, early fourth century.)

Mosaic of hunting scenes: two hunting scenes are portrayed here. In the upper register two men, one with a spear and the other with a hunting dog, are facing a fearsome tusked boar; in the lower, a horseman has already cast his spear and wounded a leopard, which is nonetheless leaping towards him with an apologetic expression. The Latin verse inscription across the top – *Siliqua frequens foveas mea membra lavacro* – is enigmatic in the extreme, but seems to refer to the pleasures of the bath. ('Abundant husk/pod, may you warm my limbs in the bath!') (El Asnam, ancient *Castellum Tingitanum*, mid fourth century.)

Part of a ***Four Seasons mosaic*** on the floor, with a bust of Dionysus in the centre. (Lambaesis, early third century.)

Circular Christian mosaic, inscribed *Pax aeclesiae catolice semper* ('Peace to the universal church evermore'). (Beni Rached, NE of El Asnam, end of fourth century).

Albertini Tablets. Examples may be on display of the remarkable find – a casual discovery near Tébessa in 1928 – of 45 wooden tablets, dated to the reign of Gunthamund (484–96). These are inscribed in ink (see p. 7 fig. 5) and document the sale of parcels of land originally belonging to Flavius Geminius Catullinus. The specific interest of these texts is the fact that Roman law (the *lex Manciana*) was continuing to be applied and that the naming of the king is the only feature which tells us that the area was under Vandal rather than Roman control.

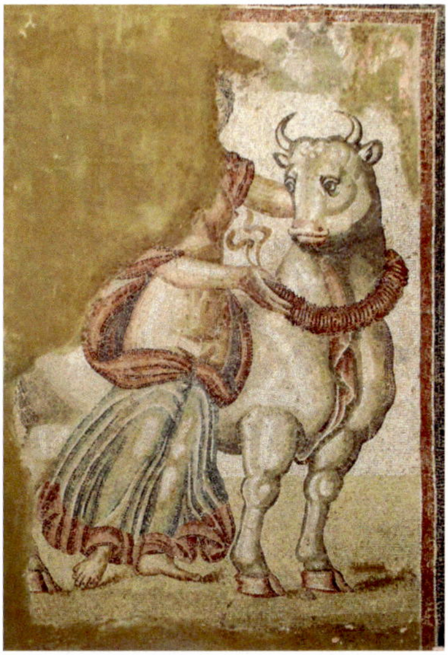

Fig. 85 (above). Algiers, National Museum of Antiquities: fragmentary mosaic of the Rape of Europa. Isn't this bull irresistible?

7. Mosaics and monumental statuary

The walls of this room are entirely covered in mosaics, the themes of which include various ***Seductions of Jupiter*** (Europa, more than once; Danaë; Antiope; Ganymede) and the ***Toilet of Venus*** (Cirta). Note also the following.

Daedalus and Pasiphaë: a small panel in a large geometric mosaic (fig. 86). Pasiphaë, Queen of Crete, had conceived a passion for a bull, and in order to help her to satisfy it, the craftsman Daedalus built her a wooden

Fig. 86 (below). Algiers, National Museum of Antiquities: mosaic of Daedalus and Pasiphaë.

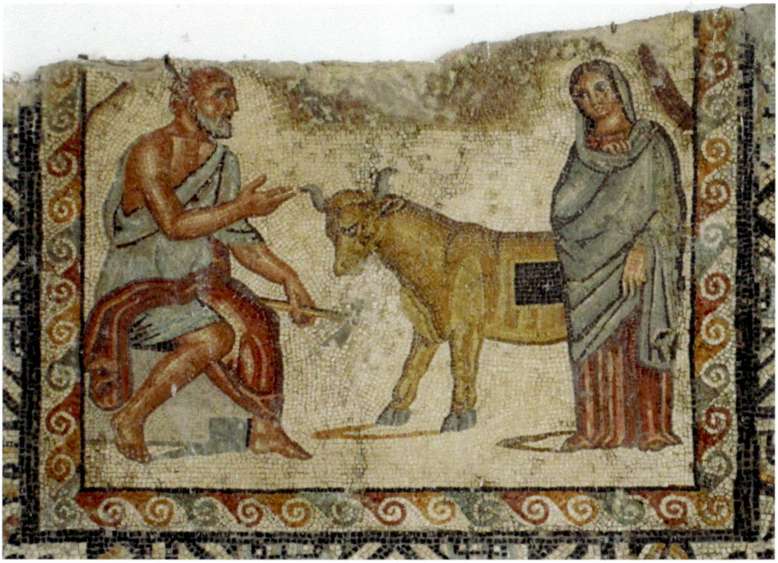

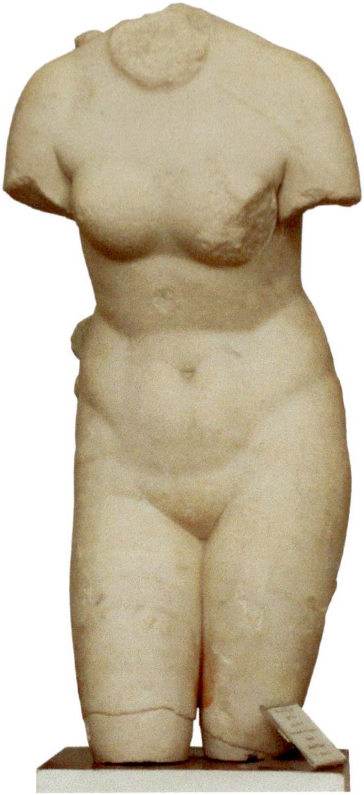

Fig. 87. Algiers, National Museum of Antiquities: Venus.

cow (shown here), which she could climb inside through a little door. The outcome of this dangerous liaison was the Minotaur, half man, half bull. (Mrikeb Thala, third quarter of fourth century.)

A single panel from a four-seasons mosaic has a fine figure of ***Winter***, carrying a hoe. (See p. 10 fig. 6, from Sour el-Ghozlane, ancient *Auzia*, beginning of fourth century?)

A huge portrait head in mosaic of ***Oceanus***. Beneath this fearsome head, surrounded by nereids in a somewhat primitive style, are three lines of Latin verse, which may be translated as follows: 'Let jealous breasts burst before this celestial visage and the idle tongue fall silent in our presence; we surpass our forebears in our zeal, and happily the crowning glory of this work shines forth in our house. Cheers!' (Ain Temouchent, near Sétif, late fourth or early fifth century.)

The statuary in this room derives mostly from early excavations at Caesarea, particularly in the West Baths (see p. 35), as do the fine marble pilasters carved with candelabra, foliage and Dionysiac motifs (first century). Gods represented here include ***Venus*** (fig. 87: body only of a fine Roman copy, like the Capitoline Venus, of a work of the fourth-century BC by Praxiteles); ***Neptune***; a very fine draped

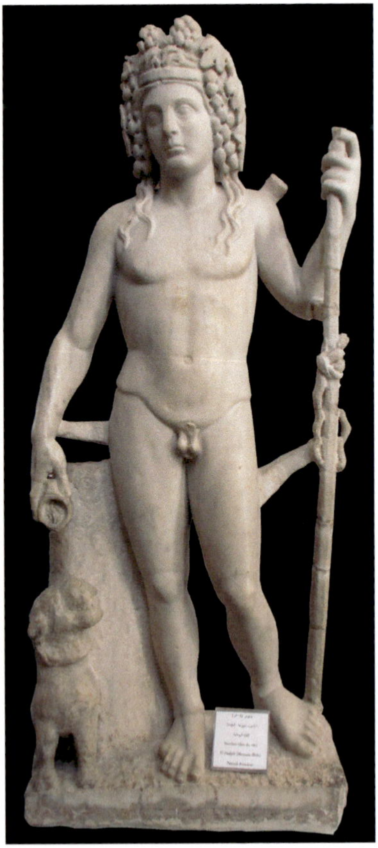

Fig. 88. Algiers, National Museum of Antiquities: Dionysus.

female, possibly **Demeter** (though the loss of the forearms and whatever she might have been holding makes precise identification impossible; again probably a copy of a work of the fifth-century BC by Phidias). There is also a fragmentary copy of another Hellenistic work, ***Hermaphroditus and Satyr.*** (Hermaphroditus, the ambiguous offspring of Hermes and Aphrodite, has been assaulted in his/her sleep by a young satyr under a misapprehension that this is a nymph. The satyr leaps away as Hermaphroditus awakes and he sees his mistake, but his leg is caught between the thighs of the other who restrains his flight.) These pieces were probably all commissioned by Juba II to embellish his capital of Caesarea 'in the Roman style' (see p. 29).

A figure of ***Antonia Minor***, the daughter of Mark Anthony and Octavia (born between 40 and 37 BC), or of her daughter ***Livilla***, is represented in the flower of her beauty. The hairstyle is characteristic of the Augustan period and this item too is from Caesarea.

A figure of ***Dionysus*** (fig. 88), holding a thyrsus in his left hand and in his right a cup of wine which he pours on the head of a panther, is from El Hadjeb (Mouzaïa, Blida province, Roman period).

A head of ***Hermanubis***, a portrait of the emperor ***Hadrian*** and a relief showing ***Mars, Venus and the deified (Julius) Caesar*** are interlopers from Carthage.

8. Courtyard

In the centre are two mosaics of the Roman period, while around the walls are tombstones and commemorative inscriptions of the medieval and Ottoman periods in Arabic and Hebrew.

Fish mosaic from the nave of the Basilica of Alexander at Tipasa (see p. 62).

Scylla mosaic: in the midst of a sea populated by marine divinities, with three nereids riding marine monsters (one of which has the head of a swan), reigns Scylla, who terrorized Odysseus and his companions. She is represented as described by the poet Virgil, with a hundred tentacles terminating in the heads of baying dogs, dashing against the rocks any passing ship and devouring the wretched sailors. We see her brandishing a steering-oar, which she has seized, and each of her legs ends in a fish tail. (Bordj el-Ksar, ancient *Sila*, fourth or fifth century).

RAPIDUM (Sour Djouab)

To the Emperors Marcus Aurelius ... and Lucius Verus ..., the veterans and villagers living next to [the fort of] Rapidum have built this wall of squared stone from the foundations up, which belongs to the veterans and villagers who live within the said wall, entirely with their own funds and resources, with the assistance and supervision of the distinguished procurator [Sextus] Baius Pudens, excellent governor, who also dedicated it.

Pair of identical inscriptions set above the E and W gates of the settlement in AD 167

The military dispositions made by Rome within and on the southern side of the Atlas Mountains are most visibly characterized by sites in Numidia (see below, pp. 99–229). The remains of the Roman fort and associated town at *Rapidum* (Sour Djouab) in Mauretania Caesariensis, to the SE of Algiers, were also part of the same frontier, somewhat further to the W, and make an interesting addition to the series.

At this point on the inland E–W road, a fort was constructed on virgin ground in the year 122, to be garrisoned by the *cohors II sardorum*, a new (nominally Sardinian) unit of 500 men, partly infantry and partly cavalry. The fort evidently soon led to the development of an adjoining civil settlement, composed partly of retired soldiers and partly of civilians, drawn there as families of soldiers or as traders benefitting from the economic attractions of soldiers with money to spend. By the year 167, this community had grown to the point of wishing to defend itself within a defensive circuit (all of Sectors A–D). The inscriptions which they set up above their gates

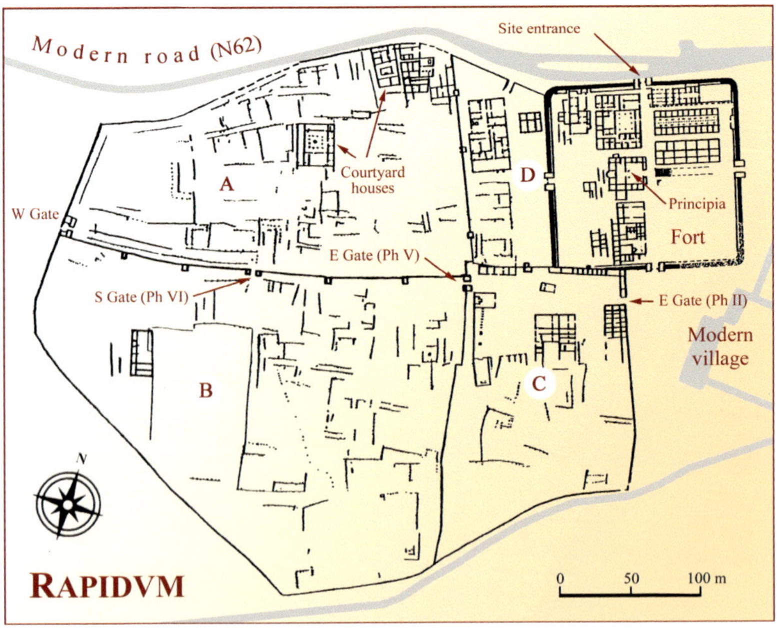

Fig. 89. Rapidum, plan of the site after J.-P. Laporte, derived from excavations and aerial photographs. The military fort and the four zones of civil occupation are indicated.

(quoted above) show that the settlement still had no formal status at this time, and that the work was undertaken entirely at their own expense. The wall, enclosing an irregular space of 11.6 ha, was well built (as they claimed), but lacked towers other than at the two gates, and seems to have been intended to discourage nocturnal prowlers rather than to resist a serious military siege or assault.

The situation changed significantly at some point between 198 and 201, when the unit was moved 450 km further W, to *Altava* (SW of Oran) and was not replaced. The settlement then lost its primary *raison d'être* and seems to have entered on a slow but inexorable decline, marked by a progressive reduction in size, with the construction of smaller defensive circuits (abandoning Sector D, then Sector C). With the departure of the army, it needed a formal status: it is described in an inscription of 297–8 as a *municipium*, and probably acquired that status around 200. The same inscription tells us that the settlement was re-founded at the later date, having long since been taken and destroyed by rebels (*ante plurima tempora rebellium incursione captum ac dirutum*); this destruction is thought to have taken place around 270.

The new settlement occupied about a third of the original area (Sector A only), with yet another reduction in the defensive circuit, but it was not a success. The inhabitants must have drawn their living from agriculture, as is shown by the many traces of oil presses across the site, but the catalogue of coins found on the site comes to a complete end with Constantine; there is no trace of Christian activity or of Christian lamps, so it must have been abandoned around 340, if not before.

The modern settlement of Sour Djouab is a French colonial foundation (formerly Masqueray); built in the second decade of the twentieth century, it was fortunately laid out beside the ancient ruins, rather than directly on top of them, which would almost certainly have been the case, had it been built in the mid-nineteenth century. Limited excavations were carried out in 1855, 1882–85, 1908–17, 1927–33 and 1948–53; these yielded a typical abundance of inscriptions, but much of the site remains unexamined.

EXPLORING THE SITE

The area enclosed by the ancient defences (but excluding the outlying necropoleis) is now a fenced archaeological zone, lying immediately on the W side of the modern town. The entrance is on the N side, and leads directly into the military fort at its N gate. Few of the internal details can now be made out on the ground, though the general disposition of the buildings is clear from the extensive scatter of squared building-stone.

The auxiliary fort

The fort formed a rectangle of 135 x 127 m, with walls faced in ashlar masonry enclosing a rubble core; it had rounded corners and a gate in the centre of each side, flanked by pairs of towers. The walls had wall-walks on the inner side, probably of timber and supported at the inner edge upon timber uprights. The main entrance was on the E side, and from this the only paved street (the *via praetoria*) led directly to the headquarters building (*principia*). This building was fronted by a four-way arch, a groma (as at Lambaesis: see p. 172) and within was a courtyard flanked by rooms on either side (stores? armouries?). On the far side was a hall with a raised tribunal at the N end and a row of five rooms on the far side of it. Four of these will have been offices or *scholae*, while the central room, with a projecting apse, will have been the Chapel of the Standards.

To the N of this building was the commanding officer's residence (*praetorium*), while to the S of it other buildings have been interpreted as workshops or as having non-residential functions. In the NW corner of the fort was a double suite of baths, with a latrine set against the inner face of the N wall. The eastern part of the fort is thought to have been dedicated to cavalry and infantry barracks, while just inside the N gate was a granary with a raised floor. In front of the granary was a fountain, fed by a raised aqueduct which brought water to the site from the source of Aïn Sahnoune, 2.5 km to the E.

The civil settlement

This grew up to the W and S of the fort, with walls which joined onto it on the W side. When the fort was built, the E–W road passed through it; but as the settlement expanded, it became necessary for the road to be diverted around the S side of the fort. A few buildings within the settlement have been excavated, but aerial photography has shown that far more can be summarily traced out. The most prominent surviving features are the defensive walls, which show the initial boundaries and subsequent shrinkage of the defended area. The history and character of the site are most readily understood in terms of four phases.

Phase I: AD 122

Construction of the fort and occupation by the *cohors II sardorum*.

Phase II: 167

The civil settlement surrounded by a defensive wall 1.14 km long, attached to the W side of the fort. A W gate has flanking towers and a circular paved court between them; the E gate also has flanking towers, but is simpler. The wall was built of good ashlar masonry (see fig. 90) and was commemorated by identical inscriptions above the two gates. Scattered blocks of one of these now lie outside the museum (see below).

Phase III: 198–201

Withdrawal of the army unit, decommissioning of the fort.

Phase IV: c. 250

Sector D abandoned and a new L-shaped section of defensive wall built, this time with interval-towers, incorporating reused materials

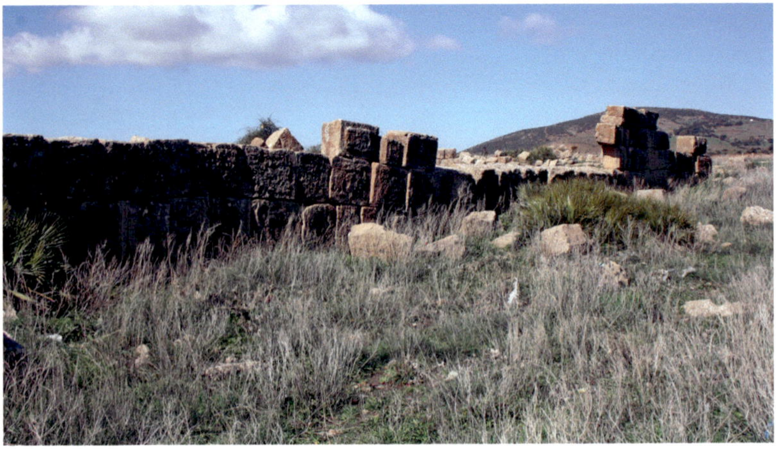

Fig. 90. Rapidum: the defensive wall 'of squared stone' on the E side of Sector C.

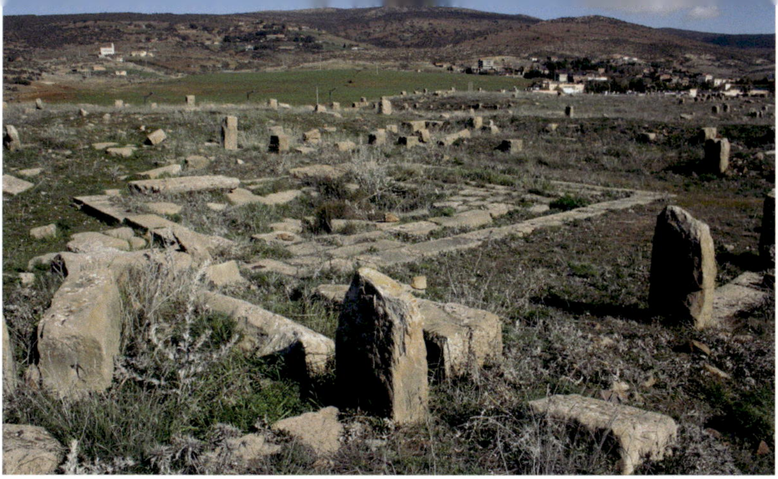

Fig. 91. Rapidum: the courtyard of the 'well-building'.

(from the fort and the abandoned area). The aqueduct which formerly fed the fountain in the fort was raised and extended to pass through the northernmost tower of this wall.

Phase V: c. 270?

Sector C abandoned, levelled and cut off by a new section of wall running N–S, to the W of it. This seems to have been done in some haste, with the abandonment at least two temples and an open space (forum?) formerly adorned with statues, of which bases were found. Also in the centre of this space are traces of a large building containing two oil presses. Evidence of haste is shown by the new E gate, built at the N end of this section of wall: it was provided with a panel for a dedicatory inscription, but the text was never carved. It is possible that the occasion was the rebel attack and destruction of the town described in the inscription of Phase VI.

Phase VI: 297–8

The reoccupation of the town at this time is described in an inscription on a marble panel (the only inscription on marble from the site) which was found at the W gate and is now in Algiers (not on display). Once again, the defensive circuit was reduced, to sector A alone, with the construction of another section of wall on the S side of it, provided with towers and built of reused materials. This wall was provided with a new gate midway along its length. The buildings in this area, largely of the fourth century but obviously overlying earlier ones, include a large quadrilateral enclosure of unknown purpose at the W end and a peristyle house in the northernmost part of the sector. In the centre of the area, it is still possible to make out a paved courtyard with a well in the centre and a surrounding peristyle, with rooms around the outside (fig. 91). This was perhaps a market building.

This phase seems to have been terminated by abandonment rather than destruction, around 340.

The museum

A small building at the NE corner of the site serves as a museum. On the ground outside are several blocks of the inscription of 167 which once stood above the W gate; the items here also include a couple of cylindrical milestones. Within the building is a collection of stelai, either funerary or dedicated to Baal-Saturn. Not here, unfortunately, is one of the more interesting funerary monuments found near the W gate in the excavations of 1948–49: this was a stele with a crude carving of a Roman infantryman, holding a lance and giving a 'modern' military salute with his right hand.

SITIFIS (Sétif)

We know little about the foundation by Nerva (97–98) of the *colonia Nerviana Augusta Martialis veteranorum Sitifensium*, established to accommodate the military veterans who were to promote the Romanisation of the high plains of the Constantine area. (The name Sitifis is of Numidian/Moorish derivation, in which language *esseddif* means 'black' – presumably referring to the soil.) The territory would be rapidly developed, thanks to the suitability of the land for cereal farming: Matidia, the niece of Trajan, owned estates in the region. The settlement soon became part of an important road network: the discovery of many milestones has shown that a marked route led from Cirta/Constantina to Sitifis and that another left from there for *Auzia* and, further on, for *Rapidum* (see fig. 1). The region of Sétif, newly colonized and therefore vulnerable, was thus linked to the valley of the Chélif to the W and to the coast.

The first settlement consisted of housing blocks which have hardly been excavated and of a necropolis of the second century. It is essentially from the end of the third century, when the city became the capital of the newly constituted province of *Mauretania Sitifensis*, that its topography is more readily understood. The major part of Sitifis was remodelled at this time, new suburban quarters were laid out to the N, a network of regular streets was established and public buildings worthy of a capital were created. This intense activity included the construction of an amphitheatre (later partly refurbished under the emperor Julian, 361–363), of a circus dated to the late fourth century and of a handsome defensive circuit which protected the

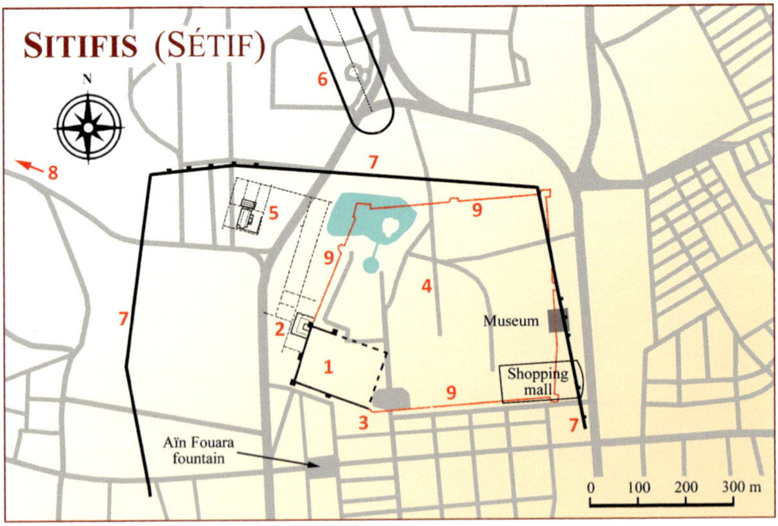

Fig. 92. Plan of central Sétif, showing the locations of antiquities (those in brackets no longer visible).

1. *Byzantine fortress*
2. *Temple of 2nd cent. AD*
3. *Fountain-house*
4. *(Roman baths)*
5. *(Christian basilicas)*
6. *(Circus)*
7. *(Line of Roman defences)*
8. *To 'Tomb of Scipio', 750 m*
9. *(Defences of French military base)*

15 ha of the central area. In the fifth century, the region which extended from Sitifis to Calama (Guelma) was recognized by treaty as subject to the Vandals, even before that people had extended their power as far as Carthage. At the time of the Byzantine reconquest, in 539, the general Solomon moved west to attack Numidia, forcing the Moor Iabdas to fall back into Mauretania. Solomon then covered the provinces of Sitifensis and Numidia with new defensive circuits and fortresses, such as those at Theveste, Calama, Madauros, Thamugadi and Sitifs and elsewhere. (It has recently been argued, very plausibly, that these fortifications were not intended to protect the local population from external marauders, but to protect the Byzantine invaders – seen by now as Greek-speaking aliens – from the local population.)

While the ruins of the ancient city were still substantially visible at the beginning of the French conquest (including defensive circuits of both the Roman and medieval periods), these were largely covered by (and plundered for) new military constructions. Even areas of extensive excavation in the 1950s around the centre of the town have now been covered by aggressive modern development. The circus and a quarter comprising two fourth-century Christian basilicas surrounded by houses have entirely disappeared. The fine local museum seeks to commemorate the ancient city of Sitifis, which is otherwise represented by the following visible monuments alone.

EXPLORING THE TOWN

Archaeological park

A part of the leisure park in the centre of the modern city has been retained as an archaeological zone. In its SW corner are the surviving walls of part of the fortress built by the Byzantine general Solomon in 539, refurbished in the nineteenth century by the French invaders as part of their large military base. (The footprint of this base, now dismantled, has otherwise provided the space for the present park.) The outlines of streets and housing may be made out on the ground outside the fortress, and its NW corner overlies the remains of a temple and

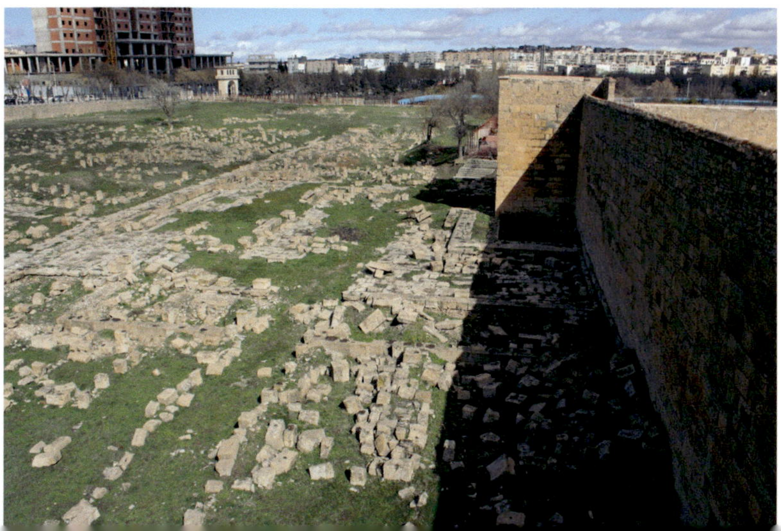

Fig. 93. Sétif: buildings of the Roman period, including the precinct of a second-century temple, seen from the ramparts of the Byzantine fortress. The uppermost parts of the fortress walls were rebuilt by the French military.

precinct of the second century (see fig. 93). In the vicinity was found the remarkable mosaic of the ***Indian Triumph of Dionysus*** which is now in the museum (see below).

Excavations in 1977–84 near the centre of the leisure park ('4' on fig. 92) exposed a Roman public bath building of two phases, of the early third century and of c. 425–430. Medieval buildings of the tenth and eleventh centuries were also found. These were all reburied.

Nymphaeum

Just to the S of the Byzantine fortress (at '3' in fig. 92) stands a remarkable survival from the Roman period. This is a monumental fountain-house, with a covered basin beneath an arcaded portico around three sides of a paved court (fig. 94). The sills beneath the arcades are worn from lengthy service, and there are (mostly broken) tethering-rings for anchoring animals in the corners of the piers. The whole building is substantially below the modern ground-level, and access stairs on the fourth side obscure the original aspect of this part. There is also a modern turret in the middle of the courtyard, and pipework which now carries away the water which once poured into the basin. It would seem, however, that this ancient water source has never fallen wholly out of use.

The pleasant adjoining garden houses a number of Roman inscriptions.

Tomb 'of Scipio'

Some 750 m beyond the road junction at the western edge of fig. 92, and just to the N of the Boulevard de Scipion amongst modern housing, there still stands a massive two-storey Roman tower-tomb (fig. 95). The construction is internally of *opus africanum*,

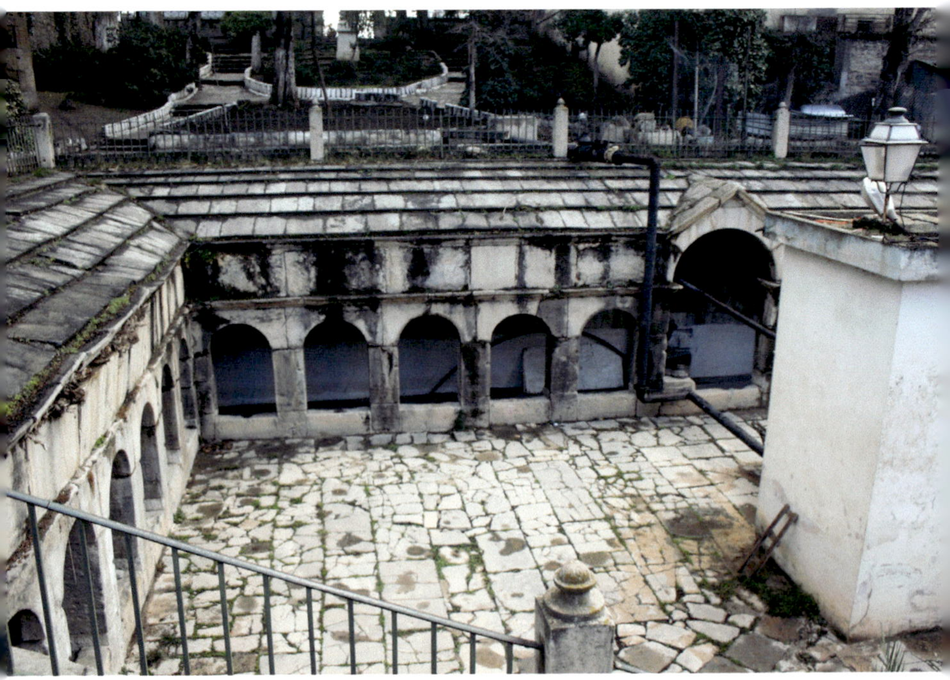

Fig. 94. Sétif: Roman fountain-house.

with a concrete barrel-vault supporting the upper floor; externally, one saw originally only ashlar masonry. The front of the building is now missing: it would have had a blank wall for the lower storey (probably with a false door in the centre) and a colonnaded porch of some sort above, in front of an arched *aedicula*. The real entrance to the tomb chamber was a small door in the rear of the building. No inscription has been recorded, and the association with the name Scipio is pure fantasy; the tomb has been ascribed to the fourth century.

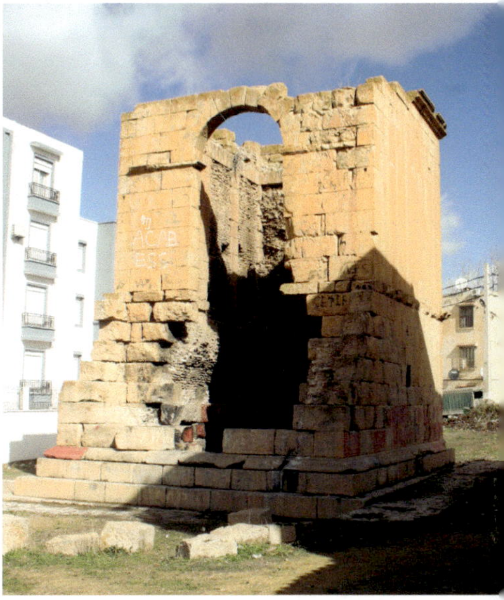

Fig. 95. Sétif: Tomb 'of Scipio'.

NATIONAL MUSEUM OF SÉTIF

As you enter this museum, which originated in 1896 but moved into its present building in 1985, you are greeted by a colossal but rather flat torso and head of Jupiter found in the Capitolium of the little settlement at Aïn Safsaf between Sétif and Djémila (ancient name uncertain, but beginning *Mopth…*). Behind this, a circuit of ground-floor rooms (going anticlockwise) takes one through the chronology of the region, passing all around the two-storey central hall dedicated to mosaics.

Hall of mosaics

The two principal mosaics here, laid horizontally, are best viewed from the first-floor gallery, accessed from a staircase to the left inside the entrance.

Indian triumph of Dionysus: this is the masterpiece of the museum, beautifully displayed, and justifies a visit to Sétif on its own. It was found in 1970 at the site of the second-century temple, following heavy rains, and the arrangement of a central figural panel surrounded by geometric designs on three sides shows that it once decorated a dining room, a *triclinium*. (There would have been couches around three sides, so there was no point in having very elaborate mosaics where they would not be seen.) The remainder of the building (beneath a modern road) has not been available for excavation. The theme of the central panel (fig. 96) is one frequently portrayed in Roman mosaic art, relating to the triumphal return of Dionysus from his conquest of India. The god is shown seated in a triumphal chariot drawn by two tigresses; he is being crowned by a winged Victory. The tigresses are being led by a satyr with cloven hooves, who is also leading two chained black slaves; one of them has had his hand cut off. The procession is composed of dancing maenads, African beasts and prisoners. Amongst the animals may be recognized two camels – one carrying prisoners, the other chalices – an elephant, a lion, and the only known representation in Roman art in Africa of a giraffe. The whole scene is surrounded by a wonderful border decorated with acanthus scrolls and flowers against a black background; this includes alternating images of centaurs battling lions and panthers, while the angles are filled by four helmeted and bearded heads. On the side

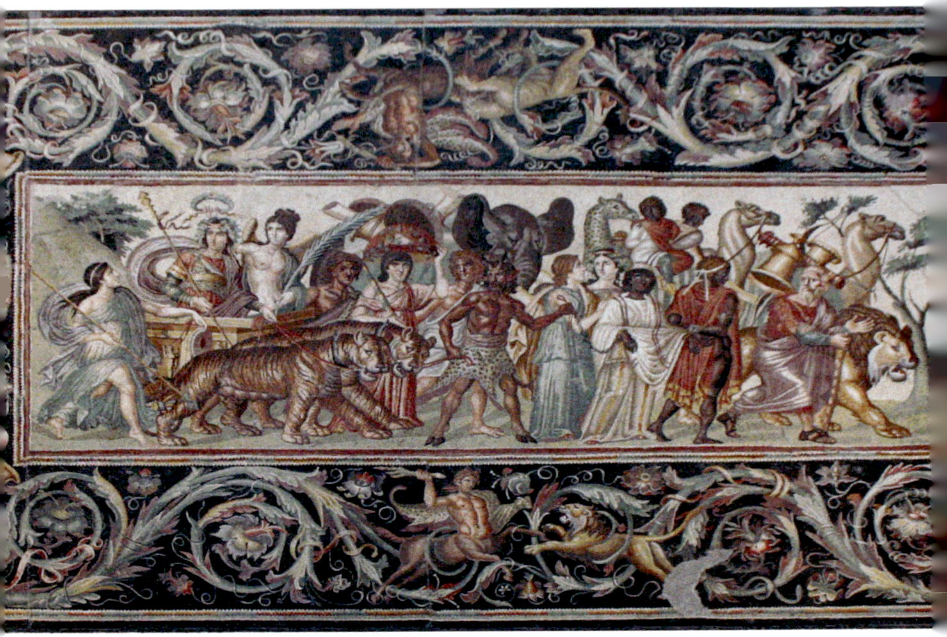

Fig. 96. Sétif: central panel of the mosaic of the Indian Triumph of Dionysus.

where the doorway into the room would have been, there is a separate hunting scene, possibly the legendary hunt of the Calydonian Boar. The whole displays a tremendous richness of colour and mastery of subtle shading. (Early fourth century.)

Toilet of Venus: this mosaic (fig. 97), attributed to the late fourth or early fifth century and found in a bath building in the vicinity of the two churches, has nothing of the quality of the Dionysus mosaic, but is nonetheless impressive for its state of preservation and the manner of its display. Venus is shown seated on a fan-shaped sea-shell supported by two tritons (one male and one female). Wearing nothing but jewellery, Venus is adjusting her hair and fixing it with a pin. Above her hover two attendant erotes, one holding a sunshade over her head and the other a mirror for her benefit. Three more erotes are portrayed in the sea below: one is driving a boat drawn by a pair of dolphins, a second is holding up a sail in order to propel himself along on a floating amphora, while in the centre a third, standing on the entwined tails of two more dolphins, offers a diadem to the goddess. The colour palette is restricted and the border is composed of geometric panels, some of which enclose images of birds.

Mosaic tomb-covers. On the left-hand wall of this room (at ground-floor level) are displayed some of the tomb-covers found in association with the churches. They name the deceased, and very often their ages. On the opposite wall are further fragments of floor-mosaics.

Chronological circuit

Beware of the very dangerous shallow steps, one set on either side of the building in the long display galleries!

Prehistory

The first room displays two main collections of prehistoric material, from Ain Hanech near El Eulma (Lower Palaeolithic, around 1.75 million years BC) and Mezloug, 12 km to the SW of Sétif (Epipalaeolithic, 7500–5000 BC).

Classical antiquity

Two rooms (right-hand side and across the far end) contain displays of pottery, glass and other small objects derived mainly from graves in the E Necropolis of Sétif and from the area of the temple, just outside the Byzantine walls. A central display shows various types of querns and millstones; there are also reconstruction models of the baths and circus found at Sétif, and of the excavated quarter of the Christian basilicas.

Medieval period

The room on the left-hand side contains medieval finds from the area of the Byzantine fortress and from the important site of Qala'at Bani Hammad 70 km to the SW of Sétif, which flourished between 1007 and 1090. There are also models of this site and of the coastal town of Bejaïa, to which the Hammadids moved their capital at the latter date.

Coin room

This houses a fine collection of Numidian, Roman and Islamic coins.

First floor

The gallery on this floor has ethnographic displays of traditional art, and provides elevated views of the mosaics below.

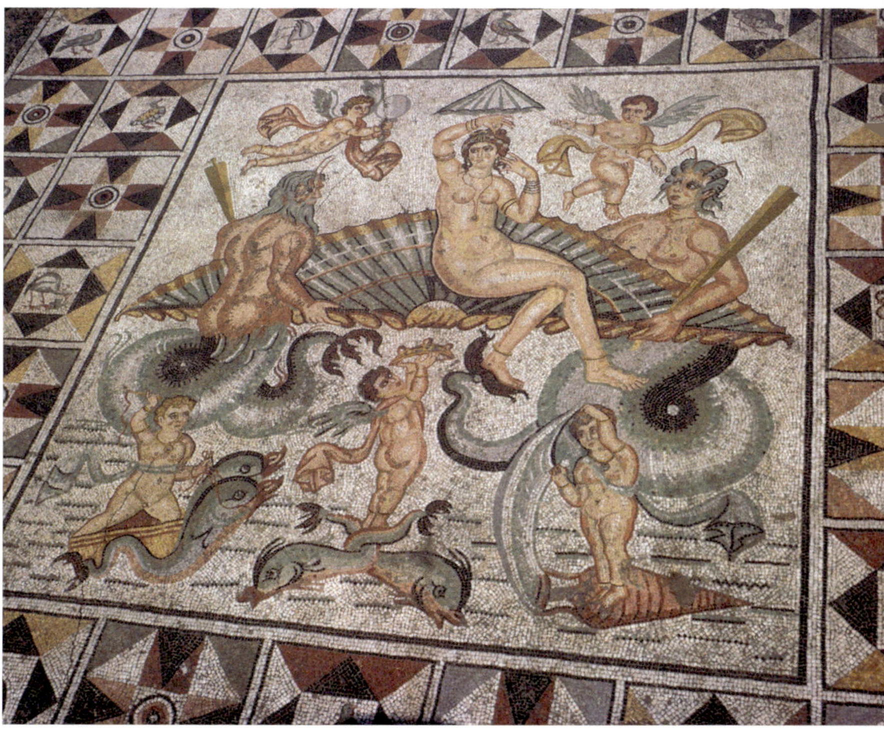

Fig. 97. Sétif: Toilet of Venus mosaic, when first discovered.

3. NUMIDIA

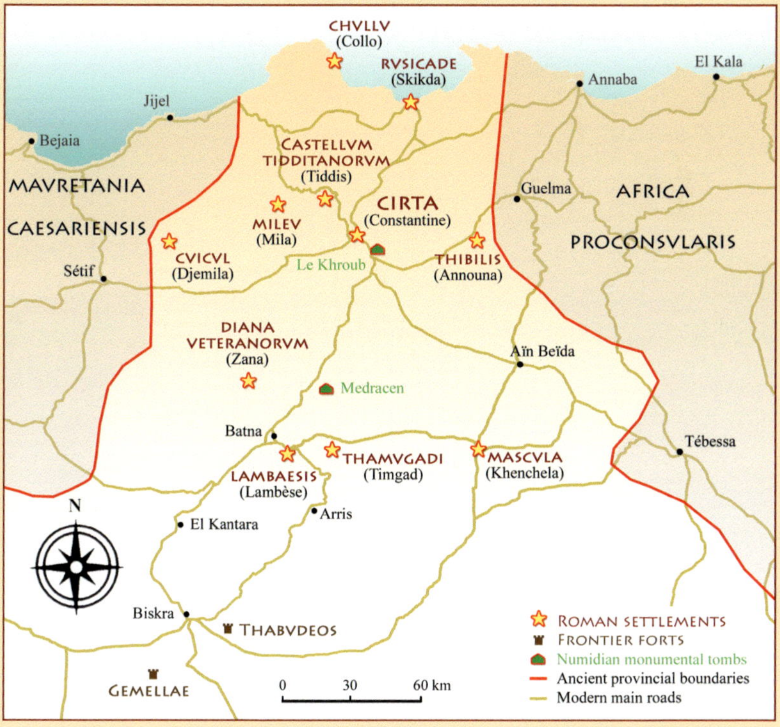

Fig. 98. Numidia in the third century AD.

CUICUL (Djémila)

And there you are, intent, faced by the stones and the silence, as the day passes and the mountains grow bigger as they turn violet. But the wind blows across the plateau of Djémila. In this great confusion of wind and of the sun which fills the ruins with light, something is forged which gives to man a sense of his identity with the solitude and the silence of the dead city.

Albert Camus

The ancient city of Cuicul derives its beauty from its location. A shelf on a rocky spur sloping southwards between the enclosed ravines of the wadis Guergour and Bétame and the surrounding hills create an austere and wild setting. In antiquity, the territory controlled by Cuicul must undoubtedly have included mountain slopes, but also more fertile terrain close to the high plains of the South. We don't know the full reason why the Romans chose to found a city here: traces of prehistoric settlement, the shadowy presence here of local tribes mentioned in ancient literature (Marchubi, Koidamousii, Todoukae) or later in inscriptions (Bavares, Suburbures, Mediani) do not alone justify the choice. It is true, however, that the city lay at an important node of communication and that the proximity of the Ampsaga river

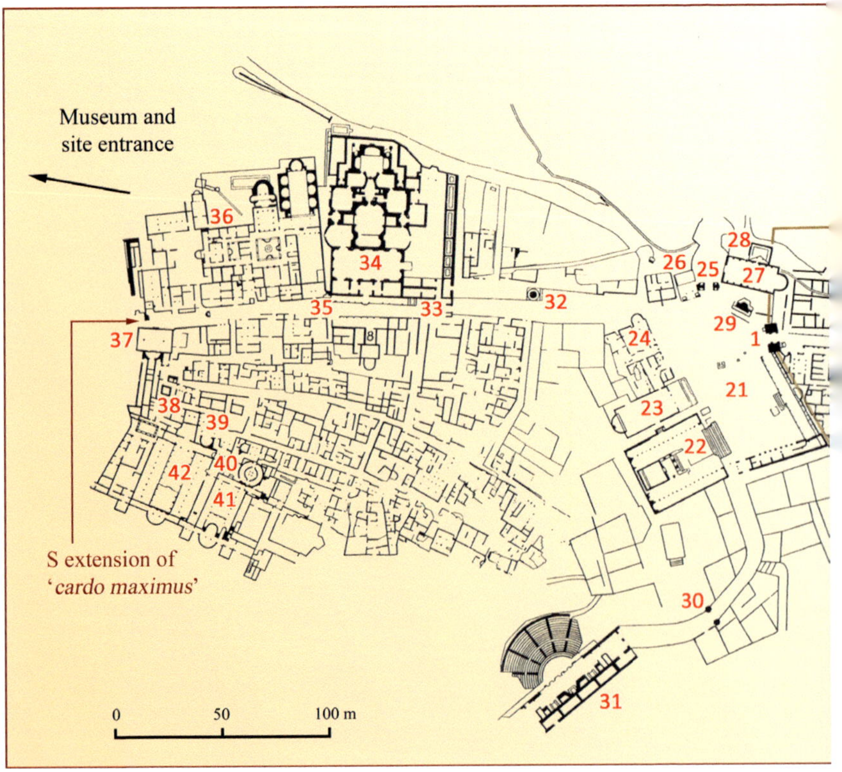

Fig. 99. Cuicul: plan of the site.

1. *South Gate and city walls*
2. *House of Castorius*
3. *Unidentified temple*
4. *House of the Ass*
5. *Western quarter and Christian basilica*
6. *Arch*
7. *Temple of Genetrix*
8. *Forum*
9. *Basilica Julia*
10. *Curia*
11. *Capitolium*
12. *Market of Cosinius*
13. *House of Europa*
14. *North Gate*
15. *Public latrine*
16. *Capitolium baths*
17. *House of brick*
18. *Baths of Terentius*
19. *House of Amphitrite*
20. *Public granaries*
21. *Severan Forum*
22. *Temple of the Gens* Septimia
23. *Fourth cent. civil basilica*
24. *House of the Hylas Mosaic*
25. *Arch of Caracalla*
26. *Small temple*
27. *Textile market*
28. *Public latrine*
29. *Nymphaeum*
30. *Arch of Julis Crescens*
31. *Theatre*
32. *Conical fountain*
33. *Late city gate*
34. *Great Baths*
35. *Tetrarchic fountain*
36. *House of Bacchus*
37. *Entrance to Christian quarter*
38. *Episcopal residence*
39. *Christian chapel*
40. *Baptistery and baths*
41. *North Basilica*
42. *Basilica of Cresconius*

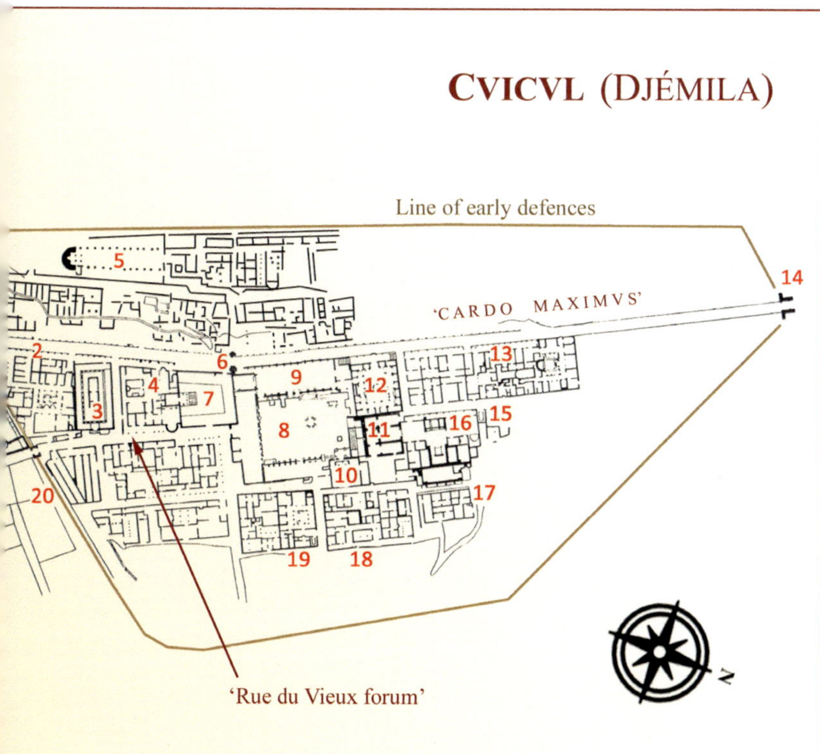

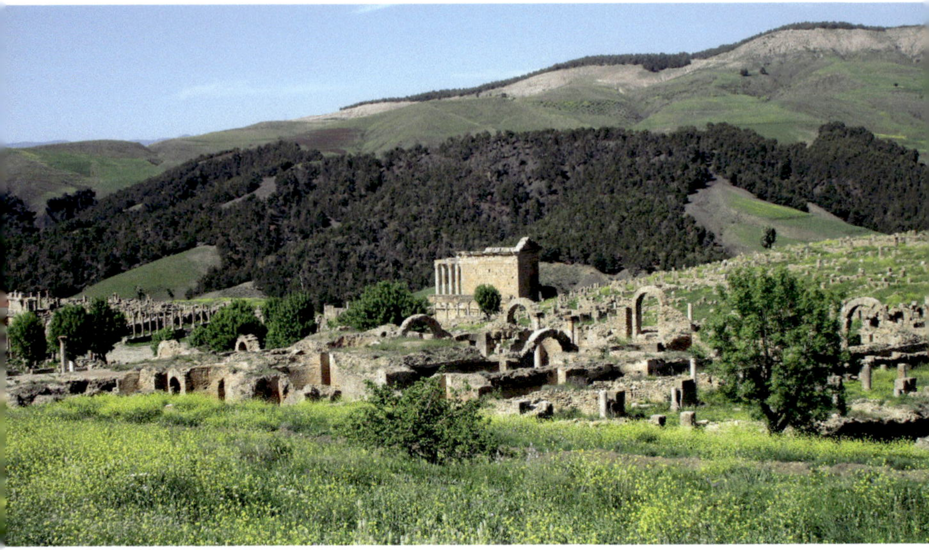

Fig. 100. Cuicul: the site seen from above, in springtime.

(now the Oued el-Kebir), the ancient natural frontier between Numidia and Mauretania, would have led to the establishment of a customs post.

The *municipium* of Cuicul was founded in AD 96 or 97 by veterans of Nerva. The place-name is of pre-Roman origin and un-latinised; the first settlers, former soldiers of the Papiria tribe, chose the god Mars as their patron. The heart of the early settlement was laid out on the shelf of the spur, where a triangular space, partly protected by the ravines on either side, was enclosed by a defensive wall. The street grid, which was cleverly adapted to the lie of the land, marked out the public and private spaces. It was in this relatively restricted zone that, in the Antonine period, the monumental appurtenances of the city were put in place: the forum, curia, capitolium, market and temples – with a theatre sited a short distance outside the walls because of its size. These expensive investments – since the materials had sometimes to be imported from great distances – demonstrate clearly the wealth of the settlement and of some of its inhabitants, a wealth that was founded largely on agriculture and trade.

Before long, the framework of the late first century could no longer contain the growth of the city, and buildings gradually accumulated outside the walls. Under the Severan dynasty, part of the defensive wall was demolished and quarters were laid out around a new forum and new streets, to the point where the urban area was substantially increased, though Cuicul was only ever a modest town. After the difficult years of the later third century, works were undertaken under Diocletian, notably to improve the water supply; it was also in the fourth and fifth centuries that the Christian topography was established. We know a little of the beginnings of the new religion here, inasmuch as we know of a first bishop, Pudentianus, in 256. A Christian basilica has been excavated on the W side of the original settlement, while an entire episcopal quarter, incorporating two basilicas, a chapel and a baptistery, was established on the high ground to the S of the Severan Forum. The dates of these buildings are not unequivocally established, but they are not thought to be earlier than the late fourth century.

Cuicul was occupied in 431 by the Vandals. Following the Byzantine reconquest a century later, the city showed renewed signs of vitality: churches were restored, wells were dug to compensate for the derelict former aqueducts and houses were restored in the southern (uphill) part of the settlement, while the northern part seems to have been abandoned. Around the end of the sixth century, the city was sacked by persons unknown and finally came to an end.

EXPLORING THE SITE

1. South Gate and city walls

The original defensive circuit forms an irregular triangle aligned NW–SE, which takes account of the lie of the land and encloses an area of 8 hectares. Preserved in places to a height of two or three metres, the rampart was constructed of an outer and an inner face of ashlar masonry, separated by a core of mortared rubble, the whole amounting to 2.50 m in thickness.

The South Gate is composed of an arch in rusticated masonry which provided a narrow passage between the road to Sitifis (Sétif) and the principal street of the town. Note the presence of several milestones at the foot of the arch, placed there during the reigns of Caracalla, Alexander Severus and their successors.

The street named *cardo maximus* in current usage (fig. 101) does not lead to the forum, but down the slope of the spur to the North Gate, with a slight bend at an arch beside the forum basilica. Averaging 5 m wide, this street was bordered on both sides by a pavement 3.50 m wide, sheltered by porticoes. The Tuscan Doric colonnade

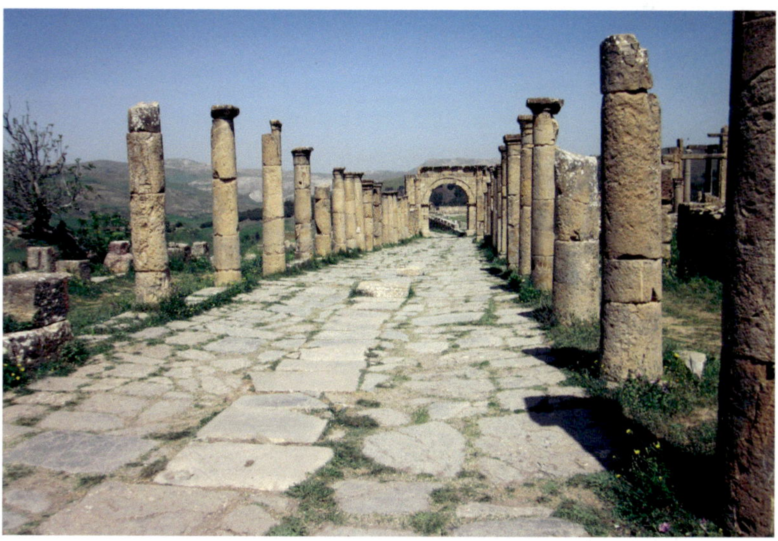

Fig. 101. Cuicul: the 'cardo maximus', *looking from the S Gate towards the forum.*

of the porticoes was interrupted only by public monuments such as the forum basilica and the Temple of Genetrix, and in front of a few large properties (House of Europa, House of the Stuccoes) where the austere Doric was replaced by the more ornate Corinthian order.

2. House of Castorius

Arranged about a large colonnaded peristyle, this wealthy residence was composed of some 27 rooms, covering an area of 1,600 sq.m. (fig. 102). The house had two entrances from the *cardo maximus* and a third from the parallel 'Rue du Vieux Forum'. The entrance just inside the city gate was embellished by two statues, of which the bases remain. They bear dedications to Victory and to Mercury, offered by L. Claudius Brutto, son of the prefect Tiberius Claudius. This entrance led into an *atrium* with an *oecus* and a corridor leading to the rest of the house. The other entrance further down the same street had an open-air vestibule with a porter's lodge, followed by a second, paved, vestibule from which one entered a large peristyle court, decorated with three semi-circular basins on the NE side and a rectangular basin in the centre. The central space was enclosed on two sides by a low wall; it could be accessed either between the columns on the SW side or through an exedra on the NW. This exedra and the porticoes were paved with undistinguished mosaics, save for two inscriptions which served to identify the owner of the property (see p. 132). Despite the absence of an obvious staircase, the solidity of the columns suggests the former presence of an upper floor. Various rooms opened off the peristyle, including a grand *oecus* and the private baths of the house. These baths were duplicated on the N side by a small, rudimentary and late bath suite; it has been plausibly suggested that this was for the slaves of the household.

As we see it today, the House of Castorius is the result of the amalgamation of two properties: a modest atrium house to the S, built under Caracalla around 211, when the rampart had become obsolete; and a larger property to the N. This was carried out by Castorius at the end of the fourth century,

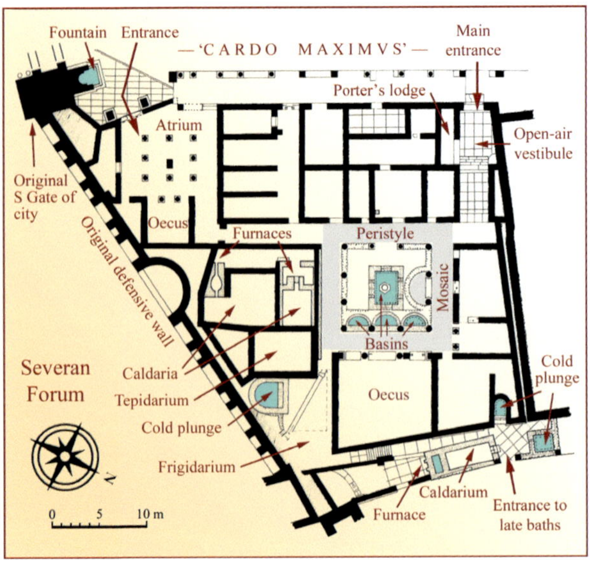

Fig. 102. Cuicul: plan of the House of Castorius.

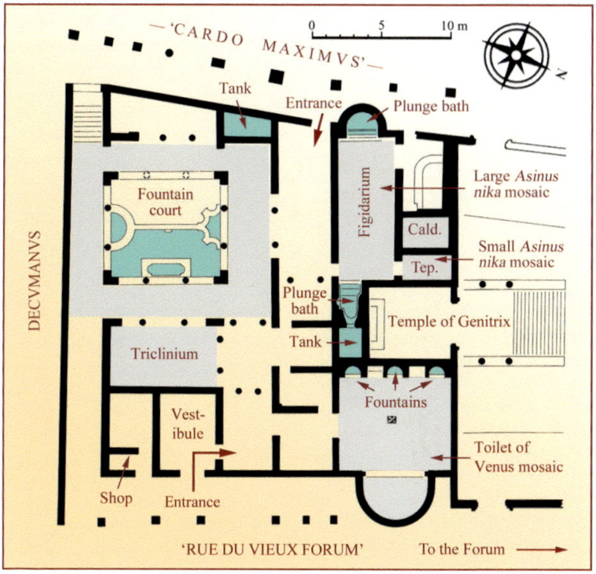

Fig. 103. Cuicul: plan of the House of the Ass.

when he also redecorated the peristyle. The little baths on the N side seem to be a yet later modification.

3. Unidentified temple

Sited between the House of Castorius and the House of the Ass, this temple, the dedication of which is unknown, stood on a podium within a peristyle. It faced towards the E, opening onto the street which led to the old forum.

4. House of the Ass

This house is dated to the middle of the fourth century, and makes use of a space behind the Temple of Genetrix at a time when the temple had surely passed out of use (fig. 103). Approached from the *cardo maximus*, a vestibule opened to the right into a peristyle court, the eastern half of which was decorated with three fountains: a rectangular one on the E side and a semi-circular one on the S which was connected to a polylobed one on the N. The remainder of the open space showed no trace of waterproof plaster and was probably laid to garden. The residential part of the property was accessed from the E side of the peristyle; at the far end of this area a large reception room with an apse had one wall composed entirely of fountains in alternating rectangular and rounded recesses, while the floor had a magnificent mosaic pavement (on display in the museum: p. 129 fig. 132 portraying the Toilet of Venus.

From the opposite side of the vestibule first mentioned, one entered the private baths of the house. The floor of the frigidarium was paved with the impressive mosaic inscribed *ASINUS NICA* ('Victory to the Ass') with its 73 medallions (visible in Room 1 of the museum: figs. 133–5), which has given its name to the house. This has been dated approximately between the early fifth and the mid-sixth centuries. Equipped with two cold-plunge baths, this room gave onto three heated rooms which it has not been possible to identify with confidence. The little room against the wall of the temple had another, smaller mosaic on the theme of the 'Conquering Ass' (also displayed in Room 1 of the museum).

5. Western quarter and Christian basilica

Situated between the original rampart and the *cardo maximus*, and difficult now to disentangle because of the steep slope, this quarter contained six blocks of houses, a temple, an apsed room described as a *schola* and a Christian basilica (see fig. 104). The following properties are worthy of note.

The House of the Stuccoes. This fine house, built at the beginning of the fourth century, was laid out on a classical plan. A lower floor, at the level of the west *cardo* from which it was entered, contained various service rooms (cellar, store rooms and baths) around a tetrastyle atrium with vaulted ceilings. A staircase led to the upper floor, which could also be entered through a porch with colonnettes on the *cardo maximus*; on that frontage, the owner had replaced the Doric columns of the street with a Corinthian colonnade. From this upper entrance, one came to two bedrooms and two large reception rooms. The largest of these rooms was richly decorated with stucco reliefs, depicting people and animals surrounded by vegetal ornament and architectural mouldings. Some of these may now be seen in Room 3 of the museum (see p. 137).

At a later date, the baths were suppressed: the frigidarium was transformed into a living space and the caldarium into an *oecus*. The whole property was subsequently destroyed by fire. In the fifth century, the ruins were reoccupied, creating a modest residence, a stable and workshops.

The House of the small basins was small (19 x 19 m) and again situated between the *cardo maximus* and the west *cardo*. From the main street, one entered a courtyard with porticoes on the N and E sides and various service rooms on the ground floor and in the basement. A staircase led to an upper floor and the residential part of the house. A heating system associated with some basins at the lower level were interpreted by the excavator as a dyeing establishment, but a recent re-examination has led to the conclusion that this was originally a bath suite, which underwent later (not readily identifiable) modifications.

The Christian basilica was built over the tomb of a martyr at the end of the fourth or beginning of the fifth century and is aligned N–S (fig. 105). Over the course of time, this cemetery church attracted a large number of burials, at first within its precincts

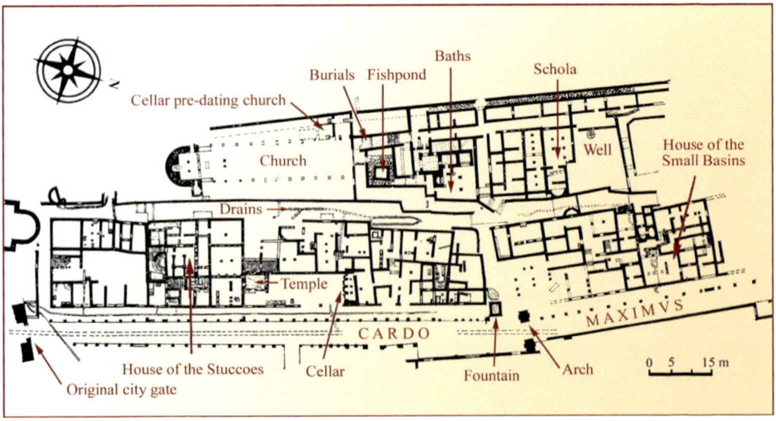

Fig. 104. Cuicul: plan of the western quarter.

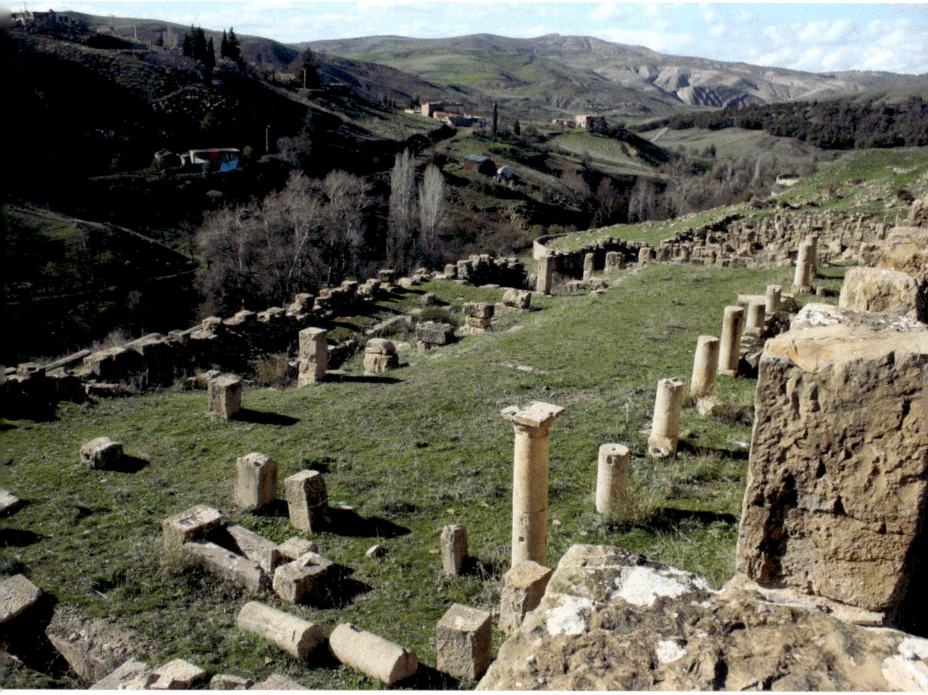

Fig. 105. Cuicul: the church in the western quarter.

and then in the area in front of its façade on the N. The cellar in its NW corner belonged to an earlier house, probably that of which the courtyard and fishpond can still be seen in front of the entrance. This cellar is very like that found beneath the peristyle of the House of Europa (13).

6. Arch

Crowned by an ornately carved cornice, this monument consists of a single archway flanked, on either face, by two engaged Corinthian columns (fig. 106). It was probably built in order to mask the angle in the *cardo maximus* at the point where it was extended towards the S.

7. Temple of Genetrix

Now backed up against the House of the Ass, this sanctuary (fig. 107) is enclosed within a trapezoidal courtyard surrounded by porticoes on three sides, with entrances from the *cardo maximus*, the S forum portico and the 'Rue du Vieux Forum' respectively. The temple itself stood on top of a podium approach by twelve steps. However harmonious it appears, the reconstructed columns have been placed arbitrarily by the excavators, without good authority. The differences of style between the granite columns of the *pronaos* (of the fourth century), those of black-veined white marble of the porticoes and those of the W façade do not therefore represent different phases of the building, but the aesthetic fancies of the 19th-century French architects responsible for their re-erection.

A single fragment of the dedicatory inscription, bearing the word *genetrix*, has been found. This is suggestive, but hardly

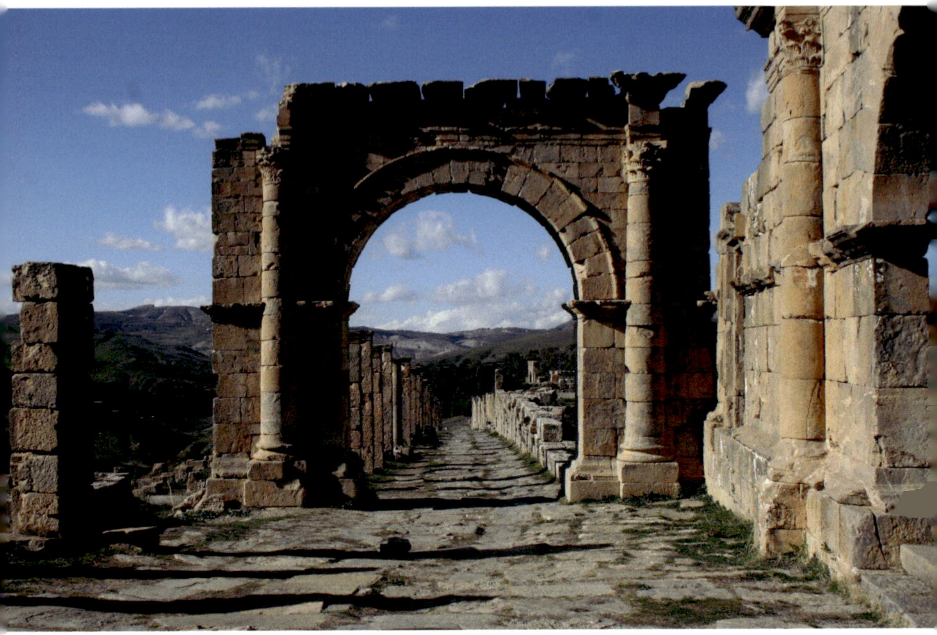

Fig. 106. Cuicul: arch on the 'cardo maximus' *next to the Basilica Julia.*

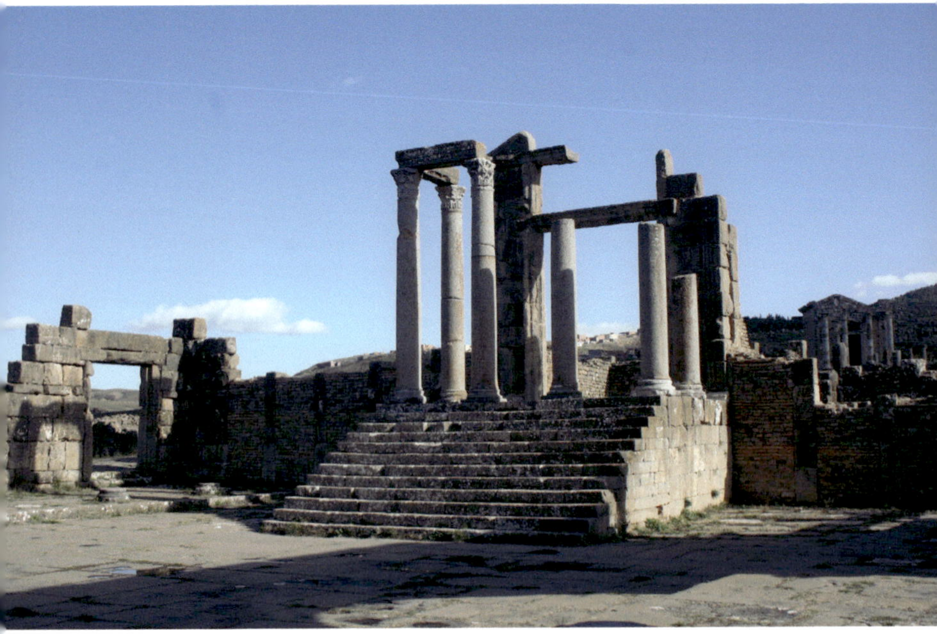

Fig.107. Cuicul: Temple of Genetrix.

conclusive for an attribution to *Venus Genetrix*, the protector of Rome since the *gens Julia*, and Julius Caesar in particular, adopted the goddess as its ancestor.

8. Forum

The heart of the original settlement is a paved square measuring 48 x 44 m, embellished with porticoes on two sides (figs. 108, 109). It was entered from the S through a monumental arch next to the enclosure wall of the precinct of Genetrix; only the base remains. As in most cities of the Roman empire (and particularly those which had the status of colonies), the forum incorporated around its perimeter the principal symbols of Romanization: the curia, the judicial basilica and the Capitoline Temple – buildings which conferred on each municipality at its own scale the senatorial, judicial and religious authority which governed the capital city. Around the square and in its centre, the many *stelai* and statue bases continue to bear witness to the largesse of the citizens of Cuicul. They include dedications to various emperors, from the second to the fourth centuries, and to the gods (Mars, Jupiter, Hercules, Mercury, divinities such as the Fortune or the *Genius* of the colony of Cuicul), but also dedications to provincial or local personalities.

In front of the steps leading to the Capitolium may be seen an altar decorated with carvings in relief (end of third century). One of its faces is decorated with a kind of 'Green Man' emanating from a chalice, a winged *genius* from whom sprout vine tendrils and ears of corn. On an adjacent face is a visual list of requirements for a sacrifice (fig. 110): fire burns on the altar, in front of which a bull is tethered to a ring in the ground while his executioner raises his double axe above his head. Also present are two other sacrificial victims, a ram and a cockerel, and three instruments of ritual: a knife, a ram's-head libation-dish and a ewer. A few paces from the altar, a recess is cut in the paving where the ring for tethering the animals used to be stapled into the stone.

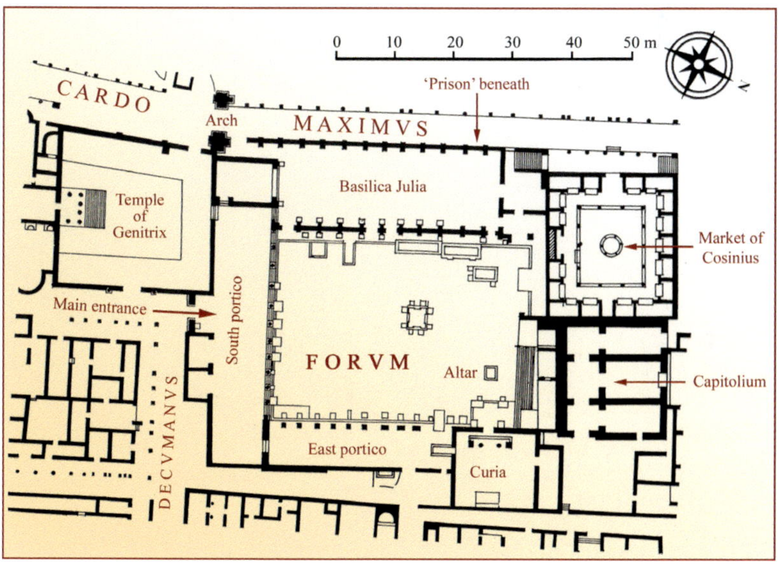

Fig. 108. Cuicul: plan of the Forum area.

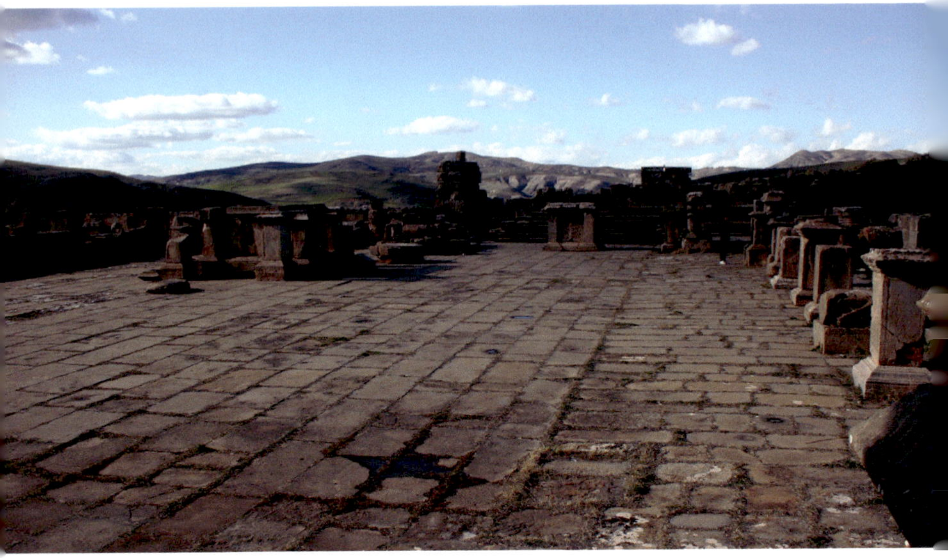

Fig. 109. Cuicul: the Forum, looking towards the steps of the Capitolium.

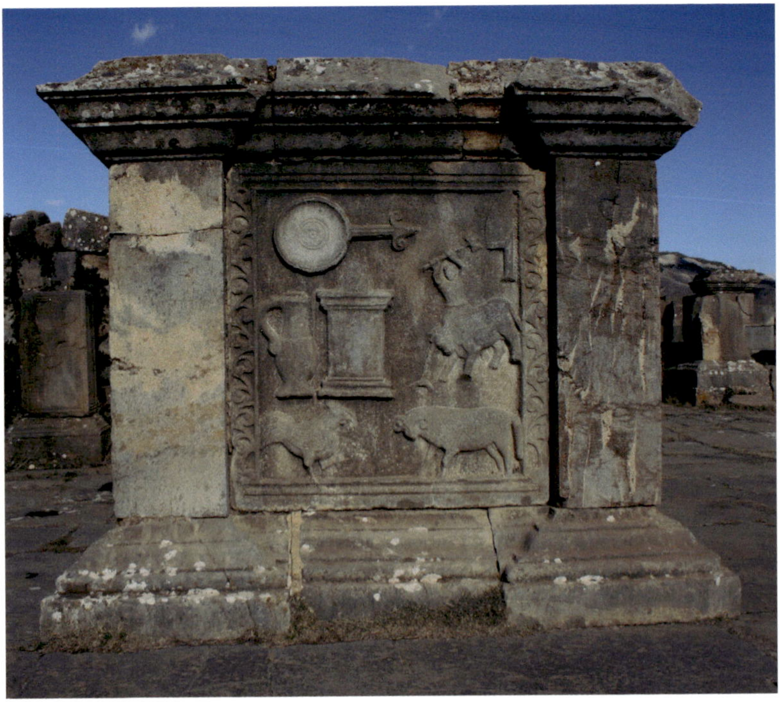

Fig. 110. Cuicul: detail of Capitolium altar, showing requirements for sacrifice.

9. Basilica Julia

Built in 169, the judicial basilica is a huge rectangular hall 38 m long and 14 m wide, with a raised dais at its southern end. On this tribunal there are still bases of statues of the joint emperors Marcus Aurelius and Lucius Verus. The building is named after the inscription on which C. Julius Crescens, perpetual *flamen* (priest) of the Four Colonies of the Cirtan Federation and perpetual *flamen* of Cuicul, declares that he has 'made, installed and dedicated in the Basilica Julia' one of these two statues at a cost of 3,000 *sesterces*.

Accessed from the forum by four doors, this building served both as the law court and as the Chamber of Commerce – or indeed as a public meeting place in bad weather.

Placed at the N end of the Basilica Julia, against the parapet of the adjoining Market of Cosinius, may be seen a broken stone block with three recesses in the top and an inscription across the front. This was a table of standard measures, with a recess for liquids (wine or oil), one for barley and one for wheat.

10. Curia

This was the meeting hall of the decurions who constituted the city council. It was entered through a porch framed by honorific inscriptions. Within, the floor was paved with a red marble with black stars (no longer visible). The platform reserved for the magistrates governing the city (*duoviri*) was paved with onyx, some of which remains in place. Also present is the dedication offered by L. Flavius Celsus to the *Genius* of the senate of Cuicul: laden with honours and responsibilities (he had just been named augur of the city), he offered three statues in gratitude.

11. Capitolium

This temple is dedicated to the Capitoline Triad, Jupiter, Juno and Minerva. Because of the fall in the slope, the temple stood on the arches and piers of a massive basement, which alone remains (fig. 111). The cella was divided into three compartments, one for each god. It was beneath one of these that was found the white marble torso in low relief of a colossal statue of Jupiter (still on site). The podium was approached from the

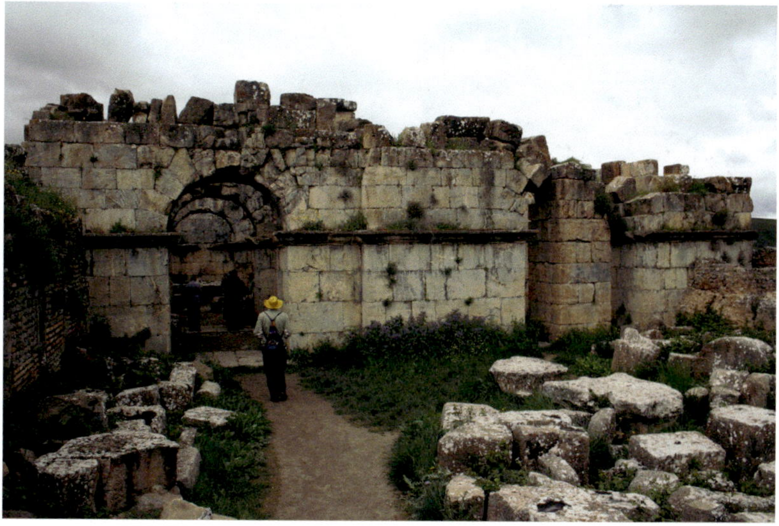

Fig. 111. Cuicul: the substructures of the Capitolium.

forum by a monumental stairway, at the top of which stood a pronaos 17.60 m wide, composed of six Corinthian columns across the façade with two on either side. Fourteen metres high and 1.50 m in diameter, these columns had stuccoed fluting and carried the triangular pediment. Some of the column drums, bases and capitals may be seen in the forum.

The Capitolium is out of alignment with the forum square and its stairway encroaches on the original N portico: these factors indicate that, as in several other North African cities, the temple was not part of the original design but was a later addition, probably in the second half of the second century.

12. Market of Cosinius

On leaving the forum by the staircase at the NW corner, one may rejoin the *cardo maximus*. Immediately beyond is the raised portico which leads into the market. Two inscribed bases tell us that the brothers C. and L. Cosinius had paid out of their own pocket for the statues voted in their honour by the Council of the Decurions of Cuicul, and that the same L. Cosinius, with the help of his brother, had spent 30,000 sesterces for the construction of the market and its portico. This generous benefactor tells us in addition that he was a prefect under the emperor T. Aelius Hadrianus Antoninus; construction therefore took place in the reign of Antoninus Pius (138–161).

On entering from the *cardo*, a doorway with a semicircular arch leads into an open space (28 x 22 m) enclosed by porticoes of monolithic marble columns (fig.112); these supported a finely worked architrave (now laid out on top of the S wall), where the dedication of the Cosinius brothers and the scale of their munificence is repeated. There was

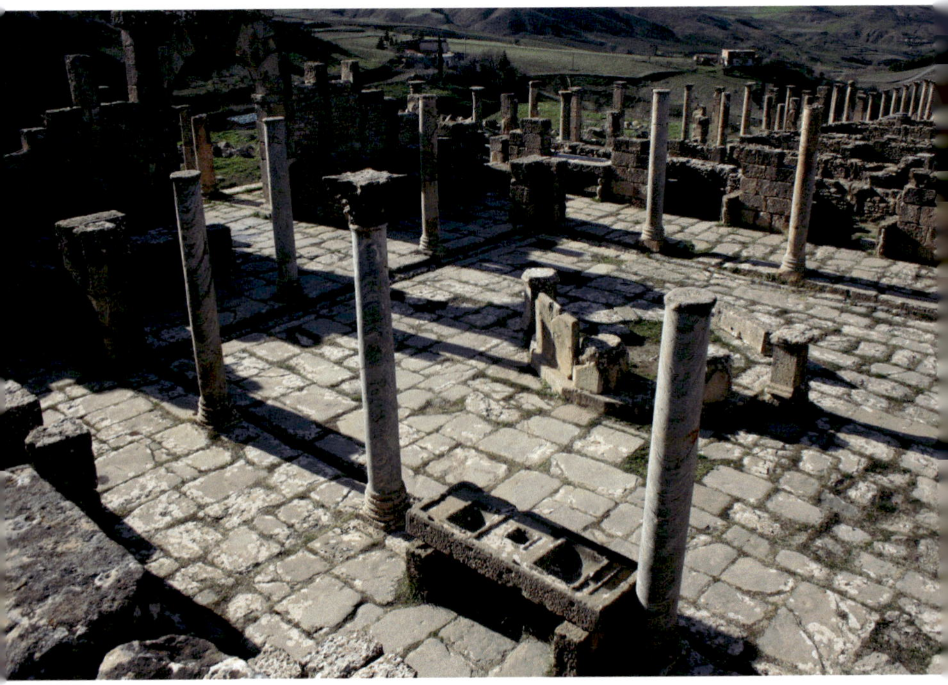

Fig. 112. Cuicul: Market of Cosinius.

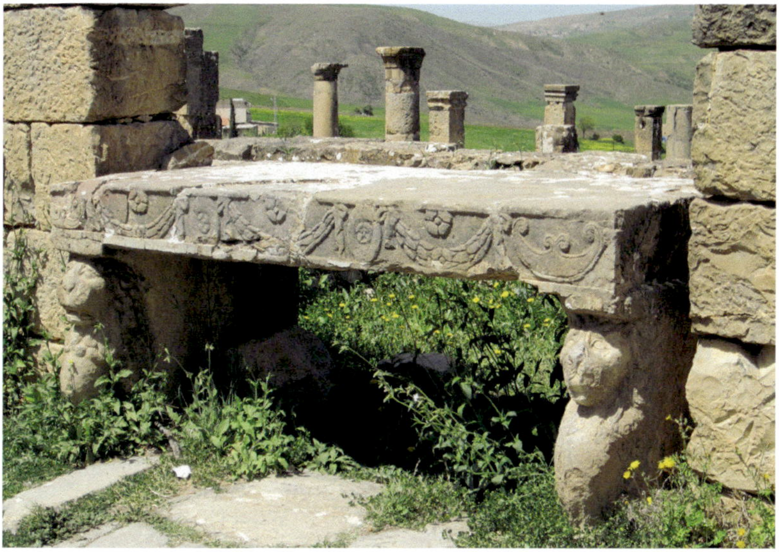

Fig. 113. Cuicul: a typical shop counter in the Market of Cosinius.

a circular kiosk in the centre of the courtyard: this was surely a fountain surmounted by a dome; the frieze of the entablature was decorated with heads and festoons. Eighteen rectangular shops are disposed around the perimeter of the market, each fronted with a stone counter. Inventive sculptures (tortoises, lions, bull's heads, garlands, various animal and marine monsters) adorn the front edges and the supports of these counters, beneath which the shopkeeper had to crawl in order to enter his shop (see fig. 113). The paving within is in small tiles of *opus spicatum* (herring-bone pattern).

In the middle of the S side, in place of a shop, is a projection from the wall, faced with a limestone panel pierced by ten circular holes. Since the inscription of the Cosinii speaks of a *ponderarium* or public set of weights, it is reasonable to suppose that these holes once held the anchorages from which the official weights were suspended. In front of this, between the columns of the portico, is a stone table carved with the corresponding approved measures of capacity.

In the SE corner, a secondary modification has resulted in a shop counter being set on edge to form a screen. The characteristic wear on the top edge shows that it must then have enclosed a water basin.

A few paces uphill on the *cardo* from the market is a doorway into a basement area beneath the Basilica Julia. This leads into what appear to be massive, vaulted strongrooms; they have been interpreted as a prison.

13. House of Europa

Created at the beginning of the fourth century by an individual of notable wealth, the House of Europa, covering 1,366 sq.m, results from the amalgamation of several earlier buildings (see fig. 114).

On the frontage of the *cardo*, the façade and the principal entrance to the house were marked by an elegant Corinthian portico (fig. 115). A large, vaulted carriage entrance and two smaller doorways led into a paved, open-air court. From this a flight of four steps led to an upper level. To the right was the *frigidarium* of the private baths of the house

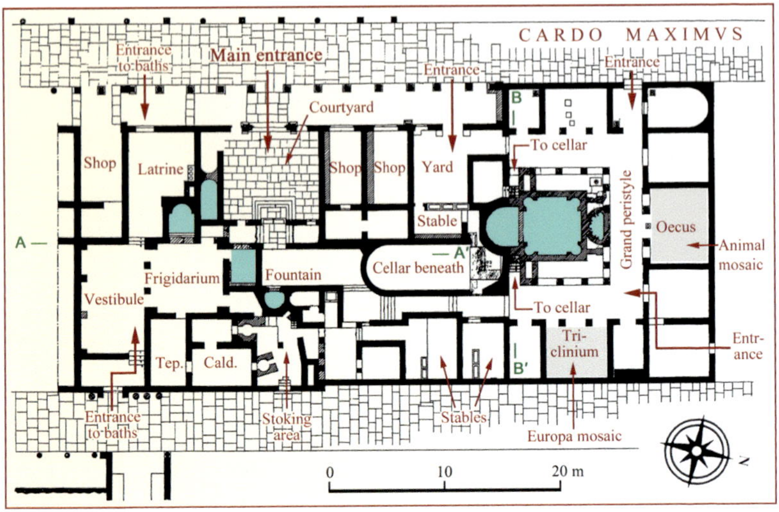

Fig. 114. Cuicul: plan of the House of Europa.

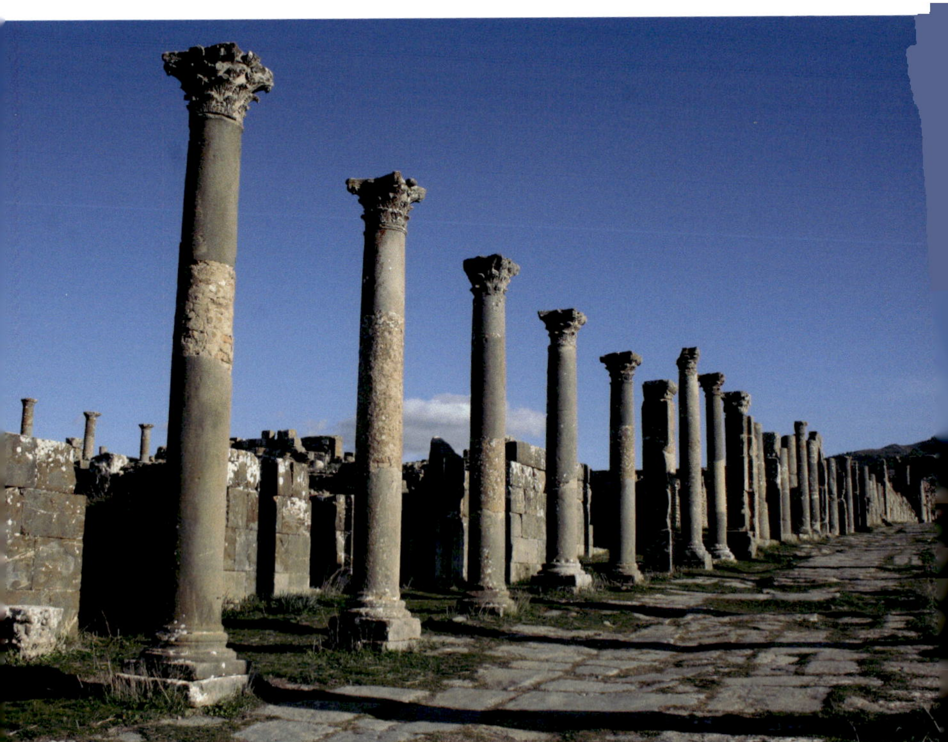

Fig. 115. Cuicul: the frontage onto the 'cardo maximus' of the House of Europa.

and to the left, beyond an ornamental fountain, was a long corridor which led to various service rooms (containing stone troughs or mangers) and to the grand peristyle of the house. To the N of the main entrance, still beneath the portico, were two shops and then a separate entrance leading to the peristyle through an open court with feeding-troughs for animals tied up there. To the S of the main entrance, a third doorway led into a latrine, and thence into an entrance-hall (with an opening from the street on the opposite side) from which one entered the *frigidarium* of the baths. This was provided with a cold-plunge bath and led in turn to the *tepidarium* and *caldarium*. Heat was provided by furnaces accessed from the street at the rear, which also served a smaller bath-suite for the slaves of the household.

At the N end of the house, the grand peristyle was surrounded by porticoes and rooms only on three sides. The central open space was filled with an elaborate pool with rounded corners; on the S side of this was a semi-circular pool at a higher level, beneath which two symmetrical staircases led down to a cellar. The hemicycle was flanked by two rectangular piers (originally 70 cm high), which were probably raised flower-beds, rather than water tanks (2 m high) as restored very speculatively by the excavator Albert Ballu. On the N side of the main basin, a third pool, smaller and semi-circular, articulated around the circumference with alternating triangular and rounded niches, was flanked by two statue-bases. Various rooms opened onto the peristyle: a large *oecus* paved with a mosaic depicting animals (in the museum), a *triclinium* with the mosaic of the Rape of Europa after which the house is named (in the museum, room 2) and several other rooms, including one in the NW corner which is apsidal.

Situated in the middle of the house, but off-centre, the cellar seems to have belonged to an earlier building. Above it was a vast apsidal hall; since only its substructure remains, it is unknown whether it was roofed or was in effect a terrace overlooking the pools. Nor is it clear how it was accessed. At many points in the rooms around the peristyle, it is possible to detect drains for washing the mosaics or emptying the pools.

Two major divisions – the walls on lines A–A' and B–B' in fig. 114 – and the vaulted cellar with its anteroom seem to represent vestiges of the earlier structures on the site. Following study of the mosaics found around the peristyle and in the baths, it has been deduced that the peristyle house was built and decorated in the Severan period; then at the beginning of the fourth century, the grand residence was created with its fine baths and street frontage, with the latest mosaic belonging to late antiquity.

14. North Gate

This marks the northern limit of the settlement; it led down into the valley to join the road to Igilgili (Jijel).

15. Public latrine

This is a well-preserved utility provided with fourteen stone seats above a drain, and with a gutter for fresh water (for cleaning oneself) running around the perimeter immediately in front of the seats (fig. 116). It is typically sited next to the baths, from which it could derive its water supply.

16. Capitolium Baths

Since the foundations of the Capitolium encroach on the plan of the baths, resulting in the asymmetry of the cold rooms, this complex probably belongs to the first half of the second century. Two doorways opening onto the 'Rue des Thermes du Capitole' on the W side led to a vestibule and then to the *frigidarium* with two cold-plunge baths framed by fluted columns. Beyond were the *tepidaria*, the *laconica* and the *caldarium*. The furnaces were on the E side, at a lower

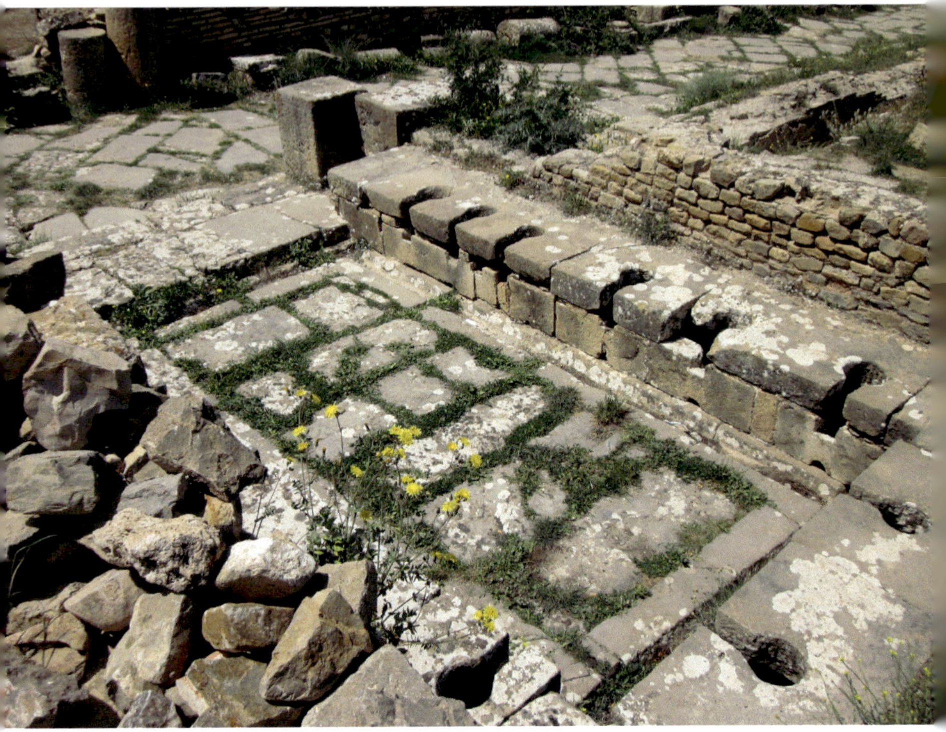

Fig. 116. Cuicul: the latrine next to the Capitolium Baths.

level, in a basement lit by a monolithic skylight block. All of the floors were paved with mosaic, and one of the cold-plunge baths preserved painted decoration of marine creatures.

17. House of Brick

This is a good example of a modest residence (120 sq.m: see fig. 117). Built of brick, or of *opus africanum* infilled with brick, this house has been dated to the fourth century. A vestibule decorated with mosaics imitating marble led to an *oecus*, also paved with mosaic and opening onto a tiny light-well. (The mosaics are displayed in Room 3 of the museum.) The base of a staircase in the NW corner of the vestibule, together with the solidity of the column which separates the *oecus* from the light-well, suggest the former presence of an upper storey above part or all of the property. Three other rooms are on different levels and must have been provided with wooden steps to link them together.

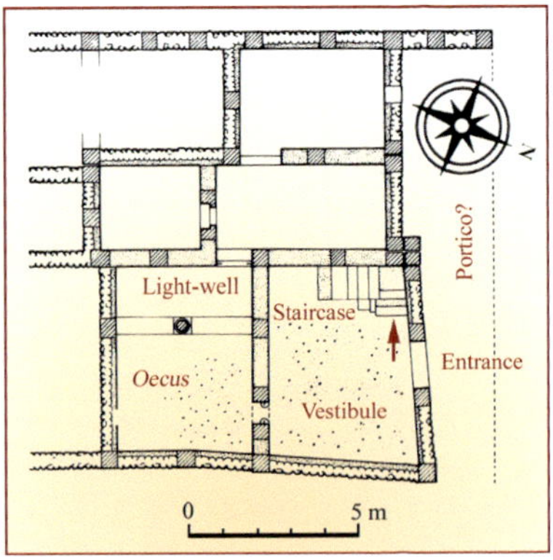

Fig. 117. Cuicul: plan of the House of Brick.

18. Baths of Terentius

An inscription in mosaic (high on the RH wall of Room 2 in the museum) reports the name of the founder of this bath building, Terentius Donatus, and that of its restorer, Longitanus. In the centre of the building, a curb cut from a single block of stone marks the head of a well 17 m deep.

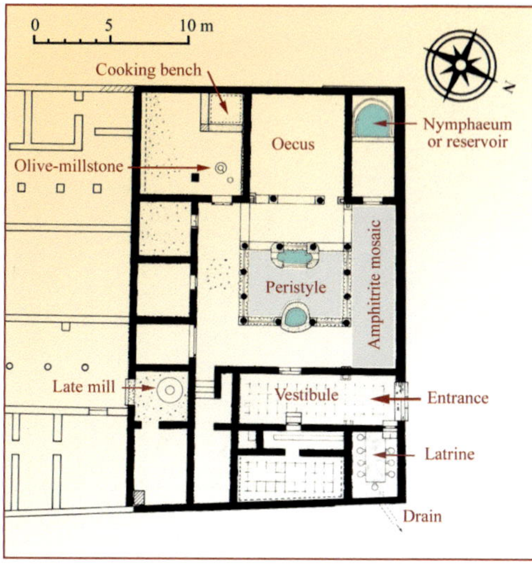

Fig. 118. Cuicul: plan of the House of Amphitrite.

19. House of Amphitrite

This mid-sized private house (28 x 18 m: fig. 118) owes its name to the mosaic of Amphitrite (in the museum, room 1), which paved the N portico of its peristyle. The house was entered from the N through a long tiled vestibule which opened on the left into an eight-seater latrine (why so lavish in this domestic context?) and then into two service rooms. On the right, a doorway led into the peristyle, which had rooms on two sides only. On the W an *oecus* was flanked on one side by a small room with a reservoir or nymphaeum, and on the other by a larger room which must originally have been a kitchen, converted at a later date for the pressing of olives. On the S side were three rooms of similar size. To the E of these, three steps descended to two narrow rooms and, on the S side of those, to two larger rooms. The latter rooms were subsequently incorporated into the adjoining house: the door sill on the S side and the olive mill belong to this late alteration. The open space in the centre of the peristyle was paved with mosaics and embellished with two basins. The colonnade is composed of reused materials: it is unknown whether this represents a refurbishment at the beginning of the fifth century, or a negligent restoration by the excavator. However, the study of the mosaics suggests that the house was originally constructed in the third century (probable date of the Amphitrite panel), at the same time as the adjoining house occupying the other half of the *insula*; and that it was then redecorated in the late fourth or early fifth century, when the geometric border surrounding the Amphitrite panel was re-done. A third phase is defined by the change of use of certain rooms for productive purposes.

For lack of any trace of a staircase, it is impossible to say whether this house, like its neighbour, had an upper storey.

20. Public granaries

These warehouses (*horrea*: fig. 119) served to store all the agricultural produce paid to the Roman state by way of tax or for the provincial contribution to the *annona*. They are divided into separate compartments (*cellae* or *granaria*), destined to house grain, oil or wine. Four parallel halls each have a raised sill, 80 cm above the ground, doubtless to facilitate the transfer of sacks of wheat from carts. In accordance with the instructions of Columella, these halls – described as *pensile* (hanging) – were provided with suspended floors in order

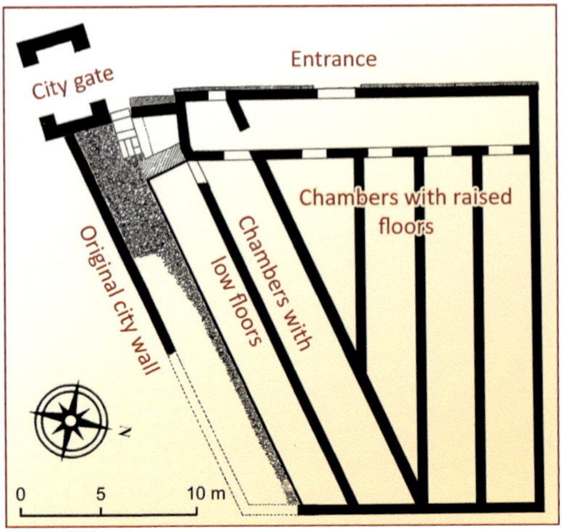

Fig. 119. Cuicul: plan of the public granaries.

to protect the grain from damp. Two further halls, adjoining on the S side at an oblique angle (because of the shape of the site) had a solid floor and a lower sill: these were probably intended for oil rather than wine.

These public granaries are possibly those referred to in an inscription found at Cuicul: this records that *horrea* of this type were built in 199 at the expense of the colony by the propraetorian legate and governor of the province of Numidia, Q. Anicius Faustus.

21. Severan Forum

This is the heart of the new city of the third and fourth centuries. Laid out outside the defences at the end of the second century or the beginning of the third, this space is an irregular quadrilateral of 3,200 sq.m, surrounded by some of the most famous monuments of the city (figs. 120, 122). It was bordered on the N side by a portico from which a flight of eleven steps led down to the square; on the E side, where the ground level falls away, the portico was adjoined by a gallery above a row of shops. The square was paved throughout; in front of the basilica (23), a dedication records that the god Mars was the natural protector of this city founded by military veterans.

22. Temple of the Gens Septimia

A monumental flight of 26 steps leads up to a platform measuring 33.65 x 39.50 m, bordered on its E and W sides by porticoes which terminate on the S in apses. On either side of the stairway, there were entrances

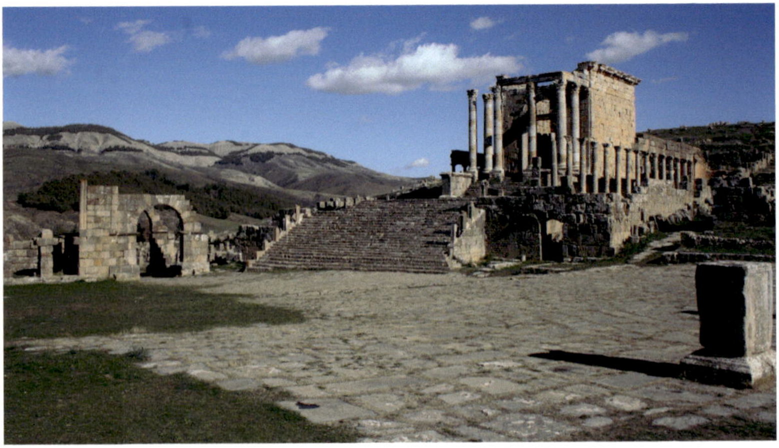

Fig. 120. Cuicul: the Severan Forum and Temple of the Gens Septimia.

to basement storerooms. The temple itself stood against the rear wall of the precinct, on top of a podium approached by a second flight of 13 steps, the uppermost of which pass between the four columns of the *pronaos* (9.99 m high, including base and capital). The *cella* was entered through double doors supported on wheels, of which the curved tracks can be seen. Above the entrance, a fragmentary inscription reveals that the temple was dedicated (i.e. completed or nearly so) in 229 in the reign of Alexander Severus, to the *Gens Septimia*, the imperial family of the Severi. The interior of the building was veneered with marble; colossal heads of Septimius Severus (p. 6 fig. 4) and of his wife Julia Domna, found within, may now be seen in front of the museum.

23. Civil basilica of the fourth century

Built in the second half of the fourth century, this single-aisled judicial basilica measures 36 m long and 14 m wide (see fig. 121). At the S end it terminates in a substantially raised apse, which was entered from one of the side rooms and served as the tribunal where the magistrates presided. On the wall between the apse and the body of the nave, an inscription records that the building was 'constructed, decorated and embellished by Publilius Caeionius Caecina Albinus, of senatorial rank, a six-fasces governor (we might say 'five-star') of the Province of Numidia (during the period 364–367), with the assistance of Cecilius Patricius, Tulius Prestantius and Pomponius Pudetianus – all perpetual *flamines* – and of Domitius Rusticus.' Another inscription, on a pedestal inside the apse, commemorates the embellishments carried out by Ulpius Egnatius Faventinus, who seems to have been the immediate successor of Caecina Albinus as governor of Numidia. A great defender of paganism, this man had a statue of Victory placed on the tribunal (two figures of this goddess were found here), corresponding to that which used to preside over the deliberations of the senate in Rome. That statue was expelled from the Curia by Constans in 357, reinstated by Julian the Apostate and then definitively removed once more, a few years later, by the emperor Gratian. The gesture of this governor was therefore highly symbolic of his loyalty to Rome and its gods, at the heart of a city where, however, Christianity was already alive and flourishing.

The fourth-century building was erected on the ruins of an earlier temple of which only traces of one of its colonnades are visible within the nave. This sanctuary was dedicated to Saturn *Frugifer*, the god of plentiful harvests. The door-sill of the basilica

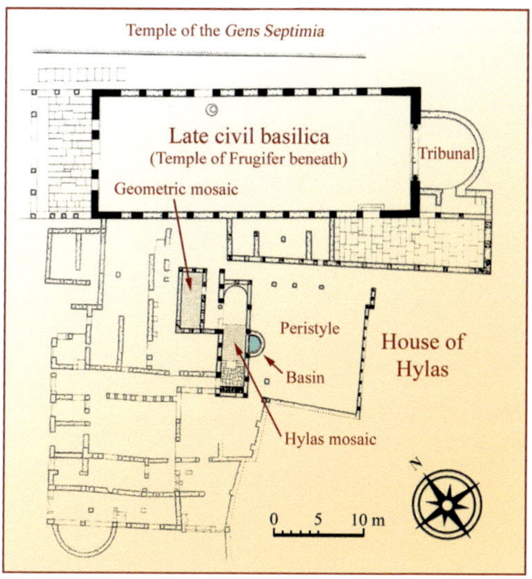

Fig. 121. Cuicul: plan of the late civil basilica and House of Hylas.

consisted of a reused block bearing the following inscription: 'Sacred to divine Frugifer, C. Popilius Felix, priest, with the assistance of his sons Seleucus and Felicianus, with his own money, has fulfilled his vow and made the dedication.' Another inscription found in the same spot was dedicated to Saturn by three freedmen of Julius Crescens Didius Crescentianus, who built the arch on the way to the theatre (29).

24. House of the Hylas Mosaic

This house is named after the mosaic which decorated the NW portico of the peristyle and represented the kidnapping of Hylas (visible in the museum, Room 3: see p. 136 fig. 139). Two other (geometric) mosaics are still *in situ*, in a long room on the N side of the peristyle (see fig. 121).

Like the adjacent basilica, this house was built between 364 and 367, partly on the site of the Temple of Saturn Frugifer. The state of the ruins makes it difficult to interpret the plan in detail, especially on the N and W where it is unclear what belonged to the house and what to the shops in front of it. It seems clear, however, that the square space to the SE, bordered by the Hylas mosaic, was a peristyle with a semi-circular fountain.

25. Arch of Caracalla

This is a structure with a single opening (fig. 122), which marked the beginning of the road to Mauretania. Measuring 12.50 m tall and 10.60 m wide, the façade on either side is embellished by two pairs of Corinthian columns, projecting in front of corresponding pairs of pilasters; each of the latter framed a niche which once housed a statue. Above, an attic storey is framed by a moulded entablature and then by two pairs of smaller columns in front of pilasters, each surmounted by a triangular pediment. Between these *aediculae*, the dedicatory inscription records that the monument was erected in 216 by the people of Cuicul, in honour of the reigning emperor Caracalla, of his mother Julia Domna and of his deceased father Septimius Severus. The statues of these persons would have stood on the three statue bases which still crown the arch.

Despite being much mutilated and encumbered, the arch was still standing in 1839 when it caught the eye of the Duc d'Orléans, who was passing by with an expeditionary force. He conceived the idea of having it transported to Paris and erected in a square with the inscription 'To France from the Army of Africa.' It is reported that three years later, when all the preparations had been made, the death of the Duc d'Orléans and the intervention of Maréchal Valée, then Governor-General of Algeria, resulted in the reprieve of the monument and its retention *in situ*. It was restored in 1921–22 by the Historic Monuments Service.

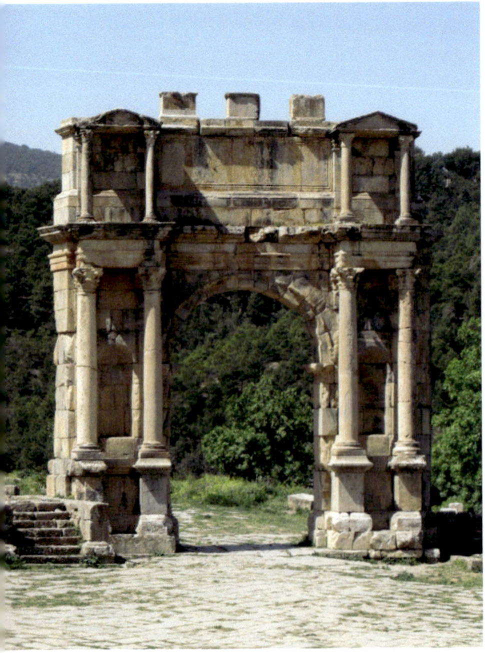

Fig. 122. Cuicul: the Arch of Caracalla.

26. Small temple

Of this temple, only the podium remains. It was once matched by another temple flanking the other side of the arch, but the second one has partly disappeared beneath the nymphaeum (29).

27. Textile market

Built between 364 and 367 by the senator Rutilius Saturninus, this large apsed hall was a *basilica vestiaria* or textile market. Known examples of such markets in the Roman world are extremely rare: there was another at Timgad (see p. 211).

28. Public latrine

Built against the W wall of the textile market, this latrine still possesses several seats and a basin, standing on a plinth in the centre. A few tens of metres to the W, on the road to Sétif, one can see a fountain erected under Antoninus Pius. Behind a rectangular basin, two Corinthian colonnettes support a pediment decorated with a head of Oceanus flanked by dolphins.

29. Nymphaeum

This ornamental fountain was decorated with statues, of which a few fragments have been found. Its basins served also as distribution tanks, with various conduits taking water to the older parts of the city. The water supply which served this structure, in addition to the many bath buildings and other fountains of the town, came from a spring in the upper valley of the Oued Gergour, 3 km away. Most of the water from this source was brought by aqueduct and then stored in huge cisterns in the outer (S) part of the city. These may be seen next to the Great Baths, with which they are contemporary: they were built in the time of Commodus, and then restored under the Tetrarchy (end of third century).

30. Arch of Julius Crescens

This monument, which framed the road from the Severan Forum to the theatre, was dedicated to the *Genius* of Cuicul. It was constructed in 161, in the reign of Antoninus Pius, by Julius Crescens and C. Julius Didius Crescentianus. The first of these nobles had left 15,000 sesterces in his will for the erection of an arch surmounted by statues of Mars and Fortuna. The second, his executor, doubled the amount and added a statue of the emperor. Today, only the foundations remain, but the presence of the inscription and of numerous architectural fragments is sufficient for a restoration to be possible.

31. Theatre

Built in the second century, the theatre was set into the side of the hill overlooking the valley of the Oued Bétame (fig. 123). Its two bands of seating (15 tiers above, nine below) could have accommodated 3,000 spectators, not counting the nobles who would have brought their own seats and placed them on the three low steps within the orchestra. These steps were separated from the seating behind by a stone balustrade (*balteus*). The top of the *cavea* was

Theatre tickets

To have access to the theatre, it was necessary to have a *tessera* or entrance ticket. This took the form of a disc of wood, bronze or ivory, issued on the authority of the *decemvir*: it gave the right to a seat for the performance. On it could be read the number of the seat, and sometimes even the title of the performance. The tesserae indicating the 'pigeon loft', the highest range of seats, were in the shape of a pigeon.

crowned by a fine moulded cornice. The stage, 33.80 x 6.00 m, was fronted by a wall decorated with small niches. These apsidal recesses were framed between pilasters, with matching colonnettes in front; they housed fountains. The whole was crowned by a cornice with vegetal decoration. Behind the stage, part of the stage building (*scaenae frons*) still survives. This supported the permanent architectural décor in front of which the plays were performed: that is to say, two or three storeys of columns with statues between them. There were three doors in this palace façade, a central one (*valva regia*) at the rear of a large apse, and two others (*valvae hospitales*) in rectangular exedrae. The leading actor entered the stage through the *valva regia* (royal door), while the secondary actors used the guest doors. On either side of the stage, a passage led to the wings. On the downhill side towards the ravine, the theatre presented a façade 60 m wide, provided with a raised portico constituting the *postscaenium*, a sheltered area which was accessible to both performers and the public.

32. Fountain

This monument takes the form of a cone 5 m high (fig. 124). Water was delivered to the apex by a lead pipe let into the stonework; from there it fell into a circular basin, the rim of which was decorated with pinecone finials.

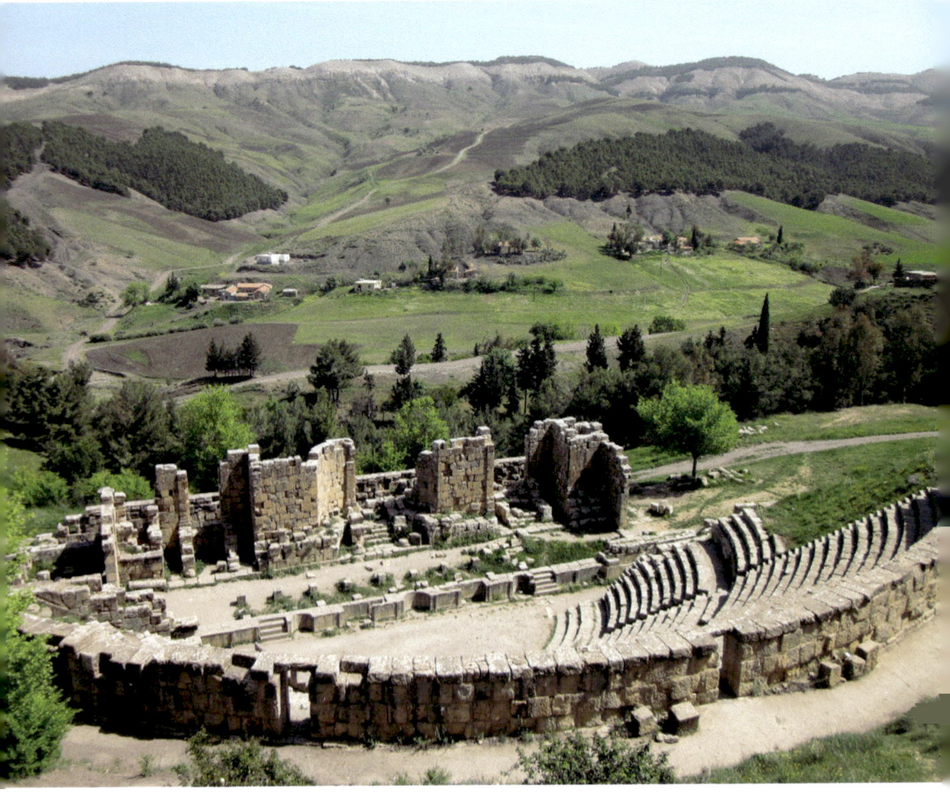

Fig. 123. Cuicul: the theatre.

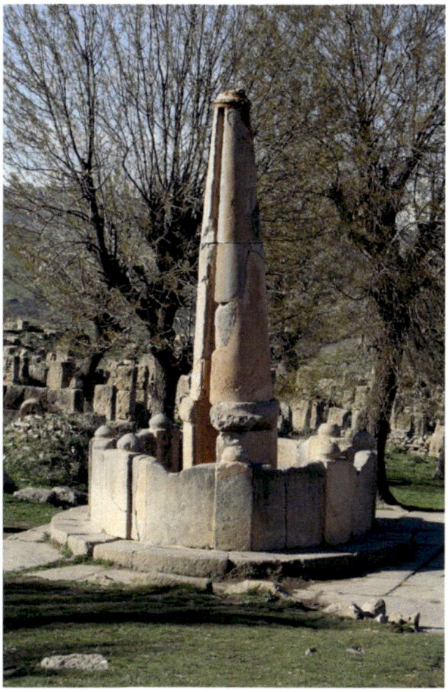

Fig. 124. Cuicul: conical fountain.

33. 'Late city gate'

This does not appear to have any defensive function, and was presumably therefore essentially a triumphal (or commemorative) arch.

34. Great Baths

These baths were built in 183, under the emperor Commodus, and therefore predate the laying-out of the Severan Forum. The complex has a symmetrical plan and covers an area of 2,600 sq.m (figs. 125, 126). Because of the slope, a stairway of 16 steps was necessary on the downhill side to reach the portico in front of the entrance. The vestibule within led to a 24-seater latrine and to an office, perhaps that of the *balnearius*, the manager of the establishment. One then passed into a vast covered gymnasium (*ephebeum*), and thence to matching changing-rooms (*apodyteria*). These two

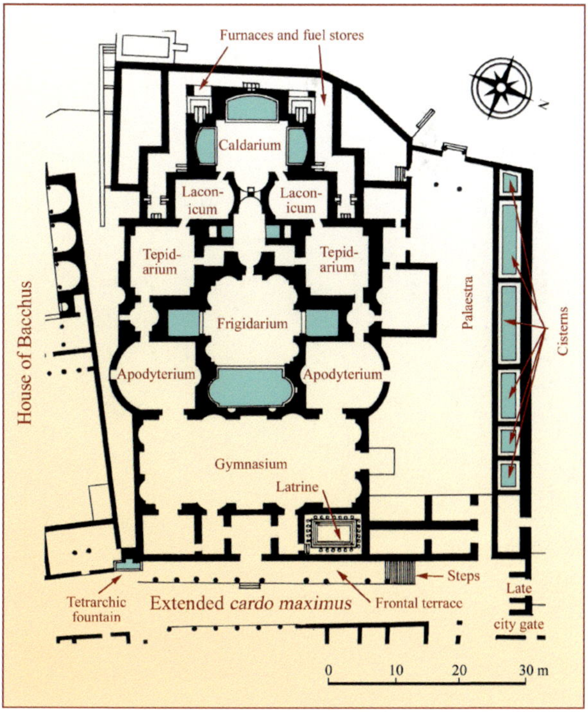

Fig. 125. Cuicul: plan of the Great Baths.

rooms led in turn into the *frigidarium* with its three cold-plunge baths. The two smaller ones are decorated with a border of black mosaic, while the larger one was framed by two Ionic columns of pink marble. This room had a mosaic pavement which has been lifted and is now in Room 2 of the museum (see p. 133). A central lobby beyond is oval, with two small plunge-baths. This is an extraordinarily baroque architectural device: from here one could proceed sideways into two large square *tepidaria*, or directly ahead through a vaulted doorway of intersecting curves, into the *caldarium*, with its three hot-plunge baths. Between the two lateral *tepidaria* and the *caldarium* are two *laconica* (hot dry sweating-rooms). On the N (downhill) side of the baths is a large paved *palaestra*, the paving of which presumably once extended over the water cisterns which line the N side. These cisterns supplied the lower part of the city: the baths themselves were supplied with water from cisterns at a higher level. From the W end of the *palaestra* steps lead down to the service areas and furnaces of the baths, which are well-preserved, together with the necessary fuel stores.

35. Tetrarchic Fountain

This takes the form of a rectangular basin in front of a high plinth surmounted by four colonnettes. An inscription tells us that M. Rutilius Felix, *Curator* of Cuicul, restored the water supply in 295, in the time of the emperors Diocletian and Maximian.

36. House of Bacchus

There was a succession of buildings on this site from at least the late second century onwards; in their latest form they constituted a single wealthy residence of the mid-fifth century (see fig. 127). Beyond a broad vestibule, three doorways led in the first half of the fourth century into a peristyle court embellished with four basins; the columns, which now appear roughly finished, were originally stuccoed. (One of the decorated capitals is now on display in Room 2 of the museum: see fig. 128.)

As in the House of Amphitrite (19), this court was paved with a mosaic that was

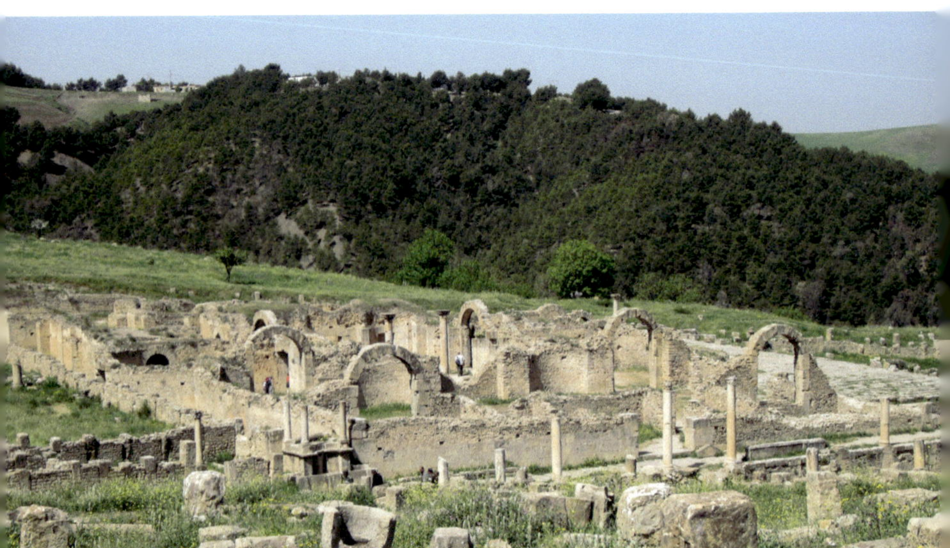

Fig. 126. Cuicul: the Great Baths.

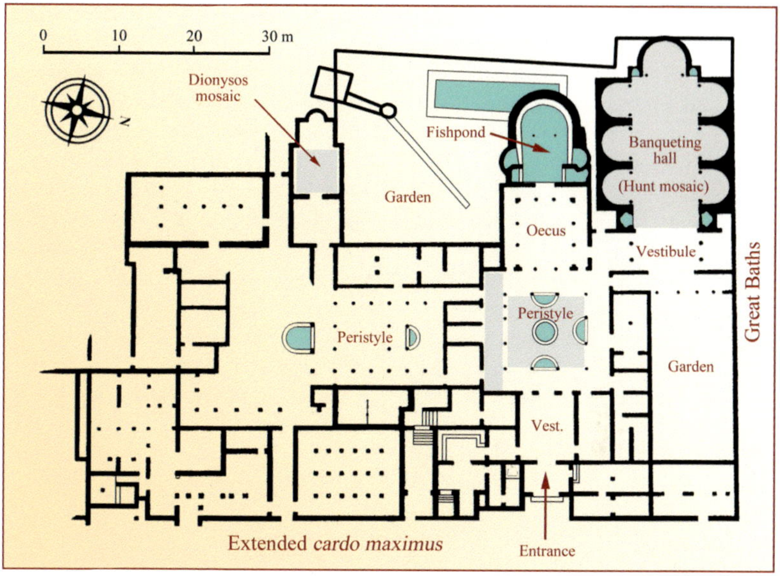

Fig. 127. Cuicul: plan of the House of Bacchus.

exposed to the open air. The S portico was decorated with a mosaic with animal motifs; the other three sides had a simple paving of concrete. On the W side was a large *oecus* lined with columns, beyond which a large apsidal pool, which served as a fishpond, was added in the mid-fifth century. This may be deduced from the presence of recesses and jars set into the walls, which were provided for the fish to spawn in.

Communicating both with this hall and with the NW corner of the peristyle, a vestibule with four columns gave access to a huge hall (21.20 x 8.90 m) with seven apses, the largest at the W end and the other six disposed symmetrically, three on each side. The construction in brick, like that of the fishpond, reveals this as one of the latest additions to the property. Comparison with the plan of the *decaenneaccubita* (dining room with 19 couches) in the imperial palace at Constantinople shows that this was a banqueting hall in which each of the apses would have housed a (semi-circular) *sigma*-couch for 13 persons, accommodating a potential total of 91 diners. Four small basins – two at the entrance and two on either side of the principal apse, provided washing facilities for the guests. Built over an earlier bath building, the hall was paved with a mosaic of hunting in the amphitheatre (in Room 3 of the museum: p. 135 fig. 138); the apses were decorated with geometric mosaics.

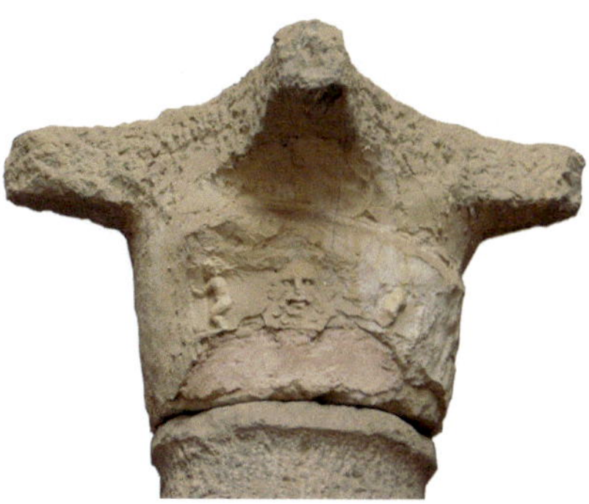

Fig. 128. Djémila Museum: stuccoed capital from the House of Bacchus.

On the S side of the principal peristyle was a second peristyle separated from the first by a range of rooms. At the SW corner of this, beyond another corridor, was an apsidal room which was paved with the mosaic of the Legend of Dionysos/Bacchus (in Room 3 of the museum: p.134 fig. 137) after which the house is named. This is the only mosaic which has been dated to the second century: it must belong to an earlier phase of occupation on the site and shows that, already in the second century, there were wealthy properties well outside the early walls.

This lavish complex included two gardens: one to the E of the banqueting hall, the other, with a rectangular pool (later encroached upon by the apsidal fishpond and perhaps by then out of use), along the whole of the W side of the property. The second of these, which was embellished also with pergolas and statues, was originally contemporary with the building with the Bacchus mosaic and possibly also with the baths beneath the banqueting hall.

37. Entrance to the Christian Quarter

By the end of the fourth century, the southern extension of the city had covered the whole of the hill behind the Severan Temple. On its summit, a cluster of religious buildings and of houses reserved for clergy constituted an episcopal complex of prime importance (fig. 129). The approach to this quarter is marked by a monumental portal built from reused materials, at the S end of the extension of the main street. This leads into an alley, now lined by some columns (restored on dubious grounds) and thence to the episcopal residence.

38. Residence of the bishop and clergy

It is very possible that this peristyle house was the residence of the bishop of Cuicul. It is composed of several rooms at different levels, but is difficult to interpret in view of the steep slope of the ground (and of the restorations carried out by the early

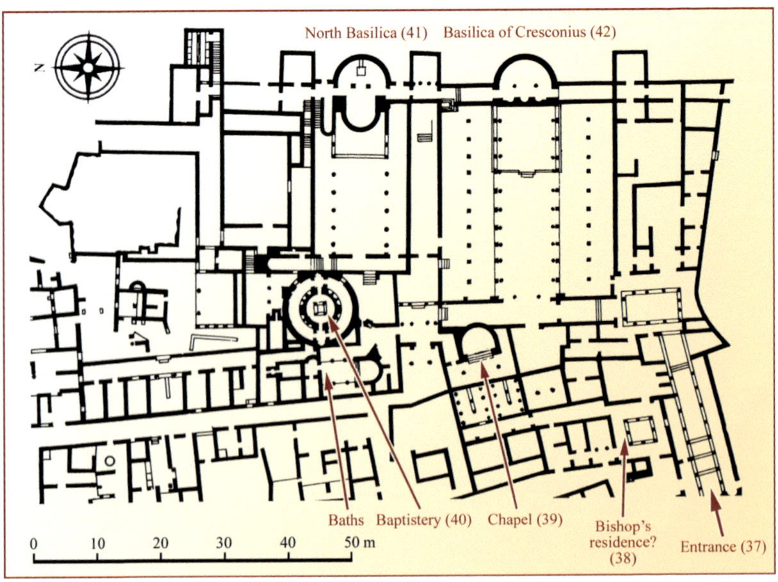

Fig. 129. Cuicul: plan of the Christian Quarter.

excavators, which have obscured the original positions of openings in walls).

39. Christian chapel

This is the smallest of the three churches in the episcopal complex. Attributed to the fourth century, it has an apse flanked by two small sacristies. Piers divided the main space into a nave and two aisles above basement rooms. This was surely the *catechumeneum* in which the final instructions were given by the bishop to candidates for baptism. From there, the catechumens proceeded to the baptistery, but the precise route is difficult to identify because of insensitive modern restoration which has closed former openings in walls and made others without authority.

40. Baptistery and adjoining baths

The baptistery is preceded by a small adjoining bath suite, where we should imagine that the catechumens came to cleanse their bodies one last time, immediately before baptism. (Typically, baptism was performed on the eve of Easter, during the night of the Resurrection.) Built of brick, the baptistery itself is a circular pavilion surmounted by a dome. Internally, it has an annular corridor around which, on either side, there are 36 recesses, originally rendered with stucco, which provided the neophytes with seats and space for clothing (fig. 130). There are also small brackets between the recesses, for lamps. On the floor is a geometric mosaic with a star design. The ceremony took place in the central rotunda with which the corridor communicates. A square basin, surmounted by a ciborium of stone (the columns are modern) provided for baptism by immersion. Within the basin, an inscription in mosaic reads 'A time will come when all people will be purified in this spring' (*[Gentes t]empus erit omnes in fonte [lavari]*). Around the edge, the floor is paved with mosaic depicting fishes, marine animals and chalices. Opposite the entrance, a niche housed the bishop's throne.

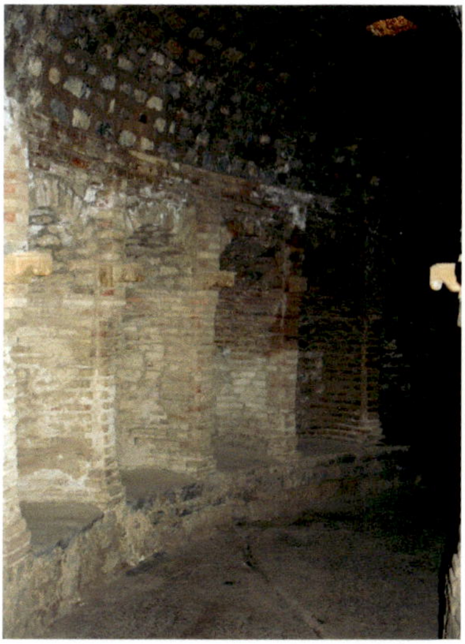

Fig. 130. Cuicul: the seating recesses around the baptistery.

The whole was lighted by means of glazed windows by day, and at night by lamps placed on brackets. A hanging lamp was suspended above the dais, fastened to a stone ring. The dome of the baptistery has been restored: the thickness of the walls suggests the presence of a dome, but its height is conjectural.

On either side of the bishop's throne, one doorway opens into an annexe of the baths (the ruins in this area are confused, partly due to the construction of a fort here by the French in the early days of occupation) and a second into a passage connected to the N basilica.

41. North basilica

Measuring 35 m long and 15 m wide, the basilica next to the baptistery has a nave and two aisles, separated by reused columns. The altar was enclosed within a chancel screen, of which only traces remain. Behind the choir, the apse – the foundations of which are preserved in the crypt which lay below – was probably roofed with a semi-dome. The nave was paved with a mosaic composed

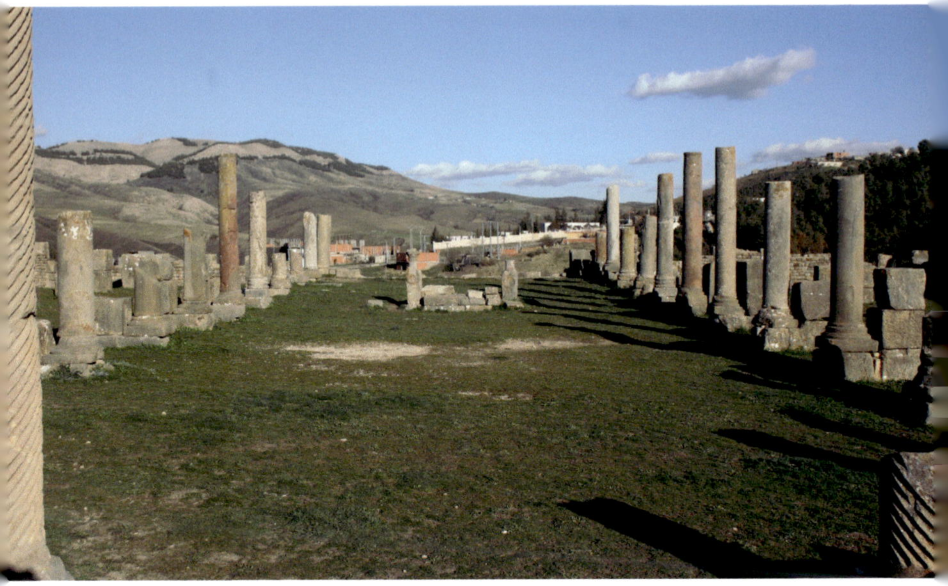

Fig. 131. Cuicul: the Basilica of Cresconius.

of cable-pattern stars enclosing animals or inscriptions identifying otherwise obscure donors, such as Pomponius Rusticus, Tulius Adeodatus, Flavius Veclus, together with more well-known benefactors such as the senator Flavius Paulus and the tribunes Flavius Uranius and Flavius Rusticianus.

It is possible that, after baptism, the Eucharist was celebrated in this church.

42. Basilica of Cresconius

This huge church (40 m x 28 m: fig. 131) has a central nave flanked on either side by two aisles, which probably had galleries above. This is suggested by the columns set against the piers between the nave and the side-aisles, but also by the base of a staircase at the end of the corridor which runs between this church and the N basilica. The choir was at the E end of the nave; the paving here bore an inscription in mosaic (on display in Room 2 of the museum: fig. 136), naming bishop Cresconius, after whom the building is named. The inscription refers to his just predecessors (*iusti priores*) and their remains, now given new prominence, thus justifying no doubt the dedication of the church to a martyr-cult. A contested reading in line 8 suggested a reference to the unification of the Church following the Donatist schism (supposedly settled at the Council of Carthage in 411, in which a bishop Cresconius from Cuicul played a part). However, the passage may refer to the healing of the 'chrism' rather than 'schism'. (See p. 132.) Beneath the apse, which has disappeared, may be seen a crypt which was reached by a staircase. The body of the nave was paved with a mosaic pattern of octagons and squares on a black background with animals (in the museum, Room 2); there were also small rectangular panels in the spaces between the columns.

The basilica of Cresconius is linked architecturally with the N basilica, both by the corridor mentioned above and by a long corridor to the E, linking the apses. These buildings must therefore be contemporary: the dating of them is, however, difficult. The mosaics of the N basilica have been attributed to the late fourth or early fifth century and the architecture would be consistent with this, but those of the S basilica (including the Cresconius inscription) to the sixth. It seems likely therefore that the buildings were constructed at the earlier date, but that the mosaics in the S basilica represent a later addition and that the Cresconius referred to may not be the bishop who was in Carthage in 411, but a subsequent bishop who was present at the Council of Constantinople in 553.

MUSEUM

In the garden in front, facing the various paths, are displayed architectural fragments, votive *stelai* dedicated to Saturn, funerary *stelai* and other inscriptions.

Between the two wings of the museum, a little courtyard houses a statue of Bacchus, one of Hercules and the colossal heads of Septimius Severus (fig. 4) and of Julia Domna from the Temple of the Gens Septimia (22).

Some large mosaics cover the external walls of the building:

E face, above the entrance: geometric mosaic, fragments from the House of Amphitrite (19) and three others from the N basilica (41).

S face: mosaic from the Great Baths (34) and, above, panel from a house on the W ravine.

W face: mosaic from the Capitolium Baths (16).

The interior of the museum is essentially a space for the display of mosaic pavements found on the site: these cover almost the whole of the wall-space, from floor to ceiling, and despite the approach of filling every space by sometimes cutting mosaics to fit awkward shapes, the effect is undoubtedly impressive.

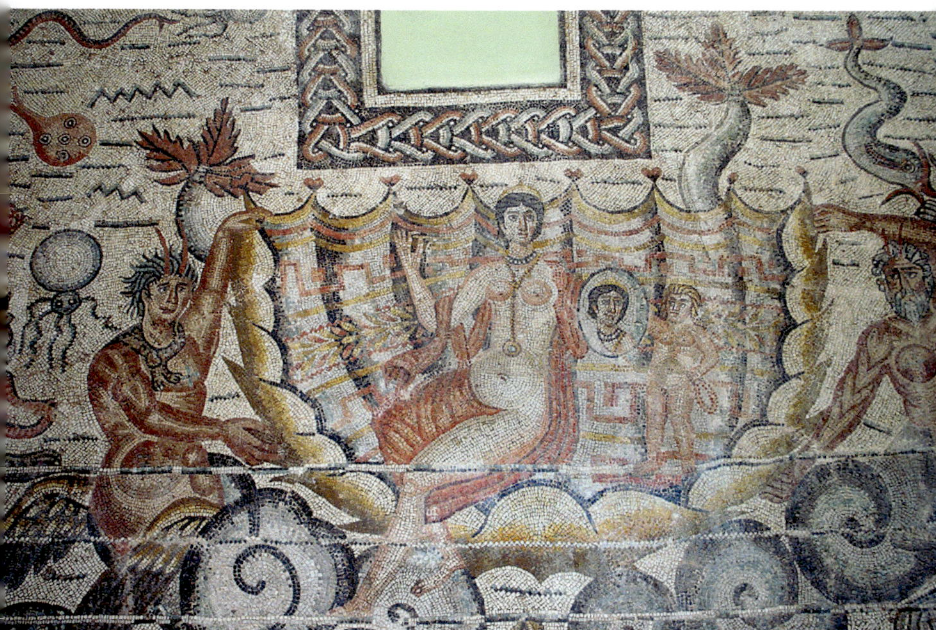

Fig. 132. Djémila Museum: central detail from Toilet of Venus mosaic, from the House of the Ass.

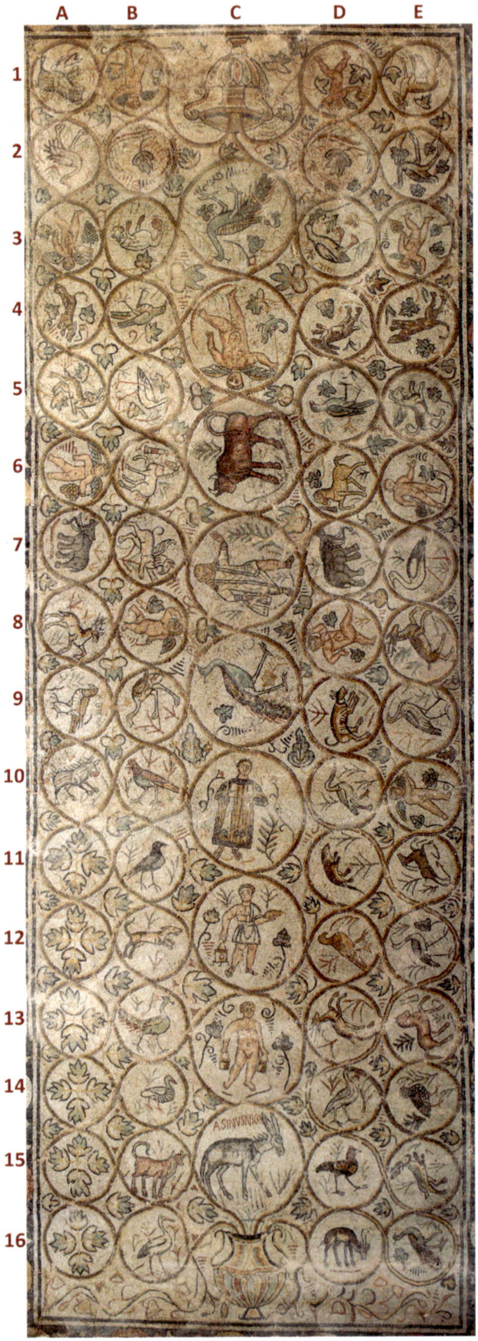

Room I

Mosaics from the House of the Ass (4)

Toilet of Venus (6.90 x 6.40 m with border 1.10 m wide: see fig. 132). Crowned with a diadem and sitting in a shell supported by two tritons, Venus contemplates her reflection in a mirror (which we see). At the four corners, nereids riding marine monsters escort the goddess. Looking down from above, a statue of Neptune surveys the procession which emerges from a marine world populated with fish. All around this scene, a border with a black background enlarges on the marine theme with various scenes of fishing and other representations of fishes and dolphins. There are also boats carrying musicians and dancers, Orpheus charming the animals (upper left corner), Perseus delivering Andromeda (upper right), Hero and Leander (lower left) and Ulysses boarding a ship on one of his adventures. (Late fourth or beginning of fifth century.)

Mosaic of the Ass (10 x 4 m: see fig. 133). This is a long panel with a vegetal border; springing from two craters at either end of the composition, vine tendrils mark out 73 circular medallions filled with animals and people, which develop the theme of cupids at the vintage. Nine of these medallions are emphasized by their larger size and their positioning along the

Fig. 133. Djémila Museum: composite photograph of the larger Mosaic of the Ass, from the House of the Ass.

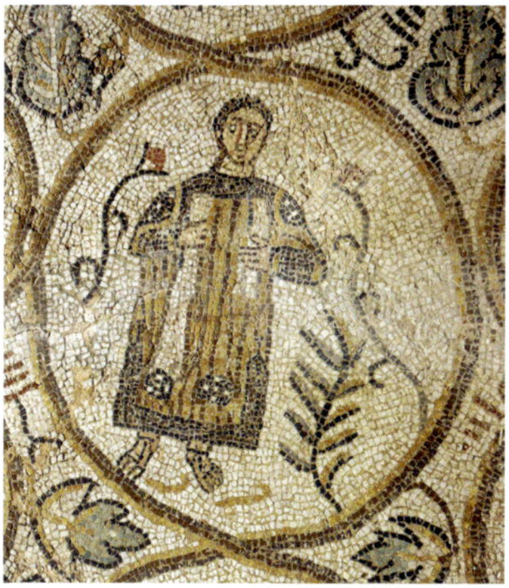

Fig. 134. Djémila Museum: detail of the Mosaic of the Ass (medallion C10/11).

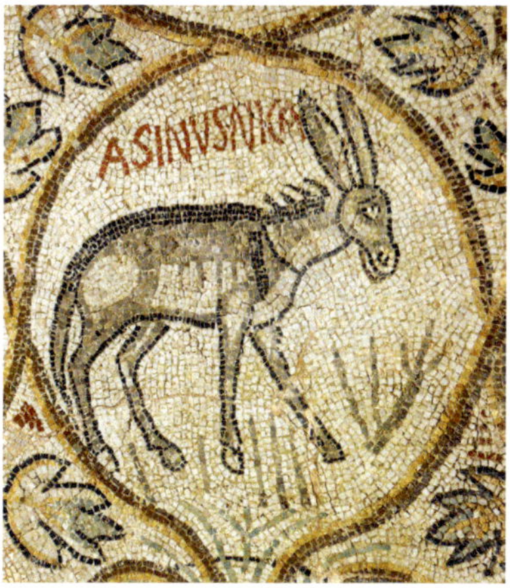

Fig. 135. Djémila Museum: detail of the Mosaic of the Ass (medallion C15).

centre of the mosaic. Amongst the subjects one may note a goose swallowing a lizard head-first (D3), some racehorses (B6, D6, E13), two elephants (A7, D7), a goose pecking at a pomegranate (B3), an ostrich (E2), various cupids carrying grapes, tendrils or pruning hooks (A3, B1, B8, D1, E3, E10) and two scenes of a dog chasing a hare (A4 + 5, E4 + D4).

Some of the more complex images in the larger central column of medallions are more difficult to interpret. A cupid holding a lizard on the end of a string (C4), like the goose (D3) or the two peacocks (C3, C9), belongs to the seasonal repertoire of autumn. Medallions C7 and C6 doubtless illustrate a *venatio* scene: a long-haired man seems to be using a cloth (*mappa*) to provoke a bull, perhaps as in modern bull-fights – or alternatively he may just be declaring the beast victorious. In C12 and 13 are depicted two slaves serving as bath-attendants. One is carrying two buckets of water, the other a lantern and a vessel which may contain perfume or a massage-oil.

The very particular dress of the figure in C10/11 (fig. 134) shows him to be a patrician of high standing: at this period in the late empire, the wearing of a stole around the neck was the mark of someone who had access to the imperial palace. This is probably the owner of the property.

As for the medallion of the 'Conquering Ass' (C15: fig. 135), this remains very enigmatic. Numerous interpretations have been advanced, but none of them is very convincing. The image of the ass may have an apotropaic symbolism, found in both Dionysiac and later Christian imagery, but that does not account for the motto *asinus nica* ('Victory to the ass'), which is hitherto without parallel. One interpretation suggests that *asinus* may be a play on the name of the proprietor (Asinius?). The expression would then be of good wishes towards him ('Victory to Asinius!'), like the *Isgunte nica* inscription at Hippo Regius (see p. 236). Apart from the fact that no one named Asinius has been recorded in Numidia, it would seem bizarre for a person of such standing to mock himself in this way. The most recent interpretation (by M. Blanchard-Lemée, who studied many of the mosaics of Djémila) is that this is a satire on the acclamation *Christos nika* ('To Christ the Victory!') and related to the accusation made against Christians in

Africa that they were donkey-worshippers (onolatry – a charge repudiated by Tertullian in his *Ad Nationes*). In this case, the panel would signify the pagan owner of the property mocking the ascendancy of Christianity at the end of the fourth century.

On the opposite wall, a smaller mosaic from the same house includes a rectangular panel which, again, depicts a donkey with the motto *asinus nica*; in this case, the donkey seems additionally to be contemplating a victor's palm.

Mosaics from the House of Castorius (2)
Panels with geometric motifs (above the Asinus mosaic and to the right of the Toilet of Venus) ***and inscriptions***. Within a laurel wreath, a first inscription reads 'We have done what we could with our means, that the house may declare: I, Castorius, have made (it)' (*Viribus | e nostris fac | tu(m) est quotcumque potimur | ut domus dicatur Castorius | feci*). A second text, inscribed in a rectangle, records that the children of Castorius had distinguished themselves by becoming assessors in the tribunals of Africa (*Libyae tribun[al]ibus [a]dsunt*). A third, enclosed in a circle, is too fragmentary to be deciphered.

Mosaic from the House of Amphitrite (19)
Wedding of Neptune and Amphitrite (2 × 6 m, above the door to Room 2). Dated to the third century, this panel shows Neptune and Amphitrite in a chariot. All that remains of the central part is Neptune's trident and a horse. The couple are flanked by two nereïds adorned with jewellery and riding on marine monsters. The rarely-seen pose of the nereïd on the right is comparable to that of the mosaic of Aspasios from Lambaesis (see p. 183). A triton holds the reins of the visible horse, and has a basket on his shoulder; above him, a torch-bearing cupid is the god Hymen who consecrates the marriage. (Third century?)

The other mosaics in this room are from the N Basilica. Also on display here are various pieces of statuary and cases with coins, objects of ivory/bone and other small items.

Room 2

Mosaics from the House of Amphitrite (19)
Mosaics from the peristyle are exhibited here: hexagons with fishes and animals on a white background (right-hand short wall); circles decorated with foliage and squares on a black ground (to the left of the door which leads to Room 3).

Mosaics from the House of Europa (13)
The Rape of Europa (4.90 × 4.05 m). Above a sea inhabited by dolphins, fishes and other marine creatures (rocks are visible in the background), Jupiter, disguised as a bull, is carrying off Europa on his back. The young Phoenician girl clasps one of the bull's horns with one hand, while the other proffers to him the basket of roses which she was picking when he carried her off. Two cupids guide the bull, one leading him by the collar, the other carrying his tail. (Late fourth or fifth century.)

Two heads of Oceanus.

Mosaic from the House of the Ass (4)
Geometric design beneath the Rape of Europa.

Mosaics from the Basilica of Cresconius (42)
Inscription of Cresconius, flanked by the letters *alpha* and *omega* and by two peacocks (on the long wall through which one enters the room: fig. 136). Twelve lines long and in verse, the text celebrates the building of the church by the bishop. It may be paraphrased as follows: 'This impressive building is the work of Cresconius, who has placed his Just Forebears in this handsome home. They shine forth once again; the crowds rush in a single mass to sing praises to God and to step over the sill of his house. They rejoice to receive through the holy sacrament the

healing of the chrism [anointing]. Cresconius (a paragon of the church, whose virtues are listed at length) has his soul in Paradise, while his body rests in peace, awaiting the Resurrection.' Much of the text is identical in its wording to that of Bishop Alexander at Tipasa (see p. 62), and both writers must have made use of a common model. The style of the mosaic has been dated to the sixth century, in which case it probably refers to and post-dates the death of the bishop Cresconius who was in Constantinople in 553.

Pavement of the nave (long wall opposite the entrance), with animals in a pattern of octagons and squares.

Panels with floral decoration from the spaces between the columns.

Mosaics from bath buildings

Also in this room is a mosaic from the *frigidarium* of the Great Baths (34: above the door which leads to Room 3), a mosaic from the Capitolium Baths (16: to the right of the same door) and a mosaic from the Baths of Terentius (18: on the opposite short wall).

There are again in this room various pieces of statuary, and cases with fragments of sculpture and smaller objects.

Room 3

Mosaics from the House of Bacchus (36)

Legend of Dionysus/Bacchus (on right-hand wall as you enter the room, second or third quarter of second century: fig. 137). This large pavement is certainly the masterpiece of the collection. It incorporates within a square composition five elements of the Dionysiac cycle, separated from one another by Victories at the four corners, from whose headgear spring interlaces of ribbons and vine tendrils, delimiting a square central scene and four segmental ones around the sides. The first scene (at the bottom) shows the suckling of the infant Dionysus by the nymph Nysa. The second (on the left) shows Dionysus as a child riding a tiger, which is led by a satyr while the nymph Nestis steadies the child. The young god has the attributes

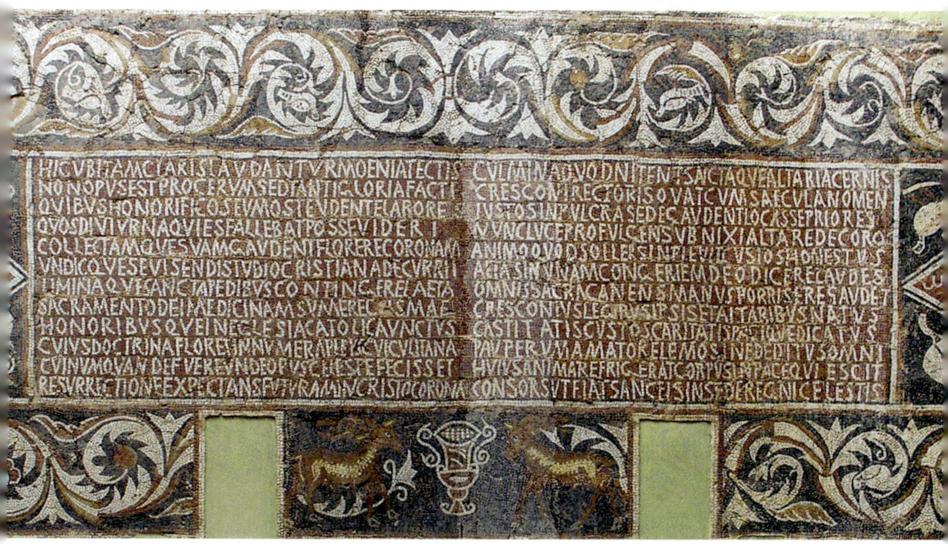

Fig. 136. Djémila Museum: mosaic inscription from the Basilica of Cresconius.

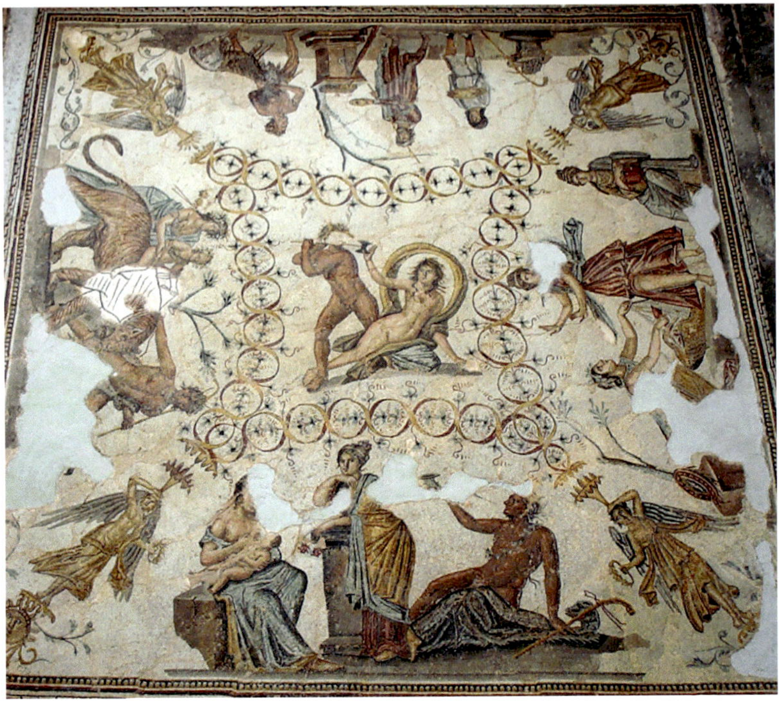

Fig. 137. Djémila Museum: Dionysus mosaic from the House of Bacchus.

of initiation: the headband, the *nebris* (fawn-skin) and the *thyrsus* (staff entwined with ivy). The scene at the top represents a sacrifice: a goat is dragged to the altar by a satyr, while a bearded figure, attended by a young servant behind whom lies a bunch of grapes on a stand, pours a libation on an altar. The interpretation of this scene is controversial: it may represent 'King' Ikarios of Attica, sacrificing to Dionysus in gratitude for the gift of wine, though another version of the legend describes Ikarios as a farmer, who was warned to keep the secret to himself but was then killed when he offered wine to two companions, who became drunk and thought that he had poisoned them. The fourth scene, to the right, shows one of the moments in the initiation into the Dionysiac cult. A winged female figure turns away with a violent gesture of rejection, as if blinded by an unbearable vision, before a phallus in a basket which is being unwrapped by a kneeling maenad. Finally, the central panel depicts the murder of the nymph Ambrosia – one of the nurses of Dionysus – by King Lycurgus. As she dies, she is transformed into a vine, the first tendrils of which may be seen about her neck. In other depictions, having already become a vine, she strangles her attacker in turn. This is therefore a mystical mosaic: it does not imply that the room in which it was found was any sort of chapel, but certainly that the person who commissioned the mosaic was a devotee, whether or not initiated, of Dionysus.

Some broken fragments to the right of the exit door are of the same date.

Images of animals next to the Dionysiac mosaic are from the main peristyle of the house.

Great Hunt (fourth or fifth century: fig. 138). This handsome mosaic, from the banqueting hall, represents a staged hunt (*venatio*) in the arena of an amphitheatre: this is represented by the portico shown at the top of the composition, with the roofs of a town projecting above it. The first hunter, at the bottom of the tableau, salutes the crowd and the sponsor of the event before the fight; he stands between two lions. Above,

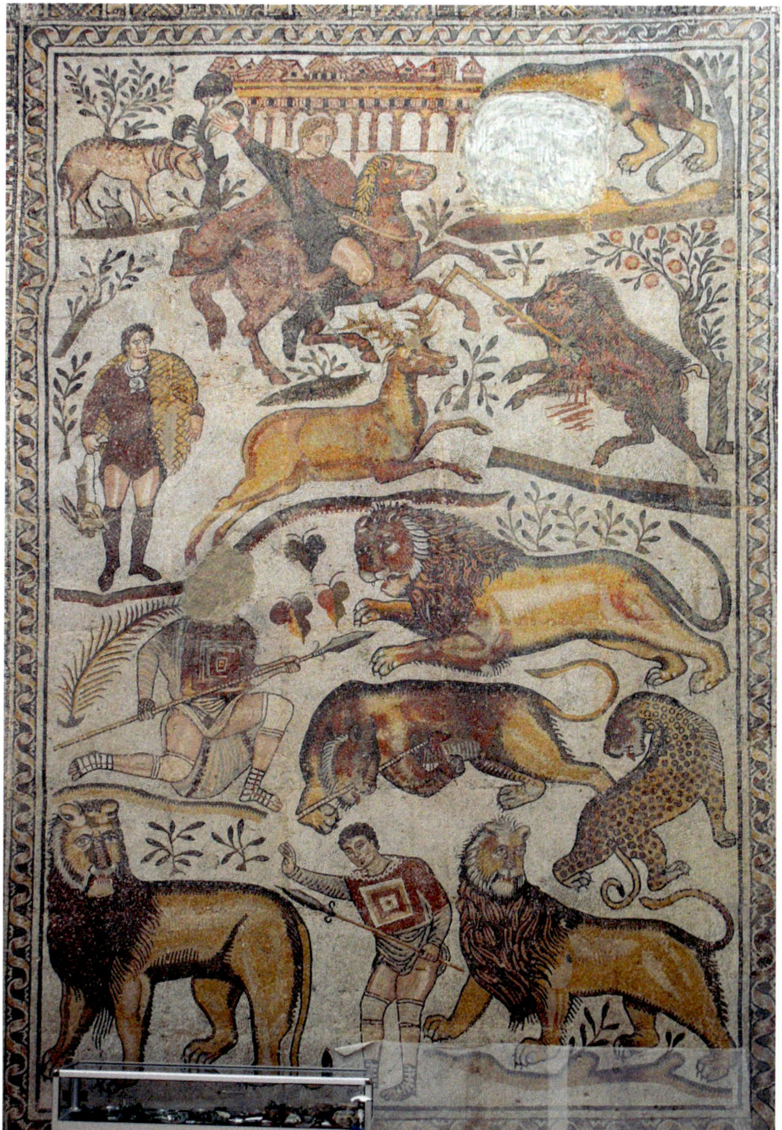

Fig. 138. Djémila Museum: Great Hunt mosaic from the House of Bacchus.

I do not nowadays go to the circus to see a dog chasing a hare; but if by chance I pass such a coursing in the fields, it possibly distracts me even from some serious thought, and draws me after it.

Saint Augustine, *Confessions*, 10.35.57.

a second hunter faces a lion with his lance; he has already wounded another animal, which is trying to pull the weapon from its flank. A leopard in a remarkably realistic attitude observes the proceedings. Between the second hunter and his opponent are three ivy leaves, the badge of the fighting troupe represented in action. In addition to this mark of identity, some of the fighters wear a coloured square motif on their chests, which must again be specific to a recognisable team. These would have enabled the spectators to understand immediately who had sponsored the games of which the beast-hunt formed part. In this way, the pavement commemorates the honour owed to the master of the house for the games which he had financed. A third register shows a leaping stag and a hunter with a net over his shoulder and a dead hare hanging from his other hand. In the topmost register, a hunter is mounted on a horse which rears before a wounded boar, in front of a lion, most of which is unfortunately missing. In the upper left-hand corner is one of the hunting dogs used in the arena, amongst

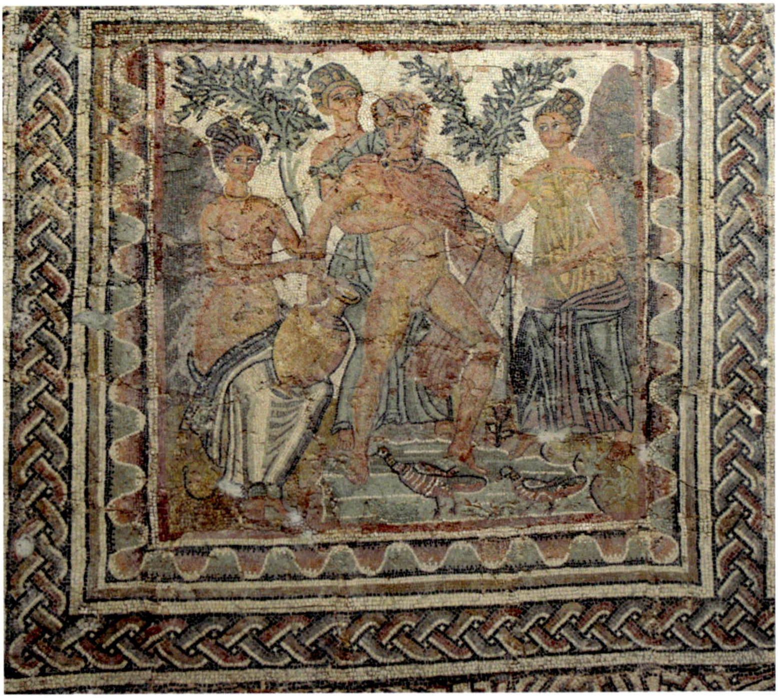

Fig. 139. Djémila Museum: mosaic of the Rape of Hylas, from the House of Hylas.

other things for the hare hunt which Augustine appreciated so much.

Semi-circular mosaics from the apses of the banqueting hall are also displayed here, together with a large rectangular mosaic with geometric decoration from one of the peristyles; placed within this is a panel showing the Legend of Hylas, from the House named after it (24: fig. 139). The story here is part of the tale of the Argonauts. Hylas, the companion of Hercules, had gone to fetch water from a river, when he was seen by some water-nymphs. Captivated by his beauty, they carried him off and he was never seen again. Also in this room (above the door to Room 2) are mosaic panels from the House of Brick (17).

Room 3 also contains a fine model of the archaeological site, made in 1937, and a number of interesting display cases. In the first part of the room are objects in iron and bronze, including tools, general ironmongery, items of plumbing and decorative sculpture (note in particular a head of

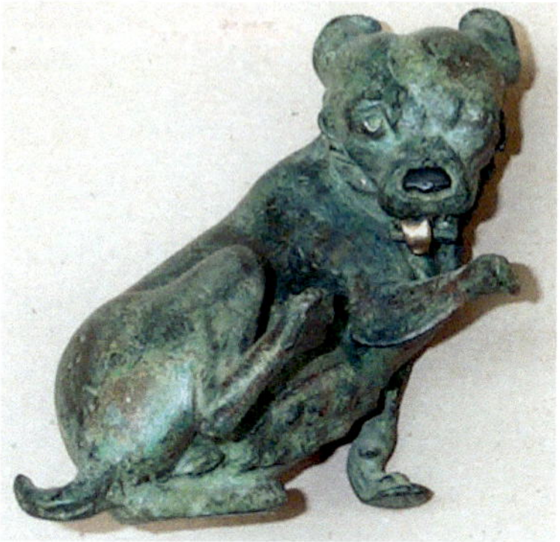

Fig. 140. Djémila Museum: bronze figure of a dog with highlights in silver and enamel.

Dionysus, a bust of a young woman and a little dog, portrayed in the act of scratching itself: fig. 140). Around the corner are displays of pottery and a collection of fragmentary stuccoes, from the house that is named after them in the W Quarter (5). A funerary *stele* portraying Dionysus and Ariadne is worthy of note, as are two large funerary statues (of a couple) in a distinctly local style beneath the Hylas mosaic.

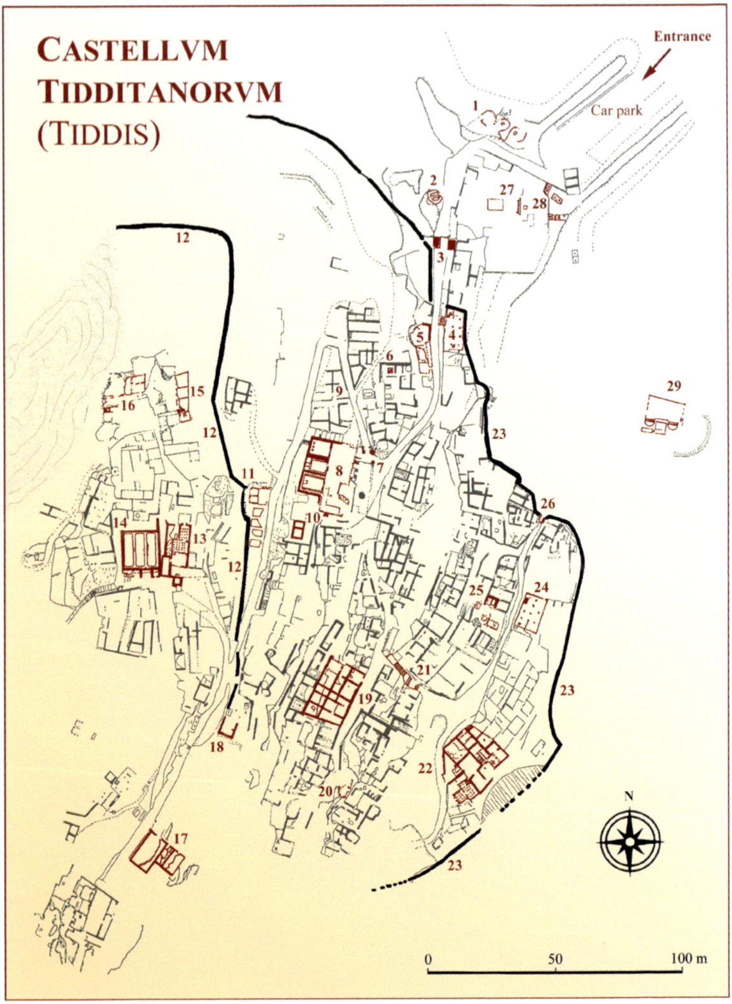

Fig. 141. Tiddis: plan of the main area of excavations.

1. *Group of bazinas*
2. *Large circular bazina*
3. *North Gate*
4. *Christian chapel*
5. *Mithraeum*
6. *Baptistery*
7. *Twin arches*
8. *Forum*
9. *'Potters' quarter'*
10. *Unidentified temple*
11. *Rock-cut houses*
12. *Defences of the Byzantine period*
13. *Small Baths*
14. *Water reservoir*
15. *'Mithraic temple'*
16. *Rock sanctuary*
17. *Sanctuary of the Cereres*
18. *Late defensive tower*
19. *'Large collegial residence'*
20. *Rock of Vesta*
21. *Stepped street*
22. *Large villa*
23. *Pre-Roman rampart*
24. *Large oilery*
25. *Potters' quarter*
26. *Pre-Roman gate*
27. *Temple*
28. *Group of fullers' vats*
29. *Great Baths*

CASTELLUM TIDDITANORUM (Tiddis)

As its Latin name (*Castellum Tidditanorum*) indicates, this community formed part, in the Roman period, of a line of *castella* – castles or, rather, fortified villages – dependant on *Cirta* (Constantine). Ancient sources make no mention of this little settlement and it is only the epigraphy found on the site which give us glimpses of the history of this community. It belonged to the Cirtan Confederation, implying a centralised administration in the capital. The site was particularly well chosen for its defensive character: a mountain encircled by ravines cut by the river Rhummel has at its summit a plateau bordered by steep cliffs, accessible only on the sloping E side. At some point, the settlement expanded from this plateau, down the steep hillside towards the valley bottom. Despite the technical challenges that one can imagine, it was on this slope and this ledge that the settlement developed over the centuries. A. Berthier, the principal explorer of the site, wrote: 'The *Castellum Tidditanorum* doesn't owe its existence to Rome alone: the site was occupied before the arrival of the Romans, and it survived their departure. Nowhere else can one find such a complete panorama of the successive civilisations which have occupied North Africa: Libyan, Punic, Roman, Christian, Muslim.' While Roman influence can be demonstrated on the site from the time of Augustus, it is particularly from the third century onwards that it is apparent in the adaptation of the relief by means of huge engineering works. By cutting into the hillside, creating ramps and terraces with retaining walls, the engineers managed to make space for public buildings, roads, sanctuaries and even a forum on the steeply sloping ground. The matter of water supply was also a serious challenge, since there were no springs. The excavations have revealed traces of an ingenious system for capturing rainwater, with surface collection, canalisations and pipes feeding every drop that fell into cisterns of various sizes.

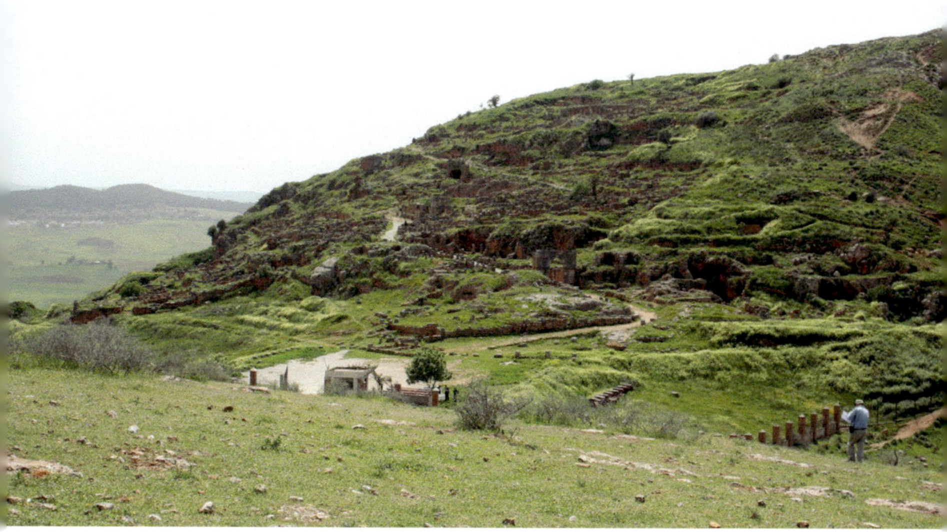

Fig. 142. Tiddis: the excavated ruins, seen from the NE.

During much of its history, Tiddis was a significant centre of pottery production: this is evident from the display in Room 5 of the National Museum in Constantine (p. 156). Of the many pottery kilns which are visible on the site, however, those which can be dated are attributable solely to the fifth to seventh centuries AD.

Although a notice dated in 484 mentions an *episcopus Tidditanus*, we know little of the Christian topography of Tiddis, limited hitherto to a chapel close to a temple of Mithras and a couple of possible baptisteries. Tiddis was provided with new fortifications in the Byzantine period, and continued to be occupied well after the Arab conquest, being finally abandoned in the twelfth century.

The description of the site which follows is necessarily dependent on the publication of the excavations by A. Berthier; however, more recent studies have suggested an extensive revision of his interpretations, which has resulted in the names of certain buildings or parts of the site being no longer fully appropriate. In such cases, Berthier's terms have been retained, but in inverted commas.

EXPLORING THE SITE

The necropolis lay to the E, on the hill across which the modern road approaches the site. Tombs have been found there of Libyan, Neo-Punic and Roman character, in three mutually distinct sectors. Both funerary enclosures and individual *stelai* may easily be made out. On top of the hill, altars still commemorate Q. Sittius Urbanus, aedile and quaestor, who died at the age of 92, and his daughter Sittia Urbana who died at only 23. Five Roman chamber tombs have been identified, also a *columbarium* with two niches.

1. Group of bazinas

These funerary monuments belong to the protohistory of Numidian tradition. They take the form of mounds with a cylindrical base (see fig. 143), which is thought to have inspired monumental mausolea such as the Medracen (p. 166) or the Mauretanian Royal Tomb (p. 75). The *bazinas* were used as ossuaries, and they have also yielded large quantities of hand-made pottery, the painted decoration of which – figured or geometric – could be the source of the motifs which are still used today on the vases produced in the Kabylie region.

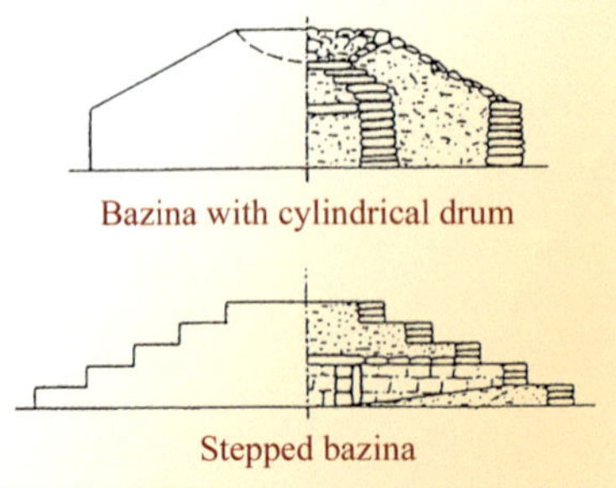

Fig. 143. Tiddis: typical sections of bazinas. *excavations.*

2. Large circular bazina

Close to the North Gate, this monument has two recesses which served as collective ossuaries. Within were found 49 painted vases which contained the bones of the hands and feet of the dead.

3. North Gate

The gate, with a single opening, is built in fine ashlar masonry (fig. 144). It had a basal moulding, a cornice and an attic; the keystone of the arch is carved with a sword in relief. A dedicatory inscription on either side (that from the inner face is now laid out on the ground) records that the gate was provided by Q. Memmius Rogatus, son of Publius, of the Quirina tribe, and that it was equipped with doors (*cum valvis*). Traces of the system

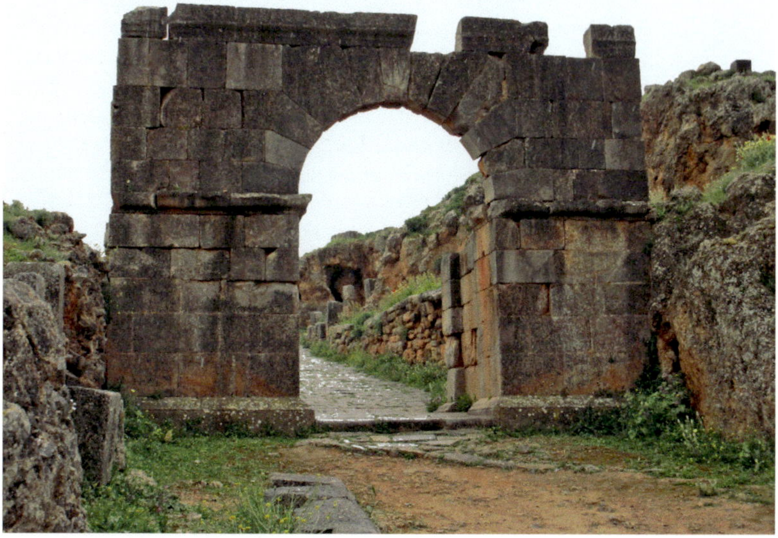

Fig. 144. Tiddis: the North Gate.

of closure may be seen on the sill. The gate marks the beginning of the *cardo*, with its paving artificially grooved in places to assist the passage of beasts of burden. On the E side, the foundations of a wide entrance and of rooms about an open yard may be the remains of a small hostelry.

4. Christian chapel

This little church has a nave and two aisles, separated by two rows of re-used columns. Four inhumation burials were found within; one of these was covered by a mosaic which mentioned the date of death and included the Christian invocation *beata in pace.*

5. Mithraeum

This building was cut into the hillside. Through a doorway, both piers of which are adorned with a winged phallus carved in relief (fig. 145), one entered a vestibule, beyond which was a ritual grotto. A stairway cut into the rock on the right-hand side provided a second means of access, from the level above. On the left of the vestibule is a deep chamber with three piers which once supported a perforated floor above. It was in this basement that initiations took place: naked above the waist, crowned with gold and with his legs clothed in silk, the initiate was spattered with the blood of a bull whose throat was cut above his head. In an adjoining room at street level, a manger cut in the rock and a suitably placed tethering-ring recall the presence of the sacrificial beast.

At the entrance to the cave at the rear, an inscription records the purpose of the complex:

I(nvicto) M(ithrae) cultore
s de suo a s
olo
aedificarun(t)

'To the invincible Mithras, his devotees built (this sanctuary) out of their own (funds).'

The god Mithras

The Mithras of the Romans, originating in a Persian sun god, is personified as a young man, wearing a Phrygian cap and a flowing cloak. From the end of the first century AD, many carved reliefs show him as tauroktonos (bull-slayer): the god kneels on the back of a bull, grasping its nostrils with his left hand and pulling the head back, while he plunges the sacred dagger in his right hand into its neck. An important element of Mithraic doctrine concerned the cosmic movements of the seven planets and the migration of human souls across the seven planetary spheres. It seems that during the initiation rites, the candidate for admission to each of the seven grades of wisdom was subjected to certain trials and then to purification rites associated with the relevant grade; however, the secret ceremonies associated with this cult are poorly understood, not least because practices certainly changed substantially with time.

The cult was particularly popular with the Roman soldiery (probably because it offered hope of an afterlife), which explains why temples and cult reliefs have been found most prolifically in garrison towns and on the frontiers of the Roman Empire (the limes). Its many similarities with the appeal of Christianity resulted in an accentuated determination to suppress it on the part of the Christian community.

Two reliefs were found here showing heads of bulls (one is visible in fig. 145), and a statue of Cybele seated between two lions (in the museum in Constantine: Cybele was closely associated with Mithras). The excavator has suggested that the sanctuary was built by Roman military veterans, who brought the cult with them, and that the cult of Cybele was introduced for their wives, who were not admitted to Mithraic worship.

To the S of this sanctuary, a small square displays three votive altars of the third century. One is dedicated to the *Genius* of the People by Q. Leptius Musteolus; the other two, one of which is decorated with an ewer and a patera, are declarations of friendship: the first was set up by L. Pescennius Sedatus in honour of his friend Q. Voltius Maximus, while the other, dedicated to his brother, Q. Voltius Natalis, was set up by a group of his friends, who presumably did not want him to be left out! On the left of the road, a base from the reign of the emperor Marcus Aurelius commemorates the institution of a market, alternating with that of *Castellum Mastarense* (near Ibn Ziad, 15 km to the W of Constantine):

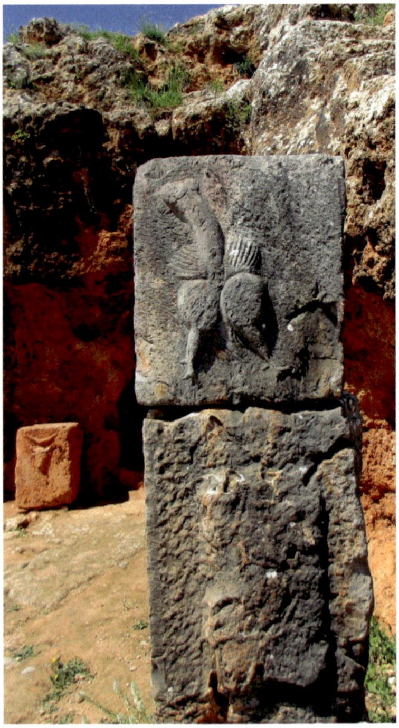

Fig. 145. Tiddis: winged phallus carved on an entrance-pier of the Mithraeum.

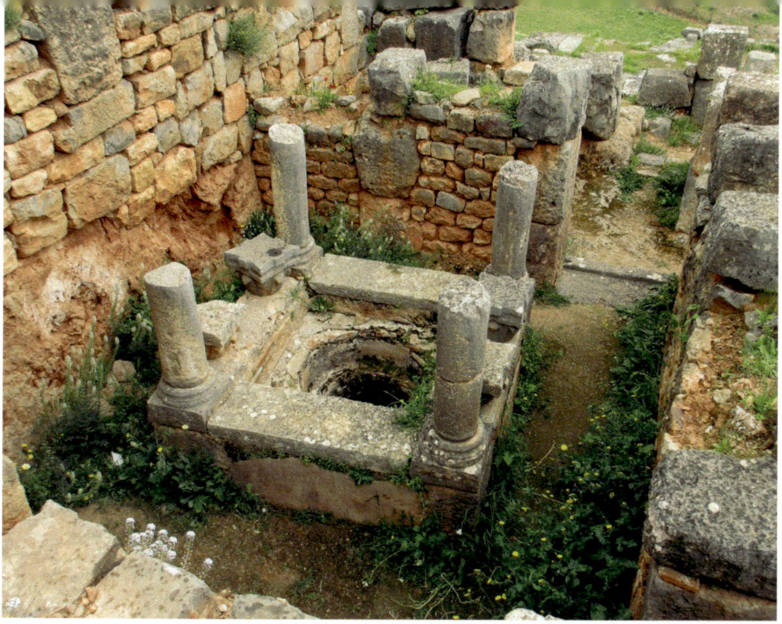

Fig. 146. Tiddis: baptistery (?) to the N of the forum.

For the prosperity of our lord, the most invincible emperor Caesar M. Aurelius Alexander Augustus, pious and fortunate, and of Julia Mamaea Augusta, mother of our emperor and of the camps and of the senate and of the country, a market will be held at the castle of the Tidditani on the eve of the Kalends and the eve of the Ides of each month, with the authority of P. Julius Julianus Martialinus, propraetorian legate of the emperor, most noble, of consular rank, governor and patron of our community, by decree of the decurions.

6. Baptistery

In a group of rooms in an angle of the main street which winds uphill is a circular basin, beneath a little ciborium supported on four columns with very simple 'Corinthian' capitals (fig. 146). This has every appearance of being

The Taurobolium

This type of expiatory offering is associated in ancient literature and epigraphy exclusively with the worship of Cybele, between the second and fourth centuries AD, though Romans had been rather shocked by her orgiastic rites when her worship was first brought to Rome in 204 BC. Since provision for the practice is regularly found in Mithraic contexts, it was clearly associated with both divinities. The essence of the rite was as described above, after which the initiate, dripping with blood, would be acclaimed by his fellows as having been purged of his sins. This was a practice decried by the writer Tertullian (c. 155–240), a Berber from Carthage and the first Christian author to have written in Latin. He declared: 'The Demon, whose aim is to corrupt the truth, thus seeks to reproduce the basis of the divine sacraments in the mysteries of idols. He has devised in his turn a baptism for his devotees and he promises, to those who believe in him, the remission of their sins through this act of ablution.'

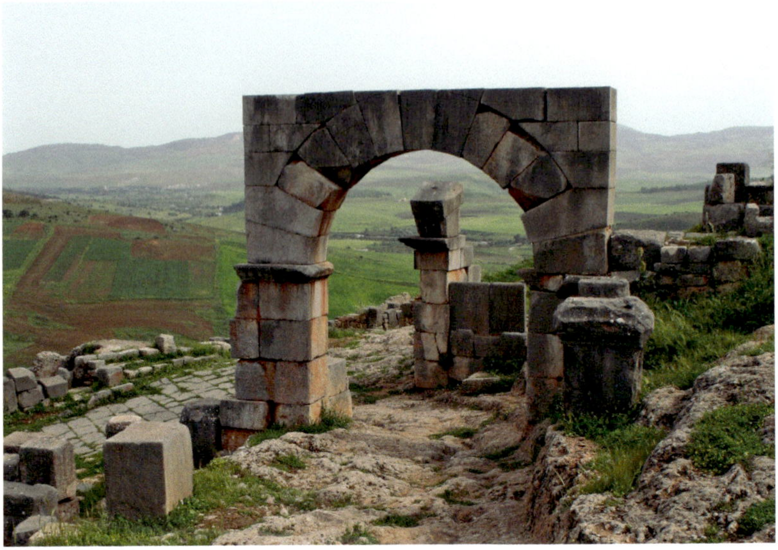

Fig. 147. Tiddis: twin arches on the approach to the Forum.

a Christian baptistery, but there is no other evidence of cult association in the immediate vicinity.

7. Twin arches below the forum

The main street from the N makes a hairpin bend at this point, as it climbs up towards the forum. The inflection is marked by two simple arches set at right-angles to one another (fig. 147). The keystone of the eastern arch was decorated with a carved wreath.

8. Forum

Below the retaining wall of the forum, a slab bears an inscription recording that Q. Sittius (he whose tombstone recorded that he lived to be 92 years old) built at his own expense a sanctuary to Fortuna Augusta (the fortune of the imperial house) together with its fittings and a statue. The paving of this space appears, however, to be late Roman or Byzantine, as is clearly the circular (baptismal?) basin which now occupies the centre of it. This was covered by a ciborium supported on four columns; curiously, there is again no trace of an associated church.

The forum above takes the form of a terrace 30 m long and 10 m wide, which must make it one of the smallest Roman fora known (fig. 148). On the uphill side and cut into the slope, three separate rooms opened onto the square. Their purpose remains uncertain, but the presence of a bench along three sides of the central one suggests that this may have been the *curia*. The room to the left has yielded an altar, and it may have been the temple of Fortuna Augusta to which the previously mentioned inscription belonged. The right-hand room has been too extensively modified for its original purpose to be clear.

Like every other Roman forum, that of the Castellum Tidditanorum was embellished with statues, of which the bases alone have survived. Marcus Aurelius and the Severi were honoured there; there is also a rare dedication to Gordian III (239). It is from these that we learn the formal name of the community: *Respub(lica) Castelli Tidditanorum.*

'Republic'

The expression *respublica* was frequently used, from the time of Septimius Severus, to indicate quasi-communal bodies. These bodies had a public purse (*ager publicus*) and might set up milestones. They were administered by an assembly which carried the title of *ordo* and whose members were known as *decuriones*.

Another pedestal is dedicated to a certain Q. Lollius Urbicus, and tells us part of his career: he distinguished himself under Hadrian in the suppression of the Jewish Revolt, was governor of Lower Germany and patron of Tiddis. A tomb dedicated to his family, some 3 km outside the village (see below, p. 151), suggests that he came from a local land-owning family. He went on to be governor of Britain, an important military province, where he is commemorated for having begun the construction of the Antonine Wall in Scotland; the apex of his career was to be governor of Rome itself (*praefectus urbis*), where he died c. 160. It is not surprising that the statue in the Forum at Tiddis honours him as patron of the community.

A further pedestal bears a dedication to L. Julius Civilis, who was Prefect of the Youth (*Juventus*) of Cirta, a militia into which young men were enrolled at an age 'when they were ready to show their independence and spirit' (Ch. Picard). Under municipal control, they were detailed to help the magistrates with the collection of the *annona* and to maintain order where there was not otherwise any military presence.

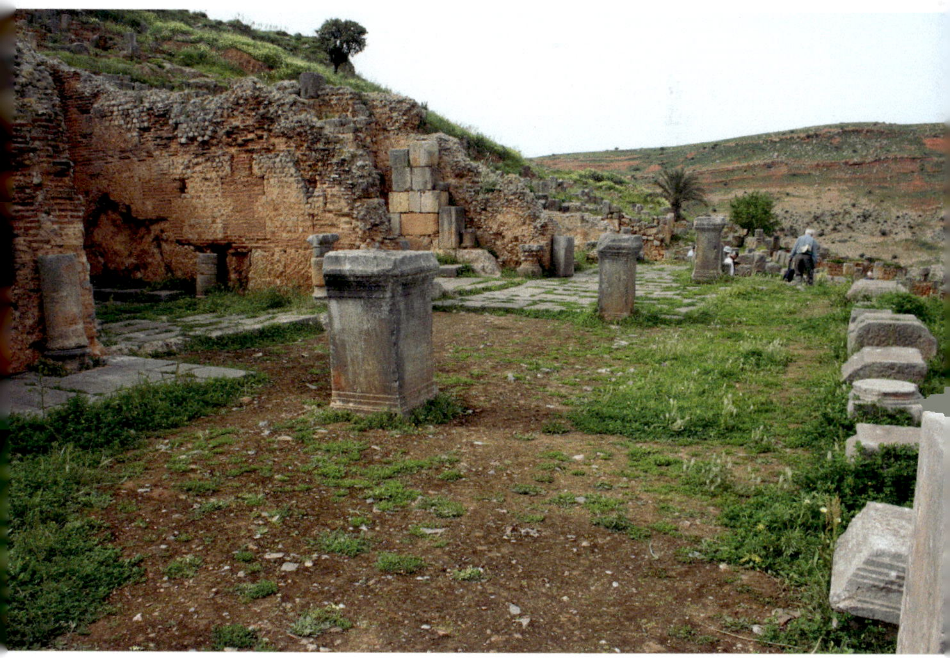

Fig. 148. Tiddis: the tiny Forum.

9. 'Potters' quarter'

Here have been found remains of kilns and semi-troglodyte habitations, including mangers and other facilities for beasts of burden. There are also fullers' vats.

10. Unidentified temple

To the S of the forum has been found a terrace and a masonry altar belonging to an unidentified sanctuary. Next to this, a cave is formed into a vault cut out of the rock.

11. Rock-cut houses

12. Defences of the Byzantine period

These walls enclose only the upper part of the settlement, presumably signifying a shrinkage from earlier times. Unlike the Byzantine defences seen elsewhere, there seems to have been no military involvement here and the walls were presumably built purely to defend the existing population.

13. Small Baths

This bath complex was supplied only with rainwater, which was collected into cisterns directly above. The narrow site is nonetheless equipped with a *caldarium*, a *tepidarium* and a *frigidarium* containing a square plunge bath. In the *frigidarium* is a bench made from a reused slab with an inscription on the front edge: the writing is primitive and irregular, but appears to record a dedication to otherwise unknown (local?) gods by a list of fourteen persons.

14. Water reservoir

This is composed of three cistern chambers which are linked together, providing a total capacity of around 350,000 litres (77,000 gallons: fig. 149). They were supplied with water solely from rain falling on the hillside above, which was directed by means of channels and conduits into the reservoir. An inscription, now to be seen against the wall on the

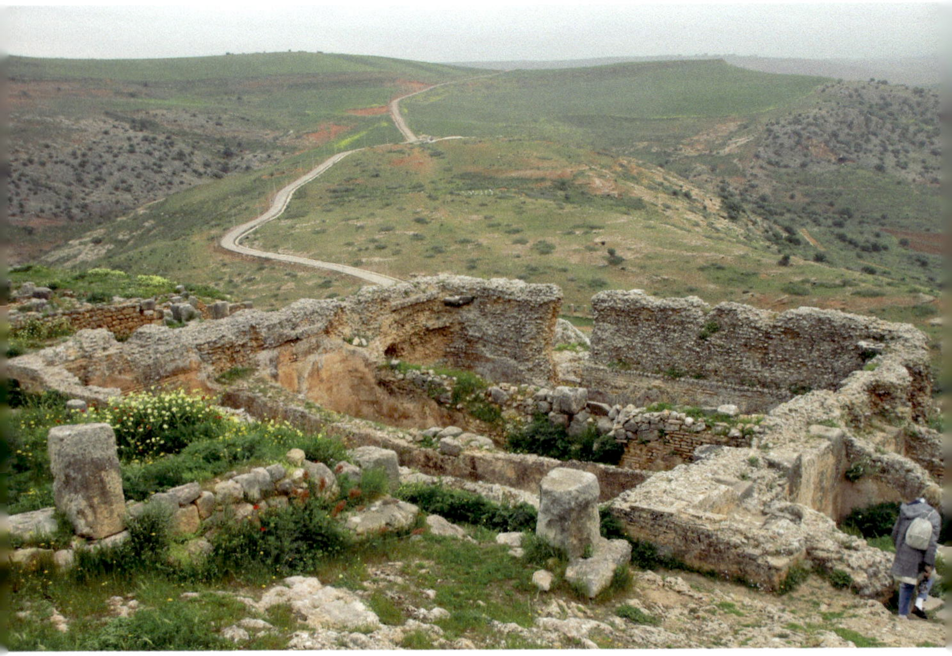

Fig. 149. Tiddis. The triple cistern above the Small Baths.

R as one climbs up beside the baths, records the construction of the system in 251:

Thanks to the indulgence and divine providence of our lords the emperors Gallus [Decius] and Volusianus [Hostilius], M. Cocceius Anicius Faustus Flavianus, consular and quindecimvir, curator and patron of the Cirtan colonies, after getting the people to remove the overlying ruins and level the bare rock, arranged for the provision of water for the health of the population.

Not far from this reservoir was found an altar decorated with staves and dedicated to *Bonus Eventus* (Success).

15. 'Mithraic temple'

This is a cave to the N of the reservoir, beyond a late quarter of the settlement which appears to post-date the arrival of Islam.

16. Rock sanctuary

Of unknown dedication, this is composed of three rooms in a row set against the rock face. It was reached from below by a sequence of four stepped platforms.

17. Sanctuary of the Cereres

This temple is composed of three adjoining rooms arranged on terraces and overlooked by a complex composed of a hall divided into three aisles by two rows of columns and a cella approached by a flight of seven steps. In this latter area were found a cistern and a rectangular pit filled with animal bones, mainly of boars.

The largest of the three terraced rooms contains an altar dedicated to the 'Fortune of the Cereres' by the priest Caecilius Rusticus. This also portrays a pregnant sow, the favoured offering to Demeter and Persephone, the two goddesses worshipped jointly in the cult of the Cereres.

It has been suggested that the separation of the three rooms reflects the rites which took place on the festal day of the Cereres, i.e. that women and men at first dined separately and then went to look for each other, their lamps extinguished, under the sign of a sexual mysticism which constitutes the original substrate of the cult.

18. Late defensive tower

This protected an entrance through the defences of the Byzantine period, which enclosed only the upper part of the settlement.

19. 'Large collegial residence'

A flight of five steps leads into a vestibule and thence into a central building with two dependant wings. Numerous architectural fragments have been found here, including column drums and capitals, some of which resemble those of the Medracen (p. 166). The northern wing consists of a succession of rooms which look like stores, while the southern wing has predominantly hydraulic installations. The withdrawn and intimate character of these buildings, together with their self-sufficiency, suggested to the excavator that they may have housed a religious community – perhaps associated with the

Cereres

These were Demeter and Persephone/Kore (Ceres and Prosperina in Latin), law-giving goddesses of Enna in Sicily, whose worship was introduced to North Africa in 396 BC by the Carthaginian general Hamilcon in expiation for having attacked their sanctuary at Syracuse. In addition to sows, both boars, rams, cranes and doves were offered to them in sacrifice.

temple of Vesta. Alternatively, this may be just a large private house.

20. Rock of Vesta

This huge rock owes its name to the little altar dedicated to Vesta which was found in the artificially enlarged cave which opens at its base. A vent sheltered from the dominant wind served for the dispersal of smoke. This was probably, therefore, a temple dedicated to the sacred flame of the goddess.

The fullers' vats here are attributable to a time when the location no longer had any religious association.

21. Stepped street

The steeper byways of this settlement are generally not well preserved. This stairway composed of 38 steps and five landings is one of the more substantially constructed.

22. Large villa

Difficult to date, this Roman house was built on pre-existing walls of the Punic period and subsequently underwent further modifications. On its W side, a door framed by two columns gave access from the street to a large room with an underground cistern of two compartments. A staircase led to the floor above. Below, a second room was paved with a pattern of rosettes and floral motifs (not visible). The small rooms to the N contain the remains of an oil-pressing installation, which went out of use in a later phase (settling tank, counterweight reused in a wall, late pier standing on a pressing-slab). The E entrance led to a vestibule with a black-and-white mosaic, partly in a chequerboard pattern, partly in opposing triangles. The house also included a private bath suite. One of the hot rooms was later reused to install a potter's kiln; another late modification was the

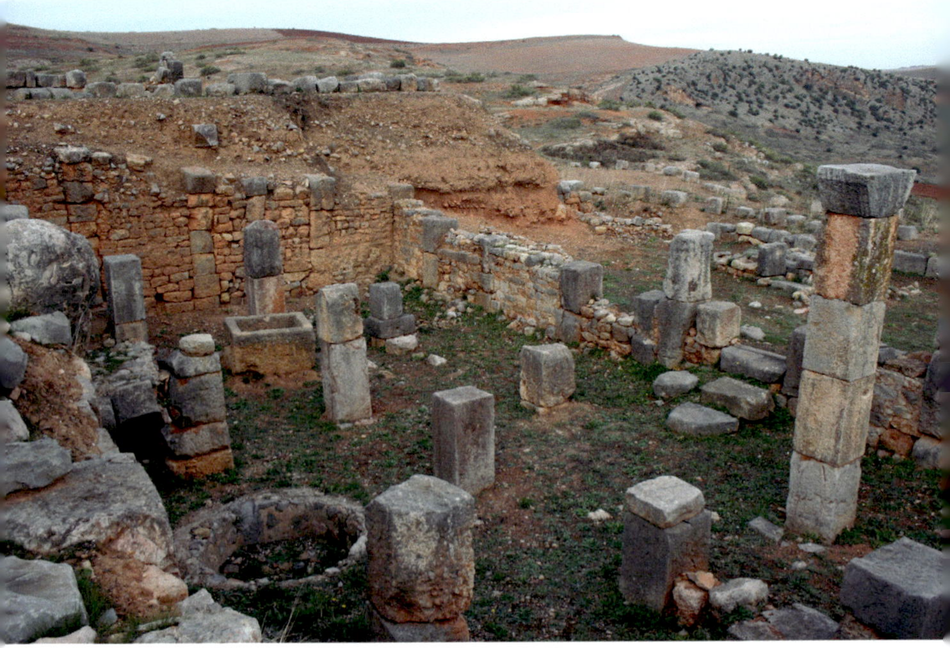

Fig. 150. Tiddis: large oilery. The original counterweight, converted into a basin, is visible in the background.

insertion of fullers' vats in the triangular room on the W edge of the property.

23. Pre-Roman rampart

This wall already enclosed the settlement before the Roman period.

24. Large oilery

The ruins of this building have been converted into a large workshop or warehouse (fig. 150). The counterweight of the press has been carved out into a basin. (Its original purpose is evident from the dovetail slots in its ends, into which the windlass would have been fastened.)

25. Potters' quarter

Displays in the museum at Constantine (see p. 156 and figs. 161, 161) show the range and vitality of the output of the potters of Tiddis. Their workshops are distributed over much of the site, often invading buildings which previously served other purposes. Kilns may be seen in this area (fig. 151); however, the ceramic vats set into tiled surfaces (fig. 152), interpreted by the excavator as basins for refining the clay, are undoubtedly (earlier) installations for the fulling (degreasing/cleaning) of woollen textiles and have nothing to do with pottery production. The kilns here are built into the ruins of earlier buildings, and have been attributed to the fifth to seventh centuries, when this area was otherwise no longer occupied.

26. Pre-Roman gate

This modest entrance through the early defences is nonetheless solidly constructed, and is protected by a carved bust (of Saturn?).

27. Temple

All that survives here is the paving and the frontal steps. Fragments of an inscription indicate that the temple was built by Q. Memmius Rogatus, who also paid for the Roman North Gate (3).

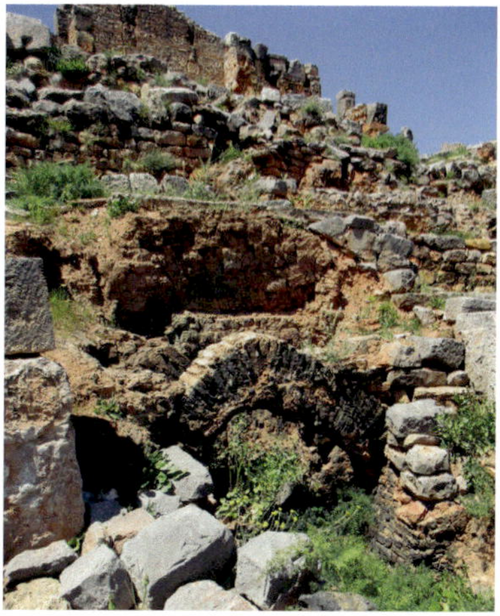

Fig. 151. Tiddis: the furnace arch of a pottery kiln above the oilery.

28. Group of fullers' vats

Here are good examples of installations which have been found in many parts of the settlement. The essential component is a ceramic vat set within a waterproof compartment (fig. 152). It is an apparently unique characteristic of the Tiddis vats that they are lined internally with abrasive grits. New woollen garments (or garments for cleaning) would be placed in the vats together with a soapy clay ('fuller's earth'), water and an alkali (often derived from plant ash) and would then be agitated by being trodden underfoot by the fuller.

29. Great Baths

Situated outside and below the settlement (and presumably with a separate water supply), this larger bath complex has been only partly excavated.

30. Summit sanctuary (Ras ed-Dar)

These very ruinous remains belong to a temple dedicated to Baal-Saturn: this is evident from the many votive *stelai* found round about. The temple was composed of a richly decorated *cella* (pilaster-capitals

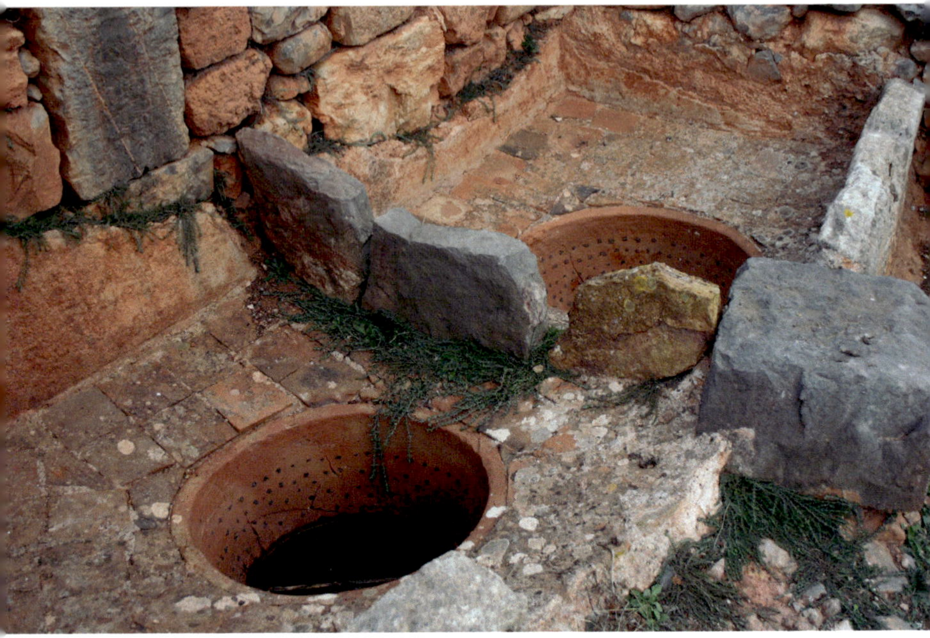

Fig. 152. Tiddis: fullers' vats near the car park.

with acanthus leaves and a six-petalled rosette have been found), a little underground room, and a terrace which may have been used for sacrifices. Below the rocky outcrop, on the N face, a natural cave reached by a small tunnel contained a number of skeletons and some coarse pottery.

31. Temple

This was a rectangular building divided into two rooms at different levels. The lower room had a bench around three sides; the two were linked by a staircase.

Some 30 m lower down, some traces of a building were found, together with a statue base dedicated to the companions of Saturn (*comitibus dei*) and to Saturn by a couple who had seen the face of the god in a dream.

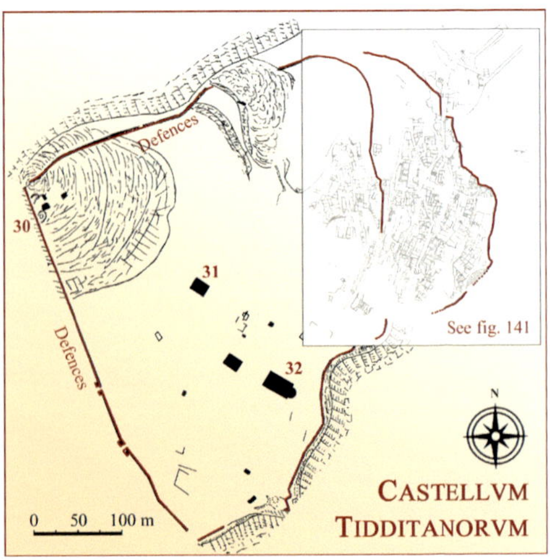

Fig. 153. Tiddis: plan of the full extent of the defended site.

30. *Summit sanctuary*
31. *Temple*
32. *Apsidal sanctuary*

32. Apsidal sanctuary

This huge rectangular monument terminates towards the E in an apse pierced by two lateral doorways. It was approached, on the W side, through two courts and a porch leading to a stairway; this descended to the rock surface within the building. The inscriptions which were recovered, consisting of four lists of names suggesting a college, and a crudely carved bust inscribed A.AVG.SAC (if correctly interpreted as *Aesculapio Augusto sacrum*) suggest a temple dedicated to Aesculapius.

Tomb of the Lollii

On leaving the site, after a distance of 2.6 km, an unmade track off to the left, beside a farmhouse, leads after a further 1.4 km to this remarkable tomb (fig. 154). From slightly farther along the asphalt road, it may also be seen away to the left, looking for all the world like a modern water tank in the middle of the fields. This is, however, a monumental family tomb of the mid-second century. It is almost intact, and takes the form of a cylindrical drum of fine ashlar masonry 10.2 m in diameter and 5.5 m high, with mouldings at top and bottom. There are inscriptions facing the four cardinal points of the compass, all with the same text:

M LOLLIO SENECIONI PATRI
GRANIAE HONORATAE MATRI
L LOLLIO SENI [F]R[AT]RI
M LOLLIO HONORATO FRATRI
P GRANIO PAVLO AVONCVLO
Q LOLLIVS VRBICVS PRAEF VRBIS

'For his father M. Lollius Senecio, his mother Grania Honorata, his brother L. Lollius Senex, his brother M. Lollius Honoratus, and his uncle P. Granius Paulus, Q. Lollius Urbicus the Prefect of the City (set this up).'

While the form of the monument may be a very distant descendant from the *bazinas* at the entrance to the village, it is more closely allied to the kind of tomb that wealthy Romans set up on the roads leading out of towns in Italy. Lollius Urbicus would have seen many of these when he was in Rome and, while he may never have returned to his family estate or to the community of which he had become patron (see p. 145), he surely sent an architect from Italy in order to build this monument as a memorial to his family, in a position where it could be seen from far afield, and especially from the family home (which has not been found). It has no close parallel in Algeria.

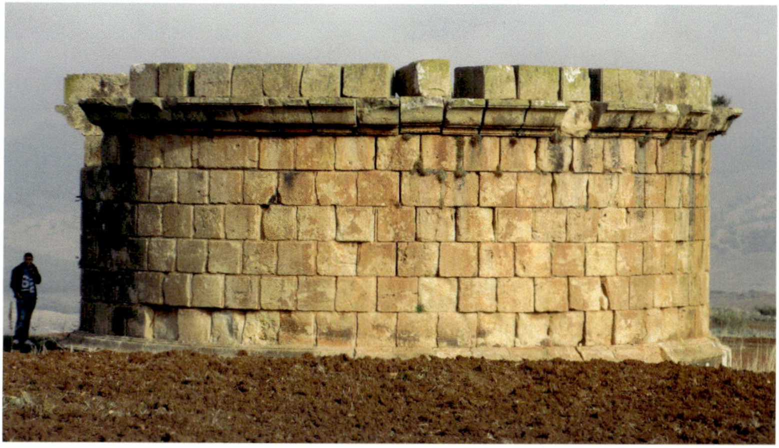

Fig. 154. Tiddis: the Tomb of the Lolli.

CIRTA-CONSTANTINA (Constantine)

I, who am now without a voice, relate my life in these verses. I have enjoyed, for a long time, a brilliant light. I was Praecilius, citizen of Cirta, where I was a goldsmith. I have always been honest and sincere. I have had the same sympathy for all, and I have had pity on everyone. I have enjoyed a happy existence amongst my dear friends. After the death of my chaste wife Valeria, I never found her equal. So far as I was able, I lived an agreeable and godly life with my wife. I have celebrated honourably one hundred times the anniversary of my birth. But the last day comes, when the spirit leaves the weakened limbs. The epitaph you now read was composed during my life, in expectation of death at the hour chosen by Fortune, which has never let me down. Follow in my steps; I await you here; come.

Funerary inscription (National Museum of Cirta, Room 6)

It is curious to note that, in a country so rich in archaeological remains, there is almost nothing to be seen of the most brilliant city of Roman times in what is now Algeria. Known to have been the eastern capital of the kingdom of the Masaesyli in the third century BC, Cirta must have been embellished by the Numidian kings who succeeded them: majestic tombs may still be seen in the region, such as the Medracen (p. 166) and El Khroub (p. 161), which was possibly the tomb of Masinissa († 148 BC) or Micipsa († 118 BC). The victory of Caesar at Thapsus in February 46 BC (over the armies of Pompey's supporters and their ally King Juba I) led to the dissolution of the Numidian kingdom and the gift of Cirta to the Campanian adventurer P. Sittius, as a recompense for his decisive support. It thus became an independent principality, known as the *Colonia Cirta Sittianorum*. Sittius, however, was murdered two years later by a Numidian prince, and by 36 BC the region had been incorporated into the province of *Africa Nova* under the name of *Colonia Iulia Cirta*. During the first century AD it was the dominant member of a confederation to which *Mileu* (Mila), *Chullu* (Collo) and *Rusicade* (Skikda) also belonged. This became formalized under Trajan as the *Respublica IV Coloniarum Cirtensium*, and included a considerable number of other villages (*pagi*) and fortified settlements (*castella*, such as *Castellum Tidditanorum*). Cirta held the common purse and managed the other towns through the intermediaries of prefects, but the precise political mechanisms which determined their relationships are not clearly understood. When the confederation ceased to function, after the reforms of Diocletian, the city retained its pre-eminence as capital of the new province of *Numidia Cirtensis*. In 311 the city was destroyed by the emperor Maxentius in the course of suppressing a revolt; it was rebuilt by Constantine as the capital of a reunited Numidia, and at this point took the name of the emperor. Under the Byzantines, Constantina, which remained the capital of Numidia, housed the residence of the military governor (*dux*) of the province.

EXPLORING THE CITY

The site, particularly well defended on three sides by the precipitous gorges of the Rhummel, has been inhabited continuously since antiquity. When the French arrived in 1837, it is known that extensive traces of the ancient city could still be seen, including several arches and a theatre (between the present law courts and the post office). They levelled the highest part of the city to build the barracks which still dominate the site, and removed all vestiges of the Capitoline temple which once stood on the spot. There are, nonetheless, traces of Roman occupation beneath many buildings in the city, and evidence that the forum lay partly beneath the

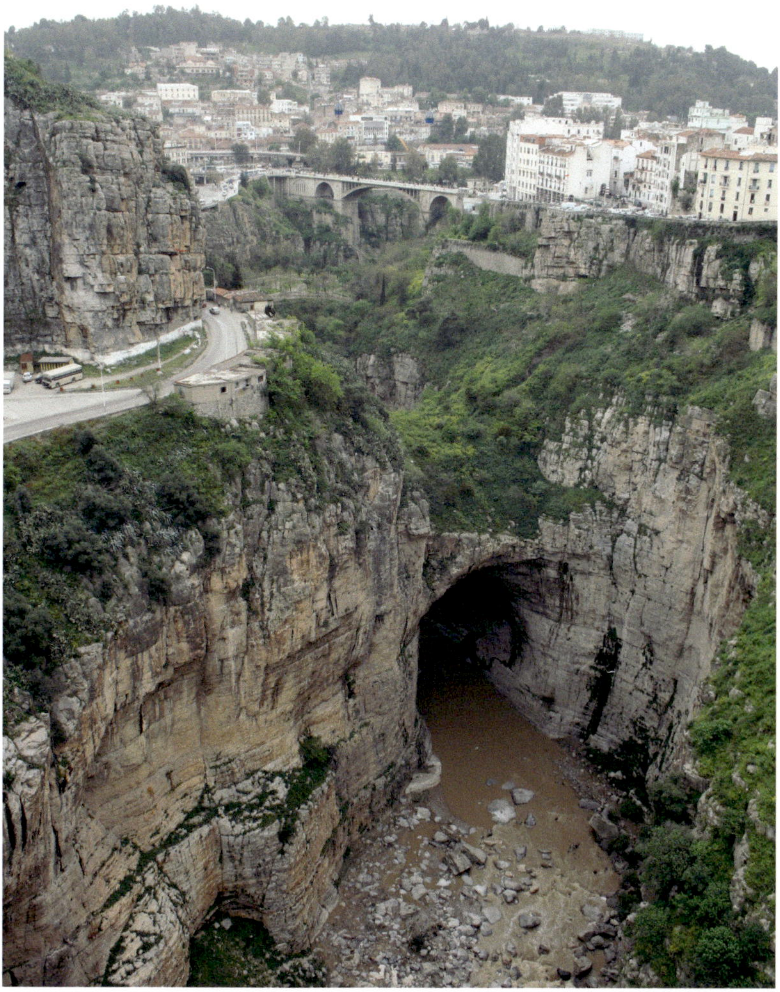

Fig. 155. Constantine: the Rhummel gorge which protects the city (on the right). The El-Kantara bridge in the distance rests on Roman foundations.

Palace of Hadji Ahmed, the last Bey of Constantine, has been demonstrated by statue bases recently found there. Almost the only vestiges from the Roman period which are visible today are the following.

El-Kantara Bridge

Deep in the gorge beneath the modern bridge (built in 1857, following the collapse of its predecessor) are the abutments of a Roman bridge, attributed to the Antonine period; the roadway was 60 m long, at a height of 65 m above the river bed. On one of the piers may still be seen a relief of two heraldically opposed elephants, with a frontal female figure (a goddess?) above.

Roman aqueduct

In the southern part of the city, on the N side of the N5 road and between it and the Oued Rhummel, may be seen five arches of an aqueduct (fig. 156) which once brought the waters of Ras el-Aïn Bou Merzoug, some 30 km to the S, to the suburb which is now Koudiat-Aty. The width of this structure suggests that it must surely have carried a road as well as a water channel.

NATIONAL MUSEUM OF CIRTA – GROUND FLOOR

Built between 1921 and 1930 by the architect Castelli, the museum of Constantine houses a particularly rich archaeological collection. The finds from the excavations at Tiddis, in particular, give a powerful impression of daily life in ancient Numidia.

1. Prehistory

This room illustrates, through a number of cases dedicated to specific sites, finds from eastern Algeria attributable to the Stone Age (Palaeolithic to Neolithic).

2. Proto-history

The wall-cases in this room display pottery from Tiddis, while in the centre of the room is a case illustrating amphorae and Hellenistic/Punic pottery from tombs at Rabta-Jijel. On the floor are numerous Punic *stelai* akin to those in the next room.

3. Numidian-Punic room

A number of Libyan inscriptions are displayed here, also more of the Punic *stelai* from the excavations of El-Hofra in Constantine. This

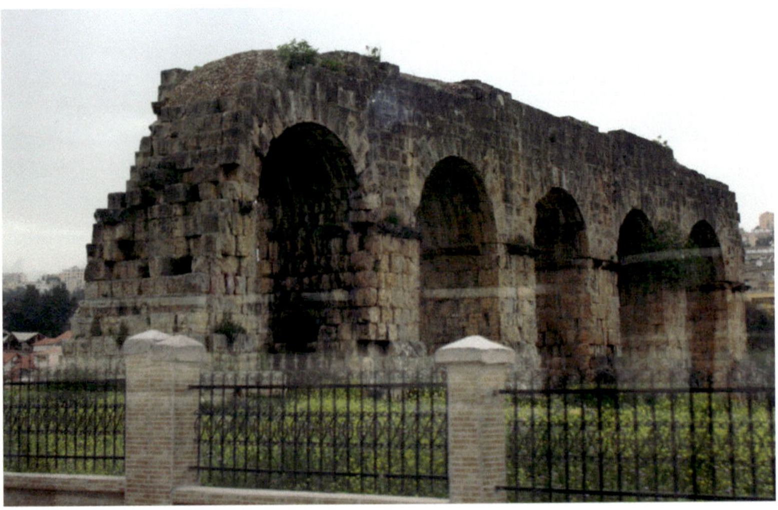

Fig. 156. Constantine: Roman aqueduct bridge.

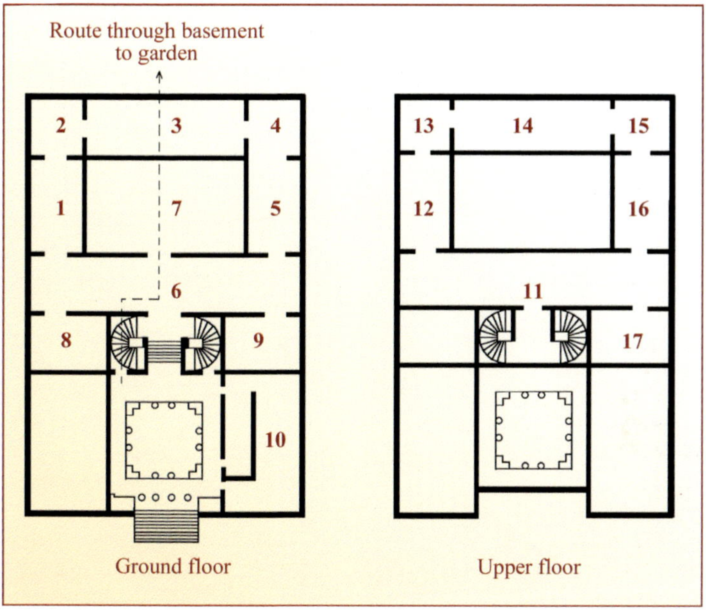

Fig. 157. Constantine: National Museum of Cirta, plan.

was the site of an important sanctuary, found in 1950 where the Hotel Transatlantique was subsequently built and now completely obliterated by the southern end of the new Salah Bey suspension bridge over the river. The site has yielded more than 830 *stelai*: with dedications to Tanit and Baal-Hammon in Libyan, Punic, neo-Punic and Greek, they underline the importance of Phoenician cults in the region of Cirta. The finds from the site range in date between the end of the third and the middle of the first century BC.

Cases in this room display some of the beautiful decorated silverware from the mausoleum of El Khroub, recovered in 1915 (in the centre of the room: see fig. 158 and p. 161), pottery and glass from burials in Constantine and other objects pertaining to the Numidian and Massylian kingdoms.

4. Roman gods

Currently, the only 'Roman' god here is a fine marble sculpture of Dionysus, identifiable by his beardless face and wreath of vine leaves and grapes (fig. 159: found in 1871 when the rue Nationale, now rue Larbi ben Mhidi, was driven through the old town). Baal/Saturn and other oriental divinities are, however, present.

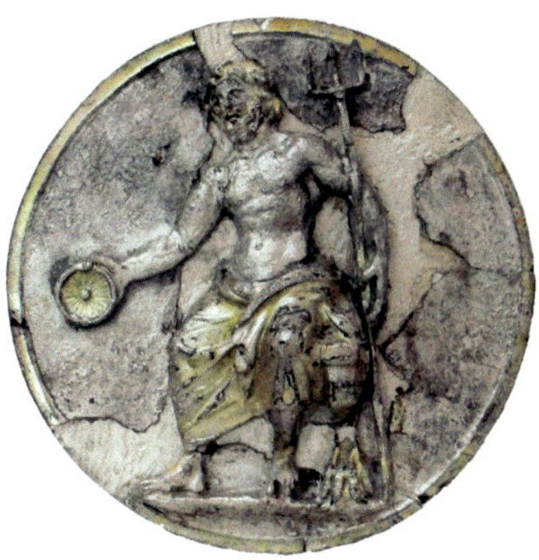

Fig. 158. Constantine/Cirta Museum: gilded silver medallion portraying Neptune, from the mausoleum at El Khroub.

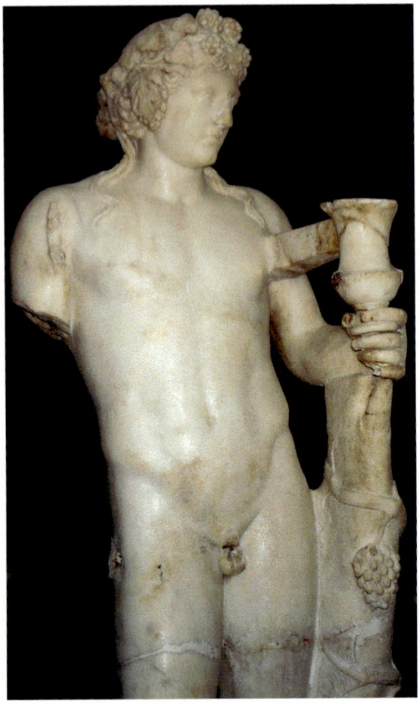

Fig. 159. Constantine/Cirta Museum: Dionysus.

5. Potters of Tiddis

This room displays many examples of the very varied output of the potters of Tiddis, often showing greater inventiveness and *joie-de vivre* than artistic skill (see fig. 160). They include a pre-Roman terracotta statuette showing a seated man, perhaps a soldier in armour, whose male attributes are carefully represented beneath his tunic (fig. 161). Tools of the potters (moulds, polishing stones, dies, stacking rings etc.) are also shown. Notice also in this room a section of terracotta water-pipe stamped *TID(D)ITAN(ORVM)* and fragments of brick and tile stamped officially by the *Legio III Augusta*, the only Roman legion stationed in North Africa. The wall-cases include fine pottery and lamps made in other parts of the Roman Empire, including Italy and Tunisia.

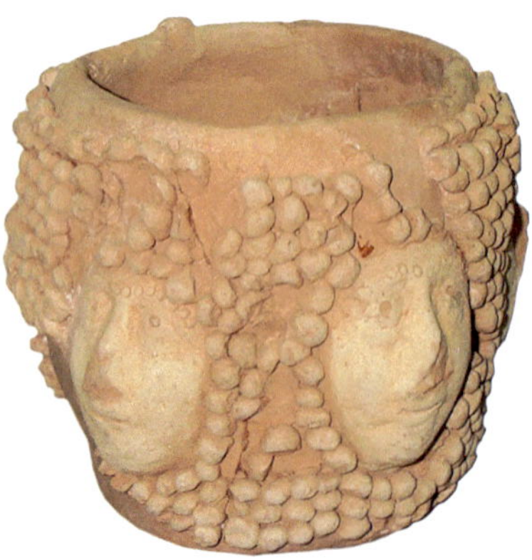

Fig. 160. Constantine/Cirta Museum: decorated pot from Tiddis.

6. Daily life at Tiddis

Thirty-one cases in this corridor display agricultural tools, articles of adornment, theatrical masks, toys, jewellery, lamps and other objects found in the excavations at Tiddis.

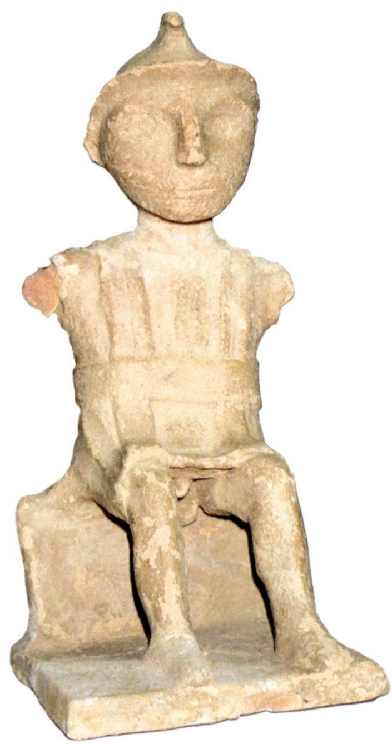

Fig. 161. Constantine/Cirta Museum: seated male figure in terracotta, from Tiddis.

Six sculptures here are of note: a portrait of the emperor Claudius, one of Antoninus Pius, a colossal head of Juno, a (headless) statue of Demeter, a statuette of a seated female figure, probably Juno and, particularly, a fine life-size statue of a woman known as the 'Lady of Djémila'. This is a patrician woman, modestly arranging her veil over her shoulder (fig. 162). This handsome and realistic piece, found at Cuicul/Djémila, has been attributed to the second century on the basis of the hairstyle, which is close to that of Faustina the Elder, wife of Antoninus Pius. Also here, on the edge of a sarcophagus lid, is the funerary inscription reported at the head of this section (p. 152).

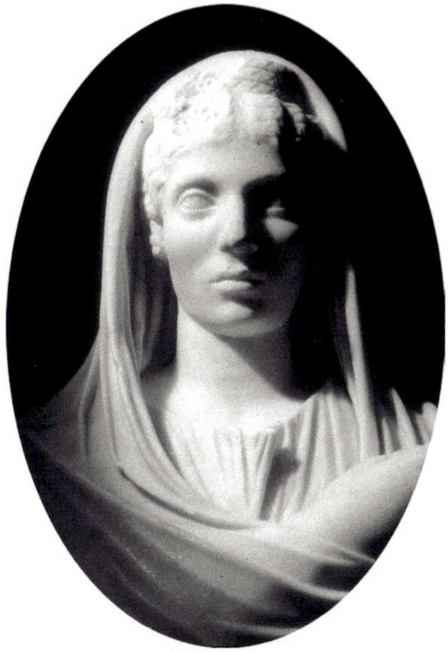

Fig. 162. Constantine/Cirta Museum: detail of the 'Lady of Djémila'.

7. Hall of mosaics

Several mosaic pavements are on display here.

Triumph of Venus (4.50 x 2.50 m, found at Khenchela, ancient *Mascula*; early fourth century). Venus is supported by two marine centaurs. In a second register below there are a hippocamp and a marine bull (taurocamp?), while in the lowest there is a fishing scene in which an elderly fisherman, lying on the rocky coast, seems to be looking enviously at the miraculous catch of his young companion. The mosaic shows originality in the unusual posture of the goddess, who is wringing out her long brown hair beneath a fringed canopy.

Mosaic of the swimmers (on the floor, from a bath-building at Sidi M'Cid, Constantine, found in 1959; late first or early second century). The central circular geometric design encloses an image of the eagle of Jupiter, clutching a thunderbolt. On one side of this is a representation of a naval battle between four ships: note the armed warriors, the decoration of the ships and the rams attached to their prows. On the opposite side is a much simpler, but pleasing, scene of two swimmers in silhouette. This is thought to be Italian

Mascula

Situated 117 km to the W of Theveste (Tébessa), and controlling the passage between the Aurès and the plateaux of Nemencha, Mascula (Khenchela) was initially a staging-post for the *Legio III Augusta* on the road between Ammaedara (Haïdra in Tunisia) and Lambaesis. Listed in the Antonine Itinerary, the city housed the Second Cohort of Thracians and the Seventh Cohort of Lusitanians, prior to a detachment of the legion under Septimius Severus. The site is today entirely overlaid by the modern town, but it has yielded on occasion some exceptional mosaics belonging to rich private houses.

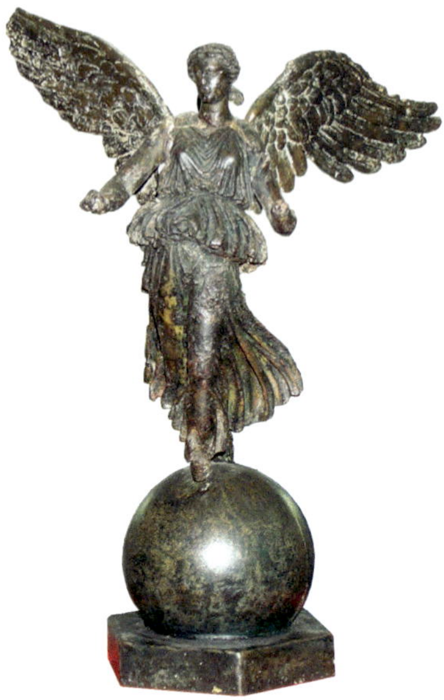

Fig. 163. Constantine/Cirta Museum: bronze statuette of Victory.

work and substantially earlier than other mosaics in the region.

Also in this room is a fragmentary mosaic with hunting scenes on the estate of a country house (found in 1928 in rue Larbi ben Mhidi, Constantine, second half of fourth century).

8. Qala'at Bani Hammad

This room displays medieval finds from this important, but short-lived, capital of a Berber dynasty, founded in 1007, largely abandoned in 1090 and last mentioned in 1185. It includes pottery, glassware, glazed tiles and architectural ornament of various kinds from the site, which lies in the mountains to the SW of Sétif. Also in this room are items of the medieval period from Tiddis, Béjaïa and Constantine.

9. Bronzes and coinage

The masterpiece of this collection is a statuette of the third century in silvered bronze, found in 1855 in the old city of Constantine (fig. 163). It represents a Winged Victory standing on a globe, which is distinguished by the beauty of the face and the fineness of the drapery. Remarkably, a fragment of an inventory found during the excavation of the Capitolium of Cirta refers to this precise item and makes it clear that it was only a small part of the cult statue that stood inside the temple:

A Jupiter Victor in silver, the head encircled by a wreath composed of thirty oak leaves and fifteen acorns in silver, holding in his right hand a sphere surmounted by a statuette of Victory, holding a palm-branch of twenty leaves and a wreath of forty leaves.

Also here is a smaller Victory, still with palm and wreath (from El Khroub), a statuette of Harpocrates, a bust of the goddess Africa (identified by her elephant headdress: from Thibilis/Announa), a number of bronze lamps, weights and various chariot fittings, such as terrets and draw-bar terminals.

10. Ethnographic display

Closed in 2017.

FIRST FLOOR

11. First floor corridor

A mosaic here from Oued Athmania, displayed in two sections, has a Dionysiac theme in its upper register (the young winged god, riding a panther, approaches a kantharos full of wine, accompanied by musicians with flute and tambourine), and a representation of the Rape of Hylas (see p. 137) in the lower (late third or fourth century). Amongst other mosaics are some from tomb-covers of the Christian period and a fishing scene of the third or fourth century. On the stairway are cases containing examples of 'Numidian' glassware and pottery of Punic derivation. At the left-hand end of the corridor are a scaled-down reconstruction of a Roman olive press and *stelai* from Tiddis.

12 and 13. Religious life at Tiddis

On the floor are *stelai* dedicated to *Saturnus Africanus* from Tiddis (like those on the floor below, found at El-Hofra), while the cases are filled with votive terracottas (horses etc.) made locally, and with oil lamps from various sources. In the second room is painted pottery of the second and first centuries BC from Tiddis, together with other varied finds from the site. In the centre of this room is a fragmentary, inventive (rather than artistic) creation in pottery which may have been an incense-burner.

14 and 15. Gallery of modern fine art

These rooms display seventeenth to twenty-first century works by French and Algerian artists.

16. Christianity in Numidia

This room displays objects pertaining to Christian worship, including lamps with Christian decorative motifs, inscriptions in memory of saints and martyrs and reliquaries.

17. City of Constantine

This room houses a fine model of Constantine (made in 1941), which recreates the appearance of the city in 1830, together with a second which represents the city in 1955. There are also architectural and decorative timbers of the Ottoman period, and the wooden doors from the Great Mosque (late twelfth century?). On the walls are pictures of the city by various artists.

EPIGRAPHIC GARDEN

The garden behind the museum should not be missed. It is reached through a door in the far left-hand corner of the initial peristyle court, from which one passes through the basement. The museum staff are not always very keen for visitors to pass this way, but it is well worth insisting. Amongst many inscriptions, in both the Libyan and Latin languages, three items are of particular note.

Menhir of Ain M'Lila. This huge stone, on the right-hand side of the garden (fig. 164), bears a very stylized carving of a Libyan warrior holding a lance. A similar, smaller stone (from Tirekbine, Foum el-Khanga) is on the left.

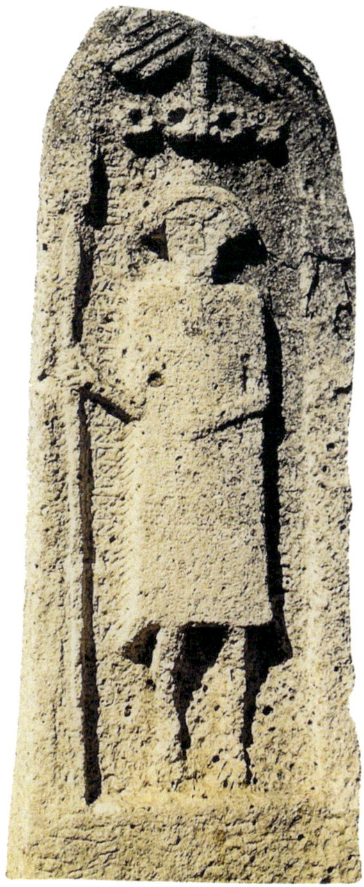

Fig. 164. Constantine/Cirta Museum: Menhir of Ain M'Lila.

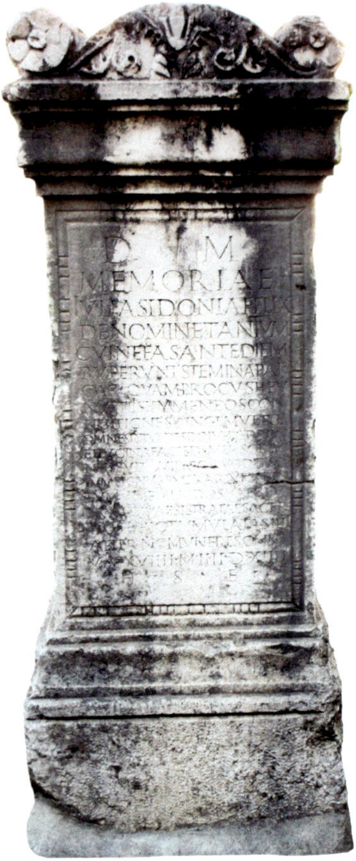

Fig. 165. Constantine/Cirta Museum: tombstone of Julia Sidonia Felix.

Epitaph of Julia Sidonia Felix. A long Latin text on a tombstone, at the far end of the garden, in the centre (fig. 165):

Happy in name alone, the Fates cruelly decided to cut the thread of her days before time. No betrothed ever had the chance to lead her to the fires of the Hymenaea. All the Dryads groaned. The young girls lamented and the goddess Lucina herself, seeing the light of her torch reversed, wept because she died a virgin, object of the tender love of her parents alone. She had been a priestess, bearer of the sistrum for the goddess of Memphis [Isis]. Buried in silence, she enjoys eternal slumber. She lived for 19 years, 4 months, 14 days.
H(ic) S(ita) E(st) *[She lies here].*

Epitaph of P. Sittius Optatus. Another (fragmentary) Latin text on a tombstone.

Passer-by, I beg you to pause briefly and learn in a few words of my life and death. I was not born of foreign stock, a Scythian, but by the banks of the Ampsaga (Oued el-Kebir) …

P. Sittius Optatus goes on to say that he owns a very agreeable property by the name of Alba,

where one enjoys the lovely aroma of maritime pines, where the chaste laurel flourishes and where the naiads gambol in water clear as glass.

He laments having lost his only daughter

carried off in the flower of her youth by an undeserved death

and concludes with a declaration of resignation:

That which Nature gives, she takes away and cannot be reproached for. Let it be no shame to say, 'May the bones of P. Sittius Optatus rest in comfort.'

THE MAUSOLEUM OF EL KHROUB

The imposing square pedestal which may be seen at El Khroub to the S of Constantine, on top of a hill with views far and wide, belonged to a monumental obelisk-tomb (see figs. 166, 167). The tradition of tombs of this type may have origins in Egypt, but it also has links with the famous Hellenistic tomb of Mausollus at Halicarnassus, and was widely used in Punic North Africa.

The stepped square base – almost the only part now standing, though the fallen blocks round about are a good guide to the original form of the upper parts – supported a lower storey with a false door on each side, flanked by embossed circular shields. The level above had a solid core with a temple façade of four columns on each side, surmounted by a pediment; finally, the whole was crowned by a spire or obelisk, bringing the total height to 25 or 30 m. The excavation of the burial chamber, beneath the basement, yielded rich grave goods in addition to the ashes of the deceased, and these are now on display in Room 3 of the National Museum of Cirta (see p. 155). The scale of the monument clearly indicates a 'royal' burial: the style of the grave goods (particularly the silverware) suggests a date after the middle of the second century BC. The most obvious candidates are therefore Masinissa, who died in 148 BC, or his son Micipsa, who died in 118 BC.

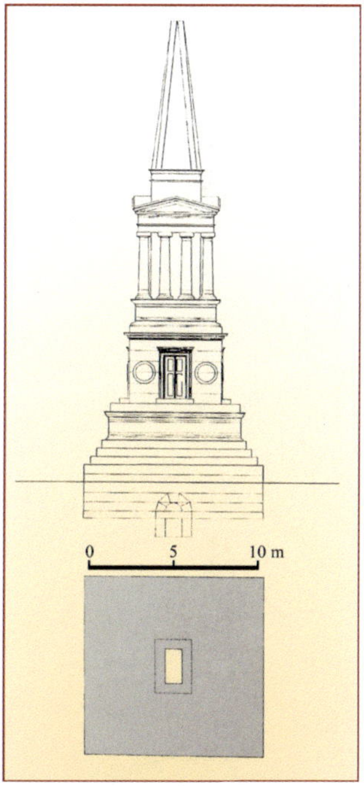

Fig. 166 (right). El Khroub: reconstruction drawing of the mausoleum.

Fig. 167 (below). El Khroub: the royal mausoleum of Micipsa?

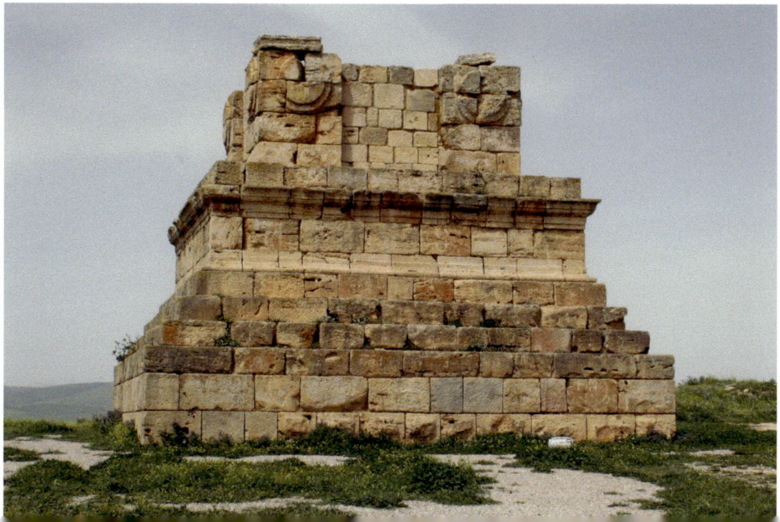

THIBILIS (Announa)

The village (pagus) of Thibilis was situated 18 km to the SW of Calama, on a narrow plateau at a height of 700 m, approachable from higher ground to the S, but protected by steep slopes which fall away on the other three sides. The settlement was a 'colony of Sittian veterans' (i.e. settled by followers of P. Sittius, who

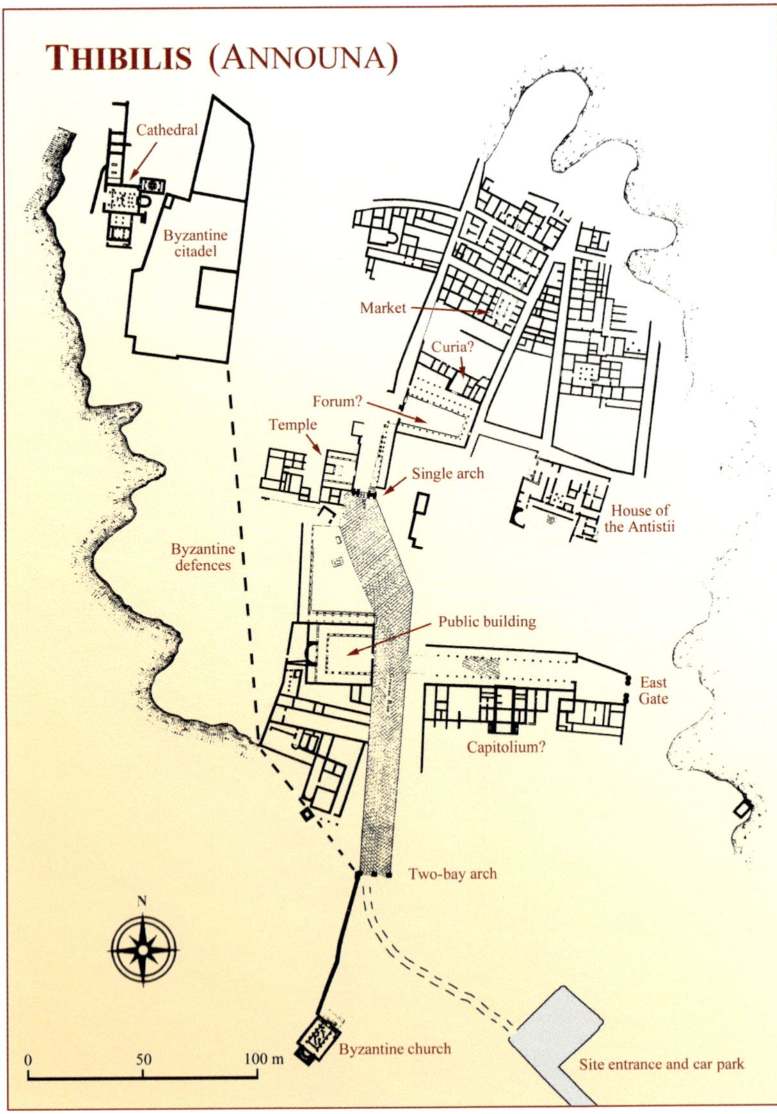

Fig. 168. Plan of Thibilis.

had supported Caesar in the civil war in 46 BC); it became a *municipium* between 260 and 268 and never possessed either a theatre or public baths. Whether in the fourth century its status had advanced to that of a formal *colonia* is uncertain, but it was the seat of a bishop in the fifth. The streets of the village run in straight lines, but only approximate to a regular grid.

Built on the S side of the settlement at the end of the third century, an ***arch of two bays*** (exceptional in Africa), framed by fluted Corinthian pilasters, led into a broad paved street (fig. 169). Part-way along, a colonnaded street on the right led to an E gate and, to the S of this and presumably facing an open square, are the concrete foundations of a substantial temple with a triple cella, presumed to have been the ***Capitolium***. There are large column drums and Corinthian capitals lying about, and there are frontal steps on the S side.

The arch of the ***East Gate*** has fallen, but one of its massive piers still stands to its full height. It had a single opening, flanked by Corinthian pilasters at ground-level. A second storey is plain, and above this an attic ran across the top of the arch. Beyond the gate, the ground falls away abruptly: the road leading away from here must have curved around to the R.

Opposite the colonnaded street stood a large building with a colonnaded internal court, terminating in three rooms, of which the central one was apsidal. The courtyard of the building was paved, there were mosaics in the porticoes and fragments have been found of a long inscription which must once have spanned the façade, dated 210/211. This was clearly a ***public building***, though its precise purpose is not clear. The far end of the paved street, which made an angle to the left, was closed by an ***arch of a single span*** framed by

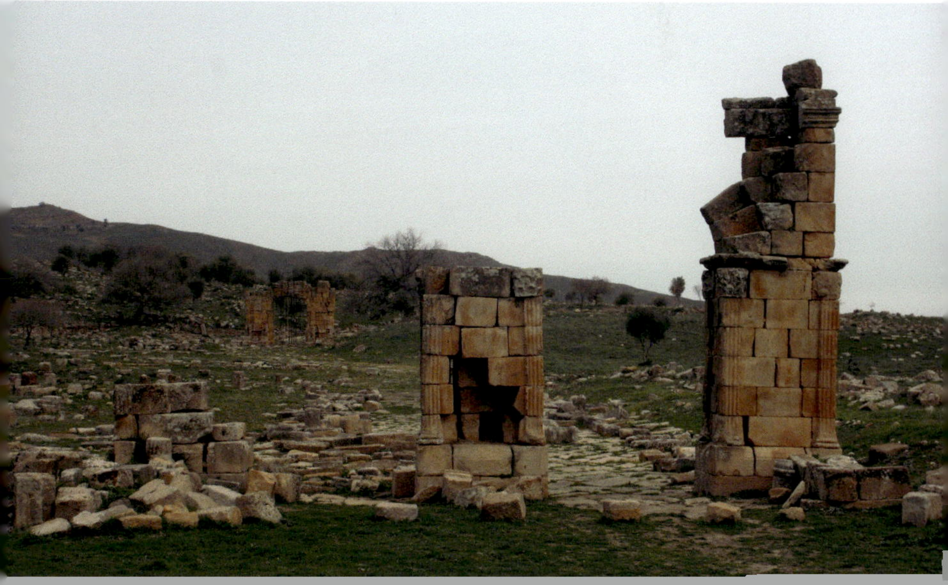

engaged columns (now sustained by rusty scaffolding and perilously close to collapse). Beyond this, a narrower street led to a little trapezoidal area on the right (27 x 12 m), accessed through a double arch (fig. 170). Because of the numerous statue bases built into late walls in this area, it has been interpreted as the ***Forum*** of the community, and a building on the N side of it as a curia, though this would have represented a very primitive manifestation of Roman culture. (The Capitolium, the scale of which surely makes its identification secure, seems a far stronger indicator that the Forum lay immediately to the S of that building. Maybe, as in so many settlements, there was both an original and a later, grander, forum.)

To the N of the trapezoidal 'forum', on the right-hand side of the next street leading to the right, a little ***market*** (15.7 x 13 m) has shops opening off a portico around a tiny paved court. In the centre lies a statue-base with a dedication to Mercury, the God of Commerce (and thieves). The market yielded a table of linear measures which is now in the theatre/museum at Guelma (see p. 254 and fig. 275).

Thibilis is known to have been the home town of a distinguished family, the Antistii, and a ***house*** excavated on the site has been identified unequivocally as belonging to this family. (An inscribed altar from this house is housed in the museum at Guelma, p. 256 and fig. 276.) However, it has yielded no mosaics and only a couple of fragments of statuary suggest any pretension to grandeur; maybe the more distinguished members of the family did not in fact return home after their social advancement. The most notable member of this family was Q. Antistius Adventus Postumius Aquilinus, a slightly younger man than Q. Lollius Urbicus of Tiddis (p. 145), but another Numidian of the second century who pursued a highly successful military career in the service of Rome (including major army commands under Marcus

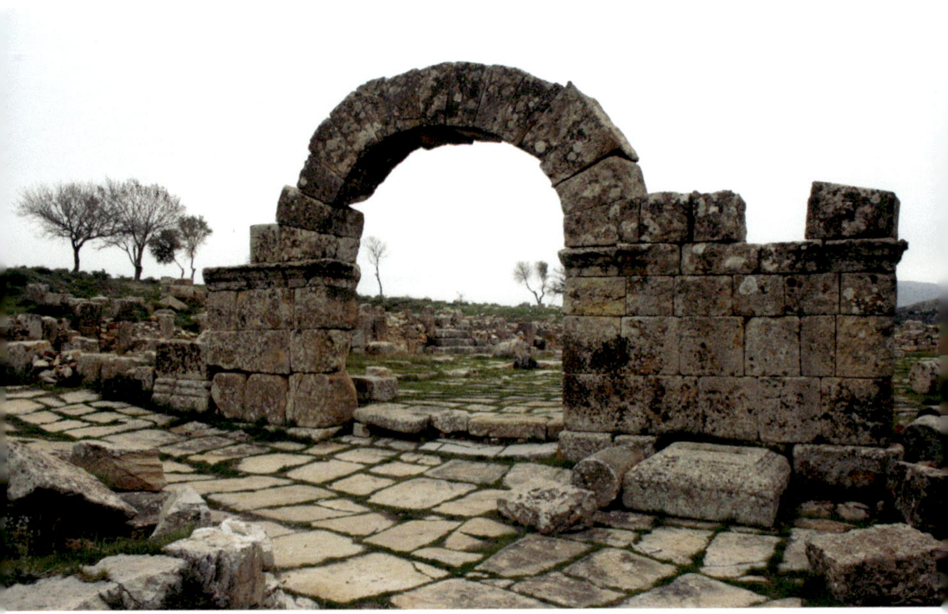

Fig. 170. Thibilis: the surviving arch at the entrance to the 'forum'.

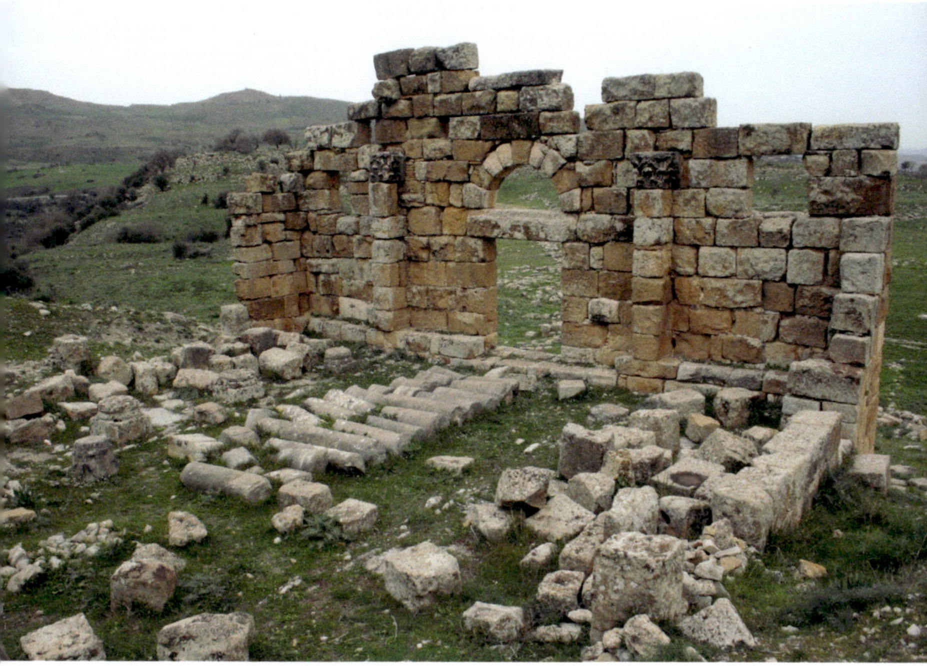

Fig. 171. Thibilis: interior of the S Church.

Aurelius and governorships of Arabia, Lower Germany and Britain). His son or nephew, L. Antistius Burrus, married the daughter of the emperor and was consul in 181.

On the highest ground on the W side of the settlement is the double enclosure of a ***Byzantine fortress***, built of reused materials. Below this, and on the very edge of the spur, is a three-aisled church, which was possibly a ***cathedral***, since it has a baptistery attached at the NE corner. The circular surround of the baptismal basin is composed in part of re-cut inscribed blocks. This complex also belongs to the Byzantine period.

On steeply rising ground, well to the S of the settlement, is another three-aisled ***church***, facing SW because of the lie of the land (fig. 171); within the apse (now once again buried beneath hill-wash) were found the semicircular steps of a *synthronon* for the clergy. The building has been attributed to the Byzantine period, based on the style of the crosses which adorn some of the architectural elements (for instance, on the keystone of the relieving arch above the main door). To the SE of the church, the discovery of numerous *stelai* dedicated to Saturn suggests the presence of a sanctuary dedicated to him.

THE MEDRACEN

Like the Mauretanian royal tomb which it resembles (p. 75), the Medracen is a mausoleum derived from the ancient Numidian type of the *bazina* (see the examples at Tiddis, p. 140), meaning that it is composed of a cylindrical base, more or less architecturally developed, with a stepped conical covering. In this instance, the drum is enlivened by sixty engaged columns of the Doric order with an exagerated Punic (or 'Egyptian') cornice above (see fig. 172). The drum is 59 m in diameter and the whole was originally 19 m high. An entrance on the E side, at foundation level and therefore hidden, leads past a blocking-slab into a funerary chamber in the heart of the structure.

There is no mention in ancient literature of this tomb, apart from an obscure reference in the *Historia*

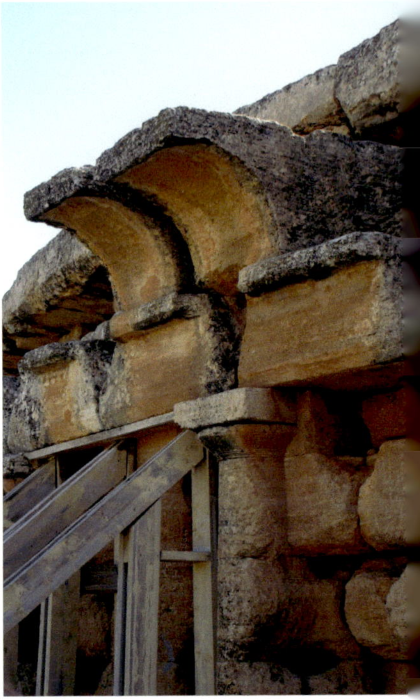

Fig. 172 (right). Medracen: detail of the architectural order.

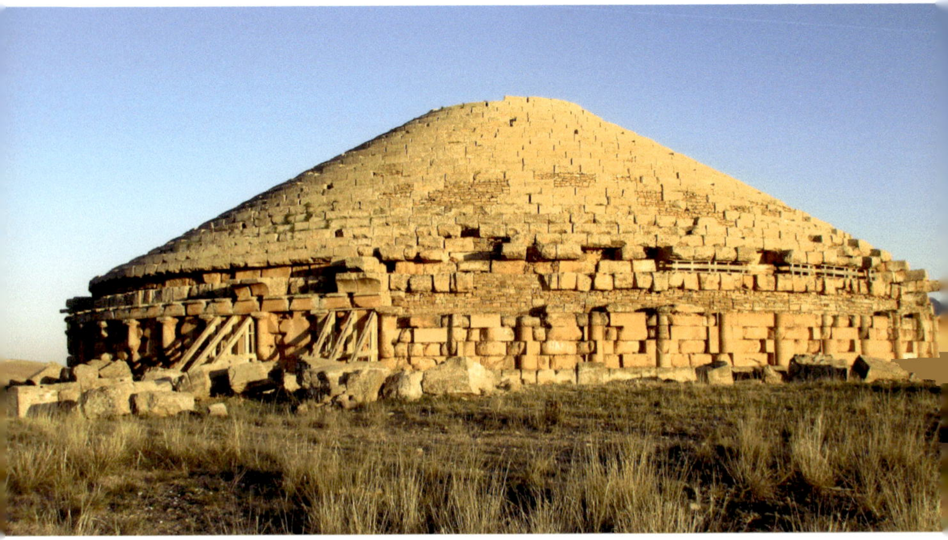

Fig. 173. The Medracen.

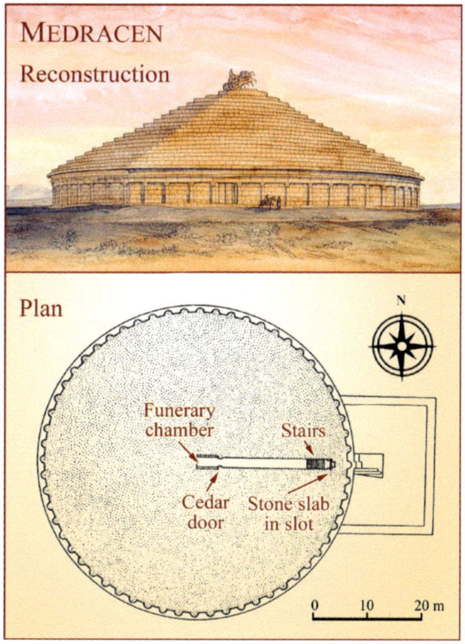

Fig. 174 (top right). Medracen: ground-plan and reconstruction drawing by J.-C. Golvin.

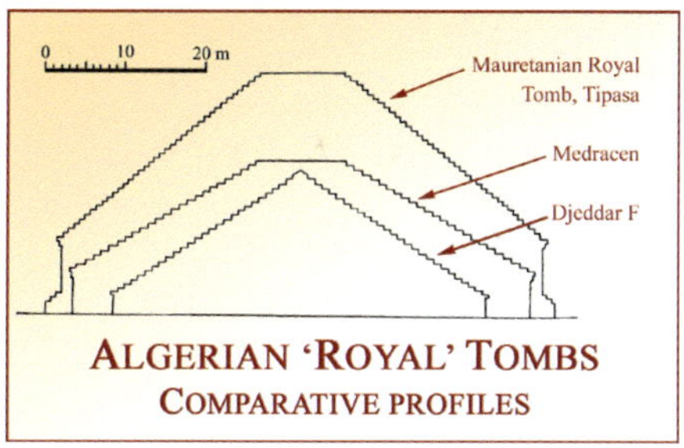

Fig. 175 (bottom right). Comparative profiles of ancient 'royal' tombs in Algeria.

Augusta, and early tomb-robbing has left no datable artefacts. However, it has been possible to obtain a carbon date from the surviving timbers in the ceiling of the corridor leading to the burial chamber. This indicates a construction date in the fourth century BC, which would not be inconsistent with the architectural details. This places it earlier than any named king that we know of, but the labour required to create such a structure leaves no doubt that it was the (intended) resting-place of a chieftain with a large population at his command.

The Berber name *Medracen* (or *imedghassen*) means 'tombs' in the plural. Within the fenced enclosure may be seen many rings of stones marking simpler graves.

THE *LEGIO III AUGUSTA*

South of Constantine, in the Batna area, the tourist in search of Classical Antiquity moves into a decidedly military zone, which justifies a brief digression into the nature of Roman military control in North Africa.

Historians have long been struck by the disproportion between the extent of the African territory and the slightness of the military forces deployed to control it. The only legion based in Numidia from the first century onwards, the *Legio III Augusta*, would have amounted to hardly more than 5,000 men, all Roman citizens, to which must be added the auxiliary troops recruited from non-Roman populations. (Note the tombstones of auxiliary soldiers at Cherchel, p. 46 and fig. 42, and Tipasa, p. 72 and fig. 68.) As in every legion, the *III Augusta* would have been under a commanding officer, the *legatus*, supported by a headquarters staff of senior officers, the *tribuni*, and would have been divided into ten cohorts, of which the first was composed of 960 men commanded by a *primipilus*, while the nine others were composed of 480 men, each under the command of a centurion. One cohort was placed at the disposition of the proconsul at Carthage to serve as an escort and police force, while the others were disposed around various posts and garrison towns. In Numidia, the Third Legion was reinforced by *alae* (wings) of cavalry or bodies described as *numeri*, the strength of which it is difficult to determine. In Mauretania Caesariensis, a military diploma of the year 107 enumerates the auxiliary forces present: ten cohorts and three *alae* from all over the empire and amounting to around 6,000 soldiers. Likewise, in Mauretania Tingitana there were only auxiliary forces: five cohorts and five alae amounting to about 6,000 men according to several diplomas. To these must be added the thousand soldiers of a first urban cohort detached from Rome to guarantee the security of Carthage. There were therefore approximately 25,000 men to carry out territorial conquest, defence and maintenance of the peace, in addition to being responsible for civil engineering, over an area measuring roughly 2,000 x 150 km. The legion was initially based at *Ammaedara* (Haïdra in Tunisia), then under Vespasian at *Theveste* (Tébessa: see p. 271) because of the siting of this town at the intersection of several roads. Under Titus, in 81, it was moved further west to *Lambaesis*, and its first base there was joined by a much larger one nearby in the time of Hadrian. The largest of the forts at *Lambaesis*, which seems to have been inspected by Hadrian in person, measured 500 x 420 m. One of the commanding officers of the legion, Capellianus, opposed the emperors Gordian I and II in the upheavals which followed the murder of Alexander Severus in 235 and, as a result, the legion was cashiered in 238 by Gordian III and suffered collective *damnatio memoriae*, for which reason its name was obliterated from many inscriptions (e.g. p. 179 fig. 189). This seems to have resulted in the partial eclipse of *Lambaesis*. The legion was re-formed in 253, but left Lambaesis in the early fourth century. We do not know where it went, though it still existed in the late fourth or early fifth.

LAMBAESIS (Lambèse/Tazoult)

July 13: 1st Pannonian Cavalry Wing

You did everything according to the book: you filled the training-ground with your wheelings, you threw spears not ungracefully, though with short and stiff shafts. Several of you hurled lancea *spears with skill. Your jumping onto the horses here was lively and yesterday swift ... You pleased equally throughout the whole maneuver.*

Part of address by the emperor Hadrian to his troops near Lambaesis in 128 (tr. M. Speidel, 2006)

To evoke the name of *Lambaesis* is to evoke the Third Legion. The site comes into existence with its arrival, expands because of its presence and goes into decline with its departure. The legion was moved in 81 from *Theveste* (Tébessa: see p. 271) to *Lambaesis*, where a first fort 200 m square was built on a favourable site: a plateau with a hill behind it, overlooking the plain. Later, a larger base was called for, this time a vast rectangle enclosing more than 2 hectares and surrounded by stone walls, set on the plain itself. An enclosed exercise-ground, probably of similar date, lies to the W; fragments of an inscription and of a commemorative column indicate that the emperor Hadrian addressed the troops here in 128.

As was often the case, a civil settlement grew up around the military facilities; the free space on the plateau was gradually built up as the urban sprawl extended around the fort. The fort was occupied by soldiers, but also by other types of personnel (the *officium*) who were at the disposal of the legate for administrative or technical tasks, such as the management of the town, survey, maintenance of roads etc. It is likely that military engineers will have been involved in the construction of civil facilities at *Lambaesis* which were financed from the funds of the legion (such as the temple of Aesculapius or the amphitheatre).

The second major period of growth for the city fell in the first half of the third century, when it became capital of the new province of *Numidia* (separated from *Africa Proconsularis* by Septimius Severus in his reorganization of the military frontier zone) and its legal status was elevated from that of *municipium* to that of *colonia*. These happy prospects were, however, soon dashed. The legion was disbanded in 238 and suffered a *damnatio memoriae* (see p. 179 fig. 189) following the troubles which resulted in the elevation of the emperor Gordian III; this deprived the city of the principal driver of its economy until the legion was reconstituted under Valerian in 253. Some time later – after serving as capital of the smaller Diocletianic province of *Numidia Militiana* ('military' Numidia) – it was deprived of its role of provincial capital in 315 by Constantine, when he reunited the two Numidian provinces (*Cirtensis* and *Militiana*) and made *Cirta*, now renamed *Constantina*, the sole capital. *Lambaesis* probably went into decline, for there are no references to it in the Vandal or Byzantine periods.

The lengthy presence of soldiers in this place seems to have left its mark, since the flanks of the Aurès mountains which overlook the site of *Lambaesis* are known even today as Djebel Askar – 'the mountain of the soldiers'.

The ancient site has suffered – and continues to suffer – more than most others from colonial and modern development, which has crept over almost its entire surface. The huge prison (still in use) was built in 1852 to house opponents of the coup d'état which took place in France in the preceding year, and the associated modern settlement has expanded at an alarming rate in recent years. Modern housing and industrial developments have exposed (and sometimes destroyed) wealthy Roman houses decorated with fine mosaics. The full extent of the ancient settlement is still far from clear.

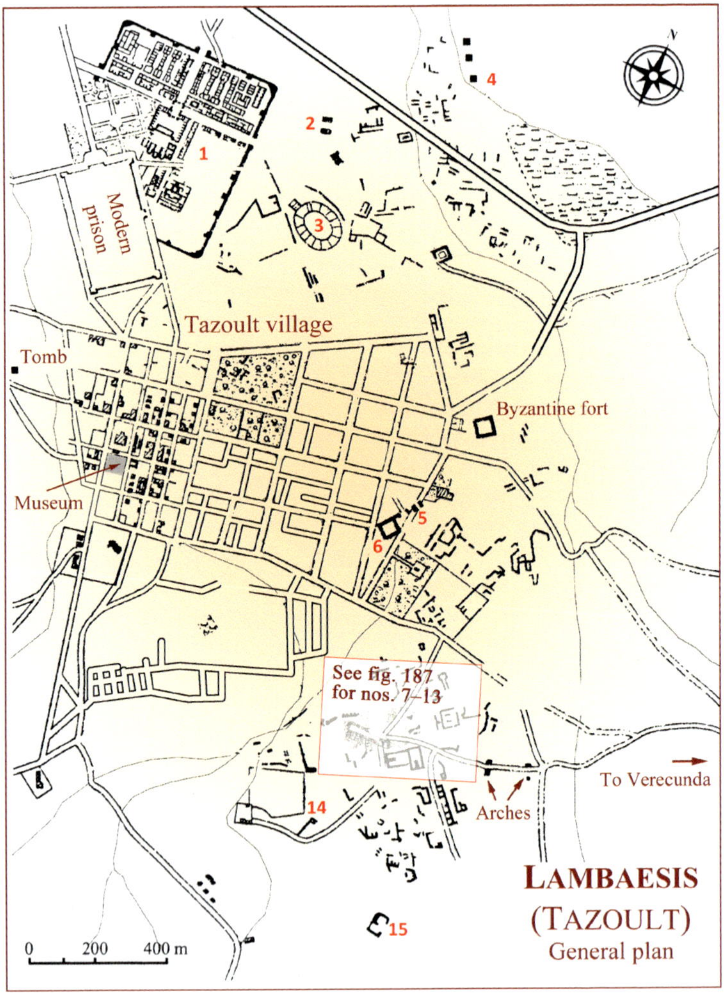

Fig. 176. Lambaesis: general plan of the ruins around the modern village of Tazoult.

1. *Hadrianic legionary base*
2. *Arch of Commodus*
3. *Amphitheatre*
4. *Necropolis*
5. *Arch of Septimius Severus*
6. *Public baths*
14. *Aqueduct*
15. *Temple of Neptune*

EXPLORING THE LOWER SITE

1. Hadrianic legionary base

Probably founded in 128, shortly before Hadrian's visit, the 'Great Fort' at *Lambaesis* (fig. 177) is one of the best preserved military complexes of its type, and this despite the unfortunate building here of a prison on the SW quarter of the site in 1852. The fort conforms to the general principles employed in the layout of permanent camps, with a defensive wall measuring 500 x 420 m and about 4 m thick, strengthened by towers and bastions and pierced by four gates. Certain parts of the defences, including towers and bastions, were restored under Marcus Aurelius.

The architects would not have started with the wall-circuit, but with the internal layout. Of crucial importance for this was the *groma*, a surveying instrument equipped with four plumb-bobs, which enabled the setting-out of right angles. This was used to mark out the N–S axis, the via *praetoria*, and the main E–W axis, the *via principalis*. At *Lambaesis*, the intersection of these roads was demarcated by a huge tetrapylon or four-way arch (fig. 178), for long mis-named the *praetorium* of the fort (the residence of the commanding

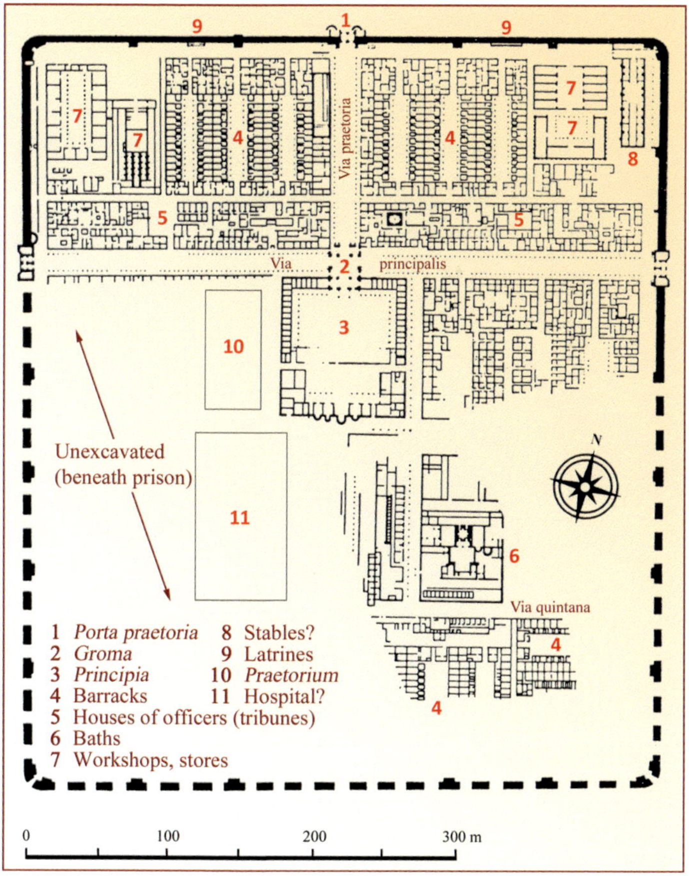

Fig. 177. Lambaesis: plan of the Hadrianic legionary base.

officer) but which we now know to have been called the *groma* – or focal point of the base – by reference to the instrument of the same name. Early travellers interpreted the building as a garage for heavy artillery or even as a stable for elephants! This rectangular monument (30.6 x 23.3 m) was covered by a pyramidal hipped roof (indicated by the four pier-bases within, which supported the cross-beams). Each of its faces, originally embellished by two storeys of pilasters and engaged columns, has a wide central opening for wheeled traffic (with a Victory carved on the keystone of the arch) and two, smaller, lateral openings for pedestrians.

The top of the lower storey is marked by a cornice running around the building, and above this there is a further arched opening on each side above the central archway. The design of the structure was rectangular rather than square, since on the S side it was extended to form an integral part of the headquarters building, the *principia*; here there is a fourth opening on the E and W sides, corresponding not to a thoroughfare but to the guardrooms at the entrance to the latter building (which are now reduced to their foundations). On the N façade, a very battered inscription immediately above the central span records a restoration carried out in 267–8, under Gallienus, presumably the culmination of works required when the base was re-commissioned in 253. The monument is there designated *groma*, as described above. Curiously, at some point between 286 and 293, the name of the emperor was erased and the names of Diocletian and Maximian inserted instead.

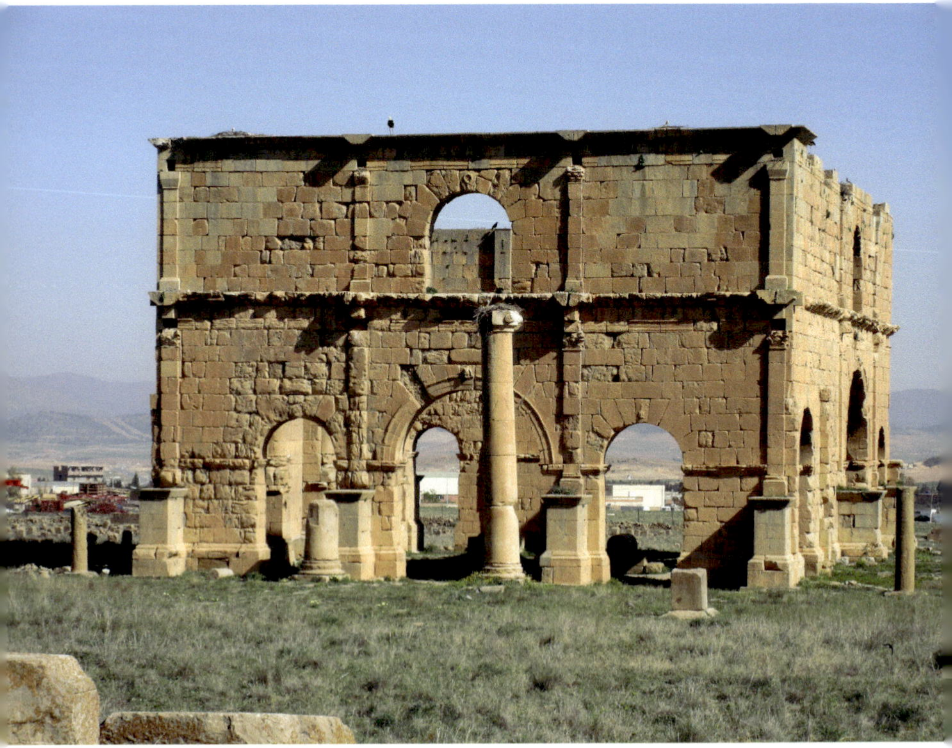

Fig. 178. Lambaesis: the groma at the centre of the Hadrianic base.

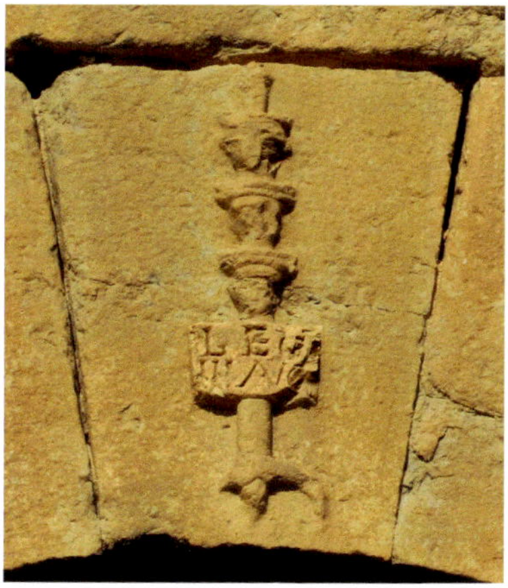

Fig. 179. *Lambaesis: the standard of the Third Legion, carved on the keystone of one of the lateral arches of the* groma.

(The new text was emphasized by red paint, but both versions can now be made out.) There was no obvious restoration at this time, and the change was presumably only honorific. Next to the E face of the *groma*, on the S side of the *via principalis*, stood a fountain, decorated with an apse fronted by a colonnade, as in theatre buildings.

The *principia*, entered through this impressive arch, was set around a huge courtyard (63 x 37.4 m) with porticoes along three sides (fig. 180). The porticoes fronted an array of small rooms, which served as offices and particularly as armouries (*armamentaria*). Thousands of slingshots, of both stone and terracotta, were found here. On the S side of the courtyard, two lateral flights of eight steps led up to a raised tribune (65 x 9.15 m), also bordered on three sides by rooms, which was converted into a basilical hall in the third century. In the centre of the S side, a room with an apse at the rear has been identified as the chapel of the standards (*aedes signorum*): this was the shrine where the bronze emblems of each cohort and other army units were deposited. Beneath this chapel, five underground chambers served as the strongroom for the treasures of the legion, together with the compulsory pension contributions of the soldiers, which they did not receive until they returned to civilian life. On either side of the chapel of the standards, other rooms, with or without apses, housed the meeting rooms (*scholae*) of the guilds of the cavalry, of the tribunes on the headquarters staff and of the armourers, as well as the archives of the legion and of the emperor. Authorised for the first time by Septimius Severus, these military guilds acquired considerable importance: they tended to take over spaces formerly reserved for the gods

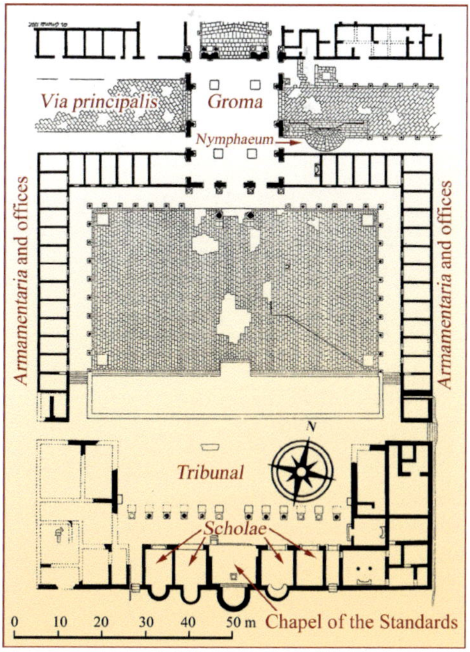

Fig. 180. *Lambaesis: plan of the* principia *of the Hadrianic base.*

(Mars, Minerva, the *genius* of the camp and Fortuna Augusta for Lambaesis) and for the emperors.

Around the headquarters building, it has been possible to identify many of the facilities of the base: the barracks for the cohorts, with dormitories for the soldiers and more generous accommodation for their centurions; the modest houses of the officers, with central courtyards; the stores; the workshop (*fabrica*) and the baths. In these last, only the heated rooms can be made out with ease. Nothing is known of the lavish residence of the commanding officer (*praetorium*) or of the hospital (*valetudinarium*), which must have been in the part of the fort that is overlaid by the modern prison.

2. Arch of Commodus

Arch of a single opening, adorned with pilasters, of which only the arch itself remains, with part of the flanking piers (end of second century: fig. 181).

3. Amphitheatre

This building, which had a capacity of between ten and twelve thousand spectators, was constructed in 169, under Marcus Aurelius, and restored in 180 and 194 (see fig. 182). Unfortunately, it was extensively quarried by the French for the construction of the prison in 1852; however, the basic features and the underground chambers and devices which were associated with the games are worthy of note. The two most famous martyrs of *Lambaesis*, James and Marian were not put to death in the amphitheatre, but beheaded on the bank of a river on 6th May 259. Reported by an eye-witness, the account of their passion is a significant historical document.

4. Necropolis and ancient tombs

The necropolis has yielded a huge number of funerary *stelai*, including some fine examples dedicated to Saturn and inscribed stones (visible in the forecourt of the museum). A mausoleum in the western part of the

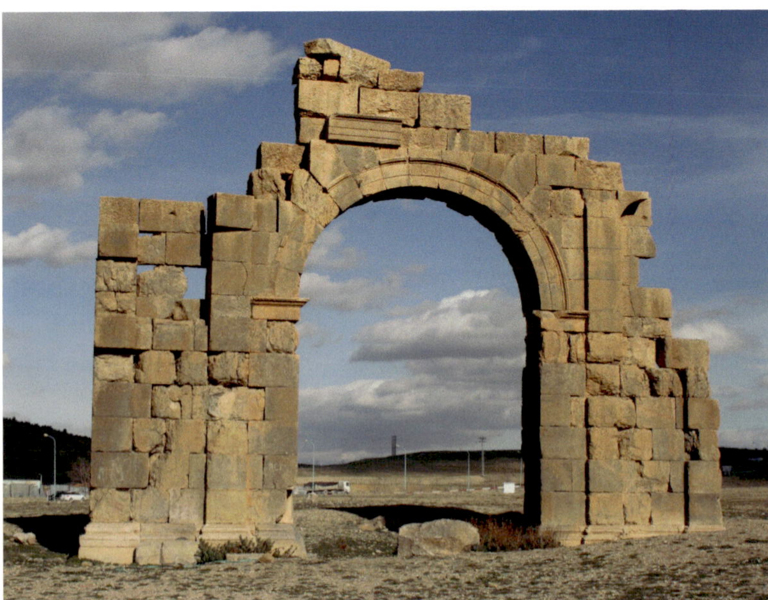

Fig. 181. Lambaesis: Arch of Commodus.

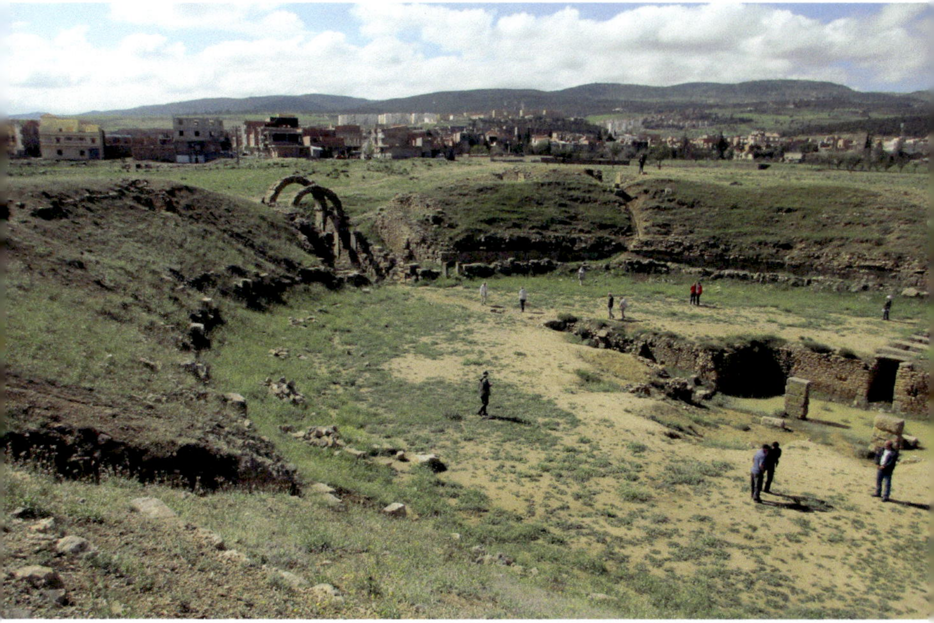

Fig. 182 (above). Lambaesis: the amphitheatre.

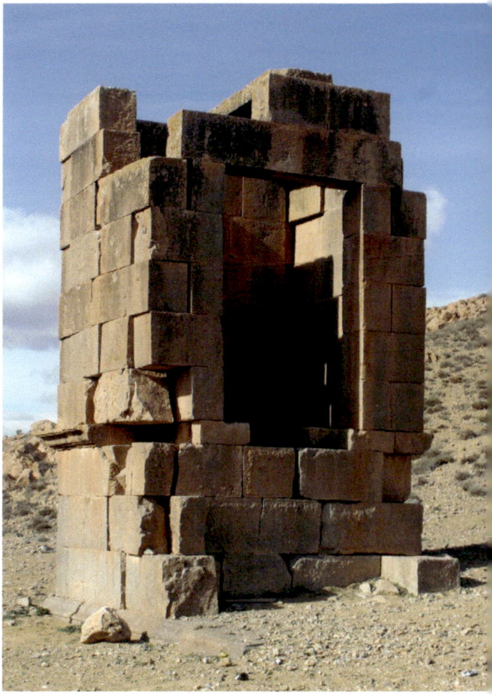

Fig. 183 (right). Lambaesis: tower tomb in the N Necropolis.

village of Tazoult (shown at the LH edge of the plan in fig. 176) is still well preserved, but disfigured by corrugated iron sheeting and rubbish; it takes the form of a high square plinth, above which is an *aedicula*, the door-frame of which is decorated with cornices and festoons. Across the valley to the N of the Hadrianic base, two plainer tower-tombs are still prominent on the opposing hillside (see fig. 183). Another such tomb has a rather poignant history. Satellite imagery (typically as publicly available through Google Earth) shows clear traces of a road leading due N from the Hadrianic base in the direction of Cirta, a few metres to the W of a modern farm track. Precisely three kilometres to the N of the *porta praetoria*, and next to the ancient road, stood a tomb with a pyramidal apex, commemorating T. Flavius Maximus, prefect of the *Legio III Augusta* in the Severan period. In 1849, Colonel Jean-Luc Carbuccia arrived at *Lambaesis* at the head of the Second Regiment of the Foreign Legion, entrusted with the 'pacification' of the region. An aesthete and man of letters, Carbuccia had a passion for local history; he informed himself on how archaeological excavations should be carried out, and soon set his men to work for this purpose. 'I could have built a town,' he wrote. 'I had in my regiment architects, engineers and artists. When I had need of a scholar, a writer or a painter, I sent for one, and the following morning the sergeant-majors would offer me ten names instead of one.' Finding the tomb of Maximus, previously intact but now threatening collapse after an earthquake, he gave orders for the monument to be restored, then filed past the tomb of this ancient brother-at-arms at the head of his troops and paid due military honours to this soldier of Rome on behalf of the soldiers of France. Fig. 184 reproduces the drawing of the re-erected tomb which Colonel Carbuccia submitted to the *Revue Archéologique* in 1850. In the context of Carbuccia's evident association of the military presence of the French in the Aurès with that of an earlier (European) occupying power, we may note the work of another academic, M. Dureau de la Malle, who translated and compressed into a very small format the best ancient sources for the use of the military, so that 'the soldier, the NCO, the junior or senior officer' could put the book in his bag and take note of what Sallust, Tacitus, Ammianus Marcellinus or Procopius had to say about the 'determination and prudent tenacity of the Romans in the conquest of Africa' (*Manuel Algérien*, 1852). The final footnote to this story, however, is that in 1983, someone pushed over the tomb once more. The tumbled blocks now remain on site in a heap, with half of the original Latin inscription visible (but none of the added French one). The tomb could presumably be restored once again, but to do so in this remote spot would hardly be worth the expense.

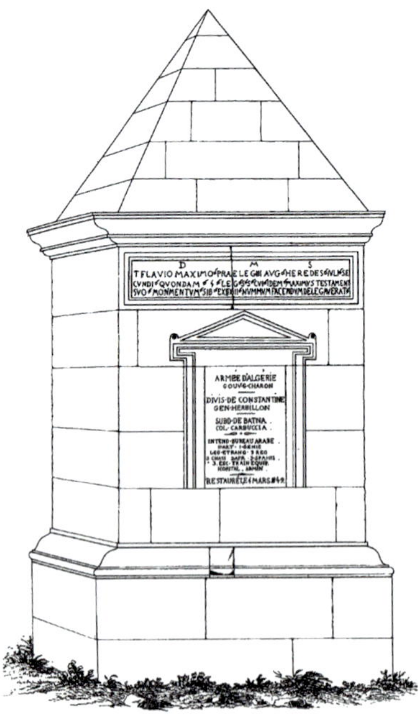

Fig. 184. Lambaesis: drawing of the tomb of T. Flavius Maximus as reconstructed in 1849.

5. Arch of Septimius Severus

To the S of a small Byzantine fort, which was much reduced by developers in the early twentieth century, stands a triumphal arch which was built by the legion in the reign of Septimius Severus (fig. 185). It is a structure of three bays, each framed by pilasters and columns. This monumental gate marked the edge of the ancient city of *Lambaesis*, a kilometre away from the big Hadrianic military base. Beside the arch, and now barely visible, was a semi-circular public latrine.

6. Public baths

Close to the arch are substantial upstanding remains of a bath complex, which has not been fully excavated. It has yielded a number of mosaics.

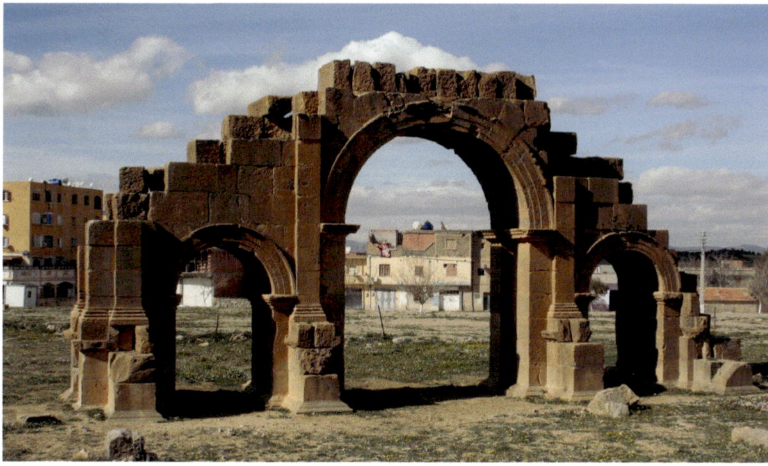

Fig. 185. Lambaesis: Arch of Septimius Severus.

THE UPPER SITE

7. Sanctuary and temple of Aesculapius

The sanctuary of Aesculapius, or Asklepieion, takes the form of a long irregular esplanade, closed at the E end by a propylaeum and at the W end by the temple itself and two linked shrines (see fig. 187). On the N edge of this complex was the camp of Titus, and at the E end of the sanctuary, in a possibly unique arrangement, access to the S gate of the camp was provided by means of a vaulted subway which passed beneath the propylaeum. This was a rectangular room entered on its S side from a paved court next to the road and opening on the W side into the sanctuary. On the N side of the sanctuary, and partly overlying the corner of the military camp, were eight small shrines dedicated to different local divinities; an extensive array of buildings on the S side (not fully published) include bath complexes, a curative establishment (connected with Aesculapius), houses and a Mithraeum.

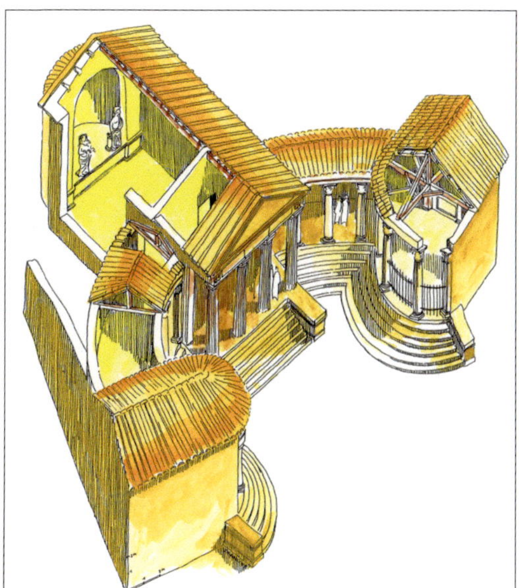

Fig. 186. Lambaesis: axonometric reconstruction of the Temple of Aesculapius by J.-M. Gassend.

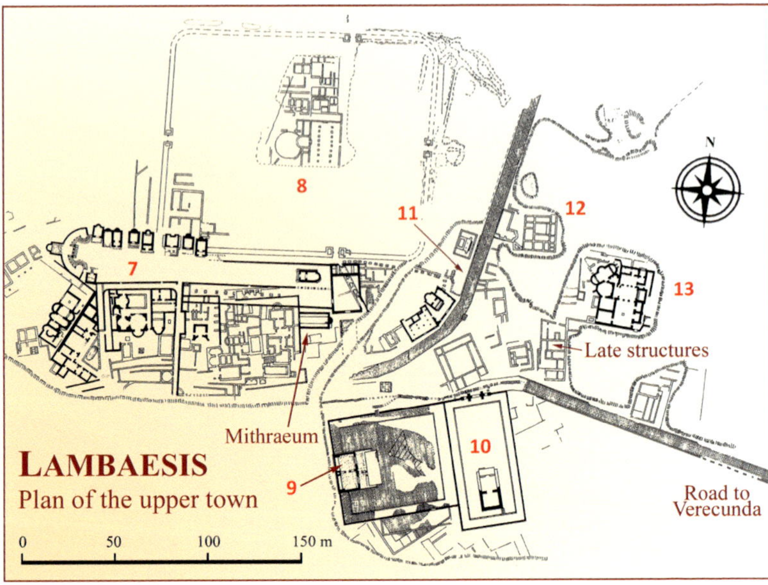

Fig. 187. Lambaesis: plan of the upper town.

7. *Sanctuary of Aesculapius*
8. *Camp of Titus*
9. *Capitolium*
10. *Unidentified temple*
11. *Septizonium*
12. *'Oilery'*
13. *Thermes des Chasseurs*

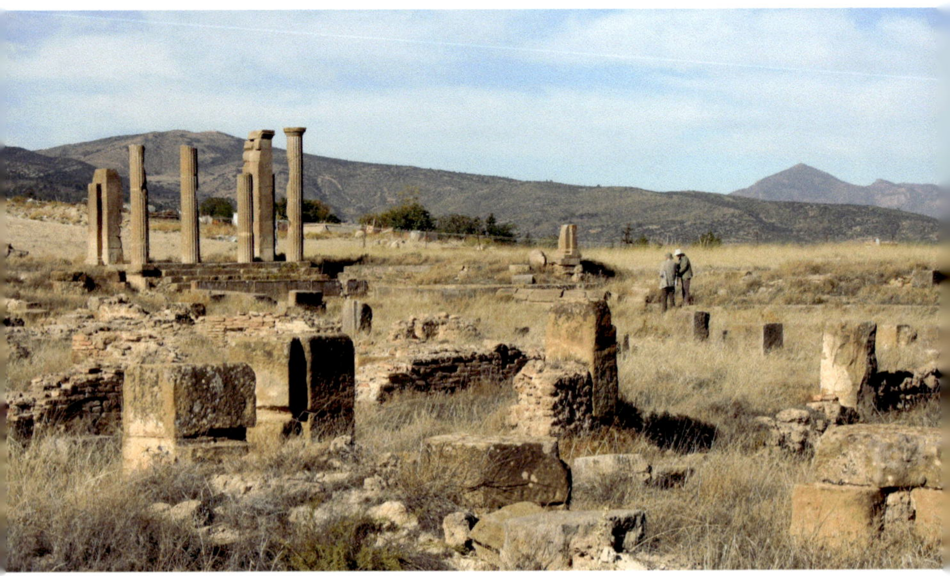

Fig. 188. Lambaesis: the Temple of Aesculapius.

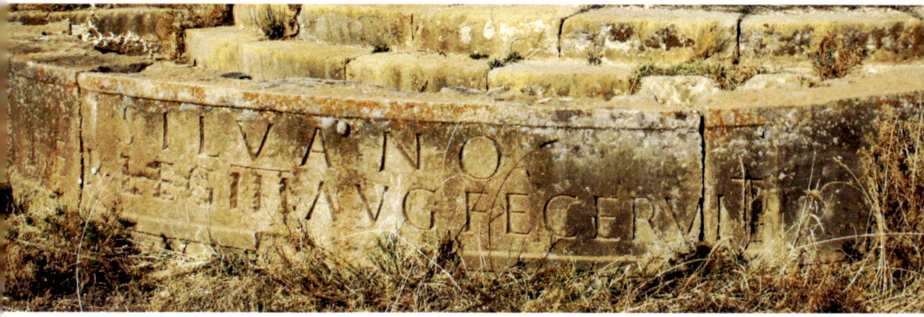

Fig. 189. Lambaesis: dedication of the shrine of Silvanus in the Sanctuary of Aesculapius, with the name of the Third Legion partially obliterated following its damnatio memoriae.

The temple itself is now reduced to its foundations, apart from the partly restored columns of its porch, but is nonetheless of considerable architectural interest (see figs. 186, 188). It was of the Doric order and dedicated by the legate of the *Legio III Augusta* in 162 to the worship of Aesculapius and Salus (*Hygeia*, the personification of Health). It was of conventional rectangular prostyle type, with a cella paved in red marble, but it was linked in baroque fashion to two flanking chapels. The linking porticoes were concave and the fronts of the chapels convex, in a clever play of intersecting curves. It may be compared to the *nymphaeum* of Herodes Atticus at Olympia, or to the temple at Zaghouan in Tunisia, which channelled the headwaters of the aqueduct which supplied Carthage. The cult statues (in the *Lambaesis* museum) stood on a tribune in the apse of the temple; the southern chapel was dedicated to *Jupiter Valens* ('valiant'), while the northern one was dedicated to Silvanus, a god of woodland associated with the Third Legion. The inscribed architraves from all three shrines now lie on the ground in front of them: note on that dedicated to Silvanus the half-hearted attempt to erase the name of the legion, following its *damnatio memoriae* (fig. 189).

Two further rectangular buildings adjoined those already described. That on the N was an adjunct to the temple, housing offerings; that on the S was a little shrine, dedicated perhaps to the *Aquae Sinuessanae*, the hot springs of Sinuessa in Italy (reported by Pliny to cure sterility in women and folly in men!). At the opposite end of the esplanade, just inside the propylaeum, are the foundations of a temple to Mercury.

The worship of Aesculapius

Two practices in particular were typical of *Asklepieia*: incubation and hydrotherapy. Devotees/patients would spend the night within the sanctuary – even in the temple itself – and their dreams would then be interpreted by the priest-physicians of the cult in order to make a diagnosis and determine a cure. The cure would take the form of dieting, fasting, emetics, bleeding and (mainly) baths of various kinds. As a complement to the medical care offered by the camp hospital, based on the rational principles of Galen, the temple of Aesculapius would offer patients divine help, by means of therapies whose benefits we would now consider to be solely psychological.

8. Camp of Titus

This camp represents the first base of the legion in this part of Numidia (see fig.187). Built between 1st July and 13th September 81 (under Titus), the camp occupies an area of 148 x 120 m. Three of the shrines associated with the sanctuary of Aesculapius encroach upon its SW corner. The enclosing wall was 2.60 m thick, composed of two faces of uncut stones with a fill of earth and rubble in between. There were two gates in the centres of the short sides and two others one third of the way along each of the longer sides. In the centre of the camp, several poorly-preserved buildings have been identified: a basilical hall (22.4 x 16.1 m) resulting from a transformation of the *principia* in the third century, some associated rooms, some barrack-buildings and a circular court 14 m in diameter which seems to be very late, and possibly even medieval.

This first camp was used for military purposes at least until the third century, despite the construction of the great fortress on lower ground and the development of civil and religious buildings around it. It is not known when the occupation of the earlier base came to an end, but a cemetery of the fourth century has been identified close to the W gate, and pottery found on the site extends as late as the sixth century.

9. Capitolium

An inscription tells us that this most unusual temple was shared between the Capitoline Triad and the *Genius* of the Colony. It stands on a high podium at the rear of a spacious porticoed precinct (fig. 190). It was built in 246 and restored in 346–7. There were eight columns across the façade. The *cella* was divided into two compartments, each with a niche for a statue, presumably corresponding

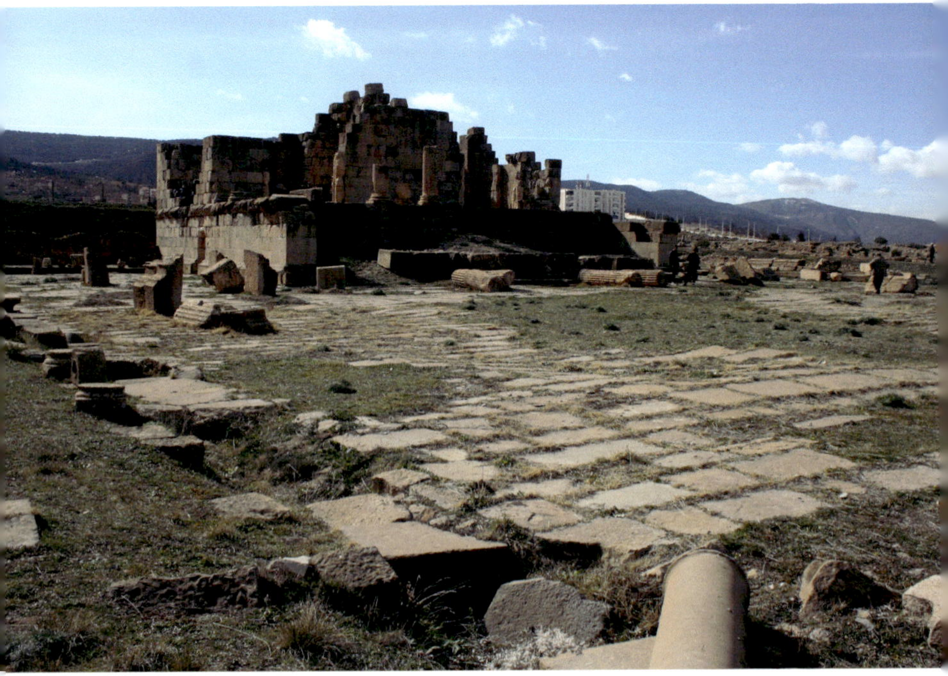

Fig. 190. Lambaesis: the Capitolium.

to the double dedication. Within the podium, and accessed at ground-level, are strong-rooms with vaults of concrete rubble.

There must have been a tall building or monument on the S side of the temple precinct, the shadow of which served as a gnomon for the sundial markings inscribed on the paving (like those in the forum at Thamugadi: see p. 192).

The forum of *Lambaesis* has not yet been identified and the lack of uniformity in the alignments of streets and buildings in this area gives no clue; but the number of official dedications found in the vicinity of the Capitolium suggests that it cannot have been far away. The space at the intersection of the road from the lower town and that from *Verecunda* may, however – as at *Cuicul* – have assumed the role of a forum in the third century. (Since *Lambaesis* started life exclusively as a military base, it would not initially have required a forum.)

10. Unidentified temple

Only the foundations of this temple remain, standing in a porticoed precinct and facing N for reasons unknown. (Greek and Roman temples faced E if not constrained by other reasons, so that the rising sun might shine into the *cella*.) It has been suggested that, if the precinct of the Capitolium served as a forum, this building may have served as a *curia*.

11. Septizonium

This was a monumental fountain in front of a header tank, composed of a hemicycle between two wings, flowing down into three basins and decorated with seven niches, with marble ornament and fluted columns. Unfortunately, little of it remains, though it belongs to a style of monument to be found at Lepcis Magna in Libya, Jerash in Jordan and – primarily – in Rome itself where Septimius Severus built such a monument (also called *Septizonium*) at the end of the *Circus Maximus*.

12. 'Oilery'

The irregularity of the masonry shows this to have been a late structure, built with re-used materials. The pressing installation (more probably for wine than for oil) succeeded a temple of unknown dedication.

13. Thermes des Chasseurs

This bath complex is so-named because it was excavated in 1880–81 by the officers of the French Chasseurs (light cavalry). It is constructed largely of brick, and many of these are stamped with the name of the Third Legion.

To the E of these baths, on the road towards *Verecunda* and Thamugadi, are two further monumental arches: the first, of three bays, was constructed of reused materials (therefore late?), while the second, with a single opening, was built in the reign of Commodus. Five kilometres further to the SE, between the modern road and the French colonial estate at Markouna, a triumphal arch marks the entrance to *Verecunda*. This was built in 172, under Marcus Aurelius, and its opening was originally framed by engaged columns on either side.

14. Aqueduct

At the beginning of the twentieth century, six arches of an aqueduct were still visible 300 m to the S of the Sanctuary of Aesculapius; the remains are now very fragmentary, with only one arch surviving. This brought water to the city from a nearby source at Aïn Drinn, the *aquae alexandrianae;* it would have fed the *Septizonium* (behind which is a row of piers which supported the conduit). Another aqueduct brought water from Ain Boubennana to the lower city.

15. Temple of Neptune

Only some fallen columns and a few terrace walls which levelled up the sloping ground remain of this temple, built close to the spring of Aïn Drinn at the beginning of the second century. An inscription indicates that the cult of Neptune was here associated with the spring. Nearby, a cistern received the water from this source, and possibly from other contributory springs.

FURTHER AFIELD

The exercise-ground

Two kilometres to the WNW of the Hadrianic base lies a feature which was formerly interpreted as a camp for auxiliaries, but which is now considered to have been an exercise-ground 200 m square, enclosed by a boundary of dry stone walling (fig. 191). This feature is not now perceptible on the ground, but the outline in the fields can still be made out on satellite imagery such as *Google Earth*, with a road leading from the entrance on the E side directly towards the Hadrianic base. The perimeter was pierced by two entrances, and was provided internally with fourteen apsidal basins: one in each corner and ten others regularly spaced around the walls. These vessels probably served as drinking-troughs for the horses and/or as sources of water for the various needs of the soldiers. In the centre of the exercise-ground where the cohorts were put through their paces, there was a platform 10 m square surmounted by a column. This was erected in 128 to commemorate the visit of the emperor Hadrian, but would have served also as a podium for the military instructors. The text of Hadrian's address to the army of Africa was inscribed on the pilasters at the corners of the plinth. Roughly one quarter of this text has been found (now in store in the National Museum in Algiers), but this is sufficient to tell us that Hadrian was here on 1st July 128 and that he briefly recounted the previous fifty years' history of the legion. He watched the manoeuvres of the infantry, and then of the cavalry of the *Legio III Augusta* under the command of the legate Q. Fabius Catullinus and congratulated those who had been promoted. We learn also that Hadrian was later at Zarai to inspect another cohort and that between the 12th and 13th July he was at an unnamed garrison to inspect an *ala* of Pannonians and the VIth mounted cohort of the Commagenians. (See the quotation at the head of this section, p. 169.)

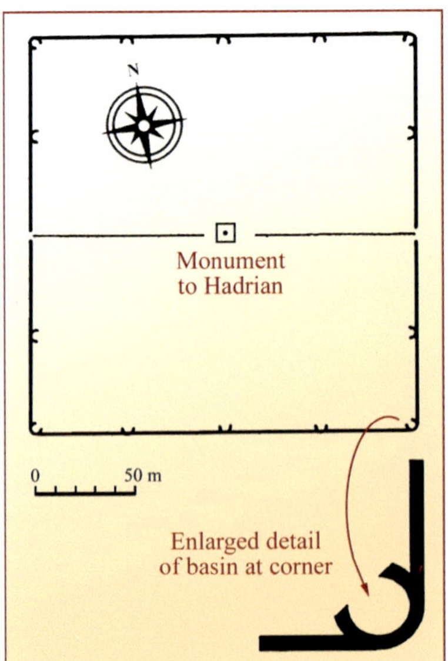

Fig. 191. Lambaesis: plan of the exercise-ground.

MUSEUM

The little museum in the centre of Tazoult should certainly not be underestimated. It is a small building in a poor state of repair, with a crowded *jardin épigraphique* in front of it; its replacement with a new building is planned, but still awaited. The inscriptions which fill the little garden and are fixed to the wall of the museum, particularly the various lists of legionaries and of military units, are a fundamental source for our knowledge of the Roman army in Africa in the third century. (See fig. 192.)

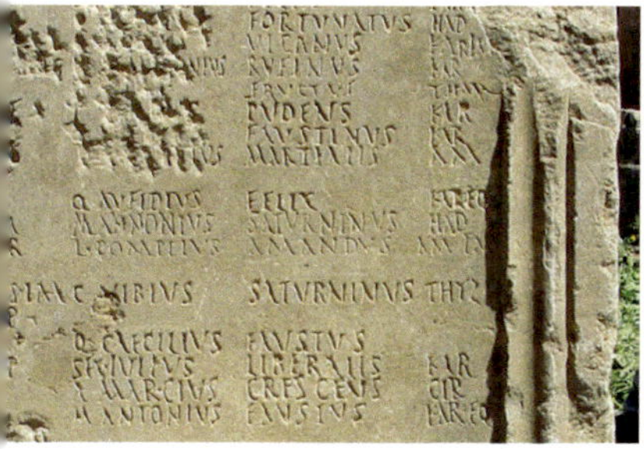

Fig. 192. Lambaesis Museum. Detail of a list of soldiers. Origins detectable here are Kar(thago), Had(rumetum), Thys(drus) and Cir(ta). Some names have been deliberately erased.

Within the building, the statues of Aesculapius and Hygeia from the *Asklepieion* are unmissable. There are also small objects of interest in cases: a cornucopia in gilded bronze and a slave collar of which the rivets are still in place (implying that the wearer died in chains). There are also examples of the thousands of slingshots which were found in the armouries of the *principia* at the Hadrianic base.

Statuary

Statue of Aesculapius. This work, 2.27 m high, was intended to be seen only from the front, and is barely roughed out at the back. Aesculapius is shown standing beside a round document box (*capsa*) with its straps, containing various scrolls (*volumina*). In his left hand he held a staff around which a snake was entwined. Derived from an original of the fourth century BC, this bastardised representation seems to belong to a typical African version of a Hellenistic model.

Statue of Hygeia/Salus. Carved in the same marble as Aesculapius and to the same scale, this statue (missing its head) is a close copy of the Hygeia from Ostia in the Kassel museum. Often reproduced in the African provinces, this example suffers, like Aesculapius, from obvious defects in execution.

Mosaics

During the existence of the huge military base, many of its senior officers lived in wealthy residences outside the forts; some very fine mosaics belonging to these have been found in various locations. Two of these, formerly set into the wall of the museum, have been removed and set on modern substrates: they are described below. Yet others derive from a villa which was the subject of a rescue excavation in recent years (close to the main road, to the NE of the Hadrianic base) and they remain in crates awaiting a suitable environment for display.

Nereids and marine monsters. At the time of writing, this magnificent mosaic is housed temporarily in the museum at Timgad and is not on public display. It portrays three nereids, attended by *erotes*, sitting on marine monsters: a marine tiger, a marine panther and a *ketos* – the sea serpent fought by Herakles and Perseus – for the third. The horizon line is visible behind them. The mosaic includes an inscription in Greek beneath the panther, reading ΑΣΠΑΣΙΟΥ Κ[ΕΤ]Η ('The monsters of Aspasios'). It has been suggested that this does not represent the signature of the mosaicist, as was first thought to have been the case, but that it is more probably a reference to the painter whose work the mosaicist has copied. This panel, of the very highest quality, is the largest known example of *opus vermiculatum*, mosaic executed in tesserae that are only between 2 mm and 5 mm across. It has nothing in common with later mosaics in the region, and was surely the work of travelling craftsmen. (Mid second century.)

The nymph Cyrene. The nymph who was loved by Apollo is shown seated in front of a tree and a building with a slit window (fig. 193). She holds a flagon in her left hand (signifying the sacred spring of Cyrene?) and a reed in her right. To the right, only the

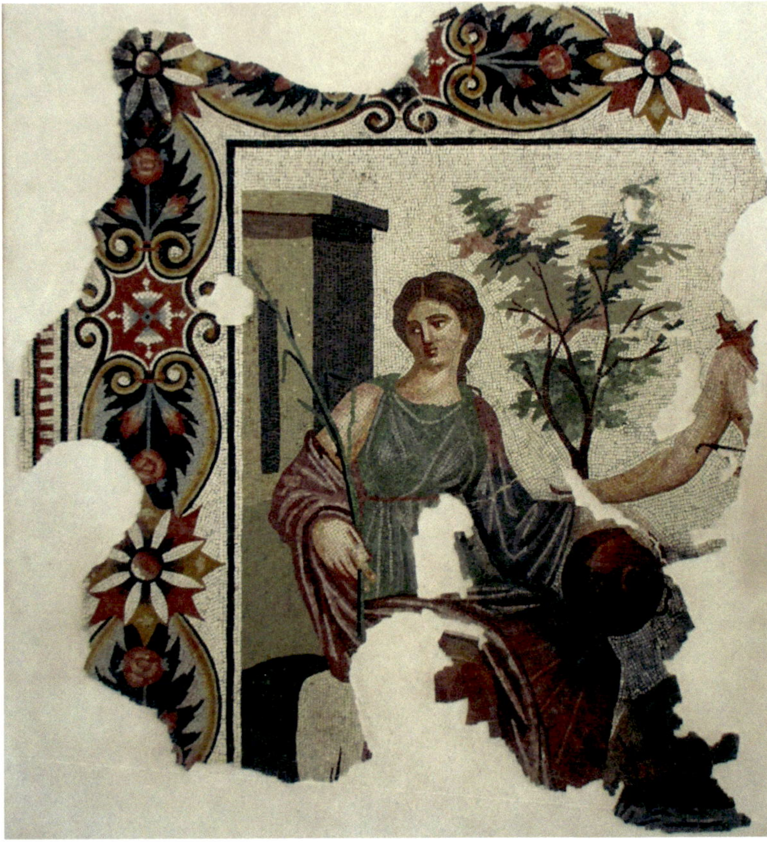

Fig. 193. Lambaesis Museum. Mosaic of Apollo and Cyrene.

naked arm of Apollo is preserved, though he is identifiable from the quiver at his shoulder. This panel (currently in the museum at Tazoult) is of similar quality to the Mosaic of the Nereids described above. It was found in the same house and was perhaps made by the same craftsmen. In this case, however, part of the border is preserved, and its patterns of hearts, octagons and floral motifs in bold colours is typical of the mosaics of the third century in southern Numidia. (Second or third century.)

THAMUGADI (Timgad)

The Emperor Caesar Nerva Trajan Augustus Germanicus, son of the Divine Nerva, High Pontiff, holding the Tribunician power for the fourth time, Consul for the third time, Father of the Country, founded the Colonia Marciana Trajana of Thamugadi, through the efforts of the Third Augustan Legion (under the command of) L. Munatius Gallus, Imperial Propraetorian Legate.

Dedication marking the founding of the city, AD 100

Situated in the heart of a savage landscape but conforming to a relentless geometry, the ruins of Thamugadi present a curious contrast: they evoke incontestably the grandeur and power of Rome while, on the other hand, the rarity of any mention in ancient sources demonstrate that this was scarcely more than a minor town with almost no impact upon history. 'It was a little town,' wrote C. Courtois in an earlier guidebook, 'like many others in the empire where veterans were willingly settled but which were never distinguished by any economic activity of consequence or stirred by any intellectual movement. To judge by what we know of it, life was entirely ordinary: only human ambition occasionally disturbed its tranquillity.'

The city is sited in a narrow plain at a mean altitude of 1,000 m; together with others such as Lambaesis (p. 169), Diana Veteranorum (p. 222) or Mascula (Khenchela: see p. 157), it formed part of a network of military settlements responsible for keeping watch on and containing the mountain people of the Aurès. These resisted Roman influence and could not easily be absorbed; they therefore constituted a threat to the development of the region. The location of the settlement was carefully chosen: well supplied with water and with building stone and surrounded by fertile lands, Thamugadi constituted a strategic node at the outlet of the routes through the mountains and an important link in the main road between Theveste and Lambaesis. These qualities have persuaded certain historians that Thamugadi might initially have been a provisional camp for the Third Legion before the unit was transferred definitively to Lambaesis towards the end of the first century; however, this hypothesis, which rests only on the presence of a poorly dated defensive circuit, remains highly speculative.

The official foundation therefore dates from the intervention of Trajan in 100 (quoted at the head of this section), with the settlement of a relatively small number of veterans. From the beginning, the regular layout and purely functional architecture of the town bore the hallmarks of the army. The army was deployed to carry out the works and applied the strictest rules of layout that were in current use for military camps. The regular grid, inscribed in a square with sides of 1,200 ft (355 m), was divided into four by two intersecting main streets which run N–S (*cardo maximus*) and E–W (*decumanus maximus*). The squares thus defined were each further subdivided into 36 blocks by secondary streets intersecting at right-angles, except that the surveyors reserved some larger spaces for public facilities, such as the forum and the theatre. (The latter made use of a convenient hillock, which involved some concession in the precision of the over-all layout.) During the second century, the rise in population (which has been estimated to have reached a maximum of 15,000) led to a quadrupling of the built-up area: the 12 ha of the original settlement

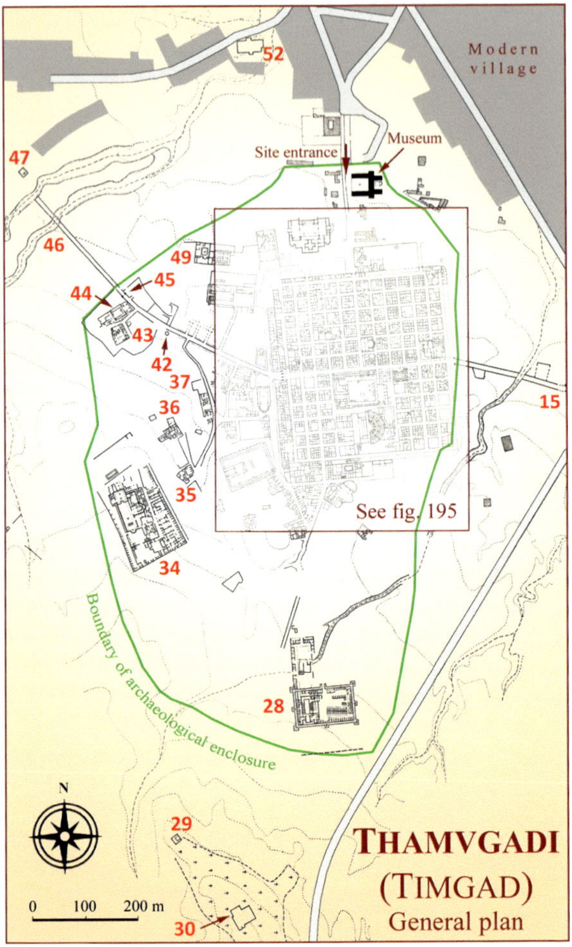

Fig. 194. Thamugadi: general plan of the site.

Key to figs. 194 and 195. Items marked with an asterisk are shown only on fig. 194.

1. *North Gate*
2. *Small North Baths*
3. *House and chapel*
4. *Public library*
5. *Shops on the decumanus maximus*
6. *Public latrine*
7. *Forum*
8. *Theatre*
9. *Theatre shrines*
10. *Temple of Mercury?*
11. *House of the Raised Flower-Beds*
12. *East Market*
13. *Small East Baths*
14. *Mascula Gate*
15.* *Triumphal arch*
16. *Great East Baths*
17. *North-East Baths*
18. *House of Corfidius Crementius*
19. *House of L. Julius Januarius*
20. *Arch 'of Trajan'*
21. *House of the Piscina*
22. *Small Central Baths*
23. *House of Sertius*
24. *House of the Hermaphroditus*
25. *'Industrial quarter'*
26. *Great South Baths*

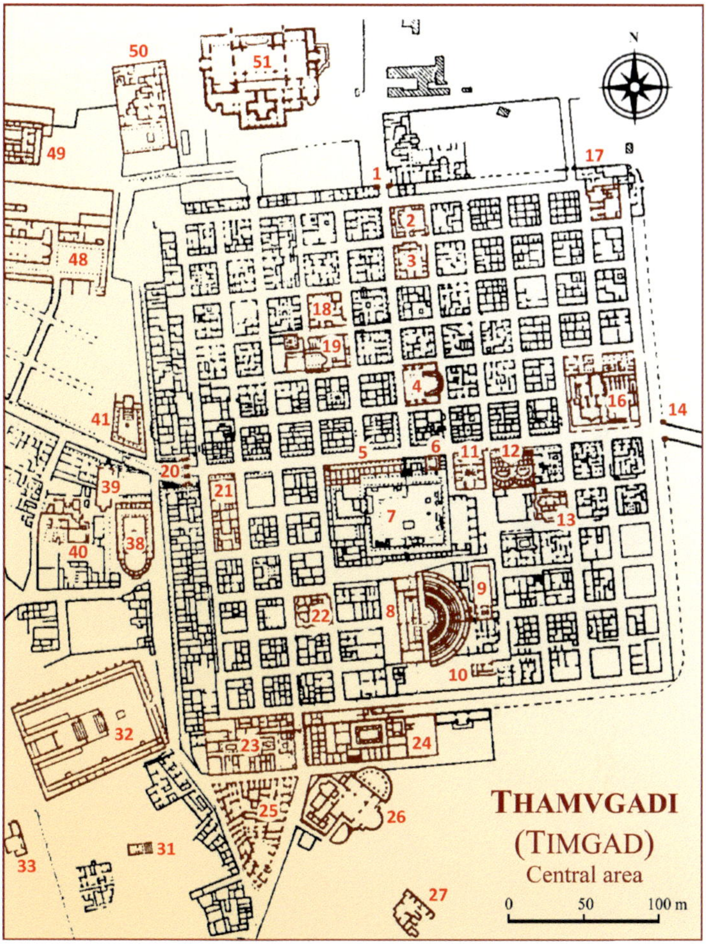

Fig. 195. Thamugadi: plan of the central area.

27. *Small South Baths*
28.* *Byzantine fortress*
29.* *Chapel*
30.* *Christian church and necropolis*
31. *Temple*
32. *Capitolium*
33. *Byzantine church*
34.* *Donatist episcopal quarter*
35.* *Capitolium Baths*
36.* *West Baths*
37.* *Hostelry?*
38. *Market of Sertius*
39. *Textile market*
40. *Bath building*
41. *Temple to the Genius of the Colony*
42.* *Fountain of Liberalis*
43.* *North-West Baths*
44.* *Private house*
45.* *Triumphal arch*
46.* *Pagan necropolis*
47.* *Church*
48. *Church complex*
49. *Private house*
50. *Baths of the Philadelphi*
51. *Great North Baths*
52.* *Temple of Saturn*

became around 50 ha, taking in the suburbs which grew up along the roads leading out of town. These new districts did not of course conform to the original layout, having grown organically in response to local needs rather than according to a predetermined plan.

The history of Thamugadi in the Christian era is similar to that of plenty of other African cities: a community well-established in the third century with a bishop at its head, persecuted and martyred under Diocletian, following which it was divided by the emergence of the Donatist schism. This sect was particularly prosperous at Thamugadi, where a schismatic Council was held in 397; its bishops were eminent

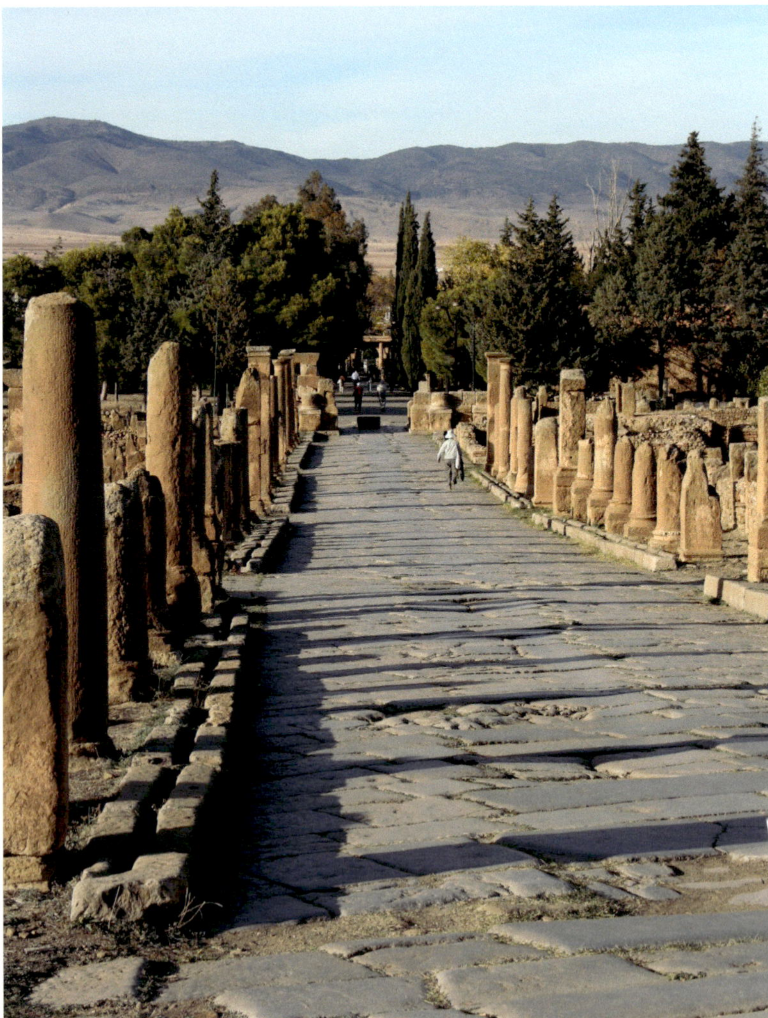

Fig. 196. Thamugadi: the cardo maximus, *looking from the Forum towards the N Gate.*

figures in the movement. Optatus was considered to be the leader of the Donatists at the end of the fourth century, and his successor Gaudentius disputed with Saint Augustine.

The historian Procopius tells us that, at the end of the fifth century, the mountain people of the Aurès ('Moors') destroyed the city and depopulated it. But Thamugadi did not disappear completely. The Byzantines built themselves a fortress, outside the former town but enclosing the all-important water supply, in the time of Justinian, and the continued occupation of the original site is attested through the construction of a chapel (19) in the mid seventh century. For how long after that anyone was living there, it is now impossible to say. The early excavators swept away without record any physical traces of post-Roman occupation in their determination to reveal the 'glory' of the Roman past; nor did they collect the modest artefacts that might have provided relevant evidence of date.

EXPLORING THE SITE

1. North Gate

Only the foundations of this gate, with two lateral guardrooms, remain. On the ground beside the gate, however, have been placed the surviving parts of the inscription which originally stood above it in 100, announcing the foundation of the colony (quoted at the head of this section). There was also a possible refurbishment in 159. This gate, which faced the road from Cirta, also marked the beginning of the *cardo maximus*, 180 m long and 5 m wide, leading to the forum (see fig. 196). The street was lined with porticoes and paved with slabs of bluish limestone, set at an angle for the practical purpose of reducing the effect of cartwheels sliding into the joints and creating deep ruts. Note the evident presence of a drain running down the centre, with occasional gratings and inspection holes.

Outside the gate, on the E side, is an array of late buildings which include two rooms with apses, an oilery and walls capped with lines of stone mangers.

2. Small North Baths

One of the fourteen public bathing establishments which have been identified in the city.

3. House and chapel

Amongst the hundred or so private houses which have been excavated at Thamugadi, this one is of note because it was reused in a late period as a church. Originally, it was equipped with private baths.

4. Public library

Built in the fourth century on the site of a pre-existing private house, this library and the famous Library of Celsus at Ephesus are the only Roman buildings of the kind

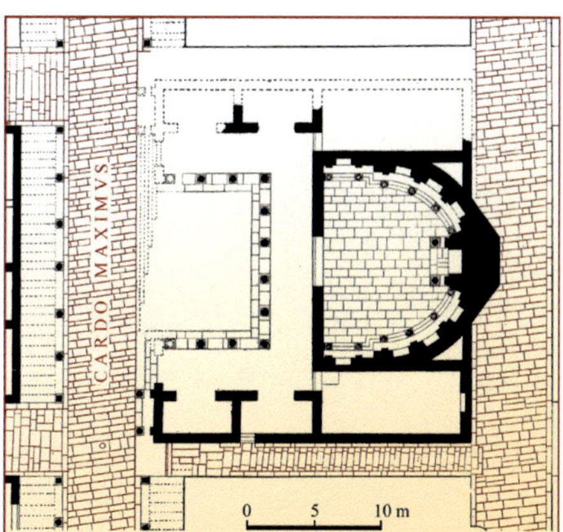

Fig. 197. Thamugadi: plan of the public library.

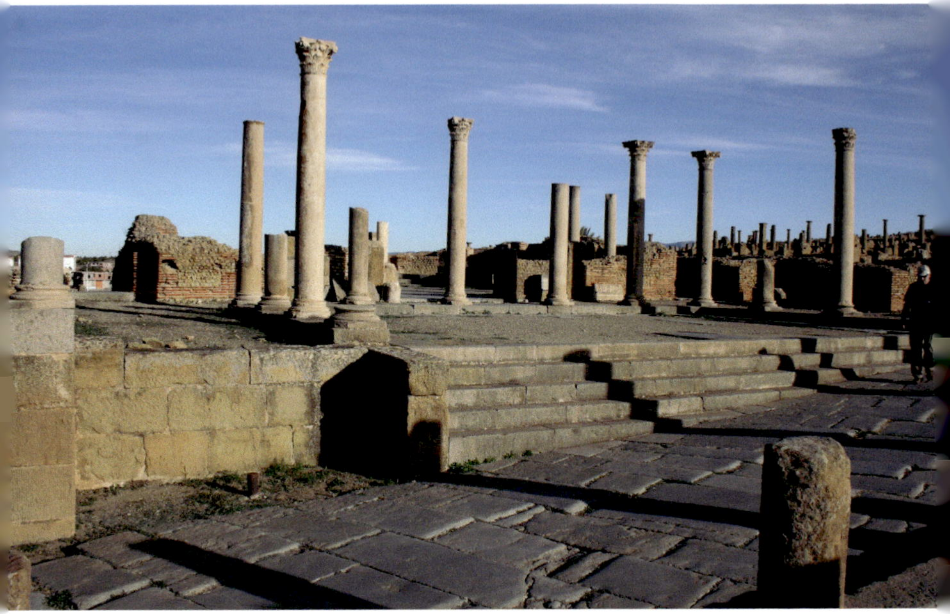

Fig. 198. Thamugadi: the public library.

to have been identified. A tapering flight of steps (fig. 198) led from the *cardo* into a courtyard bordered by porticoes on three sides. A game marked out on the portico stylobate and ancient graffiti on the columns show that not everyone came here to read! There were two offices or reading rooms on either side of the courtyard, while the books were stored in a large semi-circular room beyond (12 m in diameter), where pilasters and engaged columns framed a succession of recesses in a wall which was formerly veneered in white and green marble. It was on shelves in these cupboards that the books resided; they were reached by three steps up around the edge of the room. The scrolls (*volumina*) or bound *codices* were consulted on tables. The central niche, larger and framed between spirally-fluted columns housed a statue of Minerva – appropriately, as Goddess of Learning. The solidity of the walls is a clear indication that this room must have been roofed with a semi-dome.

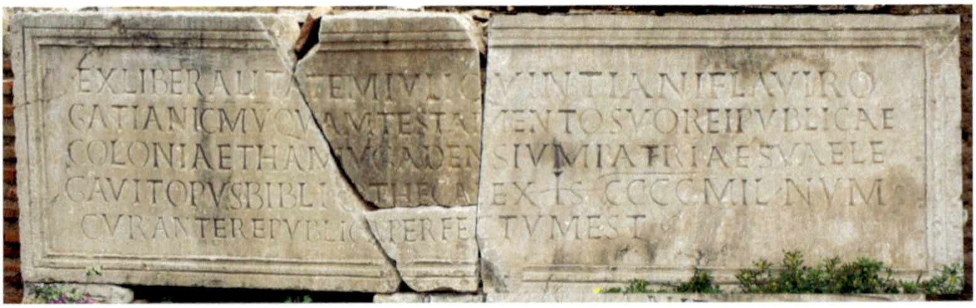

Fig. 199. Thamugadi: composite photograph of the inscription recording the building of the library.

The inscription which would once have surmounted the entrance to this building now lies against the rear wall of the courtyard (fig. 199): it records that M. Quintianus Flavius Rogatianus left the sum of 400,000 sesterces in his will for its construction.

5. Shops on the *decumanus maximus*

One block beyond the library, one meets the main E–W thoroughfare of the original settlement, also colonnaded, on the further side of which lies the Forum. The forum portico was lined on the N side by small lock-up shops, and the forum frontage was terminated at either end by a fountain.

6. Public latrine

A very well preserved public latrine may be seen at the NE corner of the forum, accessed from the *decumanus* (fig. 201). The 24 stone seats are separated at intervals by armrests carved in the form of dolphins. Not only was there a drain beneath the latrine to carry away the waste, but another essential, well seen here, is the provision of clean water, so that users could clean themselves. The water flowed from a fountain on the N side, into a channel which ran around the room in front of the seats, and finally emptied into the drain.

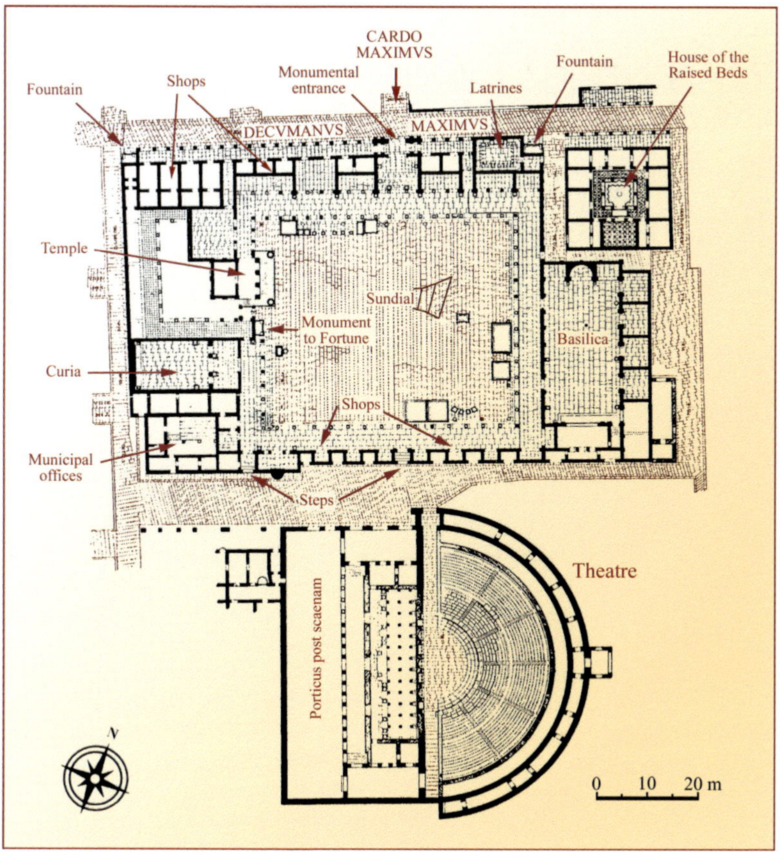

Fig. 200. Thamugadi: plan of the forum area.

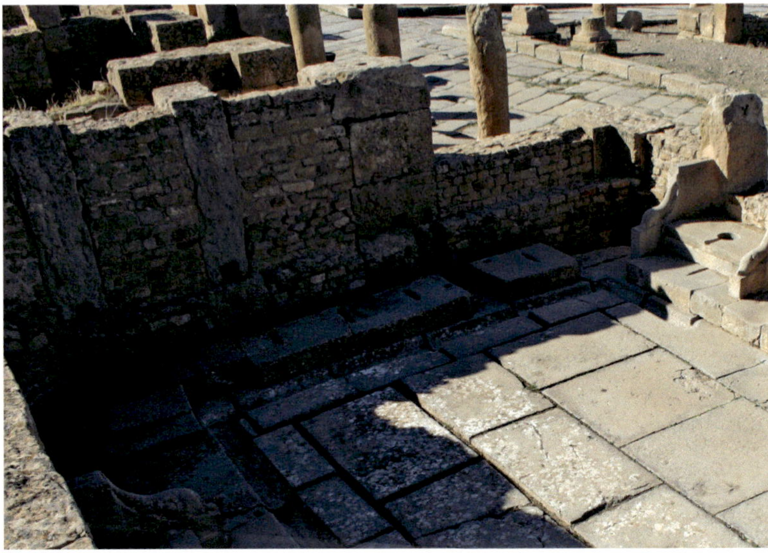

Fig. 201. Thamugadi: public latrine next to the Forum.

7. Forum

The *cardo maximus* comes to an end at a monumental entrance, beyond which was a wide flight of twelve steps decorated with statues, leading directly into the forum (figs. 200, 203). This vast square (50 × 43 m), paved with blue limestone, was surrounded on all four sides by Corinthian colonnades raised two steps above the central area. Laid out when the colony was founded, under Trajan, the construction of the forum took place progressively during the first half of the second century. Notice on the paving of the central area the markings of a huge sun-dial, based presumably on a shadow cast by a prominent building on the S side. The long curving lines trace out the course of the tip of the shadow at the summer and winter solstices, while the hours (numbered) are marked by the straight lines between them. Various games have also been chiselled into the paving of the steps or the porticoes, including a graffito crudely carved on the top step of the N portico (not far from the latrine, fig. 202): *venari lavari ludere ridere occ est vivere* – 'To hunt, to go to the bath, to play, to laugh, this is to live!' – a sentiment which was perhaps inspired by Aristippus of Cyrene, but which plenty of the empire's citizens would have subscribed to.

The N portico of the Forum is lined with rooms which are more likely to have been offices (public or private) rather than shops. The W side was occupied by a temple of unknown dedication, a building dedicated to Fortune and the *curia*. The small temple (7.0 x 4.5 m) stood upon a vaulted basement which, like the Temple of Saturn in Rome, may have housed the treasure of the colony. In front of this building was a tetrastyle portico and a platform for orators. At either end of this platform, hexagonal bases supported a pair of Victories, celebrating the triumph of the emperor Trajan over the Parthians. The dedication tells us that these statues had been given in his will by M. Annius, a former centurion of the legion at Lambaesis. Behind the podium of the temple, there was a garden, enclosed on three sides by a portico paved with mosaics. At a subsequent date, the N side of this complex was subsumed by a large paved hall, opening onto the forum portico.

Beyond a narrow vestibule and a short flight of steps, one entered the *curia* through a three-bay opening framed by two columns. The rectangular hall (14.4 x 9.8 m) was veneered in grey marble and had a dais of three steps at its W end. Four statues, of which the bases remain in position, decorated the building. Two of them flanked the central doorway: these portrayed the emperor Trajan, with a dedication indicating that the *curia* was completed in 116/7, and 'Concord of the order of decurions', that is to say the entity responsible for good relations between the members of the local senate. In this building was found the Album of Timgad, a long inscription of the year 365 in which are listed in order all the 263 decurions of that time. It includes 36 *flamines perpetui*, priests of the imperial cult who, well into the Christian era, presumably now had purely secular and municipal responsibilities.

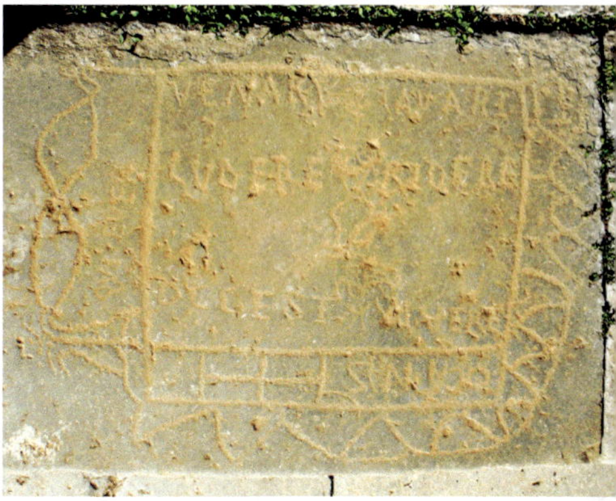

Fig. 202. Thamugadi: graffito in the N forum portico.

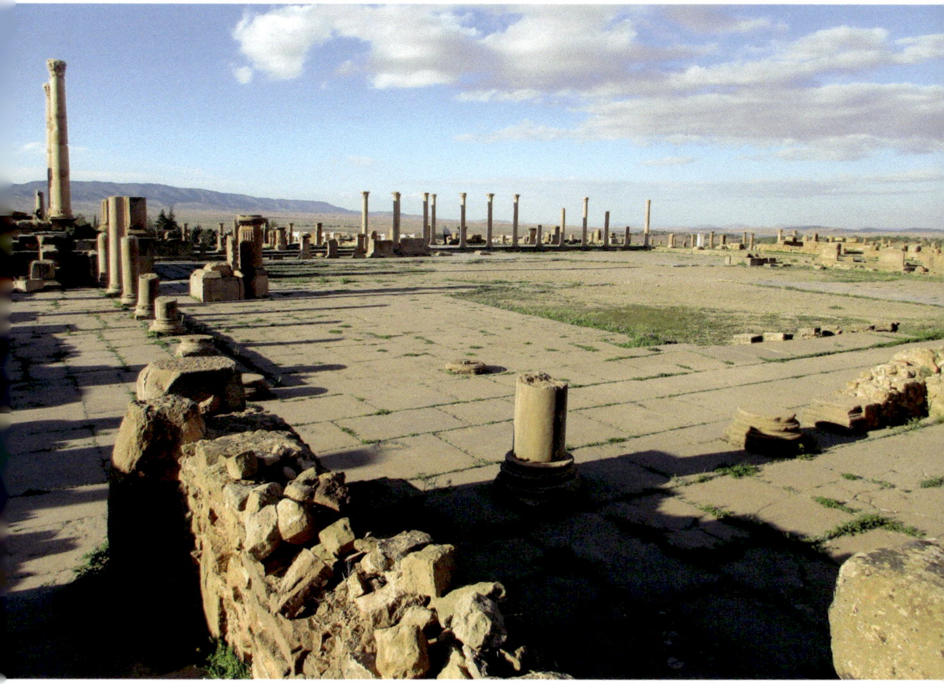

Fig. 203. Thamugadi: the Forum from the SW corner.

The Curia

This word, of obscure origin, initially designated a sector of the population of Rome, and then the place where the senate met to pass legislation. As Rome organised its empire, cities were given an administrative structure composed of a general assembly (the *comitia*, where the citizen body could exercise its political rights) and a representative assembly, equivalent to our town council, known variously as the *curia*, local senate or *ordo* of decurions. The responsibilities of this body were very wide, extending to local legislation, advising the magistrates, management of current affairs, control of entertainments, pursuing judicial cases etc., but particularly the collection of taxes, for which the members of the *curia* (the decurions) were jointly responsible. Under the early empire, the status of decurion was sought after because of the honour and prestige attached to it; but after the end of the second century, the burden became prohibitive. The centralisation of political and administrative power progressively deprived the municipal assembly of all real authority, while its role as tax collector was accentuated; the returns were underwritten by the personal wealth of members of the *curia*. Candidates for the decurionate became so hard to find that the richest citizens were compelled to undertake the office, it was made hereditary and then, as each person sought exemption, penalties for evasion were imposed.

Between the temple and the *curia*, a huge pedestal once supported a statue of Fortuna Augusta (dated to the first half of the second century), offered by members of the family of M. Annius, the rich citizen who had instructed his heirs and freedmen to set up the statues of Victory on the podium of the temple. The text runs as follows.

To Fortuna Augusta
Annia Cara Flaminica, daughter of M. (Annius), and Annia Tranquilla set up [this] statue for which Annius Protus had left the sum of 22,000 sesterces in his will. The money was provided by the said Protus and by Annius Hilarus, his father; they added from their own funds the sum of 4,400 sesterces for the construction of a shrine. They dedicated the monument, and on that occasion provided a meal for the members of the curia. *The ground was allocated by decree of the Council of Decurions.*

In front of this, a hexagonal base once bore a statue of Julian the Apostate (361–365), the emperor who tried in vain to restore the old gods and who seems to have been venerated here, even after his death and the abandonment of his reforms.

The building in the SW corner of the forum has not been identified, but it may have housed offices for public officials. The S side was bordered by shops, between which two short flights of steps led up towards the theatre. From the E portico, two doorways led into the civil basilica. The nave (29 x 15 m and 14 m high) terminated at the N end in an apse and two flanking rooms. At the opposite end, a raised tribunal fronted a room framed between two columns. Along the E wall, six offices served the administration of justice. This basilica conforms to a classic type and seems to belong either to the reign of Trajan (98–117) or to that of Hadrian (117–138). It had two orders of internal colonnades: Corinthian below and Ionic above.

The forum was full of statues, of which a number of bases remain in position. It has been possible to identify a goddess of Abundance, a Mercury, a Marsyas (symbol for the

Romans of municipal liberty, though 'speaking truth to power' did not secure him a favourable outcome), a Fortuna Augusta, a Victoria Augusta, a Concord, together with several statues of emperors, including several of Trajan, of Septimius Severus and of Caracalla. Amongst the inscriptions, of particular interest is a base dedicated to P. Flavius Pudens Pomponianus, known as Vocontius (in front of the N portico, towards the W end: fig. 204). A native of Thamugadi, this magistrate is lauded with grandiloquence for his benefactions and his oratorical talents:

To Vocontius
To Publius Flavius Pudens Pomponianus, of senatorial rank, generous supporter of his homeland and fellow citizens, who has performed his military service, whose knowledge of letters and of the Greek language is equal to that of the lustre of Rome [a play on the name of a famous orator, Romanus]

The Ordo, resident at the fount [the water source, the Aqua Septimiana, see p. 203], to its patron and its other fount – of eloquence.

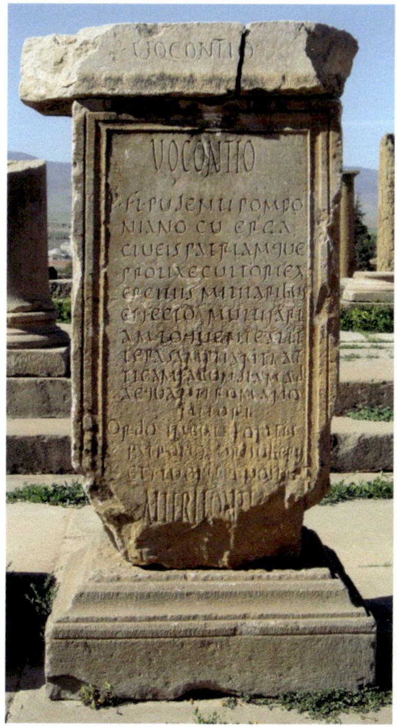

Fig. 204. Thamugadi: base of a statue dedicated to 'Vocontius'.

This inscription is also a prominent example of an innovative style of lettering, a flowing semi-uncial, far from the monumental capitals of the Augustan age. This anticipates the cursive lettering of the Middle Ages and, more particularly, the Carolingian minuscule of the ninth century. There are other examples of this original style in the city (e.g. p. 202 fig. 214, a dedication to the same man in the Great South Baths) and it seems that indeed Thamugadi, or at least this part of Roman Africa, is where it originated.

8. Theatre

This building was cut into the side of a natural hillock, and had a capacity of 3,500–4,000 spectators (figs. 200, 205). The lower part of the *cavea* is reasonably well preserved (with some restorations by the excavators), as is the *orchestra* and the steps reserved for the seats of the privileged. Of the stage (*proscaenium*) one can see the piers which once supported the floor. This is also one of the instances where there is evidence of parts of the mechanism required for the stage curtain (which rose from below, just behind the stage-front, rather than falling from above). Nothing, however, remains of the stage building (*scaenafrons*) which once provided the permanent backdrop to the action. Behind this, there was a rectangular court bordered on its E side by a portico of 16 columns (*porticus post scaenam*). The dedication on the entablature of this colonnade, to the joint emperors Marcus Aurelius (161–180) and Lucius Verus (161–169) provides a date for the complex. On a *stele* placed between the *orchestra* and the first steps of the *cavea*,

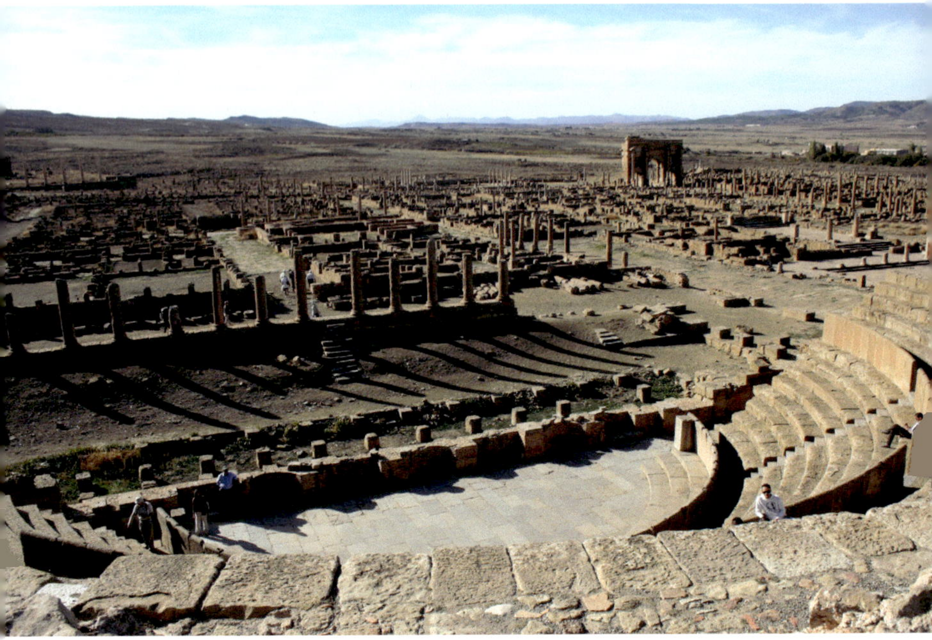

Fig. 205. Thamugadi: the theatre, with the Arch 'of Trajan' in the background.

another dedication tells us that L. Germeus Silvanus, augur, having given 21,200 sesterces to the public purse on the occasion of his elevation to this office, set up at his own expense a statue of Mercury, for the health of Septimius Severus and of Caracalla (pious and brave emperors) and for that of Julia Augusta (Mother of the Camps), and put on a theatre performance to mark the occasion.

The theatre of Thamugadi was quarried by the troops of Justinian in order to build the fortress (28) to the S of the city: hence the disappearance of the uppermost tiers of seating and of the stage building.

9. Theatre shrines

Behind the *cavea* of the theatre it has been possible to make out a temple (on the N side) dedicated to Dionysus in the reign of Marcus Aurelius. This stood within a porticoed precinct, to the W of which a stairway led to a semi-circular shrine. There were two other small temples on the top of the hillock, one of which was dedicated to Ceres.

10. Temple of Mercury?

11. House of the Raised Flower-Beds

Entered from the *decumanus maximus* next to the forum, one passed through a vestibule into a peristyle with Corinthian porticoes, off which there were various small rooms. Opposite the entrance was an *oecus* which was paved with an ornamental mosaic. The courtyard, which was equipped with a well, contained big raised flower-beds with curving sides embellished with masks in relief. The central position of this house, next to the Forum in an area which would normally be allocated to public and religious buildings, suggests the residence of a high official. It has been suggested that this was perhaps reserved for the legate of the emperor, the governor of Numidia, when he came to visit.

12. East Market

Through the portico lining the *decumanus maximus* (which slopes downhill at this point), a flight of steps led up to a semi-circular vestibule flanked on either side by three shops (fig. 206). From the vestibule, another short flight of steps led into a charming internal courtyard composed of two intersecting hemicycles, each with its own portico (fig. 207). The curved sides housed five stalls each, with three more on each of the straight sides. Each stall had a stone counter across the front, and the stallholder gained access by crawling beneath it, as in the market of Sertius (39) at Thamugadi, or the market of Cosinius at Cuicul (p. 112). The courtyard was paved in brick, with a fountain placed at the intersection of the two hemicycles.

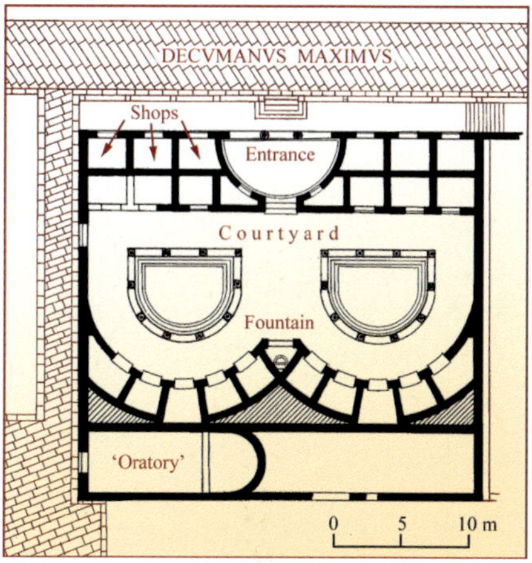

Fig. 206. Thamugadi: plan of the East Market.

13. Small East Baths

Moderately well preserved, this bathing establishment seems to be of late date. The *frigidarium* can be made out, with its cold-plunge bath, and three heated rooms.

14. Mascula Gate

This colonnaded gate, dated to 146, marked the eastern limit of the Trajanic settlement and the beginning of the road to *Mascula* (Khenchela).

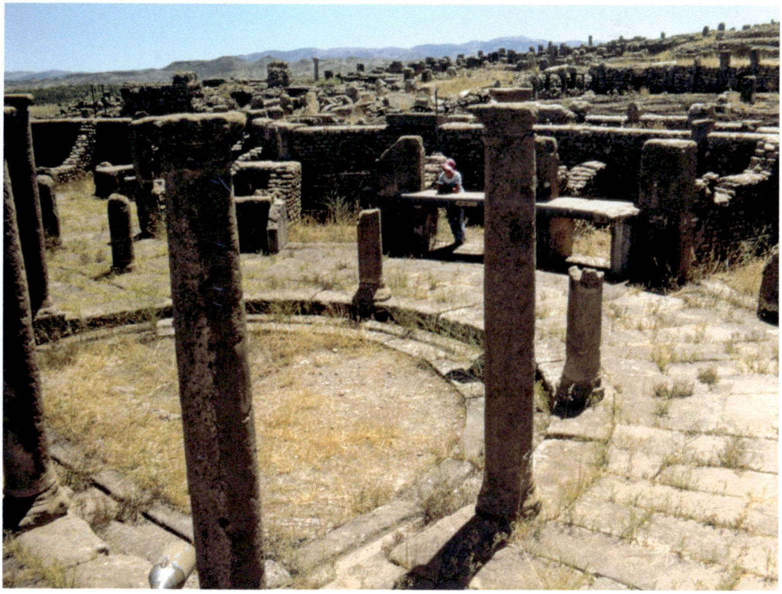

Fig. 207. Thamugadi: the East Market.

15. Triumphal arch

Like the corresponding arch in the western suburb, or Lambaesis Gate (43), and attributable to the same period (161–180), this structure marks the eastern extent of the city in the middle of the second century.

16. Great East Baths

Founded in the first half of the second century and enlarged in 167, these baths occupy four *insulae*. One can make out the vast latrines, several heated rooms and their furnaces, also the *frigidarium* in which was found the mosaic of Neptune in a chariot drawn by sea monsters (in the museum, see p. 216 fig. 231). Continuing northwards, towards the NE Baths, one passes by a modest quarter where, however, one can see an oilery and several fulling installations like those at Tiddis (p. 149), where sunken vats full of water and alkali (sometimes urine) were used for fulling (degreasing) textiles.

17. North-East Baths

This late establishment is of minor interest.

18. House of Corfidius Crementius

This house is of interest mainly for the state of preservation of its latrines, on the left of the entrance on the S side. An inscription found in the peristyle courtyard tells us that it was restored in the third or fourth century by Corfidius Crementius, who was 'saddened by its shapeless ruins and attentive to the well-being of his posterity.'

19. House of L. Julius Januarius

This wealthy property had a private bath suite. This was doubtless the setting for the statues of Aesculapius and Hygeia, which an inscription reports as having been given by L. Acilius Granianus to his father-in-law Julius Januarius to decorate his baths. The house was extensively remodelled in the Byzantine period, when a three-aisled chapel (12 x 10 m)

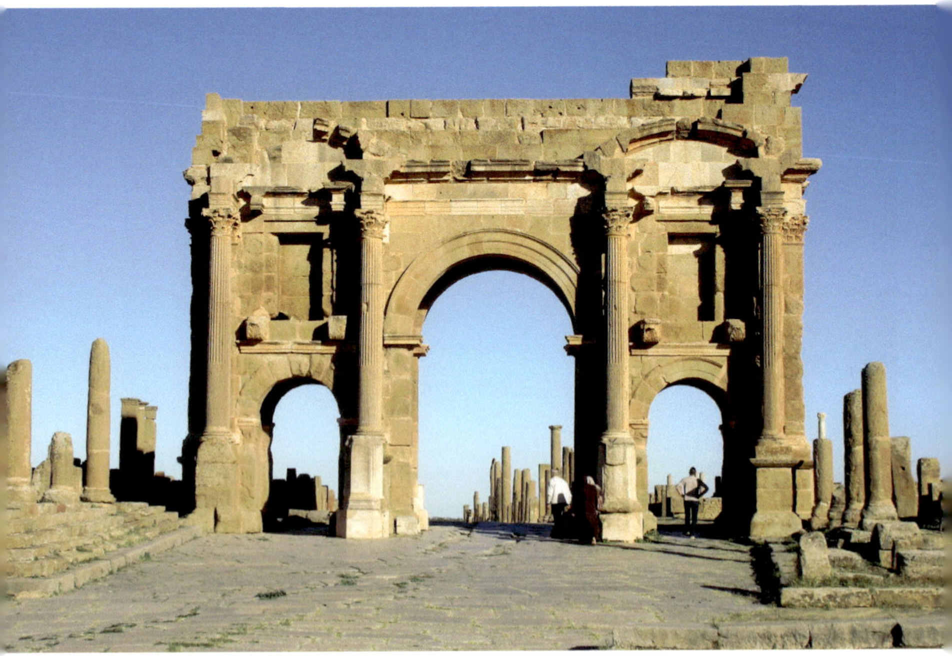

Fig. 208. Thamugadi: Arch 'of Trajan', from the W.

was inserted. The *atrium* of the church and the associated baptistery impinge on the next insula to the W.

20. Arch 'of Trajan'

This triple arch was built at the beginning of the third century (during the reign of Septimius Severus), on the site of the W Gate of the Trajanic colony (fig. 208). Its modern appellation is the result of an erroneous interpretation of an inscription at the beginning of the twentieth century. The central opening was for wheeled traffic, as is evident from the deep wheel-ruts which have cut into the paving, while the less lofty side-openings were for pedestrians. Above the lateral openings were niches framed by red marble colonnettes and surmounted by low curved pediments, which once housed statues. In front of the piers of the arch, four Corinthian columns on each face supported the projecting entablature. (Note that the capitals above these columns on the face towards the city have eagles clutching thunderbolts, in place of the usual volutes at the corners.) The structure was crowned by an attic, which doubtless supported imperial statues.

The arch was designed to be seen primarily by travellers approaching the city from Lambaesis, since from the E (inside the city) the lateral bays were masked by the porticoes of the *decumanus maximus*. Also, in front of the columns flanking the main passageway on the W side, there are two octagonal bases which once supported statues of Mars (on the left) and the Concord of the Emperors (on the right: fig. 209). According to the dedication, they were offered by L. Licinius Optatianus at a cost of 35,000 sesterces, in recognition of his nomination as *flamen perpetuus* (a priest of the imperial cult) in the time of Septimius Severus. Ironically, the concord celebrated here between the members of the imperial house (Septimius Severus and his sons Caracalla and Geta) was broken immediately after the death of Severus when

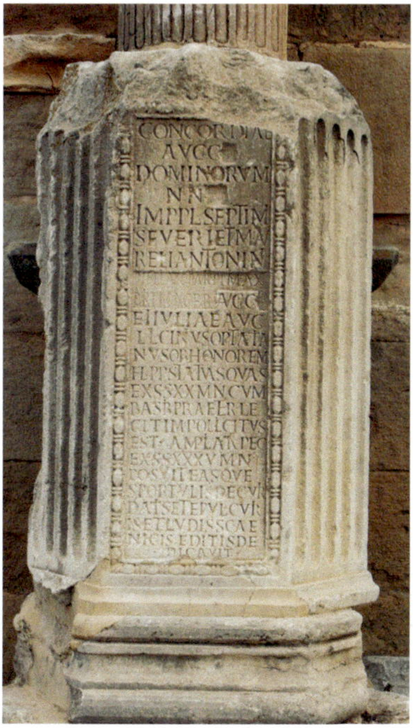

Fig. 209. Thamugadi: statue-base dedicated to the Concord of the Emperors, in front of the Arch 'of Trajan'.

Caracalla murdered his younger brother and issued a *damnatio memoriae*, requiring the obliteration of all written references to Geta. The name of Geta has been chiselled out and replaced by further titles of Caracalla, while the triple plural abbreviations (AVGGG, NNN, for *augustorum, nostrorum*) have been reduced to twin plurals.

21. House of the piscina

This wealthy residence covered two *insulae*. In the exposed part of its peristyle courtyard one can see a handsome basin of blue granite with a rounded end, adorned with nine columns of pink marble. The *oecus* facing this basin on the S side was decorated with a magnificent mosaic with a vegetal design of flowers and tendrils (the mosaic 'of the acanthus rosettes' in the museum).

22. Small Central Baths

This has yielded a mosaic of the Four Seasons, now in the museum. Opposite the baths, a fountain built of sandstone blocks the road which led from the theatre towards the Capitolium; this arrangement perhaps signifies the merging of two *insulae* at a late date under the same ownership.

23. House of Sertius

This sumptuous residence (fig. 210) occupies an area of 2,500 sq.m. A paved vestibule on the E side was flanked on the right by a porter's lodge and a small private bath suite, and on the left by two rooms which open only to the street. From the vestibule one passed into a peristyle with a rectangular basin in the centre; recesses in the walls indicate that this was a fishpond. (The recesses were for the fish to spawn in, as seen in the House of Bacchus at Cuicul, p. 125.) There are bases there for statues of Aesculapius and Hygeia, dedicated by Plotius Faustus Sertius, a former cohort commander in the *Legio III Augusta* who had retired to his home town, and by his wife Cornelia Valentina Tuccia. It was this couple who sponsored the market named after them at the W Gate of the city (p. 211), and possible even the huge capitolium (p. 206).

On the opposite side of the peristyle from the vestibule is a large *oecus*, once paved with a floral mosaic (now in the museum), while on the left are a number of rooms which appear to have been offices (one of them heated). Towards the W, the residential part of the house was arranged around a second peristyle, with a raised flower bed. A marble basin was found here, on which was carved a nautical scene. A further *oecus* faced this second peristyle, where there was also a *triclinium* and adjacent kitchen.

24. House of the Hermaphroditus

Of comparable size to the House of Sertius, this property takes its name from a mosaic representing the toilet of Hermaphroditus (now in the museum, p. 218). On the W side, the *insula* frontage took the form of a portico, behind which was a range of five shops. The house was entered from the street on the S side. A vestibule, with a guardian's lodge, led into a long gallery (30 x 7 m) and then to a room with a black and red mosaic pavement. The heart of the house was a peristyle (23 x 19 m), around which were the residential rooms. The columns of the peristyle were linked by balustrades, while the mosaic flooring was decorated with gaming layouts. The plans of both this house and the neighbouring House of Sertius recall those found at Pompeii.

25. 'Industrial quarter'

This mostly triangular area (fig. 211), the base of which is parallel to the house of Sertius, was interpreted by the excavator as a commercial and industrial district, but seems now to have contained a range of activities and occupations no different from any other part of the city. The only 'industrial' activity for which there is clear evidence was a bronze foundry at the southern tip. This contained 300 kg of bronze and quantities of glass, pitch and resin when it was

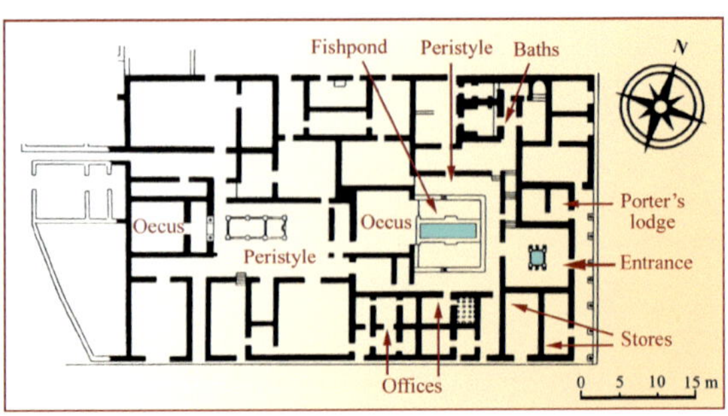

Fig. 210. Thamugadi: plan of the House of Sertius.

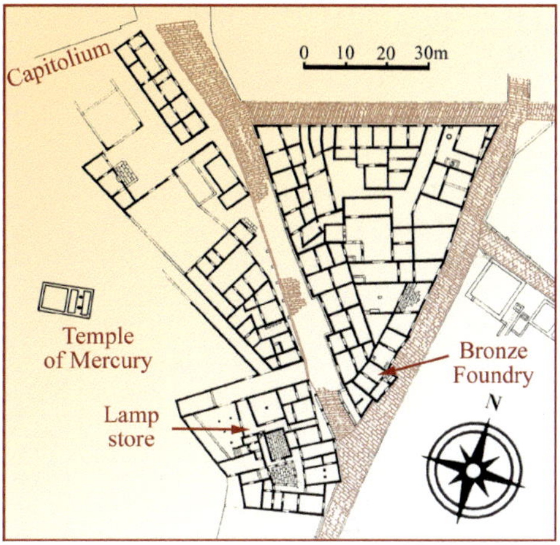

Fig. 211. Thamugadi: plan of the 'industrial quarter'.

destroyed by fire, probably in the fifth century. Across the road to the W, a building containing quantities of (mostly) unused lamps of the Christian era was thought to have been a production site – but in the absence of any kiln is more likely to have been simply a warehouse or shop. The road towards the Capitolium was lined with shops on both sides, in one of which was found a hoard of almost six thousand bronze coins of the fourth century.

26. Great South Baths

This complex (figs. 212, 214) was built in the second century and enlarged in 198, by decree of the decurions (dedicatory inscription found in the *apodyterium*). Its unusually asymmetrical layout is probably due to the constraints of the site. The building is embellished with a fountain on its blind side, at the street intersection where the southbound *cardo* bends more to the W. There were three entrances. The two on the NE side led into a semi-circular colonnaded portico, while that on the SW side led past a grandiose latrine, also semi-circular. This was originally paved with a fine mosaic of aquatic creatures; it had 28 seats, separated from one another by little ornamental fountains (providing the essential cleansing water).

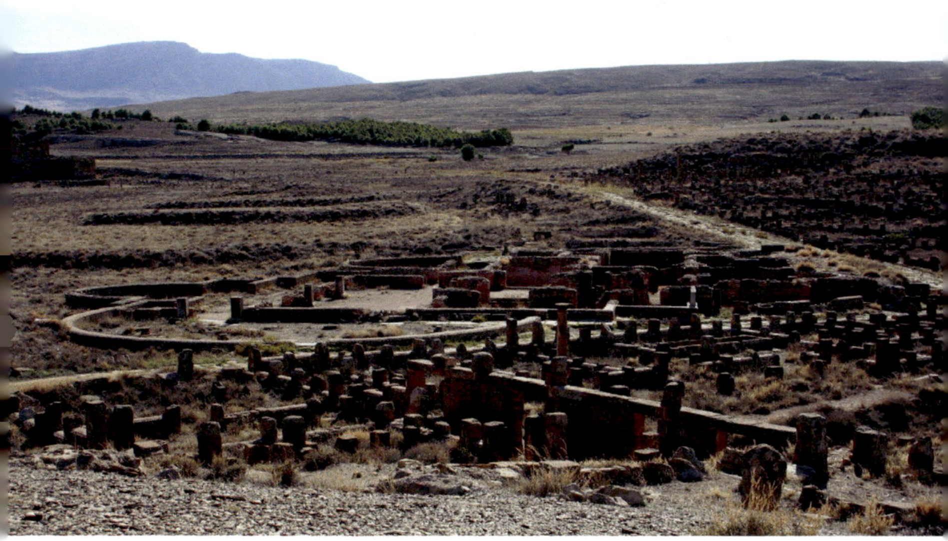

Fig. 212. Thamugadi: the Great South Baths from the theatre hillock.

The opposing entrances were linked by a dog-leg corridor, on the S of which was an apsidal social space and on the N a vast lobby. From this, one accessed the changing-room (*apodyterium*) and the *frigidarium*, decorated with statues of the *Genius* of Thamugadi, of Fortune and of Victory and equipped with two cold-plunge baths. Here too was a statue of P. Flavius Pomponianus, the Vocontius commemorated in the Forum, recording his public career which had included governorships of Crete with Cyrene and of Aquitania. (See fig. 213.)

From the *frigidarium*, one might pass into the heated rooms, but also into the elaiothesium, where oiled massage and perfumed scrubs took place. The subterranean furnaces, fuel stores and service corridors are particularly well preserved here (fig. 215). Water for the complex came from the *Aqua Septimiana Felix* (see below).

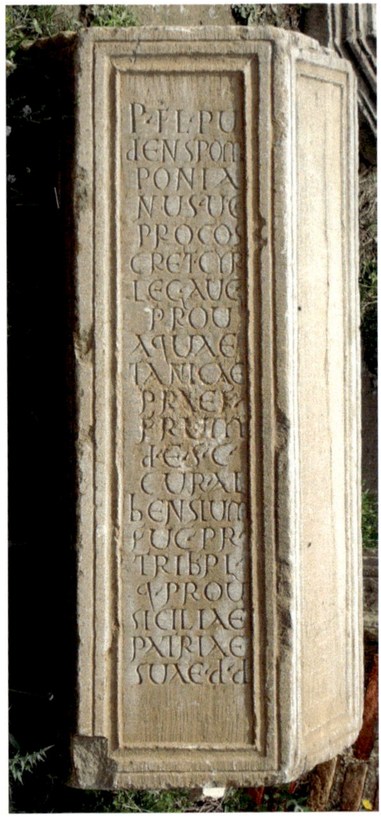

Fig. 213 (right). Thamugadi: statue-base in the Great South Baths, dedicated to Pomponianus (cf. fig. 204).

Fig. 214 (below). Thamugadi: plan of the Great South Baths.

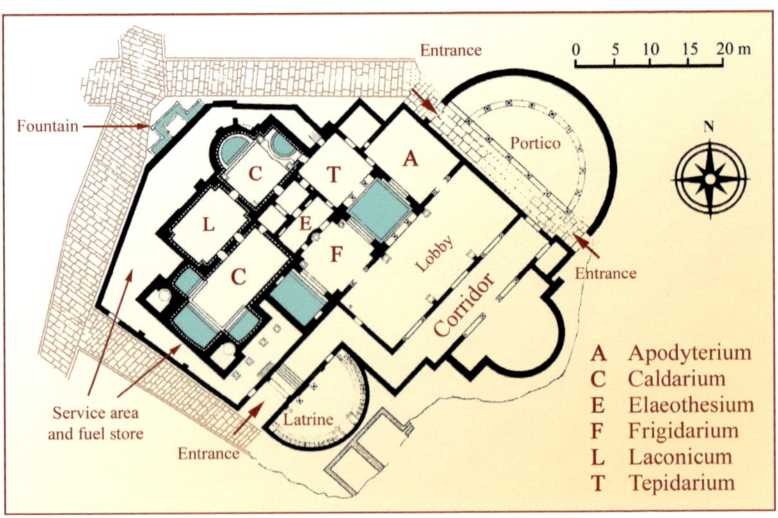

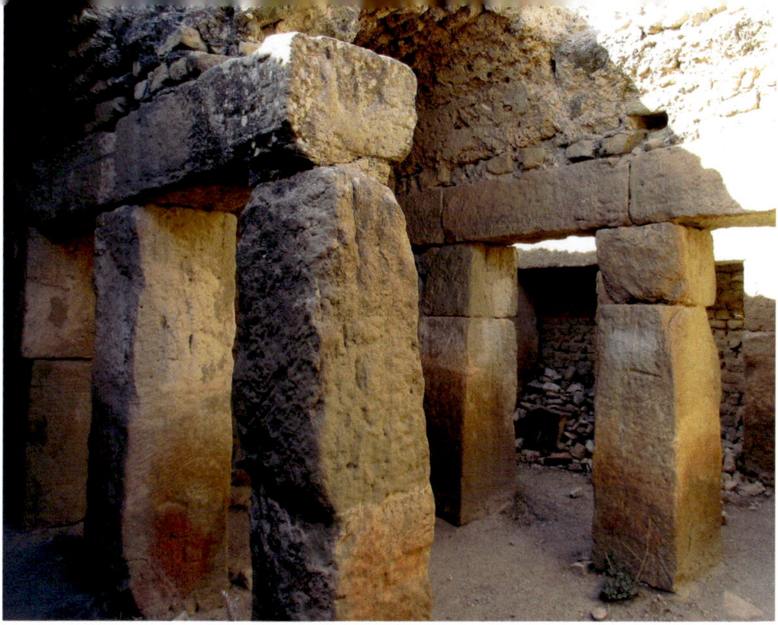

Fig. 215. Thamugadi: the fuel store beneath the Great South Baths.

27. Small South Baths

28. Byzantine fortress

This was constructed on the site of three earlier temples which shared a common podium and were associated with the spring of the *Aqua Septimiana Felix*, a curative water source which was certainly once abundant but has long since disappeared (figs. 216, 217). The central temple (9.8 x 7.5 m) was paved in white and green marble, and had in front a vestibule paved in mosaic. It was dedicated to the *Genius Patriae* (the patron spirit of the city), merged with the *Dea Africa* (personification of Africa) and perceived as the spirit of the source. The divinities to

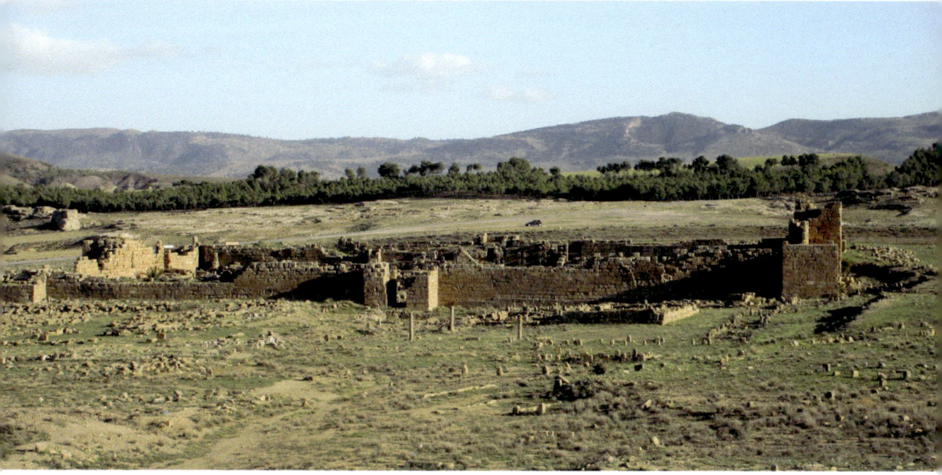

Fig. 216. Thamugadi: the Byzantine fortress from the N.

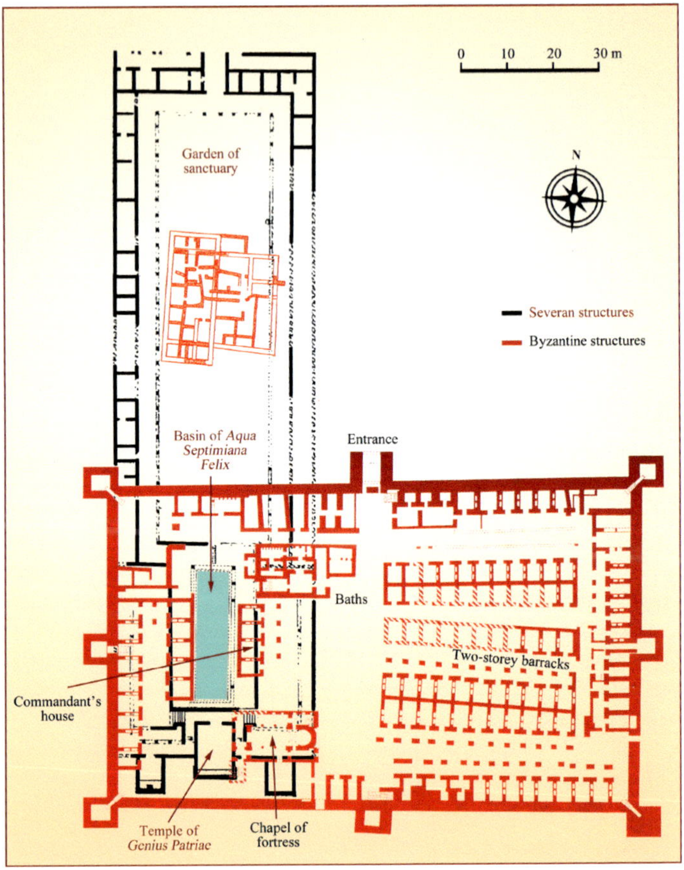

Fig. 217. Thamugadi: plan of the Byzantine fortress, overlying the earlier precinct of the Aqua Septimiana Felix.

which the smaller lateral shrines were dedicated (7.1 x 5.1 m) have not been identified, though a head of Serapis was found there. In front of these temples, to the N, was a huge basin, 27 x 7 m and 1.7 m deep (fig. 218), which was fed from the S by the sacred water source. An inscription found at the N end records that under Caracalla the basin was enclosed by a peristyle with a bronze balustrade. To this was added a monumental entrance with arches framed within two square bays, and on the N side of this a porticoed garden decorated with (wall-) paintings.

It was probably the existence of this source and of the basin (serving as a reservoir), which caused Justinian's *magister militum*, Solomon, in 539 to choose this location for the construction of the fortress visible today. (The dedicatory inscription lies on the ground by the entrance.) This immense rectangle (112 x 67 m) is flanked by square towers which project at the four corners and at the centre of each side (that on the N enclosing the sole entrance). The wall, 2.5 m thick, is composed of two faces of reused blocks (many of them seats taken from the

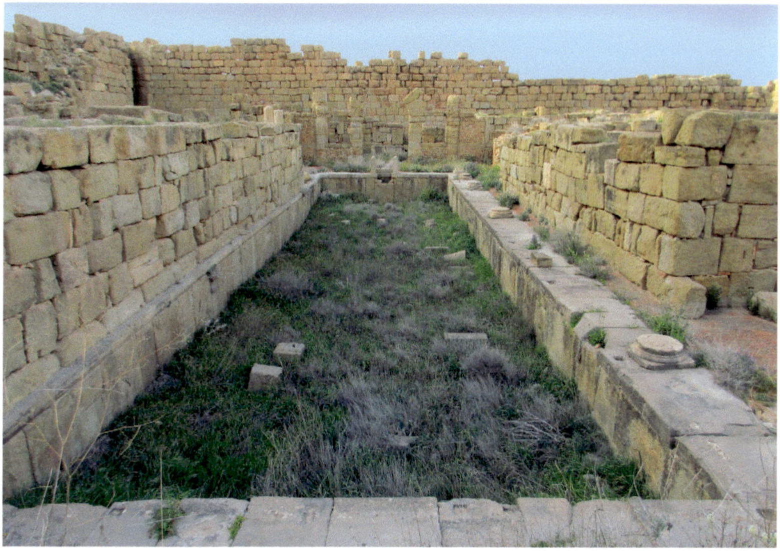

Fig. 218. Thamugadi: the basin of the Aqua Septimiana Felix, *within the Byzantine fortress.*

theatre) with an infill of earth and rubble. At its greatest preserved height today, it still rises 15 m above the ground. Against the inner faces of the wall, staircases provided access to the wall-walk.

Two separate parts may be distinguished: the western half was reserved for the officers and the general staff, while the eastern half was filled with barracks for the troops. In the western part, the headquarters building had four rooms on the ground floor, while the commandant's residence was probably on the floor above. This was flanked on either side by a bath-building and a chapel. The baths had a *frigidarium* with two plunge-baths and several heated rooms, also with plunge-baths. In the bottom of one of these plunge-baths was found the inscription naming the *Aqua Septimiana Felix.* The small size of the brick-built chapel suggests that it served the senior staff rather than the garrison as a whole. It was composed of a narthex, a nave and two aisles, separated by columns, and an apse which shows evidence of two phases: initially there was a *synthronon* for the elders of the church, subsequently replaced by paving over a sarcophagus. A second sarcophagus (surely belonging to an earlier period, and reused), shows a partly opened door into the tomb: this was discovered near the apse and is now in front of the museum (fig. 219). The altar is recognizable, as is a small baptistery.

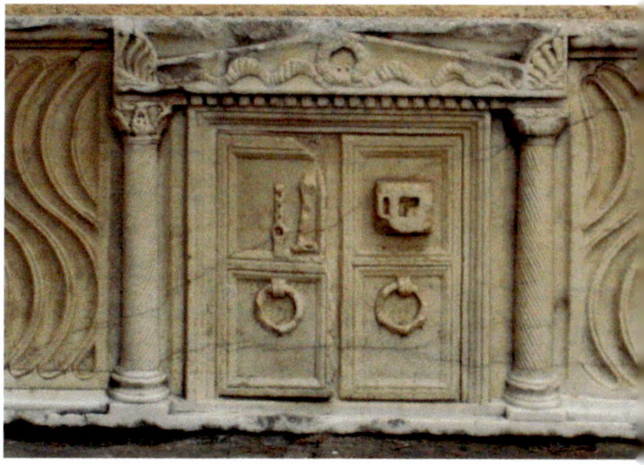

Fig. 219. Timgad Museum: detail of sarcophagus from the chapel of the Byzantine fortress.

Along the N side of the western part were offices, storerooms, latrines and kitchens serving this part of the fortress.

In the eastern half there were further offices and three ranges (two double and one single) of barracks, aligned E–W. The rooms in these quarters, together with others along the walls, were all of uniform size (5 x 3 m), provided with two cupboards set into the dividing walls and fronted by porticoes. Ninety such cells have been counted, and knowing that the buildings had an upper floor – certainly two against the outer walls – and calculating that each cell would have accommodated two or four men, one arrives at a potential garrison strength of 1,000 soldiers. The fortress must therefore have served as a base of operations – like the earlier military base at Lambaesis – for securing regional communications and controlling the tribes of the Aurès.

29. Chapel

Though the plan is not clear, this three-aisled church was built between 641 and 647 by John, *dux* of Tigisis, at the time of the exarch Gregory (who died in battle against the Arabs in 647). Its principal entrance made use of a carved frame from an earlier building, which has now been reused again to enliven the doorway of the modern museum.

30. Christian church and necropolis

This church (aligned SE–NW) has only two aisles, since the NE aisle has, in effect, been extended into a large rectangular court surrounded by a portico. A second court on the NW side, where there should have been the *atrium*, was filled with burials and in the surrounding cemetery ten thousand individual and collective tombs have been identified.

31. Temple

The foundations of a small prostyle, tetrastyle temple here are possibly to be associated with an inscription found nearby, which records the restoration at the beginning of the fourth century of a ruinous temple dedicated to Mercury (suited to a commercial quarter).

32. Capitolium

The date of this temple (fig. 220), dedicated to the Capitoline triad of Jupiter, Juno and Minerva (fragments of colossal statues of all

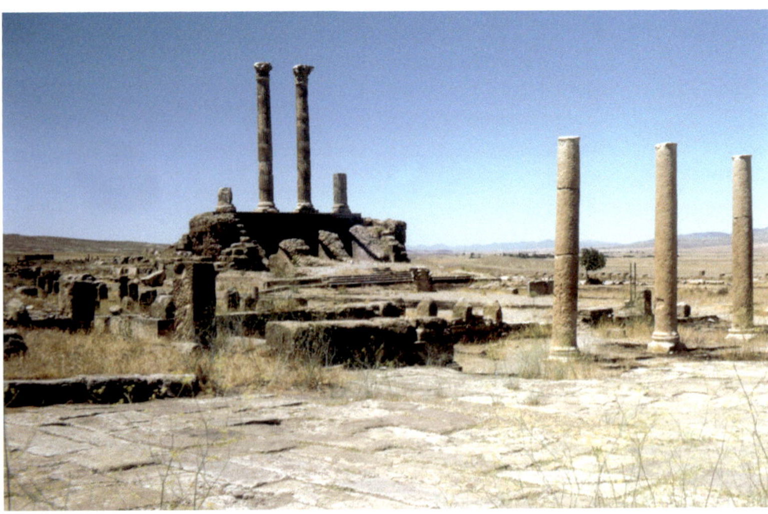

Fig. 220. Thamugadi: the Capitolium from the E.

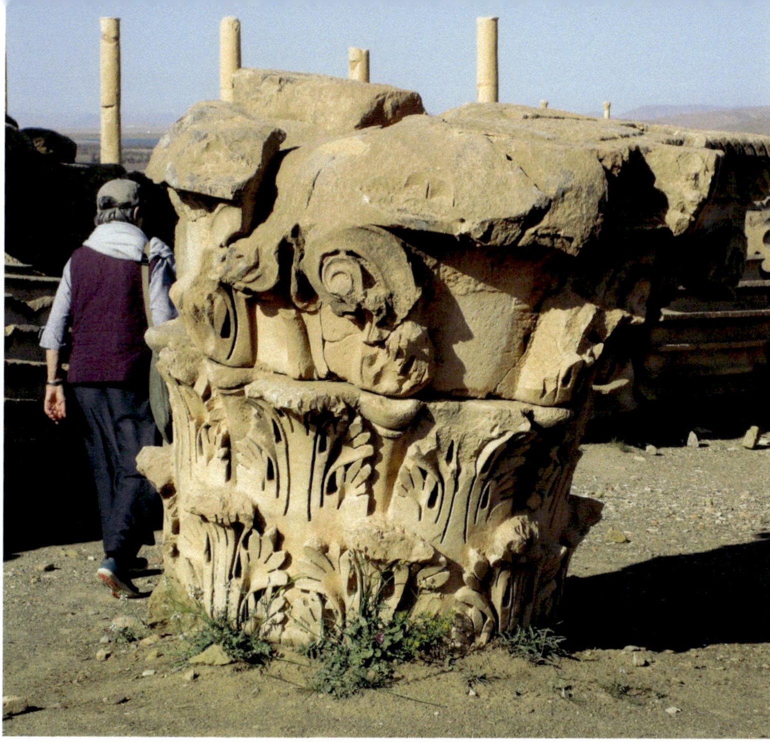

Fig. 221. Thamugadi: one of the capitals from the Capitolium.

three have been found), is not firmly established. Its position and orientation clearly indicate that it was not part of the original layout of the city. Arguments based on the style of the carving have favoured a mid-second century date, but the reuse here in late paving of a monumental inscription recording a benefaction of the Sertii (see pp. 200, 211) suggests that the portico (and therefore the temple) may have been built at their expense at the beginning of the third. The sanctuary is composed of a vast precinct 105 m long and with an average width of 66 m: its size is therefore greater than that of the forum. It was entered from the E by a short flight of steps. The architrave of the E portico carried an inscription which recorded that the four surrounding porticoes, 'ruined by age and collapsed to their foundations,' were restored under Valentinian I and Valens (364–367) through the munificence of the governor of Numidia Publilius Ceionius Caecina Albinus and under the supervision of the *curator* of the city Aelius Julianus. This marks a time of changing attitudes to religion, since the governor (responsible also for the late basilica at Cuicul, p. 119) appears to have been a pagan, while we know that Aelius Julianus was a Christian. It is possible that here, as in other cases now recognized, the portico was rebuilt in order to *hide* the ruins of the old temple. The temple itself stood on a massive podium (53 x 23 m in plan and 6.7 m high) approached by a flight of 38 steps, supported on sloping concrete vaults. The *cella* (17 x 11 m), of which only the foundations remain, was preceded by a pronaos which has also disappeared, but two of the columns of which were re-erected at the beginning of the twentieth century. The cella was surrounded on three sides by columns 14 m high, on top of which were huge Corinthian capitals (in two parts) 1.6 m high: several of these now lie on the ground (fig. 221).

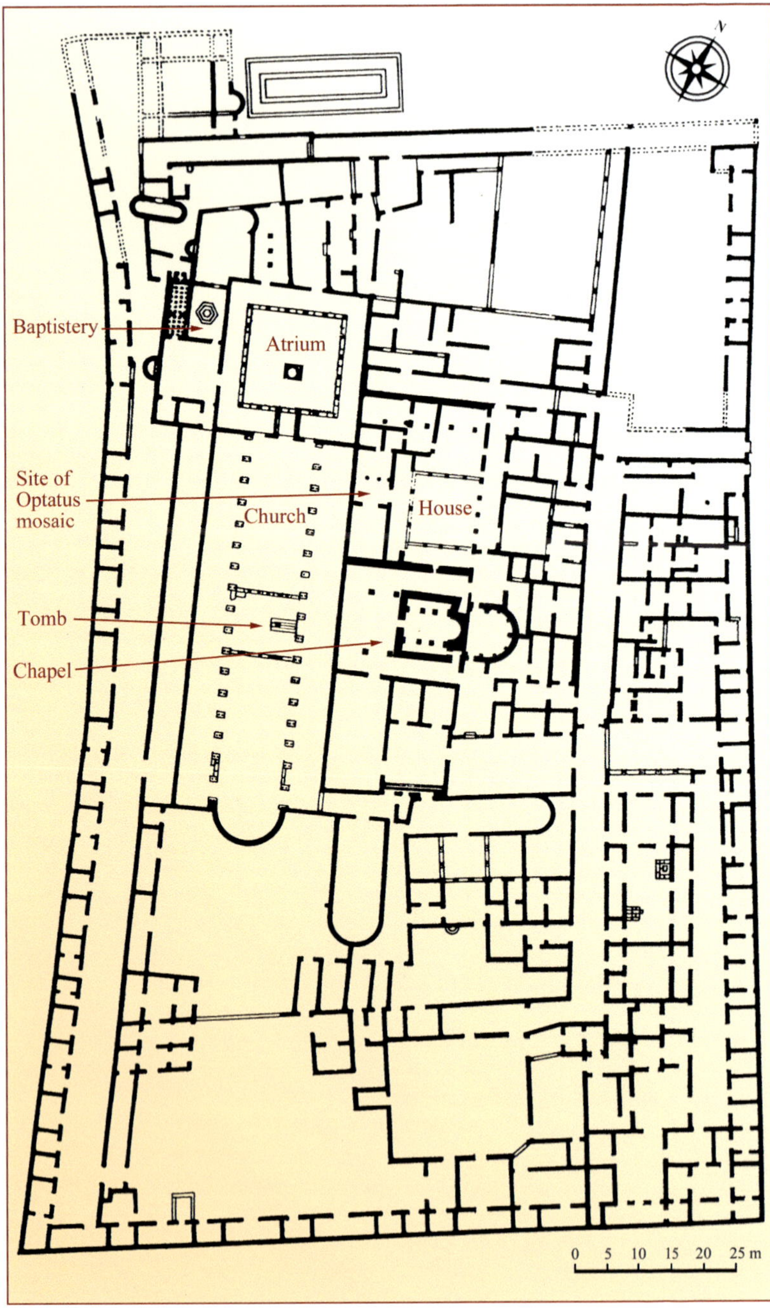

Fig. 222. Thamugadi: plan of the Donatist episcopal quarter.

Against the W wall of the *cella*, a staircase led to three cellars (favissae) which served as strong-rooms for the safe deposit of articles belonging to (or entrusted to) the cult. An altar stood in the precinct in front of the temple.

An interesting (and rare) feature of this temple is the demarcation of the sacred area in the street which passes in front of it. At either end of the zone, the normal paving is interrupted by a stripe of darker grey slabs running across the width of the street.

33. Byzantine church

This is a three-aisled basilica which made use of second-hand columns.

34. Donatist episcopal quarter

This self-contained enclosure lies in a part of the extended city which has not yet been fully explored. It consists of a basilica and its dependencies (fig. 222), assumed to have belonged to the Donatist sect. This church was the largest in Thamugadi (63 x 22 m) and was divided into three aisles by paired columns. It is aligned towards the S, at which end it terminates in an apse. The body of the church was entered by three doorways from a peristyle *atrium* equipped with water basins (for ablution: surviving marks in the paving indicate the presence of two). On the W side of the *atrium* was a baptistery, together with the often associated small bath suite. The baptismal basin, hexagonal in shape and formerly covered by a ciborium supported by colonnettes, still possesses its wonderful mosaic decoration of floral and geometric motifs. There are chi-rho symbols on its outer face. (A modern cover building has been erected over the baptistery, but in 2018 this was not accessible.) The church is thought to have been built in the fourth century.

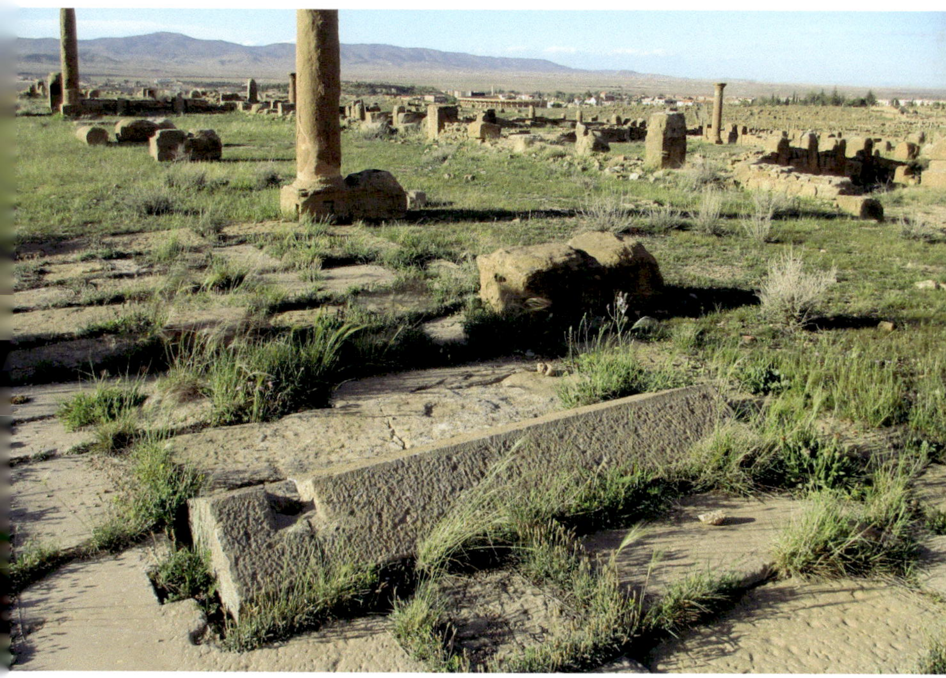

Fig. 223. Thamugadi: tomb in the nave of the Donatist church.

Attached to the E side of the church, and perpendicular to it, was a chapel facing E. There are two phases to this building: the earlier (and larger) structure had three aisles and is contemporary with the main church, while the later phase, considered Byzantine, was altogether smaller. It still had three aisles and an apse, but was fitted wholly within the nave of the earlier chapel. The construction of the later chapel was much more solid, suggesting that it may have had a vaulted roof. Two burials are associated with these chapels. There was a tomb beneath the floor of the earlier chapel, at its W end; there is also a more prominent tomb opposite the chapel but in the nave of the main church (fig. 223). This tomb has a ridged cover which projects above the paving, and is pierced at one end by an opening with a kind of strainer. This probably contained the remains of a saint or martyr: the opening may represent a persistence of the libation tubes found in earlier pagan burials (through which offerings of food and drink might be poured to refresh the dead), or it may reflect the Christian practice of the faithful bringing there pieces of cloth, 'to become impregnated with the miraculous virtues' of the incumbent.

In the peristyle house which occupied the angle between the church and the smaller chapel was found an inscription in mosaic which reads 'I have done this work on the instructions of the priest of God Optatus' (*haec iubente sacerdote Dei Optato perfeci*). This has been taken to refer to bishop Optatus of Thamugadi, the principal spokesperson for Donatism in Africa at the end of the fourth century. However, both Catholic and Donatist bishops of that name are known, and the term *sacerdos* does not necessarily imply a bishop.

In 411, after the condemnation of Donatism, it was perhaps here that bishop Gaudentius, ardent defender of total religious liberty and apologist for voluntary martyrdom, threatened to set fire to himself and his family rather than to hand over the church of Optatus to the Catholics.

The numerous covers of pagan tombs in this area suggest that it was a necropolis prior to the construction of the ecclesiastical buildings.

35. Capitolium Baths

36. West Baths

37. Hostelry?

This house, with its own bath suite, was the source of the big mosaic with still-life images of food which is now in the main hall of the museum (p. 216 fig. 230), and several other mosaics with marine subjects; indeed it yielded such a rich variety of mosaics (even in the smaller rooms) that it seems to differ in this from typical private houses. It was perhaps a hostelry.

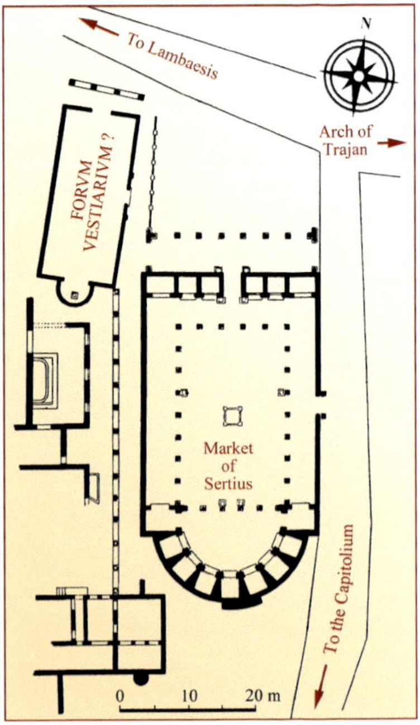

Fig. 224. Thamugadi: plan of the Market of Sertius.

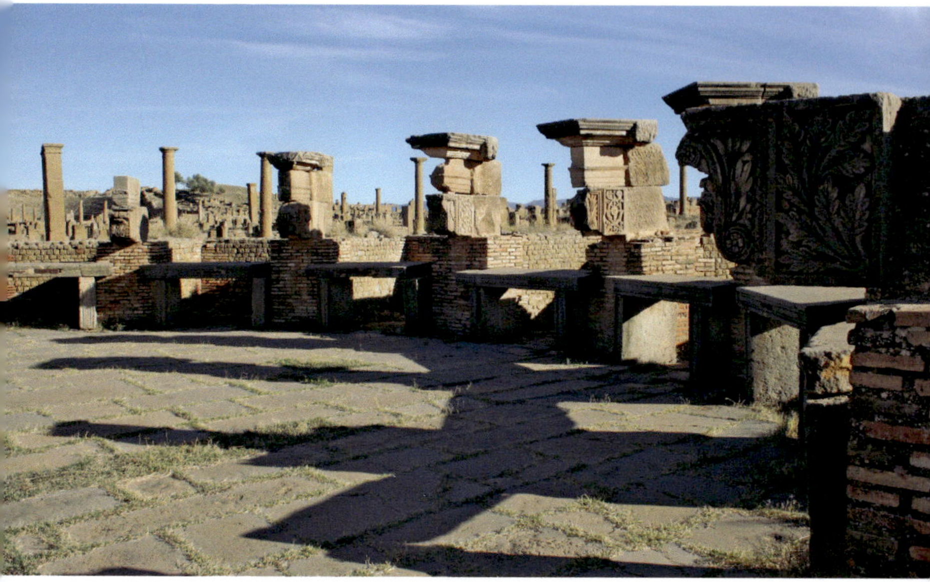

Fig. 225. Thamugadi: shop counters in the apse of the Market of Sertius.

38. Market of Sertius

This new market formed part of the extension of the city at the beginning of the third century. Its construction was due to M. Plotius Faustus Sertius, the Roman knight (*eques*) and *flamen perpetuus* whose house has been described (23). The market is composed of a rectangular peristyle court, terminating in an apse at the S end (figs. 224, 225). There was a square basin in the centre of the open space. The market had entrances on the N and E sides; the doorway on the N was flanked by two statues: on the right stood Sertius, and on the left his wife Cornelia Valentina Tucciana Sertia. Not averse to self-promotion, the sponsor placed two further statues of himself and his wife inside the building, and in order that his largesse should not be in any doubt, the letters of his name, S–E–R–T–I–U–S, were carved on the individual springer-blocks of the surrounding arcades, which have been partly re-erected.

Three permanent stalls with stone counters stood on either side of the entrance at the N end, while nine more were arranged around the apse (fig. 225). The roof of the apse was carried by the columns of the main portico across the diameter, and around the hemicycle by engaged colonettes and architraves supported on elaborately carved console brackets. The rich decoration, including vine-scrolls, cornucopiae, leafy masks and Bacchic figures reflect the baroque tendencies of the third century.

39. Textile market

The building next to the Market of Sertius is contemporary with, and closely resembles, the textile market found at Cuicul (p. 121). As a result, it has been associated with two inscriptions found in the vicinity (both re-used) which refer to a *forum vestiarium*, and has been interpreted as having served a similar purpose. It was built under Valentinian I and Valens (364–367) in the governorship of Publilius Caeionius Caecina Albinus, who restored the porticoes of the Capitolium. The building is a hall of 24 x 10 m,

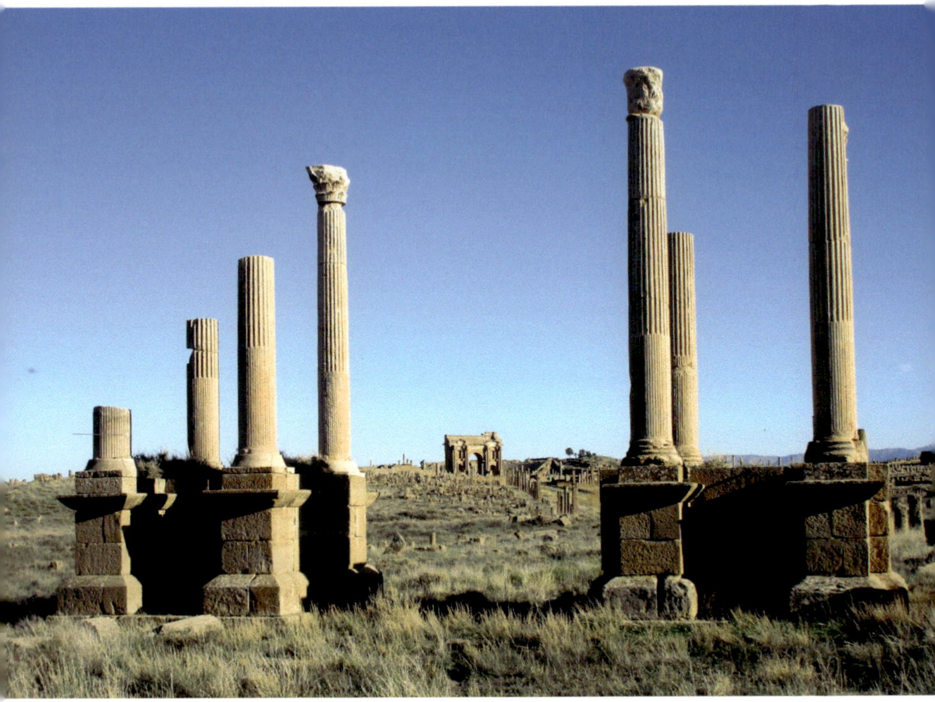

Fig. 226. Thamugadi: triumphal arch at the western approach to the city, with the Arch 'of Trajan' in the background.

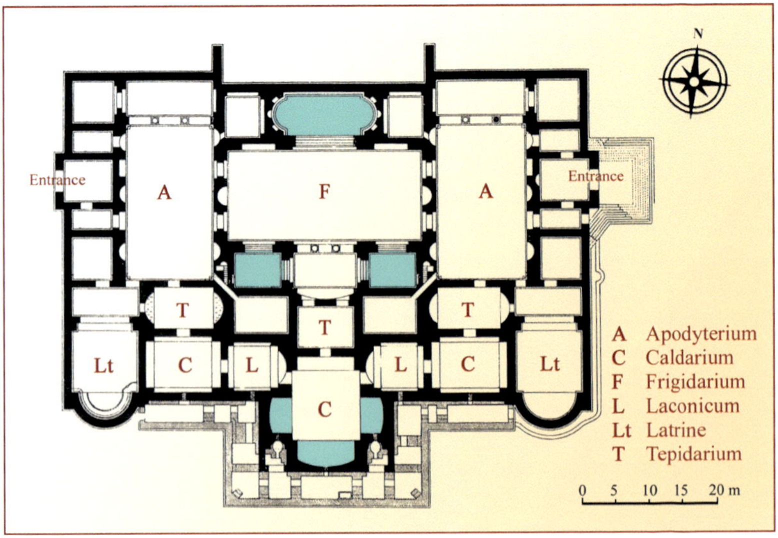

Fig. 227. Thamugadi: plan of the Great North Baths.

terminated at the S end by an apse, in which stood a statue of Concord. The hall was paved with slabs of bluish limestone, enlivened in the centre by a chequer-pattern of pink porphyry and black limestone. This hall was later absorbed into the Market of Sertius next door.

40. Bath building

This yielded a fine mosaic portrayal of the head of Oceanus, on display in the museum (p. 218, fig. 233).

41. Temple to the *Genius* of the colony

This temple, built in 169 under the emperor Marcus Aurelius, was dedicated to the protecting spirit of the colony of Thamugadi. It stands at the rear of a porticoed precinct which is an irregular quadrilateral, accommodating itself to the angle at which the road for Lambaesis leaves the city. The cella (8.5 x 7.0 m) had a porch of the Corinthian order and stood on a podium fronted by a flight of 16 steps.

42. Fountain of Liberalis

This fountain, with an octagonal basin, was a gift to the city from P. Julius Liberalis, at a cost of 32,348 sesterces. It was embellished with statues and colonnettes.

43. North-West Baths

44. Private house

This includes both a bath suite and a pressing installation (probably for wine) in its facilities.

45. Triumphal arch

Built between 166 and 169 (in the time of Marcus Aurelius and Lucius Verus) this arch (fig. 226) is the western counterpart to its pair on the eastern side of the city (15). It was an arch of a single bay, with masonry piers framed by Corinthian columns, which greeted travellers arriving from Lambaesis.

46. Pagan necropolis

Here may be seen a great diversity of inhumation and cremation burials, where sarcophagi, inscribed *stelai* and *mensae* for funerary feasts jostle with modest burials *a capuccina* (covered by tiles leaning against one another to form a pitched roof).

47. Church

This is a church with nave and two aisles, separated by lines of re-used (and re-erected) columns. In the nave was a recess containing a sarcophagus, and at the SE end an apse above a crypt. The apse was flanked by two sacristies, of which that on the right also had a crypt beneath. The church was preceded by a porch of six columns, and the whole is attributable to the Byzantine period.

48. Church complex

The church here (39 x 17 m) has three aisles, separated by ranges of ten paired columns; the raised apse was once paved with mosaic and was accessed from steps at either side. There were sacristies on either side of the choir, that on the N being itself apsidal. The entrance to the church at the W end was by means of a corridor which passed by a baptistery on the right and another room on the left. On the S side of the church, a porticoed passageway led to a large peristyle court of uncertain purpose, located behind the apse. It has been suggested that this complex could have been the seat of the Catholic bishop of the city.

49. Private house

The source of a fine mosaic in the 'vegetalised' style of Thamugadi, now in the museum (p. 217 fig. 232).

50. Baths of the Philadelphi

The entrance to this complex (on the S side) led into a peristyle court with a central basin, and then to a passageway leading to the *frigidarium* of the baths, with its cold-plunge bath. Beyond this was the usual succession of heated rooms. The name given to the baths derives from the mosaic found in the *caldarium* (in the museum: see p. 219 fig. 234), which includes the salutation *Filadelfis vita* ('Long live the Brotherhood').

51. Great North Baths

Like the South Baths of Cuicul or the Hadrianic Baths at Lepcis Magna, this complex, set in open ground to the N of the original settlement, has an entirely symmetrical layout (fig. 227). Whether one entered on the E or the W side, one passed through a vestibule into a large meeting hall or *apodyterium* with a colonnaded recess on the N side. From each of these halls, two doorways communicated with the central *frigidarium* (30 × 14 m); either from here or from the lateral meeting halls, one could proceed southwards into the heated rooms. In general, the bather would undress in the *apodyteria* and then pass through the lateral *tepidaria* towards the *caldaria*, where he or she would be rubbed down and washed by slaves before taking a hot bath in the central *caldarium* or sweating in a *laconicum* (hot dry room). On the return, through the centre of the building, he or she would be rubbed down again and massaged before taking a plunge in the cold bath in the *frigidarium* or spending time in social conversation. The whole complex, including the two lateral latrines, would have been veneered with marble, paved with mosaics and enlivened with statues, though none of these have been found.

52. Temple of Saturn

This poorly preserved sanctuary, outside the main archaeological zone and now surrounded by modern buildings, was composed of three *cellae* at the W end of a court (48 × 22 m) surrounded by porticoes on three sides, with a monumental altar in the centre. The altar seems to have taken the form of a tower, with a sacrificial area in front of it (indicated by a tethering-ring at the E side of the altar, for the sacrificial animal). Little of this can now be made out on the ground. Associated finds indicate that this was a temple of Baal-Saturn.

MUSEUM

Various pieces of statuary are arranged around the courtyard in front of the entrance. These include a statue of Tucciana Sertia, the wife of the benefactor M. Plotius Faustus Sertius, a statue of Fortuna, a torso of Lucius Verus, the heads of Aesculapius and Serapis which were found in the Byzantine fortress (28), a marble vase portraying Eros and Psyche from the House of Sertius (23) and fragmentary inscriptions. Also here is a strigilated marble sarcophagus, found in the chapel of the Byzantine fortress (28), showing in the centre the door of a tomb which is slightly ajar (p. 205 fig. 219). The doorway to the museum is framed by the door-frame found (already in its second incarnation) in the chapel to the S of the Byzantine fortress (29).

Beneath the portico and along the pathway leading to the site are many *stelai*, both funerary and dedicated to Saturn, together with *mensae*, carved offering-tables which were placed on top of burials (figs. 228, 229). They show interesting vernacular traits derived from Punic tradition. The *stelai* dedicated to Saturn are generally carved in three registers: at the top is the bearded figure of Saturn, often flanked by the Sun and Moon; beneath this is/are shown the dedicant(s), making an offering on an altar, while the lowest register portrays the animal(s) offered in sacrifice. (See also the examples in Algiers: p. 80 and fig. 78.)

The museum is an elderly building, suffering from ground movement which has created damaging cracks, not only in the walls but in the mosaics which have been robustly cemented into them (a technique which is not approved today, for this reason amongst

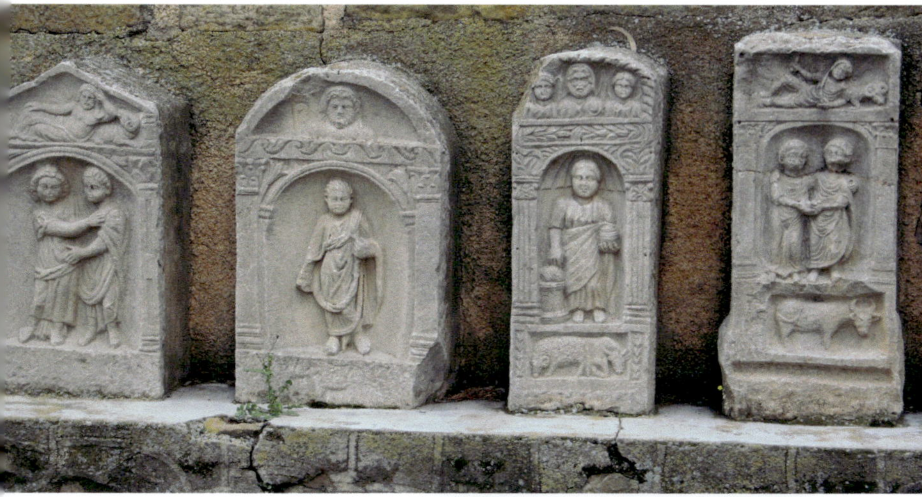

Fig. 228 (above). Timgad Museum: stelai *dedicated to Saturn.*

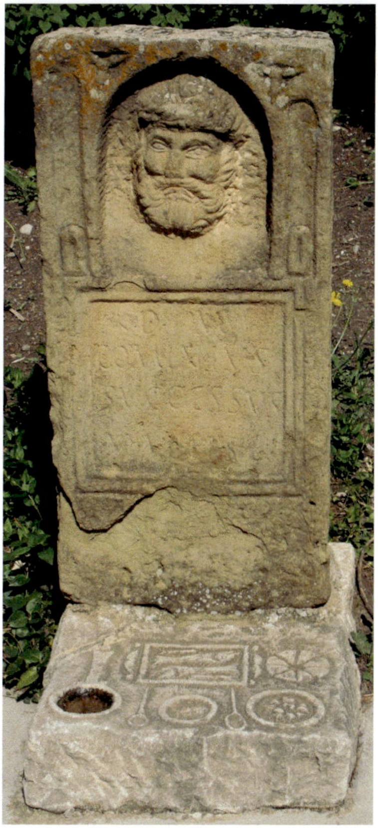

Fig. 229 (right). Timgad Museum: tombstone and mensa *of Cominius Successus. The portrait is presumably of Saturn, rather than of the deceased.*

others). In 2018 it was definitively closed for repairs, hopefully not for too long. The museum was designed for the display on its walls and floors of some 235 panels or fragments of mosaic, which make an unforgettable impression if access can be obtained. There is space to describe only a few of these below.

Central Hall

Large still life with images of food from the hostelry (37: fig. 230). This dining-room mosaic represents the elements of a lavish meal. Within a border of laurel leaves and fruits, twenty medallions in five rows represent a variety of dishes, including snails, lobsters, pastries, partridges, a kid, bunches of grapes, a tethered hare, apples, a sea-urchin, hens and thrushes, fruits and bread. (Third or fourth century.)

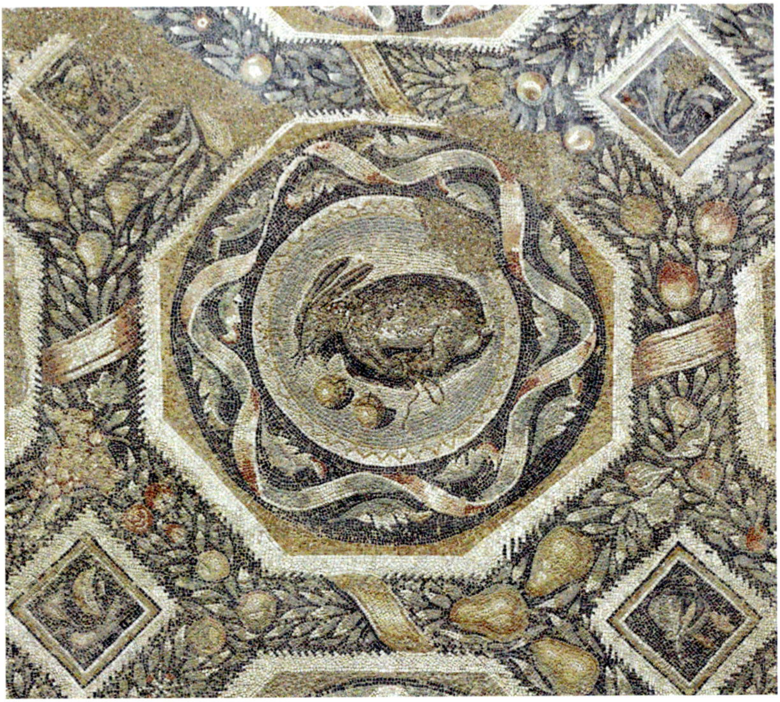

Fig. 230. Timgad Museum: detail of still life with hare, from the hostelry.

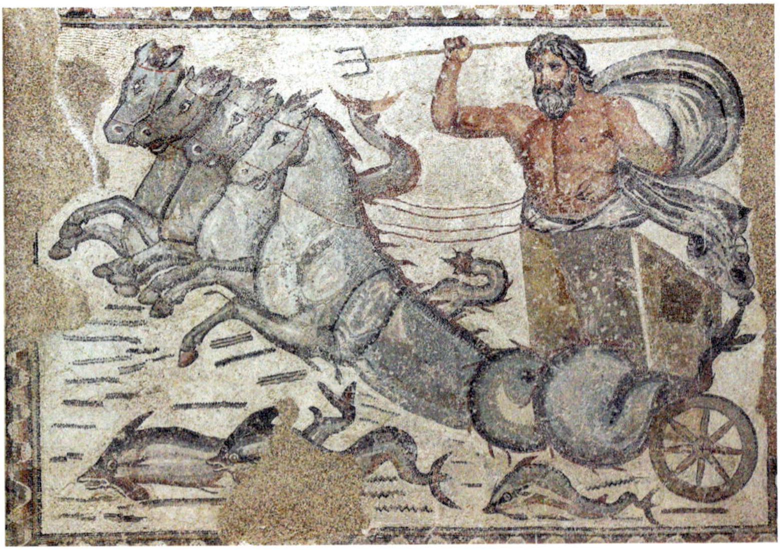

Fig. 231. Timgad Museum: Neptune mosaic from the East Baths.

Neptune in his chariot from the East Baths (16: fig. 231). The god brandishes his trident as he stands in his chariot, which is drawn across the sea by four sea-horses and accompanied by dolphins. (Third century.)

Geometric design from a private house (49: fig. 232). A pleasing square composition of vegetal elements, showing off the best colouristic effects of the local style: a central, concave-sided octagon containing an acanthus rosette is surrounded by a pattern of interlaced hearts and spades. (Third century.)

Head of Oceanus from the baths by the Market of Sertius (40: fig. 233). This very fine square panel is placed immediately above the entrance door. It was originally set in a black surround on the bottom of the cold-plunge bath and the eyes seem always to be directed towards the observer.

Right-Hand Hall

Marine Venus from a private house. In a square panel, a naked Venus is shown resting on two marine centaurs, one of whom she crowns with laurel. The head of the goddess, and part of that of the centaur on the left, has been restored in antiquity. (First half of second century, with third-century repairs?)

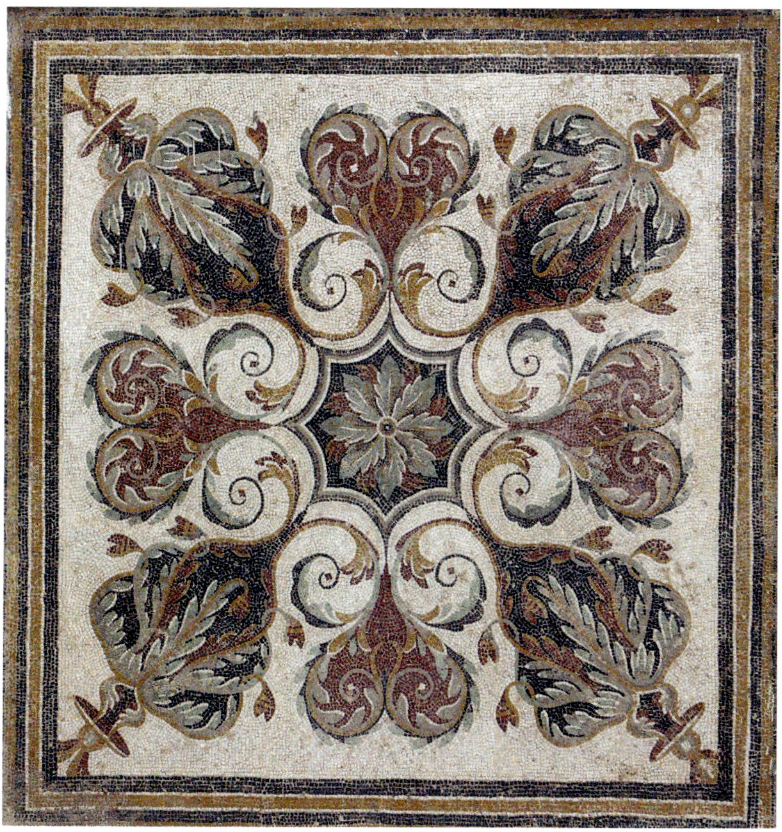

Fig. 232. Timgad Museum: vegetal mosaic design from a private house.

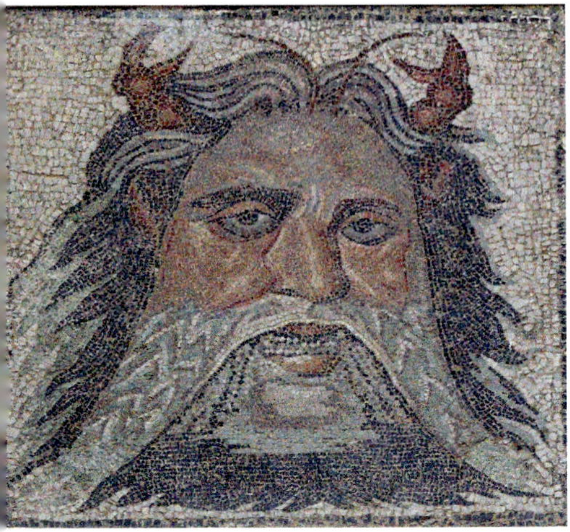

Fig. 233 (left). Timgad Museum: Head of Oceanus from the baths next to the Market of Sertius.

Mosaic of the Philadelphi from the baths named after them (50: fig. 234). In the centre of a lively polychrome pattern of vegetal scrolls – one of the best examples of the 'vegetalised' style created by the workshops of Thamugadi and Lambaesis – is a panel superscribed *FILADELFIS VITA* which portrays the pursuit of Antiope by Zeus, who is disguised on this occasion as a satyr. The scene has a Dionysiac flavour. Antiope has stumbled onto one knee, but still holds the tambourine of a dancing meaenad, while Zeus carries a shepherd's crook (rather than a *thyrsus*). The mosaicist has also used a *trompe l'oeil* effect to conflate the left arm of Antiope, raised to defend herself, with the right arm of Zeus, who is about to lay hands on her. (Beginning of third century.)

Left-Hand Hall

Marine Venus from a private house (fig. 235). A relatively small figured panel occupies the centre of a luxuriant pattern of vegetal motifs set against a black background. The goddess is shown naked, sitting on the back of a marine centaur; he, together with another centaur, holds a drape above her head while she wrings out her hair. The contrast between the pedestrian character of the figured panel and the virtuosity of the vegetal pattern surrounding it is extraordinary. (Third century.)

The toilet of Hermaphroditus from the house named after it (24). This ambiguous scene is rendered all the more so for its fragmentary state. The youth Hermaphroditus, offspring of Hermes and Aphrodite, was wooed unsuccessfully by the nymph Salmacis, who then begged the gods that she might be permanently united with him. They granted her wish, changing the youth into an androgynous figure with the face and breasts of a woman, but with male genitals beneath. Here, the clothed figure (with decidedly female legs) lifts up her dress to reveal her male genitals. He/she is accompanied by two women (proffering toiletries?). (End of third century.)

Artemis and Actaeon from a private house (fig. 236). This is a Greek myth which takes many forms. The kernel of the story is that the hunter Actaeon saw the goddess Artemis bathing naked in a pool, in return for which she turned him into a stag and he was torn to pieces by his own hounds. What we see here is Artemis, crowned and with a *nimbus* (the halo was not a Christian invention) taking her bath; a naked attendant on one side redirects water from a waterfall into the pool, while a second on the other side pours water (or perfumed oil?) from a jug. Actaeon, peering over a rock at the upper left, is now missing, but his reflection in the water, already growing horns, is clearly depicted. At the top of the picture is a rare artist's signature:

Fig. 234 (opposite). Timgad Museum: mosaic of Zeus and Antiope from the Baths of the Philadelphi.

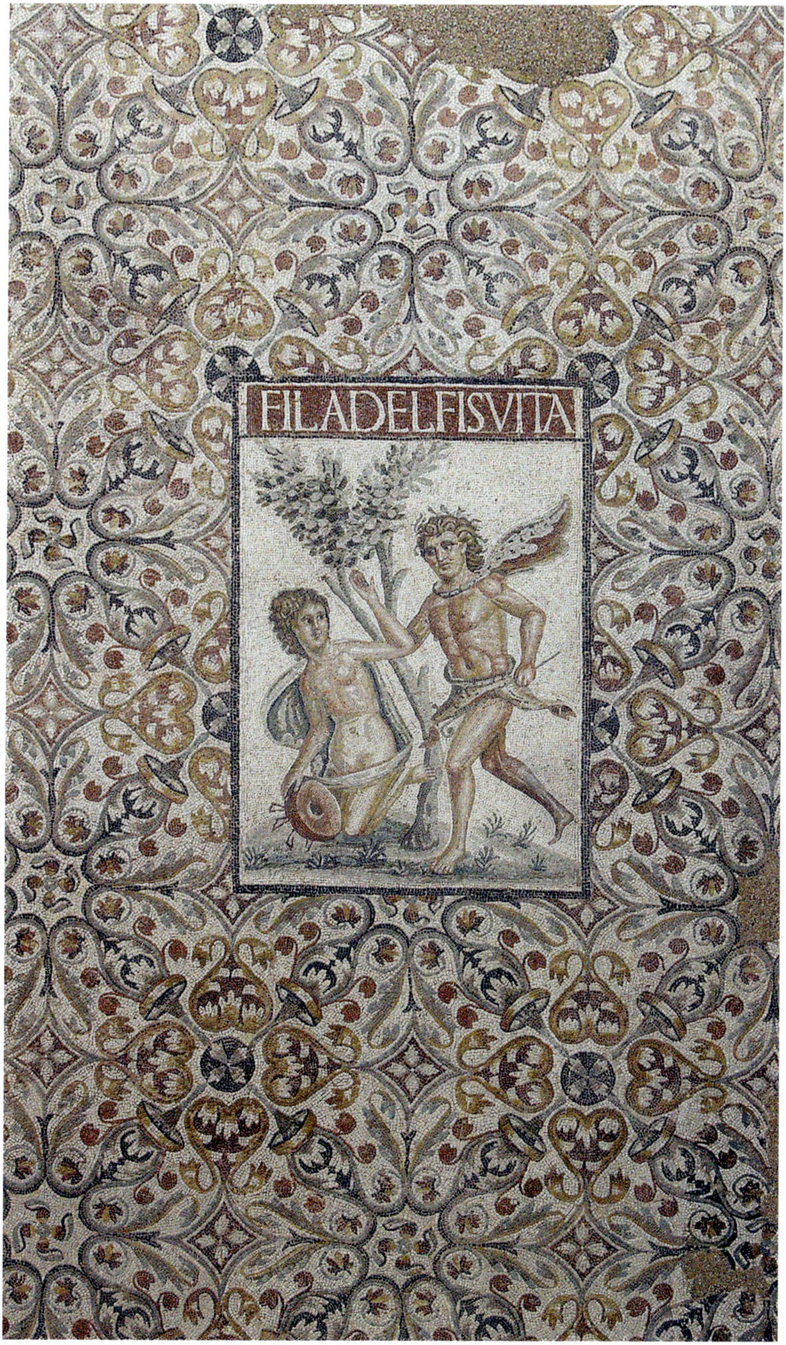
FILADELFISVITA

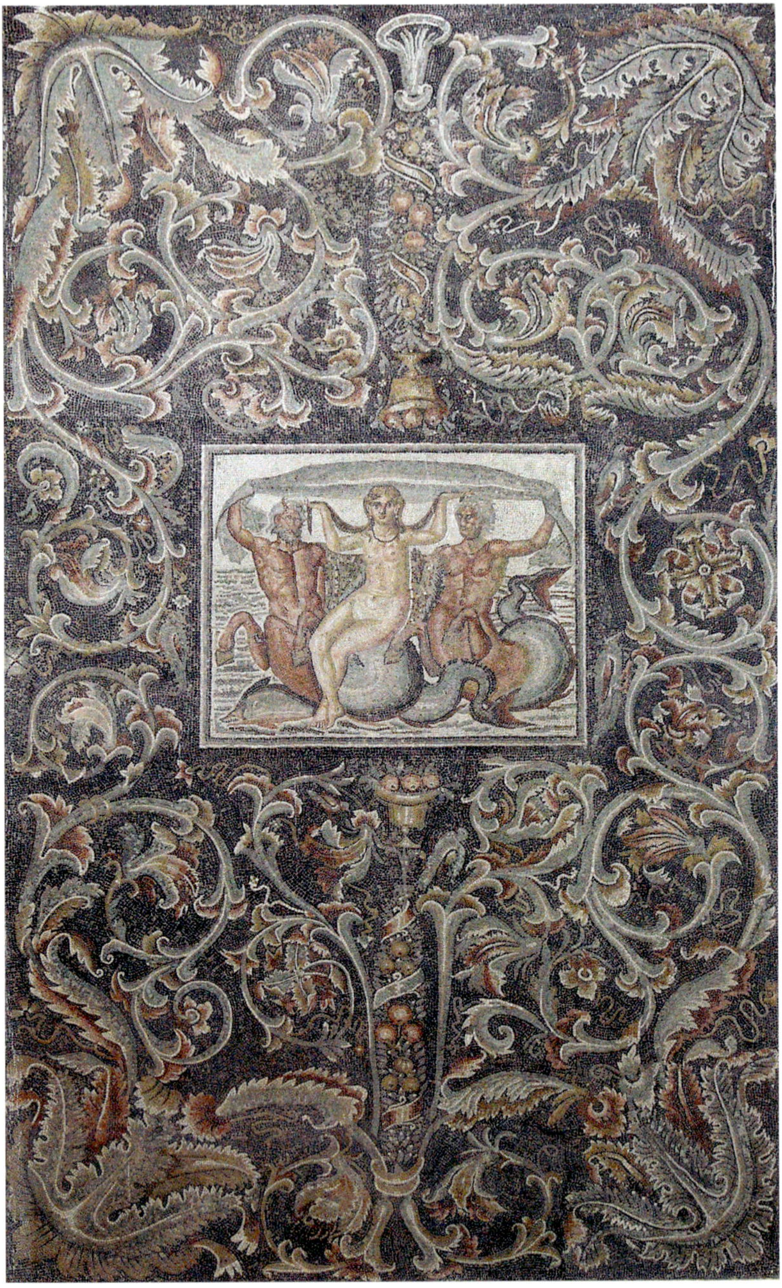

Fig. 235. Timgad Museum: mosaic with Marine Venus panel.

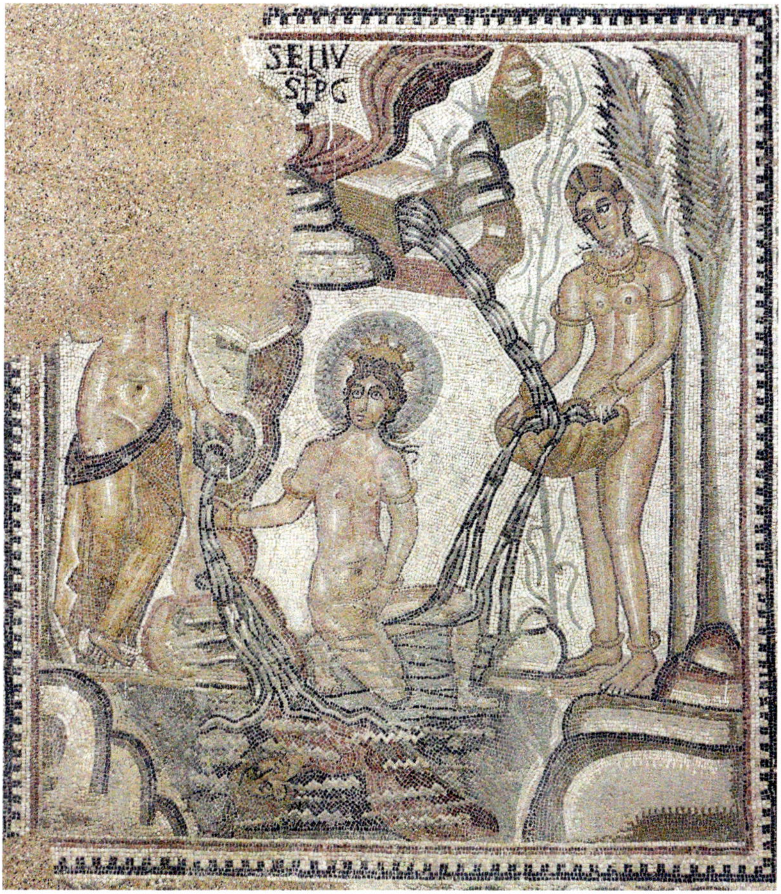

Fig. 236. Timgad Museum: mosaic of Artemis and Actaeon.

SELIV / S P C (possibly 'Selius pictor' – painter). Note the combination of marble with glass paste tesserae and the style of the vine-scroll border (not shown in fig. 236), which is unlike anything else at Thamugadi. This mosaic has perhaps been imported in its entirety from somewhere in the eastern Mediterranean. (End of third century.)

Two further rooms at the rear of the building house cases of small objects, including pottery and terracotta lamps.

DIANA VETERANORUM (Zana)

At the end of the first century and during the first half of the second, an important trend towards urbanisation is detectable in the regions which were now under the control of the Roman army, that is to say the S and W parts of North Africa. Fieldwork and epigraphic studies have shown that settlements, of varying legal status, followed the establishment of military control. It is also clear that the purpose of this colonisation was not so much the control of the mountainous regions as the exploitation of the richer soils and regard for the future of the veterans of the Third Legion. The establishment of *Diana Veteranorum* (Zana) was linked to this global scheme: soon after the camp at *Lambaesis* was made permanent and a city grew up around it, villages and small towns such as *Verecunda*, *Lambafundi*, *Diana*, *Casae*, *Lambiridi* and others began to spring up in the vicinity. *Diana* probably acquired the status of *municipium* under Trajan. A water supply was brought from the spring of Aïn Soltane by means of an aqueduct.

Diana was the seat of a bishopric in the third century and must have had a significant Donatist community, since a bishop of this persuasion, Fidentius, was present at the Council of Carthage (at which Donatism was definitively condemned) in 411. From the Byzantine period, two forts and a church survive. The settlement was finally destroyed by the Fatimids in the tenth century.

Limited excavations have been carried out on the site at different times, but no measured plan has been published and, essentially, Zana is an ancient site which still awaits systematic exploration. The following buildings are identifiable.

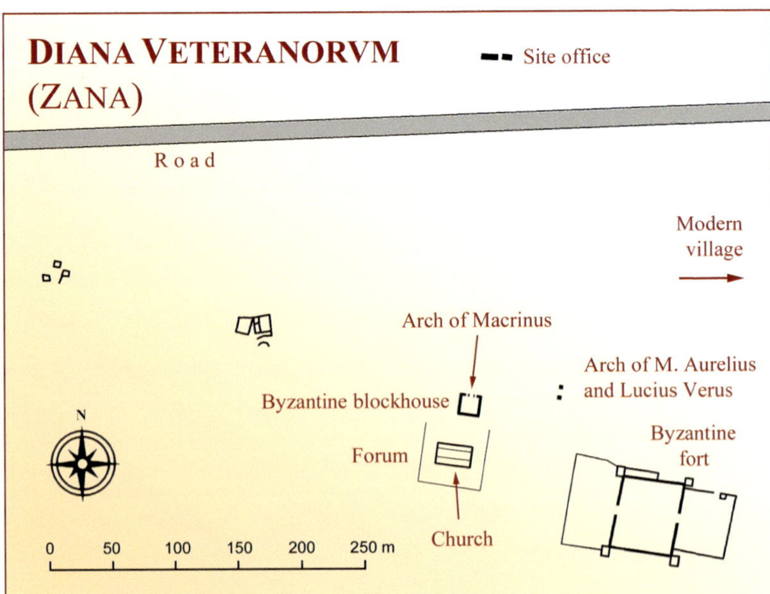

Fig. 237. Sketch-plan of the central area of Diana Veteranorum.

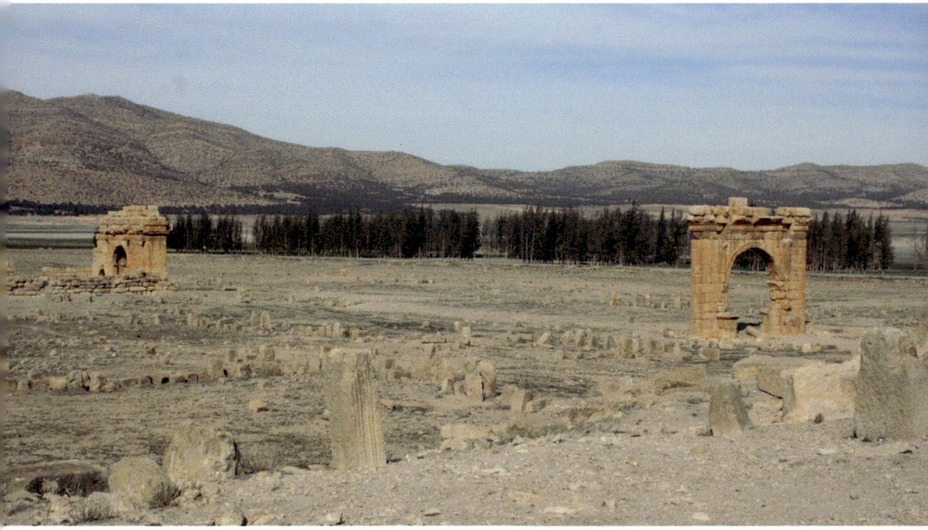

Fig. 238. Diana Veteranorum: the two arches seen from the Byzantine fort.

Arch of Marcus Aurelius and Lucius Verus

This is an arch of a single opening, embellished on either side by engaged columns and with fine coffering beneath its narrow span. It was built in 165 at the expense of the community when C. Maesius Pacatianus was Governor of Numidia.

Arch of Macrinus

This is an arch of three bays which led into the forum (fig. 239). It is extremely unusual, in having been dedicated to the emperor Macrinus and his son Diadumenianus, who reigned briefly in 217–8 after procuring the death of Caracalla. He was perhaps honoured because he was a native of Cherchel (a Moor?). In the Byzantine period the arch was incorporated into a small blockhouse; its main opening became the entrance and the lateral ones were sealed up.

Forum/church

The original paving of the forum has been partly exposed, but the surrounding buildings have not been explored. In the Byzantine period, when the forum was in ruins and, indeed, buried to a depth of perhaps a metre, a church was constructed in the centre (fig. 240). The building is inscribed in a rectangle, with a nave and two aisles, and a central apse between double sacristies. The church is (unusually) oriented towards the W and has been attributed to the second half of the sixth century on the basis of a carved cross containing an undeciphered monogram on a block in the centre of the apse (still present, in pieces). When excavated, the floor level was not recognized (in the absence of paving) and the irregular lower courses of walling show that these were in fact foundations.

There is now a mass of inscriptions lying loose in the forum area, some of considerable size and clearly from public buildings. These have probably been extracted from the Byzantine structures.

Byzantine fort

To the E of the forum, on slightly higher ground and therefore with extended views, stand the walls of a Byzantine fort measuring 61 x 53 m, with projecting square towers at

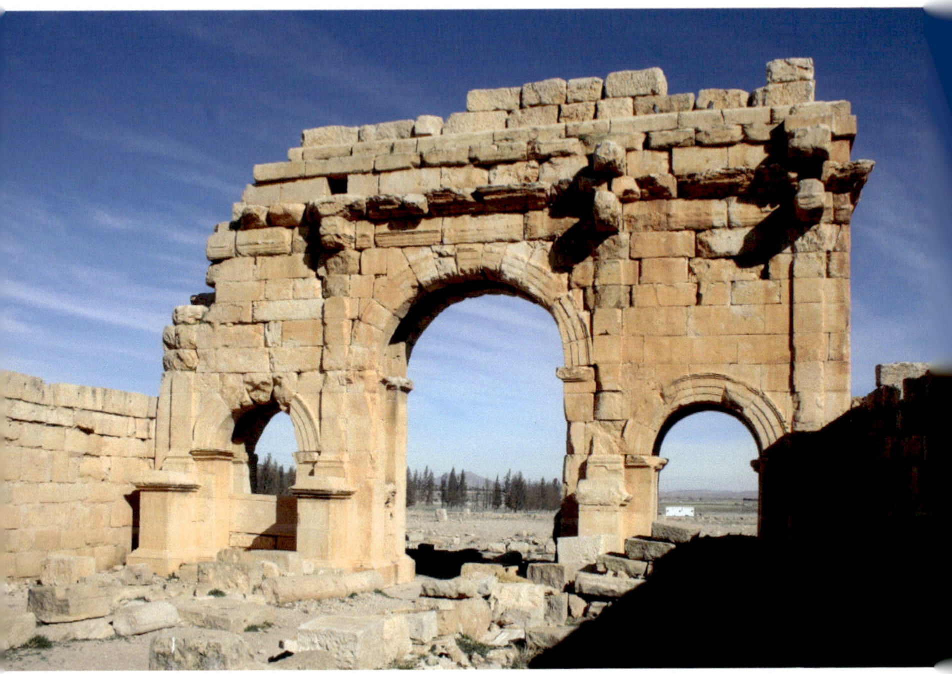

Fig. 239. Diana Veteranorum: Arch of Macrinus, S side.

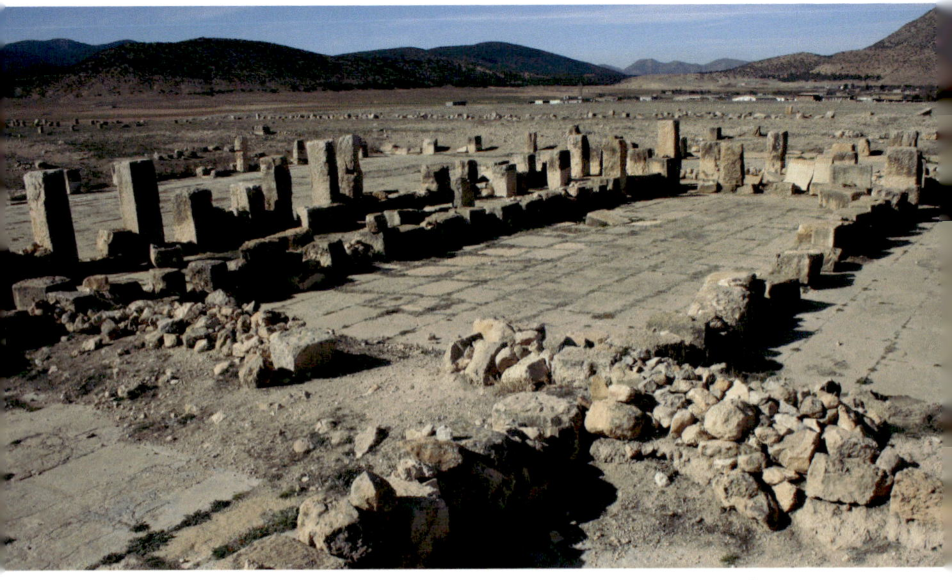

Fig. 240. Diana Veteranorum: the foundations of the Byzantine church in the Forum.

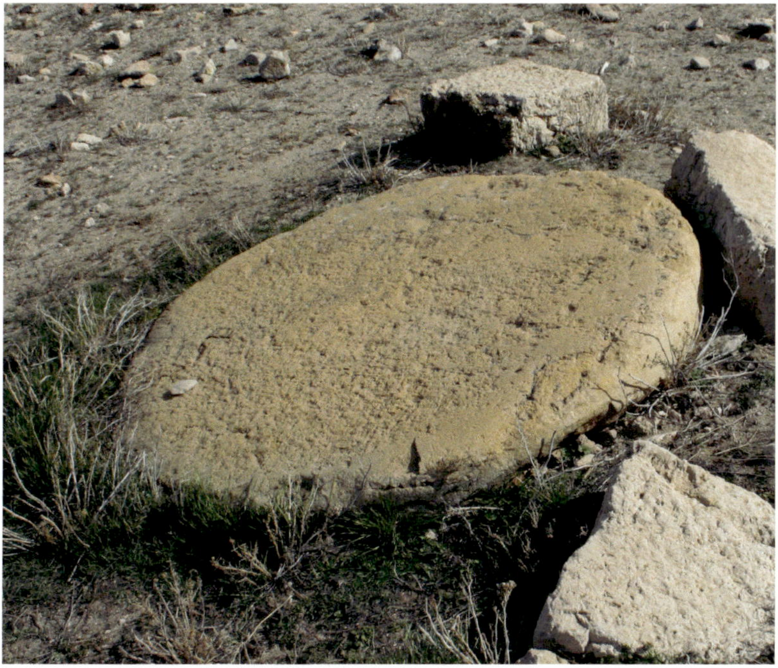

Fig. 241. Diana Veteranorum: rolling-stone door by the Byzantine fort.

the corners. It had entrances on the E and W sides, and appears to have had annexes on both sides (though that on the W may be no more than a later animal pen). The eastern annexe appears to have an entrance on the N side, flanked by a guard-room. Lying on the ground nearby is a large stone disc with rounded edges (fig. 241): a typical rolling-stone closure for small doorways in the Byzantine period.

A temple of Diana has also been identified in the SE quarter of the site – though nothing is now visible.

THE FRONTIER ZONE

As Roman control over the fertile coastal regions and the High Plains was progressively established, it became necessary to establish both routes of communication and military posts further south; not so much to resist incursions by hostile nomads as simply to control population movements. To the S of the legionary base at Lambaesis, two routes through the Aurès massif led to the edge of the Sahara at Biskra (ancient *Vescera*, of which nothing is visible). The first – still today the main route of the N3 highway – followed the valley of the Oued el-Ksour past the little explored ancient settlement of *Lambiridi* to a point where the valley narrows and the river cuts through the dramatic gorge of El-Kantara. The modern road and railway depart from the ancient route just at this point, and no longer pass over the river where

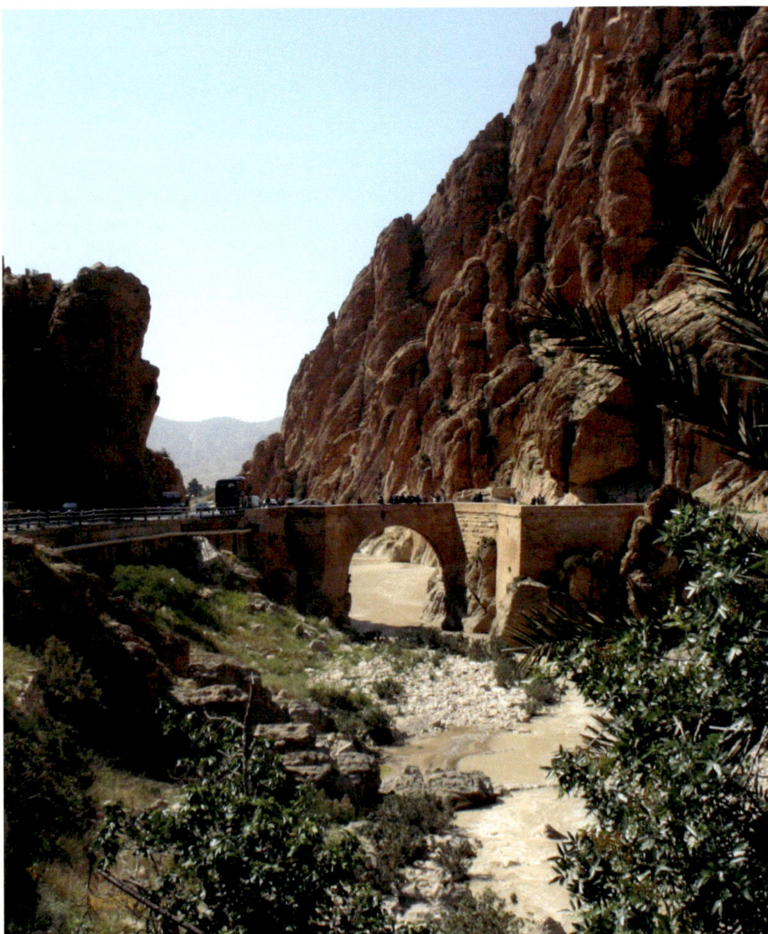

Fig. 242. The reconstructed bridge in the Gorge at El-Kantara.

they did in Roman times. The Romans named the place *Calceus Herculis* (the Boot of Hercules) and constructed a road through the gorge. The abutments of the original bridge are still in place, and the Roman work is distinguishable from the restoration by the French *Génie Militaire*, which was carried out in 1862 and celebrated Napoleon III (fig. 242). During the second and third centuries the passage was guarded by a force of Syrian archers from Palmyra and Emesa.

Another route through the mountains, a little further to the E, passed by *Verecunda* (between Lambaesis and Thamugadi) and then descended the valley of the Oued el-Abiod. Here again, the river makes an abrupt change of course half-way along its length, carving a narrow defile through a mountain ridge at Tighanimine (fig. 243). Just above the modern road through the gorge is a Latin inscription cut into the rock face, commemorating the construction of a road in 145 by a detachment of the *Legio VI Ferrata* (fig. 244). The particular curiosity of this is that, when the inscription was discovered by a French expeditionary force in 1850, there was no passage through the gorge other than along the river bed. (The tunnel used by the present road was cut only in 1936.) However, mortises cut into the rock may once have supported a narrow timber walkway, cantilevered out from the rock face; such a solution is known from other parts of the Roman world.

Gemellae

This military post, 30 km to the SW of Biskra and just on the S side of the Oued Djedi at Ourelal, was established in the Hadrianic period, presumably to secure the fertile oases of the Oued Djedi (known as the Zibans) which benefit from the rains draining southward

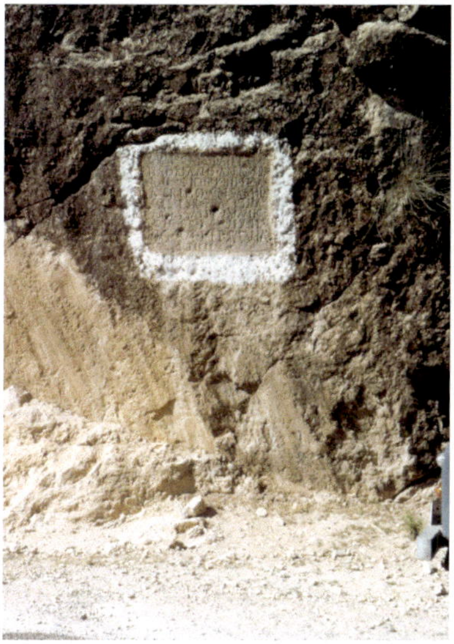

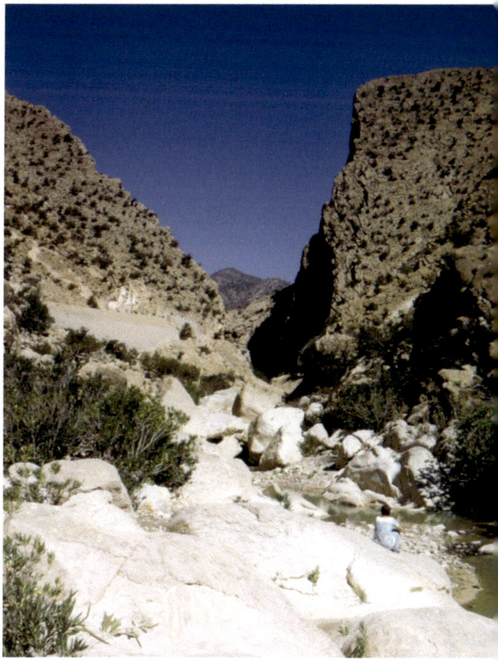

Fig. 243 (above). The Gorge of Tighanimine.

Fig. 244 (left). Rock-cut Latin inscription in the gorge of Tighanimine.

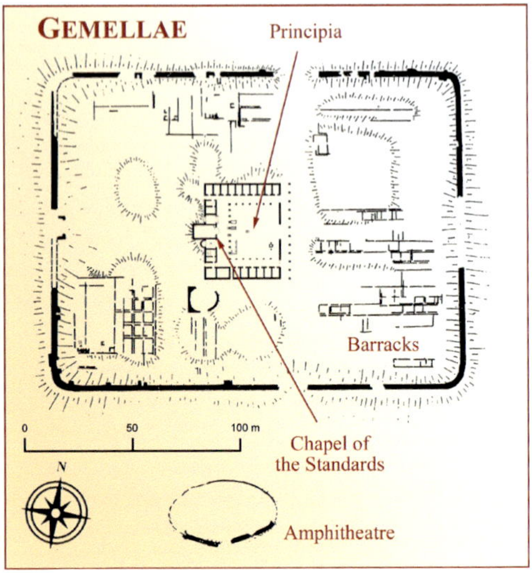

Fig. 245. Plan of the fort at Gemellae.

off the Aurès Mountains. The fort and the various military works in this region were identified from the air by Col. Jean Baradez immediately after the Second World War, and excavations were carried out in the fort in 1947–50. (See fig. 245.) These showed that the first Roman unit to be stationed here, in 126, was the *Cohors I Chalcidenorum*, a force of mounted Syrian archers. The stone-built fort (190 × 150 m) was established a few years later, in 132, by a detachment of the Third Legion. The long-term garrison, however, seems to have been the *Ala I Pannoniorum*, a cavalry unit (addressed by Hadrian at Lambaesis in 128: see p. 169). Cavalry units were essential in such posts, because of the huge extent of territory that they had to manage. No inscriptions later than 258 have been found, but there are other reasons to suppose that the fort was garrisoned at least until the advent of the Vandals in the fifth century.

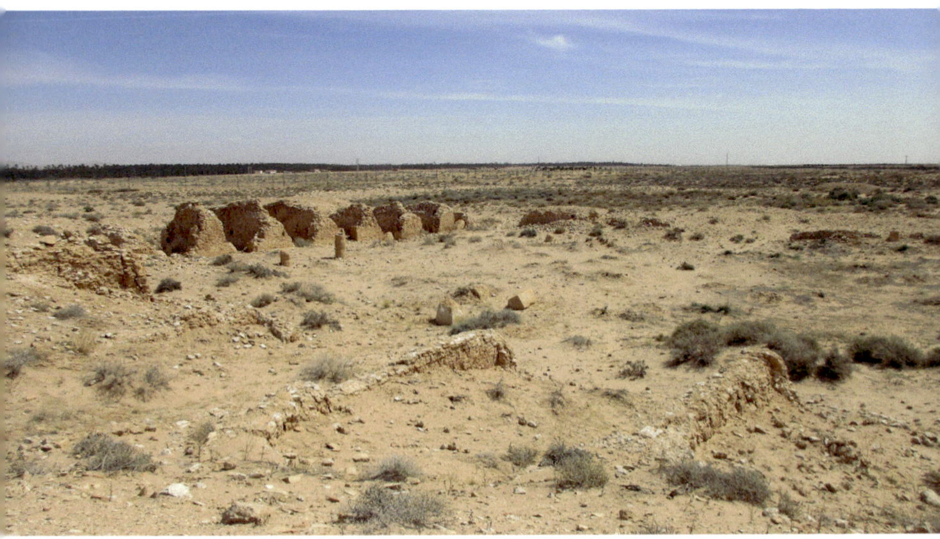

Fig. 246. Gemellae: the principia, with the Chapel of the Standards in the foreground and armouries/offices around the courtyard beyond.

As at *Rapidum* (p. 88), an extensive civil settlement grew up that came to have its own defensive circuit, some 2.8 km long, which here completely enveloped the fort. Within this space was a bath building, an amphitheatre (on the S side of the fort) and a parade-ground, which has not been located but which is attested by two dedications to the *dii campestres* (gods of the parade-ground).

On the ground today, the outlines of the fort may readily be made out, with its rounded corners. In the centre, the headquarters building (*principia*) remains exposed (fig. 246). The plan reflects, on a smaller scale, the corresponding building at Lambaesis (see p. 173 and fig. 180), with a central colonnaded courtyard flanked on either side by armouries. Opposite the entrance was the Chapel of the Standards, with a strong room beneath and *scholae* or offices on either side of it. These rooms were all vaulted and several were plastered and adorned with painted floral decoration. In the centre of the courtyard once stood an altar to Discipline. The headquarters building was surrounded by the other buildings typical of such a fort: some of the barracks were excavated, but little of these is now apparent.

Fossatum Africae

This term is known only once in ancient literature, in a letter of 409 to the Vicar of Africa (the over-all governor of the provinces now composing the Diocese of Africa), telling him to see to its proper maintenance. Extensive traces of a linear work were identified from the air by Jean Baradez in the 1940s, and it was at first thought that this was something akin to Hadrian's Wall in Britain. Now it is clearer that along the African frontier there were various – discontinuous – barriers of this kind and that they were intended, not so much to resist an organized military invasion, as to control the movements of transhumant pastoralists and their flocks and generally to police movement on the desert fringes. The dating of these works is difficult to establish, and they may belong only to the late Roman empire: we simply do not know.

One of the longest sections of such a barrier lies a few kilometres to the S of Gemellae, and is some 60 km long, running E–W. It was composed of a bank and ditch with occasional watch-towers and gateways and, though much denuded, it can still be detected on the ground. In the medieval period a legend grew up which attributed the work to a Queen Bent el-Khrass and described it as a canal which led, ultimately, to Mecca. It hence became known as the Séguia Bent el-Khrass.

4. AFRICA PROCONSULARIS

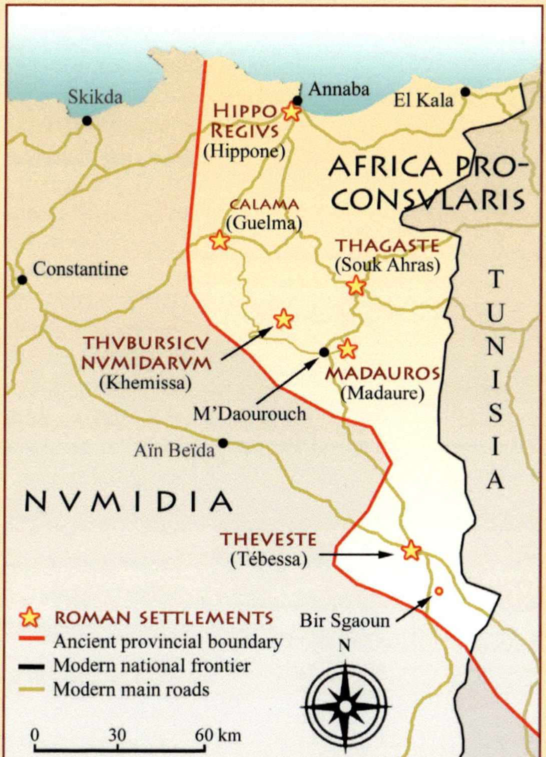

Fig. 247. The western part of Africa Proconsularis in the third century.

HIPPO REGIUS (Bône, Annaba)

Of the innumerable churches [of Africa] he saw only three survive, namely those of Carthage, Hippo and Cirta, which by God's favour were not demolished. These cities too still stand, protected by human and divine aid, although after Augustine's death the city of Hippo, abandoned by its inhabitants, was burned by the enemy. Amid these calamities he was consoled by the thought of a certain wise man who said: 'He is not to be thought great who thinks it strange that wood and stones should fall and mortals die.'

Possidius, *Life of Saint Augustine*, chap. 28 (translation by H. T. Weiskotten, 1919)

The site of Hippo – a particularly well sheltered bay, fresh water in profusion, a rich hinterland – certainly caught the attention early on of sailors looking for good anchorages along this often inhospitable coast. However, for lack of early sources, the evidence for the earliest settlers is tenuous: it has been suggested that Cretans came in the third millennium BC, then Phoenicians and Numidians, but these hypotheses are based on very little.

On the other hand, it is clear that in the Punic period the city was under the domination of Carthage, whose administrative character it seems to have adopted, with two *sufetes* as their leading magistrates. There followed a very troubled period during the Punic Wars between Rome and Carthage: Hippo changed hands several times, becoming eventually a Numidian royal residence, from which it acquired the epithet *Regius* ('royal'). After the destruction of Carthage in 146 BC, it enjoyed considerable independence until Juba I became embroiled in the Roman civil war between Caesar and Pompey. The last of the ships loyal to Pompey were captured at Hippo by the fleet of Caesar's supporter P. Sittius in 46 BC, resulting in the suicides of Metellus Scipio and of Juba. The kingdom of Juba was annexed by Rome and became the province of *Africa Nova*, resulting in a return of peace and prosperity. Hippo became a *municipium* under Augustus and a colony under Trajan; it played an important role as a commercial hub, but particularly as the point of departure of ships carrying the *annona*, the corn supply for the city of Rome. There were therefore official grain-stores and the residence of the officer-in-charge, the imperial *procurator annonae*.

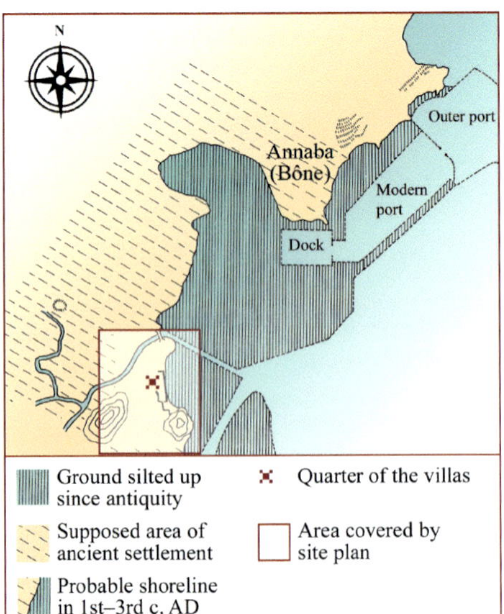

Fig. 248. Hippo Regius: plan showing the relationship between the site of Hippo and the later town of Annaba, together with the supposed ancient shoreline.

The first manifestations of Christianity and the first records of martyrs belong to the third century AD. (Bishop Theogenes was put to death at Hippo in 259.) As elsewhere, the Donatists established a firm hold in the second half of the fourth century; Augustine, appointed priest at Hippo in 391 before becoming bishop in 395, found the city almost entirely under their control. A significant part of his ministry would be dedicated to the refutation of the Donatists' positions; in addition to his writings and sermons, Augustine organized three councils in the city dedicated to this question (in 393, 397 and 427). 'But a short time after this,' wrote his disciple and friend, bishop Possidius of Calama,

it came about, in accordance with the divine will and command, that a great host of savage foes, Vandals and Alans, with some of the Gothic tribe interspersed, and various other peoples, armed with all kinds of weapons and well trained in warfare, came by ship from the regions of Spain across the sea and poured into Africa and overran it. And everywhere through the regions of Mauretania, even crossing over to others of our provinces and territories, raging with cruelty and barbarity, they completely devastated everything they could by their pillage, murder and varied tortures, conflagrations and other innumerable and unspeakable crimes, sparing neither sex nor age, nor even the priests or ministers of God ...

All these evils Augustine deplored bitterly every day, and it added to his grief that the city of Hippo, hitherto spared, now also fell under siege. He died in August 430 before this 14-month siege came to its conclusion, at the age of 76 years; almost forty of these had been spent in the priesthood or episcopate. After his death, Hippo fell to the besiegers, who put it to the torch. It recovered in some measure from this disaster; Possidius reports the presence of some ecclesiastical authority under the Vandals and some sources, such as the *Thronos Alexandrinus* or Leo the Wise, mention Hippo Regius in the eighth and ninth centuries. Its successor, Buna (a corruption of 'Hippone'), built on higher ground to the north, has a mosque which goes back to the ninth century, and was equipped with walls in 1058. Buna was described at that time as 'New Buna', three miles to the N of the old town, which was presumably still inhabited even then. In the sixteenth century it received the Arabic name Annaba (= 'buckthorns').

Saint Augustine of Hippo

Augustine was born in 354 at *Thagaste* (Souk Ahras). He was educated at Madauros and then at Carthage, where he led the dissolute life of a young man of means, fathering an illegitimate son when he was 17. He became a professor of rhetoric at Milan in 384. There, he fell under the influence of Saint Ambrose and was baptised as a Christian in 387. Returning to Africa, he became a priest at Hippo in 391 and then served there as bishop from 395 until his death in 430. During his ministry in Africa, he travelled and argued tirelessly against the proponents of the Donatist Schism, and wrote prolifically. He is regarded as one of the Fathers of the Christian Church; his most influential writings were *On Christian Doctrine*, *The City of God* and *Confessions*.

EXPLORING THE SITE

The entrance to the site is on the E side, immediately beneath the hillock on which the museum stands. The condition of the ruins has been influenced very heavily by the interests of the principal excavator, E. Marec, who typically sought to expose the vestiges of the classical period and swept away any overlying traces of early medieval occupation without record.

1. Quarter of the Villas

This area (figs. 251, 252) was on the seafront of the city at a time when the silts of the Oued Seybouse – the ancient *flumen ubus* – had not yet filled up the space between the visible ruins and the coastline of today (see fig. 248). A feature which strikes the eye immediately on entering the site is a wall of large rusticated ashlar blocks, against

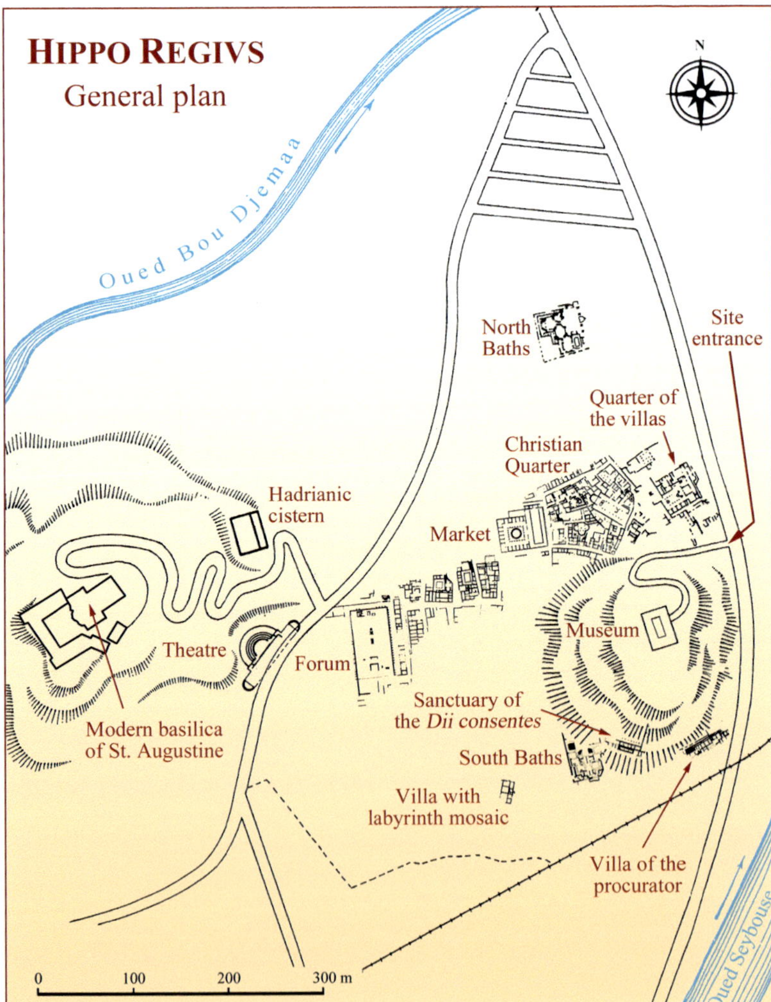

Fig. 249. Hippo Regius: general plan of the site.

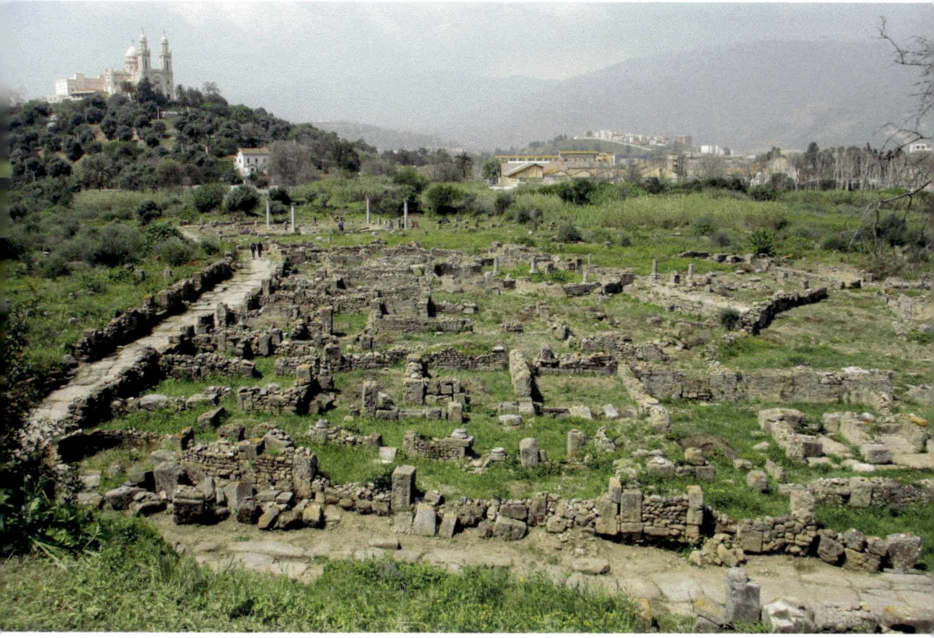

Fig. 250. Hippo Regius: view from the museum, across the site to the 19th-century Basilica of Saint Augustine.

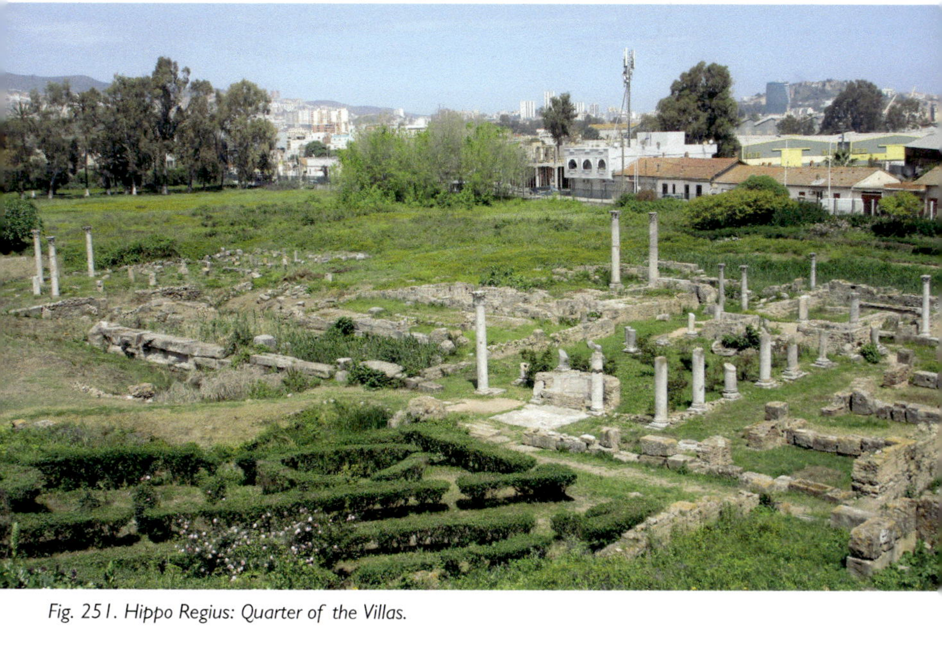

Fig. 251. Hippo Regius: Quarter of the Villas.

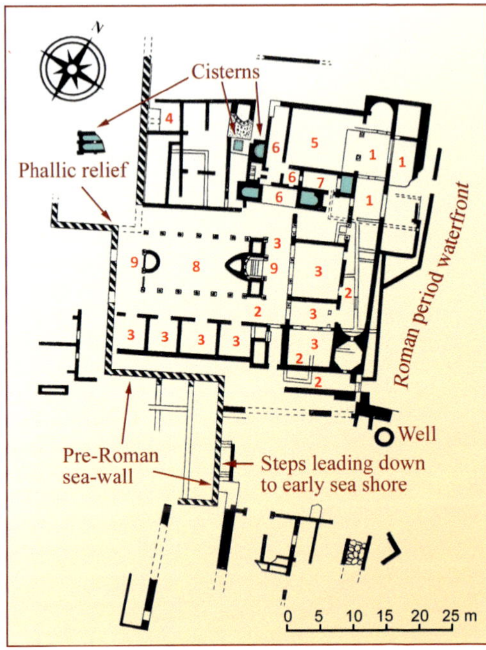

Fig. 252. Hippo Regius: plan of the Quarter of the Villas.

1. *Villa of the Punic caduceus mosaic (1st period)*
2. *Villa of the 'Isgunte Nica' mosaic (2nd period)*
3. *Villa of the Hunt (3rd period)*
4. *Mosaic of Aion (3rd period)*
5. *Villa of the Triumph of Amphitrite (4th period)*
6. *Heated rooms*
7. *Frigidarium of private baths*
8. *Peristyle of Villa of the Hunt*
9. *Fountains (Villa of the Hunt)*

which have been built several seaside villas. Five metres high and 75 m long, this wall (with massive foundations 6 m deep) was in the first century BC a sea-wall. On it can be seen (at a low level, and therefore only after the luxuriant vegetation has died down) a triple phallus to ward off evil. Note also four trapezoidal springer-blocks decorated with lotus leaves in high relief (fig. 253). These are not *in situ*, but have been placed on top of the wall: they presumably belonged to the Punic trading-post and were re-used in the Roman period.

On the E (seaward) side of this breakwater are the ruins of a succession of private houses, which has built up over several centuries. It is difficult to say exactly how many or of what date, but the study of their mosaic pavements has made it possible to distinguish four separate phases ranging from the late second to the fourth century.

The earliest of these is situated at the NE angle of the quarter. It had a mosaic pavement composed of a lozenge pattern surrounded by a border of flaming hearts, including also a head of wheat and a Punic caduceus. A later house yielded the mosaic with a panorama of Hippo (p. 248 and fig. 265) and the *Isgunte Nica* mosaic (a motto which appears to be a victory salutation – to the owner of the property, Isguntus?) with a rich pattern of stylized double tulips; also from this building was a marine mosaic with a head of Oceanus at each corner (see p. 248 and fig. 266). In the centre of the area, and partially on top of the *Isgunte nica* villa, was the peristyle of a much larger property, known from one of its mosaics as the Villa of the Hunt. The base of a staircase at the SE corner of the peristyle indicates that it had an upper floor. All of the rooms opening onto the courtyard (small rooms on the S side and an *oecus* on the E) were paved with mosaic. The floor of the *triclinium*, at the SE corner of the villa, was divided into panels illustrating all the foodstuffs which

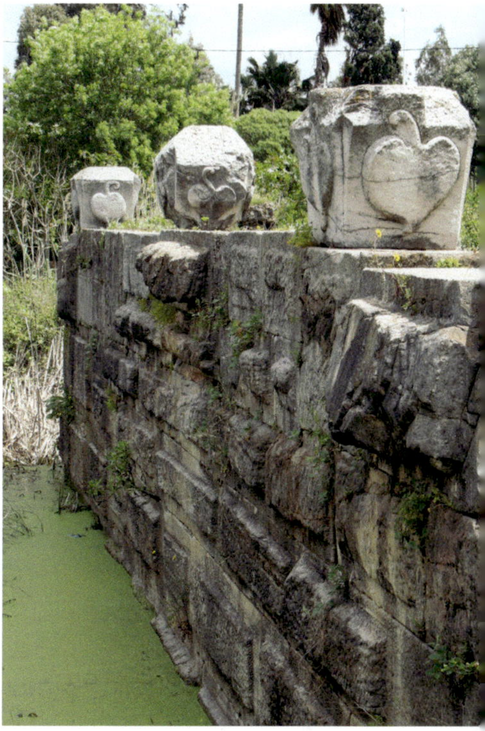

Fig. 253. Hippo Regius: carved springer-blocks on top of the sea-wall. (The water-table on this site is never far below the surface.)

might have been set before the diners arranged around this room: duck, partridge, lobster, bream, a bunch of asparagus and the like. The rectangular room between the *triclinium* and the *oecus* produced the Hunt Mosaic which is one of the masterpieces of the site museum (p. 248 fig. 264). It was the lifting of this mosaic that led to the discovery of the *Isgunte Nica* mosaic beneath.

A mosaic at the NW corner of this quarter (not currently visible) has been attributed to the same period. The central *emblema* portrays a figure carrying a cornucopia full of grapes and the Circle of the Zodiac, in which the signs of the spring and summer months (*Aries* to *Virgo*) are shown. Around this youth, who may be identified as Aion (Eternal or Cyclical Time), are medallions within laurel wreaths, four ellipses portraying Seasons as musicians or athletes, and four circles containing theatrical masks. To the right of the cornucopia are branches and fruits of the jujube or buckthorn, a plant which grows abundantly and which gave its Arabic name (*annâb*) to the medieval successor of Hippo.

Finally, in the NE corner of the area, there was a house equipped with private baths, one of whose rooms was decorated with a large mosaic of the Triumph of Amphitrite. The long gallery with apses at either end which extends across the E edge of the area, and the associated hexagonal room at its S end, seem to belong to a bathing establishment which enveloped the whole area in Late Antiquity.

2. 'Christian Quarter'

The principal feature of this quarter (fig. 254: nos. in brackets refer to this plan) is a large basilica (1), divided into a nave and two aisles by rows of columns on plain square bases (fig. 255). Measuring 42 x 20 m, the building terminates towards the NW in a raised apse (2), lined internally by a solid bench (*synthronon*), interrupted in the centre by an episcopal throne. The apse was flanked by two sacristies (3), and in front of it was a chancel enclosed by screens. All of the floors were paved in mosaic (now covered). The SW aisle housed eleven tombs, including that of a priest named Egyptzuius, adorned with a cross between the letters alpha and omega and the formula *fidelis in pace* ('faithful in peace'). In the NE aisle there were seven further tombs: these included a certain Victoria, with doves rendered in mosaic, and a Suebian – Ermengon, wife of Ingomar – from the Vandal period. Two tombs with richly decorated mosaics enjoyed pride of place in the central nave, where there was also a crypt which made use of a pre-existing cistern (4).

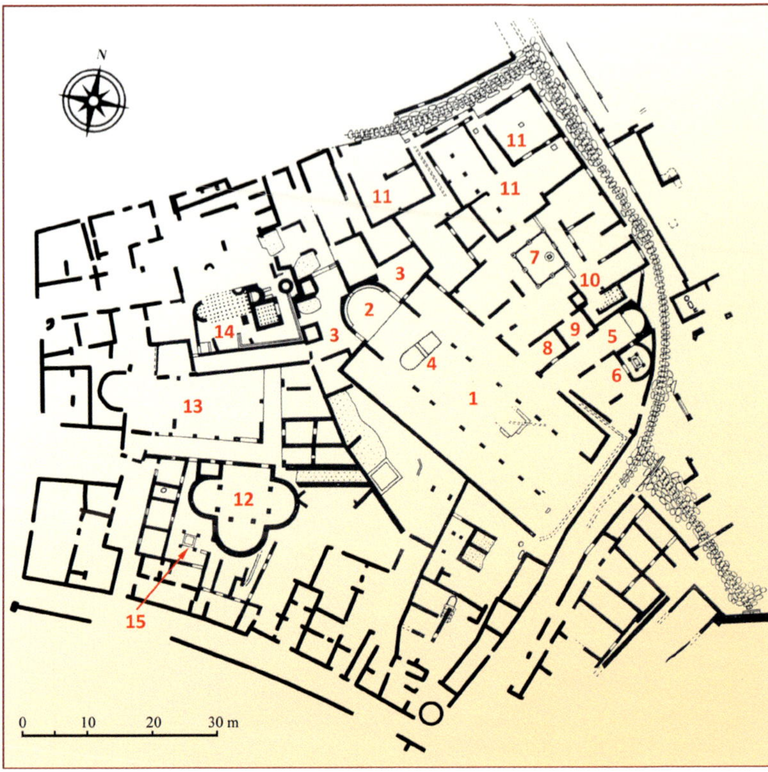

Fig. 254. Hippo Regius: plan of the 'Christian Quarter'.Augustine.

1. *Basilica*
2. *Apse*
3. *Sacristies*
4. *Cistern/crypt*
5. 'Consignatorium'
6. *Baptistery*
7. *Peristyle of earlier house*
8. *Site of mosaic of the Muses*
9. *Site of mosaic of cupids at the vintage*
10. *Bath suite*
11. *Parts of house later used as store-rooms(?)*
12. *Triconch*
13. *Mosaic-paved courtyard*
14. *Former bath complex*
15. *Courtyard with* impluvium

Roughly perpendicular to the church and opening into the first third of the E aisle, an apsed chapel 18 m long (5) was perhaps the *consignatorium* associated with the adjoining baptistery (6). The rooms on the NE side of the church are, however, difficult to interpret. The church was inserted into an irregular *insula* which was already fully built up. The NE part of the space was occupied by a peristyle house (7) which has yielded pavements of Antonine date, representing the Nine Muses (of which only History and Lyric Poetry survive: 8) and cupids at the vintage (on display in the museum: 9). During the Christian period, this may have served as the residence of the bishop, and the baptistery seems to represent a (very modest) conversion of one of the rooms of the house. The

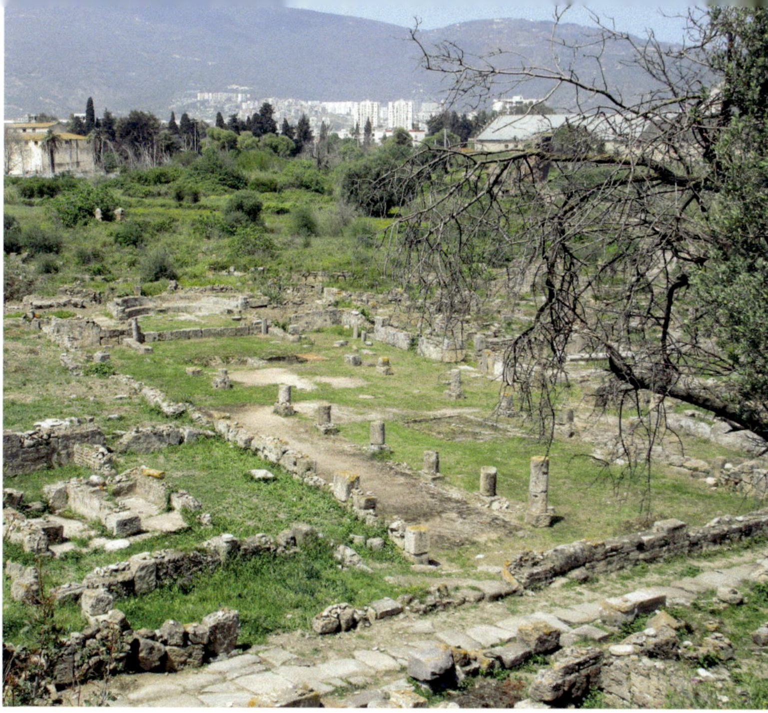

Fig. 255. Hippo Regius: basilica in the 'Christian Quarter'.

adjoining *'consignatorium'* (including its apse) was also part of the pre-existing house, for which reason its ecclesiastical function is far from certain. A small bath in this corner (10) was part of the furnishings of the house, and had gone out of use before the baptistery was inserted.

Mosaics belonging to houses underlying the church suggest that it was built in the second half of the fourth century. Could it have been the Church of Peace of which Augustine was the famous bishop? There is no archaeological evidence in this regard and we cannot even exclude the possibility that this was a Donatist cathedral. The association is plausible, to the extent that we know Augustine's church faced W; also that he was bequeathed in 425, by a certain Julianus, an adjoining house which he had wanted to acquire for many years in order to enlarge his church. It is at least certain that the famed bishop of Hippo would have preached here

The churches of Hippo

There were at Hippo at least seven churches: the Church of Peace, in which the Council of 393 was held; the chapel of Saint Stephen, the vault of which was embellished with four verses composed by Augustine to summarise the story of the first martyr; the basilica of Leontius (on the 4th May, the anniversary of the founding bishop, there were licentious feasts which Augustine had tried to forbid in 395); the basilica of the Eight Martyrs built by Augustine; the chapel of the Twenty Martyrs; the chapel of Saint Theogenes; and the Donatist cathedral, whose boisterous celebrations in honour of Saint Leontius were a theme for censure in the sermons of the bishop of Hippo.

at some point, since after 412 all of the Donatist churches were confiscated and handed over to the Catholic authorities.

The western part of the *insula* is filled with walls and some fine mosaics (not currently visible), belonging to other houses which pre-date the church and have nothing to do with it (for which reason it is misleading to refer to the area as a whole as a 'Christian quarter'). Recent researches have suggested that there were several distinct properties with open spaces between them. One such house (12) has a 'triconch' reception room opening off a mosaic-paved courtyard. Another property (14), behind the apse of the church, displays the heated floors and plunge-baths of a former public bath.

3. Market

This poorly-preserved complex (figs. 256, 257) consisted of a first rectangular peristyle court (37 x 11 m) on the E side, paved with a black-and-white mosaic with swastika decoration, and a second, square court (16 x 16 m) with shops around three sides and a central circular *tholos*, surrounded by columns and raised on three marble steps. The building was constructed in the first century AD and refurbished in the fourth.

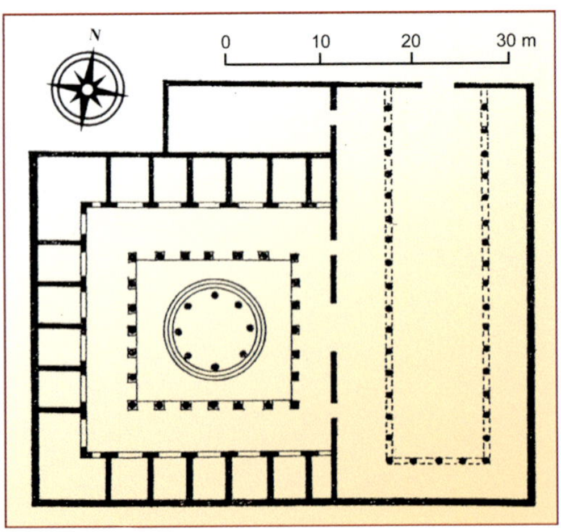

Fig. 256. Hippo Regius: plan of the market.

4. Forum Quarter

Aligned N–S, the Forum of Hippo Regius is a rectangular paved area measuring 76 x 43 m, one of the largest in North Africa (fig. 259: nos. in brackets refer to this plan). It was surrounded by elegant porticoes of the Corinthian order, raised on two steps. In front of the steps ran a gutter to carry away rainwater, a feature found also in the market. The whole complex, including the porticoes, was paved in marble (fig. 258). The principal entrance (2), framed by two columns and with a latrine next to it (3), was at the NE corner where the adjacent *cardo* formed a T-junction with the *decumanus* approaching from the E (if such terms can properly be applied to the irregular, pre-Roman layout of this town). The latter was given a monumental aspect at this point for some 20 m, by porticoed pavements along either side (4). The gateway into the Forum could be closed at night by a double grille. Two other entrances have been identified: one immediately to the N of the main entrance and the other at the S end of the E portico (also possibly provided with a latrine). As with the sill of the main entrance, there are traces there of the anchorages of a grille.

A dozen small rooms (5) opened off the E portico, and the lavish use of marble here suggests shrines rather than shops. Two large rooms identified at the NW corner of the Forum (6), also embellished with marble, may have housed the *curia* of the city. Beneath the paving in this corner was found an early type of Ionic capital, implying the existence of an earlier forum, or at least of an earlier phase of its decoration.

A long inscription, extending in two lines across the entire width of

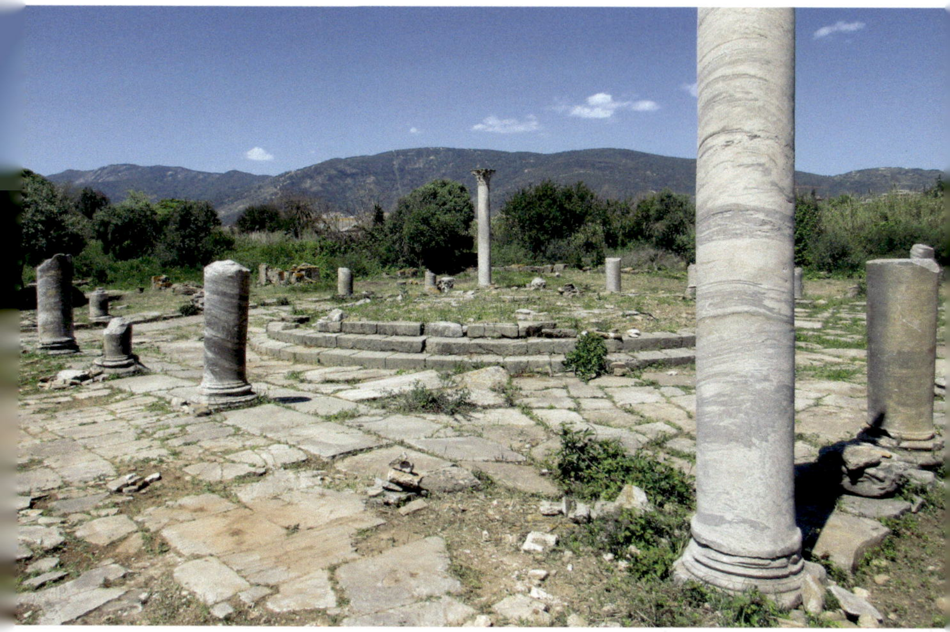

Fig. 257. Hippo Regius: the market.

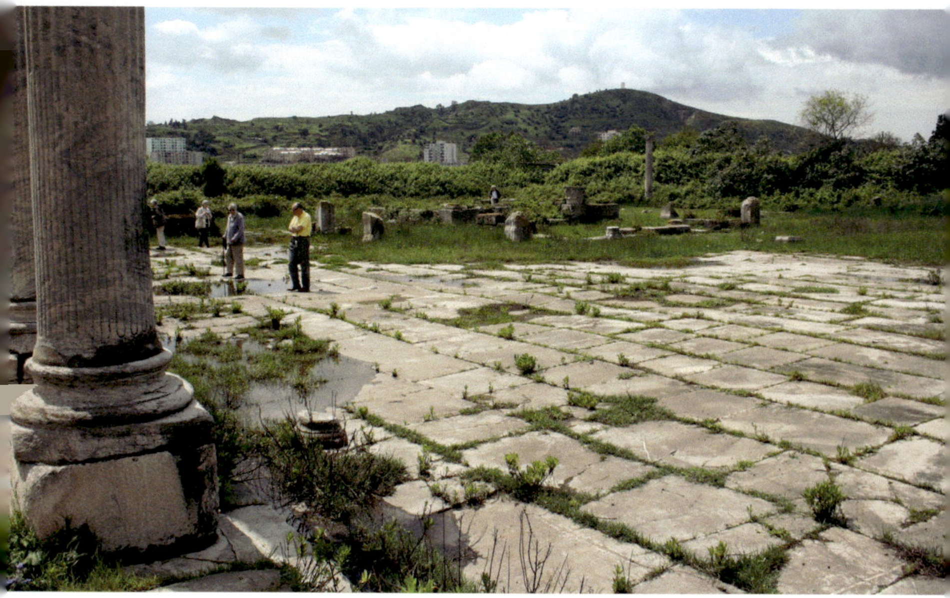

Fig. 258. Hippo Regius: the Forum. This part of the site is still regularly flooded at certain times of the year.

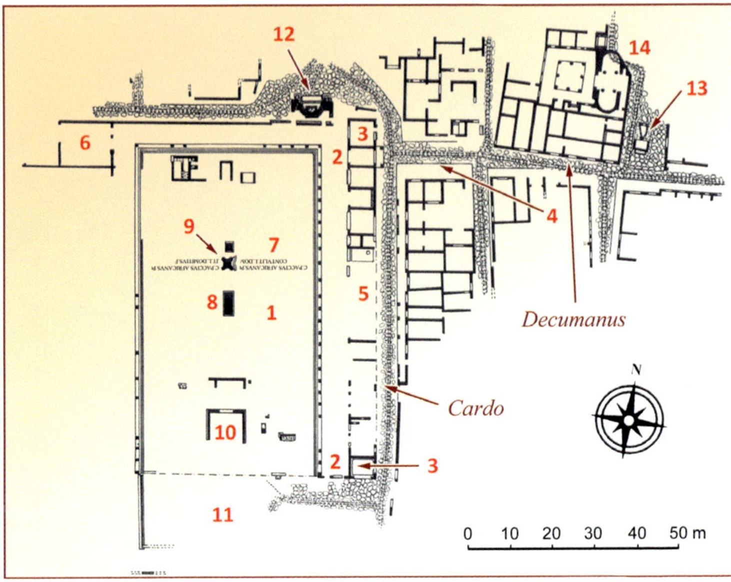

Fig. 259. Hippo Regius: plan of the forum area.

1. *Forum square*
2. *Entrances*
3. *Latrines*
4. *Colonnaded* decumanus
5. *Shrines?*
6. *Curia?*
7. *Inscription in paving*
8. *Statue base*
9. Aedicula
10. *Capitolium?*
11. *Forum extension?*
12. *Nymphaeum*
13. *Fountain with Gorgon mask*
14. *Funerary chapel*

the Forum (7) is now represented by letters which are hollowed out of the paving: originally the hollows were filled with bronze and the letters would have shone from the constant polishing of passing feet. The text records that the paving was dedicated by C. Paccius Africanus, *pontifex*, consul, proconsul and patron of the *municipium* of Hippo – known to us through Tacitus as a senator under Nero, and subsequently Vespasian. We also know (from an inscription at Lepcis Magna in Libya, where he dedicated a triumphal arch) that he was proconsul of Africa Proconsularis in 78.

The possibility that earlier phases of the Forum may go back as far as the third quarter of the first century BC is suggested by the discoveries both of a statue base dedicated to the emperor Claudius in 42 and of an exceptionally rare bronze trophy which was on display in the Forum and may now be seen in the museum (see p. 250 and fig. 268): the latter has been attributed to the time of Julius Caesar, when the Numidian kingdom fell under Roman control after the defeat of Juba I.

In the centre of the square is a large base (8) which presumably supported an equestrian statue, and another smaller one. Between them, a square *aedicula* with concave sides (9) was decorated with colonnettes and, perhaps, reliefs of captives. To the S of these, some foundations (10) fronted by those of a monumental stairway, with fragments of architectural decoration (including capitals like those of the Capitolium at

Thamugadi), belong to a temple which seems to have been too small to have accommodated the Capitoline Triad. Scattered about the Forum, there are numerous statue bases dedicated to the emperors Titus, Vespasian, Hadrian, Septimius Severus, Gordian and Valens, as well as to notables of the city (such as a certain Celer, who immortalized himself by the composition of bad hexameter verses forming an acrostic). A very fragmentary tablet, found re-used in the late paving of a shrine on the E side of the Forum, bears a dedication to the historian C. Suetonius Tranquillus (c. 75–130, author of the *Twelve Caesars*), who was perhaps, therefore, a native of Hippo. The over-all impression given by this forum, with its gates and its shrines and the absence of shops is one of an exclusively sacred and non-commercial space. The latest datable inscription found here belongs to the year 364.

A monumental nymphaeum (12) was sited close to the NE corner of the Forum, facing the street which approached from the N. This fountain was composed of a broad exedra veneered with marble, flanked on either side by smaller basins.

To the E of the Forum, excavations have revealed parts of six *insulae*, on either side of the *decumanus*: these were high-status private houses with marble door-sills and many traces of mosaics. On the N side, the junction with a wider side-street is marked by another public fountain, with its header-tank behind (13). The water once flowed from the mouth of a marble Gorgon mask (which may now be seen in the National Museum in Algiers: see p. 81 and fig. 80). To the NW of this fountain is a late antique funerary chapel with two apses (*memoria*; 14) which leads into a small peristyle courtyard.

5. Theatre

This building (fig. 260), tentatively ascribed to the first century AD, was set into the E side of a hill which was once dominated by a temple of Baal-Hammon (equated with Saturn) and where now stands the modern Basilica of Saint Augustine. Cut into a fine cipollino limestone rock, the *cavea*, 55 m in diameter, had two tiers of seating separated by a horizontal landing (*diazoma*). The *orchestra* was separated from the seating above by a balustrade, and paved in marble with three steps, so as to accommodate the portable chairs of the privileged. The stage-front (*pulpitum*) had lavish marble decoration. In the centre, facing the *orchestra*, was a succession of rectangular and semi-circular niches with alternating statues and reliefs. The only two reliefs that have been recovered portray, above a drum and rattles, a maenad carrying on her shoulder a quarter of a kid, torn apart in a Dionysiac orgy; and Apollo *citharoedos* (playing the lyre) with a griffin and, beneath his feet, the quiver which is one of his habitual attributes. (These may be seen in the museum: see p. 251.) One of the statues from within the semi-circular niches has also been found: a clean-shaven god with hair tied back, doubtless another Apollo.

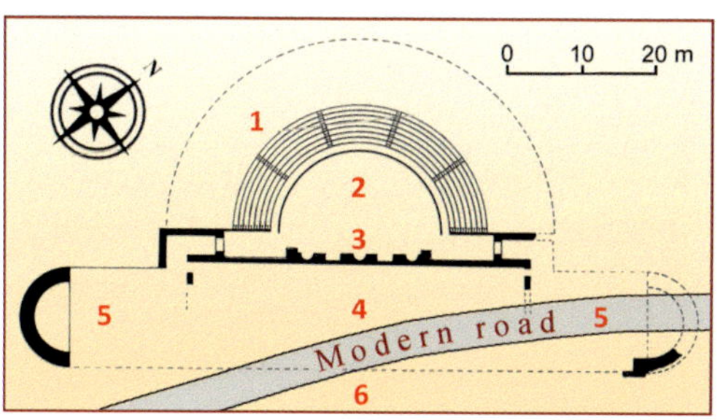

Fig. 260. Hippo Regius: plan of the theatre.

1. *Cavea*
2. *Orchestra*
3. *Pulpitum*
4. *Stage (scaena)*
5. *Wings*
6. *Position of stage building (scaenafrons)*

On either side of these elements, two moulded plinths framed panels that were richly carved with geometric and symbolic motifs; these included the steering-oar and cornucopia which are ordinarily associated with the goddess Fortuna.

The stage, at 40 x 14 m one of the largest in Africa, had a suspended floor, beneath which was a row of huge terracotta vessels (*dolia*, 1.20 m in diameter), variously arranged parallel to the stage-front. This was a device described by the Roman architect Vitruvius (*De Architectura*, 5.5.1), intended to amplify the voices of the actors. This is an archaeological rarity, known otherwise only from the Roman theatre of Nora in Sardinia; there is no sign of them in the theatre at Corinth, cited by Vitruvius, nor in any other Greek building.

Another singular aspect of the theatre at Hippo is the exceptional dimensions of the theatre wings. These huge rooms (13 x 14 m plus apses), which perhaps served as foyers, were faced in marble and embellished with statues, while their vaults were decorated with mosaic. Their proportions give the theatre of Hippo Regius a total width of 100 m – absolutely exceptional for a building of this type in antiquity. Of the stage-building itself (*scaenafrons*), nothing is known.

To the N of the theatre, part-way up the hill towards the modern Basilica of Saint Augustine, cisterns built in the time of Hadrian (see fig. 249) were supplied from an aqueduct built by Trajan, which brought water from a spring in the Edough, 11 km away. (These cisterns have been brought back into service in modern times.) To the SE of the cisterns has been found a little sanctuary dedicated to the *Cereres* (Demeter and Persephone), which is no longer visible; a dedicatory relief from here is on display in the museum (see p. 247 and fig. 263).

6. Great North Baths

This majestic bathing establishment (fig. 261) was dedicated in the name of Septimius

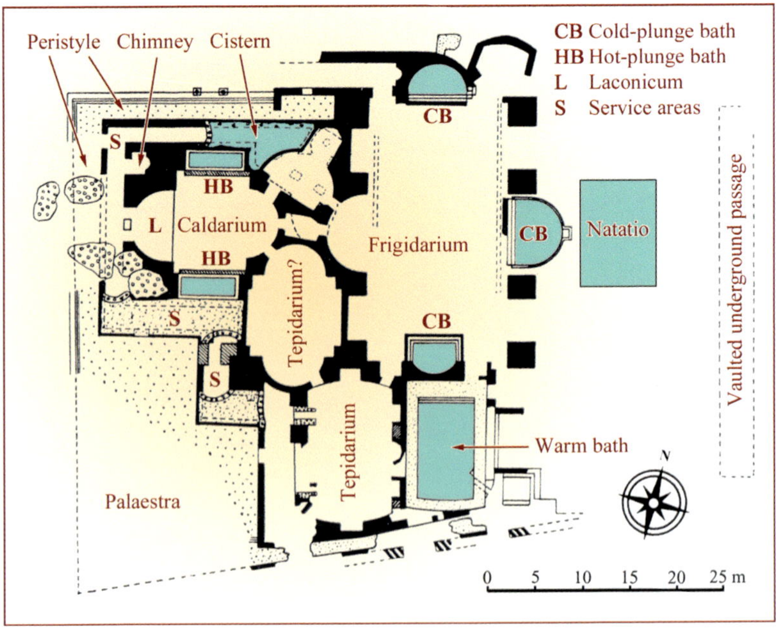

Fig. 261. Hippo Regius: plan of the Great North Baths.

Severus under the reign of his son Caracalla. The plan is asymmetrical, covering an area of 4,500 sq.m. It was enclosed by a peristyle, of which only the N and W arms survive, raised by two steps above a marble-paved *palaestra*. On the N side, a corridor led into the *frigidarium*, equipped with three cold-plunge baths. This hall was richly decorated, as one would expect: its floor was of white marble, its walls veneered with yellow breccia, its vaults covered in polychrome mosaic enlivened by gilded, silvered and enamelled tesserae. In addition, there were numerous statues: six bases indicate statues bequeathed by L. Asellius Honoratus; another base belonged to a statue of Domitius Fronto of Hippo, a Stoic philosopher known only from this stone. Statues found here included an Aesculapius, a Minerva signed by L. Plotus Clemens, a veiled Aphrodite, a fine head of Dionysos, a torso resembling the *Doryphoros* of Polykleitos and – notably – a Hercules 2.60 m tall which is a copy of the fourth-century BC masterpiece of Lysippus (like the Farnese Hercules in the National Museum in Naples, which once adorned the Baths of Caracalla in Rome). Most of these are in Parian marble and demonstrate, if not the competitive spirit of the people of Hippo, at least their desire to show refined taste. Several of them are on display in the museum (see p. 247). To the E of the *frigidarium* was a natatio, beyond which may be seen a vaulted underground passage 6 m wide. This has been described hesitantly as a *cryptoporticus*, but it is often filled with water and has undoubted well-heads along its length: it is surely a cistern.

From the *frigidarium* one could pass directly, through a small lobby, to the *caldarium* or, at the S end into the *tepidarium* (or suite of two *tepidaria*, communicating at the far end with the *caldarium*?). The *caldarium* was provided with two hot-plunge baths; an apse at the farther end provided with a basin (*labrum*) has been interpreted as a *laconicum*, though this usually took the form of a separate room. The *caldarium* also communicated with the *frigidarium* by a northerly route through another semi-circular room with a recess in it, the precise function of which is not clear. In the angle between the S end of the *frigidarium* and the *tepidarium* is a much larger pool, interpreted as a warm-plunge bath.

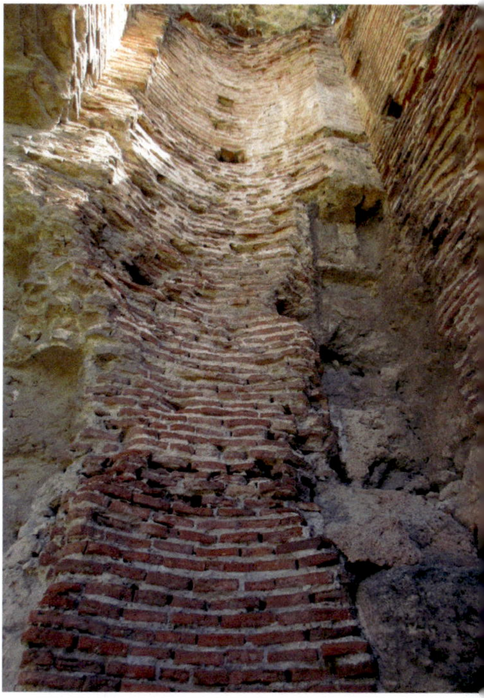

Fig. 262. Hippo Regius: the 'chimney' at the NW corner of the Great North Baths.

The service areas of this bath complex are well preserved: from the *palaestra* one may descend into the corridors and furnaces on the W side. At the NW corner there is an unusual vertical flue or chimney (fig. 262) in front of one of the furnaces; there was possibly a second one in the more ruinous SW corner. Beyond the NW corner, the service corridor returns along the N side, terminating in a large cistern which probably received the water supply for the baths.

7. The S side of the museum hill (Gharf el-Atran)

In this area (now largely overgrown: access is not encouraged) a second ***public bath complex*** has been summarily excavated and even more summarily published; the ruins can barely now be made out. The complex was symmetrical, and its size was comparable to that of the Great North Baths. Inscriptions found in the South Baths indicate that they were built (or repaired) in 198 and that they received further attention under Caracalla.

Some 75 m to the SW of these baths, a ***private house*** was excavated which possessed a marble-lined pool and three rooms with mosaics, one of which was (at the time of discovery) a fine representation of the Minotaur at the centre of a labyrinth enclosed within ramparts. In the opposite direction, 35 m to the E of the South Baths are the foundations, in heavy rusticated masonry, of a ***sanctuary*** built in the time of Augustus. Its dedication to the *Dii Consentes* (the twelve major gods of the Classical pantheon) is shown by a little cylindrical altar set up here between 164 and 167 by C. Lutius Priscus of Forum Livii (Forlì in Emilia-Romagna, Italy) and L. Octavius Serenus of Brixellum (Brescello in the same region), now in the left-hand room of the museum (see p. 250). In front of the sanctuary was a cistern associated with the South Baths.

Sixty metres further to the E and close to the modern railway line are the remains of the two-storey ***'Villa of the Procurator'***. Once on the coast, this wealthy private property had its own bath suite and an upper floor which opened, behind the house, onto a paved road running beneath the edge of the cliff above. The ruins were irreparably damaged between 1832 and 1836 by General d'Uzer, who deliberately made use of the visible remains to construct a house for his gardener. Only fragments – too fragile for conservation – have been recovered of the sumptuous mosaics which once adorned some of the floors. The excavator of Hippo, Erwan Marec, succeeded, however, in reconstructing some of the patterns, which show baroque characteristics that are exceptional for this site. He had the good fortune, on the other hand, to find the large Mosaic of the Nereids (now in the museum: see p. 249 and fig. 267) which had been believed lost in the refurbishment of the ruins. This work, attributed to the third century, portrays four nereids riding marine monsters through the waves, accompanied by dolphins, eels, wrasse and mullet. Of excellent quality, this scene is enclosed in a border of acanthus scrolls on a black background.

Various epigraphic sources suggest that this house may have belonged to the imperial procurator T. Flavius Macer, appointed by Trajan to supervise the *annona*, the purchase of corn for the supply of Rome, and as head of the estates of Hippo Regius and Theveste. Later, in the second century, it would have become the official residence and offices of his successors in the office of *procurator annonae*.

THE MUSEUM

This stands on the hill of Gharf el-Atran, one of the two eminences of the ancient city, which surely would have accommodated some monument of note. Nothing of such character has been recorded, but the modern building was erected by military authorities in the nineteenth century, long before it came into the custodianship of the Service des Antiquités in 1954. A well-head in the centre of the courtyard gives access to a large cistern beneath, which is certainly of Roman date.

Numerous ***votive and funerary stelai*** are now displayed, both in the courtyard of the museum and on the bank opposite the entrance. Some are dedications to Saturn, but of particular note is a large funerary stele on this bank with a triangular pediment

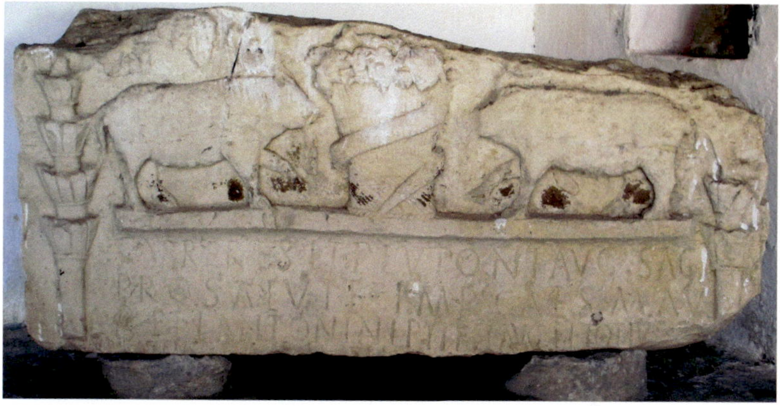

Fig. 263. Hippo Regius Museum: relief dedicated to the Cereres.

decorated with an array of religious symbols beneath the outlines of the sun and moon. This was found about 50 km to the E of Annaba in 1868. A Latin text within a *tabula ansata* reads 'Sactut son of Ihimir [buried here] lived 72 years' while a text in Libyan characters below names the same person and commits him to the care of Amun.

In the SW corner of the courtyard is a ***relief dedicated to the Cereres*** from the Hill of Saint Augustine (fig. 263; see p. 244): on either side of a basket of fruits around which a serpent is entwined, are two sows and two candelabra. In the middle of the S wing is the torso of the *Doryphoros* from the Great North Baths. Also of note – since it implies the existence of an amphitheatre – is an inscription which records that a statue of a certain priest had been erected by each of the electoral colleges of Hippo to thank him for having arranged for his fellow-citizens a wonderful three-day presentation of gladiatorial fights. It was often the case, in regard to such honours, that the person honoured paid for the statue himself! On the W side of the courtyard are further stelai, mainly dedicated to Saturn, while on the opposite side (flanking the entrance to the indoor displays) are inscriptions and tomb-markers of Christian date.

The entrance to the indoor displays leads into a lobby with a staircase. Here may be seen a head, with part of the torso, of a fine marble statue of ***Dionysos***, found in the Great North Baths. From here one may proceed to exhibition rooms on either side, with a third upstairs.

Ground floor, right-hand room

This is dedicated primarily to mosaics, but houses also two further statues from the Great North Baths: a colossal ***Hercules*** and an equally large (but now headless) ***Minerva***, the latter signed on the base by the sculptor, L. Plotus Clemens. The mosaics in here are the following.

Hunt mosaic (left-hand wall, from the Quarter of the Villas: fig. 264, see also p. 237). This is probably one of the earliest examples of a scene which was much reproduced in African mosaics, and most notably in the villa at Piazza Armerina in Sicily. Wild animals are being rounded up for transport to games in the arena, exactly as described by the poet Oppian in the second century. The wild beasts are driven into a net camouflaged with brushwood by beaters armed with flaming torches and shields (with which they make a noise). One of the hunters has

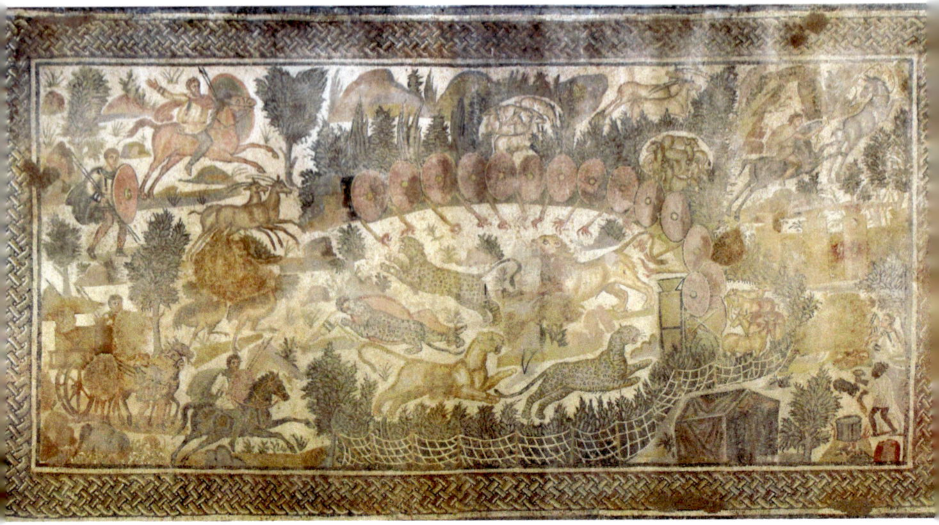

Fig. 264. Hippo Regius Museum: Hunt mosaic.

been surprised by a leopard and downed by him; within the net, tethered domestic animals serve as bait. Above the main scene, at left and right, separate hunts on horseback are taking place, directed against antelopes, ostriches and wild asses. At lower left, a wagon approaches with a crate for a captured animal while, at right, hunters recline at ease while a black cook is preparing their meal. (Early fourth century.)

Fishing mosaic with panorama of Hippo (right-hand wall, from the Quarter of the Villas: fig. 265, see also p. 236). This large tableau, unfortunately missing its upper part, portrays a marine scene in the foreground, including fishermen hauling a net into a boat, while nearby a boat under sail tows a dinghy. The scene is full of detail, and on the left is represented a wide assortment of buildings, including a wooden bridge and a temple with a *quadriga* on top. At the extreme right is a rocky headland. There is no attempt at perspective, and it is possible that the various motifs are arranged at random; but it is not implausible that the artist was trying to portray the landscape of Hippo, with a bridge over the river Seybouse and, on the other side, the headland of the Rocher du Lion which encloses the bay. (First half of third century.)

Mosaic of cupids at the vintage (far wall, from the house E of the church in the 'Christian Quarter'). This is fundamentally a Dionysiac theme, pleasingly composed with the vines springing from kraters, not in the corners, but in the centre of each side. The cupids are typically accompanied by birds, who are also appreciating the fruit. The Christian symbolism of the vine may have assured the continued enjoyment of this mosaic when the house became attached to the church. (Third century.)

Mosaic of the Heads of Ocean (above the door, from the Villa of the *Isgunte nica* mosaic: fig. 266, see also p. 236). Only part of this mosaic has been lifted; part of the opposite edge was exposed on site in 2018. More or less square, with a border of shells and crossed dolphins, the central field was divided into four semicircles (not unlike the mosaic in fig. 137, p. 134) around a central motif (a divinity?) which is lost. The semicircles were occupied by nereids riding on sea-monsters, while in the corners were four heads of Ocean, rendered in very fine detail. Above one of these (and perhaps all) was a representation of the monster Scylla, with her tentacles ending in heads of baying dogs. (Third century.)

Ground floor, left-hand room

This room houses a couple of mosaics of note and various pieces of monumental sculpture.

Mosaic of the Nereids (on the wall immediately inside the door, from the Villa of the Procurator: fig. 267; see also p. 246). Four nereids are portrayed, riding on various marine monsters; the central scene is surrounded by a border of acanthus scroll against a black background, very similar in style to those found at Timgad and Lambaesis (e.g. p. 220 fig. 235). (First half of fourth century.)

Mosaic of animal protomes (on the floor, from house with triconch room in the 'Christian Quarter': see p. 240). A pattern composed of 'portraits' of the foreparts of animals in medallions within a geometric frame.

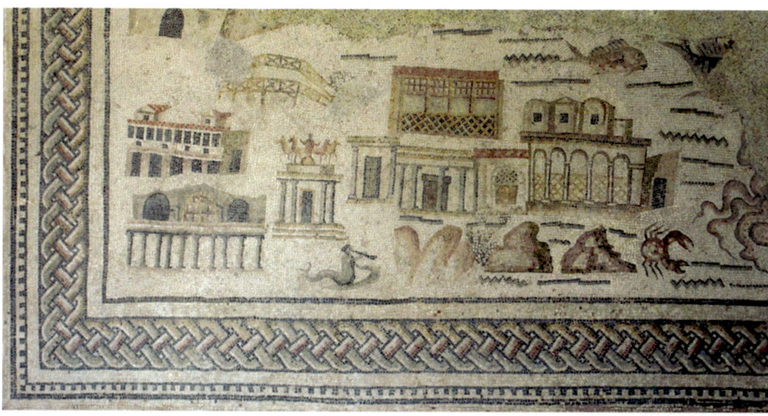

Fig. 265. Hippo Regius Museum: left-hand part of Panorama of Hippo mosaic.

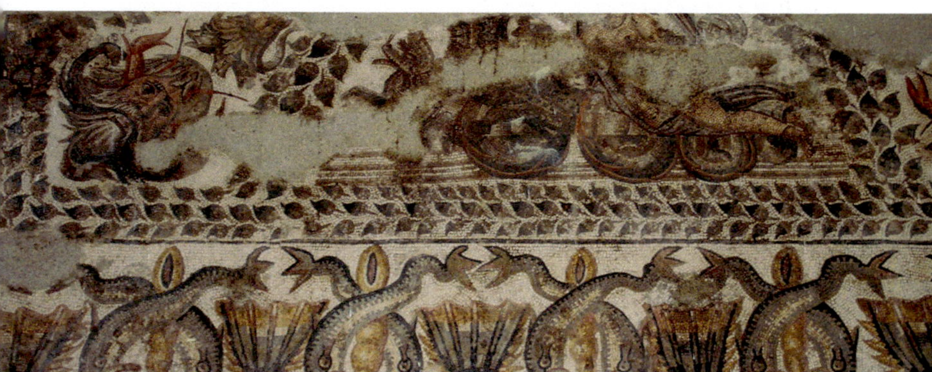

Fig. 266. Hippo Regius Museum: part of the Heads of Ocean mosaic.

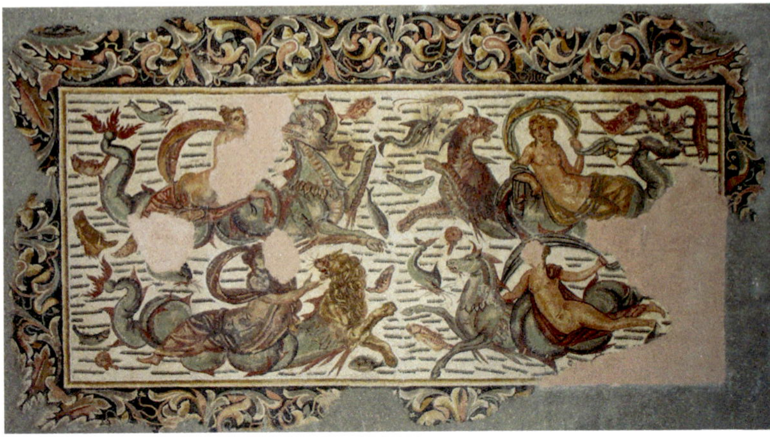

Fig. 267. Hippo Regius Museum: Mosaic of the Nereids.

***Dedication to the* Dii Consentes.** This is inscribed on a small cylindrical altar which is currently standing in front of the mosaic of animal protomes; it was found in a sanctuary on the S side of the museum hill (see p. 246).

Bronze trophy (fig. 268). This unique and impressive piece of cast bronze, 2.44 m high and weighing some 240 kg, was found in the forum in 1948, near the NE corner, lying on its back on top of the Flavian paving. Its date has been disputed, with some asserting that it belongs to the third century AD, but opinion now generally places it at the time when Julius Caesar defeated that last of the Pompeian faction in 46 BC and brought the kingdom of Numidia under Roman control. The form is that of a suit of armour and cloak, hung on a timber frame to celebrate a military victory.

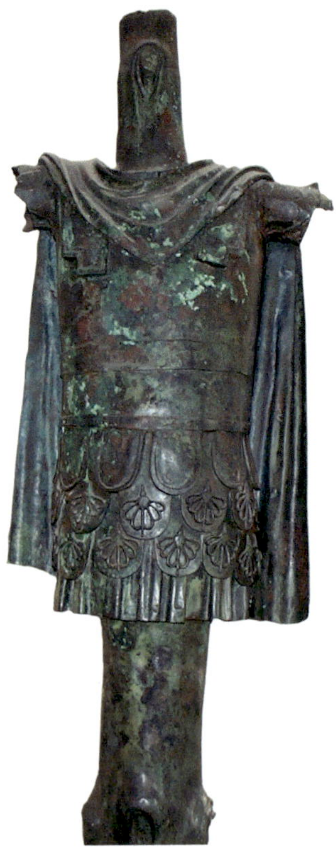

Fig. 268. Hippo Regius Museum: bronze trophy.

Sarcophagus of Greeks fighting Amazons (found in the late nineteenth century at Souk Ahras, *Thagaste*). The scene, which extends across the front of the sarcophagus and both ends, is full of action and movement in which, on the whole, the Amazons seem to have the upper hand. The sarcophagus is carved in white marble, and remaining traces show that it was originally gilded: a very lavish repository for someone in the middle Roman period.

Decorative panels from the theatre stage. At the far end of the room, amongst various *stelai*, are fragments of two panels carved in low relief, representing Apollo and a dancing maenad, and a third with purely geometric decoration in relief (see p. 243). (First century AD?)

There are two large statues, of Apollo (from the theatre) and of Aphrodite (a fine copy of the Vénus de Milo or draped type, originally by Praxiteles in the fourth century BC), also a number of smaller pieces, including heads of emperors (e.g. Augustus, a fine Vespasian, found near the Forum, and perhaps Hadrian) and a comic mask, found in the theatre.

First floor

Here is displayed a wide variety of small objects, from Hippo itself and from Annaba (including objects recovered from the sea when dredging the port). They include pottery (tableware, cooking and storage wares, lamps), bone, iron, bronze, glass and stone; some are decorative items, others (such as steelyards and weights) primarily functional.

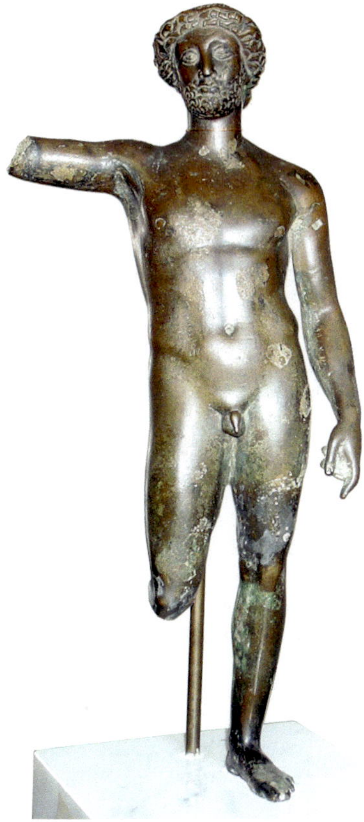

Fig. 269. Hippo Regius Museum: bronze statuette of a god.

Of particular note are two items of bronze, both from the sea; these are in a case in the centre of the room. One is a statuette of a naked, bearded man, probably either Jupiter or Neptune (fig. 269); the other is a charming (though sadly headless) representation of a small girl, seated on the ground (fig. 270).

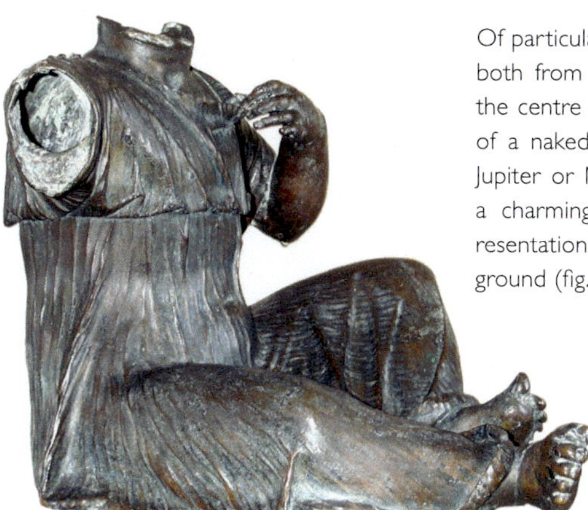

Fig. 270. Hippo Regius Museum: bronze figurine of a seated girl.

CALAMA (Guelma)

Situated 55 km to the SW of Hippo Regius, the settlement originally named *Malacca* was a prosperous city in the kingdom of Masinissa. Both the name (meaning 'salt') and the fact it was governed, like Cirta or Macomades (Aïn Beida), by *sufetes* on the Carthaginian model suggest a Punic or Phoenician foundation. The name Calama was adopted under Roman domination, and the town became a *municipium* in the reign of Trajan and was attached to the province of Africa Proconsularis. It is not however mentioned by Pliny the Elder or by the geographer Ptolemy. Neither does the name appear in the Antonine Itinerary or the Peutinger Table. In 283, the city had the status of a colony.

In the reign of Diocletian, the Christian community (as elsewhere), was fiercely persecuted. A later bishop, Possidius, is famous as the friend and biographer of Saint Augustine. The city was taken and sacked by the Vandals in 429, and recovered to the (Byzantine) Empire in 533 by Paulus, on the orders of the patrician Solomon. It was then equipped with a wall circuit with thirteen towers, on the lines of an earlier rampart, and became one of the fortress-towns of Byzantine Numidia. It disappears from history with the Arab conquest, apart from a single mention in the twelfth century. When the French army under Maréchal Bertrand Clauzel arrived in 1836, it had long been no more than a vast field of ruins (albeit, some of them very well preserved until then).

These remains have subsequently been almost completely enveloped by the modern settlement which grew up with the colonial military base. The ***theatre***, built in 201 or 203, was set into a hillside and built up with ashlar-faced rubble. It was a benefaction of a certain Annia Aelia Restituta: an inscription tells us that she paid out 400,000 sesterces for the entertainment of her fellow-citizens, and that she was honoured by them with the award of five statues (which she probably paid for also).

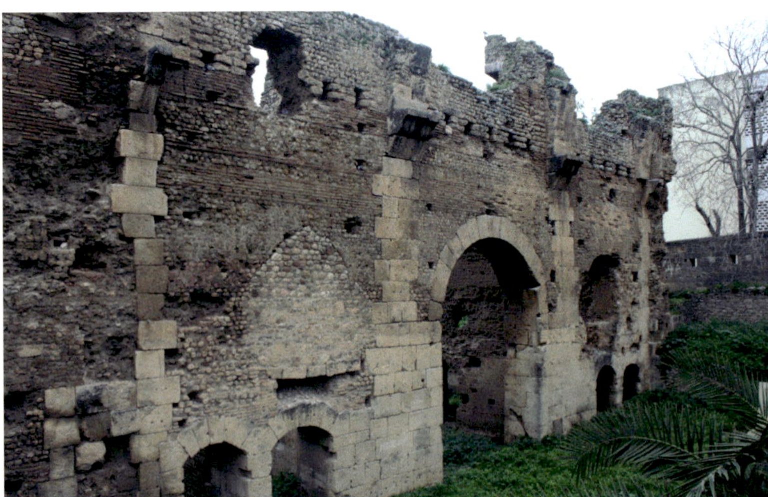

Fig. 271. Guelma: the remains of a Roman public bath inside the ancien caserne.

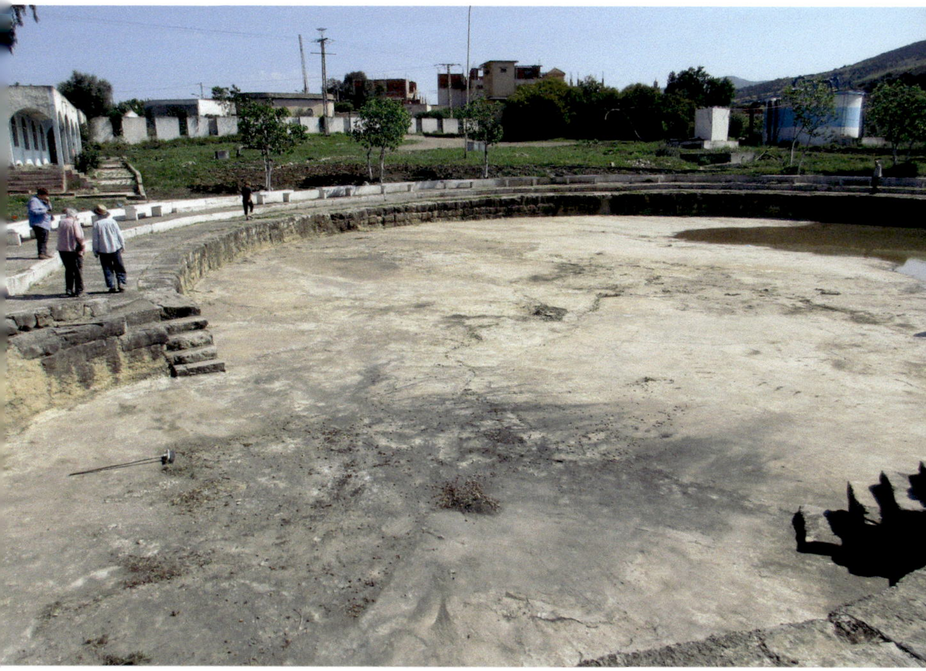

Fig. 272. The Roman thermal spring at Hammam Berda.

The building was well-preserved in 1836, but was then completely dismantled to provide building materials for new barracks. Between 1902 and 1918, by which time archaeologists had become appalled by the earlier depredations of the military, a replica was built on site by Charles Joly. This now serves as the local museum, with a *jardin épigraphique* above, but none of it is original.

The most substantial genuine relic of antiquity which is visible in Guelma today is part of a ***Roman bath complex***, built probably in the second century (fig. 271). This was later incorporated into the Byzantine citadel and then into the French military base (of which it stands just inside the entrance on the SE side). A huge barrel-vaulted hall is apparent, said to have been the *tepidarium* of the baths.

Near to Guelma there were thermal springs which were well known in Roman times. Some 7 km to the N of the town, immediately on the E side of the N21 road to Annaba, at ***Hammam Berda***, is a fine circular basin 35 m in diameter, lined with ashlar masonry, which is still (sometimes) fed by a hot spring from a semicircular recess on one side (fig. 272). Much more dramatic and copious hot springs are also to be found 22 km to the W of Guelma (via the N20 and W122) at ***Hammam Debagh*** (formerly known as Hammam Meskoutine). The principal interest of this site is in the natural phenomena and the striking calcareous deposits (not unlike those at Pamukkale in Turkey) and since the site has been extensively built over in modern times, remains of the Roman period are not readily distinguished. The name of the location in Roman times was *Aquae Thibilitanae.*

MUSEUM

The rebuilt theatre (fig. 273) functions as the local museum, with many sculptures and inscriptions housed in the open air, while more precious or vulnerable objects are housed in the covered halls on either side of the stage.

Stage

Two colossal statues from Khamissa (*Thubursicu Numidarum*; fig. 274): ***Aesculapius*** (left) is a cloaked figure, bearded and crowned; he leans on a staff around which a serpent is entwined, while his right hand once held the strap of the bucket beside him, which is full of scrolls. ***Neptune*** (right) is represented naked, holding a small dolphin in his right hand and accompanied by a (headless) sea-monster; in his left hand he originally held a trident. At the right-hand side of the stage is a ***table of linear measures*** found in the market at Thibilis (see p. 164) and set up there by the aedile (market officer) M. Marius Aemilianus (fig. 275). The uppermost measure corresponds to the Egyptian royal cubit, adopted by the Phoenicians and widely used in N Africa; the second measure is just slightly shorter, and must represent another cubit in local use, while the third represents a Roman foot.

In the vaulted *parodoi* to either side of the *orchestra* are displayed numerous *stelai* dedicated to Saturn: these are mostly from Aïn Nechma (ancient *Thabarbusis*), where a Roman temple to Saturn was found, overlying an earlier sanctuary to Baal-Hammon.

Hall at stage-left *(used as office space and not usually open to the public)*

Triumph of Venus mosaic (from Khamissa, fourth century): Venus is seated on a large shell held aloft by two marine centaurs.

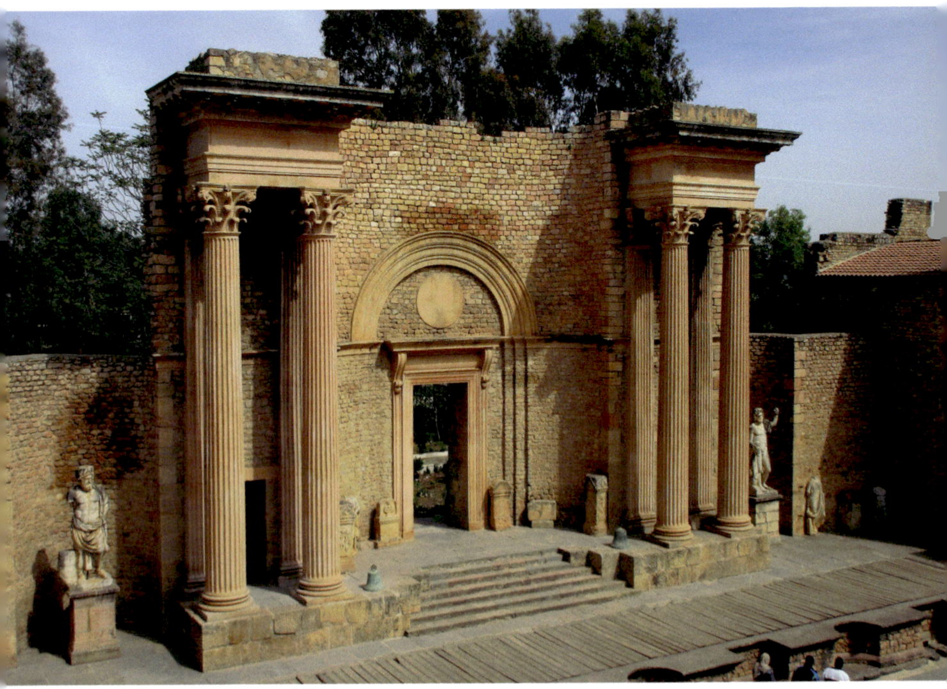

Fig. 273. Guelma: the stage of the rebuilt Roman theatre.

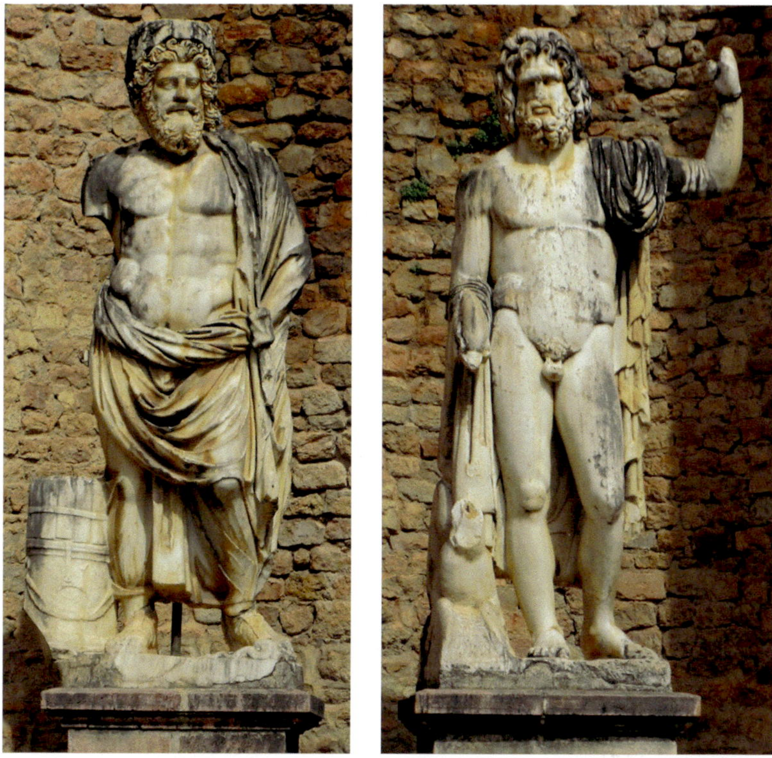

Fig. 274. Guelma theatre: statues of Aesculapius (left) and Neptune (right), from Khamissa.

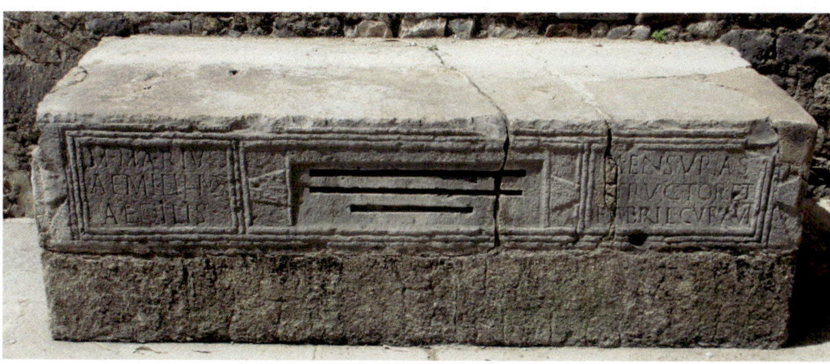

Fig. 275. Guelma theatre: table of linear measures, from Thibilis.

Around her, on a sea populated with fish, are shown various fishing scenes. Above right, a young man prepares to cast his net, while below he is shown hauling it back in full of fish. Above left, another fisherman is putting into a net the octopus or cuttlefish that he has just harpooned. To the left of the shell, a fisherman with a rod has caught a small grouper. The central panel is set within a border of garlands and theatrical masks.

Hall at stage-right

This space is mainly devoted to sculpture, amongst which the following are of note.

Statue of Jupiter: a fine piece, in Carrara marble from Italy.

Monumental bust of Jupiter from Khamissa.

Statue of Hermes: this piece, attributed to the third century, has been modified in the Byzantine period by the addition, on the chest, of a chi-rho Christian symbol.

Statue of schoolboy (plaster cast): this striking representation of a young child was found at Madauros, for which reason it was immediately inferred (without any evidence) to be a portrayal of the young Augustine, since he had spent part of his childhood there.

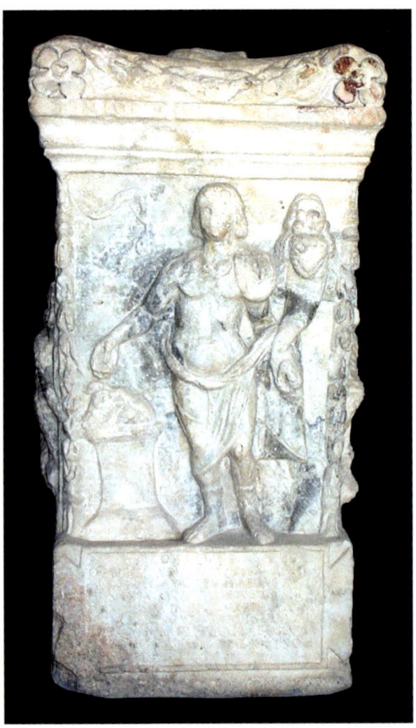

Fig. 276. Guelma theatre: domestic altar of the Antistii.

Domestic altar of the Antistii. This altar, of remarkable interest (fig. 276), was found in the 'House of the Antistii', named after it, at Thibilis (see p. 164). On one of its faces, where traces of added colour may still be made out, the protecting spirit of the family (*Genio domus sacrum* is the dedication) offers a libation: he holds a cornucopia in his left hand, and in the other a dish, the contents of which he pours onto a small altar. Next to the altar is the head of a snake, whose coils are on the adjoining face, entwined around another decorated altar. The inscription tells us that the altar was dedicated in 164 to the wellbeing of Q. Antistius Adventus Postumius Aquilinus, of his wife Novia Crispina, of L. Antistius Mundicius Burrus, of his mother Antonia Prisca and of his children and household by the freedman Antistius Agathopus. The first-named, a native of Thibilis, had had a brilliant career in the imperial service: he had been successively legate of the province of Africa, imperial legate of the *Legio VI Ferrata*, of the *Legio II Adiutrix*, then legate of the province of Arabia. He held a special position as a general in the German expedition of Marcus Aurelius in 168; from this he moved on to the governorship of Lower Germany, and finally to the governorship of Britain (in the 170s). His relationship to L. Antistius Mundicius Burrus is not clear: it has been suggested that this was his brother and that Mundicius was the father of the L. Antistius Burrus who married the daughter of Marcus Aurelius and sister of the emperor Commodus. This man served as consul in 181, but was involved in a failed conspiracy against Commodus in 188, which resulted in his execution. These men, together with Q. Lollius Urbicus of Tiddis (see p. 145) and the orator and tutor to Marcus Aurelius, M. Cornelius Fronto of Cirta, are examples of persons originating far from the centre of Roman power who, in the second century, could nonetheless rise to positions of great responsibility and prestige.

THUBURSICU NUMIDARUM (Khamissa)

Situated in a dramatic landscape 40 km to the SE of Calama and at a height of 950 m, the town is doubtless the *Thubuscum castrum* where, according to the historian Tacitus, the unsuccessful siege of the town by Tacfarinas in AD 24 heralded the abrupt end of a revolt against Roman rule which had lasted for eight years.

Some historians have thought that the town had a Numidian origin, particularly because of an inscription which mentions a *princeps gentis numidarum* ('chief of the Numidian people') and the name of the place, which clearly identifies it as a tribal centre of the *Numidae*. However, the episode when it was besieged by Tacfarinas implies that it was seen in the early first century AD as a Roman settlement. A dedication dated to AD 100 shows that Trajan had accorded municipal status to it, as *municipium Ulpium Traianum Augustum Thubursicu.* The Old Forum and surrounding buildings, and possibly the theatre, belong to this period. Shortly before 270 the town acquired the honorary status (i.e. without receiving a settlement of military veterans) of *colonia*. There was significant building activity in the fourth century under the emperors Constans II and Julian the Apostate. At this time also, there was a substantial Donatist community: one of its bishops, Fortunius, argued publicly with Augustine in 395, when the bishop of Hippo was on his way to Cirta. Augustine visited the town for a second time in 407, as part of an episcopal commission. The town continued to be occupied at least until the Arab conquest, but probably disappeared then or soon after.

The revolt of Tacfarinas

This African noble, probably of the *Musulamii* tribe, had initially served in the auxiliary forces of the Roman army under the emperor Tiberius. In AD 17 he defected and gathered around him a loose confederation of *Musulamii* and other native tribes, whom he instructed in Roman military practice. However, while he was never strong enough to stand up to set-piece battles against Roman forces, the Roman army was equally ill-equipped to handle his guerrilla tactics and his resilience in defeat. In the course of the conflict, three successive governors were awarded triumphal honours in Rome for their successes, but still failed to bring the revolt to an end. Finally, in 24, the governor P. Cornelius Dolabella, faced a situation in which Tacfarinas had larger forces than ever at his disposal (due in part to discontent in Mauretania when Ptolemy acceded to the throne on the death of Juba II). Tacfarinas embarked on the siege of Thubuscum, but was driven off by Dolabella. The rebels then withdrew into forested country near *Auzea* (Sour el-Ghozlane, SE of Algiers and well outside the Roman province). Their location was discovered by Dolabella's scouts, and a rapid strike force made a surprise attack at dawn. This resulted in a massacre of the Numidians. In the knowledge that only the death of Tacfarinas himself would bring the revolt to an end, the Roman attackers soon surrounded him and his entourage. Seeing his bodyguards killed and his son taken prisoner, he hurled himself upon the spears of his attackers.

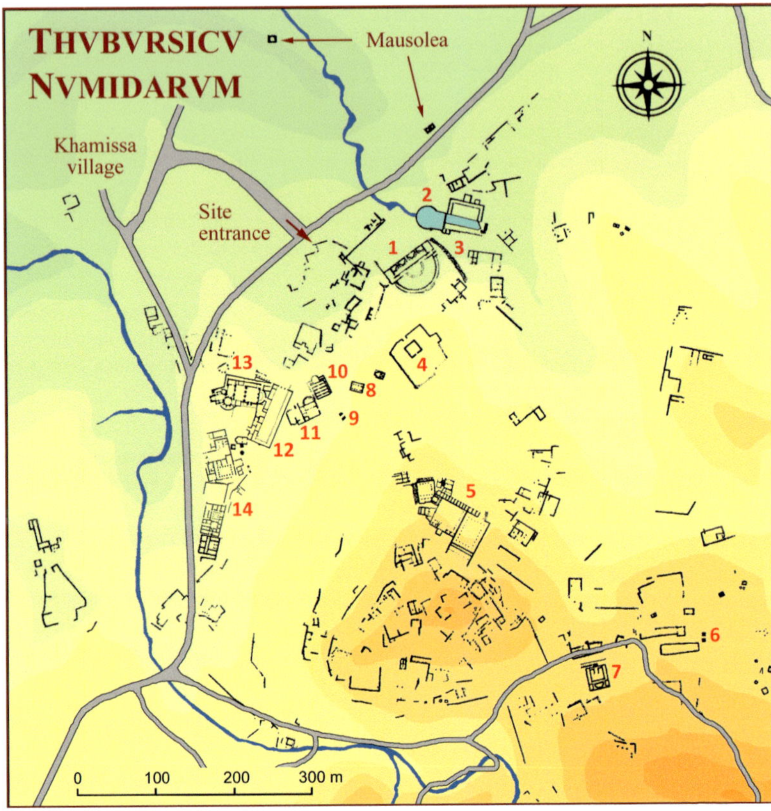

Fig. 277. Thubursicu Numidarum (Khamissa): plan of the site

1. *Theatre*
2. *Spring complex (Aïn el-Youdi)*
3. *Paved street*
4. *Ksar el-Kebir*
5. *Old Forum* (platea vetus)
6. *Town gate*
7. *Funerary enclosure*
8. *'Byzantine chapel'*
9. *Monumental arch*
10. *Cisterns*
11. *Public baths*
12. *New Forum and market*
13. *Public baths*
14. *'Recent' excavations*

Limited excavations were carried out on the site between 1900 and 1922, and little has been done since. Some of the finds from the site are now in the museum at Guelma. It is clear however, both from the site-plan published in 1914 (upon which fig. 277 is based) and from walking over the ground, that there is much still to be learned about the extent and detailed layout of this unwalled town. The high ground above the Old Forum is likely to have been the core of the earliest settlement.

EXPLORING THE SITE

1. Theatre

The theatre of Khamissa is exceptionally well preserved (having not been pillaged by the French in the early years of the occupation: fig. 278). It is slightly smaller than that of Cherchel (p. 34). The stage building is rather plain: given the state of preservation, the absence of any traces of columns or elements of the entablature suggests that the building may never have been completed as planned. (There are foundations for a *porticus post scaenam*, but again no sign of any superstructure.) It has also been remarked that its proportions are not 'canonical' and that maybe the settlement did not have access to an architect of great calibre. The sleeper walls which supported the wooden floor of the stage are apparent, but there is no slot for a curtain. Opinions on the date of the theatre range from Trajanic to Severan.

2. Spring complex: Aïn el-Youdi

Immediately to the NE of the theatre, at the foot of a steep re-entrant, is a monumental double water basin and a sanctuary, built to celebrate the supposed source of the river *Bagradas*, the modern Medjerda which flows into the sea between Tunis and Bizerta (fig. 279). (In point of fact, this spring – known today as Aïn el-Youdi – is the source of a minor tributary: the Medjerda itself rises in the mountains a little to the N of Khamissa.). The complex is composed of two connected basins, one rectangular and the other horse-shoe-shaped, which are fed by the brackish

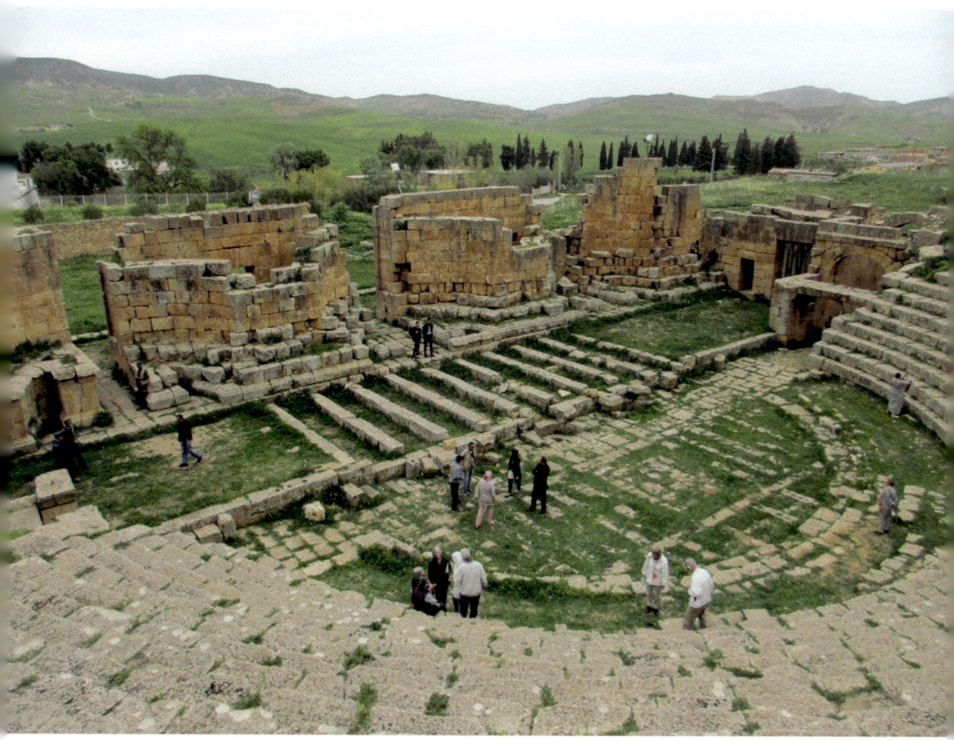

Fig. 278. Thubursicu Numidarum: the theatre.

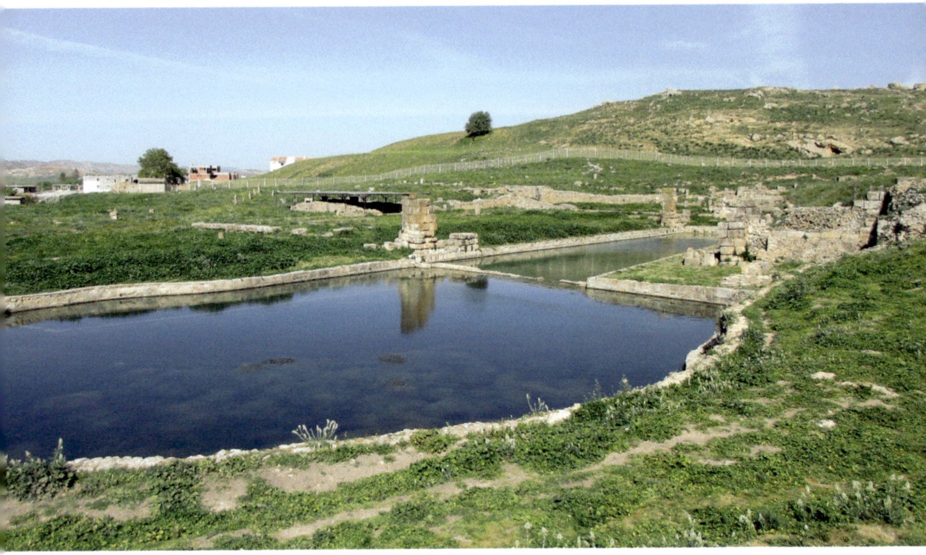

Fig. 279. Thubursicu Numidarum: the spring complex.

waters of Aïn el-Youdi; they are joined, however, in a third narrow basin between the two, by the sweet water of Aïn el-Bir. The long basin is bordered on the S side by a quay, with a room at the W end in which fragments of statuary were found. On the N side of the basin was a colonnaded courtyard, with a central temple on the N side. Raised slightly higher at the E end was a small temple containing a colossal statue of Neptune, now in the theatre-museum at Guelma (see p. 254 and fig. 274, right).

3. Paved street

A solidly-built and well-paved street rises up the hillside between the theatre and the sacred spring.

4. Ksar el-Kebir

'The Big Castle' is the name given to a small Byzantine redoubt which stands on the spur above the theatre, with a commanding view over the lower part of the town. It stands within a larger enclosure of earlier date (which is now barely detectable).

5. Old Forum

Higher still, but still on steeply sloping ground beneath the more level area at the top of the spur (surely the heart of the earliest settlement) is a piazza identified as the *platea vetus* or Old Forum of the town (figs. 280, 281). The central space, including the colonnades on three sides, was approximately 35 m square; on the downhill side considerable terracing was necessary in order to create a large enough level space, and this enabled the provision of shops facing outwards on the lower level. Conversely, on the uphill side the rock had to be cut back to make space for offices (?) and a temple to the Spirit of the Numidian people (*Genius gentis numidiae*), behind which was a strong room or treasury. On the SE side was a civil basilica (built in AD 113), which was adorned with limestone paving and columns, yellow marble veneer on the walls and numerous statues. The presence of yellow marble from Chemtou (*Simitthus*) in Tunisia indicates a date no earlier than the second century. On the NW side of the forum was a capitolium, a public latrine and other buildings.

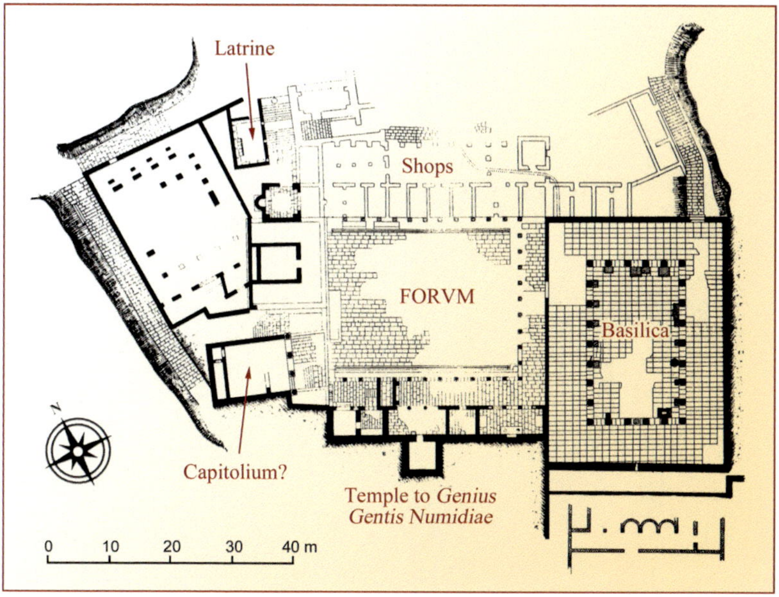

Fig. 280. Thubursicu Numidarum: plan of the Old Forum.

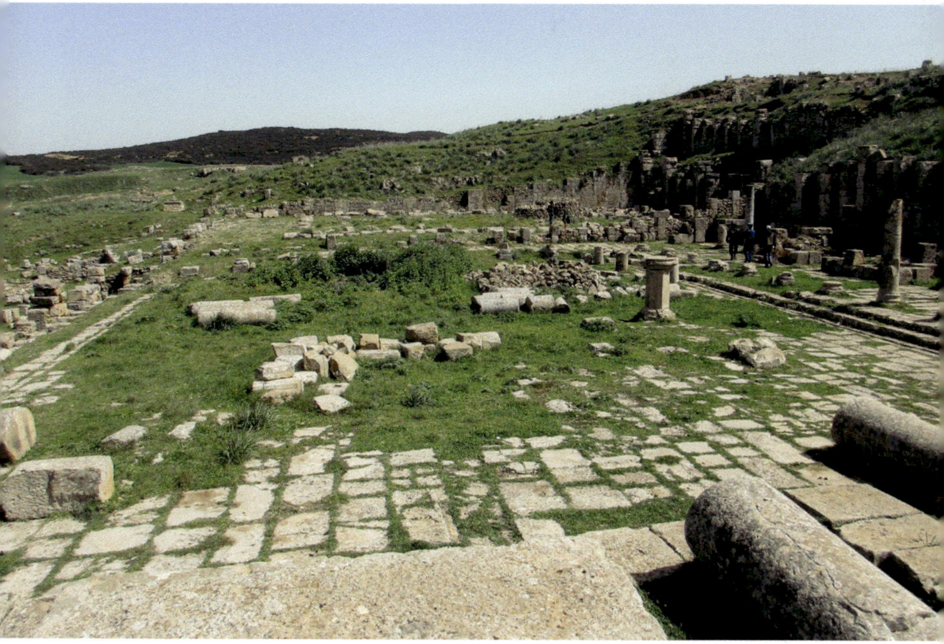

Fig. 281. Thubursicu Numidarum: the Old forum from the NW, looking towards the basilica.

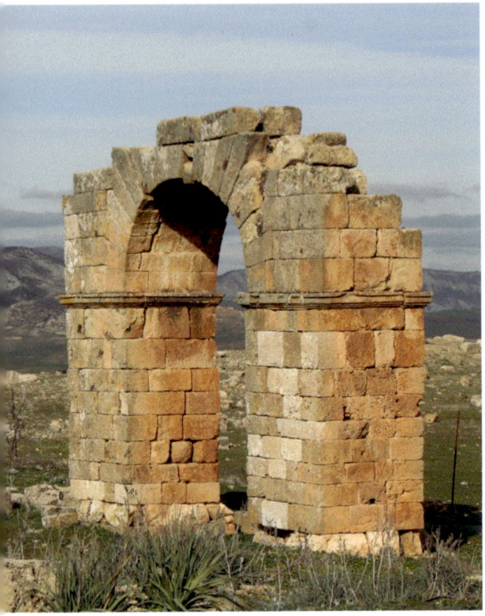

Fig. 282. Thubursicu Numidarum: town gate.

In this area was found a table of measures, but the measures do not correspond to any known Roman unit and they may have represented a local system, suggesting, like the theatre, that the community was only partially 'Romanised'. The paving of the forum was repaired between 323 and 333, but only a generation later the complex was superseded by a 'New Forum' at the bottom of the hill.

6. Town gate

On the high ground, towards the SE corner of the site, stands a well-preserved monumental arch, relatively plain and with a single opening (fig. 282). To the E of it, the line of the ancient road heading towards *Tipasa Numidarum* can easily be made out. About 100 m beyond the gate the base of a rectangular mausoleum is visible, while nearby Roman tombstones still mark ancient burials (fig. 283).

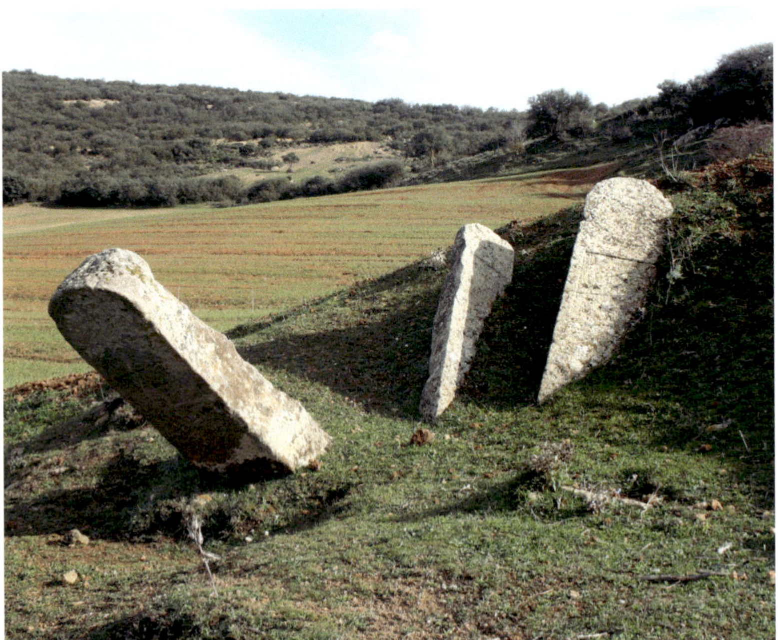

Fig. 283. Thubursicu Numidarum: tombstones beside the ancient road.

7. Funerary enclosure

Not far to the W of the town gate, just above the modern track which skirts the outside of the fenced archaeological zone, are the lower courses of what has been interpreted as a funerary enclosure. A semi-circular exedra in fine ashlar masonry faces onto what appears to be a rectangular courtyard (or garden?) within a larger rectangular enclosure. The enclosing walls were built in small-rubble masonry.

8. 'Byzantine chapel'

This is a building of modest size but very solid ashlar masonry construction (from reused materials). It is rectangular externally, with three aisles internally, separated by piers, and an apse inscribed in the (SE) end of the nave. There is no direct evidence of date, but the massive, defensive nature of the construction suggests that it post-dates the Byzantine reconquest. There is no visible evidence (such as carved Christian motifs) for a religious function.

9. Monumental arch

Here stand the piers alone of a single-bay monumental arch, similar in style to the town gate (6). It must have spanned a road which wound down the hillside from the Old to the New Forum.

10. Cisterns

This is a massive reservoir with five parallel vaulted chambers. It presumably provided water to the two substantial bath-buildings in the vicinity.

11. Public baths

The presence of hypocaust heating systems shows that this massive structure was a public bath complex. It seems a little surprising that it should have co-existed with an equally large complex less than 100 m away, on the other side of the New Forum; but maybe these were baths for different seasons, as at Madauros. (See p. 265.)

12. New Forum and market

On the low ground to the SW of the theatre is a long rectangular piazza which was the *Forum Novum*, constructed between 360 and 370 (figs. 284, 285). This is the last significant case of a late antique forum in North Africa

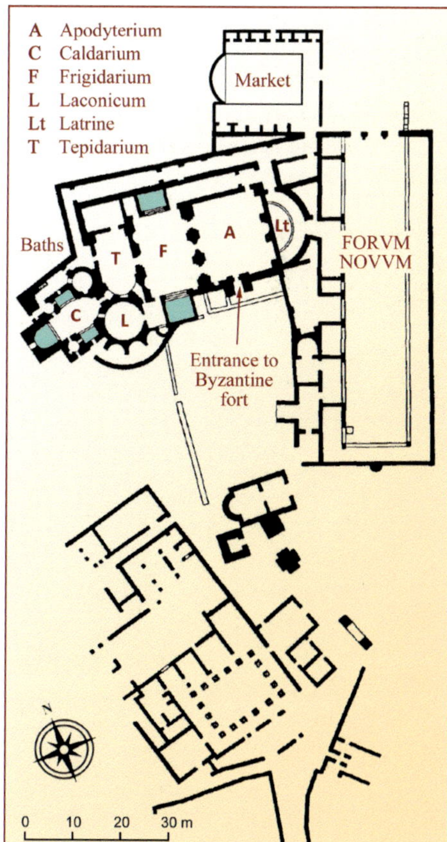

Fig. 284. Thubursicu Numidarum: plan of the New Forum and adjoining buildings.

supplied with a good range of statues, including emperors (even if these were brought from other parts of the site). The forum was entered through a triple arch at the N end. Surviving statue bases have dedications to Trajan and to Constantine, and report specifically that they had been brought from the old 'ruined' forum (*de ruinis ablatum/translatum*, barely a generation after the Old Forum had been repaved – abandoned due to earthquake?). Fragments of two colossal statues which stood at the S end of the piazza have been identified as representing Marcus Aurelius and Lucius Verus, though the bases did not identify them as such. Was it no longer known who they were?

Immediately to the N of the New Forum, a rectangular market building has been exposed, which seems to have had stalls around a rectangular colonnaded courtyard.

13. Public baths/Byzantine fort

On the W side of the New Forum is a monumental public bath complex (see fig. 284) with a semi-circular latrine and the usual sequence of cold and heated rooms, including a circular *laconicum* on the S side. This is probably earlier in origin than the New Forum, the alignment of which it does not share; however, the appreciation of its structure is complicated by the fact that the ruins were refurbished in the Byzantine period to form a blockhouse. This is evident from reused (carved) blocks in the wall on the S side [and elsewhere?] and from what seems to be a high window on the S side of the *apodyterium*, but is in fact the entrance into the blockhouse from what was then the contemporary ground level.

14. 'Recent' excavations

To the S of the New Forum, other buildings have been excavated, some of which were already shown on a plan published in 1919. Detailed descriptions of this area do not, however, appear to exist. On the ground, it appears that there was a number of substantial peristyle houses along the road which heads towards the SW. Some of these have undergone modifications in the late Roman period, when mangers hollowed out of tombstones were inserted.

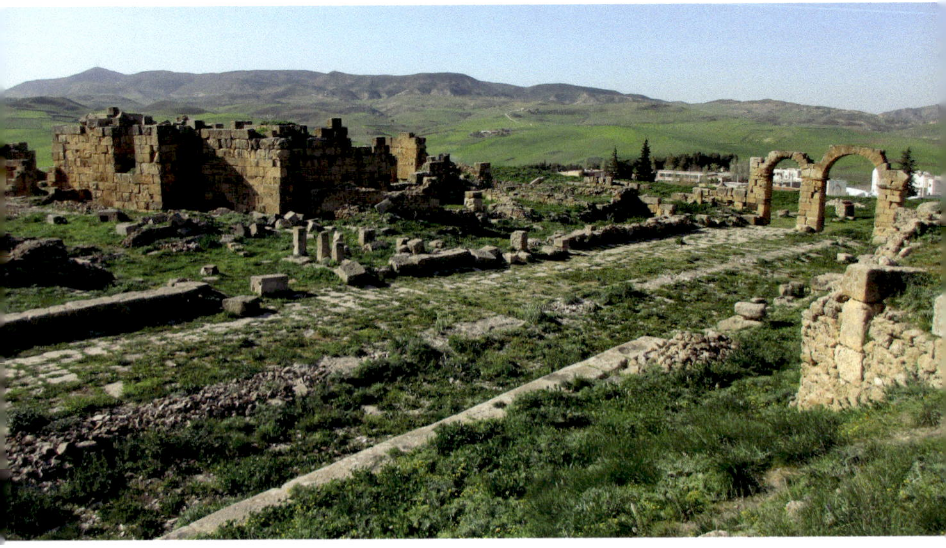

Fig. 285. Thubursicu Numidarum: the New Forum from the S, with baths/Byzantine fort beyond.

MADAUROS (M'Daourouch)

In the said market-place [of Madauros] Mars is represented in two images, the one unarmed, the other armed, and a statue of a man placed over against these restrains with three extended fingers the fury of their demonship from the injuries which he would willingly inflict on the citizens.

Saint Augustine, *Letter 17* (to Maximus of Madauros, AD 390), tr. P. Schaff

The author of *The Golden Ass*, Apuleius, is the most famous son of Madauros. In the witty speech he made in his defence, when on trial for witchcraft at Sabratha in 158, he described it thus:

As to my birthplace, [it lies] right on the marches of Numidia and Gaetulia ... Even in the time of Syphax we were a township. When he was conquered, we were transferred by the gift of the Roman people to the dominion of King Masinissa, and finally as the result of a settlement of veteran soldiers, our second founders, we have become a colony of the highest distinction.

This settlement of ancient Numidian origin, today 7 km to the E of the modern village of M'Daourouch and at a height above sea level of 900 m, was chosen as a home for military veterans (i.e. colony) in the Flavian period. Although it was not directly on the principal routes of the region, the settlement served to exploit the agriculture of the high plains and, at the same time, to reinforce the 'Roman' character of the area close to the recalcitrant tribe of the *Musulamii*. The quality of education offered by the schools of Madauros was renowned: Augustine, for instance, born in *Thagaste* (Souk Ahras), studied there before moving on to Carthage. The city also counted amongst its citizens the noted grammarians Maximus (to whom Augustine's letter cited above was addressed) and Nonius. A Christian presence is detectable in the third century, and churches were constructed within the city and in its vicinity in the fourth and fifth centuries. Following the Byzantine conquest, in 535 the general Solomon built here, as in other cities of the region, an imposing fortress incorporating the theatre and part of the forum. It is thought that the settlement did not long survive the Arab conquest in the seventh century.

EXPLORING THE SITE

1,2. Bath buildings

At the N edge of the site, next to the modern road, are two public bath buildings of the third century, set only some 20 m apart. They have been identified as 'summer' and 'winter' baths, and possess the usual sequence of cold and heated rooms. The larger establishment, which has a large semi-circular latrine, is assumed to have been the Summer Baths (*thermae aestivae*, attested in an inscription). The *frigidarium* of the smaller complex was converted at an unknown date into a church ('Church 3'). Sockets in the centre of the hall for a chancel enclosure are visible; others around the cold-plunge bath on the SE side (not readily detectable now) are supposedly the remains of a raised wooden floor to create the presbytery.

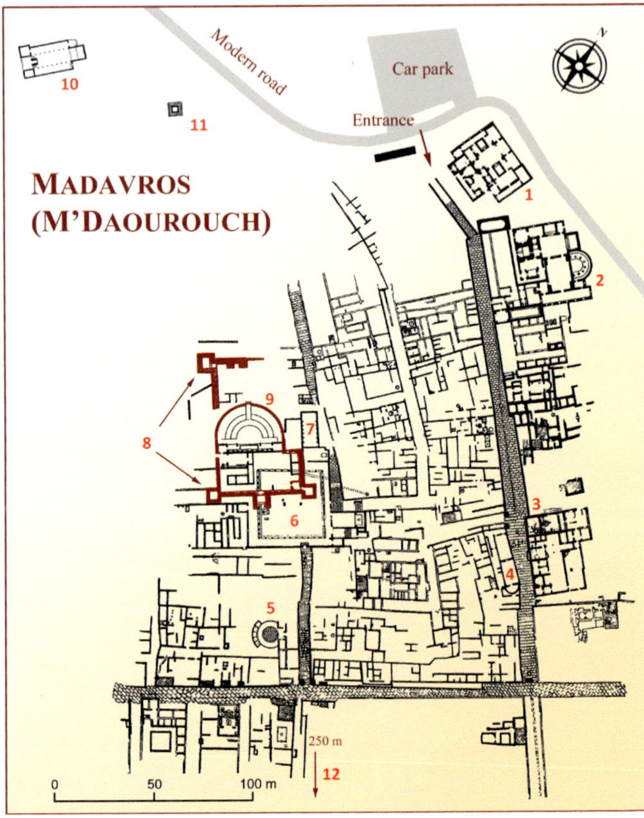

Fig. 286. Madauros: plan of the site.

1. Winter Baths	*5. Market*	*9. Theatre*
2. Summer Baths	*6. Forum*	*10. Church 2*
3. Oilery	*7. Basilica*	*11. Mausoleum*
4. Church 1	*8. Byzantine fortress*	*12. Mausoleum*

3. Oilery

There are many oil-processing installations amongst the houses of Madauros, and they seem generally to conform to a uniform design (see figs. 287, 288). They may typically be identified from the large pressing-stones, carved with a circular channel which caught the liquid squeezed out of the olives. The olives underwent a primary crushing in a rotary mill; the pulp was then placed into baskets which could be stacked one upon another on the pressing-stone. This stack was then compressed by means of a huge timber lever, anchored at one end into the wall and pulled down at the other by a windlass attached to a big stone anchor-block by means of dovetail sockets. The liquid which ran out from the press would be a mixture of oil and water. This would be collected in one or more settling-tanks, from which the oil could be drawn off separately.

Fig. 287. Madauros: plan and section of a typical oilery.

1. *Pressing stone*
2. *Baskets of crushed olives*
3. *Press beam*
4. *Receiving tank for oil*
5. *Anchor block for windlass*
6. *Windlass*
7. *Block and tackle to raise press beam*

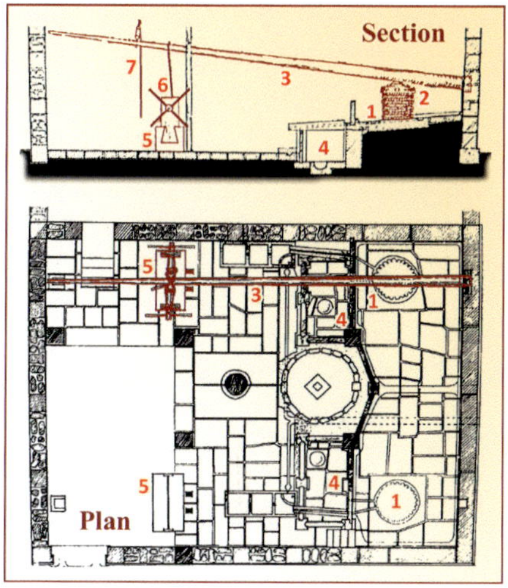

4. Church I

About 120 m to the SE of the baths is a church which has been attributed to the second half of the fifth century. It lies alongside the street leading from the baths and appears, from its long, narrow shape, to have been adapted from an earlier building. It is entered through a porch at the NW end, framed between two columns and next to an arch marking the departure of a side-street. The body of the church is long and narrow, without aisles; at the SE end is a raised apse containing the steps of a stone *synthronon*. The nave has been divided in two, half-way along its length: it is unclear whether this was because it was found to be inconveniently long or for some other reason. The floor paving shows sockets for altars in both halves.

There is a baptismal basin in the corridor which runs along the SW side of the church.

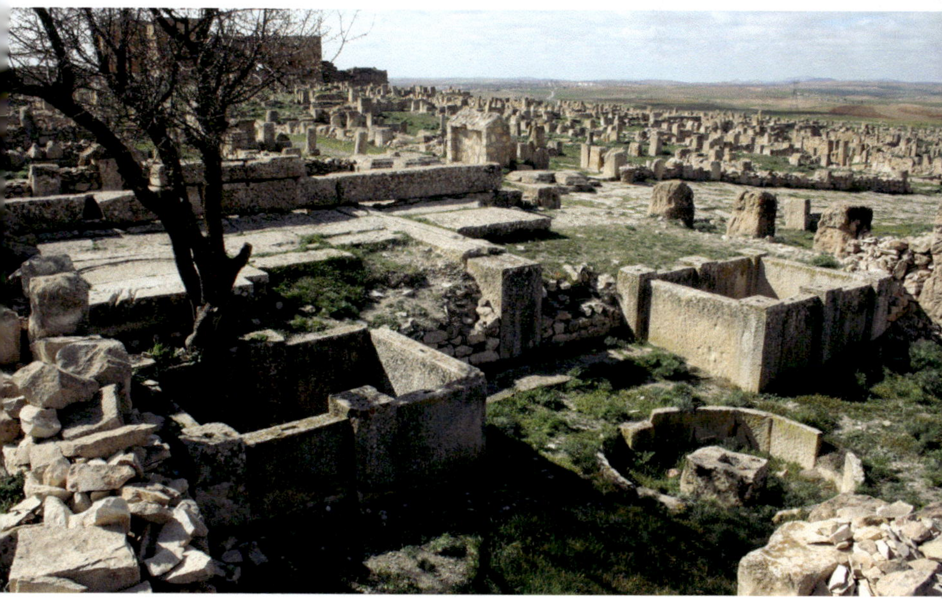

Fig. 288. Madauros: two-press oilery opposite Church I.

5. Market

This market had a circular, paved central space (fig. 289), surrounded by a portico sheltering radial market stalls.

6, 7. Forum and basilica

Built on a terrace, the Forum (32.4 x 27/28.5 m) was surrounded by porticoes (fig. 290). A refurbishment of the paved surface, which is almost intact, is commemorated by an inscription which ran across its width in bronze letters; these have been removed, leaving corresponding hollows in the paving slabs. The work cost 200,000 *sesterces* and was done at the expense of a certain M. Aurelius (not the emperor). The adjoining basilica (a simple hall without aisles) lay not along one of its sides, but extending lengthways from the N corner: this is of late imperial date, and may have succeeded an earlier and more conventional arrangement. (Mangers in the building also suggest a change of use at some point to stables.) The building on the NE side of the Forum was probably the *curia*. Bases of statues found in the Forum evoke those referred to by Saint Augustine (see above); one seems to have supported a statue of the writer Apuleius: *[ph]ilosopho [Pl] atonico [Ma]daurenses cives ornament[o] suo d(ecreto) d(ecurionum) p(ecunia) [p](ublica)* ('To the Platonic philosopher, their ornament, the citizens of Madauros [set this up] by decree of the decurions at public expense').

8. Byzantine fortress

This strong-point, intended as a rectangle with square corner-towers and a central gate-tower in the SE side, was overlaid in 535 on part of the forum, the whole of the theatre and part of the lower ground to the NW. (See figs. 289, 290; the inscription, in both Greek and Latin, naming Solomon as the constructor, is still in place above the entrance.) It seems, however, that construction was abandoned part-way through and that at a later date, perhaps after 539, the

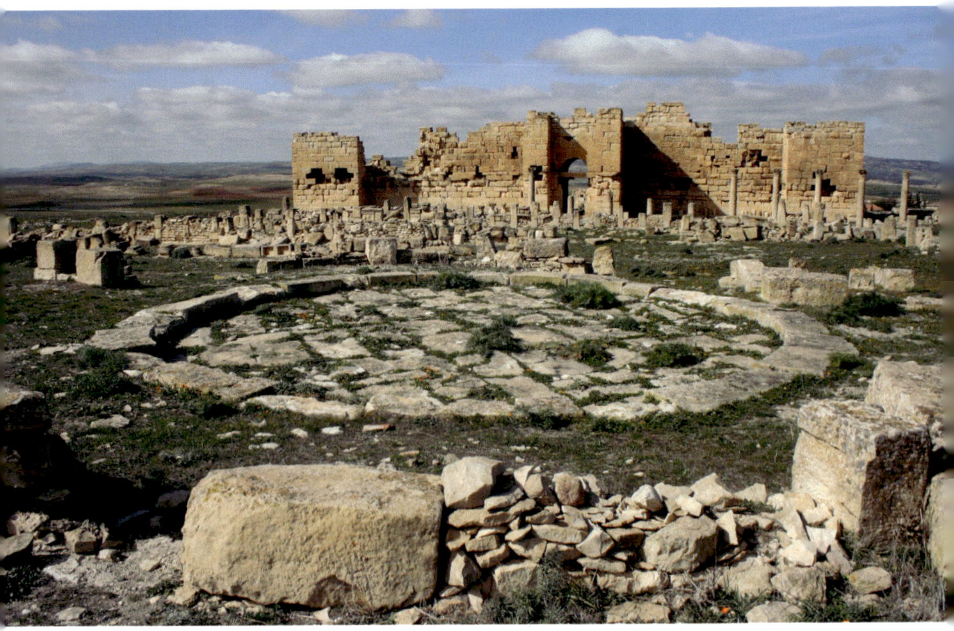

Fig. 289. Madauros: the market, with the Byzantine fortress beyond.

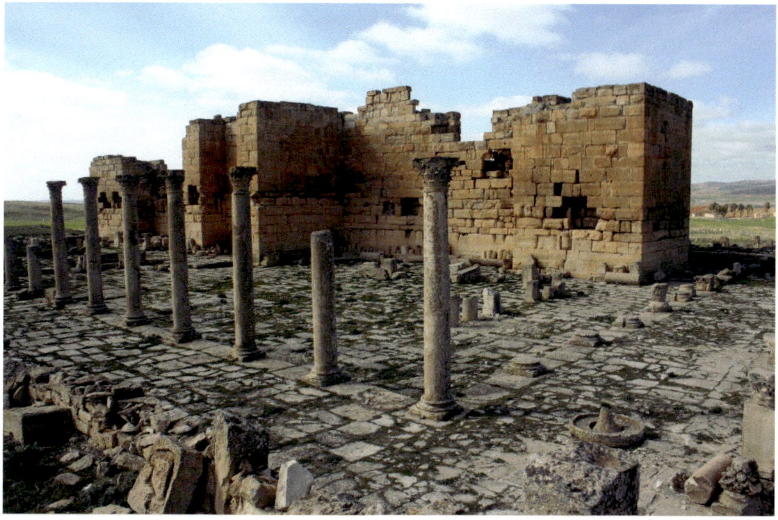

Fig. 290. Madauros: the Forum from the E corner, partially overlaid by the Byzantine fortress.

project was reduced on the NW side to adding a wall on top of the perimeter of the theatre and blocking the doorway below. This has resulted in the isolation of the W corner-tower and lengths of adjoining wall. Part of its circuit still stands however to a height of 10 m, and it is composed extensively of re-used materials (including inscribed blocks and statue-bases) from the immediate surroundings. On the NE side, a concealed underground passage, roofed with re-used slabs, extends outside the fortress for some 30 m to reach a well.

9. Theatre

This faces the Forum on the same side as the basilica. It was built in the Severan period by the *flamen* M. Gabinius Sabinus at a cost of 375,000 sesterces – a lot, for a relatively small theatre with a seating capacity of about a thousand (fig. 291). (The blocks composing this inscription are laid out on the ground behind the stage building. Statue bases found in the theatre show that Gabinius Sabinus commemorated at least six members of his family here.) Instead of making use of the natural slope to accommodate the seating, the *cavea* has surprisingly been constructed to face the other way, with the result that the seating rests entirely on a masonry substructure. A portico ran around the top. Another unusual feature (unique in North Africa, though found in the theatre of Ostia in Italy) is a central entrance through the seating into the *orchestra*.

10. Church 2

This lies some 200 m to the NW of the Byzantine fortress, away from the main conurbation and close to the modern road. It is aligned towards the NE, has a nave and aisles separated by columns and a rectangular presbytery rather than an apse. At the opposite end, it was entered through a narrow porch between flanking rooms (sacristies?), with steps up to the higher level within. The building was constructed very largely from reused materials, and has been dated to the fourth century or later. The many funerary inscriptions found in the vicinity range in date from the fourth to the sixth centuries. Those now in the church included both pagan and Christian texts.

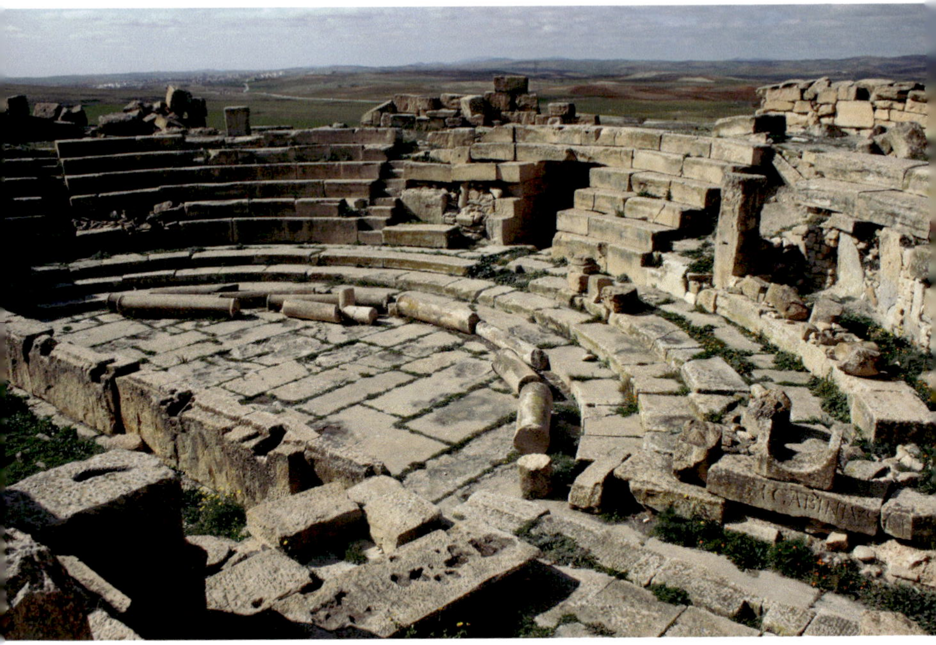

Fig. 291. Madauros: the theatre.

11. Mausoleum

Not far from Church 2 is the stepped base of what must once have been a square tower-tomb. There is no sign of the blocks of the superstructure: these were perhaps removed in order to build the church.

12. Mausoleum

A much more fully preserved tower-tomb stands on higher ground above the settlement, approximately 250 m to the SE of the street intersection by the market (fig. 292). This is a square two-storey building, originally with a pitched roof. The burial chamber, with three recesses in the far wall for cinerary urns, was on the ground floor and entered through a doorway in the front with mouldings around the frame. Above a projecting cornice, the upper storey is framed by an arch resting on square piers, set back between the flanking walls. This would presumably have housed a statue.

This is clearly in a necropolis, outside the town, as there are many tombstones to be seen in the vicinity.

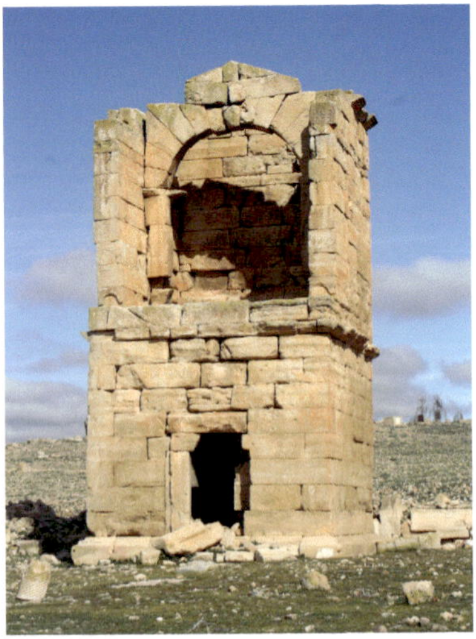

Fig. 292. Madauros: tower-tomb.

THEVESTE (Tébessa)

And Solomon ... ruled with moderation and guarded Libya [= North Africa] securely, setting the army in order ... and removing those of the Vandals who were left and especially all their women from the whole of Libya. And he surrounded each city with a wall, and guarding the laws with great strictness, he restored the government completely. And Libya became under his rule powerful as to its revenues and prosperous in other respects.

Procopius, *History of the Wars* 4.19, tr. H. B. Dewing

Tébessa is situated at the foot of Djebel Amor, close to abundant sources of water. This zone, sparsely populated today, was densely inhabited in prehistoric times: this is demonstrated by the number of occupation sites that have been found in the vicinity. It is possible that the native settlement on this site is to be identified with the grandiosely-named *Hecatompylos* ('with a hundred gates') which was brought under Carthaginian rule in 247 BC by the general Hanno. This must have been a substantial conurbation, since Hanno was able to take 3,000 hostages. However, apart from a few tombs of Punic date, nothing is known archaeologically of the pre-Roman settlement.

Its layout first becomes apparent with the arrival of the Romans: the core of the native site seems to have developed a few years before the change of era, on either side of the Oued Zarour. The lie of the land did not permit the imposition of a regular rectangular grid, as later at Thamugadi and elsewhere, but we know that the course of the wadi was carefully managed, with quays and seven bridges.

Theveste acquired real importance when the *Legio III Augusta* moved its headquarters there from *Ammaedara* (Haïdra in Tunisia, 35 km to the NE) in AD 75, shortly after the war against the *Musulamii*. Given municipal status, the town acquired a forum and an amphitheatre, while the surrounding countryside was organized for the systematic cultivation of cereals, and later olives (in the Severan period). Olives were particularly well suited to the stony terrain of the high plateaux, and this led to the establishment of intensive semi-industrial processing installations, the most spectacular of which is the oilery of Bir Sgaoun (p. 13 fig. 8 and figs. 288–90).

Despite the departure of the legion for Lambaesis, just six years later, the town, raised to the rank of a colony, was provided with a theatre and public baths. As in many other cities in North Africa, its greatest prosperity came in the Severan period.

The rise of Christianity also followed a pattern common to other cities of the region: timid first shoots in the early third century, sporadic persecutions with which certain named martyrs were associated (Crispina and the conscientious objector Maximilian being the most famous at Theveste) and troubles due to the Donatist schism. The city seems to have been an important Donatist stronghold, since a schismatic council was held there in 350. However, the Catholic community was clearly both vigorous and rich, since it built one of the largest churches in Africa.

The appearance of Theveste was profoundly altered in the Byzantine period. Whereas there had never before been a defensive circuit, Solomon, who succeeded Belisarius in command of the African campaign in 534, expelled the Vandals, rebuilt

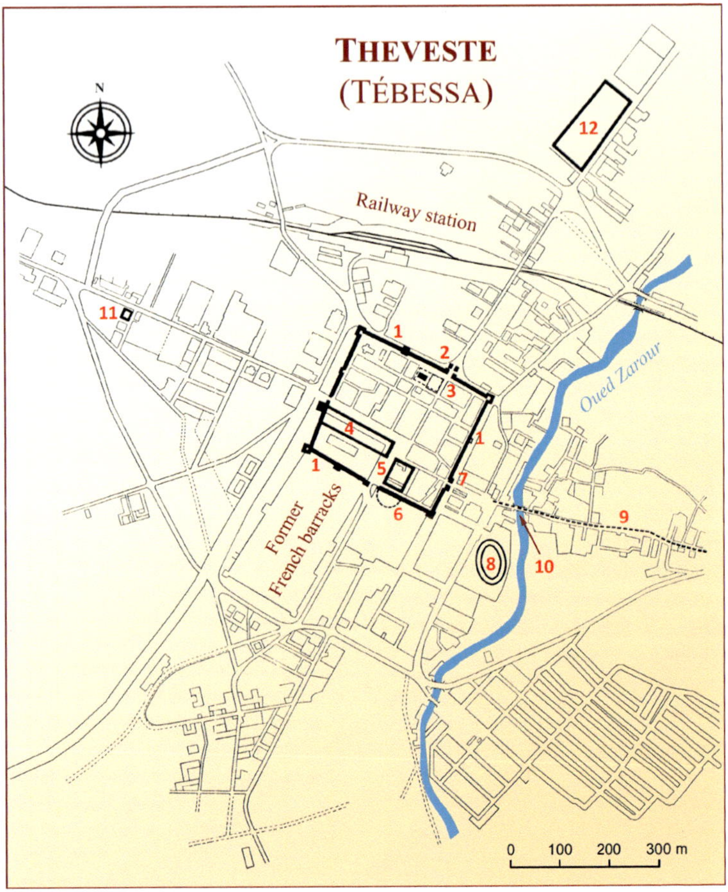

Fig. 293. Theveste: the location of antiquities in the modern town of Tébessa.

1. *Byzantine walls*
2. *Arch of Caracalla*
3. *'Temple of Minerva'*
4. *Forum*
5. *Roman building*
6. *Theatre*
7. *'Gate of Solomon'*
8. *Amphitheatre*
9. *Aqueduct*
10. *Aqueduct bridge*
11. *Arch on Constantine road*
12. *Pilgrim church of St. Crispina*

the city from its ruins and enclosed it within a massive wall, parts of which are still remarkably well preserved, imposing their character on the modern town centre (figs. 294, 295). This ushered in the last century of the settlement's 'Roman' existence. Following the arrival of the Arabs in 647 it continued, nonetheless, to survive, since it is mentioned by Arab geographers several times between the eleventh and fourteenth centuries. As in other cases, the arrival of the French led, in the early years of occupation, to the dismantling of ancient structures in order to build new military facilities on the same site.

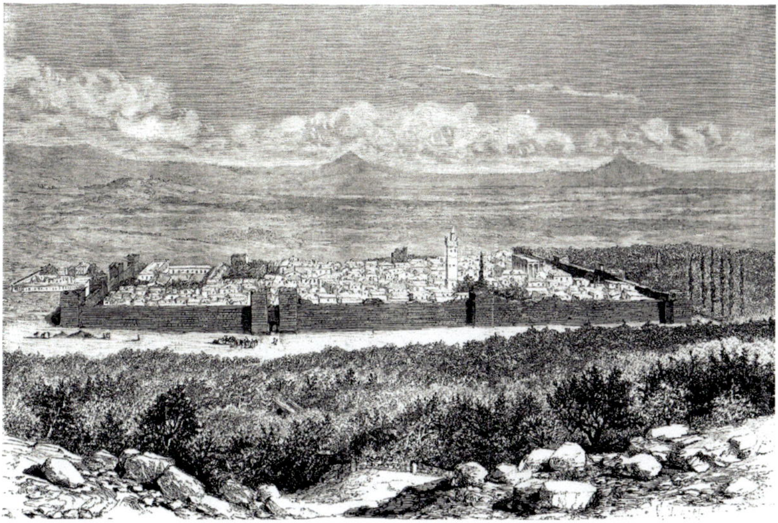

Fig. 294. Tébessa in 1880: the Byzantine defences and the 'Gate of Solomon' still define the town.

EXPLORING THE TOWN

1. Byzantine defensive circuit

It was in 540, during his second governorship of Africa, that the general Solomon had the surviving walls of Theveste constructed, using materials robbed from the monuments of the city. Column drums from the theatre, seats from the amphitheatre, mouldings, capitals, inscriptions – all were pressed into service. The rampart was more than 2 m thick and 9 or 10 m high – sufficient not to require an external ditch – forming a rectangle of 320 x 280 m; it still preserves 14 towers (once 18 m high), capable of covering one another, and three of its original four gates. A wall-walk, accessed by four stairways close to the gates, enabled the defenders to move between the towers. The ground floor of each of these was vaulted, as was the upper floor opening onto the wall-walk. The upper floor supported an artillery platform and was reached by means of a stairway set against the inner face of the tower. On either side of each tower, a look-out point with two loop-holes facilitated surveillance of the adjoining curtain wall and the countryside beyond.

2. Arch of Caracalla

This triumphal arch has the form of a *quadrifrons*, that is to say that it is square in plan (11 x 11 m) and with four essentially identical faces (fig. 296). It is one of the best-preserved examples in Africa. Each face has a single arched opening between flanking piers, which are embellished by paired engaged Corinthian columns on either side. The keystone of each opening was to have been carved with a portrait of a member of the Severan family in a medallion: Septimius himself was on the E face, his wife Julia Domna as protectress of the city on the W face and Caracalla (mutilated) on the S face (inside the city). The medallion on the N side was never carved: there should presumably have been a likeness of the younger son, Geta, who was murdered by his brother after the death of Septimius. Above each arch was an entablature and attic which projected forwards on either side above the columns. The architrave is highly decorated with vegetal

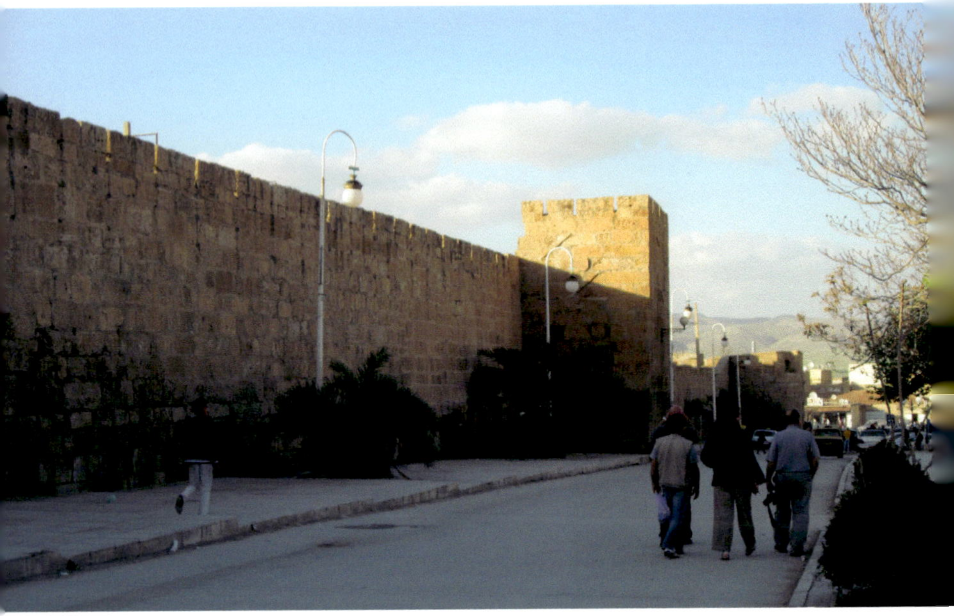

Fig. 295. Theveste: the Byzantine walls on the E side today.

motifs. On the very top were originally two *aediculae*, of which one alone survives, framed by columns and pilasters and housing statues of Caracalla and his brother Geta. Each face of the attic bore an inscription relating to the individual portrayed on the keystone beneath. That on the E side is dedicated to the 'divine' (i.e. dead) Septimius Severus, that on the opposite side to Julia Domna, while that on the S side (restored) gives the titles of Caracalla; these enable the date of construction of the arch to be placed in 214.

The arch was originally roofed by a coffered dome (now fallen), but two inscriptions in the interior give the further information that the arch was due to the largesse of a rich citizen of Theveste, C. Cornelius Egrilianus, prefect of the *Legio XIV Gemina* in Pannonia, who left 250,000 sesterces in his will for the its erection, with two tetrastyle *aediculae* for the statues of the two *Augusti* (Caracalla and Geta), and two further statues of the 'divine' Septimius and the goddess Minerva. He left a further 250,000 sesterces for the provision of bath oil to his fellow citizens (*ut … gymnasia populo publice in thermis praeberentur*), to be dispensed on sixty-four precisely defined days of the year.

The N face of the attic, corresponding to the uncarved medallion of Geta, remained likewise uninscribed, but French engineers placed there a Byzantine inscription found out of context, but interesting nevertheless for its commemoration of the restoration of Theveste by Solomon:

By Divine will, in the happy times of our pious masters the Emperor Justinian and the Empress Theodora, after the Vandals had been driven out of Africa and the entire race of the Moors had been destroyed by Solomon, most glorious and excellent Master of the Troops, former Consul, Prefect of Africa and Patrician, the city of Theveste has been rebuilt from the ground up through the attentions of this most eminent person.

The irony of this inscription will not be lost when it is recalled that in 544 Solomon was killed nearby at *Cillium* (Kasserine in Tunisia) in attempting to suppress a Moorish rebellion.

3. So-called 'Temple of Minerva'

This temple of the early third century AD is one of the best preserved in the whole of North Africa (see figs. 297, 298). It stands on a podium 4 m high, originally approached by a stairway of 20 steps. It stood within a porticoed precinct, the E side of which, with its principal entrance, can be detected in the marabout of Sidi Ben-Saïd, some 30 m away on the line of the former *cardo maximus*.

The temple itself resembles the famous Maison Carrée of Nîmes. It consists of a *cella* which extends to the edges of the podium, embellished with Corinthian pilasters, fronted by a *pronaos* with four similar columns across the façade and two on either side. The columns are monolithic, in

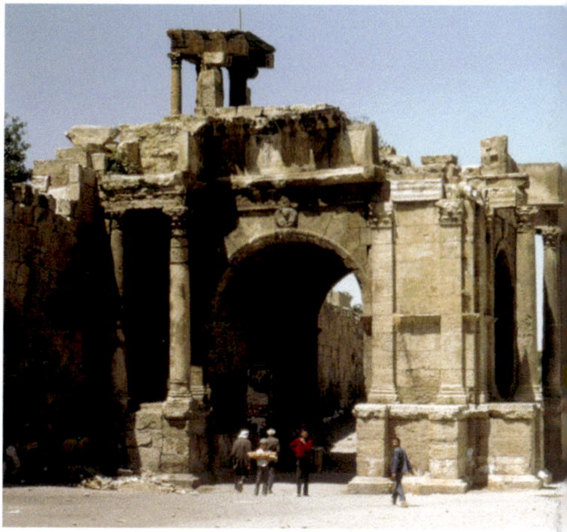

Fig. 296. Theveste: the Arch of Caracalla, serving as a gate through the Byzantine walls.

a blue-veined marble. The *cella* and *pronaos* are crowned by a richly decorated architrave, cornice and attic (fig. 298). The frieze

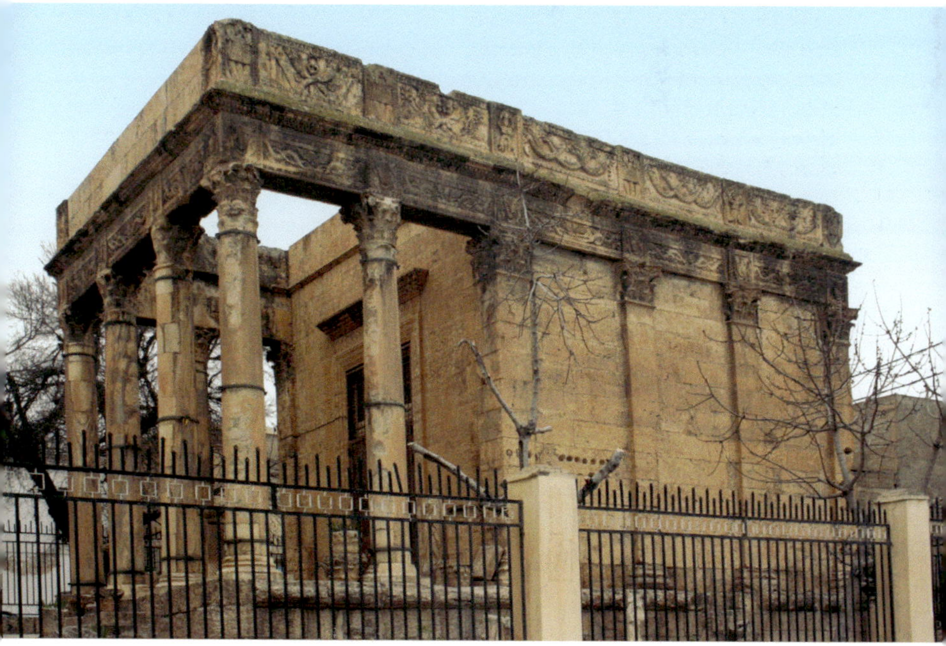

Fig. 297. Theveste: the 'Temple of Minerva'.

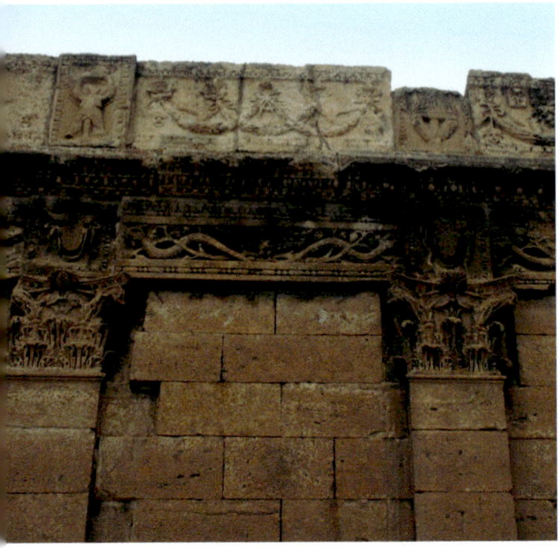

Fig. 298. Theveste: detail of the carved decoration on the cella of the 'Temple of Minerva'.

is composed of a succession of eagles with their wings outspread, holding in their talons two snakes (associated with Heracles) entwined with vine tendrils. Between these long panels, the projecting rectangular plaques above each capital are decorated with *bucrania* (ox sculls) hung with ribbons. Above the cornice, equally richly decorated, the attic repeats the same scheme: the long panels are decorated with festoons, *cornucopiae*, rosettes and a pair of Medusa heads at either end. The smaller panels contain military trophies composed of shields, axes, helmets and breastplates, in addition to representations of Heracles with his club and Dionysus with a crown of ivy. The undersides of the architraves in the portico are also elaborately carved with flowers and baskets of fruit. The attic across the façade is completely plain and presumably was faced with marble bearing a dedicatory inscription (or should there have been letters of bronze dowelled into the stonework?). The absence of a pediment shows that the roof of the building was flat; there may have been additional statuary above the attic across the façade, or indeed all the way round.

A misreading of the eagles on the frieze as owls resulted in the early attribution of the temple to Minerva. It is more likely that the temple was dedicated to Heracles and Dionysus, the divine protectors of Septimius Severus, and that the eagles symbolized the imperial power.

The building became a church in the Byzantine period, a house under the Ottomans, an office, a canteen and then a prison at the beginning of the French occupation; after that it was again a church until 1873. It has served since then as the local archaeological museum (see below), but this function is currently in the process of being transferred to a new location roughly 2 km to the N.

4. Forum

Laid out under Vespasian, the forum suffered first from the building of the Byzantine defences and then disappeared wholly beneath the annexes of the French barracks. 'The ruins of the forum,' reported A. Héron de Villefosse, 'were still visible when our first expeditionary columns arrived. The tree-lined avenue which leads from the Constantine Gate to the entrance to the Casbah occupies their position, of which no trace now remains. Finds made in the course of levelling the ground and preparing the surface for the plantations included architectural elements, fragments of sculpture, marble capitals ... It seems that the destruction of these ruins was essential to the creation of the square!'

It seems entirely plausible that the *cardo maximus*, passing along the E side of the pilgrim church to the NE of the town, should have entered through the Arch of Caracalla and thence run alongside the barracks. The *decumanus maximus* approached from the E alongside an aqueduct, passed through the Gate 'of Solomon', along the edge of the forum and thence westwards as far as the arch on the Constantine road (11), where until a few years ago, its paving could still be made out.

5. Roman building

This notable building, constructed in ashlar masonry and with a marble entablature and cornice on its façade, still stands between six and eight metres high. It had an upper floor and flanked a building with arcades. Part of an architrave found nearby was inscribed with the beginning of a dedication to Vespasian and Titus. This inscription, and particularly the quality and style of the masonry, suggest a public building – perhaps part of the civil basilica which once adjoined the forum – rather than a private house. This intriguing building is still inhabited and has never been subjected to archaeological investigation, so it remains an enigma.

6. Theatre

To the S of the Roman Building, the inner face of the Byzantine rampart may be seen to incorporate the lower parts of seven piers decorated with pilasters; the space between them is bridged by arcades supporting the wall-walk. These are the reused substructures of the former theatre stage-building, attributed to the Antonine period. Some column bases were found in front of the piers, together with some column drums which were gathered up and mortared into the spaces beneath the arcades in 1886, by an officer of the Engineers who wished to protect them. Nothing survives of the *cavea* of the theatre: its components were dismantled to build the Byzantine defences, and anything remaining went into the barracks of the French expeditionary force.

7. So-called 'Gate of Solomon'

The E Gate, or 'Gate of Solomon', was strongly protected by twin towers which flanked a narrow passageway into the city. Above this gateway, the curtain between the bastions was provided with machicolations (murder holes for dropping objects on an enemy).

The S Gate is modern, while the W Gate has disappeared; the N Gate is composed of the (re-used) Arch of Caracalla (2).

8. Amphitheatre

This structure of modest size (80 x 76 m) has been estimated to have had a maximum capacity of around 7,000 spectators. Many times remodelled and then pillaged over the course of the centuries, its origin is likely to go back to the first century AD. In 1859 it was studied by a Captain A. Moll of the Military Engineers, who was able to establish its plan and the fact that it had two entrances at opposite ends of its shorter axis. The lowest tiers of seating were in soft stuccoed limestone, while the upper tiers were in more solid squared blockwork. The wall around the edge of the arena dates from the late third or early fourth century, and on its balustrade could be read the names of prominent families of the city.

Much of the masonry of the amphitheatre was quarried to built the Byzantine defences and, then or later, the area was given over to habitations. The area is fenced and the main outlines are visible, but it is a constant struggle for the authorities to keep it clear of rubbish.

9, 10. Aqueduct

Built in limestone tuff and carried on massive arcades, the aqueduct brought to the city from some 700 m to the E the waters of the spring of Aïn el-Bled and that called the 'garden' spring, both of which still serve the city. Its route was deliberately sinuous in order to reduce the gradient of its bed.

Little of the aqueduct is now detectable, apart from the bridge upon which it crossed the wadi (beneath the narrow modern road bridge).

11. Arch on the Constantine road

When the French arrived, all that remained of this arch of a single opening was the lowest course of its S pier. To this they added a socle in the form of a cube and a truncated column, transforming it into a monument commemorating the Tunisian expedition of 1882. The paving of the decumanus maximus, on the other hand, was well preserved, with ruts where it passed beneath the arch.

All of this has disappeared following recent building development.

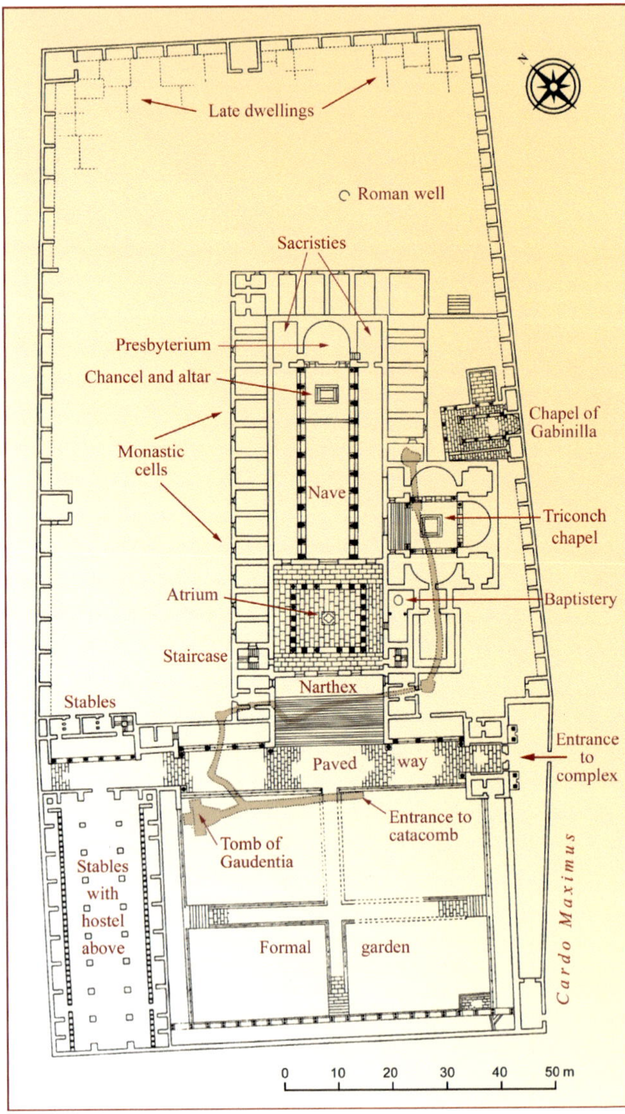

Fig. 299. Theveste: plan of the church complex of Saint Crispina.

12. Pilgrim church of Saint Crispina

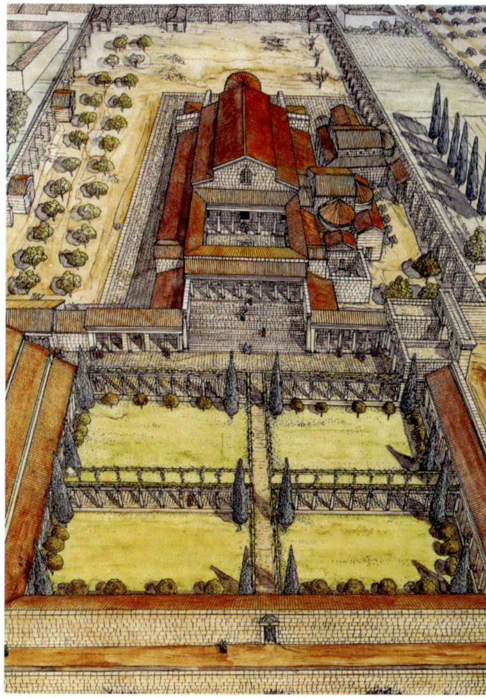

Fig. 300. Theveste: reconstruction by J.-C. Golvin of the church complex of Saint Crispina.

This huge church, dated to the end of the fourth century AD and dedicated to Saint Crispina (executed at Theveste in 304), lies in the centre of a complex which includes gardens, a hostel, several associated chapels and some catacombs which predate the construction of the church (see figs. 299, 300). The whole was enclosed within a boundary wall, provided with towers and a (timber) wall-walk supported on buttresses. The complex is aligned towards the NE, but for the sake of simplicity, this will be described conventionally below as if it faced the E.

An entrance from the *cardo maximus*, in the form of an arch flanked on either side by two engaged columns in front of corresponding pilasters, led into a broad paved way (52 m long and 7.5 m wide) with a drain beneath, which originally terminated on the far side in a similar archway. On the inner sides, each of these entrances was flanked by a single column on either side of the arch. On the W side of this paved area, two narrower paved pathways served to divide a large garden into four formal parterres enclosed within wooden balustrades, set between stone pillars like the slabs of a chancel screen. The other three sides of the garden were delimited by raised walks, that on the W offering in addition the shade of a portico.

Opposite the grand stairway that leads to the basilica, on the W side of the paved way, an opening leads into a long underground gallery (averaging 9 m deep over a length of more than 200 m) which constituted a catacomb. The first section leads to a crypt, the central chamber of which contained an anonymous sarcophagus and the tomb of Gaudentia 'who lived thirty years', behind which two tombs of marble together formed an altar at the rear of an *arcosolium*. These two graves housed the remains of martyred families: the body of an adult accompanied by two children, and of a second adult with another child, had all been buried together. Other tombs, two of them inscribed, occupied chambers on either side. The second section of the tunnel, deliberately blocked when the basilica was built, forks off to the E and then turns back beneath the grand stairway, continuing to beneath the triconch chapel on the S side of the basilica. Several Christian tombs were found within it.

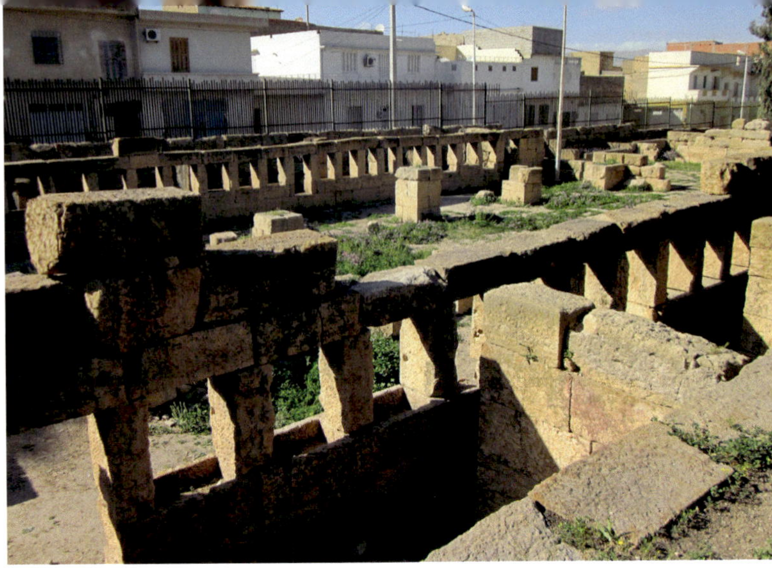

Fig. 301. Theveste, Church of Saint Crispina: the hostel.

To the N of the formal garden was a hostel for pilgrims (fig. 301). The living quarters were on the upper floor (not preserved), supported by massive piers. The ground floor was used to house carriages and for stabling: along the long sides of the building were small stalls, fronted by low walls supporting about eighty carved stone troughs. In many cases, it is possible still to see the chiselled anchor-points for the animals (fig. 302). Opposite the front of the building, across the paved way, are two separate, smaller stables, perhaps for the mounts of superior visitors.

On the E side, the grand stairway (20 m wide, composed of 15 steps with a landing at every fourth step) led to a *narthex*, beyond which further flights of two steps led through three doorways into a peristyle *atrium* in the Corinthian order (fig. 303), which had vases and statues set between the columns. On the S side a doorway led into a baptistery; the bottom of the baptismal basin was formed of a slab of marble with twelve recesses around the edge. In the corners of the *atrium* on either side of the entrance, two staircases provided access to the floor above, and thence to upper galleries in the basilica. In the centre of the peristyle, a four-lobed basin provided for the ritual ablutions of the early Christians – a practice later adopted by the Muslims, but now represented only symbolically in Christian churches by holy-water stoups. On the E side of the *atrium*, three doorways led into the nave and aisles of the basilica.

The body of the church, measuring 46 x 22 m, was divided into a nave and two aisles by two rows of twelve square piers, each with an engaged Corinthian column in front (fig. 304); the richness and diversity of these – in various marbles, multicoloured breccias, granite and even onyx – bear witness to the prosperity of the region at the time. Purely decorative in function, these columns supported two further tiers of diminishing height, fronting the galleries above the aisles and the clerestory windows above those. The piers behind, linked by semicircular arcades, alone bore the weight of the superstructure. The framework of the tiled roof rested on elaborately carved corbels, decorated with shells, rosettes, heraldically opposed fishes and the like, and these in turn were supported by similarly carved console brackets set into the wall (fig. 305).

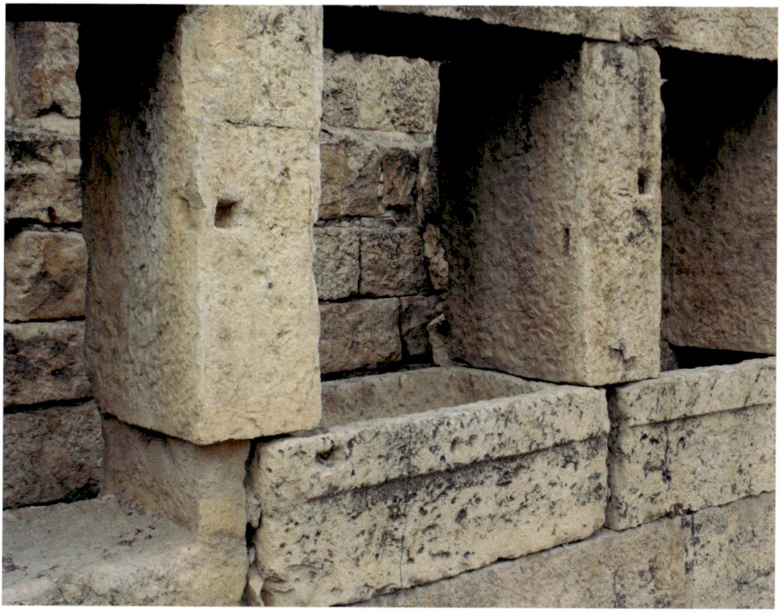

Fig. 302. Theveste: detail of the stables beneath the hostel, showing the mangers and chiselled anchor-points for tethering the animals.

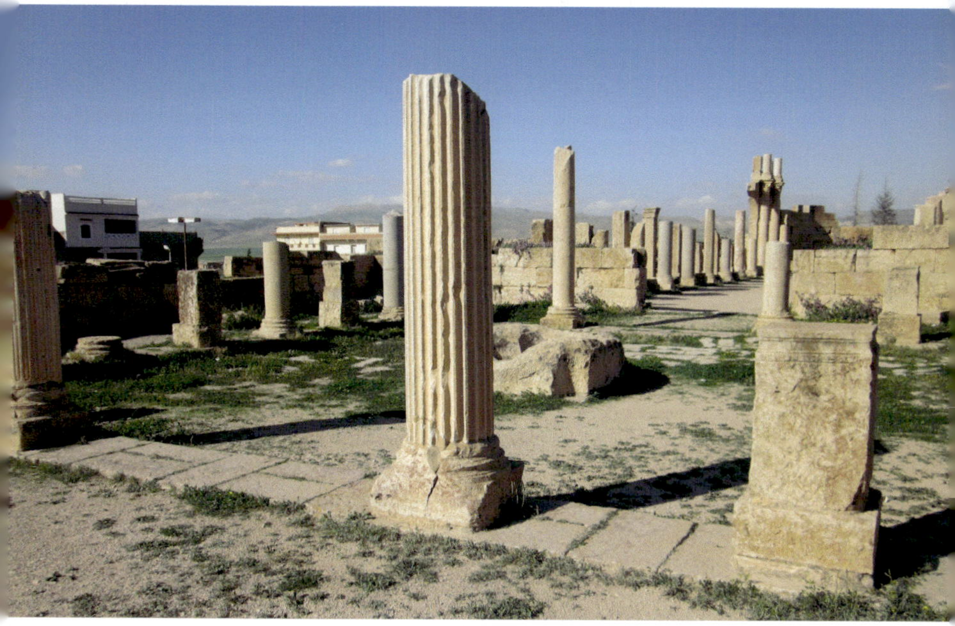

Fig. 303. Theveste, Church of Saint Crispina: atrium, with the nave beyond.

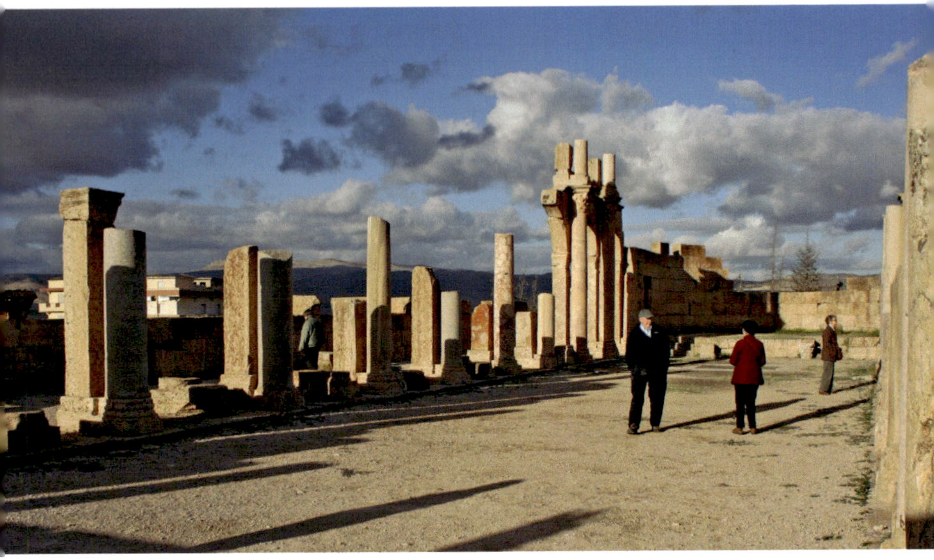

Fig. 304. Theveste, Church of Saint Crispina: the nave.

The nave ended in an apse, raised 80 cm above the floor, constituting the *presbyterium* of the church. This space would have housed an episcopal throne, and on either side were two sacristies. In front of the apse, the last three bays of the nave formed a square chancel around the high altar, enclosed by marble screens.

At the W end of the S aisle, a monumental staircase led down to a triconch chapel (*trifolium*: fig. 306), built on the traces of the early church which was contemporary with the catacombs described above (p. 279). A funerary mosaic paving (not visible) covers a considerable number of Christian burials. The central apse housed a *memoria* dedicated to seven persons, with an inscription placed by the deacon Novellus threatening divine retribution on any violator of the tombs. The western apse enclosed burials of children, and the eastern one contained sarcophagus burials. On the W side of this chapel, a rectangular room beyond a little vestibule, presumably a *martyrium*, contained several burials beneath mosaics: these were bishop Palladius, who had come from Idicra and died at the house of his friend, bishop Felix; a poor Marcella who had died at the age of three; a young Petronius, and a priest aged thirty named Quodvultdeus ('Will of God'). A fine marble sarcophagus, decorated with Christian motifs, was found at the foot of the staircase; the body of it was taken to serve as the altar in the modern church of Tébessa within the N corner of the ancient city (now the museum reserve: see below) but part of its lid, decorated on the end with a chi-rho monogram and the letters alpha and omega remains on the site. In the centre of the triconch chapel is the base of an altar which was once surrounded by mosaics. The whole basilica was once similarly enriched by mosaics with geometric patterns, the surviving parts of which are now covered with gravel for protection.

To the E of the triconch chapel, a separate building rests partly against it and partly against the boundary wall of the complex. This was another chapel of 11 x 9 m, divided into a nave and aisles by two rows

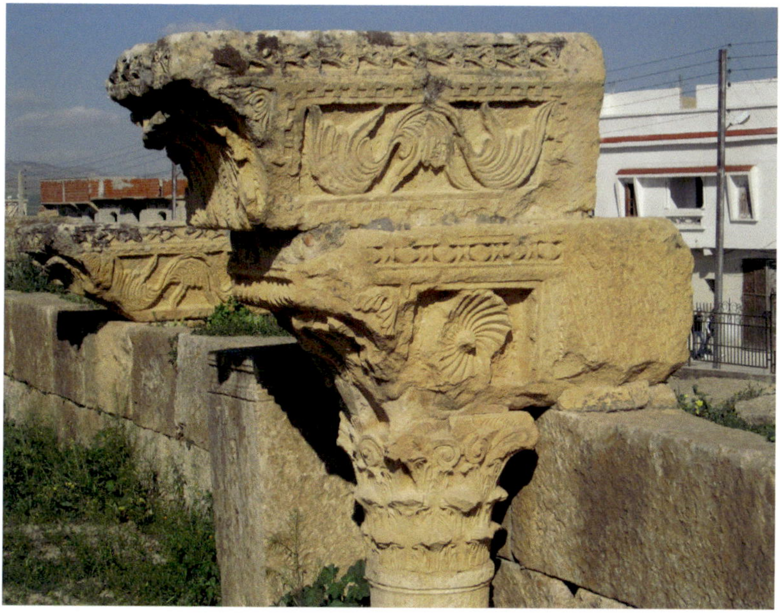

Fig. 305. Theveste, Church of Saint Crispina: re-assembled roof-support brackets.

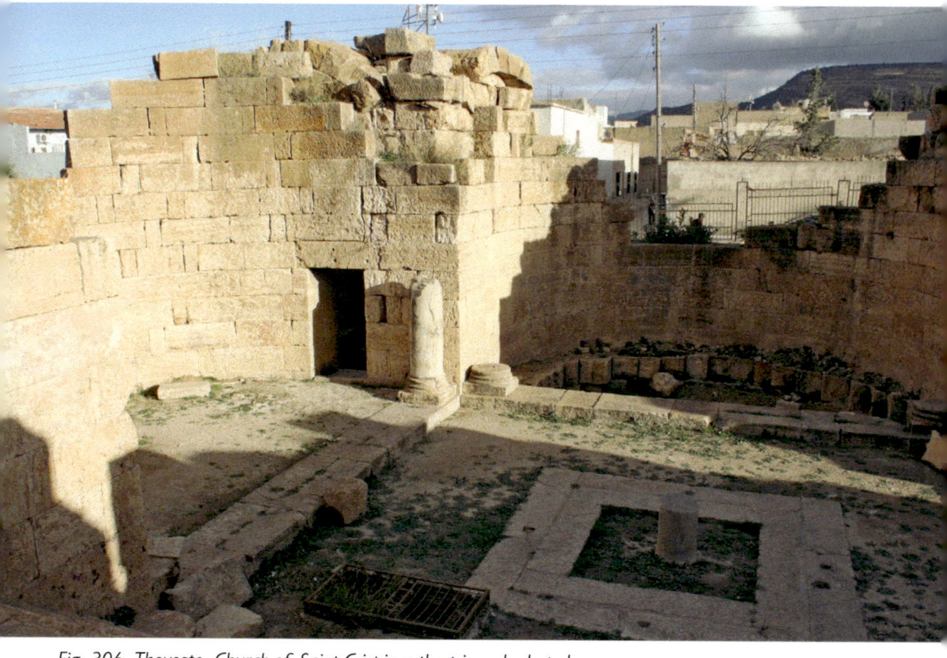

Fig. 306. Theveste, Church of Saint Crispina: the triconch chapel.

of columns. The apse and flanking sacristies are accommodated between the buttresses of the boundary wall. Close to the choir, an inscription in mosaic, embellished with a chi-rho monogram together with alpha and omega, commemorates a certain Celia Domitia Gabinilla, who died at the age of thirty-eight. The large number of burials clustered around the entrance suggests the presence of especially venerated relics – perhaps those of Gabinilla. This building is the only element of the entire complex which is demonstrably secondary – but the date of its insertion is unclear.

Finally, the exterior of the main church is entirely surrounded by what are surely monastic cells.

THE MUSEUM

The 'Temple of Minerva' has long served this purpose, but a fine new museum on the N side of the town was under development in 2018 (at N 35° 25.23' E 8° 7.01'). It is likely, therefore, that many objects will move. The temple, however, has several mosaics of interest, which will be less easy to remove. The most notable are the following.

Triumph of Venus (7 m x 9 m, opposite the entrance: fig. 307). The goddess, of whom only the head survives, in the centre of the composition, was carried by a marine centaur. A cortège of Nereids riding marine monsters (panthers, dragon, hippocamp etc.) accompany her upon a sea populated with cupids and fishes. Note the very careful rendering of the jewellery worn by the Nereids. (From the baths in the SW quarter of the town, sacrificed to the construction of the French cavalry barracks: early fourth century.)

Fortuna redux (2.98 x 3.40 m, to the R of the Triumph of Venus). Two fragments alone of this mosaic now survive: when first recorded there was rather more: see fig. 308.) A merchant ship loaded with amphorae sails amongst dolphins and other sea creatures; above this are the words *fortuna redux* (loosely translated as 'The fortune that brings one home'). Below, in the same panel, were

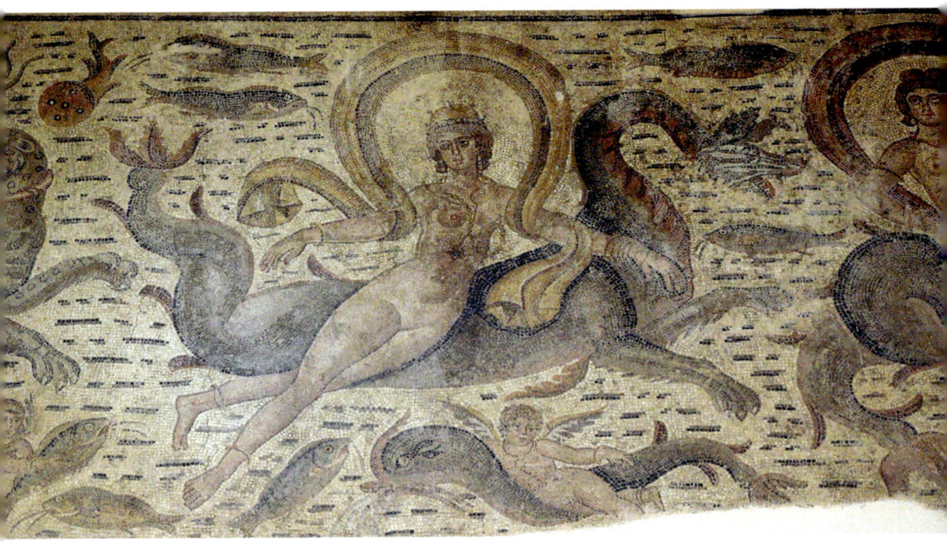

Fig. 307. Theveste: detail of the Triumph of Venus mosaic.

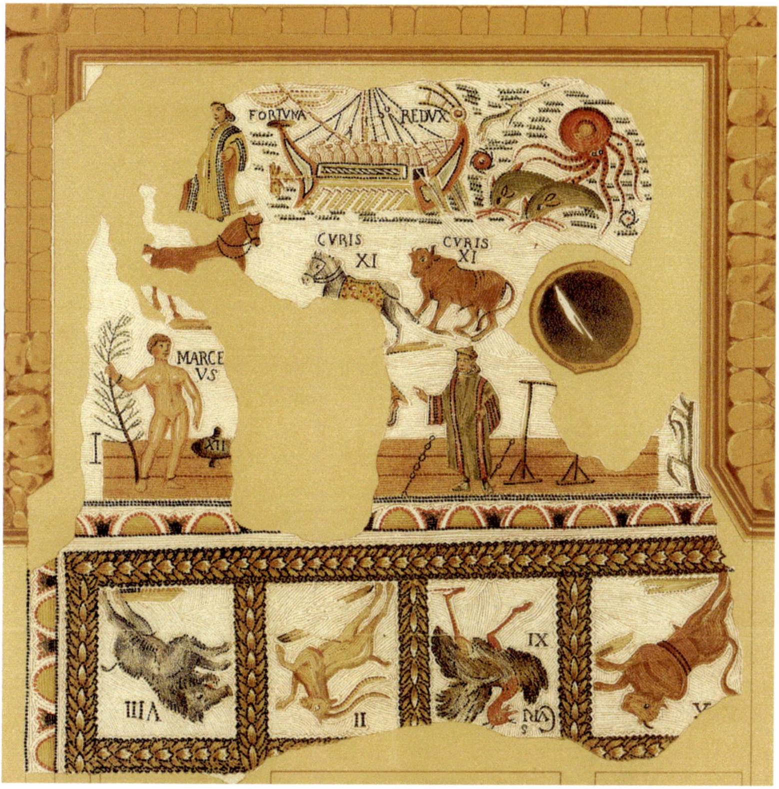

Fig. 308. Theveste: drawing of the Fortuna Redux mosaic made at the time of discovery.

formerly a bull and two horses, and below them an athlete (named Marcellus) holding a victor's palm and with a bag of prize money beside him (labelled 'XII'). Facing the athlete is possibly a judge, declaring his victory. Adjoining the main panel was a grid of (sixteen?) smaller panels separated by bands of laurel; each contained a figure of a leaping animal with a number next to it. The survivors are a bull (X), an ostrich (CVRIS XI), a gazelle (I) and a boar (VIII); there was formerly also a bear (XVIII). The whole is decidedly enigmatic, and possibly even without a common theme. It has been suggested, however, that it could commemorate a festival of athletic competitions and parades of animals (with the number of each displayed) on the occasion of a safe return from a particularly successful commercial venture. (From the same context as the preceding: early fourth century.)

Apollo and Daphne (to the L of the Triumph of Venus). The nymph is shown at the moment when, in answer to her prayer for an escape from the pursuit of Apollo, she is transformed into a bay tree.

Neptune and marine motifs (on the floor); fragments with ***hunting and amphitheatre scenes*** on either side of the doorway.

Polychrome chi-rho mosaic. This is a poor replica of the mosaic found on the altar in the triconch chapel in the Saint-Crispina complex; the original was unfortunately stolen and later destroyed.

Both within and around the museum, there is also a rich collection of small finds, inscriptions, architectural fragments, tombstones, Christian *mensae* and other objects.

A similar plethora of objects in stone is stored in the former parish church and its garden within the N corner of the Byzantine walls, which functions as a further reserve. There are there some complete *mensae* in a clearly vernacular style and some of the funerary mosaics which were lifted from the church of Saint Crispina. Also there is the sarcophagus-altar from the triconch chapel (p. 282), which on one side shows a crude representation of 'Christian Rome' wearing an Amazon's helmet, with her right breast exposed and holding in her left hand a chalice.

TÉBESSA KHALLIA

Three kilometres to the SW of the ancient city (now on the edge of the Cité el-Mzeb) is a hillock covered with extensive ruins that have been only partially excavated, known as Tébessa Khállia ('Tébessa the Abandoned': see fig. 309). There is here a complex of late buildings including a large rectangular enclosure, measuring approximately 117 x 100 m which had a colonnaded well-head within. Immediately to the NW of this are the remains of a very curious bath-building which was entered from a monumental circular feature 16.40 m in diameter, built in handsome ashlar masonry (fig. 310). This room is lined with a bench around the inside, and has a fountain or plunge-bath in a recess on the SE side. A small plunge-bath here is lined with mosaic, patterned to resemble ashlar blockwork.

In this area are also two triconch buildings (of which neither shows signs of having

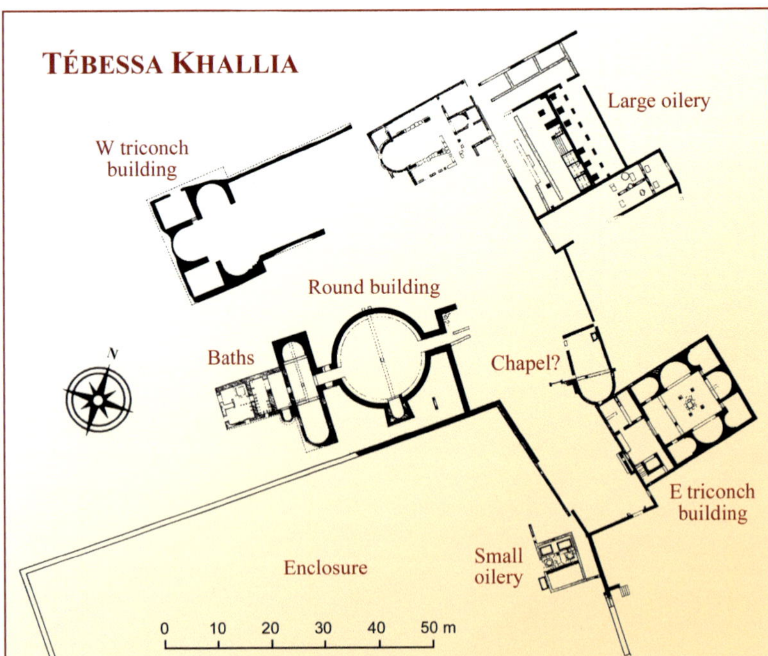

Fig. 309. Plan of excavations at Tébessa Khallia.

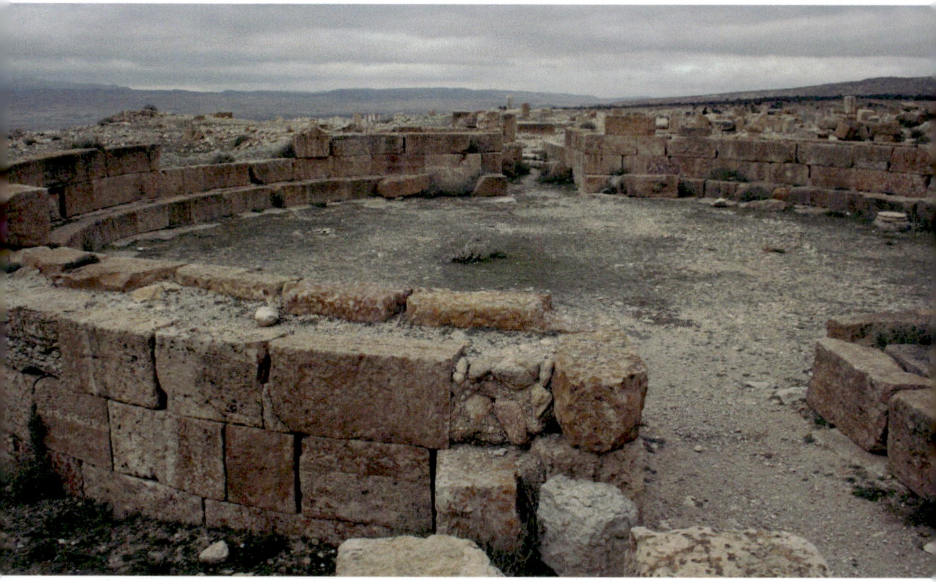

Fig. 310. Tébessa Khallia: the round building leading to the baths.

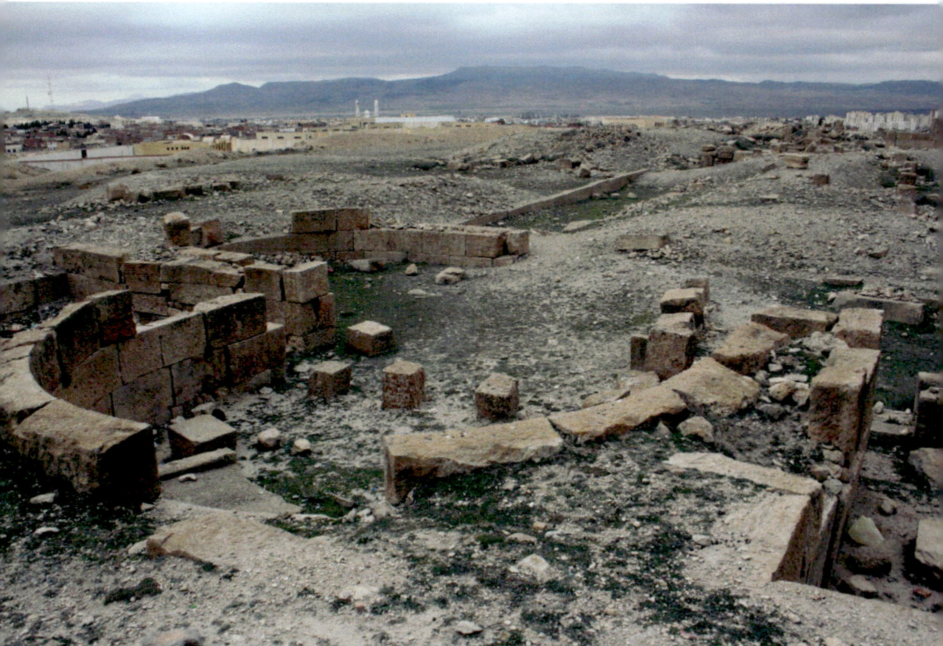

Fig. 311. Tébessa Khallia: W triconch building.

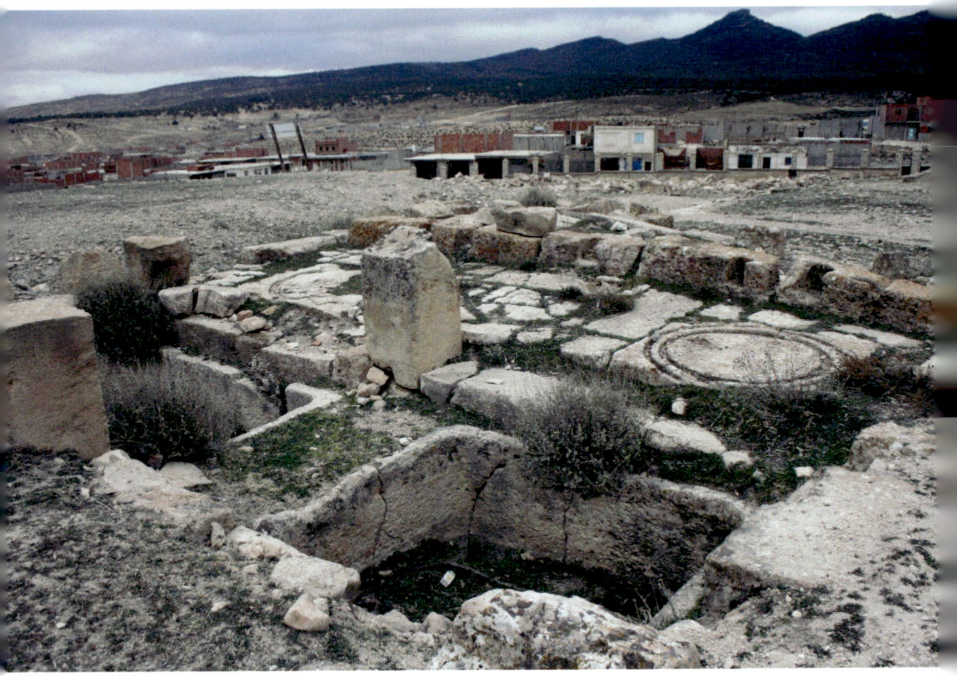

Fig. 312. Tébessa Khallia: the small oilery.

been a church: see fig. 311) and two oileries. One of these had six presses and was very similar in design to the installation at Bir Sgaoun (see below); the other had two, almost identical in design to those at Madauros (compare figs. 288 and 312). The E triconch building was elaborately decorated with mosaic floors and marble veneer on the walls; in the forehall are two mangers and a staircase, leading either to an upper storey or to the roof. The whole resembles a place of entertainment. At a later date, it was converted into a defensible blockhouse and provided with a door-closure in the form of a rolling stone, 1.8 m in diameter and 25 cm thick; unfortunately, this was stolen in 1943. (Such a rolling-stone closure may be seen at Diana Veteranorum: see p. 225 and fig. 241.) Next to it is a small apsed building which may, in contrast, have been a Christian chapel. The structural details of most of what has been found on this site show close similarities to those observed in the Saint Crispina complex, and it has been suggested that this site was perhaps a farm belonging to the church.

OILERY AT BIR SGAOUN (BRISGANE)

The countryside of North Africa, from Tripolitania in Libya, through Tunisia to Algeria, is dotted with evidence of intensive olive cultivation in the Roman period. This was managed both by small producers (as at Madauros: see p. 266) and by very large industrial-scale farm estates, which have left remains of massive oil-pressing installations. One of the most interesting of these, though far from the largest, lies at Bir Sgaoun, approximately 38 km to the S of Tébessa and just 900 m to the E of the

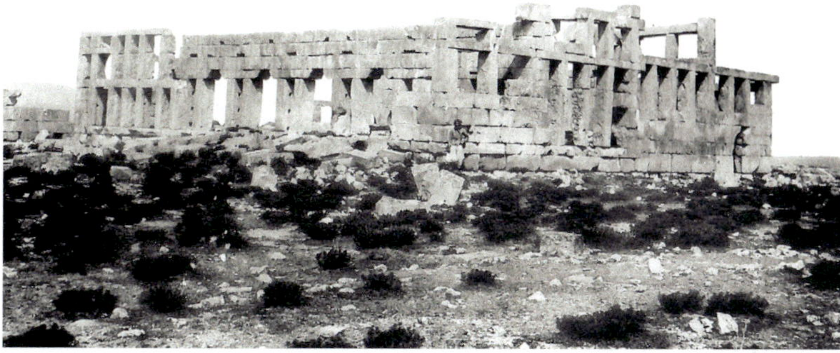

Fig. 313 (above). Bir Sgaoun: the press building at the end of the nineteenth century.

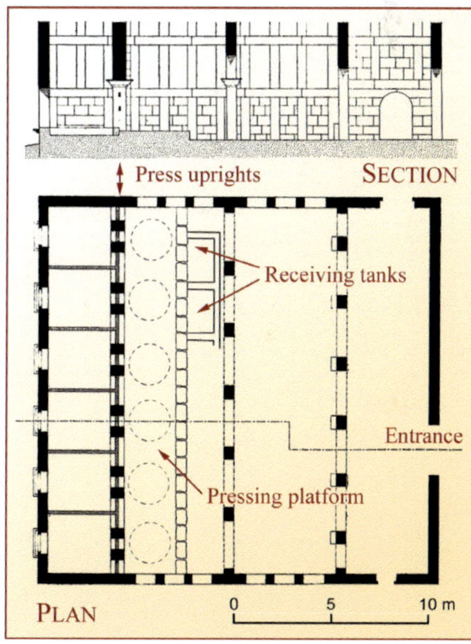

Fig. 314 (right). Bir Sgaoun: plan of the press building.

N16 (the road to El Oued). It may be most easily located now (and seen in *Google Earth*) by means of its geographical co-ordinates: N 35° 7.26' E 8° 13.07'. The press building was still in an extraordinary state of preservation at the end of the nineteenth century (figs. 313, 314), but has progressively collapsed (or been quarried?) since then. Even so, the upstanding remains constitute a remarkable example of the *opus africanum* building technique (see p. 13 fig. 8 and fig. 315).

The structural frame of the building is made of long limestone beams, the interstices of which were originally filled in with small mortared rubble. The small stones have entirely disappeared, leaving something which looks like a giant's climbing-frame. The building was rectangular (20.2 x 18.6 m), with a main arched entrance, presumably for carts, on the N side (fig. 315). There were other pedestrian entrances on the E and W sides. Along the S side, inside the rear wall, were the stone uprights and lintels of six huge oil-presses. (See p. 13 fig. 8: only two sets remain standing.) These have sockets in their internal faces at several different heights, so that the timber press-beam could be anchored at a suitable height for the stack of baskets to be pressed. In front of the presses was a corresponding row of tanks which received the oil (fig. 315). The pressing area was separated from the storage and handling space in front by a fine stone arcade (supporting an upper floor?), still standing until the middle of the twentieth century but now, sadly, lying on the ground.

This building was only one component of a large farm complex: there has been no

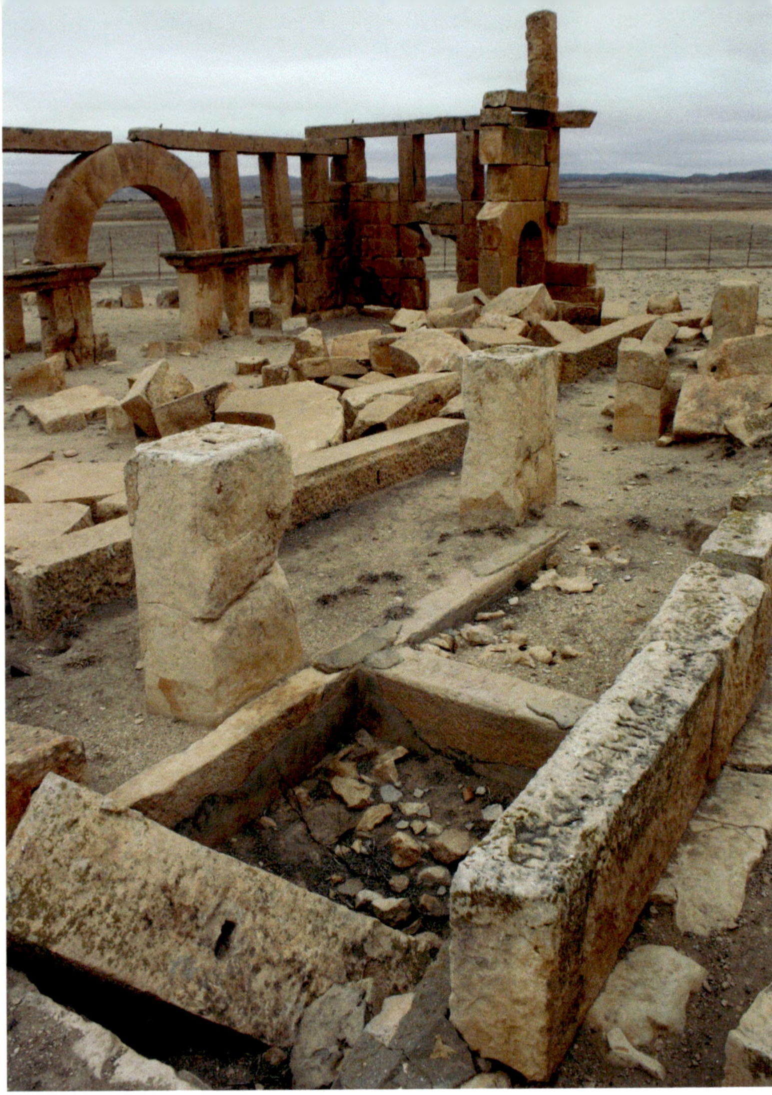

Fig. 315. Bir Sgaoun: two of the oil-collecting tanks in front of the presses. The arch of the main entrance may be seen in the background.

excavation on the site, but scattered traces of other buildings are visible, including one with two Christian cross-monograms carved on its stone door-posts. A dozen Roman funerary inscriptions have been recorded in the vicinity, including one from a monument dedicated to his dearest sister Julia Thegusa (?) by Julius Victor, who had served as a *beneficiarius* (an adjutant to the commanding officer) in the *Legio XX Valeria Victrix* in Britannia Superior.

CHRONOLOGY

BC	
11th cent.	First contacts of the Phoenicians with the African and Iberian coasts and with the major islands of the Mediterranean.
814	Traditional date for the foundation of Carthage by the Phoenicians.
753	Traditional date of the foundation of Rome.
6th–5th cent.	Punic coastal settlements at Cherchel, Algiers, Annaba and elsewhere founded.
3rd cent.	Masaesyli with capital at Cirta (Constantine) control much of W Algeria and Morocco.
264–241	First Punic War.
218–202	Second Punic War. Syphax of Mauretania allies himself with Rome, but then changes sides, is defeated and taken prisoner.
203–148	Reign of Masinissa over Numidia. This king, allied to Rome, was given control of all of Numidia and Mauretania. With the encouragement of Rome, he harassed Carthage unceasingly – until the Romans realized that they were in danger of replacing one powerful enemy with another. When he died, Scipio Aemilius divided his possessions between his three sons, Micipsa, Gulussa and Manastabal.
154	Birth of Jugurtha, son of Manastabal; brought up at the court of Micipsa, on whose death his kingdom was divided between his two sons and Jugurtha.
149–146	Third Punic War and destruction of Carthage. Establishment of the Roman province of *Africa (vetus)*.
118	Death of Micipsa, succeeded by nephew Jugurtha (virulently anti-Roman).
112–105	War between Jugurtha and Rome. Jugurtha handed over to the Romans by his father-in-law Bocchus of Mauretania, who acquired his possessions as a reward for this betrayal. This part of Numidia now known as eastern Mauretania.
48–46	Fighting in N Africa during the civil war between Caesar and Pompey; Juba I of Numidia sides with Pompey, reforms his army after the defeat at Pharsalus, but is defeated again and commits suicide. His kingdom is annexed by Caesar, who in 46 creates the province of *Africa nova* and a buffer state to the W in the hands of his supporter P. Sittius.

44	Assassinations of Caesar and of Sittius.
43?	Establishment by Octavian of *Legio III Augusta*, based at Ammaedara (Haïdra, Tunisia)
33	Death of King Bocchus of Mauretania; Mauretania taken over by Roman administrators, and Roman colonies founded there.
27	The two African provinces combined to form *Africa proconsularis.*
25	Juba II installed by Augustus as king of Mauretania.

AD

23	Death of Juba II, succession of Ptolemy.
37	The frontier zone of Numidia administered by the legate of the *Legio III Augusta.*
40	Murder of Ptolemy on the orders of Caligula.
42	Full annexation by Claudius of Mauretania and creation of the provinces of *M. Tingitana* and *M. Caesariensis.*
c. 70–72	Promotion by the proconsul T. Curtilius Mancianus of the *lex manciana*, a law to encourage small tenant farmers, to extend the reclamation of uncultivated land and to raise the standard of living in the countryside.
81	Headquarters of *Legio III Augusta* moved to Lambaesis.
96/97	Foundation of *Cuicul* (Djémila).
100	Foundation of *Thamugadi* (Timgad) by Trajan.
128	Vast new legionary base constructed at Lambaesis, visited by Hadrian.
197	Creation of the province of *Numidia.*
212	Edict of Caracalla, extending Roman citizenship to all free men throughout the Empire.
238	Dissolution of the *Legio III Augusta* following its opposition to the first two Gordians.
253	Re-formation of the *Legio III Augusta.*
258–260	Serious insurrections on the borders of Numidia and Mauretania.
c. 300	Reorganization of the administration of the entire Empire by Diocletian. Africa now divided into eight provinces, all but *Mauretania Tingitana* in the Diocese of Africa.
303–5	Persecution of Christians by Diocletian.
311/2	Beginning of the Donatist Schism, following the end of the Diocletianic persecution.
354	Birth of Augustine at Thagaste.
355	Death of Donatus in exile.
371–375	Rebellion of Firmus: sacking of Caesarea and Icosium; successful resistance of Tipasa.

395	Augustine, having been ordained in 391, becomes Bishop of Hippo Regius.
411	Council of Carthage: Augustine finally discredits the Donatists.
429	Vandals cross to Africa at the invitation of the *comes* Boniface.
430	Augustine dies during the (unsuccessful) siege of Hippo by the Vandals.
439	Carthage taken by the Vandals without a fight; established as their capital.
455	Vandals take possession of Tripolitania; Rome sacked; Berber chief Masties proclaims himself Emperor in the Aurès.
476	Abdication of the last emperor at Rome (Romulus Augustulus); Odoacer becomes King of Italy.
493–6	The Albertini Tablets demonstrate the continuation of Roman property law under the Vandals.
533–534	Reconquest of the African provinces by Belisarius on behalf of Justinian, ('Byzantine') emperor in Constantinople.
534–536, 539–544	Solomon in command of the Byzantine forces in Africa.
641–645	Arab armies under Amr Ibn al-Aasi invade Egypt, Cyrenaica and Tripolitania.
647	Byzantine forces under the exarch Gregory defeated at Sufetula (Sbeïtla in Tunisia) by an Arab army.
670	Conquest of Byzacena by Okba ibn-Nafi and establishment of a permanent Arab capital at Qayrawan in Tunisia.
683	Okba reaches the Atlantic coast, but is overstretched. On his return he is defeated and killed at Thabudeos near Biskra by Kosayla. Arab possessions abandoned, mostly to Berber chieftains rather than Byzantine rule.
698	Carthage taken by Hassan, Byzantines expelled. Resistance to Arabs by Berber queen Kahena.
709	Byzantines driven from their last African possession at *Septem* (Ceuta on the Moroccan coast).

SELECTIVE TABLE OF ROMAN EMPERORS

Julio–Claudians

31 BC–AD 14	Augustus
AD 14–37	Tiberius
37–41	Gaius (Caligula)
41–54	Claudius
54–68	Nero

68–69	Galba, Otho, Vitellius

Flavians

69–79	Vespasian
79–81	Titus
81–96	Domitian

96–98	Nerva
98–117	Trajan
117–138	Hadrian

Antonines

138–161	Antoninus Pius
161–180	Marcus Aurelius
161–169	L. Verus
180–192	Commodus

192–193	Pertinax
193	Didius Julianus

Severans

193–211	Septimius Severus
211–217	Caracalla
217–218	Macrinus
218–222	Elagabalus
222–235	Severus Alexander

235–238	Maximinus Thrax
238	Gordian I
238	Gordian II
238–244	Gordian III
244–249	Philip the Arab
249–251	Decius
251–253	Trebonianus Gallus
253–260	Valerian
253–268	Gallienus
268–270	Claudius II Gothicus
270–275	Aurelian
275–276	Tacitus
276–282	Probus
282–285	Carus, Numerianus, Carinus
284–305	Diocletian
285–305	Maximianus Herculius
(293–313	'Tetrarchy': rule of four)
293–306	Constantius I Chlorus
293–311	Galerius
305–313	Maximinus Daia
306–312	Maxentius
306–337	Constantine I
308–324	Licinius
337–340	Constantine II
337–350	Constans I
337–361	Constantius II
361–363	Julian (the Apostate)
363–364	Jovian
364–375	Valentinian I
364–378	Valens
367–383	Gratian
375–392	Valentinian II
378–395	Theodosius I the Great

Western Empire

393–423	Honorius
425–455	Valentinian III
455–465	Petronius Maximus, Avitus, Majorian, Libius Severus
467–472	Anthemius
472–476	Olybrius, Glycerius, Julius Nepos, Romulus Augustulus

Eastern Empire

395–408	Arcadius
408–450	Theodosius II
450–457	Marcian
457–474	Leo I
474	Leo II
474–491	Zeno
491–518	Anastasius
518–527	Justin

527–565	Justinian I	641–668	Constans II
565–578	Justin II	668–685	Constantine IV
578–582	Tiberius II (I) Constantine	685–695	Justinian II
582–602	Maurice	695–698	Leontios
602–610	Phocas	698–705	Tiberius III Apsimar
610–641	Heraclius	705–711	Justinian II (restored)

GLOSSARY

Aedicula: Niche or recess with an architectural frame, such as a pediment supported on a pair of columns.

Aedile: Minor public official in the Roman administration, usually a young man early in his career. Aediles would typically be responsible for the maintenance and conduct of public facilities, such as markets and baths.

Album: Stretch of a wall or other surface covered in white (*albus*) plaster, on which was written edicts from the praetor, public announcements and a list of the decurions.

Algeria/Algiers: The name 'Algeria' was given to the country only following the French invasion in 1830. It is derived from the name of the capital, which was founded in the eleventh century as al-Djazaïr (Arabic: *the islands*) because of the rocks lying off the coast (which were later incorporated into the mole which now encloses the historic port).

Amphitheatre: Place of entertainment (usually oval), with tiered seating all around a central arena (like a football-ground), for watching gladiatorial combats and wild-beast fights. NOT to be confused with a theatre, for watching plays on a stage.

Anadyomene: Attribute of representations of Venus/Aphrodite: 'arising (from the waves)'.

Anastylosis: Re-erection of ruins.

Annona: The supply of free (or heavily subsidised) foodstuffs to the population of Rome; the foodstuffs provided for this purpose (mainly grain and oil) by way of tax.

Antonine Itinerary, The: A list of routes of the Roman Empire, probably compiled in the reign of Caracalla (211–217). It gives lists of roads, the settlements along them and the distances between them.

Apodyterium: Part of a Roman bath complex: the undressing-room.

Apotropaic: Adjective used to describe objects or carvings intended to avert evil, such as an amulet worn around the neck or a carved phallus at a street-corner.

Architrave: Horizontal lintel which spans a doorway or the space between columns in a colonnade.

Arcosolium: Form of tomb, usually rock-cut, which was widely used in the Roman period. A rectangular recess, of a size to hold a coffin (or in the form of a coffin) roofed with a barrel-vault. [*Pictured*]

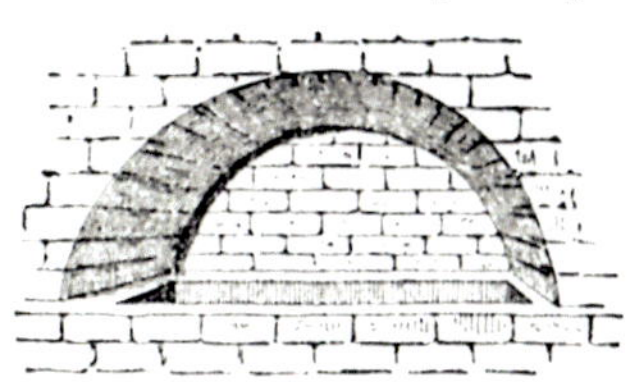

Area (*pl.* areae): Sacred area or courtyard.

Arianism: Heresy preached by Arius (280–336) who denied the equal status of the Persons of the Trinity (see p. 16).

Ashlar: Masonry cut in regular rectangular blocks and laid in horizontal courses; a block of such masonry.

Atrium: Central hall of a Roman house of Etruscan type.

Attic: Box- or plinth-like uppermost element of a Roman building or triumphal arch, above all other architectural ornament.

Augur: Priest whose role was to interpret the will of the gods through the flight of birds ('taking the auspices').

Bestiarius: Fighter trained to fight wild beasts (also *venator*, 'hunter').

Byzantine: This is a chronological and cultural term used by modern scholars, which would not have been understood by those to whom it is applied. It signifies the ambit of Roman rule from Constantinople, established as a second capital alongside Rome by Constantine the Great. In the Maghreb, it is applied to the period and the regime between the expulsion of the Vandals by Belisarius in AD 533 and the Arab conquest in the seventh century.

Caldarium: Part of a Roman bath-building: a hot, humid room with hot plunge-bath(s).

Capitoline Triad: The gods Jupiter, Juno and Minerva.

Capitolium: Principal temple of a Roman city, dedicated to Jupiter, Juno and Minerva (named after the hill on which their temple stood in Rome).

Cardo and **Decumanus**: Terms freely employed by modern archaeologists (on the authority of ancient surveyors) to name the streets of Roman towns. The **cardo** (pl. *cardines*) should run N–S and the **decumanus** E–W; the principal street in either direction would be the **cardo/decumanus maximus.**

Catachumen: A convert to Christianity who is under instruction but has not yet been baptised.

Cavea: Seating area of a theatre or amphitheatre.

Cella: Of a Roman temple, the central chamber, housing the cult statue (sometimes also referred to by the Greek term **naos**, q.v.).

Chancel: That part of an early church containing the altar, usually within the E end of the nave. The space was typically enclosed by a screen of decorated marble slabs and was reserved for the clergy.

Chi-rho monogram: Christian symbol composed of the first two letters of 'Christos' in Greek (XP), often accompanied by the letters alpha and omega (symbolizing Christ as the Beginning and the End).

Ciborium: A regular architectural feature of early churches, in the form of a canopy supported on four columns which enclosed the altar.

Cipollino: Type of marble, quarried in antiquity at Carystos on the Greek island of Euboea and widely used in Roman buildings. It has alternating stripes of green and white colour and has a high content of mica, which sparkles in the light.

Circus: Track with spectator seating for the presentation of chariot-races. Identical to a hippodrome.

Cist: Of graves, a simple cutting in the natural bedrock to contain a body.

Colonia: Initially a term for a new settlement of Roman military veterans. This came to symbolize full assimilation to the administrative structure of Rome itself, a status much sought after by pre-existing communities and *municipia* (q.v.).

Columbarium: Funerary structure resembling a dovecote, in which there are multiple recesses for cinerary urns.

Comes: A late Roman title for various imperial officials. The *comes Africae* was responsible for the military defence of

Africa. The original meaning of the word is a 'companion' (of the emperor), and it is the root of the medieval title of 'count'.

Consignatorium: In the early Church, a room or chapel in which the bishop confirmed those who had been baptised.

Corbel: Stone bracket, projecting from a wall in order to take the weight of a beam or arch above.

Corinthian: An order of architecture for Greek and Roman public buildings, in which the capitals of the columns are formed like the base of an acanthus plant, with three tiers of leaves. The columns usually have narrow vertical flutes and the entablature above is decorated with a frieze based on a continuous acanthus scroll. [*Pictured*]

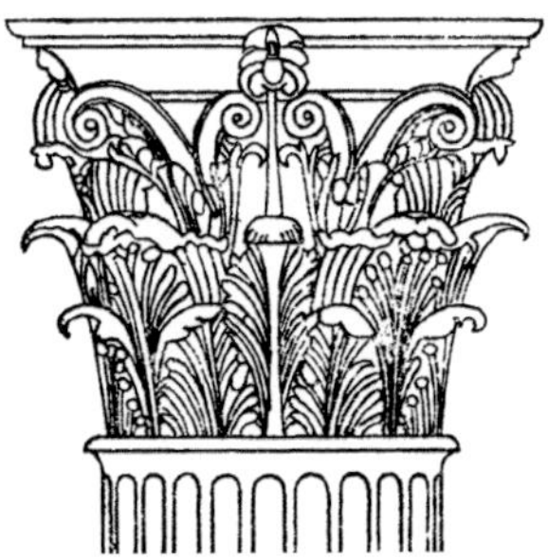

Cryptoporticus: Partially underground portico, designed to provide protection from the heat of summer.

Curia: The building in which the municipal council met.

Damnatio memoriae: The erasure of a name from public inscriptions and documents, as if the individual (or body, since it was applied in AD 238 to the *Legio III Augusta*) had never existed. See figs. 189 and 209.

Decemvir: Member of a college of ten persons; magistrate responsible for the administration of justice in the absence of the praetor.

Decumanus: See **Cardo**.

Decurion: Member of a Roman town-council (a position of prestige, held for life, but one in which one was expected to use part of one's private wealth for the public good).

Dii consentes: The twelve divinities under the presidency of Jupiter constituting the supreme council of the gods. In the order immortalized by the poet Ennius, these are Juno, Vesta, Minerva, Ceres, Diana, Venus, Mars, Mercury, Jupiter, Neptune, Vulcan and Apollo.

Dolium (*pl.* dolia): A Latin term for a large storage jar, such as would normally be a permanent fixture in a storeroom.

Domus (= 'house'): Used typically of a private house belonging to a single owner and occupied by him and his family.

Doric: An order of architecture in Greek (and occasionally Roman) buildings identified by the absence of bases beneath the columns and by very plain capitals in the form of squat inverted cones. The columns have wide vertical flutes and the frieze above takes the form of alternating metopes and triglyphs (q.v.). [*Pictured*]

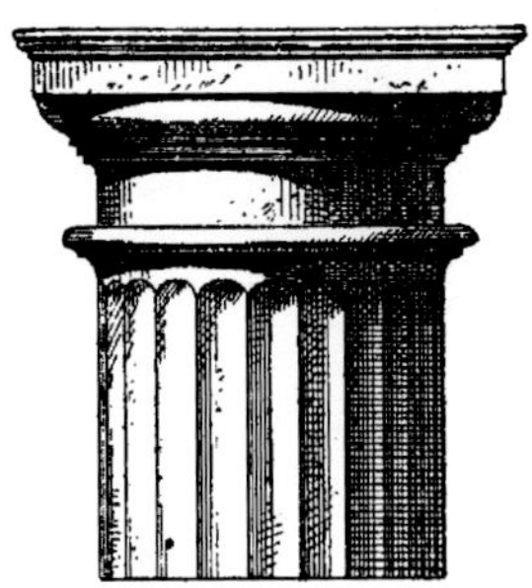

Duumvir: One of the two supreme magistrates in the administration of a Roman town (corresponding to the two consuls at Rome itself).

Emblema (-ata): Small mosaic panel, usually not more than about 60 cm. square, with a picture in fine mosaic (*opus* *vermiculatum*). This would have been assembled in a workshop as a complete panel, which a less skilled craftsman could then place in the centre of a floor with simpler (and coarser) decoration around it.

Emporium: Overseas trading-post.

Engaged (column): See under **Pilaster**.

Entablature: The totality of the architectural elements which properly surmount a colonnade, composed therefore of an architrave, a decorative frieze and a projecting cornice. [*Pictured*]

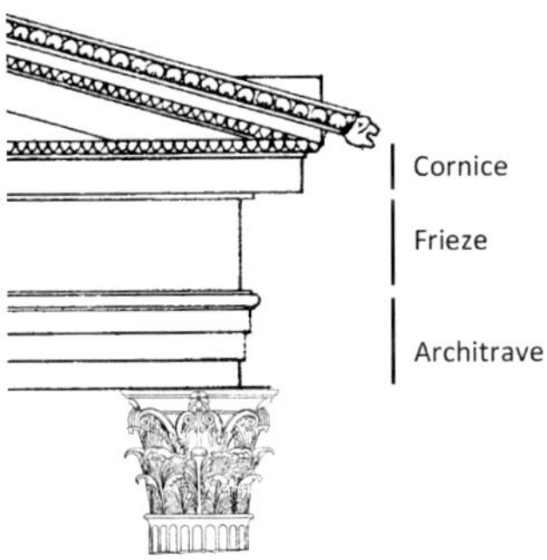

Exedra: Semicircular or rectangular recess ('for sitting out in').

Flamen: A Roman priest attached to a particular cult. In the imperial period a *flamen perpetuus* was a priest of the cult of the emperor (and thus of the state), only a quasi-religious position which continued to have secular responsibilities (e.g. for the urban fabric) after the triumph of Christianity.

Forenames (praenomina) of Roman citizens: these are always indicated by the same abbreviations, such as

C.	Caius
L.	Lucius
M.	Marcus
P.	Publius
Q.	Quintus
Sex.	Sextus
T.	Titus
Ti.	Tiberius

Frieze: Horizontal band above the architrave (q.v.) in a colonnade, usually decorated in relief with either some sort of vegetal scroll or with figure scenes.

Frigidarium: Part of a Roman bath-building: the cold room, usually with a cold plunge-bath.

Garamantes: A Libyan people based in the Fazzan in southern Libya.

Garum: Much-favoured condiment based on the fermented entrails of fish (see p. 60).

Genius: Spirit.

Gens: Family or race.

Hippodrome: Track with spectator seating for the presentation of chariot-races. Identical to a circus.

Hypocaust: Under-floor Roman heating system, used particularly in bath-buildings and (in colder climates) for general room-heating. The floor of the room is raised on small piers (*pilae*), and the exhaust gases from an external furnace are conducted beneath the floor and up flues set behind the wall-surface.

Hypogeum: An underground chamber, typically a tomb.

Insula (*pl.* insulae): Conventionally used by modern scholars to indicate a city block bounded by streets.

Ionic: An order of architecture for Greek and Roman public buildings, in which the capitals of the columns are decorated like a scroll which is rolled up (or rather, downwards) on either

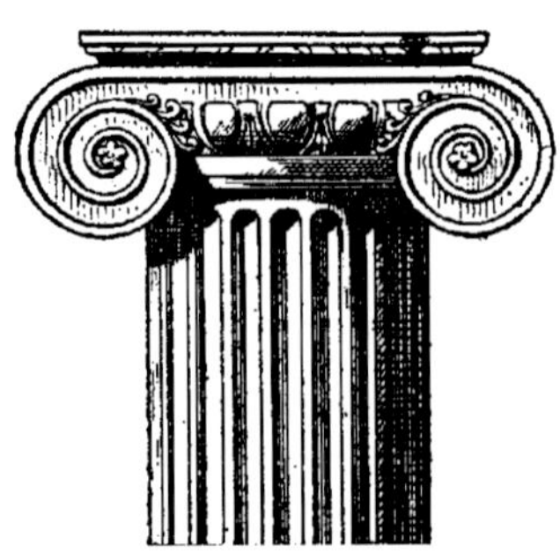

side of a 'cushion'. The columns usually have narrow vertical flutes and the entablature above is decorated with a frieze based on a continuous acanthus scroll. [*Pictured*]

Kantharos: Two-handled drinking-cup with a pedestal-foot. [*Pictured*]

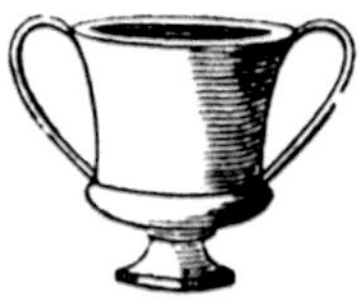

Kore (*pl.* korai): Sculpture of a standing female figure, clothed and typically with the feet together. Introduced into Greek art in the Archaic period, the pose is initially stiff and formal; it becomes more realistic and relaxed with time.

Laconicum or **sudatorium:** Part of a Roman bath-building: a particularly hot room without plunge-baths, intended to generate a dry heat for sweating.

Lanista: Trainer of gladiators, who would then rent them out to organizers of games. (Lit. 'butcher')

Lavacrum: Water-basin for daily purification and ablution (a term originally related to Roman baths but adopted by early Christians).

Legion: The largest single infantry unit in the Roman army, nominally about 5,000 strong.

Limes: Frontier zone of the Roman Empire.

Loculus: Niche or recess (typically for a burial).

Maenad: A female devotee of the god Dionysus, always represented in an ecstatic dance and holding a thyrsus, a kind of staff with a finial in the form of a pine-cone entwined with ivy-leaves.

Maghreb: Term used in Arab sources for North African territories to the W of Egypt (and more particularly to the W of the Syrtic Gulf).

Magister militum: In the late Roman Empire, a supreme regional military command (= 'Master of the soldiers').

Marabout: Tomb of a Muslim holy man.

Martyrium: A church or chapel housing the relics of a venerated holy person or saint (dedicated to their veneration).

Memoria: Funerary monument or a small chapel commemorating someone.

Mensa: Semicircular dining couch in a cemetery for feasts in honour of the dead. (See p. 64.)

Metope: Part of the frieze above a Doric colonnade: a more-or-less square panel with relief decoration (typically either a rosette or a human figure).

Mithraeum: A temple for the worship of the oriental god Mithras (see p. 142).

Monolith: A term for an architectural element (such as a column or pier) which takes the form of a single block of stone.

Municipium: A town in the Roman Empire enjoying local autonomy under a municipal charter, whose citizens had the status of Roman citizens.

Munus (*pl.* munera): A present or favour: hence a gladiatorial spectacle offered to the public by a rich sponsor.

Naos: The building within the colonnade of a Greek temple, often subdivided into a *pronaos* (porch), *naos* (principal chamber, like the *cella* of a Roman temple) and either an *adyton* (inner chamber for the cult statue) or *opisthodomos* (blind rear porch). See also cella.

Narthex: Vestibule or outer room at the entrance to a church. (Catachumens and penitents would be confined to this area.)

Natatio: Swimming pool.

Nereids: Sea-maidens, daughters of Nereus, the Old Man of the Sea.

Nebris: Skin of a fawn, worn by Dionysos and his followers. [*Pictured*]

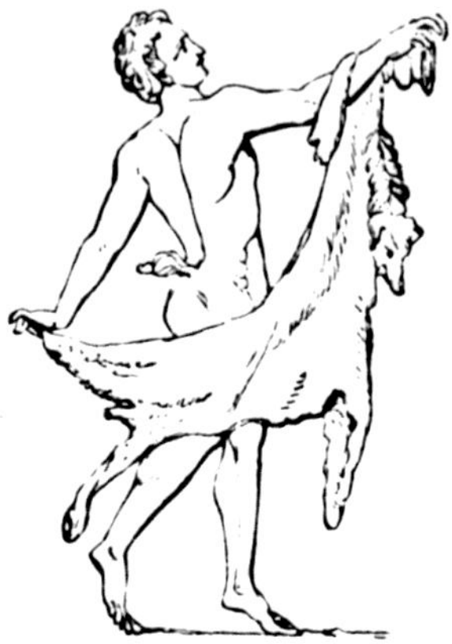

Nymphaeum: A monumental public fountain or water source (originally dedicated to the Nymphs).

Oecus: Large covered reception room.

Opus africanum: A building technique, particularly characteristic of North Africa in the classical period. The main framework of a wall is composed of tall vertical blocks with spaces between them which are infilled with small rubble masonry.

Opus sectile: A decorative treatment, mostly of floors, in which a pattern is composed of shaped tiles of different coloured marbles.

Opus tessellatum: Coarse mosaic paving.

Opus vermiculatum: Extremely fine mosaic decoration, consisting of up to 60 stones per sq. cm., usually reserved for small *emblemata* (q.v.).

Orchestra: The semicircular space in a theatre between the spectator seating (*cavea*) and the stage. Originally used in Greek theatres as a performance space for dancers, in Roman times it was occupied by the (portable and comfortable) seats of the wealthier citizens.

Orthostat: An upright stone block (see *opus africanum*).

Palaestra: An exercise-ground.

Patera: Shallow dish, typically used for pouring liquid offerings (libations) on an altar to a god.

Pelta: Decorative motif in the form of a crescent, usually with an additional central lobe, named after an early Greek type of shield. [*Pictured*]

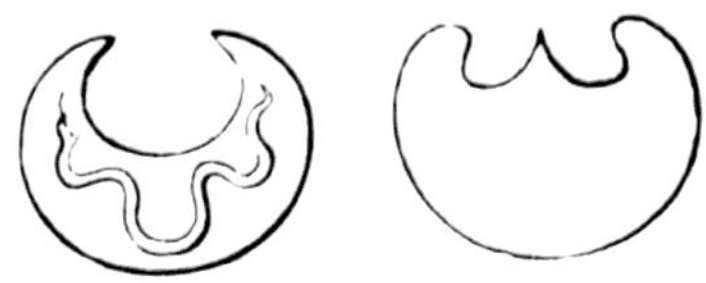

Pentelic (marble): A warm white, almost honey-coloured marble from the quarries of Mount Pentelikon near Athens.

Peplos: Sleeveless woman's cloak, worn over the tunic and fastened at the shoulder with a brooch.

Peristyle: Courtyard or garden surrounded by a colonnaded portico.

Peutinger Table, The: A twelfth- or thirteenth-century copy of a map of the later second century AD, covering the world known to the Romans. It shows named locations (with a variety of conventional symbols), the roads joining them and the distances between them.

Phoenician: A cultural term for the inhabitants of Phoenicia in the Middle East (approximating to the Lebanon of today). Extended to the Phoenicians who settled at Carthage and elsewhere in the western Mediterranean and sometimes used interchangeably with 'Punic' (q.v.).

Pila: Small pier up to 50 cm high and usually composed of square or circular bricks, used to support the suspended floor of a heated room in a Roman bath-building.

Pilaster: Flat-faced, barely projecting, representation of a column on the face or end of a wall. (To be distinguished from an engaged column, which is fully rounded but against the wall and linked to it above and below; and an engaged semi-column, half of which projects from the face of the wall.)

Podium: The platform upon which a temple or monument stands to raise it above its surroundings.

Praenomen (*pl.* praenomina): see **Forenames**.

Praeses: 'President,' a widely-used title under the late Roman Empire, sometimes applied to the civil governor of a province.

Praetor: High-ranking administrative official with judicial responsibilities.

Praetorium: Residence of the praetor in a town or residence within a military camp of the commanding officer of the unit.

Proconnesian (marble): A grey and white veined marble quarried at Proconnesos, an island in the Sea of Marmara near Istanbul.

Proconsul: The civil governor of a province in the early years of the Roman Empire, notionally appointed by the Senate of Rome.

Pronaos: see **Naos**.

Propraetorian legate *(legatus pro praetore)*: Official appointed by the emperor, governing a province with military forces or commanding a legion.

Propylaeum: Monumental entrance (to a precinct rather than to a building).

Prostyle: Of a temple, with columns only across the front.

Protome (in sculpture, painting and mosaic): the forepart of an animal, usually including the front legs.

Pulpitum: The front wall of a theatre stage.

Punic: An adjective used by scholars to describe the culture originating from the (Phoenician) settlement at Carthage after the fall of Phoenicia itself under Persian domination in 539 BC.

Quadrifrons: See **Tetrapylon**.

Quadriga: Four-horse chariot.

Quaestor: Relatively junior Roman public official, usually with financial responsibilities.

Rusticated masonry: Stonework of which the edges are dressed smooth, but the major face is left rough and projecting as a decorative device.

Satyr: Mythical attendant of the god Dionysos, of human form but with pointed ears and a horse's tail; lustful and always represented with an erect phallus.

Scaenafrons: The elaborately decorated façade of the stage-building of a Roman theatre.

Schola: Professional association (typically within the military, e.g. of cavalry officers, armourers); by association, the room or building in which such an association met.

Sestertius (*pl.* sesterces): Roman unit of currency, abbreviated 'HS' in inscriptions. When costs of buildings and statues are mentioned in inscriptions, the intention is surely to impress the reader with the donor's largesse: see the text-box at the end of the glossary.

Silenus: A balding, drunken old man, sometimes with pointed ears, supposedly the tutor of the god Dionysos.

Sistrum: An Egyptian musical instrument in the form of a bronze rattle, particularly associated with the worship of Isis. [*Pictured*]

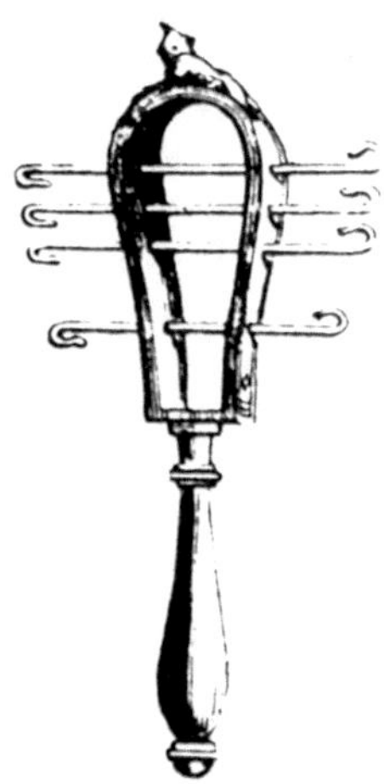

Spina: The central spine running the length of a circus, around which the chariots raced: terminated at either end by a monumental turning-post (*meta*), decorated with statues, fountains and the like and supporting the tallies indicating the number of laps completed.

Standard: Symbol of military unit: a long pole surmounted by bronze emblems (eagle, wreath, medallions), carried into battle and serving as a rallying-point for the troops. (See fig. 179.) [*Pictured*]

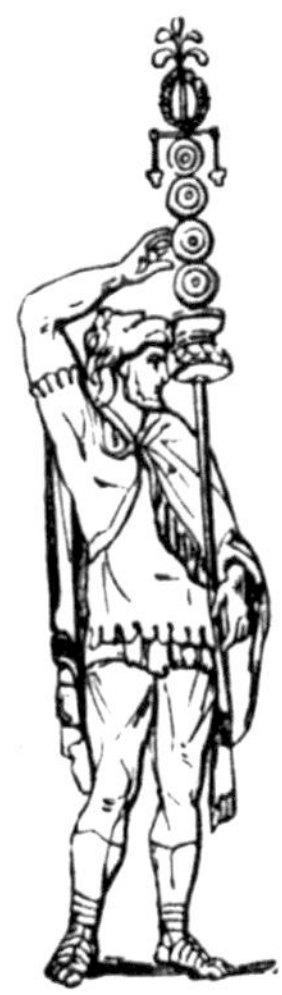

Stele (*pl.* stelai): A vertical stone marker (similar to a tombstone).

Strigil: Bronze or iron curved scraper with which athletes and bathers would scrape oil, sweat and dirt off their skin.

Strigilated: A form of decoration on sarcophagi composed of repeated S(trigil)-shaped flutes.

Stylobate: The linear foundation for a colonnade.

Sudatorium: see **Laconicum**.

Sufes: Phoenician/Punic title for a civil magistrate.

Synthronon: Semi-circular seating around the central apse of a church, providing seating for the higher clergy.

Taberna: Stall or shop.

Tabula ansata: Frame for an inscription or the like which is rectangular with projecting dove-tails ('handles') at either side.

Tepidarium: Part of a Roman bath-building: the warm room which provided a transition between the hot and cold rooms.

Tessera: Small stone cube of which mosaics are composed.

Tetrapylon or **Quadrifrons:** Arch (over a cross-roads) which faces four ways.

Tetrarchy: 'Rule of four', a short-lived experiment in government of the empire introduced by Diocletian in 293, whereby there would be two senior emperors (*augusti*) and two juniors (*caesares*).

Tetrastyle: Of a temple, with four columns across the façade. (Thus 'hexastyle' = six columns across).

Theatre: A place of entertainment with a raised rectangular stage and a tiered semi-circular auditorium (or *cavea*), for the presentation of plays.

Thiasos: The assembled mythical followers of Dionysos (satyrs, maenads etc.)

Tholos: A circular pavilion or monument.

Thyrsus: Staff with a finial in the form of a pine-cone entwined with ivy-leaves (an attribute of Dionysos and his followers). [*Pictured*]

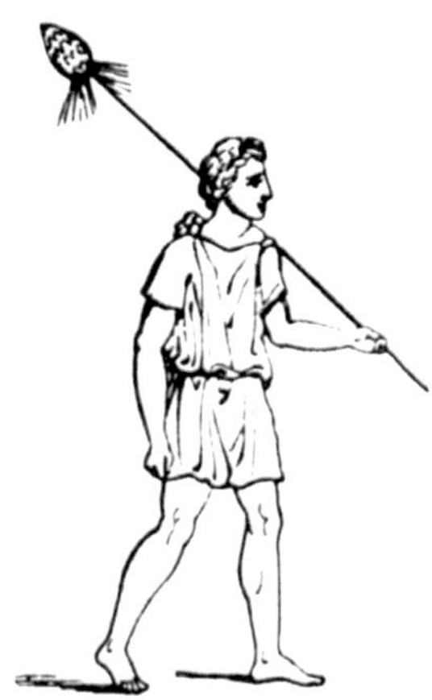

Tophet: Open-air Punic sanctuary and place of sacrifice (typically dedicated to the goddess Tanit), in which are found urns containing the remains of sacrifice – at an early date human infants, but more usually remains of newborn animals or birds.

Tribunal: A raised dais from which judges presided over judicial proceedings (in a civil basilica), or from which a commanding officer might address his troops (in a military fort).

Triclinium: The dining-room of a Roman house. The word means a room with three couches, and typically a decorated (mosaic) floor will reflect this arrangement, with the principal decoration in the area immediately inside the door and simpler patterns around the three sides, which would largely have been covered by furniture.

Triconch: An architectural feature in the form of a square or rectangular room with projecting apses on three sides.

Triglyph: An element of a frieze above a Doric colonnade, composed of three vertical ribs (thought to have originated as a representation in stone of the ends of the roof-beams).

Triton: A merman, fish-shaped from the waist down.

Uraeus: Cobra decorating the headdress of Egyptian pharaohs as a symbol of authority.

Venatio: Hunting of wild beasts, either genuinely in the countryside or as a staged spectacle in the amphitheatre. Also (in the latter), staged fights between animals.

Vir clarissimus ('very famous man'): Title used under the High Empire and in the Late Roman period to indicate a member of the Roman Senate.

The value of money

Public benefactors often liked to emphasize their generosity by stating in inscriptions exactly how much they had spent on their community. It is almost impossible now to convert these values into contemporary figures (which are not themselves stable anyway). Inflation has not been confined to the modern world and the value of the *sestertius* – the unit of currency generally quoted, abbreviated 'HS' – also changed during the Roman period. In the first century AD, a legionary soldier is estimated to have earned HS 9–1,200 per year, while in the early third century this had risen to HS 2,700 per year. Some of the figures quoted in this book are reproduced in the table below.

Page	*Location*	*Date*	*Purchase*		*Value*
30	Nicomedia	100	Wasted on abortive aqueduct	HS	3.2 million
35		50	6.5 litres of *garum*	c. HS	1,000
61	Cuicul	161–9	Statue	HS	3,000
62	"	138–61	Market of Cosinius	HS	30,000
67	"	161	Arch of Julius Crescens	HS	15,000
95	Thamugadi	4th cent.	Library	HS	400,000
96	"	1st half of 2nd cent.	Statue of Fortuna	HS	22,000
"	"	"	Provision of shrine to Fortuna	HS	4,400
97	"	161 +	Statue of Mercury	HS	21,200
99	"	Early 3rd cent.	Two statues	HS	35,000
105	"	?	Fountain	HS	32,348
133	Calama	201–3	Theatre	HS	400,000
141	Madauros	3rd cent.?	Repaving of forum	HS	200,000
142	"	Early 3rd cent.	(Small) theatre	HS	375,000
144	Theveste	Early 3rd cent.	Quadrifrons arch and 2 additional statues	HS	250,000
"	"	"	64 days of free public bath use	HS	250,000

FURTHER READING

Since the archaeology of Algeria has been studied almost exclusively by Francophone writers (one of the most important of whom was Stéphane Gsell), the vast majority of the relevant literature is in French: for this, the reader is referred to the 2003 French edition of this work, to which three important additions may be made:

S. Germain, *Les mosaïques de Timgad: étude descriptive et analytique* (Paris 1969).
X. Delestre, *Hippone* (Aix-en-Provence 2005).
T. Amraoui, *L'artisanat dans les cités antiques de l'Algérie (Ier siècle avant notre ère – VIIe siècle après notre ère)* (Oxford 2017).

For the wider historical and archaeological background, the following (listed in order of publication) are informative:

K. Dunbabin, *The Mosaics of Roman North Africa: Studies in Iconography and Patronage* (Oxford 1978).
P. MacKendrick, *The North African Stones Speak* (London 1980).
D. Pringle, *The Defence of Byzantine Africa from Justinian to the Arab conquest: an account of the military history and archaeology of the African provinces in the sixth and seventh centuries* (Oxford 1981).
S. Raven, *Rome in Africa* (3rd edn., London 1993).
K. Dunbabin, *Mosaics of the Greek and Roman World* (Cambridge 1999).
D. Roller, *The world of Juba II and Kleopatra Selene: Royal scholarship on Rome's African frontier* (New York & London 2003).
B. Rogerson, *North Africa: a History from the Mediterranean Shore to the Sahara* (London 2012).
D. Mattingly et al., *Frontiers of the Roman Empire: the African Frontiers* (Edinburgh 2013).
A. Leone, *The End of the Pagan City: Religion, Economy and Urbanism in Late Antique North Africa* (Oxford 2013).

For one of the few British-Algerian excavations (1977–81), see the readable account

T. Potter, *Towns in late antiquity: Iol Caesarea and its context* (Oxford 1995).
(Others took place in the same period at Sétif and Lambaesis, but were not published in English.)

INDEX

Where an entry is followed by more than one reference, that in **bold type** points to the principal description of the topic.